D1488485

Directions in Sexual Harassment Law

EDITED BY
CATHARINE A. MacKINNON
AND REVA B. SIEGEL

Directions in Sexual Harassment Law

Yale University Press
New Haven &
London

Published with assistance from the Louis Stern Memorial Fund.
Copyright © 2004 by Yale University. Chapter 13 copyright © 2004 by Janet
Halley. Chapter 14 copyright © 2004 by Marc Spindelman. Chapter 16 copyright
© 2004 by Judith Resnik. Chapter 30 copyright © 2004 by Sally F. Goldfarb.
Afterword copyright © 2004 by Catharine A. MacKinnon.

Set in Sabon type by Keystone Typesetting, Inc.
Printed in the United States of America.

Library of Congress Cataloging-in-Publication Data
Directions in sexual harassment law / edited by Catharine A. MacKinnon and
Reva B. Siegel.
p. cm.
Includes index.
ISBN 0-300-09800-6 (alk. paper)
1. Sexual harassment—Law and legislation—United States. 2. Sexual harassment
—Law and legislation. I. MacKinnon, Catharine A. II. Siegel, Reva B.
KF4758 .D+   2003050086

A catalogue record for this book is available from the British Library.

The paper in this book meets the guidelines for permanence and durability of the
Committee on Production Guidelines for Book Longevity of the Council on
Library Resources.

10 9 8 7 6 5 4 3 2 1

Contents

Preface

On February 27–29, 1998, a symposium at the Yale Law School commemorated the twentieth anniversary of the publication of *Sexual Harassment of Working Women* (Yale, 1979). To mark the occasion and look forward, the group considered how the legal claim for sexual harassment as a form of sex discrimination had evolved from its origins and theorized its further development. As Catharine MacKinnon noted in opening the symposium, "Books, unlike children, only grow old, they don't grow up, except like this."

The event turned out to be more timely than anticipated when originally planned, taking place at a moment of broad national debate and deep national crisis over the sexual conduct of the then President with a former White House intern, a context that marked many of the talks. The resulting volume is published as *Sexual Harassment of Working Women* reaches its 25th year in print.

Many people helped bring this book into the light of day. Deborah Sestito, Rita Rendell, Sharon Renier, and Yvonne Squeri tackled with impressive skill, energy, and resourcefulness the often massive tasks of materially birthing a book written by thirty-nine people. Rachel Farbiarz, Shoshana Gillers, Kristen Jackson, Leondra Kruger, Brian Lehman, Diane Marks, Liz Theran, Rebecca Tushnet, Elizabeth Wydra, Michelle Foster, and Jane Yoon brought ideas and energy as well as concern with detail to the research, editorial, and production work they performed for the collection. Owen Fiss, Rebecca Tushnet, and Ariela Dubler helped us imagine and organize the symposium itself. Kimberle Crenshaw, George Priest, Kendall Thomas, and Kenji Yoshino contributed substantially to the quality of the symposium but chose not to write for the book. They all have our gratitude.

Most of all, we thank our contributors for their commitment and their patience. Their contributions exemplify the deep and wide-ranging work that has grown out of this quarter-century struggle to take seriously questions of gender inequality in law.

C.A.M.
R.B.S.

A Short History of Sexual Harassment

REVA B. SIEGEL

Some two decades after the federal courts first recognized sexual harassment as a form of sex discrimination, debate still continues about what sexual harassment is, why it might be sex discrimination, and what law can and should do about it. Many voices take up these questions in the pages to follow. In this introduction I will describe the historical foundations of this conversation, a conversation that continues without sign of diminishing, in the workplace and the popular press, as well as in such academic fora as the conference from which this book grew.

What can history bring to our understanding of sexual harassment? Sexual harassment is a social practice. Social practices have lives, institutional lives and semiotic lives. And so social practices like sexual harassment have histories. Considering sexual harassment in historical perspective allows us to ask some fundamental questions about the nature of the practice, the terms in which it has been contested, and the rules and rhetorics by which law constrains — or enables — the conduct in question.

My object in these pages is to invite reflection, not only about sexual harassment, but also about the law of sex discrimination itself. It is only quite recently that sexual harassment acquired the name of "sexual harassment" and was prohibited as a form of "sex discrimination." By examining the process through which a persistent and pervasive practice came to be recognized as discrimination "on the basis of sex," we learn much about what law does when it recognizes discrimination.

Clearly, this act of recognition was a momentous one. For the first time in history, women extracted from law the means to fight a practice with which they had been struggling for centuries. And yet, when we consider this development from a historical vantage point, it becomes plain that legal recognition of sexual harassment as sex discrimination was at one and the same time a process of misrecognition — involving a sometimes strange account of the practice in issue. On a moment's reflection, this is not terribly surprising. When law recognizes the harms inflicted by social practices, it is intervening in the social world it is describing, both enabling and constraining challenges to the social order of which the practices are a part.

For this reason, the language of discrimination is a specialized language, one that describes the social world in selective ways. When we in turn talk about a practice in the language of discrimination, we are viewing the world through this conceptual filter. Recourse to history supplies one way in which we can think about the languages in which we characterize the social world, to consider what work they are doing, and to ask again what work we might have them do.

It is in that spirit that I offer the following short history of sexual harassment, as a prelude to a much larger conversation, and as a provocation of sorts: an invitation to meditate, yet again, on what we mean when we say that a practice discriminates "on the basis of sex." The longer I think about what that proposition might mean, the more I appreciate how its elusive meaning is the very source of its power — its maddening capacity to excite and to deaden curiosity, to challenge and to legitimate the social arrangements that make men men and women women.

It is with a view to continuing a several-decades-old conversation about what discrimination "on the basis of sex" might mean that I begin my short history of sexual harassment at a time well before anyone dreamed of describing the practice in such terms. I begin my story, quite self-consciously, with a provisional account of what sexual harassment might be and end by speculating about some ways that the practice seems to be changing in our own day. In this way, I hope to survey the terrain of the debate that the essays in this book join — a debate about what sexual harassment is and what law should do about it, a debate about the terms in which we describe and remedy the wrongs we have only recently come to call "discrimination."

Some Historical Perspectives on the Practice, Protest, and Regulation of Sexual Harassment

The practice of sexual harassment is centuries old — at least, if we define sexual harassment as unwanted sexual relations imposed by superiors on subordinates at work. For example, sexual coercion was an entrenched feature of chattel slavery endured by African-American women without protection of law.[1] While there were crucial differences in the situation of free women employed in domestic service, they, too, commonly faced sexual advances by men of the households in which they worked.[2] Surviving accounts of women employed in manufacturing and clerical positions in the late nineteenth and early twentieth centuries also point to a variety of contexts in which men imposed sexual relations — ranging from assault to all manner of unwanted physical or verbal advances — on women who worked for them.[3]

Nor was this sex shrouded in silence. Since the antebellum period, there has been public discussion of women's vulnerability to coerced sexual relations at work. To be sure, Americans often blamed women's sexual predicament on women themselves; both slaves and domestic servants were often judged responsible for their own "downfall" because they were promiscuous by nature.[4] Yet an equally powerful line of public commentary condemned men for sexually abusing the women who worked for them. The abolitionist press, for example, "was particularly fond of stories that involved the sexual abuse of female slaves by their masters"[5] as such stories directly put in issue the morality and legitimacy of slavery. And sexual relationships between women and the men for whom they worked as domestic servants were, if anything, even more volubly discussed. Over the decades, governmental hearings and reports, as well as all manner of commentary in the public press, delved into this and other aspects of the "servant problem."[6] Thus, by the close of the nineteenth century, we find Helen Campbell's 1887 report on *Women Wage-Workers* invoking the common understanding that "[h]ousehold service has become synonymous with the worst degradation that comes to woman."[7] Campbell also described in some detail the forms of sexual extortion practiced upon women who worked in factories and in the garment industry.[8] Along similar lines, Upton Sinclair's 1905 exposé, *The Jungle*,[9] dramatized the predicament of women in the meat-packing industry by comparing the forms of sexual coercion practiced in "wage slavery" and chattel slavery:

> Here was a population, low-class and mostly foreign, hanging always on the verge of starvation, and dependent for its opportunities of life upon the whim of men every bit as brutal and unscrupulous as the old-time slave drivers; under such circumstances immorality was exactly as inevitable, and as prevalent, as it

was under the system of chattel slavery. *Things that were quite unspeakable went on there in the packing houses all the time, and were taken for granted by everybody; only they did not show, as in the old slavery times, because there was no difference in color between the master and slave.*[10]

As public commentators such as Campbell and Sinclair and the abolitionists before them well appreciated, the American legal system offered women scant protection from sexual coercion at work. Rape was, of course, punishable by law; but the criminal law did not protect slaves from rape,[11] and it defined the elements of rape so restrictively that most free women sexually coerced at work would have little reason to expect the state to sanction the men who took advantage of them.

Few women were willing to endure the damage to reputation and prospects for marriage that followed from bringing a rape complaint, and if they did, the prospects for vindication of their complaint were remote indeed. The common law required a woman claiming rape to make a highly scripted showing that sexual relations were nonconsensual; she had to show that sex was coerced by force and against her will[12] — that she succumbed to overpowering physical force despite exerting the "utmost resistance."[13] Economic coercion did not suffice, nor was most physical resistance enough to satisfy the common law requirement of "utmost resistance." New York's high court explained in 1874, as it rejected a rape prosecution of a man who forcibly assaulted his fourteen-year-old servant girl, after sending away her younger siblings and locking her in his barn: "Can the mind conceive of a woman, in the possession of her faculties and powers, revoltingly unwilling that this deed should be done upon her, who would not resist so hard and so long as she was able? *And if a woman, aware that it will be done unless she does resist, does not resist to the extent of her ability on the occasion, must it not be that she is not entirely reluctant?* If consent, though not express, enters into her conduct, there is no rape."[14]

In short, the law assumed that women in fact *wanted* the sexual advances and assaults that they claimed injured them. Unless women could show that they had performed an elaborate ritual of resistance, perfect compliance with the legally specified terms of which was necessary to overcome the overwhelming presumption that women latently desired whatever was sexually done to them, they could expect little recourse from the criminal law. Rape law's protection was further vitiated by the fact that prosecutors and judges relied on all kinds of race- and class-based assumptions about the "promiscuous" natures of the women in domestic service and other forms of market labor as they reasoned about utmost resistance.[15]

Tort law was only marginally more effective as a weapon against sexual coercion at work. Initially, tort law gave women no right to recover damages for sexual assault. At common law, sexual assault gave rise to an action for damages insofar as it inflicted an injury on *a man's property interest in the woman who was assaulted;* thus, a master might have a claim in trespass against a man who raped his slave,[16] or a father might bring a seduction action against an employer who impregnated or otherwise defiled his daughter.[17] When American law eventually began to recognize a woman's right to recover for sexual injury in her own right — whether through an action for seduction or indecent assault — tort law developed a specialized body of law on "sexual" touchings that incorporated doctrines of consent from the criminal law of rape.[18] By the early twentieth century, some jurisdictions moderated the consent requirement in actions for indecent assault, but none seems to have relinquished it.[19] The tort action for seduction, by contrast, seems to have been more plastic, as it evolved from an action designed to recompense a father's economic injury (when it focused on his daughter's out-of-wedlock pregnancy) to an action designed to recompense injuries to a father's honor (when it focused his daughter's loss of virginity) to an action designed to recompense women directly for injuries suffered in "sexual connexion."[20] In this newly configured form, Lea VanderVelde reports, by the late nineteenth century there were at least some seduction cases in which "the coercive force of words of economic threat were sufficient to render the sexual predation redressible."[21] But this development was by no means uniform across jurisdictions[22] and was, moreover, short-lived: by the early twentieth century, many states began legislatively to repeal the tort of seduction along with other "heart-balm" actions.[23]

The law's failure to protect women from sexual predation at work did not, of course, pass unnoticed; it has been a subject of protest since the days of the antislavery movement. We might count in this tradition abolitionist Henry Wright's description of South Carolina as "one great legalized and baptized brothel,"[24] or Harriet Jacobs's *Incidents in the Life of a Slave Girl,*[25] or the petitions of Henry McNeal Turner and other African-American men in the aftermath of the Civil War who protested the sexual violation of black women in domestic service: "All we ask of the white man is to let our ladies alone, and they need not fear us."[26] As the story of Turner's petition reminds us, the parties most interested in achieving law reform in such matters were for the most part disfranchised. Petition thus emerged as a crucial weapon in the campaign. For example, even before the movement for woman suffrage emerged in the 1840s, women's moral reform societies had begun to wage petition campaigns designed to persuade state legislatures to enact legal penalties for seduction.[27] The campaign to reform tort law had both practical and expressive purposes. Abolitionist Lydia Maria Child described the dignitary affront of a tort regime that recognized the sexual injury of women as an economic loss to men. She protested the common law of seduction as it denied to women the legal subjectivity to sustain sexual injury and the legal agency to secure its redress, and argued that women had internalized their devaluation and objectification by law: "[A] woman must acknowledge herself the *servant* of some-body, who may claim *wages* for her lost time! . . . It is a standing insult to womankind; and had we not become the slaves we are deemed in law, we should rise en masse . . . and sweep the contemptible insult from the statute-book."[28]

With the rise of the woman's rights movement in the decade before the Civil War, some of its more vocal spokespersons began to discuss the socioeconomic conditions that made women susceptible to sexual coercion. The portrait they painted of heterosexual interaction was completely at odds with the common law's, insofar as it presented coercion as the normal rather than deviant condition of heterosexual relations. On this account, restrictions on women's labor market participation ("crowding") and the systematic depression of their wages left women as a class dependent on men for economic support, and it was in this condition of "pecuniary dependence" that men could extract their sexual compliance, in and out of marriage.[29] As Ernestine Rose explained at an 1856 woman's rights convention: "What was left for her but to sell herself for food and clothing either in matrimony or out of it; and it would require a wise head to determine which was the worse."[30]

In this critique of marriage as "legalized prostitution"[31] the woman's rights movement had begun to analyze the political economy of heterosexuality in a way that took as structurally interconnected the institutions of marriage and market. This socioeconomic understanding of sexual relations shaped the movement's response to the trial of domestic servant Hester Vaughn in the aftermath of the Civil War. Vaughn was fired by her employer when she became pregnant by him; she gave birth alone, ill, and impoverished, and was found several days later with her dead infant by her side, adjudged guilty of infanticide, and sentenced to death.[32] As Elizabeth Cady Stanton, Susan B. Anthony, and other woman's rights advocates publicized the Vaughn case, they pointed to a variety of gendered injustices that cumulatively sealed Vaughn's fate — an analysis that started with the gender and class restrictions that drove Vaughn to domestic service, and the sexual vulnerability her economic dependency engendered.[33] For the woman's rights movement, the Vaughn case presented an occasion to protest the economic arrangements and social understandings that visited the judgment of death on Vaughn for a predicament the woman's movement judged society as a whole — and men in particular — culpable.

The woman's rights movement responded to Vaughn's case with wide-ranging social critique and an equally wide-ranging remedy. The movement drew on Vaughn's case to protest the injustice of women's exclusion from jury service and suffrage and, after persuading the governor of Pennsylvania to pardon her, turned the Vaughn episode in the direction of its larger quest for political empowerment.[34] During the late nineteenth century, only the Woman's Christian Temperance Union mounted a sustained effort to reform laws protecting women from sexual predation; as Jane Larson has recounted, their effort took the form of a national campaign to raise the age of consent for statutory rape law.[35] While the campaign spoke the language of moral purity, Larson has shown that it was centrally preoccupied with the failure of rape law to protect women from sexual predation, and at least some of its centrally publicized cases involved the sexual exploitation of young women workers.[36]

For the most part, efforts to protect working women from sexual coercion in the early twentieth century focused, not on law reform, but on other modes of collective self-help. For example, in 1908, settlement workers Grace Abbott and Sophonisba Breckinridge took a saloon-keeper to court who fired a young barmaid when he discovered that she was about to bear a child by him; after losing the case, Abbott and Breckinridge they turned to organizing immigrant protective associations to provide young working women alternate bases of community support.[37] Outside the settlement movement, various labor activists addressed the issue of women's vulnerability to sexual coercion at work as part of a more wide-ranging effort to organize working women.[38] But as Lisa Granik relates, there were pressures on women workers struggling to organize that caused them to defer gender-specific demands — such as protection from sexual coercion — in favor of traditional union demands such as seniority rights.[39]

Even so, the fusion of labor and feminist advocacy agendas in the progressive era bore critical fruit. In 1916, for example, socialist-feminist Emma Goldman elaborated the "legal prostitution" critique of the nineteenth-century woman's rights movement in her influential essay "The Traffic in Women": "*Nowhere is woman treated according to the merit of her work, but rather as a sex. It is therefore almost inevitable that she would pay for her right to exist, to keep a position in whatever line, with sex favors.* Thus it is merely a question of degree whether she sells herself to one man, in or out of marriage, or to many men. Whether our reformers admit it or not, the economic and social inferiority of woman is responsible for prostitution."[40]

Women in the early feminist and labor movements never managed to organize a sustained assault on the set of practices we have come to call "sexual harassment," but they did articulate an indictment of the practices that anticipated many of the arguments that women in the modern feminist and labor movements voiced in the 1970s.

The Rise of Sexual Harassment Law: Regulating Sexual Harassment as Sex Discrimination

As we have seen, the practice and protest of sexual harassment have a long history, in which we can situate developments of the 1970s as a recent and relatively short chapter. But these developments nonetheless represent a dramatic turning point in social and legal understandings of the practice.

In the 1970s Catharine MacKinnon and Lin Farley and the many other lawyers and activists who represented women in and out of court were able to mount a concerted assault, of unprecedented magnitude and force, on the practice of sexual harassment. Responding on many fronts to the demands of the second-wave feminist movement, the American legal system began slowly to yield to this challenge, and for the first time recognized women's right to work free of unwanted sexual advances.

How did this come about? Sexual harassment law arose, first and foremost, from women acting as part of a social movement speaking out about their experiences as women at work; the term "sexual harassment" itself grew out of a consciousness-raising session Lin Farley held in 1974 as part of a Cornell University course on women and work.[41] But more was required for the American legal system to recognize this experience of gendered harm as a form of legal injury, when for centuries it had refused. We could speculate for a long time about the convergence of social forces and social understandings that enabled legal recognition of the sexual harassment claim—a story involving differences in the movements for race and gender emancipation in the nineteenth and twentieth centuries, shifts in women's labor force participation, and much more. But for present purposes I would like to consider the question in rather modest terms. What new ways of talking about the harms of a centuries-old practice enabled its recharacterization as unlawful conduct?

FEMINIST ACCOUNTS OF SEXUAL HARASSMENT AS SEX DISCRIMINATION

As we know, the practice of subjecting employees to unwanted sexual advances at work was made legally actionable under a particular legal regime, Title VII of the Civil Rights Act of 1964.[42] During the 1970s, lawyers, advocates, and theorists had to persuade the American judiciary that sexual harassment is "discrimination on the basis of sex." For this to happen, the injuries inflicted on women by sexual coercion at work had to be presented to courts in terms that could be assimilated to a body of law adopted to regulate practices of racial segregation in the workplace. Catharine MacKinnon's analysis in *Sexual Harassment of Working Women*[43] — a stunningly brilliant synthesis of lawyering and legal theory — played a crucial role in this process.

I want now briefly to revisit the 1970s campaign, with a view to understanding the legal system's "reception" of the sexual harassment claim, its translation into antidiscrimination discourse. By considering how MacKinnon and Farley described the injury of sexual harassment, and how judges interpreting federal employment discrimination law explained the harm of the practice, we learn much, not only about sexual harassment, but, just as important, about what law does when it recognizes claims of discrimination.

Writing in the 1970s, MacKinnon and Farley had only sketchy knowledge of the history we have just surveyed; much of this scholarship was produced as an outgrowth of the same set of social transformations that gave rise to the sexual harassment claim in the 1970s. Nevertheless, there are certain striking parallels between their arguments, and arguments advanced by Child, Rose, Stanton, Anthony, and Goldman before them. Like these early advocates, MacKinnon and Farley understood the sexual coercion women encountered at work as part of the larger political economy of heterosexuality, a social order that situates sexual relations between men and women in relations of economic dependency between men and women, an order in which marriage and market play reinforcing roles in the reproduction of women's social subordination as a class.[44] As MacKinnon wrote in 1979: "Sexual harassment perpetuates the interlocked structure by which women have been kept sexually in thrall to men and at the bottom of the labor market. Two forces of American society converge: men's control over women's sexuality and capital's control over employees' work lives. *Women historically have been required to exchange sexual services for material survival, in one form or another. Prostitution and marriage as well as sexual harassment in different ways institutionalize this arrangement.*"[45]

Farley and MacKinnon each then proceeded to read the sexual advances constituting harassment within a semiotics of status inequality. Farley defined sexual harassment as the "unsolicited nonreciprocal male behavior that asserts a woman's sex role over her function as a worker."[46] Drawing on sources as diverse as Adrienne Rich and Erving Goffman, Farley asserted that the practice of sexual harassment was properly understood within the "micropolitics" of "the patriarchy." She drew upon psychologists and sociologists to decode the practice as part of "the communication of power between persons," insisting that "sex is hardly the real meaning of much male behavior at work."[47] MacKinnon, in a now-familiar voice, tersely remarked: "Sexual assault as experienced during sexual harassment seems less than an ordinary act of sexual desire directed toward the wrong person than an expression of dominance laced with impersonal contempt, the habit of getting what one wants, and the perception (usually accurate) that the situation can be safely exploited in this way—all expressed sexually. It is dominance eroticized."[48] MacKinnon located this relationship within a system of social relations that divided the workforce into gender-marked roles that sexualized inequality on the model of marriage: "Work relationships parallel traditional home relationships between husband and wife" so that "women's employment outside the home tends to monetize the roles and tasks women traditionally perform for men in the home."[49]

Looking back at Farley and MacKinnon's arguments, we can discern the basic outlines of a social account of gender. Social stratification along lines of gender has material and dignitary dimensions; it is produced by the interaction of social structure (institutions, practices) and social meaning (stories, reasons);[50] sexual harassment is part of the relations of distribution and recognition both.[51]

This set of understandings played a central role in MacKinnon's argument that sexual harassment was sex discrimination: "Practices which express and reinforce the social inequality of women to men are clear cases of sex-based discrimination in the *inequality* approach."[52] She then illustrated how sexual harassment expressed and reinforced sexual inequality as a matter of social structure and social meaning: for example, "Sexual harassment is discrimination 'based on sex' within the social meaning of sex, as the concept is socially incarnated in sex roles. Pervasive and 'accepted' as they are, these rigid roles have no place in the allocation of social and economic resources."[53] Of course, in so arguing, MacKinnon was engaged in a creative act of resistance, couching the claim that sexual harassment was sex discrimination in terms that expressed the experiential and theoretical understanding of harassment that had emerged from the women's movement, even as her arguments diverged from the conceptual framework in which the American legal system had come to apprehend race and sex discrimination by the mid-1970s.

This set of more conventional legal understandings MacKinnon termed the "differences approach": "The basic question the differences approach poses is: how can you tell that this happened because one is a woman, rather than to a person who just happens to be a woman? The basic answer . . . is: a man in her position would not be or was not so treated."[54] Employers may take all kinds of adverse employment actions against women; what they may not do is treat women employees differently than they treat, or *would* treat, male employees. Note how, on this conception of discrimination, the harm of sexual harassment no longer involves interaction of social structure and social meaning, but instead reduces to an inquiry into the criteria by which an employer sorts employees. MacKinnon offered a variety of arguments that sexual harassment was sex discrimination on the differences approach, while at the same time conducting a detailed diagnosis of how the antidiscrimination tradition was misrecognizing status harm in the course of recognizing discrimination.[55] Without rehearsing the different iterations of disparate treatment and disparate impact arguments MacKinnon and others offered in briefing the sexual harassment claim in more conventional legal terms, I would like, in the interests of concision, to consider how, as a matter of history, the American legal system made sense of the proposition that sexual harassment was sex discrimination within the meaning of Title VII. Much was gained, and lost, in this act of "recognition."

RESISTANCE AND (MIS)RECOGNITION:
HOW COURTS TRANSFORMED SEXUAL HARASSMENT DISCOURSE

At first, courts simply refused to acknowledge that sexual harassment had anything to do with employment discrimination on the basis of sex. Sexual harassment was rejected as a personal matter having nothing to do with work[56] or a sexual assault that just happened to occur at work.[57] Alternatively, judges reasoned that sexual harassment was natural and inevitable and nothing that law could reasonably expect to eradicate from work.[58] But the central ground on which courts resisted recognizing the claim was simply that sexual harassment was not discrimination "on the basis of sex." It could happen to a man or woman or both;[59] even if its harms were inflicted on women only, they were not inflicted on all women, only those who refused their supervisors' advances.[60] It is worth examining the objections to recognizing sexual harassment as sex discrimination set forth in these early cases, and the legal arguments that ultimately prevailed against them. By reconstructing the process through which courts came to reason that that sexual harassment discriminates "on the basis of sex," we learn much about the ways that antidiscrimination law selectively constrains practices that sustain social stratification.[61]

Courts initially offered two reasons to support the judgment that supervisors who subjected employees to unwanted sexual advances did not discriminate on the basis of sex. The first objection was that the practice did not systematically differentiate among employees by sex. As one district court reasoned: "In this instance the supervisor was male and the employee was female. But no immutable principle of psychology compels this alignment of parties. The gender lines might as easily have been reversed or even not crossed at all. While sexual desire animated the parties, or at least one of them, the gender of each is incidental to the claim of abuse."[62] This objection was answered, famously, in the 1977 case of *Barnes v. Costle*,[63] by Judge Spottswood Robinson, when he located the act of class-categorical discrimination in the presumed sexual orientation of the harasser: The plaintiff in that case, he noted, alleged her supervisor had conditioned "retention of her job . . . upon submission to sexual relations *an exaction which the supervisor would not have sought from any male,*" and, Robinson noted, "there is no suggestion that appellant's allegedly amorous supervisor is other than heterosexual."[64] On this model, Robinson explained,

> a similar condition could be imposed on a male subordinate by a heterosexual female superior, or upon a subordinate of either gender by a homosexual superior of the same gender. In each instance, the legal problem would be identical to that confronting us now: the exaction of a condition which, but for his or her sex, the employee would not have faced. These situations, like that at bar, are to be distinguished from a bisexual superior who conditions the employment opportunities of a subordinate of either gender upon participation in a sexual affair. *In the case of the bisexual superior, the insistence upon sexual favors would not constitute gender discrimination because it would apply to male and female employees alike.*[65]

In this strange juridical moment, we see sexual harassment defined as sex discrimination through a narrative of sexual orientation. Monosexual harassers discriminate on the basis of sex, bisexual harassers do not.[66] Judge Robinson notes the status inequality between the supervisor and subordinate pressured for sexual attention, yet does not emphasize it in explaining why the supervisor's sexual attentions are sexually discriminatory. Instead, Judge Robinson reasons about discrimination as differentiation, arguing that harassers who are interested only in members of one sex discriminate on the basis of sex as they select subordinates from whom to demand sexual relations. The harasser's sexual orientation thus supplies the act of group-based differentiation that makes the sexual overture between supervisor and subordinate sexually discriminatory. So framed, there would seem to be no further ground of dispute, with a dare posed to the harasser: "Well, you're not going to claim you're that kind of man . . ."

The sexual orientation argument advanced in *Barnes* would ultimately prove persuasive to many. But, at the time of the decision, there was yet another ground on which defendants argued and courts held that sexual relations between supervisors and their employees did not amount to discrimination "on the basis of sex." In the words of the district court in *Barnes*, "The substance of plaintiff's complaint is that she was discriminated against, not because she was a woman, but because she refused to engage in an affair with her supervisor."[67] Even if the plaintiff's sex was a "but-for cause" of the relationship on the "orientation" account above, her sex was not the *sole* ground of distinction; the employer selected among women employees, using some criterion in addition to and putatively distinct from the plaintiff's "sex."[68] Because the supervisor had targeted some, but not all, class members for sexual attention, his harassing conduct did not amount to discrimination "on the basis of sex."

The Supreme Court itself gave stature to such arguments when it ruled in 1974 that statutes regulating employees on the basis of pregnancy were not sex-based for purposes of Fourteenth Amendment equal-protection analysis, a rule that the Court then applied to the interpretation of federal employment discrimination law in 1976.[69] In the Court's reasoning, a policy refusing employment disability benefits to pregnant women discriminated on the basis of *pregnancy,* not on the basis of sex: "[t]he program divides potential recipients into two groups—pregnant women and nonpregnant persons. While the first group is exclusively female, the second includes members of both sexes."[70] In other words, it was not enough for the plaintiff to show that the challenged policy affected members of one group only; the plaintiff would have to show that the challenged policy affected *all* members of the targeted group before the court would characterize the policy as discriminating "on the basis of sex."

During the 1970s, the federal judiciary invoked this formalistic conception of discrimination to explain why some sex-dependent practices were not "sex-based" and relieve defendants of the obligation to justify them under constitutional or statutory antidiscrimination laws. Employers eagerly seized upon the defense. Businesses argued that employers were not discriminating on the basis of sex (so did not have to supply a "bona fide occupational qualification"[71] defense) when they refused to give employment benefits to women who were pregnant,[72] or to hire women with pre-school age children,[73] or women who were married,[74] or men with long hair,[75] or women in pants suits,[76] or gays and lesbians[77] or men with effeminate mannerisms[78]—or to retain women who wouldn't sleep with their supervisors.[79] All these policies singled out members of one sex and imposed conditions on their employment that preserved traditional gender roles in the workplace. Yet courts applying Title VII law did not characterize the policies as openly discriminating on the basis of sex and so require employers to supply business justifications for the policies that would meet the rigorous "bona fide occupational qualification" exception to Title VII's antidiscrimination norm. Instead, courts characterized the challenged practices as "sex-plus" policies, policies that discriminated on the basis of "sex" "plus" some other putatively *neutral* criterion (hair length, type of dress, mannerisms, orientation, or "willingness to furnish sexual consideration").[80] Courts elaborating sex-plus doctrine reasoned that the statutory prohibition on policies that discriminate "on the basis of sex" applied to policies that affected (1) *only* class members and (2) *all* class members. A challenged practice would have to sort all employees into two perfectly sex-differentiated groups before the sorting operation amounted to discrimination on the basis of sex.[81]

The court that dubbed this area of Title VII law the "sex-plus" doctrine was quite frank about the larger social concern animating the doctrine. "We must decide . . . whether Congress intended to include all sexual distinctions in its prohibition of discrimination (based solely on sex or on 'sex plus'), or whether a line can legitimately be drawn beyond which employer conduct is no longer within reach of the statute."[82] After consulting the legislative history of the Civil Rights Act of 1964, the court concluded that Congress had added the prohibition on sex discrimination to the statute without much deliberation, and thus, "in all probability did not intend for its proscription of sexual discrimination to have significant and sweeping implications."[83] In short, the declared object of sex-plus doctrine was to protect traditional ways of doing business from disruption by the antidiscrimination statute.[84] With this goal in view, the court held that only certain sex-plus policies discriminated "on the basis of sex" within the meaning of Title VII—those that discriminated on the basis of sex "plus" an immutable trait or fundamental right (e.g., marital status or having children).[85]

Given these developments in Title VII law during the 1970s, sexual-harassment defendants advanced a plausible claim when they argued, as the federal agencies defending early cases did, that sexual harassment was not discrimination on the basis of sex, but instead discrimination on the basis of "willingness to furnish sexual consideration."[86] The two federal courts that first rejected this defense waded in long-winded fashion through a maze of Title VII precedents, searching for grounds on which logically to separate sexual harassment from the other "sex-plus" practices that federal courts had already declared did not discriminate on the basis of sex.[87] In the end, Judge Robinson, writing for the D.C. Circuit in *Barnes*, simply asserted: "A sex-founded impediment to equal employment opportunity succumbs to Title VII even though less than all employees of the claimant's gender are affected."[88]

But Robinson did not simply decide the matter by fiat. Reading the opinion more closely, one uncovers a normative justification for the holding in *Barnes* that sounds in a different tenor than the "bisexual harasser"—a justification

rooted in the experience and animating commitments of this civil rights pioneer.[89] (The *Barnes* opinion is written with a particularly rich consciousness
of race/gender intersections as, not only the judge, but also the plaintiff and
her alleged harasser, the director of the equal employment opportunity office
for the Environmental Protection Agency, are black.)[90] *Barnes* concludes its
discussion of the sex-plus problem by pointing to cases where employees had
been dismissed for engaging in interracial sexual relations, and notes that in
each of these cases "a cause of action was recognized although it did not
appear that any other individual of the same gender or race had been mistreated by the employer."[91] At one and the same time, the *Barnes* opinion
demonstrates that there are formal inconsistencies in the ways that Title VII
law defines "discrimination on the basis of sex," and insists that questions
about how to characterize practices under the statute should be resolved on
normative rather than formal grounds. Just as prohibitions on interracial sexual relationships play a role in the perpetuation of racial inequality, *Barnes*
suggests, coerced sexual relations in the workplace play a role in the perpetuation of gender inequality. Thus, in taking the momentous step of recognizing
sexual harassment as sex discrimination, the court reasoned about the practice
as perpetuating group status inequalities and not simply group-based differentiation. Robinson concludes his opinion in *Barnes* — the first appellate opinion
recognizing the sexual harassment cause of action — by quoting from *Rogers v.
EEOC*,[92] the first appellate to recognize a hostile environment claim of *racial*
harassment under Title VII: Congress deliberately left the language of Title VII
open-ended, " 'knowing that constant change is the order of our day and that
the seemingly reasonable practices of the present can easily become the injustices of the morrow.' "[93]

While the first cases recognizing the sexual harassment claim as a form of
sex discrimination under Title VII labored mightily with the "sex-plus" problem,[94] the issue simply disappeared thereafter. Federal courts still use sex-plus
doctrine to remove a variety of sex-specific policies from Title VII scrutiny
(employers may refuse to hire women who wear pants, men who wear dresses,
women who date women, men who display "effeminate" mannerisms),[95] yet
no one remembers that sexual harassment was once legally grouped with these
practices, disaggregated into a policy based on "sex plus refusal to furnish sexual consideration." Plainly, if we are to account for the different doctrinal
analysis of sexual harassment and sex-specific grooming codes under Title VII
today, we would have to seek an explanation in the domain of social, not formal, logic. Today, under Title VII employers may not fire women who refuse
to sleep with them, but they may fire women who sleep with other women.
The gender transformations of the 1970s persuaded the federal judiciary that

some, though surely not all, features of heterosexual social practice were at odds with the nation's egalitarian commitments.

We can thus read the formal distinctions in the 1970s case law as remnants of a larger social struggle, doctrinal residue of a wide-ranging debate about whether and how law would intervene in a field of contested gender relations.[96] (We might liken this dispute to arguments about whether separate-but-equal was discrimination on the basis of race that took place in the thirteen years spanning *Brown*,[97] the per curiams,[98] and the Court's ruling in *Loving v. Virginia*[99] that antimiscegenation laws unconstitutionally discriminated on the basis of race—a decision the Court did not hand down until 1967, the same year that *Guess Who's Coming to Dinner?* won the Academy Awards. In our own day, we can see a similar dynamic at work as social movement protest pressures federal courts to decide whether the state's use of race in suspect descriptions amounts to discrimination "on the basis of race"—a dispute over the meaning of the equal protection clause in which a version of "race-plus" figures.)[100] In short, judgments about whether practices discriminate "on the basis" of sex or race may depend on evolving social intuitions about whether a practice unjustly perpetuates a status regime, rather than formal characteristics of the practice itself, as antidiscrimination discourse leads us to believe.

But if judgments about whether practices discriminate on the basis of race or sex are social constructions, shaped by social-movement protest and the like, we do not, of course, generally experience them or discuss them in such terms. Antidiscrimination doctrine selectively internalized changes in gender norms during the 1970s without acknowledging the project in which it was engaged. Even as the *Barnes* opinion recognizes that sexual harassment is discrimination on the basis of sex, it still clings to the fiction that it is merely analyzing discrimination as the practice of sorting sexed bodies: sexual harassment involves "a treatment differential allegedly predicated upon an immutable personal characteristic gender which subjected appellant to a marked disadvantage in comparison with men employed at the agency."[101] Sex discrimination law, like race discrimination law, pretends that it analyzes distinctions on the basis of physiologically, rather than sociologically, defined aspects of identity.[102] In this way, antidiscrimination law represses the social history, social structure, and social meaning of the practice of sexual harassment in the very act of declaring the practice a legal wrong.

Consider again the way that doctrine reasons its way to the conclusion that sexual harassment is sex discrimination. At first, courts viewed the conduct constituting sexual harassment as completely distinct from practices the law calls sex discrimination; then cases such as *Barnes* tie the practice of sexual harassment to the concept of discrimination by means of a narrative that finds discrimination in the way that persons of monosexual sexual orientation select sexual objects (on this account, discrimination is an act of differentiation, a species of taste or desire, and its objects are particular kinds of sexed bodies). Antidiscrimination law explains how sexual harassment is sex discrimination in terms that are fundamentally uninterested in the social circumstances of the harasser's target (for example, her position in an employment hierarchy, her other economic alternatives if she does not stay employed at this job). It also excludes from the formal account of why harassment is discrimination "on the basis of sex" the particulars of what the harasser does to his targets once he selects her.[103]

Finally, and most important, the law's account of sexual harassment as discriminating "on the basis of sex" does not address the particular kinds of harm that sexual harassment inflicts on its targets — the ways that it *engenders* them. When the sex discrimination in sexual harassment is conceptualized as a form of desire (selecting appropriately sexed bodies given the nature of one's orientation), the act of differentiation that makes sexual harassment sex discrimination would appear to be a normal, natural, and fundamentally benign feature of social life. On this account, the harm of sexual harassment is somehow incidental to the practice of sex discrimination; the harm arises from an act of sexual coercion that just happens to be inflicted on a person with a body sexed female. (This is exactly the understanding expressed by sex-plus doctrine when it conceptualizes sexual harassment as "sex" "plus" the "neutral" criterion of "unwillingness to furnish sexual consideration.") What is more, as antidiscrimination law begins to recognize sexual harassment as sex discrimination, it treats the sexual coercion in sexual harassment as a harm so obvious as not to need explanation or account. But this very failure to explain "the obvious" means that antidiscrimination law rather unselfconsciously incorporates a gender-conventional understanding of why harassment harms women (it is a form of socially inappropriate conduct, "not a nice way to treat a lady").

And so, as antidiscrimination law recognizes sexual harassment as sex discrimination, it never acknowledges the power dynamic that women over two centuries have described: the way that men extracting sex from economically dependent women reiterate a coercive relationship that organizes heterosexual relations in marriage and the market both. Sexual harassment would be sex discrimination on this account, not because of how it sorts sexed bodies, but because of how this form of coercion, iterated across social institutions, constructs the dignitary and material meanings of sex. Sexual harassment would be sex discrimination on this account because it engenders as it coerces, because it is a practice that "makes" women women and men men.

Thus, looking back at the 1970s, we can see that antidiscrimination law intervened, selectively, in a system of social stratification that elaborated "sex" in a series of institutions, practices, stories, and reasons that cumulatively made reasonable, natural, and just a world in which women were (so to speak) on the bottom and men on the top. But antidiscrimination law explained its decision selectively to disestablish elements of this social order without describing the system of status relations in which it was intervening; the law instead asserted that it was prohibiting arbitrary and irrational distinctions on the basis of immutable characteristics that denied persons equal opportunity.

This is not at all surprising. Antidiscrimination law intervened in the practices sustaining gender stratification in much the way it intervened in practices sustaining racial stratification — that is, without providing a systemic account of the social order sustained by "discrimination" on the basis of immutable physiological traits (like race or sex). Silence about the structure of the larger social order was, in an important sense, a precondition of the disestablishment dynamic, a narrative necessity if antidiscrimination law was going to persuade those with privilege voluntarily to cede (some of) it. Just as antidiscrimination law gave only the thinnest account of why discriminating on the basis of race was a wrong (silences that are the subject of ongoing interpretive struggle today),[104] so too did it give a terribly thin account of the harms of sex discrimination, in matters of sexual harassment and elsewhere. Garbling the story of the harms in issue was in an important sense a creative, enabling act, one that facilitated characterization of sexual harassment as unlawful conduct.

To summarize: even as antidiscrimination law recognized sexual harassment as a species of sex discrimination, it did so without acknowledging the larger social arrangements within which the practice of sexual harassment acquired dignitary meaning and distributive consequence. As we will see, this silence has proven consequential in various ways — especially because the practice of sexual harassment seems to have been undergoing important changes in the very era that courts began to recognize it as a form of sex discrimination under Title VII.

Contemporary Transformations in the Practice of Sexual Harassment

To this point in our story, we have considered sexual harassment as a relatively stable social practice that is an integral part of a variety of heterosexual economic relationships, from slavery to secretarial work. Of course, we could identify differences in the practice of sexual harassment in these various institutional settings. For example, when the harassed worker and any off-spring she might bear are the property of the harasser, different social under-standings and economic incentives structure the practice than when harasser and harassee face each other as master and servant or employer and employee. Still, certain features of the practice seem relatively fixed over time and across social and legal settings: men pressure women who are working for them into sexual relations the women do not want. Antidiscrimination law describes the practice of sexual harassment as performing "desire"; feminist critics describe the practice of sexual harassment as performing "power" of a sort iterated throughout the social order. On both accounts, the harasser is using his greater economic authority and resources to secure sexual access to women he other-wise would not have.

So understood, we could say that the practice of sexual harassment persisted in relatively stable terms over the centuries prior to its recognition as an injury under Title VII. But in the very era that the courts began to recognize the sexual harassment claim, the practice itself was going through striking changes.

During the 1970s, following a period of relative stability in occupational sex segregation, women began to break into a variety of traditionally male jobs.[105] Different factors account for these changes, among them long-term shifts in women's labor force participation[106] as well as the federal govern-ment's growing commitment to enforce the sex discrimination provisions of the Civil Rights Act of 1964.[107] In fact, these changes in the degree of occupa-tional sex segregation were relatively small, and restricted to certain occupa-tional categories. (For example, from 1970 to 1980, the percentage of women in administrative positions increased by 11.9 percent, while the percentage of women in construction work increased by only 1.3 percent to about 1 percent of the jobs in the industry.)[108] But however small these changes, they were fraught with symbolic import. An active second-wave women's movement was energetically asserting women's right to partake in traditionally male practices, preserves, and prerogatives, especially in matters of work. Against this backdrop even marginal shifts in workplace integration resonated with larger social import. At stake was the gendered character of work itself.

There was a quite varied repertoire of tactics that men in different occupa-tional positions used to frustrate women's efforts to participate in forms of work that were traditionally gendered male. Sexualized attention emerged as a weapon in this turf war, a means of making women feel so unwelcome that they would eventually leave. In short, the practice of sexual harassment — which we have thus far defined as unwanted sexual relations imposed by superiors on subordinates at work — began to play a new role in political economy of heterosexuality.

Note how, in this new context, the social meaning of the "sex" in sexual harassment changes. As early as 1978, Lin Farley — an avid student of Heidi Hartmann's work on occupational sex segregation — described how sexual attention shifted semantic registers when directed at women in traditional and nontraditional forms of employment: "*The function of sexual harassment in nontraditional jobs is to keep women out: its function in the traditional female job sector is to keep women down.*"[109] We have already seen that sexualized conduct in different socioeconomic settings can express different kinds of social relationships, including relations of inequality. Farley was simply taking the point a step further: depending on the background conditions (women in traditional or nontraditional job category) sexualized attention could express gender inequality of different sorts, communicating messages of institutional subordination (sexualizing hierarchy) or institutional exclusion (gender-marking work spaces and roles).

A number of sociologists have analyzed the ways men use sexualized conduct to enforce segregation of the workplace. Barbara Bergman describes how harassment works when directed at women who have invaded traditionally male jobs or work spaces: "The sexual harassment of women already in male-dominated occupations appears to take the form of insults, which may include mock propositions to engage in sexual relations. Such behavior appears to be motivated by a desire to wound and embarrass the woman, to demonstrate the men's contempt for her unfeminine behavior in invading their territory, to show her that they will not accept her as 'one of the boys,' and out of a hope that she will be made sufficiently uncomfortable to abandon the job."[110]

Barbara Reskin and Heidi Hartmann add: "When work groups are integrated, gender becomes salient for the male occupants, who may subject the women to remarks calculated to put them in their place by emphasizing their deviant gender status. These may take the form of profanity, off-color jokes, anecdotes about their own sexual prowess, gossip about the women's personal lives, and unwarranted intimacy toward them."[111]

To see how the social meaning of the sex in harassment changes when sexual harassment is directed at women in traditional and nontraditional jobs, we can simply compare the facts of the Supreme Court's first two sexual harassment decisions. *Meritor Savings Bank v. Vinson,*[112] decided in 1986, presents the classic sexual harassment scenario involving work roles that conform to gender conventions. In the *Vinson* case, a bank teller complained that shortly after she was hired (and while she was still on probation), her supervisor invited her out to dinner, and then "suggested that they go to a motel to have sexual relations";[113] after resisting, she capitulated. According to her complaint, she then had sex with her supervisor some forty or fifty times in the next several years, and on several occasions was raped by him.[114] The Court's next harassment case, *Harris v. Forklift Systems*,[115] handed down in 1993, presents the "new" sexual harassment scenario involving work roles that do not conform to gender conventions. Here the plaintiff worked as a manager of a company that rented heavy equipment to construction companies. Hardy, Forklift's president, harassed the plaintiff in terms that differ in important particulars from the harassment at issue in *Vinson*. For example, Hardy continually made the plaintiff the target of comments such as: "You're a woman, what do you know" and "We need a man as the rental manager," and at least once, he told her she was "a dumb ass woman."[116] These comments were interspersed with a variety of sexualized interactions. As the Supreme Court relates: "In front of others, he suggested that the two of them 'go to the Holiday Inn to negotiate [Harris'] raise.' . . . Hardy occasionally asked Harris and other female employees to get coins from his front pants pocket. . . . He threw objects on the ground in front of Harris and other women, and asked them to pick the objects up. . . . He made sexual innuendos about Harris' and other women's clothing."[117]

In both *Vinson* and *Harris* employers ask their female employees to go to a motel, but this "proposition" does not have the same meaning in the two cases. It does not appear from the facts of the *Harris* case that the employer is the slightest bit interested in consummating sexual relations with the plaintiff, as an expression of "desire" or "power." Rather, the "proposition" he makes reiterates his claim that "we need a man as the rental manager." Like the other sexually demeaning performances that Hardy exacts of Harris and the other women in his employ, Hardy's mock proposal is intended to humiliate, sending the message that, by trying to fill a man's job, Harris has made herself contemptible: a failure, both as a woman and as a man.

Sexual harassment in nontraditional job settings communicates anxiety about male authority not as visible in harassment in traditional job settings. The harasser — who may stand to harassee in the role of superior, coworker, or subordinate — uses harassment as an informal way to exclude women he lacks formal legal or institutional authority to fire. The woman has violated gendered work spaces or roles, and, as the *Harris* facts illustrate, sexualized conduct aims to restore the gendered order of work by expressing all the ways a woman invading male work space is out of her proper role and place.

As Vicki Schultz has recently emphasized, harassment in nontraditional job settings can involve many kinds of conduct, much of it not typically characterized as sexual; she demonstrates that judges in some circuits have failed to recognize the ways that sexual harassment can enforce occupational segregation, so have refused to analyze harassing conduct that is *non*sexual in nature — or have "disaggregated" sexual and nonsexual harassing conduct in ways that obscure their interactive exclusionary dynamics.[118]

But as this discussion should suggest, differences in the harassment dynamic in traditional and nontraditional job settings can produce confusions about the sexual elements of harassment as well. As the *Harris* case illustrates, harassment in nontraditional job settings is often accomplished by sexualized conduct. (In fact, one study reports that women in male-dominated work settings "were generally more likely than other women workers to report a variety of different kinds of social-sexual behavior in their current jobs.")[119] Because of the different dynamics of harassment in traditional and nontraditional job settings, there may be confusion about the kind of injury the "sex" in sexual harassment inflicts. Is the harm of sexual harassment sexual coercion? Or occupational exclusion?

In the classic harassment scenario — the kind Catharine MacKinnon first analyzed in the 1970s — a woman is forced to participate in sexual relations she does not want in order to keep her job; in these circumstances, sexual coercion enforces a traditionally gendered form of subjection that is fraught with the kinds of dignitary meanings and distributive consequences that women have protested since the first critique of marriage as legalized prostitution in the decade before the Civil War.

This classic form of harassment continues to flourish. But, as *Harris* illustrates, alongside it, there are newer forms of harassment, in which economically leveraged sexual coercion does not play the same central role. In these kinds of cases, men are not using economic power to secure sexual access to women they otherwise would not have; rather, in this new kind of harassment case that arises as women enter nontraditional jobs, men use sexualized and nonsexualized conduct to communicate to women their outsider status in the workplace. In this new scenario, the harm of sexual harassment is not a traditional kind of sexual coercion but a new cousin of it. Harm occurs — not through the traditional pathway in which the harassed woman lacks capacity to refuse an unwanted sexual relationship, — but instead because the harasser uses sexualized and nonsexualized conduct to construct the harassed woman as an outsider in the workplace — de-authorized and denigrated, in her own eyes and in the eyes of others. As *Harris* illustrates, the harm here involves forms of gender-role policing,[120] often accomplished through sexualized attention of a denigrating or mocking sort, rather than classic forms of sexual coercion.

Consider the facts of *Harris* again. When Harris' boss suggested that he go with her to the Holiday Inn to discuss a raise, Harris was perfectly able to say no; but the moment Hardy propositioned Harris (in front of her subordinates), he inflicted harm as directly as when he uttered the "nonsexual" remarks he was in the habit of directing her way ("You're a woman, what do you know?" "We need a man as the rental manager," "[You're] a dumb ass woman"). The mock "proposition" here communicates to the plaintiff, "You're a woman, what do you know?" "We need a man as the rental manager," and "[You're] a dumb ass woman — but it interpellates gender *by invoking the sexual prerogative performed in Vinson and in countless scenes like it for centuries prior*. By invoking this social memory — in the form of the mock proposition and the various commands to assume sexually compromising positions — the president of Forklift seeks to assert masculine authority over his "dumb ass woman" rental manager that she has challenged by her very presence in a traditionally male occupation.

In *Oncale v. Sundowner Offshore Services*,[121] a case involving "same sex" sexual harassment, the Supreme Court acknowledged the existence of different scenarios or paradigms in sexual harassment case law. In *Oncale*, a group of men on an oil platform in the Gulf of Mexico harassed a male coworker, in ways Justice Scalia was too uncomfortable to discuss, but which, according to the plaintiff, involved different forms of assaultive sexualized conduct: not only threats to rape the plaintiff, but part- or mock-performances of the act (holding the plaintiff down while placing their penises up against his body, grabbing him in the shower and doing the equivalent, or more, with a piece of soap).[122] The Court held that the plaintiff could sue his employer for sexual harassment under Title VII so long as the plaintiff could show that the conduct in question amounted to discrimination on the basis of sex. The Court's discussion of the different ways that sexual harassment plaintiffs can demonstrate sex discrimination provides a revealing account of the case law:

> Courts and juries have found the inference of discrimination easy to draw in most male-female sexual harassment situations, because the challenged conduct typically involves explicit or implicit proposals of sexual activity; it is reasonable to assume those proposals would not have been made to someone of the same sex. The same chain of inference would be available to a plaintiff alleging same-sex harassment, if there were credible evidence that the harasser was homosexual. *But harassing conduct need not be motivated by sexual desire to support an inference of discrimination on the basis of sex. A trier of fact might reasonably find such discrimination, for example, if a female victim is harassed in such sex-specific and derogatory terms by another woman as to make it clear that the harasser is motivated by general hostility to the presence of women in the workplace. . . .* Whatever evidentiary route

the plaintiff chooses to follow, he or she must always prove that the conduct at issue was not merely tinged with offensive sexual connotations, but actually constituted "*discriminat[ion]* . . . because of sex."[123]

This passage in *Oncale* acknowledges that there is a divide running through the sexual harassment cases, a difference between "desire" and "hostility" cases. There do seem to be different dynamics at work in the sexual harassment cases, and recognizing some of these differences could well help clarify why certain cases and not others should be actionable. But dividing the cases into harassment that concerns "desire" and harassment that concerns "hostility to women in the workplace" may obscure as much as it illuminates. However we characterize the cases — and there is no reason to think that there are only two paradigms to be found in them — it will not help to ground the enterprise in an account that views the classic harassment scenario as a scene of "desire."

As feminist commentators have been emphasizing since the marriage-as-"legalized prostitution" arguments of the nineteenth century, heterosexual "desire" has a political economy: a set of institutions, rules, and roles governing the exchange of sex and money that gives men power over women in marriage and market both. It is only by considering the larger social order that is the background condition for the "desire" expressed in classic sexual harassment cases that we can begin to read the power dynamics expressed through the sex, in either the classic or newer harassment scenarios. The sex in *Vinson* is performed in gender-traditional roles and expresses the inequality in power and status that sex coerced under those background conditions would. And, when women take or challenge men's traditional roles at work, *Harris* illustrates how harassment tries to restore a gender-traditional order, with sex summoning the "memory" of the gender-traditional scene, a scene in which men's power over women is secure. With no appreciation of this connection, the sex in *Harris* is merely offensive, as in, crude, a breach of good manners, not a nice way to treat a lady. With an appreciation of this connection, the sex in *Harris* becomes a particularly visceral way of reminding women of their proper place in matters of work and sex — at the bottom, where gender conventions of the traditional order would have them be.

There is a risk, of course, in overemphasizing the genealogical connection between the sex "scenes" in *Vinson* and *Harris*. The harassment cases quite wonderfully illustrate how the sex in sexual harassment morphs in meaning as gender bends at work. Constructing a set of rigid legal presumptions about the meaning of sex in sexual harassment would entrench a set of understandings that is quite literally contested, in every sense, in the harassment cases. At the same time, there is a danger in underreading the sex here, in ways that sever it from its genealogical referents. Sex between men and women is part of the semiotics of status between men and women — surely as expressive as "You're a woman, what do you know?" and "We need a man as the rental manager." If sex has been taken up in the defense of gender-traditional work roles, as a mechanism for enforcing the code that marks some work roles "male" and others "female" — it would make little sense to ignore it because there was no real risk of sexual coercion in the traditional-scenario sense.

Which brings us back to the "rape" scene in *Oncale*. Where, if at all, do we find sexual harassment on these facts? The Court seems confident that there is sexual harassment on these "same-sex" facts, if Oncale's harassers are gay. Then, by the Court's logic, what Oncale's harassers are doing to him reflects "desire" and, by reason of the harassers' orientation, would count as an act of discrimination "on the basis of sex." If, however, Oncale's harassers are not gay, then, by the Court's logic, it is unlikely that what they are doing is "discrimination on the basis of sex" unless it reflects "hostility to women in the workplace." The Court's aversion to contemplating the facts of this case and considering how they might enact discrimination on the basis of sex (even as the *Oncale* opinion insistently — and somewhat remarkably for a discrimination case — reminds us that sexual harassment doesn't arise in every act of gender differentiation but instead requires context-attentive interpretation of the facts)[124] suggests that the Court doesn't in fact see harassment on these facts, unless the men harassing Oncale are gay.

But our reading of *Harris* reveals how sexualized conduct can parodically "recall" the traditional gender order and mark certain work roles "male." Suppose the men harassing Oncale are straight. The male-male harassment in *Oncale* could well be assimilated to the male-female harassment in *Harris*. On this view, Oncale's harassers would be deploying sexualized conduct to gender-mark work roles, even though no women are on the scene — in some important sense *to ensure that no women ever appear on the scene*. Oil platforms in the Gulf of Mexico, just like construction-equipment rental companies, are "male" space, and performing certain masculinities in the course of performing one's work is apparently an important mechanism for keeping them so.

Suppose, by contrast, the men harassing *Oncale* are gay. The hypothetical case the Court seems to thinks an easy case of "sex discrimination" in *Oncale* — the case involving "credible evidence that the harasser was homosexual"[125] — is one that we would have to think about much harder. On these facts, involving an attempted rape, there would be no doubt whatsoever in calling the conduct an actionable assault — but do we want to call it sex discrimination? If we vary the facts some, and substitute a scene involving a sexual overture or advance in the workplace rather than an attempted assault, would we want to say that, *as between persons of the same sex,* the overture presents the same harm as a classic heterosexual scenario? Would its meanings be the same, along the axis of either sexual coercion or gender-role policing? Can we make sense of same-sex relations by assimilating them to the hetero-sexual model, or do same-sex relations have independent semantic structure? Even if they might, how far is it possible to disaggregate gender and sexuality in this way? And should we do so by dividing the social world along lines of "orientation," or are there queer alternatives that would subvert these con-structions of the sexual?

Sexual Harassment Law: Future Directions

Sexual harassment is now unlawful under Title VII, yet remains a seem-ingly unending source of controversy.

Americans who agree that harassment of the sort alleged in *Vinson* and *Harris* is sex discrimination disagree about the reasons why this is so. As this discussion demonstrates, disagreement about the normative basis of the pro-hibition on sexual harassment in turn produces dispute about the range and types of practices the prohibition constrains. Debate is not restricted to law-yers, but can take heated form in workplaces, in the media, and on the streets. Nor is it likely to abate any time soon. As we have seen, the practice of sexual harassment is evolving, assuming new forms as groups formerly excluded from positions of economic authority seek equal access to the workplace. At the same time, the regulation of sexual harassment, and debates over it, imbue workplace interactions with new significance. These macro and micro trans-formations in the ecology of work change the meaning of particular overtures, actions, and utterances.

Harassment continues to have enormous dignitary and distributive conse-quences, but the practices through which it is accomplished may well vary, across workplace settings and over time. In some settings, sexual invitations continue to function in the political economy of heterosexuality as they long have, as coercive threats. Yet sexual proposals in work relationships do not always coerce. The speaker may lack supervisory authority over the addressee, or may wear it in such a way as to assure the addressee that she is free to refuse his attentions without adverse consequence. Such utterances and overtures may nonetheless denigrate the addressee, deprive her of authority, exclude her, or undermine her competence in the workplace. Or they may not. Employees may experience a sexual invitation as harmless — an occasion of social discomfort, or instead of deep delight. In some workplace settings, sexualized attention may have little dignitary or distributive consequence, and nonsexualized utterances and actions may play a more important part in gendering work than the sexual interchanges that are most commonly understood to harass.

Americans debating the proper contours of sexual harassment law invoke all these scenes, countering story with story, and harm with harm. Just as discrimination "on the basis of sex" shifted in meaning during the 1970s and 1980s as courts began to recognize harassment as discrimination, it continues to evolve in our own day as advocates and critics of the sexual harassment claim argue about how law can best secure liberty and equality in work, education, and other arenas of civic importance.

The chapters in this volume engage this conversation from a variety of vantage points. In Part I, *Contexts*, Andrea Dworkin, Guido Calabresi, Anne Simon, Pamela Price, and Gerald Torres offer brief observations on the law's role in regulating sexual harassment; some speak of their pioneering work in litigating early cases; others reflect on the aspirations of this body of law as it has matured. Thereafter the chapters address points of deep normative conflict in the law of sexual harassment today.

In Part II, *Unwelcomeness*, Carol Sanger, Louise Fitzgerald, Kathryn Abrams, Jane Larson, and Robin West address the role of consent. Under current case law, when will courts find that sexual relations to which a plaintiff has consented are nonetheless harassing? In what ways must plaintiffs communicate that sexual attention is unwelcome for the conduct to be actionable? Does requiring a showing of unwelcomeness make sense where the harassment does not take the form of sexual overtures? Or where the sexual overture itself is openly denigrating? Can mutually desired sexual relations ever serve as the basis of a harassment claim?

What kinds of same-sex sexual overtures ought law proscribe as sex discrimination under Title VII? Is sexual or nonsexual denigration directed at persons of same-sex orientation ever sex discrimination? In Part III, *Same-Sex Harassment*, William Eskridge, Katherine Franke, Janet Halley, Marc Spindelman, and Christopher Kendall debate such questions in ways that expose profound disagreement about the relation of gender and sexuality, and the role that law plays in regulating sexual relations. Is sexual interaction at work a field of latent harm from which law can emancipate employees? Or is it a valued form of performance or expression that law threatens to muzzle?

Even if we can agree about the kinds of conduct law should prohibit as sexual harassment, there are still deep questions about the ways the state should attempt to vindicate these commitments. Who should be sanctioned for harassing conduct, and how? In Part IV, *Accountability*, Judith Resnik, David Oppenheimer, Deborah Rhode, Ann Scales, Cass Sunstein, and Judy Shih explore questions of institutional responsibility for sexual harassment in both employment and education settings. Should liability vary with forms of harassment, or with changes in institutional context? How ought considerations of efficiency and justice shape the ways law endeavors to deter or remedy harassment?

Part V, *Speech*, considers how, if at all, law ought take account of speech values in the ways it defines and regulates sexual harassment. Frederick Schauer, Dorothy Roberts, Robert Post, Kingsley Browne, Janine Benedet, and Jack Balkin address the question. There has been remarkably little discussion of how the First Amendment constrains antidiscrimination law, with most attention devoted to the speech implications of harassment law itself. What does this pattern — of attention and inattention — reveal about the underlying structure of First Amendment doctrine? How does wrestling with the question alter the way we understand speech or equality law? Should we modify antidiscrimination law to vindicate speech values in the harassment context? If not, why not?

Sexual harassment doctrine has inaugurated profound changes in the ways we understand questions of gender justice, racial justice, and values of equality more generally. In Part VI, *Extensions*, Sally Goldfarb, Adrienne Davis, Tanya Hernández, Lea VanderVelde, and Diane Rosenfeld trace the life of the sexual harassment paradigm in a variety of contexts. How does harassment illuminate the intersection of race and gender inequality? In what ways might the sexual harassment paradigm provoke us to reconceive other relationships? What new kinds of law reform might it prompt?

Part VII, *Transnational Perspectives*, considers sexual harassment law in comparative perspective. Orit Kamir, Susanne Baer, Abigail Saguy, Yukiko Tsunoda, Martha Nussbaum, and Christine Chinkin, respectively, analyze sexual harassment law in Israel, German, France, Japan, India, and in international human rights law. As the harassment paradigm crosses borders, it assumes new forms, simultaneously illuminating the features of other legal cultures and our own.

An afterword by Catharine MacKinnon concludes the volume by assessing the changes wrought by sexual harassment law in the past quarter century. Anchoring her case in the national debates spanning the Thomas-Hill hearings and the Clinton impeachment, MacKinnon charts the norms and practices this body of law has transformed — as well as the entrenched understandings and arrangements that it has yet to disturb.

Notes

1. Slave women were subject to sexual coercion by masters and overseers. *See* Elizabeth Fox-Genovese, *Within the Plantation Household: Black and White Women of the Old South* 49, 297–99, 325–26 (1988); Jacqueline Jones, *Labor of Love, Labor of Sorrow: Black Women, Work, and the Family from Slavery to the Present* 20, 28, 37–38 (1985); Melton A. McLaurin, *Celia, A Slave: A True Story* 24–25 (1991). For a discussion of the literature on the sexual exploitation of slave women, *see* Catherine Clinton, "Caught in the Web of the Big House: Women and Slavery," in *The Web of Southern Relations* 19–35 (Walter Fraser, Jr., et al., eds. 1985). For sources discussing the law governing slave rape, *see infra* note 11.

2. On the sexual exploitation of African-American women working as domestic servants in the South in the decades after emancipation, *see* Paula Giddings, *When and Where I Enter: The Impact of Black Women on Race and Sex in America* 86–87 (1984); Tera W. Hunter, *To 'Joy My Freedom: Southern Black Women's Lives and Labors After the Civil War* 34, 106 (1997); Jones, *supra* note 1, at 150; Bettina Berch, " 'The Sphinx in the Household': A New Look at the History of Household Workers," 16 *Review of Radical Political Economics* 105, 115–16 (1984). On the predicament of women in domestic service generally, *see* Kerry Segrave, *The Sexual Harassment of Women in the Workplace, 1600–1993,* at 23–39 (1994) (analyzing sexual abuse of women working in domestic service and comparing practices in United States and various European countries); *see also* Faye E. Dudden, *Serving Women: Household Service in Nineteenth-Century America* 213–19 (1983) (discussing prevalence of sexual relations in domestic service, focusing on seduction and abandonment); Gerda Lerner, *The Majority Finds Its Voice: Placing Women in American History* 57 (1979), quoted in Giddings, *supra*, at 48–49 ("Victorian morality applied to the 'better class' only. It was taken for granted during the period and well into the twentieth century that working-class women — and especially Black women — were freely available for sexual use by upper-class males").

3. For an overview of factory working conditions in the United States and several other nations in the period from 1800 to the mid-1900s, *see* Segrave, *supra* note 2 at 40–73; *see also* Mary Bularzik, "Sexual Harassment at the Workplace: Historical Notes," 12 *Radical America,* 25, 28–38 (1978). On clerical workers, *see* Ruth Rosen, *The Lost Sisterhood: Prostitution in America, 1900–1918,* at 152–55 (1982) (discussing prostitutes who reported sexual harassment in previous employment as domestic or clerical workers); Bularzik, *supra*, at 25; *see also* Alice Kessler-Harris, *Out to Work: A History of Wage Earning Women in the United States* 102 (1982) (quoting report of the U.S. Commission on Industrial Relations) (" 'A good many girls in department stores have got to give in to the demands . . . of certain . . . buyers, managers, and floor walkers . . . if they want to hold their positions' ").

4. For sources discussing how sexual exploitation of slave women was rationalized as an expression of the natural promiscuity of African-American women, *see* bell hooks, *Ain't I a Woman: Black Women and Feminism* 52 (1981) ("White women and white men justified the sexual exploitation of enslaved black women by arguing that they were the initiators of sexual relationships with men"); Deborah Gray White, *Ar'n't I a Woman: Female Slaves in the Plantation South* 61 (1985); Regina Austin, "Sapphire Bound!" 1989 *Wisconsin Law Review* 539, 570 (1989) ("Jezebel was the wanton libidinous black

woman whose easy ways excused white men's abuse of their slaves as sexual 'partners' "); Peter Bardaglio, "Rape and the Law in the Old South: 'Calculated to Excite Indignation in Every Heart,' " 60 *Journal of Southern History* 749, 757. On domestic servants, *see* Dudden, *supra* note 2, at 217 ("Some observers thought that prostitution recruited many ex-servants because service was filled with 'low' women"); Segrave, *supra* note 2, at 26–27 (discussing reputed promiscuity of servant girls).

5. *See* McLaurin, *supra* note 1, at 81; *accord* Kristin Hoganson, "Garrisonian Abolitionists and the Rhetoric of Gender, 1850–1860," 45 *American Quarterly* 558, 571–73 (1993) ("[T]he many images of slave women as victims of seduction and rape that permeated abolitionist publications contradicted Southern images of the slave woman as Jezebel"); *see also* Karen Sanchez-Eppler, *Touching Liberty: Abolition, Feminism, and the Politics of the Body* 83–104 (1993) (analyzing account of sexual exploitation in Harriet Jacobs's *Incidents in the Life of a Slave Girl*).

6. *See* Dudden, *supra* note 2, at 213–19.

7. Helen Campbell, *Prisoners of Poverty: Women Wage-Workers, Their Trades and Their Lives* 234 (1887), quoted in Lin Farley, *Sexual Shakedown: The Sexual Harassment of Women on the Job* 39 (1978).

8. *See, e.g.,* Campbell, *supra* note 7, at 22–29, 87, 135–56.

9. Upton Sinclair, *The Jungle* (1960) (1905).

10. *Id.* at 109 (emphasis added).

11. Masters who raped their female slaves were not held legally accountable. *See* McLaurin, *supra* note 1, at 93; Bardaglio, *supra* note 4, at 756–60; Margaret A. Burnham, "An Impossible Marriage: Slave Law and Family Law," 5 *Law and Inequality Journal* 187, 219–22 (1987); A. Leon Higginbotham, Jr., and Anne F. Jacobs, "The 'Law Only as an Enemy': The Legitimization of Racial Powerlessness Through the Colonial and Antebellum Criminal Laws of Virginia," 70 *North Carolina Law Review* 969, 1055–58 (1992) (describing the legal impunity with which white men raped black women).

12. 2 Joel Prentiss Bishop, *Commentaries on the Criminal Law* 607–16 (5th ed. 1872).

13. As one nineteenth-century treatise explained the "utmost resistance" requirement, "Nature has given her hands and feet with which she can strike and kick, teeth to bite and a voice to cry out—all these should be put in requisition in defense of her chastity"; the treatise went on to explain that there should be "some marks of violence upon the person of the alleged ravished woman, and her statement is greatly strengthened if the marks are found to have been present and seen by others immediately after the commission of the offense." Ira M. Moore, *A Practical Treatise on Criminal Law and Procedure in Criminal Cases Before Justices of the Peace and in Courts of Record in the State of Illinois* 299–301 (1876), quoted in Lea VanderVelde, "The Legal Ways of Seduction," 48 *Stanford Law Review* 817, 856 (1996). For additional nineteenth-century commentary on the utmost resistance requirement, see *id.* at 855–58.

14. *People v. Dohring*, 14 N.Y. 374, 384 (1874) (emphasis added).

15. For instance, in *Christian v. Virginia*, 23 Grattan 954 (Va. 1873), a black man was acquitted for attempted rape of a black woman, even though he had "laid hold of her, pushing her down on a pile of lumber, choking her, and trying to pull up her cloths." *Id.* at 955. The court reasoned that the burden of proof varies from case to case, depending on "the character and condition of the parties." *Id.* at 958. Even though such actions would

have been a "shocking outrage toward a woman of virtuous sensibilities . . . how far it affected the sensibilities of the prosecutrix does not appear," since the defendant's actions might simply have been an attempt to "work upon her passions." *Id.* at 959. Racial bias in rape cases persists today. *See* Elizabeth M. Iglesias, "Rape, Race, and Representation: The Power of Discourse, Discourses of Power, and the Reconstruction of Heterosexuality," 49 *Vanderbilt Law Review* 869, 880–86 (1996) (discussing studies in Gary D. LaFree, *Rape and Criminal Justice* [1989], showing that conviction rates depend on the victim's race as well as on the defendant's).

16. *See* Bardaglio, *supra* note 4, at 756–57 (observing that, according to an influential treatise on slave law, "only the master could seek compensation in the courts because 'the violation of the person of a female slave, carries with it no other punishment than the damages which the master may recover for the trespass upon his property'") (quoting Thomas R. R. Cobb, *An Inquiry into the Law of Negro Slavery in the United States of America* 99 [1858]).

17. *See* VanderVelde, *supra* note 13, at 837–41 (1996) (quoting Chitty's 1832 edition of Blackstone as stating that "In no case whatever, unless she has had a promise of marriage, can a woman herself obtain any reparation for the injury she has sustained from the seducer of her virtue"). Where touching was sexual, the common law incorporated the assumptions of rape law, including presumptive consent; moreover, the common law resisted commodifying what it understood as a "moral" rather than "economic" injury. On the understandings underlying the common law's failure to provide victims of rape a private action for recovery, *see* VanderVelde, *supra*, at 842–67. On the tort claim available to fathers alleging loss of their daughters' services by reason of their seduction, *see id.* at 867–91. On the use of the tort to redress sexual injury inflicted on women employed outside their own household, *see id.* at 837 n.90 (noting that of 287 nineteenth-century reported seduction cases studied, forty-six indicate that the seducer was either the woman's employer or his son).

18. *See id.* at 854–67 (analyzing tort of seduction as elaborated in nineteenth-century treatises and case law); *see also* Lisa Granik, "Running in Hermeneutic Circles: Challenging/Embedding Social Hierarchies Through Litigation" 198–210 (J.S.D thesis, Yale Law School, 1997) (analyzing tort actions for indecent assault filed by women against their employers from the mid-nineteenth century to the mid-twentieth century).

19. *See* Granik, *supra* note 18, at 205–208.

20. *See* VanderVelde, *supra* note 13, at 883–97 (charting the evolving meaning, and legal elements, of the seduction action over the course of the nineteenth century).

21. *Id.* at 895. Even after statutory reforms nominally accorded women in some states the right to sue for seduction, courts continued to reject their claims on the ground that a woman's "consent" to intercourse defeated her seduction action. *See* M. B. W. Sinclair, "Seduction and the Myth of the Ideal Woman," 5 *Law and Inequality* 33, 51–52 (1987); *see also* Thomas M. Cooley, *The Elements of Torts* 86 n.1 (1895) (noting that a woman could not recover if she was "equally guilty with the man"); Right of Seduced Female to Maintain Action for Seduction, 121 *American Law Reports* 1487, 1487–92 (1939) (citing statutory rape cases, where consent was a legal impossibility, as exceptions to a general policy of disallowing women's seduction suits).

22. *See* VanderVelde, *supra* note 13, at 896.

23. *See* Michael Grossberg, *Governing the Hearth: Law and the Family in Nineteenth-Century America* 51–63 (1985); Ariela R. Dubler, "Wifely Behavior: A Legal History of Acting Married," 100 *Columbia Law Review* 957, 1002–1003 (2000) (comparing anti-common law marriage statutes to anti-heartbalm legislation); Jane E. Larson, "'Women Understand So Little, They Call My Good Nature "Deceit"': A Feminist Rethinking of Seduction," 93 *Columbia Law Review* 374, 393–401 (1993); Sinclair, *supra* note 21, at 72–98.

24. Hoganson, *supra* note 5, at 571.

25. Harriet Jacobs, *Incidents in the Life of a Slave Girl, Written By Herself* (L. Maria Child ed., 1861).

26. Hunter, *supra* note 2, at 34 (protesting sexual assaults on women in domestic service in year after war ended).

27. *See* Barbara J. Berg, *The Remembered Gate: Origins of American Feminism* 211–12 (1978) (describing petition drives for statute criminalizing seduction in New York that collected nearly 20,000 signatures in 1840, and another involving almost as many signatures that same year in Ohio); Larry Whiteaker, *Seduction, Prostitution, and Moral Reform in New York, 1830–1860*, at 142 (1997) (reporting that by 1841 Moral Reform Society had forwarded "some 40,000 petitions" to the state legislature seeking a law criminalizing seduction); Larson, *supra* note 23, at 391.

28. *American Female Moral Reform Society, Advocate of Moral Reform* 41 (1844), quoted in Berg, *supra* note 27, at 210 (1978).

29. *See* Reva B. Siegel, "Home as Work: The First Woman's Rights Claims Concerning Wives' Household Labor, 1850–1880," 103 *Yale Law Journal* 1073, 1121–22 (1994) [hereinafter Siegel, "Home as Work"].

30. "Woman's Rights Convention in New York," *Liberator*, Dec. 5, 1856, at 196; *see also id.* (reporting that Henry Blackwell asserted that "[h]alf the marriages [which] were now contracted would not be, were women pecuniarily independent").

31. For accounts of the legalized prostitution argument, *see* Rosen, *supra* note 29, at 55–57; Siegel, "Home as Work," *supra* note 29, at 1121–22 & n. 166; *see also* Reva B. Siegel, "Reasoning from the Body: A Historical Perspective on Abortion Regulation and Questions of Equal Protection," 44 *Stanford Law Review* 261, 308–14 (1992) (describing claims about marriage as legalized prostitution in nineteenth-century debates about abortion); Jill Elaine Hasday, "Contest and Consent: A Legal History of Marital Rape," 88 *California Law Review* 1373, 1455 (describing claims about marriage as legalized prostitution in nineteenth-century debates about marital rape).

32. *See* Ellen Carol DuBois, *Feminism and Suffrage: The Emergence of an Independent Women's Movement in America, 1848–1869*, at 145–47 (1978); Segrave, *supra* note 2, at 29–30.

33. DuBois, *supra* note 32, at 146.

34. On pardon, *see* Segrave, *supra* note 2, at 30. On the location of the Vaughn case in the postwar movement's advocacy agenda, *see* Pillsbury, "The Hester Vaughn Meeting at Cooper Institute," *Revolution*, Dec. 10, 1868, at 361; *see also* Elizabeth Pleck, "Feminist Responses to 'Crimes Against Women,' 1868–1896," 8 *Signs* 451 (1983).

35. Jane E. Larson, "'Even a Worm Will Turn at Last': Rape Reform in Late Nineteenth-Century America," 9 *Yale Journal of Law and Humanities* 1 (1997).

36. *See, e.g., id.* at 15. In her investigation of Alameda County, California, records of statutory rape prosecutions from 1910 to 1920, Mary Odem found a disproportionate number of forcible assault cases involving male employers of domestic servants. *See* Mary E. Odem, *Delinquent Daughters: Protecting and Policing Adolescent Female Sexuality in the United States, 1885–1920,* at 58–59 (1995).

37. *See* Bularzik, *supra* note 3, at 36.

38. *See* Segrave, *supra* note 2, at 52–60 (discussing instances where sexual harassment became "one of the issues, or the major issue, that precipitated a strike"); Bularzik, *supra* note 3, at 34–35 (observing that "sexual harassment was addressed in *Life and Labor,* the publication of the National Women's Trade Union League").

39. *See* Granik, *supra* note 18, at 213–20.

40. Emma Goldman, *The Traffic in Women and Other Essays on Feminism* 20 (Alix K. Shulman, ed. 1970) (emphasis added).

41. *See* Farley, *supra* note 7, at xi–xiii (recounting first use of term in 1974).

42. 42 U.S.C. § 2000e (2000). For an account of some of the other legal fora — notably state unemployment insurance systems — in which advocates pressed the sexual harassment claim during the 1970s, *see* Farley, *supra* note 7, at 125–33; Catharine A. MacKinnon, *Sexual Harassment of Working Women: A Case of Sex Discrimination* 77–81 (1979) [hereinafter MacKinnon, *Sexual Harassment*].

43. MacKinnon, *Sexual Harassment, supra* note 42.

44. *See, e.g.,* Farley, *supra* note 7, at 49 ("Depression of female earning power reinforces the domestic division of labor, which in turn reinforces job segregation, which in its own turn reinforces depressed female wages").

45. MacKinnon, *Sexual Harassment, supra* note 42, at 174–75 (emphasis added); *see also id.* at 58 ("If women's sexuality is a means by which her access to economic rewards is controlled, relations between the sexes in the process of production affect women's position throughout the society, just as women's position throughout the society makes her sexuality economically controllable").

46. Farley, *supra* note 7, at 14–15.

47. *Id.* at 15–16, 17.

48. MacKinnon, *Sexual Harassment, supra* note 42, at 162.

49. *Id.* at 18.

50. *See* Reva B. Siegel, "Discrimination in the Eyes of the Law: How 'Color Blindness' Discourse Disrupts and Rationalizes Social Stratification," 88 *California Law Review* 77, 82–83 (2000), *reprinted in* Robert Post et al., *Prejudicial Appearances* (2001) [hereinafter "Discrimination in the Eyes of the Law"].

51. *See* Nancy Fraser, *Justice Interruptus: Critical Reflections on the Postsocialist Condition* (1997).

52. MacKinnon, *Sexual Harassment, supra* note 42, at 174 ("Sexual harassment of working women is argued to be employment discrimination based on gender where gender is defined as the social meaning of sexual biology").

53. *Id.* at 178.

54. *Id.* at 192.

55. As MacKinnon dryly remarked, "The central conceptual difficulty (which often occurs as a difficulty of proof) arises because of the necessity to infer from a context, a

frequency distribution, a single event, or proximate circumstances that a given discrimination is sex-specific, without deeply investigating the concrete social meaning of gender status." *Id.*

56. *See Corne v. Bausch and Lomb*, 390 F. Supp. 161, 163 (D. Ariz. 1975) (supervisor's conduct was "nothing more than a personal proclivity, peculiarity or mannerism"; supervisor was "satisfying a personal urge" and "no employer policy [was] involved" nor was the company "benefited in any way").

57. *See Tomkins v. Public Service Electric & Gas Co.*, 422 F. Supp. 553, 556 (D.N.J. 1976) ("Title VII is "not intended to provide a federal tort remedy for what amounts to physical attack motivated by sexual desire on the part of a supervisor and which happened to occur in a corporate corridor rather than a back alley.")

58. *See Miller v. Bank of America*, 418 F. Supp. 233, 236 (N.D. Cal. 1976) ("The attraction of males to females and females to males is a natural sex phenomenon and it is probable that this attraction plays at least a subtle part in most personnel decisions"); *cf. Corne v. Bausch and Lomb*, 390 F. Supp. 161, 163–64 (D. Ariz. 1975) ("The only sure way an employer could avoid [sexual harassment] charges would be to hire employees who were asexual").

59. *See infra* notes 62–66 and accompanying text.

60. *See infra* notes 67–100 and accompanying text.

61. *See generally* Siegel, "Discrimination in the Eyes of the Law," *supra* note 50 (analyzing this question with respect to the law of race discrimination).

62. *Tomkins v. Public Service Electric & Gas Co.*, 422 F. Supp. 553 (D.N.J. 1976); *see also Corne v. Bausch and Lomb*, 390 F. Supp. 161, 163 (D. Ariz. 1975) ("It would be ludicrous to hold that the sort of activity involved here was contemplated by the Act because to do so would mean that if the conduct complained of was directed equally to males there would be no basis for suit").

63. 561 F.2d 983 (D.C. Cir. 1977).

64. *Id.* at 989–90 and n.49 (emphasis added).

65. *Id.* at 97 n.55 (emphasis added). *See also Williams v. Saxbe*, 413 F. Supp. 654, 659 (D.D.C. 1976) (similar analysis, incorporating bisexual harasser exception, as basis for finding that sexual harassment discriminates on the basis of sex).

66. For a remarkably astute discussion of this turn in sex discrimination discourse from the early days of sexual harassment law, *see* Kerri Weisel, Note, "Title VII: Legal Protection Against Sexual Harassment," 53 *Washington Law Review* 123, 134 (1977). And for a provocative account of the lacunae in our sexual self-accountings that the figure of the bisexual threatens to reveal, *see* Kenji Yoshino, "The Epistemic Contract of Bisexual Erasure," 52 *Stanford Law Review* 353 (2000); *id.* at 432–58 (discussing bisexuality and sexual harassment law).

67. *Barnes v. Train*, 13 F.E.P. Dec. 123 (D.D.C. 1974), 1974 WL 10628, *1 (D.D.C.) ("This is a controversy underpinned by the subtleties of an inharmonious personal relationship. Regardless of how inexcusable the conduct of plaintiff's supervisor might have been, it does not evidence an arbitrary barrier to continued employment based on plaintiff's sex").

68. The federal government mounted this defense to sexual harassment charges leveled

against its employees in at least two cases in the early 1970s. *See Barnes v. Costle*, 561 F.2d 983, 990 (D.C. Cir. 1977) (ground of discrimination not sex, but refusal "to furnish sexual consideration"); *Williams v. Saxbe*, 413 F. Supp. 654, 657 (D.D.C. 1976) ("since the primary variable in the claimed class is willingness *vel non* to furnish sexual consideration, rather than gender, the sex discrimination proscriptions of the Act are not invoked").

69. *Geduldig v. Aiello*, 417 U.S. 484, 496–97 n.20 (1974); *Gilbert v. General Electric Co.*, 429 U.S. 125 (1976). Note that *Gilbert* was statutorily "overruled" by Congress when it enacted the Pregnancy Discrimination Amendment to Title VII in 1978. *See* Pregnancy Discrimination Act, Pub. L. No. 95–555, 92 Stat. 2076 (1978) (codified at 42 U.S.C. § 2000e(k) (1994).

70. *Geduldig v. Aiello*, 417 U.S. 484, 496–97 n.20 (1974). *See Gilbert*, 429 U.S. at 135 (quoting this passage as a basis for holding that, under Title VII, employment policies that discriminate on the basis of pregnancy do not discriminate on the basis of sex).

71. *See* 42 U.S.C. § 2000e-2(e) (2000).

72. *Gilbert v. General Electric Co.*, 429 U.S. 125 (1976); *Nashville Gas Co. v. Satty*, 434 U.S. 136 (1977)

73. *Phillips v. Martin Marietta Corp.*, 400 U.S. 542 (1970) (holding that policy violates Title VII).

74. *Sprogis v. United Air Lines*, 444 F.2d 1194 (7th Cir. 1971) (striking down policy forbidding female, but not male, flight attendants to marry).

75. *Willingham v. Macon Telegraph Publ'g. Co.*, 507 F.2d 1084 (5th Cir. 1975).

76. *See, e.g., Lanigan v. Bartlett & Co. Grain*, 466 F. Supp. 1388, 1391 (W.D. Mo. 1979) (applying "sex-plus" doctrine to uphold discharge of female employee who violated dress code by wearing a pantsuit) ("plaintiff's affection for pantsuits is not an 'immutable characteristic' "); *cf. Devine v. Lonschein*, 621 F. Supp. 894, 897 (S.D.N.Y. 1985) ("At least until that dreadful day when unisex identity of dress and appearance arrives, judicial officers . . . are entitled to some latitude in differentiating between male and female attorneys, within the context of decorous professional behavior and appearance").

77. *See, e.g., DeSantis v. Pacific Tel. & Tel. Co.*, 608 F.2d 327, 331 (9th Cir. 1979) ("We must again reject appellants' efforts to 'bootstrap' Title VII protection for homosexuals. . . . [W]hether dealing with men or women the employer is using the same criterion: it will not hire or promote a person who prefers sexual partners of the same sex. Thus this policy does not involve different decisional criteria for the sexes").

78. *Smith v. Liberty Mutual Ins. Co.*, 569 F.2d 325 (5th Cir. 1978).

79. *See Barnes v. Costle*, 561 F.2d 983, 990 (D.C. Cir. 1977) (ground of discrimination not sex, but refusal "to furnish sexual consideration"); *Williams v. Saxbe*, 413 F. Supp. 654, 657 (D.D.C. 1976) ("[S]ince the primary variable in the claimed class is willingness *vel non* to furnish sexual consideration, rather than gender, the sex discrimination proscriptions of the Act are not invoked").

80. *See, e.g., Stroud v. Delta Air Lines, Inc.*, 548 F.2d 356, 1977 WL 25929, at *2 (5th Cir. 1977) (unpublished opinion) (holding that in an all-female pool, discriminating against married women does not violate Title VII) ("[C]ertain women — stewardesses who

are unmarried — are favored over certain other women — stewardesses who are married. As one of the all-female group of flight attendants employed by Delta, plaintiff suffered a discrimination, but it was based on marriage and not sex"); *Knott v. Missouri Pacific Railroad Co.*, 527 F.2d 1249, 1252 (8th Cir. 1975) (upholding different grooming standards for men and women) ("While no hair length restriction is applicable to females, all employees must conform to certain standards of dress. Where, as here, such policies are reasonable and are imposed in an evenhanded manner on all employees, slight differences in the appearance requirements for males and females have only a negligible effect on employment opportunities"); *Willingham v. Macon Tel. Publ'g Co.*, 507 F.2d 1084, 1092 (1975) (upholding different grooming standards for men and women) ("This frame of analysis removes Willingham's complaint completely from the Sec. 703 (a) 'sex-plus' category, because both sexes are being screened with respect to a neutral fact, i.e., grooming in accordance with generally accepted community standards of dress and appearance").

81. *Cf. Geduldig v. Aiello*, 417 U.S. 484, 496–97 n.20 (1974) ("The program divides potential recipients into two groups — pregnant women and nonpregnant persons. While the first group is exclusively female, the second includes members of both sexes").

82. *Willingham v. Macon Tel. Publ'g Co.*, 507 F.2d 1084, 1090 (5th Cir. 1975) (en banc).

83. *Id.*

84. *See id.* at 1092.

85. *See id.* at 1091–92.

86. *See supra* note 67 and accompanying text.

87. *See, e.g., Williams v. Saxbe*, 413 F. Supp. 654, 657–61 (D.D.C. 1976) (distinguishing pregnancy cases and "so-called 'hair cases'" and insisting that "[t]he requirement of willingness to provide sexual consideration in this case is no different from the 'preschool age children' and 'no-marriage' rules" in cases where a sex-plus policy was held to be sex discrimination in violation of statute).

88. *See Barnes v. Costle*, 561 F.2d 983, 993 (D.C. Cir. 1977).

89. Robinson played a key role in litigating *Shelley v. Kraemer*, 334 U.S. 1 (1948), and was part of the NAACP team that argued *Brown v. Board of Education*, 347 U.S. 483 (1954). He also served as dean of Howard University Law School, where he and his colleagues and students developed many of the central legal theories of the civil rights movement. *See* Richard Kluger, *Simple Justice: The History of Brown v. Board of Education and Black America's Struggle for Equality* 253–55, 485–505, 667–69 (1976).

90. *See id.* at 984. A number of the early sexual harassment plaintiffs were African-American women, some suing white male supervisors. *See, e.g., Miller v. Bank of America*, 418 F. Supp. 233 (N.D. Cal. 1977) (black female clerk suing white male supervisor); *Munford v. James T. Barnes & Co.*, 441 F. Supp. 459 (E.D. Mich. 1977) (black female assistant manager suing white male employer). Other early cases, like *Barnes*, involved intraracial harassment. For discussions of several of the early cases and their racial dynamics, *see* MacKinnon, *Sexual Harassment, supra* note 42, at 61–62, 65–68; Elvia R. Arriola, "'What's the Big Deal?' Women in the New York City Construction Industry and Sexual Harassment Law, 1970–1985," 22 *Columbia Human Rights Law Review* 21, 41–42 (1990).

91. *Barnes*, 561 F.2d at 993–94 (footnotes omitted).

92. 454 F.2d 234 (5th Cir. 1971).

93. *Barnes*, 561 F.2d at 994 (quoting *Rogers v. EEOC*, 454 F.2d 234, 238 (5th Cir. 1971)).

94. *See, e.g.*, Weisel, *supra* note 66, at 129–32.

95. *See generally* Mary Anne Case, "Disaggregating Gender from Sex and Sexual Orientation: The Effeminate Man in the Law and Feminist Jurisprudence," 105 *Yale Law Journal* 1 (1995).

96. For an account of how sexual harassment was discussed in popular magazines during the 1970s (and the ways that account deviated from feminist criticisms of the practice), *see* Arriola, *supra* note 90, at 44–47.

97. 347 U.S. 483 (1954).

98. For a summary of the per curiam Supreme Court opinions invalidating segregation policies in noneducational contexts, *see* Derrick Bell, *Race, Racism and American Law* 118–19 (3d ed. 1992).

99. 388 U.S. 1 (1967).

100. At present, the American judiciary is relying on a version of "race-plus" to argue that the state can conduct searches using suspect descriptions containing race without engaging in race-based state action of the sort that would trigger heightened scrutiny. *See, e.g., Brown v. City of Oneonta*, 221 F.3d 329, 337–38 (2d Cir. 2000) ("This description contained not only race, but also gender and age, as well as the possibility of a cut on the hand. In acting on the description provided by the victim of the assault — a description that included race as one of several elements — defendants did not engage in a suspect racial classification that would draw strict scrutiny"). *See generally*, Richard Banks, "Race-Based Suspect Selection and Colorblind Equal Protection Doctrine and Discourse," 8 *U.C.L.A. Law Review* 1075, 1095 (2001) ("This sole factor/one-of-many-factors distinction is undeniably prominent in many discussions of racial discrimination, including the Supreme Court's recent redistricting decisions"). Courts exempt suspect descriptions from strict scrutiny on the grounds that race is only one of several selection criteria employed, hence the practice is said not to discriminate on the basis of race. But there is no general equal-protection rule to this effect. Courts often apply strict scrutiny to practices that employ race along with several other selection criteria; the classic case is affirmative action.

101. *Barnes*, 561 F.2d at 991 n. 57.

102. *See* Siegel, "Discrimination in the Eyes of the Law," *supra* note 50, at 90–91, 98–102 (discussing race discrimination case law).

103. These particulars are regulated through the remaining doctrinal criteria that define the elements of harassment. For instance, EEOC guidelines provide that "Unwelcome sexual advances, requests for sexual favors, and other verbal or physical conduct of a sexual nature constitute sexual harassment when (1) submission to such conduct is made either explicitly or implicitly a term or condition of an individual's employment, (2) submission to or rejection of such conduct by an individual is used as the basis for employment decisions affecting such individual, or (3) such conduct has the purpose or effect of unreasonably interfering with an individual's work performance or creating an intimidating, hostile, or offensive working environment." 29 C.F.R. 1604.11 (1999). The requirement that the plaintiff communicate to her harasser that his attentions were

"unwelcome" is one much-criticized definitional element. *See, e.g.,* Susan Estrich, "Sex at Work," 43 *Stanford Law Review* 813, 815–16 (1991) (arguing that the law of sexual harassment imports many of the "rules and prejudices" endemic in traditional rape law, including a misplaced emphasis on the victim's conduct).

104. *See* Siegel, "Discrimination in the Eyes of the Law," *supra* note 50, at 109–13 (analyzing how dynamic interaction of antidiscrimination rhetoric and status-enforcing practices gave rise to dispute about whether civil rights law was best understood to embody an "antidiscrimination" or an "antisubordination" principle).

105. In a much relied upon study of sex segregation in employment, Andrea Beller reports that occupational segregation from 1972 to 1981 experienced "a rate of decline almost three times as large as that during the 1960s." *See* Andrea H. Beller, "Trends in Occupational Segregation by Sex and Race, 1960–1981," in *Sex Segregation in the Workplace* 12 (Barbara F. Reskin ed., 1984).

106. *See* Barbara F. Reskin and Patricia A. Roos, *Job Ques, Gender Ques: Explaining Women's Inroads into Male Occupations* 3–90 (1990) (examining socioeconomic factors that might account for changing sex composition of occupations during 1970s and 1980s).

107. *See id.* at 64. The EEOC was at first extremely reluctant to enforce Title VII's prohibition on sex discrimination. *See* Cynthia Harrison, *On Account of Sex: The Politics of Women's Issues, 1945–1968,* at 187–205 (1988). Under pressure from the National Organization for Women (NOW), formed partly in response to the EEOC's foot-dragging, the commission gradually became more responsive to feminist concerns. *See* Hugh Davis Graham, *The Civil Rights Era: Origins and Development of National Policy, 1960–1972,* at 205–32 (1990). By the early 1970s, enforcement of Title VII's sex discrimination provision had become a more significant priority for the EEOC. *See* Reskin and Roos, *supra* note 106 at 54–55 (describing sex discrimination litigation during the 1970s involving nontraditional job categories such as banking and insurance).

108. *See* Reskin and Roos, *supra* note 106, at 17–19 tbls. 1.6, 1.7. While in many jobs, such as managerial, administrative, and clerical work, there was a significant increase in sex integration (*see id.* at 17), other occupations, such as construction and other traditionally male blue-collar work, remained overwhelmingly male, with women making up only 1 or 2 percent of the field — percentages that remained static or dropped during the period in question. *See id.* at 19. *See also* Barbara R. Bergmann, *The Economic Emergence of Women* 70 (1986) (tables demonstrating that the percentage of women in the Occupational Group of "Operators, fabricators, and laborers" rose only from 24 percent in 1972 to 25 percent in 1985, whereas women rose from 33 to 42 percent of the "Managerial and professional specialty" workers over this same period).

109. Farley, *supra* note 7, at 90 (emphasis added).

110. Bergmann, *supra* note 108, at 106.

111. Barbara F. Reskin and Heidi I. Hartmann, eds., *Women's Work, Men's Work: Sex Segregation on the Job* 53 (1986).

112. 477 U.S. 57 (1986).

113. *Id.* at 60.

114. *Id.*

115. 510 U.S. 17 (1993).

116. *Id.* at 19.

117. *Id.*

118. Vicki Schultz, "Reconceptualizing Sexual Harassment," 107 *Yale Law Journal* 1683 (1998).

119. Barbara A. Gutek and Bruce Morasch, "Sex-Ratios, Sex-Role Spillover, and Sexual Harassment of Women at Work," 38 *Journal of Social Issues* 55, 67 (1982). ("For all seven categories of social-sexual behavior assessed, women in nontraditional occupations and jobs reported more experiences of them on their current jobs than were reported by working women in general or by women in sex-integrated work who also interact predominantly with men." In this study, "31.5 percent of the women in male-dominated occupations and jobs reported being touched sexually compared to 15 percent of working women in general"). Gutek and Morasch observe that these results may reflect the fact that these nontraditionally employed women actually did experience more social-sexual behaviors than the average working woman. However, it may also be an indication of their awareness of such behavior." *Id.*

120. *See* Katherine M. Franke, "What's Wrong with Sexual Harassment?" 49 *Stanford Law Review* 691 (1997). On Franke's account, "sexual harassment — between any two people of whatever sex — is a form of sex discrimination when it reflects or perpetuates gender stereotypes in the workplace." *Id.* at 696. Franke argues that sexual harassment should be reconceptualized as "gender harassment." "Understood this way, sexual harassment is a kind of sex discrimination not because the conduct would not have been undertaken if the victim had been a different sex, not because it is sexual, and not because men do it to women, but precisely because it is a technology of sexism." *Id.*

121. 523 U.S. 75 (1998).

122. *See id.* at 76–77.

123. *Id.* at 80 (emphasis added).

124. *See id.* at 81–82 ("The real social impact of workplace behavior often depends on a constellation of surrounding circumstances, expectations, and relationships which are not fully captured by a simple recitation of the words used or the physical acts performed"; judgments in sexual harassment cases require "[c]ommon sense, and an appropriate sensitivity to social context").

125. *Id.*

PART I

Contexts

What Feminist Jurisprudence Means to Me

ANDREA DWORKIN

It is a great pleasure to be here to celebrate with you the twentieth anniversary of Catharine A. MacKinnon's *Sexual Harassment of Working Women*. To most of us, twenty years has been a lifetime. For twenty or twenty-five years we have been working to change the fact of male dominance over women. The question is: how do we do that? And in this conference, the question becomes: how does sexual harassment law do that?

So, I would like to say that when I look at feminist jurisprudence I expect to see two things. The first is that the law has to recognize real injuries to real women, concrete ways in which women are turned into second-class citizens, acts that hurt women, and the lexicon through which women's bodies are colonized for sexual exploitation. The law has to, in some way, be about something real that is helping to keep women under, to keep women accessible for sexual exploitation or sexual abuse. The second thing that law must do is exactly what law does not want to do: which is, the law has to undermine or sabotage male dominance. Now, I understand that I am talking to the legally enfranchised here, but in political terms when I and my colleagues look at law, we want to see that in addition to redressing real grievances the law makes a difference in the distribution of power between men and women.

We also want the law—not tangentially but at its heart—to make a difference in other social hierarchies, all of which are infused with aspects of sexual domination. I mean white supremacy, which we usually call racism in this country; class inequities, which in this country are becoming worse and worse such that whole parts of our population are being thrown away. And we sit here. We are not being thrown away. I cannot tell you what it is like for me to visit rooms like this one: because I work with the people who do not get into these rooms. They do not know if they will live tomorrow. They do not have a sense of well-being or welfare or shelter or food. They are women who have to sell their bodies.

Catharine MacKinnon and I have talked over the last fifteen years—since the ordinance recognizing pornography as a form of sex discrimination was passed in Minneapolis—about why it was that sexual harassment law was basically accepted, but why, when we try to go after a bunch of pimps who are exploiting the most marginalized women in our society, everyone rears up and says, "No, no, no, no! Life stops today! The Constitution is null and void!" If we do anything for the equality rights of women in offices, okay; but if we do anything for the equality rights of women on street corners, we must be crushed and destroyed. I'm not positing something as simplistic as: sexual harassment has worked for middle-class women, in their interests, therefore sexual harassment has worked as a legal strategy. This would be the same as saying: sexual harassment law recognizes a real grievance but has not undermined male dominance. I think, in fact, that in both its origins and where we stand now, sexual harassment law has been part of the process of undermining male dominance. As lawyers you are not supposed to think about this. I am asking you as an activist and a theorist and a not-lawyer—but just as a citizen—to think about this all the time.

When Lin Farley wrote her early book on sexual harassment, which I think was in 1976, she was among the women who could not envision in any way a legal action based on the reality she documented: that sexual harassment made women into vagabonds in the workplace; that women changed jobs, lost seniority, had to physically move their families. She was talking about waitresses and secretaries and women who had no concept that there ever would be a glass ceiling. Sexual harassment law in fact did begin to be used by women who had a very tenuous hold on being middle class: African-American women in offices. I think that it was only when white middle-class men understood that this new law was really going to have something to do with them that we began to see extraordinary backlash, which went as follows: "Sex equals sexual harassment." You've heard it many times. "Those women are trying to stop us from having sex in the workplace." Well, it was certainly news to all of us that actually millions of men wanted to have a young woman in their place of work to suck their cock. We did not really think that was what we were up against. We did not understand that it was that literal, that specific, that real.

So, then, sexual harassment law serves middle-class women. This law shows us the potential when women who can — women who have some right to the place that they have in society, not the earliest black litigants but later white litigants — use this law; when white middle class women say, "Yeah, this law is about me, too." Then the middle-class men say, "Oh my God! What have we done?" They mean: we should have squashed the black women, cut this insurrection off at its roots; now it has taken hold, what can we do now?

Now, I am here because I want to talk to you — to feminist lawyers — about jobs in which the job is to be sexually harassed. I point you to Hooters, for instance, which gets around sexual harassment law by saying, "But these women are entertainers. They're hired because they have big breasts. This is the entertainment. They don't just serve food. The breasts bounce and that's entertainment." Or, where the job is to be sexually abused over and over and over again: for instance, prostitution. Or when women are used in pornography and the woman's body is colonized and the injuries to her are real — and those injuries themselves provide the entertainment, create a huge profit because men consume the material made from the injuries of these women and the exploitation of these women and the abuse of these women. I think that you have to make these women matter. You have to see what is happening to them in relation to the fact that it continues second-class status for all women. If you won't or don't, they will be left out in the cold, left on the street corners, left for the pimps forever.

I want to know: is there a difference yet in the male vocabulary after twenty or twenty-five years of us working to articulate and clarify the elements of sexual exploitation and sexual abuse: is there a difference between sex and sexual harassment, between sex and sexual exploitation, between sex and forced sex? Or, are these all pairs of synonyms? Do they mean exactly the same thing? If they continue to mean exactly the same thing to men in real life then we have not done our work. We have not succeeded even with the great power of the law. With respect to sexual harassment, the law has actually been with us for some small period of time. We need to ask — what has moved and what refuses to move?

I need to say this very clearly: I am not a lawyer. I don't know how to talk the way you all do. I have the burden of having to say what I mean. So, understand that I mean this: we need, we must, you must find ways to destroy male power over women whether that power is institutional or in fact it is acted out in what appear to be isolated and individual cases of sexual abuse.

We need, you need to destroy the hierarchies that are premised on the sexual availability of women and girls. We need to destroy both the implicit rights and the excess of rights that men now have over women. I think this is a part of feminist change that women do not want to face. Academics do not have to face it. All their degrees are a buffer. But women who have food and shelter, who are not being battered, who are not being raped in their homes have an obligation: they have an obligation to the women who are enduring all of that.

Women are afraid of confrontation. As lawyers you learn to be adversarial including not to tell the truth, not to know the difference between telling the truth and lying, not to know the difference between right and wrong, not to know the difference between being fair and not being fair. What I am saying to you is that if we do not solve this problem of learning how to confront male power in the work that you do, there really is no hope for the rest of us who are not in here but who are out there.

2

Perspective on Sexual Harassment Law

GUIDO CALABRESI

I would like to go back to the beginning question that Catharine Mac-Kinnon put, "How do we end the inequality of the sexes?" That may seem a very broad way of speaking, but I think that it is the key question that we must ask about sexual harassment. The issue is not only how do we end inequality, but what kind of equality do we want. I go back to this, even though it is the broadest of perspectives, because I am old and I have been struggling with this question for many years. Indeed, I first began to address it when Catharine was in my torts class and teaching me.

I think my problem is at the core of what is discrimination in sexual matters. Because if it is discrimination that we are talking about, then equality would seem to be the answer. But it is not the answer unless we ask what kind of equality should be strived for.

The traditional way in which equality is offered is the equality of the melting pot. You will get equality, you whoever are unequal and dominated now, if you adhere to the stereotype of the dominant culture. In the melting pot it is, "You will be equal, immigrant, if you become a white, Anglo-Saxon Protestant." In other words, you will get equality on our terms. You will get equality if you become like us. Note, that I said "offered," not "given." There is no guarantee that even that equality will be achieved. But this is the equality that is proposed.

By and large, immigrants could not help adhering to this offer. They were minorities; they had no possibility of power. And so, until very recently, they melted-in and tried to buy equality by forgoing who they were. And though this is sad, tragic even, when one dealt with the "taking in" of immigrants, it was not something that ultimately was threatening to society. If Italians came and were offered equality only if they gave up that particular sense of individual relationships that is the essence of that Latin society, too bad. And if, when they tried to reestablish themselves three generations later, all they found was pizza, and not those individual relationships, it would be unfortunate. But it would not be the end of the world; many societies have survived quite well without those relationships.

That same proposition is being made, "offered," to women today. You will be equal, perhaps — anyway, we offer equality to you — if you adhere to male stereotypes. And we often offer this kind of equality thoughtlessly, that is, without even thinking about it. One of my favorite examples is the difference in toilets — which, in the past, usually were called "men's room" and "ladies' room." That is not equal, for the words "men" and "ladies" don't connote the same thing. When equality was offered, they almost always became men's room and women's room. They didn't become ladies' room and gentlemen's room. Now, I'm not sure that gentility in toilets is a very important notion. What interests me is not that, but rather how thoughtlessly, when we give formal equality, we adhere to the stereotype of the previously dominant group.

More on point for sexual harassment law, if we end the sexual double standard, if everyone behaves the way men stereotypically behaved, even if we achieve equality in some sense, have we gotten anything that we truly want? Suppose that we end sexual harassment by moving to a world in which there are women bosses who are powerful and who grope and feel men subsidiaries. But there are also men bosses who continue to grope and feel women subsidiaries. What have we gotten? What have we been fighting for if that is where we end up?

What is more, if we gain equality by demanding that women behave as, stereotypically, men did, we do something that is far more dangerous than when we did the same with respect to immigrants and the melting pot. This is so because, culturally, with all the deprivations to which women have been subjected, women have nevertheless represented all sorts of things that have been essential to our society. If we lose what is good in what women have stood for by making women behave stereotypically like men in order to melt them into an equal society, we will have lost things without which a society cannot survive.

I'm not saying that women only should continue to look after children, but I am saying that if we become a society in which no one looks after children, because women behave the way men — who stereotypically did not look after children — do, we will be a dreadful society. Similarly, in sexual matters, if we all become as nonsissy men were supposed to, we will have achieved very little indeed. That melting-in is fundamentally dangerous, and it is also not necessary, in the way that it may have been necessary for immigrants, because women are, after all, a majority. In fact, women can demand, and we all should demand, that equality be offered, and given, now, not according to the stereotype of the previously dominant group, but thoughtfully and taking into account what there is and has been that women have stood for that must be preserved and must become the way both men and women behave.

But, what is the effect of that? Equality is always offered grudgingly, and given rarely. But it is given even more grudgingly if achievement of it requires that the rulers change their ways. If it means that the dominant groups stop doing what they have always wanted to do — which is having sex in the workplace and so forth — it is almost impossible to come by. There is no doubt about it; to ask for equality that is worth having delays equality, and this was my discussion with Catharine, twenty-five years ago.

When she was a student Catharine said to me, "You are just saying that we must ask for equality on our terms, because to do so will slow equality down and that is what men want." But I persisted, and a few years later she said, "Damn it! I think you are right." Having said that, she went beyond both her and my position of twenty-five years ago to become the dominant scholar that she is. She asked the right question and she saw the problems that are at the root of what we are asking today. We can adhere to the dominant stereotype so long as it is applied equally. Or we can demand that the values of those who have been dominated play a significant or preeminent role in the equality that we strive for. Or, finally, we can (occasionally) even say: treat people equivalently, rather than equally, rather than in the same way. We can admit cultural differences, if we want. That is very dangerous, and especially difficult in the United States because it sounds like separate but equal, which is usually plenty separate, but not equal. And yet it is something that cannot be completely ruled out as we try to figure out what really is the equality that we wish to strive for.

Which of these is wanted in the workplace, and, specifically, as to sexual harassment, sexual relations and language in the workplace? Do we want a workplace in which men and women are equally free to talk like swine and to demand sex from those who are below them? Or do we want equality of a sort that says, "I have respect. You must respect me for what I am"?

I hope that we do not settle for that first, cheap, equality. But if we do not settle for that, then as Andrea Dworkin said, "We have to work an awful lot harder, an awful lot harder, because the equality we are looking for is going to be given, if at all, only after the most crucial, bitter, and often demeaning fight."

3

Alexander v. Yale University
An Informal History

ANNE E. SIMON

The writing of *Sexual Harassment of Working Women* was not exactly an academic exercise. As it was being written, many of the practical and theoretical problems of sexual harassment litigation were emerging in the work of the New Haven Law Collective,[1] when we sued Yale University in the spring of 1977. More specifically, we represented five women students and one male faculty member in a lawsuit asserting that sexual harassment of women undergraduates by male faculty members, without any mechanism for students to complain or for Yale to do anything about the complaints, was sex discrimination in violation of Title IX of the Education Amendments of 1972.[2]

The case developed from the work of women undergraduates at Yale who delved into the rumors and discussions about widespread sexual harassment and the unwillingness of the Yale administration to do anything about it. Their knowledge that something was very wrong, even if they did not have a name for it, was the basis of all that followed.

The women students who came forward to be plaintiffs ran the gamut of the problems of sexual harassment in higher education. Central to their claims was their understanding that, because of sexual harassment, none of the plaintiffs received the education she had come to Yale to get. Ronni Alexander's claim was that her flute teacher had forced her into sexual intercourse, that she had no one to talk to or go to in order to complain about it, and that as a result she had abandoned both majoring in music performance and playing the flute. Pamela Price reported that a professor of political science, her major field, offered her an A in exchange for sex. She refused. She got a C in the course. Lisa Stone stated that she had spent a good deal of time with a friend who had been sexually harassed and had not been able to do anything about the harassment. Stone concluded that if she were sexually harassed she, too, would be left on her own by Yale; as a result, she began to fear and shun interaction with male faculty members. Margery Reifler, manager of the field hockey team, asserted that her life had been made miserable by sexual harassment from the male coach of the team. Ann Olivarius was one of the members of the Yale Undergraduate Women's Caucus who had been most active in investigating the persistent reports of sexual harassment at Yale. She had been told by a senior Yale administrator that if she did not stop saying those things about faculty members, she would get sued for defamation — and Yale would not help her. The late Jack Winkler was a classics professor who concluded that he could not do his job as a teacher if his women students were in a constant state of anxiety about male faculty members because the university provided no way for them to make complaints about sexual harassment and have them resolved.

Ann Olivarius felt threatened by Yale's warning. Being a good student of Kitty's, she decided she needed a lawyer. She walked into our office one afternoon and talked to Kent Harvey, who rapidly decided that there was a serious problem. Initially, it looked as though we would be seeing that problem from the defense side of a defamation case. Soon, however, it became clear that it would be much more worthwhile to go on the offensive than to wait for Olivarius to be sued. As the details of more incidents of sexual harassment came to light, we saw that there was a widespread pattern of sexual harassment, well represented by the courageous women who would become plaintiffs. They would present a great case. There were just two problems: we had no cause of action, and we had no private right to sue.

The claim that sexual harassment in employment was sex discrimination that violated Title VII of the Civil Rights Act of 1964 was not doing well in the courts in early 1977. The decisive turn in the recognition of the validity of the claim did not begin to occur until the summer of 1977, after we filed *Alexander*.[3] We were trying to raise for the first time the claim of sexual harassment as sex discrimination in education, and we were basing the claim on an analogy to what was then still a losing cause of action in the employment context.

The statutory basis for the claim of sex discrimination in our case against Yale was Title IX, which prohibits sex discrimination in federally funded educational programs. The regulations implementing Title IX provided that "a recipient shall adopt and publish grievance procedures providing for prompt and equitable resolution of student and employee complaints alleging any action which would be prohibited by this part."[4] Our legal claim was that Yale's actions and policies were violating that mandate. This formulation of the claim was consistent with the students' understanding of the issue. From the beginning, and throughout the litigation and its aftermath, the women students wanted to be able to take their complaints of deprivation of equal educational opportunity to the university itself, not an outside judge or agency. They reasoned that the university was the site of their education, and thus the university was responsible for ensuring that they could actually obtain it.

The conceptual and political appropriateness of Title IX did not, however, get us very far in itself. The explicit enforcement mechanism provided in the law was the ability of the federal funding agency (at that time, the Department of Health, Education and Welfare) to cut off funding to the noncomplying institution.[5] Only one federal court of appeals had ruled on the question of whether individual students could bring suit to enforce Title IX, and had decided it the wrong way.[6]

Here, as in many other circumstances, life imitated baseball. An opposing pitcher once said of Wade Boggs, the third baseman and brilliant hitter for the Boston Red Sox and later the New York Yankees, "When you have two strikes on him, he's got you exactly where he wants you." This is also an apt description of the Catharine MacKinnon approach to legal problems. There we were, with no cause of action and no right to sue, and Kitty was convinced we were going to win.

We brought the case in federal court in New Haven. Yale, naturally, moved to dismiss it. The question of the private right of action under Title IX got most of the attention. Yale treated enforcement of Title IX as an encroachment on its prerogatives at a time when many women's rights organizations were fighting for effective implementation of Title IX. The Project on the Status and Education of Women of the Association of American Colleges was following Title IX enforcement closely around the country. Litigation against the Department of Health, Education and Welfare, asserting that HEW was failing to enforce any of the statutes requiring equity in educational programs receiving federal financial assistance, was moving ahead.[7] The Women's Equity Action League (a plaintiff in the case against HEW) and the NOW Legal Defense and Education Fund, represented by the National Women's Law Center, took the unusual step of filing an *amicus curiae* brief on the motion to dismiss in *Alexander*, in support of a private right of action under Title IX.

This activity on the private right of action issue, welcome though it was, addressed only one of our two problems. On the issue of whether sexual harassment was sex discrimination under Title IX, we were more on our own. Fortunately, part of the manuscript of *Sexual Harassment of Working Women* was available to help us formulate our arguments. We pulled out the arguments most likely to be persuasive in the context of undergraduate education, updated the status of the employment cases, and explained the allegations in *Alexander* in order to file an effective opposition to the motion to dismiss the case.[8]

In deciding the motion to dismiss, the district court broke new ground by concluding that sexual harassment in education would, if proved, be actionable sex discrimination under Title IX, at least in the form of the trade of a grade for sex given in Price's claim.[9] Alexander's claim was held to be mooted by her graduation, "absent sheer conjecture that [she] may in the future wish to resume study in [the] field." [10] It is natural to wonder whether a court would have been so cavalier about a man's claim that misconduct by a university professor had destroyed his career plans.

The trial court dismissed Reifler's claim on the ground that she had not complained to the university, although it simultaneously accepted the legal sufficiency of the allegation that Yale did not have a grievance procedure for complaints under Title IX.[11] The claims of Stone, Olivarius, and Winkler were said to be "untenable," because "no judicial enforcement of Title IX could properly extend to such imponderables as atmosphere or vicariously experienced wrong."[12] Today, we would understand those as claims of hostile environment sexual harassment. More than fifteen years after this ruling, Price, as a lawyer in Oakland, California, won a published decision on behalf of high school students, affirming that hostile environment sexual harassment was illegal under Title IX[13] and demonstrating yet again that litigants often know more than judges.

Price's claim was tried before a judge without a jury in 1978. It wound up looking a lot like an individual tort case after the court denied class certification and refused to admit any evidence of sexual harassment at Yale outside of the facts of Price's situation. These rulings made it difficult, if not impossible, to prove that there was a systemic problem for which an institutional grievance mechanism would be at least part of the solution. The judge then decided that she did not believe that the underlying sexual harassment had occurred. Here, too, the court failed to see the true nature of the injury alleged.[14] The judge concluded that if she did not believe that Price had been sexually harassed, Yale had no legal obligation to have a grievance procedure to investigate whether this incident (or any other instance of sexual harassment) had occurred. This conclusion ignored the text of the Title IX regulations, which required "grievance procedures . . . for prompt and equitable resolution of . . . *complaints alleging* any action which would be prohibited by this part."[15]

The students' claims were appealed to the Second Circuit.[16] The court decided that, since everyone had graduated, it did not need to bother.[17] The court was also not inclined to spend its time considering alleged deprivation of educational opportunities in "an activity removed from the ordinary educational process," such as flute lessons or field hockey. This view has since been repudiated in the Title IX cases addressing unequal athletic opportunities.[18]

Two other factors probably influenced the appellate outcome. One was not explicitly acknowledged in the opinion: all three of the men named in the complaint were no longer at Yale, since the last had departed a couple of weeks before oral argument. The other factor was extensively discussed by the court: by the time the appeal was heard, Yale did finally have a grievance procedure designed to deal with complaints of sexual harassment. The Second Circuit thus felt able to opine that "it appears that the major relief sought in this suit has already been granted."[19] The court made no mention of *how* Yale had acquired a grievance procedure, though everyone at Yale knew. It had not been "granted"; the grievance procedure was the result of persistent and continuous pressure, and a great deal of work, by the Undergraduate Women's Caucus and the Council of Third World Women at Yale, as well as several other student organizations, both undergraduate and graduate.

Nevertheless, it is fair to conclude that *Alexander*, through the decision on the motion to dismiss upholding the legal sufficiency of the Price claim, established that sexual harassment of students by teachers was illegal sex discrimination under Title IX. A brief check of the legal citation services reveals that the case, in either its trial or appellate form, has been cited in thirty-nine reported cases in the past twenty years. Twenty-eight of them, almost all in the Second Circuit, cite it for mootness, standing, or related procedural barriers to plaintiffs in a wide variety of contexts. Eleven cite *Alexander* in some decision on the merits about sexual harassment in education. Only one of those cases involved undergraduates; one, high school students; one, junior high school students; three, elementary school students; four, graduate or professional students; and one plaintiff was a junior faculty member.[20] These are not particularly impressive citation statistics for a case that announced an important new legal principle.

The relative skimpiness of the later legal history of *Alexander* has at least three sources. First, it remains very difficult for students to sue for sexual harassment. It requires time, energy, commitment, and willingness to endure the nastiness of litigation and the risks to future educational and employment opportunities from being labeled a troublemaker. And you need to find a lawyer.[21]

Second, the doctrinal development of the sexual harassment claim under Title IX, unlike that under Title VII of the Civil Rights Act of 1964,[22] has not been the subject of extensive common law interpretive argumentation.[23] The idea that sexual harassment was illegal sex discrimination in education went from being impossible before *Alexander* to being obvious after it with virtually no intermediate doctrinal steps — at least as to the most direct forms of harassment.[24] When the Supreme Court decided in 1992 that compensatory damages could be awarded under Title IX, it did so in a sexual harassment case brought by a high school student who alleged she had been subjected to coercive intercourse by a teacher, and that the school administration discouraged her complaints and ultimately took no action on them.[25] The Supreme Court devoted all of two sentences to the question of whether the behavior alleged was sex discrimination under Title IX. Relying on its 1986 decision in *Meritor Savings Bank, FSB v. Vinson*, 477 U.S. 57 (1986), the Court stated: "Unquestionably, Title IX placed on the Gwinnett County Public Schools the duty not to discriminate on the basis of sex, and 'when a supervisor sexually harasses a subordinate because of the subordinate's sex, that supervisor "discriminate[s]" on the basis of sex. . . .' We believe the same rule should apply when a teacher sexually harasses and abuses a student."[26]

Which leads to the final point: the biggest impact of *Alexander v. Yale University* was not in the development of legal doctrine in the courts, but the creation and institutionalization of grievance procedures for complaints of sexual harassment and other forms of discrimination in educational institutions. The impact of the legal principle was seen almost immediately in the explosion of sexual harassment policies and procedures. This, more than anything else, is what *Alexander* made happen. Within two years of the appellate decision, institutions of higher education as various as the University of Minnesota, Brown University, Tulane University, and the University of California at Santa Cruz had formal policies and procedures about sexual harassment.[27] Within five years, hundreds of colleges and universities had them.[28]

Sexual harassment in education was a widespread problem long before *Alexander*. Once we started work on the issue at Yale, we started hearing from faculty wives, administrators, women faculty members, graduate students, about the years of "gossip" and rumors and facts about sexual harassment. It was widely discussed — but not in public. It was as if women in higher education saw a solid wall when they looked for a way out of the sexual harassment dilemma. The feminist ferment of the 1970s suggested that there ought to be something that could be done about sexual harassment. Kitty's work identified where women might look for a handle. We looked, we found it, we pushed and kicked at it, and a door opened. As soon as it did, everyone looked at it and thought, "Oh, that's a door, not a wall," and began walking through it — as they have continued to do ever since.

Notes

1. At that time, we were Judith Berkan, Kent Harvey, Rosemary Johnson, Catharine MacKinnon, and Anne Simon. Phyllis Crocker and Charles Pillsbury came into the group later in the history of the case.

2. "No person in the United States shall, on the basis of sex, be excluded from participation in, be denied the benefits of, or be subjected to discrimination under any education program or activity receiving Federal financial assistance." Numerous exceptions follow. 20 U.S.C. § 1681(a) (1997). The statute has had an uneven history in the Supreme Court. In *Cannon v. University of Chicago*, 441 U.S. 677 (1979), the Court held that Title IX is enforceable through an implied private right of action. In *North Haven Board of Education v. Bell*, 456 U.S. 512 (1982), the Court held that Title IX covered employment discrimination in federally funded educational institutions. In *Grove City College v. Bell*, 465 U.S. 555 (1984), the Court narrowed the scope of Title IX's application so drastically that Congress overturned the decision in the Civil Rights Restoration Act of 1987, Pub. L. No. 100–259, 102 Stat. 28 (1988), codified with respect to Title IX at 20 U.S.C. § 1687–88. Returning to its less restrictive views, in *Franklin v. Gwinnett County Public Schools*, 503 U.S. 60 (1992), the Court recognized a right to compensatory damages for violations of Title IX. It remains to be seen whether the decisions in *Gebser v. Lago Vista Independent School District*, 524 U.S. 274 (1998), and *Davis v. Monroe County Board of Education*, 526 U.S. 629 (1999), inaugurated a move back toward restrictiveness.

3. *See* chapter 4 of Catharine A. MacKinnon, *Sexual Harassment of Working Women* (1979).

4. 45 C.F.R. § 86.8 (b) (1978). When the Department of Education was created in 1980, it took over and recodified various regulations of the former Department of Health, Education and Welfare. The grievance procedure regulation now appears at 34 C.F.R. § 106.8 (b) (1997).

5. 20 U.S.C. § 1682 (1997). The Department of Education has applied its regulations on funding termination under Title VI of the Civil Rights Act of 1964, found at 34 C.F.R. Parts 100–01, to Title IX. 34 C.F.R. § 106.71 (1997).

6. *Cannon v. University of Chicago*, 559 F.2d 1063 (7th Cir. 1977). This decision was reversed by the Supreme Court two years after we filed suit. *Cannon v. University of Chicago*, 441 U.S. 677 (1979).

7. The litigation began in 1970, as a suit against HEW for failing to cut off federal funds to racially segregated higher education systems. *Adams v. Richardson*, 356 F. Supp. 92 (D.D.C. 1973). Groups seeking more vigorous HEW enforcement of Title IX and of section 504 of the Rehabilitation Act of 1973, 29 U.S.C. § 794 (1997), later joined the case. A consent decree was entered at the end of 1977. The case ended with the decision in *Women's Equity Action League v. Cavazos*, 906 F.2d 742 (D.C. Cir. 1990).

8. This effort, somewhat revised, eventually made its way back into the book, as "Appendix B: *A Brief.*"

9. *Alexander v. Yale University*, 459 F. Supp. 1, 5 (D. Conn. 1977).

10. *Alexander*, 459 F. Supp. at 3.

11. Compare *Alexander*, 459 F. Supp. at 3 with *Alexander*, 459 F. Supp. at 6.

12. *Alexander*, 459 F. Supp. at 4.

13. *Patricia H. v. Berkeley Unified School District*, 830 F. Supp. 1288 (N.D. Calif. 1993). Some of the cases making hostile environment claims under Title IX are collected in *Brzonkala v. Virginia Polytechnic Institute and State University*, 132 F.3d 949, 958–59 (4th Cir. 1997), *affirmed by U.S. v. Morrison*, 529 U.S. 598 (2000).

14. For a discussion of sexual harassment specifically in higher education, *see* Phyllis L. Crocker and Anne E. Simon, "Sexual Harassment in Education," 10 *Capital University Law Review* 541 (1981).

15. 34 C.F.R. § 106.8(b) (1997) (emphasis added). The U.S. Department of Education thinks this means what it says: "regardless of whether harassment occurred, a school violates this requirement of the Title IX regulations if it does not have those procedures and policies in place." U.S. Department of Education, Office for Civil Rights, "Revised Sexual Harassment Guidance: Harassment of Students by School Employees, Other Students, or Third Parties" (Jan. 2001), p. 19.

16. The appeal was argued by Nadine Taub, Women's Rights Litigation Clinic, Rutgers — Newark School of Law, as a cooperating attorney for the Center for Constitutional Rights.

17. *Alexander v. Yale University*, 631 F.2d 178, 184 (2d Cir. 1980).

18. *Alexander*, 631 F.2d at 184. *See Cohen v. Brown University*, 101 F.3d 155 (1st Cir. 1996), *cert. denied*, 520 U.S. 1186 (1997); *Haffer v. Temple University*, 678 F. Supp. 517 (E.D. Pa. 1987).

19. *Alexander*, 631 F.2d at 184.

20. Undergraduate: *Bougher v. University of Pittsburgh*, 713 F. Supp. 139 (W.D. Pa. 1989). High school: *Patricia H. v. Berkeley Unified School District*, 830 F. Supp. 1288 (N.D. Cal. 1993). Junior high school: *Doe v. Petaluma City School District*, 54 F.3d 1447 (9th Cir. 1995). Elementary school: *Canutillo Independent School District v. Leija*, 101 F.3d 393 (5th Cir. 1996); Does: *1, 2, 3, and 4 v. Covington County School Board*, 969 F. Supp. 1264 (M.D. Ala. 1997); *Davis v. Monroe County Board of Education*, 120 F.3d 1390 (11th Cir. 1997), *reversed*, 526 U.S. 629 (1999). Graduate and professional schools: *Micari v. Mann*, 481 N.Y.S.2d 967 (Sup. Ct. 1984); *Moire v. Temple University School of Medicine*, 613 F. Supp. 1360 (E.D. Pa. 1985); *Lipsett v. University of Puerto Rico*, 864 F.2d 881 (1st Cir. 1988); *Bilut v. Northwestern University*, 645 N.E.2d 536 (Ill. App. Ct. 1994). Junior faculty: *State University of New York at Albany v. State Human Rights Appeal Board*, 438 N.Y.S.2d 643 (App. Div. 1981).

21. See the observations of Louise Fitzgerald about the further damage plaintiffs can suffer from litigation, and the comments of Pamela Price about the costs of litigation and the scarcity of lawyers willing to represent plaintiffs, in this volume.

22. 42 U.S.C. § 2000e *et seq.* (1997).

23. *See, e.g., Oncale v. Sundowner Offshore Services, Inc.*, 523 U.S. 75 (1998) (same-sex harassment); *Faragher v. City of Boca Raton*, 524 U.S. 775 (1998) (employer liability standards); *Burlington Industries, Inc. v. Ellerth*, 524 U.S. 742 (1998) (nature of discriminatory injury).

24. As Pamela Price points out in this volume, this has sometimes made it difficult for lawyers to find cases to cite when they are presenting new sexual harassment claims in the education context.

25. *Franklin v. Gwinnett County Public Schools*, 503 U.S. 60 (1992).

26. *Franklin*, 503 U.S. at 75.

27. These early efforts are collected and evaluated in Phyllis L. Crocker, "Analysis of University Definitions of Sexual Harassment," 8 *Signs: Journal of Women in Culture and Society* 696 (1983).

28. Louise F. Fitzgerald, "Institutional Policies and Procedures," in Bernice Lott and Mary Ellen Reilly, eds., *Combatting Sexual Harassment in Higher Education* (1996), p. 130 (citing Claire Robertson, Constance E. Dyer, and D'Ann Campbell, "Campus Harassment: Sexual Harassment Policies and Procedures at Institutions of Higher Learning," 13 *Signs: Journal of Women in Culture and Society* 792 [1988]).

4

Eradicating Sexual Harassment in Education

PAMELA Y. PRICE

In the new millennium, where do we take the struggle for equality and the right to exist without sexual harassment? The front lines continue to be as vivid and significant in education as in the workplace. The controversies that surround the development of the law and its efficacy are nowhere more vibrant and thought-provoking than in the context of education. Questions that arise in the context of sexual harassment in employment — questions about definitions, prohibitions, personal liability, and personal relationships — are also the subject of concern in education and carry the added angst of judgments and attitudes about youth and sexuality.

The question of accountability these issues raise touches upon our basic notions of the purpose and role of education in our society. It also raises issues such as whether "good intentions" really matter in the interpretation and enforcement of the law, what remedy the law provides for victims of sexual harassment in education, and whether the standards developed under Title VII work for victims under Title IX. These remarks will address how far we have come since 1977 in holding anyone accountable from a historical perspective, and whether we should insist that the law of sexual harassment is developed until it absolutely *does* work.

The Personal Herstory

In the spring of 1976, I was nineteen and naive when a Yale professor offered to give me an A in his course if I would "make love" to him and implied that my refusal would result in a C.[1] In 1977, I joined the landmark lawsuit *Alexander v. Yale*.[2] Our goal was to require Yale to establish a Title IX[3] grievance procedure to redress complaints of sexual harassment. Since that time, I've been, in essence, "living my making."

I graduated from U.C. Berkeley School of Law (Boalt Hall) in 1982, and have been practicing law in California since 1983. In 1993, sixteen years post-*Alexander*, I argued *Patricia H. v. Berkeley Unified School District*[4] in the United States District Court for the Northern District of California. The case established that a hostile environment created by the abuse of sexual power violates Title IX.[5] This decision was the first time that a court accepted and applied Title IX's prohibition against sex discrimination to the "hostile environment" type of sexual harassment. I relied on *Alexander* and the experience of that litigation. I found it incredible, disturbing, and quite sobering that there simply wasn't much other authority in the law.

My husband, Vernon Crawley, and I have also developed a course on sexual harassment and liability prevention for educators, managers, and employees. What I have found in my law practice and in our teaching is that many school districts still don't have Title IX officers, don't have grievance procedures, and some don't even know what Title IX is. With so little knowledge and no experience in enforcing the law, *it is still 1977 in most parts of America*.

The Assault on the Law

In early 1998, one commentator announced that the law of sexual harassment is "mired in muck."[6] In my view, that's the kind of propaganda you hear when they want to get rid of the law, and it clearly presaged the death of Title IX. In June 1998, the United States Supreme Court, in an opinion by Justice O'Connor, dealt a mortal blow to Title IX in *Gebser v. Lago Vista Independent School District*,[7] by redefining the cause of action for sexual harassment and decimating twenty years of jurisprudence. The Court continued this evisceration of the law less than a year later in *Davis v. Monroe County Board of Education*.[8]

Gebser held that a damages remedy "will not lie under Title IX unless an official who at a minimum has authority to address the alleged discrimination and to institute corrective measures on the recipient's behalf has actual knowledge of the discrimination."[9] The Court suggested that the "basic objective" of

Title IX's enforcement scheme is to "avoid diverting education funding from beneficial uses where a recipient was unaware of discrimination in its programs and is willing to institute prompt corrective measures."[10]

Justice Stevens correctly pointed out in his dissent that, as a matter of policy, the Court ranked protection of the school district's purse above the protection of the potential victims for whose special benefit Congress enacted Title IX.[11] Moreover, the majority's analysis is repeatedly inconsistent and confusing. While the Court referred to the "deliberate indifference" standard defined in 42 U.S.C. § 1983 jurisprudence as a "rough parallel"[12] to the deliberate indifference showing required for Title IX liability, it actually did not adopt § 1983 jurisprudence nor explain in any real detail the particulars of Title IX's new brand of "deliberate indifference."

While the Court avoided the "deliberate indifference" issue in *Gebser*, it came back and dealt a second deadly blow to Title IX in *Davis*. There, the Court fashioned its own unique deliberate indifference standard, requiring the plaintiff to prove that the harassment has "the systemic effect of denying [her] equal access to an educational program or activity,"[13] and that the defendant's response to the harassment was "clearly unreasonable"[14] in light of the known circumstances. The Court concluded that the District's conduct must, at a minimum, cause students to undergo the sexual harassment or make them liable or vulnerable to it.

A major argument for why the law of sexual harassment won't work in education is that issues of sexuality can't be regulated (similar to the debate in employment) or that adolescent behavior is too unpredictable to be legally controlled. That argument sounds like "boys will be boys" or "it's much too difficult to resolve these issues so let's just do nothing." In fact, let's just go back to the way things were—things were so much easier then. The real question is for whom? The concern appears to be that, if we intercede in the developing sexual identities of adolescents, or unduly interfere in their sexual behavior, we will somehow warp their notions of sexuality. This concern is writ large in discussions of the application of the law of sexual harassment in education, but appears completely muted when discussing issues of teen pregnancy, date rape, and related problems, where the law intervenes aggressively. Surely, victims of sexual harassment should be entitled to the same legal protections albeit in the context of civil justice.

What is the purpose and role of education? It is to impart knowledge (enlightenment) and socialize individuals (how to get along with others in the society). What better place to teach our children how to respect each other than in school? What better thing to teach our children than that the victimization of women is not appropriate behavior?

Why We Can't Quit: Things Are Gonna Change

As Title IX has been effectively neutralized, the victims whom it was intended to protect are being victimized a second time by the judicial system.[15] In the wake of *Gebser*, I lost two Title IX cases in short order.[16] As a matter of course, the sexual harassment plaintiff can expect to be maligned, defamed, invaded, and harassed. In *Nicole M.*, the fourteen-year-old victim, who fled her junior high school where peer-to-peer sexual harassment was absolutely rampant, was repeatedly told that she was the only one who complained and who "couldn't handle it."[17]

In *Catherine M.*, the questioning of the two plaintiffs by defense counsel was so hostile, heartless, and relentless that one of the plaintiffs suffered recurring nightmares that included the rape of one of the defense counsel (a female attorney). This harsh and demeaning treatment occurred in a case in which the District itself concluded that its co-defendant, a community college professor, had an extensive and well-known history of sexual harassment of his female students. Indeed, it had fired him based upon the plaintiffs' allegations.

As a matter of practice, I warn potential plaintiffs that their privacy and reputation cannot be protected or preserved. One client's childhood sexual assault by a family member became the subject of discovery in her mother's deposition; this is a relatively routine experience. In *Catherine M.*, defense counsel subpoenaed every possible medical record of the plaintiffs, persisting even after a court order restricting discovery was issued.

We still fall short in providing a reasonable remedy, particularly given the time that these cases can take. In 1977, even if we had won at trial, there would have been no effective remedy for me for "quid pro quo" sexual harassment; by the time the court would have gotten around to "fixing" my college grade, I had graduated from law school. In 1998, I was still representing Nicole M. as she graduated from high school in a case filed in 1993.[18] The *Catherine M.* case was commenced in 1994 and finally resolved with a settlement with the defendant professor in 1999. In the meantime, both plaintiffs had fled the community college and abandoned their education.

Should the educational institution's "good intentions" matter in the interpretation and enforcement of the law? The answer is a resounding no. The procedures and protection mandated by Title IX offer specific protections to victims and could deter others from violating it. Experience has shown that one danger of accepting "good intentions" in lieu of compliance is that the victim too easily becomes the thing that needs to be fixed.

Should educators and administrators be held accountable for sexual harassment in the schools? The answer must unequivocally be yes. Unless and until individual school administrators are held *personally* liable for either failing or refusing to do their job, nothing will change.[19] In the real world, without personal liability for those responsible and in control of the institutional response, sexual harassment in education will remain an injury without a remedy.

One of the more disturbing trends in the backlash against the eradication of sexual harassment is the denigration of lawyers who prosecute these cases. You hear terms like "windfall for lawyers" or "bonanza for lawyers." There is no windfall or bonanza. This work is hard and demanding and *often* sacrificial. The victims are branded as troublemakers and pariahs; it is thus not surprising that their lawyers are vilified. In the real world, equal access to justice for most victims of civil rights violations is an insidious myth. The sexual harassment plaintiff is no exception to the rule. The costs to prepare and try a case are absolutely exorbitant. Most individual plaintiffs simply cannot afford to pay the price to protect or vindicate their rights.

Furthermore, there are only a few brave attorneys who dare to take these cases and fewer still who can afford to finance them to achieve a fair result for the plaintiff. After only ten years in private practice, my firm regularly has a waiting list of fifty people seeking representation; that number has soared as high as one hundred and twenty. One client contacted as many as fifty attorneys over a period of six months before he found us. Two years later, following a three-week trial, a San Francisco federal jury awarded him more than $501,000 as compensation for racial and religious discrimination.[20]

In May 1993, Maria Blanco, then an attorney with Equal Rights Advocates in San Francisco, remarked that "the trump card in this society is the lawyer." For the sexual harassment plaintiff, the lawyer qua "trump card" is what makes people accountable. That is what made the difference in 1977 and it continues to make the difference today. In 1977, Ann Olivarius and Ronni Alexander had no one to turn to. Their trump cards were Catharine MacKinnon, Kent Harvey and Anne E. Simon. In due time, they became mine. Today, I'm proud to be the trump card for my clients, who often tell me that they appreciate what we're doing and wish there were more like us. We desperately need more lawyers willing to take the risks, who understand what it takes to win a case and are committed to eradicating sexual harassment.

Melba Beals, one of the Little Rock Nine, tells the story that, when Thurgood Marshall came to Little Rock, he told the children and parents seeking to integrate Central High School that "things are gonna change."[21] According to Ms. Beals, lawyers were the heroes of the civil rights movement in the integration of the schools. For female students in America, things were changing for the better before *Gebser* and *Davis*. The spate of sexual harassment lawsuits in education between 1992 and the Supreme Court's devastating handiwork in

1998 and 1999 — including *Patricia H.*,[22] *Doe v. Petaluma*,[23] *Nicole M.*,[24] and *Nabozny v. Podlesny*[25] make it clear that things have changed and eventually again are "gonna change." During that brief time, we advanced from the quid pro quo concept to defining and beginning to address peer-to-peer hostile environment sexual harassment. The judicial backlash against Title IX reflects in no small measure the breadth and scope of our progress.

So don't be discouraged by those who say the law of sexual harassment doesn't work. Dr. King told his followers that justice doesn't take long "because truth crushed to the earth will rise again."[26] He said it won't take long "because the arc of the moral universe is long, but it bends toward justice."[27] Most people don't understand how difficult it is to accomplish change through the judicial system. For every case you win, there are ten other good ones that are lost. Most, if not all, of the time, the companies, institutions, and lawyers who defend these cases are better financed, better staffed, and in better control of all of the witnesses to the events.[28] So don't blame the law itself; blame the odds.

Lawyers and legal scholars alike, in the path created by Catharine MacKinnon and in her image, have the opportunity to become heroes and sheroes in the eradication of sexual harassment. In the process of fulfilling the legacy created by MacKinnon, Simon, and Harvey, you undoubtedly will be fulfilled yourself.

Notes

1. Following a trial in the winter of 1979, Judge Ellen Bree Burns decided that I had not proven that Professor Raymond Duvall propositioned me on that fateful day in his office in 1976. *Alexander v. Yale*, 631 F.3d 178, 183 (2d Cir. 1980).

2. 459 F. Supp. 1 (D. Conn. 1977), *affirmed* 631 F.2d 178 (2nd Cir. 1980).

3. 20 U.S.C. § 1681 (2001).

4. 830 F. Supp. 1288 (N.D. Cal. 1993).

5. The abusive conduct in *Patricia H.* was the repeated sexual molestation of two young sisters by Berkeley High School teacher Charles Hamilton.

6. Tom Brokaw, February 1998.

7. 524 U.S. 274 (1998).

8. 526 U.S. 629 (1999).

9. *Gebser*, 524 U.S. at 290.

10. *Id.* at 289.

11. *Id.* at 306.

12. *Id.* at 290.

13. *Davis*, 526 U.S. at 652.

14. *Id.* at 649.

15. Another very disturbing consequence of the dismantling of Title IX is the impact of the Court's decision on Title VI as an antidote for racial discrimination. The similarities

between Title VI and Title IX are clear and time honored; hence, it appears that a funeral for Title VI as well may be in order. *See Cannon v. University of Chicago*, 441 U.S. 677, 694 n.16 (1979) ("This is identical language, specifically taken from title [*sic*] VI of the 1964 Civil Rights Act") (citing statement of Sen. Bayh); *Franklin v. Gwinnett County Public Schools*, 503 U.S. 60 (1992); *Gebser*, 524 U.S. at 286.

16. *Nicole M. v. Martinez Unified School District*, 964 F. Supp. 1369 (N.D. Cal. 1997), a peer-to-peer sexual harassment case, went to trial in September 1998; under the weight of jury instructions based on *Gebser*, the jury exonerated the district and all of its officials. *Catherine M. v. San Francisco Community College District* was on appeal when *Gebser* was decided; on August 27, 1998, in an unpublished decision, the California Court of Appeal, citing *Gebser*, affirmed the grant of summary judgment on totally unrelated grounds by the lower court. *Catherine M.*, Nos. A078308 and A079443 (Cal. Ct. App. Aug. 27, 1998).

17. *Nicole M.*, 964 F. Supp. 1369.

18. *Id.*

19. The possibility of suit against individual school officials appears to remain a viable option after *Gebser* in light of the Court's statement that "[o]ur decision does not affect any right of recovery that an individual may have against a school district as a matter of state law or against the teacher [Waldrop] in his individual capacity under state law or under 42 U.S.C. § 1983." *Gebser*, 524 U.S. at 292.

20. *Reissner v. California Department of Corrections*, No. C96–2508 (N.D. Cal. Dec. 19, 1997). Claude Reissner was a Jewish nurse working at Pelican Bay State Prison when he became the focus of racial slurs and anti-Semitism because he treated the African-American inmates with basic human respect. He left Pelican Bay when one of the racist officers who had targeted him spat on him in full view of the inmates as he was leaving an exercise yard.

21. Melba Beals, *Warriors Don't Cry* (1994).

22. 830 F. Supp. 1288 (N.D. Cal. 1993).

23. 54 F.3d 1447 (9th Cir. 1995).

24. 964 F. Supp. 1369.

25. 92 F.3d 446 (7th Cir. 1996).

26. Martin Luther King, Jr., *Our God Is Marching On!* (March 25, 1965), *http://www.mlkonline.com*.

27. *Id.*

28. In defending *Alexander v. Yale* through trial, Yale had all of these advantages: more money, more staff, more experienced defense counsel, and control of most of the witnesses. Additionally, the trial judge was a Yale graduate. Ultimately, we lost the case for a whole lot of reasons that had nothing to do with the truth. The miracle was that Anne Simon, Kent Harvey, and Catharine MacKinnon even got the case to trial. And, in the process, we established that sexual harassment violates Title IX.

5

The Ecology of Justice
The Relationship Between Feminism
and Critical Race Theory

GERALD TORRES

For this symposium I had wanted to provide a detailed account of the many ways in which the book *Sexual Harassment of Working Women*[1] had changed the legal and social landscape. I especially had wanted to illustrate the deep connections between the feminist and structural analysis of the book and the critical race theory movement. That detailed study will have to wait. Instead I want to offer a more personal account. Like many who spoke at this gathering, I feel as though I was present at the creation. Catharine MacKinnon and I were in law school together and the ideas that ultimately took shape in the book were also part of our many deep conversations. Those discussions, as well as the book itself, had a profound impact on my own thinking and activism.

The book is rooted in the lives of women and in the social life that we all are part of constructing. Legal expertise may have been required to make the arguments at the core of the book, but its reality and texture emerged from the act of translating the lived experience of working women into a form legal experts could comprehend. This approach marked the book as a work of feminist theory, but also fundamentally as a work of critical theory. MacKinnon advanced a methodology that rested on the assumption that women would determine and express their own interests. She argued that the act of doing so is self-enabling in that it frees women from specific forms of naturalized social coercion. Importantly, MacKinnon also described the cognitive content of this methodology. The critical epistemology at the heart of the translative function of the book was an attack on the "ways of knowing" that were accepted indiscriminately in conventional legal discourse.

The use of critical reflection was essential to the legal method MacKinnon employed. Her legal theory began with a clear understanding of the historical specificity of our cultural practices. This effort aimed at bringing the practices of the legal discipline and the discourse of law into opposition with the forms of cultural and legal domination that feminist theory had identified.

In light of MacKinnon's important contributions to critical theory, it seems appropriate to link feminism with another critical legal discourse, critical race theory, and ask how these two approaches have helped change our understanding of the contours of equality in the law. Both critical race theory and feminist legal theory focus on the question of equality, especially the social basis of inequality and the law's role in perpetuating or reducing that inequality. Their focus highlights the disjunction between continuing social inequality and the triumph of formal legal equality, which took issues of continuing material inequality off the table. Critical race theory and feminist theory suggest that the social consequences of this victory are clear when we examine how formal equality theory and theorists converted notions of social equality to notions of legal equality. The consequence of that process is that it substitutes an individualized diagnosis and remedy for structural collective problems. The problem of gender or racial inequality is located not in the bad hearts of individual people, but in the ways in which observable inequality has been naturalized into the normal workings of social institutions. For example, Lani Guinier and I have defined racism "as acquiescence in and accommodation to racialized hierarchies governing resource distribution and resource generation. Racism treats the inequitable distribution, generation, and transfer of resources as normal, natural, and fair."[2]

One of the goals of critical theory was to put issues of material inequality back on the table. The first step in this critical inquiry was to challenge the essential absence of perspective from which questions about equality were commonly asked. Both MacKinnon's critical theory and critical race theory noted that, by changing the perspective from which the question is asked, or the social phenomenon is observed, a couple of things happen. Within the domain of law, you ask, "What is the meaning of equality?" You are also obliged to ask, "What is the idea of justice that grounds the inquiry into equality?" In fact, both MacKinnon's critical feminist theory and critical race theory require that you link conceptions of equality to conceptions of justice. Ideas of justice in this inquiry are informed by commitments to equality as a concrete social event, a social moment, rather than to formal, abstract ideas about what equality means. Formal equality built on a base of structural inequality condemns legal equality to the role of guardian of privilege.

The extent of the victory of the doctrine of formal equality—and Reva Siegel's point on this is quite sound[3]—has meant the elimination from the repertoire of necessary tasks the inquiry into the social basis of inequality merits. For purposes of assessing the justice of a particular state of affairs, the required inquiry has been reduced to the question of whether two abstractly constructed legal persons are sufficiently similarly situated to even warrant an exploration of the complained-of inequality. If, in fact, that is the legal definition of inequality, then the very idea that law itself can function as the vehicle for justice is implicated and has to be criticized. Understanding the linkage between equality and justice and the continued forms of racialized and gendered justice forces you to understand the formidable tension in the idea that law itself is a vehicle for justice.

Yoking equality to justice compels you to understand the way in which the pressure of doctrine reduces legal claims for relief to abstractions. Formal neutrality, said to stand for the highest articulation of justice, merely reinforces the social reality of inequality. So, faith in law creates a double bind. To pursue issues of justice and equality as though they are merely questions of doctrine creates a psychological trap—and a real political trap as well.

Critical race theory suggests that an ecological model of justice is necessarily required for grasping the relationships between all of the elements we claim to be the component parts of justice. Equality is the central and most important element, but it is not the only one. When the focus is exclusively on equality—especially equality as the law has understood it—as the sole proxy for justice, even the understanding of equality itself becomes anemic. Legal examination of the issues is reduced to abstracting individual claims of equality from their social context.

Feminist theory, especially MacKinnon's feminist theory, points out very clearly how current notions of formal equality transform our understanding of systemic injustice into an isolated, acontextual case of individual prejudice or discrimination. The formalized notion of equality that has emerged doctrinally eliminates the possibility of understanding discrimination, whether it is gender discrimination or racial discrimination, as the mere precipitate of the working out of normalized institutional practices. What *Sexual Harassment of Working Women* did was to expose and reveal those processes.[4]

Methodologically, feminism started with consciousness-raising. Critical race theory adopted this methodology and turned to story telling. Story telling refocuses on the lived experience of the subject. It accomplishes this not in opposition to individuals, but rather by situating individual instances of injustice in a larger social context and bringing disparate narrative objects into conjunction to highlight this context. Story telling reestablishes the linkage between individuals and their environment.[5]

Let me tell one story. In Texas, we are subject to the *Hopwood* decision.[6] *Hopwood* and the state attorney general's interpretation of it outlaw all forms of race-conscious affirmative action in higher education in Texas. The expected result was a serious reduction in the number of African-Americans and Mexican-Americans matriculating at the elite public universities. A remarkably large cross section of Texans recognized that the long-term political stability and economic health of the state rested on continued access to the institutions of social mobility, especially the University of Texas.

Without the conventional tools of affirmative action to manage racial inequality, a group of people devised an alternative plan. It would be based strictly on merit and reward for conventional values of grit and hard work. Under the leadership of a coalition of Mexican-American and rural white legislators, the state made all high school graduates in the top 10 percent of their class automatically eligible for admission to the University of Texas. The social reality of residential segregation in Texas means that there are more African-Americans and Mexican-Americans students eligible for enrollment at the University of Texas than were eligible for enrollment under affirmative action. That fact alone raises the question: what was affirmative action for, anyway?

Of course, the fact that more students of color would be eligible for admission does not explain why conservative rural white politicians supported the plan. The key to their support lay in their realization that students from poorer rural school districts were also systematically disadvantaged. A white student from rural west Texas was likely to be in the same boat as a Mexican-American student from the Rio Grande valley. Advocates for the plan pointed out that traditional important values like hard work were being undermined by over-reliance on statistical predictors like standardized admissions tests. Moreover, advocates noted that success on these standardized tests was tied more closely to parental income and family wealth than to whether the graduating senior would make good use of state-supported higher education. As one populist supporter of the plan put it: "No one from Princeton, New Jersey ought to be deciding whether a hardworking kid from Levelland can go to college."[7]

The plan was not without its critics. They pointed out that the uniform admission standard means that some kids who finished, say, in the top 15 percent of a very good high school are denied automatic admission, whereas someone who graduated in the top 10 percent of a bad high school gets in.

How, the question was asked, is this fair? It became suddenly apparent to those who could ignore it before that there is a social dimension to the sameness theory of equality. Here it cuts a little differently. Perhaps these kids are not similarly situated. Maybe when you start talking about equality, you actually have to look at the real social context of the people to whom you are applying notions of sameness.

The idea that there is a social dimension to the sameness theory caused people to focus on the "real" meaning of equality within the context of public education. People then also had to ask, "how is it that someone who graduates in the top of their class from a high school in Texas is incapable of doing college level work?" This inquiry triggered a debate about what it means to prepare high school students to enter college and the workforce. The debates about quality began at a different point from the past. The budget is not the starting point, as it was before, since dollars spent is no longer the measure of quality. Performance is. The quality of public education, while tied importantly to a willingness to spend money on schools, is more closely linked to the capacity of the schools to prepare students for post-secondary education or employment. In Texas, schools are constitutionally obligated to provide equal or efficient education. Now that there is a specific way that obligation can be measured other than in dollars, people start to ask about curriculum. Why, for example, are there fewer advanced placement courses at some high schools that happen to be all black or all brown?

The old answer was that fewer students at those schools could take advantage of them. What the new law throws into relief is how advanced placement courses are a continuing subsidy to people who are already well off. They have operated historically as a form of advanced financial aid not quantified on the basis of need. For example, if, as a result of access to advanced placement courses in high school, a student enters college as a sophomore, his or her family saves a year's tuition. If the policy goal is to equalize education without spending more money, the conjunction of curricular reform with subsidy is one place to start. The Texas 10-percent plan illustrates the connection between equality and justice by connecting social facts with legal ones and by allowing the privileged to see the connection.

What the debate about the 10-percent plan revealed is that an exclusive focus on race obscured class injustice. This story tells us that an exclusive focus on congealed status obscured the content of the social roles people play. Additionally, it highlights the fact that each of us occupies many roles and that they are connected to and replicate the structure of the culture within which we are embedded. In this sense, legal challenges can be understood as cultural challenges: law is one tool to contest cultural values and to force them into the debates over economics and politics. The dominant legal discourse struggles to maintain a deculturized discursive framework. Applying an ecological model requires that the limitations of such a deculturized framework be revealed as limitations on understanding.

To limit the field of understanding is to risk the legitimacy of the discourse itself. The challenge to the formalized conception of both equality and justice is also, then, a challenge to the legitimizing norms of legal discourse. To be legitimate, an institution must reflect a generally accepted system of norms. Conventional legal discourse assumes that the system of norms that it represents is capable of conferring legitimacy because it stands in the right relation to the basic world-picture of the society that it regulates. The challenge critical feminism and critical race theory have posed is contained in the question "generally accepted by whom?" This challenge to the conventional picture is a basic challenge to the legitimacy of the enterprise. The way in which legitimacy is retained is not through suppression of the challenge, but through engagement with it. It also requires, disturbingly for many, opposition to the extant distribution of power.

Feminist legal theory is related to critical race theory in other ways, of which I want to suggest, but again not develop, one more. One largely overlooked focus of these critical theories has been the question of property. Property was, in many ways, the central organizing doctrine during the formative period of our legal culture, raising the question of the extent to which conceptions of property affect the doctrinal evolution of other areas of the law. Marriage, after all, began as a property relationship. The marital rape exception and the idea of common law marriage take on a different valence when conceived as extensions of that basic property relationship. Is the marital rape exception a form of property reasoning extended to another domain of social relations? What is the legal history of the commodification of women's sexuality in relation to men? Are its historical antecedents to be found as deeply rooted in property doctrine as anywhere else?

Consider, also, the significance of property doctrine to race. The history of race in this country is in important ways the history of how a people emerged from a property relationship into a relationship of personhood and humanity. Every constraint, every drag, every bit of friction can be found as much in the antecedents of that relationship as in the associational desire to be with those like ourselves. That women emerged from a property status much earlier than African-Americans should not obscure this historical doctrinal linkage. Feminist and critical race theories converge at the point of such linkages.

One of the most important sentences in *Sexual Harassment of Working Women* is the very first one. What has happened in the years since its publication is the gradual disproving of that sentence: "The intimate violation of women by men is sufficiently pervasive in American society as to be nearly invisible."[8] That insight announced the project: "Let's make it visible." That was a *critical* project and — I want to be very clear about this — it was not a therapeutic version of law reform. MacKinnon was not asserting that bringing sexual harassment to consciousness was sufficient. The purpose was, and is, to change social reality, not to make people feel better. She was saying, "Let's make it visible," meaning, "let's make it political," which is why I originally thought I would entitle this essay: "The Personal Is Not Political Enough." The challenge to men, which is like the challenge to white people, is that you can learn something about the way a society is constructed by viewing the world through the lens of gender or the lens of race. By being feminists, men can learn something about their world that they could not learn otherwise, things that, MacKinnon argues, in critical ways, they cannot see. However, the upshot of those insights is not, "once blind, now I see." Instead, our practice must be aimed at making visible what these insights expose — the nexus of equality and justice, perspective and norms, social roles and legal protection — and at enabling people to make the political rather than the therapeutic response.

Notes

1. Catharine A. MacKinnon, *Sexual Harassment of Working Women: A Case of Sex Discrimination* (1979).

2. Lani Guinier and Gerald Torres, *The Miner's Canary: Enlisting Race, Resisting Power, Transforming Democracy* 292 (2002) (internal footnotes omitted).

3. *See* Reva Siegel, "Why Equal Protection No Longer Protects: The Evolving Forms of Status-Enforcing State Action," 49 *Stanford Law Review* 1111 (1997).

4. That, of course, is what has caused many people to turn away. If the normalized working out of relations between the sexes both produces and is premised on inequality, then without a critical theoretical approach it is impossible to conceive of what equality might look like. As the blindness is made more evident, you are forced to concede that you cannot see as far as you imagined that you could.

5. In this way, it is consistent with my theme of an ecology of justice.

6. 78 F.3d 932 (5th Cir. 1996).

7. *See* William E. Forbath and Gerald Torres, "Merit and Diversity After Hopwood," 10 *Stanford Law and Policy Review* 185 (1999).

8. MacKinnon, *supra* note 1, at 1.

PART **II**

Unwelcomeness

6

Consensual Sex and the Limits of Harassment Law

CAROL SANGER

An enormous achievement of the campaign against the harassment of working women has been to establish a set of facts about sex at work that had previously been denied, mocked, and misunderstood. As a result of Catharine MacKinnon's early theorizing, brave public story-telling by Anita Hill and others, and concerted, ongoing litigation by many, it is now understood that sex can be unwelcome, that unwelcome overtures are neither harmless nor fun, and that consent to sex demanded on the job does not shift the behavior from the category of unwanted sex to the category of the welcome.

At the same time, one of the most ferocious complaints against the establishment of sexual harassment as a legal wrong — a complaint hurled with particular zest against "feminists" — is that now everything is spoiled. "Everything" usually refers to relationships at work or in the academy, and "spoiled" has often meant little more than the very accomplishments celebrated above — legal recognition that sex can be unwelcome and that unwelcome sexual advances may harm women and constitute harassment.

Recently, however, new and more sophisticated critiques of harassment law have made their way into the debate. Unlike earlier opposition, the newer critiques do not deny the *existence* of harassing behavior but focus instead on its scope and particularly its relation to sexual activity. One concern, articulated by Vicki Schultz, is that the early focus on sexualized harassment ("the prevailing sexual desire-dominance paradigm") may now divert attention from unwelcome but nonsexualized forms of discrimination faced by women workers.[1] A second complaint also takes aim at the law's focus on sexual relations but, in contrast to the concern about nonsexual harassment, it directs attention at behavior that is explicitly and, it would seem, *agreeably* sexual. It is this second issue, the place of consensual sexual relations in the larger scheme of workplace regulation, that is my topic here. Can such relationships constitute harassment or is there a limit to law's domain over this category of personal interaction? In thinking through these questions, I focus particularly on consensual (or amorous, as they are sometimes called) relations within the academy, acknowledging that most of the case law comes from the commercial workplace. Even if not the only locus of this problem, the academy is a particularly interesting one, because of the diversity and context of the power issues that it raises: not just power between supervisors and subordinate employees; but power among professionals in a loosely structured hierarchy (tenured versus untenured, famous versus nonfamous, and so on) and, most acutely, power between teacher and student.

Certainly the existence of consensual relations between workers with some power and workers with less has increased in recent years. Institutions, whether schools or workplaces, that were once the bastion of one or the other sex — secretarial pools, the trades, the Ivy League — are now open to both men and women. And indeed many professors have chosen the pleasure of reading (and shopping), trying out ideas (and doing the dishes), editing (and climbing into bed) with another academic. There is also a more energized, nonacademic model of attraction: "A lot of work today is like the movie 'Speed': a man and a woman in a high-pressure situation where they have to solve a problem together. So it's no surprise they become romantically involved."[2] So, while falling in love with someone you know from nine to five may not be inevitable, it happens often enough to attract attention and provoke concern.

The concern derives not just from the new demographics but from new sensibilities. All the players in these situations — professors and students, employers and employees, supervisors and subordinates of all sorts — are adjusting to a new and still developing institutional ethic regarding gender relations. Indeed, there is now an entire phalanx of human relations officers whose very job it is to figure out and guide internal policies on exactly what kind of behavior is harassing and what appropriate individual and institutional responses should look like. But while there is still much to work out about sex-based behavior as a matter of law and as a matter of workplace norms, many now argue that *consensual* relations are a no-brainer. By definition, they say, relationships that are welcome cannot constitute harassment: consent negates the unwelcomeness requirement. On this account, consensual sex simply falls outside the proper scope of harassment law and policies. The view is something of a corollary to modern law's general disinterest in affairs of the heart. Over the last century, a variety of once robust causes of action that sought to remedy romantic wrongdoing fell into disuse and disapproval. In consequence of "anti-heartbalm statutes," wounded parties could no longer find legal comfort for alienation of affection or breach of the promise to marry, as those actions were removed from the books. The nonregulation of consensual relations, it might be argued, sensibly follows this trend, as falling within neither the letter nor the spirit of the law.

Others tell a more complicated story about the nature of superior-subordinate sex and about the fit between consensual relations and law. They argue that consent between people of differing power within the same institution is only an illusion: no one in the weaker position ever *really* consents freely. There are two common explanations for this. The first is the "Kissinger as conqueror" phenomenon: in Henry's phrase, power is the great aphrodisiac. (Though it may work both ways. As Jean Baudrillard remarked, from the perspective of power, "[t]here is no aphrodisiac like innocence.")[3] On this account, the student succumbs dreamily to her professor; the secretary, trancelike, to her boss; while legislative aides and interns swoon or whatever at the feet of elected officials. In each of these cases, the underling consents, but her consent is somehow disconnected from will. Casting bosses as Svengalis may overstate the view, but a slightly less mystical look at student-professor relationships, to focus on the academic example, captures the gist of the dynamic. Few dispute that the appeal of the professor has something to do with power; ask any participant-observer (we all know someone). There is the professor's institutional authority, his charismatic command of the class, his intellectual grasp of subject. (Not to mention the age difference, the tie, and the phenomenon of transference.)[4] There is also, for many women students, the added draw of the long-awaited, seemingly genuine interest in the student's *mind:* "Those of us who fell for the professor cast ourselves as Cinderella intellectuals, waiting for the phrase — rather than the slipper — that fit us perfectly. We waited, at fourteen, at nineteen, at twenty-five or even thirty-five, for the figure who would see what was hidden and special and glorious in us, who would love us for our smart selves alone and not for our yellow [or brown] hair — or so we thought."

The second explanation for doubting the integrity of student or employee consent is not that power hypnotizes, but rather that it creates a threat or fear of reprisal in subordinates who might otherwise prefer to decline. It is sometimes necessary to look behind consent to the options available to the consenter. Choice, after all, is always relative to background conditions of constraint, and with a choice like this, background constraints are particularly interesting. Indeed, as the Supreme Court made clear in *Meritor Savings Bank v. Vinson*, "the fact that sex-related conduct was 'voluntary,' in the sense that complainant was not forced to participate against her will, is not a defense to a sexual harassment suit brought under Title VII. The gravamen of any sexual harassment claim is that the alleged sexual advances were 'unwelcome.' . . . The correct inquiry is whether respondent by her conduct indicated that the alleged sexual offenses were unwelcome, not whether her actual participation in sexual intercourse was voluntary."[6] T. S. Eliot provides a powerful illustration of the difference:

> He, the young man carbuncular, arrives,
> A small house agent's clerk, with one bold stare,
> One of the low on whom assurance sits
> As a silk hat on a Bradford millionaire.
> The time is now propitious, as he guesses,
> The meal is ended, she is bored and tired,
> Endeavors to engage her in caresses
> Which still are unreproved, if undesired.
> Flushed and decided, he assaults at once;
> Exploring hands encounter no defence;
> His vanity requires no response,
> And makes a welcome of indifference.[7]

If, as *Meritor* established, consent to sex is a precarious defense to harassment, it makes sense for institutions to choose a default rule that at a minimum creates a highly rebuttable presumption regarding the validity of employee consent to sex. Many institutions, including a number of universities, have made exactly this move. Under such policies, consensual relations between people of unequal institutional rank only *seem* welcome. Relationships are only "ostensibly" consensual and consent is only "apparent." These policies split the difference regarding respect and suspicion so far as consent is concerned. Consensual relations are not *prohibited*, but employee consent cannot be used as a defense if the employee later claims she said "Yes" for fear of saying "No" to someone with greater institutional power. The policy of New York University Law School is instructive. It creates only a rebuttable presumption that consensual sexual relations between persons of unequal institutional power are consensual. If, however, the relationship is challenged, it is up to the professor to demonstrate the true voluntariness of the student's consent.[8] In cases where everyone lives happily ever after—whether together or apart—burdens of proof never arise. Where, however, the relational result is less agreeable, "it is almost always the case that the individual with power of status advantage will bear the burden of accountability."[9]

Putting the burden on the party in greater control of the transaction is a familiar method of allocating risk. We know this from contract and tort law, and the same sort of reasoning would seem to apply to institutional relationships. The professor or boss is surely better able to protect himself from the consequences of intimate involvement: he has superior information; he knows how the institution works; he may be a repeat player in the consensual sex game or at least will have heard the war stories of others. In addition, the boss (or his institution) may have more to lose financially or reputationally if he has misjudged the transaction; this provides an added incentive for supervisorial prudence.

Consensual relations policies that discourage workplace relationships on the grounds that consent is presumptively suspect have, however, drawn fire from two separate groups. The first are those who see such policies as just the latest step in the feminist plot to wipe out all sex of any kind for everyone everywhere. As University of Massachusetts professor William Kerrigan declaimed in a forum on consensual relations on campus, "[There is] a generation of academic feminists who push this legislation because in an era where a leer constitutes rape, they believe they are powerful enough to punish womanizing male colleagues."[10] (This is the same Professor Kerrigan who explained, in public, that "there is a kind of student I've come across in my career who was working through something that only a professor could help her with. I'm talking about a student who, for one reason or another, has unnaturally prolonged her virginity. . . . There have been times when this virginity is presented to me as something that I, not quite another man, half an authority figure, can handle—a thing whose preciousness I realize.")[11]

The issue has produced interesting bedfellows. Many feminists also oppose consensual relation policies on the familiar and appealing ground that to deny grown women the right to engage in personal relations of whatever kind with fellow workers of whatever status is a giant and dangerous step backward toward the very paternalism the movement has worked so hard to obliterate. As Jane Gallop argues in her provocative defense of faculty-student sex, *Feminist Accused of Sexual Harassment*, consensual relation policies are based on the protectionist assumption "that when a student says yes she really means no. I cannot help but think that this proceeds from the same logic that according to which when a woman says no she really means yes."[12] Gallop concludes that this is just a reprise of the old rules of gender control, applied with special relish in regard to sex, that "women do not know what we want, that someone else, in a position of greater knowledge and authority, knows better."[13] The feminist case against consensual relations policies is based on respect for women's decisional autonomy. Sherry Young summarizes the view: for administrators "to ignore a woman's own perceptions and stated preferences about her life and her exercise of her own sexuality is deeply anti-feminist."[14] Young takes no position on the subjective wisdom of a woman's stated preferences for sex with superiors at work. What is protected, she says, is the decision, not the woman.

Gallop goes much further and argues that, at least with regard to students, sleeping with superiors can be highly beneficial, both intellectually and sexually. Basing her advice on her own exuberant experience as a graduate student who seduced two (count them, two!) of her male dissertation advisers, Gallop's campaign against consensual relations policies is part of her commitment to "transmit the experience that brought me as a young woman out of romantic paralysis and into the power of desire and knowledge."[15] (A 1992 book is dedicated to "my Students: The bright, hot, hip (young) women who fire my thoughts, my loins, my prose.")[16] Despite her flamboyant formulation, Gallop's argument offers a crucial insight into the nature of student-professor relations. Teaching, she argues, is, at is its best, a passionate enterprise. That the participants should ignite one another intellectually may quite understandably derive from or turn into sexual passion. This should come as no surprise, says Gallop, and it should not be stamped out. Whether *all* sexual relations between supervisors and subordinates are a positive good inherent in the joint undertaking or whether such benefits transfer across institutional settings is not entirely clear. What works at State U. may not hold for Union Bank and Trust. And, as I shall soon discuss, Gallop's argument is, for my money, an insufficient account of passion on the job. Not everyone flourishes, and some are harmed.

While I disagree with Gallop's conclusions about the benefits of sleeping with the boss, derived as they are from her sample of one, feminists are surely right to insist on a very high threshold before we accept that a woman's consent can be invalidated on the ground that it is unwise or that she is incapacitated by virtue of a power differential. Sherry Young usefully reminds us that "life occurs under conditions of inequality"[17] and that that fact is not regularly invoked, at least in few noncommercial settings, to limit or qualify consent.

Let us assume then that the agency of an adult woman is not abandoned simply by virtue of her status as employee or student. That is, despite the fact that professors (I cannot speak for all bosses) regularly treat students like children, students and workers still retain the capacity to decide what personal or sexual relationships to take up. Still, voluntariness is only part of what the law looks at when deciding the validity of consent. The law also requires that consent must be *informed;* indeed, information is understood to enhance and secure voluntariness. Thus even grown-up consumers perfectly capable of saying yes or no must get disclosures of all kinds before they can buy items on credit or in their homes. Disclosures are also sometimes required in more personal areas of decision-making. Birth mothers, for example, must receive information — on counseling, on financial support, on revocation — before they may consent to the adoption of their child. Indeed, the failure to reveal certain crucial information to a fiancé — impotence, for example, or misrepresentations about the sincerity of one's religious beliefs — may be grounds for a later annulment.

And just what information might be useful to the employee who seeks or accepts a relationship with a superior at work? The facts that might best inform such a decision are, of course, rather hard to come by. How can the employee know if her boss *really* finds her the most interesting person he has ever come across or if he is *really* going to leave his wife? These are risks that all lovers have to take on faith.

There is, however, information regarding the law of sex discrimination that might be useful for subordinates to have at least in the back of their minds before enrolling. This information concerns not so much what one might like to know going into the relationship, but rather what can happen, as far as the law is concerned, after the relationship ends, as some inevitably will do. I draw attention here to a pattern that often emerges "after the dance is over," to borrow from an old melody. Does the subordinate party know (do either of the parties know) what happens, as far as the law is concerned, when an employer or professor finds it more difficult than he had imagined to be near the once admired employee or student after they have broken up? For despite the common promise that no matter what happens with regard to the personal relationship, there will never be any professional repercussions for the subordinate, hardened feeling and some form of retaliation after the relationship is over are not uncommon. What then does the law have to say about cases in which the consensual lover with the greater institutional power later has the consensual lover with less power transferred, demoted, or fired?

Three employment cases provide a sobering answer. The starting point is *Huebschen v. Department of Health and Social Services.*[18] There David Huebschen, a probationary employee, developed a close friendship with his supervisor, Jacquelyn Rader. Their friendship blossomed temporarily into romance and a brief liaison in a motel, but "after Rader had made a sexually insulting remark to him, Huebschen told her that "he just wanted to be a friend."[19] Rader soon informed Huebschen that there were problems with his job performance and by the end of the year, on her recommendation, Huebschen's probation was terminated. He sued for sexual harassment and sex discrimination, and lost.

His claim failed because, as the court explained, the plaintiff "must show intentional discrimination against him because of his membership in a particular class, not merely that he was treated unfairly as an individual."[20] Thus while there was no question that Rader acted spitefully, what mattered was her *specific* motivation for spite. And her spite, said the court, was not triggered by Huebschen being a man, but rather his being "a former lover who had jilted her."[21] Accordingly, "the proper classification, if there was one at all, was the group of persons with whom Rader had or sought to have a romantic affair,"[22] a group unprotected by the equal protection clause.

Huebschen was elaborated in *Keppler v. Hinsdale Township High School District 86*.[23] In *Keppler*, school principal Dr. Miller had a four-year consensual sexual relationship with Ms. Keppler, the director of special services. Not long after they broke up, Keppler was demoted to a mere special education teacher. She then sued the school district for sexual harassment and discrimination. Or, as the court restated in its opening paragraph, she "alleges [those causes of action] but what she really wants is to make others pay for her mistakes. She will not succeed here."[24]

The reason for her failure was the prior consensual relationship with her boss. As the court explained, "an employer who seeks retribution because his former lover has jilted him may be reacting not to the rejection of copulation per se, but to the change in the status quo—that is, the termination of the intimate physical and emotional relationship."[25] The court acknowledged that Title VII prohibits sex discrimination in the workplace, but concluded that

> an employee who chooses to become involved in an intimate affair with her employer . . . removes an element of her employment relationship from the workplace and in the realm of private affairs people *do* have the right to react to rejection, jealousy and other emotions which Title VII says have no place in the employment setting. . . . [That] employee cannot then expect that her employer will feel the same as she did about her before and during their private relationship. Feelings will be hurt, egos damaged or bruised. The consequences are the result not of sexual discrimination, but of responses to an individual because of her former place in her employer's life.[26]

A third case further underscores the predicament of plaintiffs punished on the job on account of the wounded feelings of former lovers. In *Campbell v. Masten*,[27] Susan Campbell, a research biologist, was fired from her job after her boss heard critical comments about her from Jeffrey Masten, a coworker with whom she had had an affair. Campbell argued that Masten wanted her fired because he believed her continued presence at work threatened his new marriage.[28] Aware of the earlier cases, Campbell argued that her termination was clearly based on her sex: Masten would not have initiated an affair with her "but for her gender as a woman."[29] The court refused to buy this link to sex discrimination. It found that Masten's animosity toward his former lover was based on her relational status, not her sex. "In the absence of such a distinction," warned the court, "any workplace affected by consensual workplace romances gone sour, and the concomitant workplace politics, could spawn Title VII claims."[30] The court then gave a sobering glimpse into permissible workplace politics, noting that while

> Masten's criticism of Campbell's work after their relationship ended may have detrimentally affected [her boss's opinion of her], it is hardly uncommon for a friend to demonstrate loyalty through a showing of allegiance and support after [a] friend ends a romantic relation with another. While such behavior may cause divisiveness among co-workers as a result of blurring the line between one's private life and one's workplace, it does not add up to, or even approach, sex discrimination.[31]

These cases clarify two points. The first is that unless there is something more — a quid pro quo threat or a request for sex after the consensual relationship has ended — existing harassment law provides no relief at all for whatever professional vindictiveness follows the break-up of the relationship. The employee's consent not only prevents the possibility of a claim for harassment, as many argue it should, but it obliterates the case for subsequent retaliation as well.[32] Second, despite the prominence of sexual harassment in the media where it is suggested that every slight now counts as harassment, an employee's right to recover is in fact enormously limited by the framework in which recovery must be sought. It is not enough to show there has been unjustified retaliation; one has to show that the retaliation falls exclusively within the category of sex-based discrimination and that there is no other explanation.

Thus it appears that before consenting to much of anything, would-be employee or student sweethearts might benefit from accurate information, not about the state of their superior's heart, but about the state of the law. Indeed, a number of companies are now protecting their employees (and themselves) by offering consensually involved employees "consensual relation agreements" along exactly these lines.[33] In these agreements, the superior party affirms that "I want to assure you that under no circumstances will I allow our relationship or, should it happen, the end of our relationship, to impact on your job or our working relationship."[34] This assurance is then countersigned by the "object of affection." The agreement is intended to convert an assurance with no purchase whatsoever in harassment law into an enforceable promise. Under this scheme, demoting one's beloved now becomes an actionable breach of contract.

There are, of course, a few problems with disclosure statements as a corrective mechanism for personal relationships. (There may also be problems with consideration in these agreements.) With the exception of communicable diseases, sweethearts are not normally required to disclose much of anything else to one another as a matter of law. Moreover, we know that even when relevant negative information is known about the duration or aftermath of personal relationships, most people don't believe that the statistically likely event will ever happen to *them*. As Lynn Baker and Robert Emery's study on divorce denial among the newly married suggests, love means never having to work percentages: almost no respondents thought *they* would ever be included within the prevailing 50 percent divorce rate.[35] In short, consensual relation agreements aside, mandatory disclosure requirements seem off the mark as a way of redressing institutional power imbalances between lovers. For now then, the retaliating or wounded boss cases serve only as pointed reminders that the course of true consensual love does not always run smooth and that when it goes off track, it is every subordinate for herself.

If postrelationship retaliation is not harassment, what about the consensual relationship itself? I agree with Gallop and the others that the relationships as such should not fall within harassment policies. Consensual relations may be many other things: unwise, misguided, unnecessary, and at times perhaps irresistible. But characterizing them in the first instance as harassment does too much too quickly. As Kathy Abrams and Jane Larson have done, one must at least puzzle through the hard question of whether consent is valid, even when taken under the auspices of institutional or societal constraint.[36] In addition, including consensual relations within harassment policies may well distract attention from the kinds of quid pro quo cases and nonsexualized discrimination that continue to plague women workers. One sees a pronounced, almost delighted tendency in public discourse to seize marginal, eccentric, and inappropriate applications of harassment policy — the occasional "kindergarten kisser," for example — to demonstrate once and for all how foolish and repressive the whole project really is.[37]

But although consensual relationships at work may not be harassment, they may still constitute a category of behavior about which institutions are properly concerned. Putting aside concerns about the professional well-being of the more vulnerable of the pair, in an institutional setting the members of the happy couple are not the only ones affected by their relationship. Even if we assume perfect consent in every case, there is still the matter of employer conflict of interest: the reasonable concern regarding the appearance of favoritism in the eyes of underlings not attractive or attracted to their supervisors.

In this regard, consensual relations policies simply extend rules against fraternization which are already used in a number of familiar settings such as business, government, the military, and the family. Such policies rely not on the (contested) frailty of employee consent, but on the impact of consent to sex, even among adults, for others. The case of *Allen v. Farrow* is instructive in this regard. There, a father (Allen) had an affair with the adopted adult daughter (Previn) of his wife (Farrow). In denying his request for custody of Previn's siblings, the court observed that Allen's insistence that the relationship with Previn was between two consenting adults "demonstrates a chosen ignorance of his and Ms. Previn's relationships to Ms. Farrow, his three children and Ms. Previn's other siblings. His continuation of the relationship . . . shows a distinct absence of judgment . . . and an absence of any parenting skills."[38] To borrow language from law and economics, consensual relations, whether in families, universities, or the workplace, may involve situations where the externalities of personal attraction cannot be internalized to the parties concerned. The idea that promotions, letters of recommendation, and work schedules are based on merit or seniority is seriously compromised when someone's sweetheart moves up (or after the break-up, down) the professional food chain. Maybe justice is still done in such cases, but it will seldom *seem* to be done.

Policies based on fairness differ in kind from those rooted in incapacity. Where the objection is based on favoritism, the focus moves from concerns about the trustworthiness of consent to the integrity of a broader enterprise. Under this rationale, companies may require disclosure of consensual relations to a designated officer to minimize whatever supervisory role is implicated, or they may prohibit such relationships outright, as Yale has recently done.[39] That is because even overwhelmingly consensual relationships may still, in the words of the Yale policy, "jeopardize the integrity of the educational process by creating a conflict of interest and may lead to an inhospitable learning atmosphere for other students."[40] Indeed, the more consensual the relationship is, perhaps the greater the fairness threat to others.

In all this, the articulation of the institutional rationale for a consensual relation policy is important. Rules that burden consent may have the desired effect of closing down consensual relations, but they do so by indirection. A rationale focusing directly on the integrity of the institution and on potential unfairness to third parties avoids the category mistake of trying to redress all workplace disadvantages under the headings of consent and incapacity. On this account, consensual relationship policies are not concerned with the employee or student's inability to fall in love, but on the consequences of doing so for everyone else. Policies based on environmental concerns situate workplace romances in their fuller context, a familiar aspect of feminist analysis. Rules that insist on supervisory neutrality — what we used to call professionalism — do not aim to thwart desire or deny agency (at least in the case of schools) for longer than a semester. They do, however, aim to permit working and learning to proceed in a way that is less mired, influenced, or tainted by the inevitable complexities of private entanglements, however satisfying or consensual they may be for the participants.

This is not to pretend that consensual relation policies are without their own complexities, as operational details are put in place. What *kind* of consensual involvements trigger the policy? Close friendships as well as relationships? Good buddies as well as sweethearts? What counts as superiority in rank and supervision? May the student editor-in-chief of the *Transnational Journal of Legislative Intent* date a cite-checker? Are there provisions for "work-outs," as alternatives to requiring one member of the couple to quit the institution are called? Consensual relations policies and their implementation must be sensible as well as sensitive: not every shared sandwich need result in a transfer to another department, or deferring Advanced Con Law until the second semester.

There is also the potential problem of uneven enforcement, with some concern that policing may more often be directed at same-sex faculty-student couples, as well as worries about mentoring. Male partners in law firms have expressed hesitation in taking on women associates for fear of overstepping some vague or invisible line of impermissible conduct. [41] When raised with regard to consensual relations, however, such concerns may be misdirected or overstated. A number of policies specify what relationships count; "intimate familial or close personal relationships" at the University of Michigan, to give one example.[42] Moreover, deciding whether particular facts fall within particular definitions is not an unfamiliar task for lawyers, professors, and the captains of industry. And, as noted earlier, a number of policies resolve the problem, should a dispute later arise with regard to the consensual nature of the relationship, by assigning the burden of persuasion to the party with greater power.

Assigning the allocation of risk to the boss is not just a convenient, appropriate tie-breaker. It reinforces the conception of professionalism that underlies why sleeping with students is a bad idea, even though, as Gallop rightfully insists, teaching is an enterprise laced with passion. While Gallop takes the call to passion literally, others may at least agree with the proposition that "the educational process involves an emotionally suffused link between human beings. Its intimacies form a tangled web of intellectual aspiration and erotic desire."[43] But if teaching edges so close to the erotic, might a tumble into the occasional student bed seem, if not inevitable, then at least understandable? (Let us put middle-age boredom and opportunity aside.)

Professor Michele Barale explains the crucial importance for teaching of steadying oneself against a tumble into real sex: "Since neither the material of the classroom nor the pedagogy itself ever can or should be made off-limits for erotic pleasure, the students must be. The boundary that separates our sexual desire from that of our students has to be intentionally established to allow no negotiation. . . . [Otherwise] it will be only too easy to use the classroom as a way to feel good about ourselves."[44]

Without question, we already feel rather good about ourselves even without sex. Consider John Glavin's description of what it is professors get to do:

> Society licences the teacher to do what virtually no other adult in the real world can. He or she stands up several times a week for fifty, seventy-five, ninety minutes to exhibit with unconditional authority the self. This is not the self enveloped in a role or in a part, not wearing a uniform or enclosed in a vestment, and certainly not playing by any sort of rules. The teacher is there simply and obviously to improvise the self, and to carry off that self-improvisation without inhibition until the class comes, by the teacher's consent, to an end. (Isn't that why so many of us prolong class just that extra minute after the period officially ends, to confirm exactly how much our narcissism controls this particular site of exhibition?) The successful teacher . . . enjoys — needs, also — more than anything else that sheer power to exhibit the self untrammeled that insists that everything s/he thinks and feels and knows ought to be interesting and relevant to everyone who listens. And that enjoyment guarantees in turn the student's enchantment.[45]

Professionalism for a teacher might therefore include an appreciation of how much of the self we already put out, and what the effect, intended or otherwise, is on students. That in turn might lead to a recognition not simply of the phenomenon of transference (why *they* fall in love with *us*), but of counter-transference, the projection of the professor's own emotional resonances back onto the student. Putting student adoration to personal use betrays the professional role that enabled the professor to become an object of desire in the first place. (Do professors really think students would fall in love with them if they met outside the academy, say, standing behind one another on a checkout line?)

South African novelist J. M. Coetzee captures a hint of professional self-awareness in the protagonist of *Disgrace:*

> "I wanted to say, I know I've missed a lot of classes, but the production is taking up all my time."
>
> "I understand. You are telling me your drama work has priority. It would have helped if you had explained earlier. Will you be in class tomorrow?"
>
> "Yes, I promise."
>
> She promises, but with a promise that is not enforceable. He is vexed, irritated. She is behaving badly, getting away with too much; she is learning to exploit him and will probably exploit him further. But if she has got away with much, he has got away with more; if she is behaving badly, he has behaved worse. To the extent that they are together, if they are together, he is the one who leads, she the one who follows. Let him not forget that.[46]

The one who leads — the educator — knows more. He knows, or intuits, what is happening, why it is happening, and in many cases, what is going to happen. It is likely that colleagues and classmates will also appreciate the realities of the relationship, if not the atmospherics. Colleagues, whether impressed, jealous, or furious, will also have to deal with (call on, grade, recommend) the student lover.[47] Classmates, whether impressed, jealous, or furious, may reasonably wonder whether the possibilities of intellectual excitement and exchange play out quite the same when both parties to a consensual relationship come to class. Surely this is not the stuff of admissions brochures.

It may also not be the stuff of sexual harassment law, with its current emphasis on unwanted advances as the prerequisite to recovery. But structures of aspiration and restraint within institutions need not always be statutorily imposed: There are still issues susceptible to resolution by private ordering. Private policies and codes aimed at establishing standards of conduct not required as a matter of law may be such a solution with regard to consensual relationships at work or in the academy. As one court has urged in the context of a repeat player professor, "[i]n the absence of a statutory prohibition on such behavior, the Court would hope that colleges and universities would take steps . . . to set higher standards than those required by law so as to insure an academic environment which is utterly devoted to the goals of learning and education."[48]

Such policies may seem heavy-handed when they are treated or discussed as though they were part of a criminal code. But the purpose of consensual relationship policies is something different than arrest. It is to frame a set of relationships within a context of professionalism rather than to regulate them externally. The limits of law in this area are clear, and to some, disappointing. As a New York court explained, "Although surely antithetical to good business practices, discrimination against an employee on the basis of a failed voluntary sexual relationship does not of itself constitute discrimination because of sex."[49] Nonetheless, conduct "surely antithetical to good business practices" or the "distinct absence of judgment" decried in the family law setting are matters of importance to institutions and to players up and down the relevant hierarchy, independent of the prod of law.

Notes

1. *See* Vicki Schultz, "Reconceptualizing Sexual Harassment," 107 *Yale Law Journal* 1683 (1998).

2. Philip Weiss, "Don't Even Think About It. (The Cupid Cops Are Watching)," *New York Times Magazine*, May 3, 1998, at 43, 45.

3. Jean Baudrillard, *Cool Memories* 185 (1987, translated 1990).

4. For a good discussion along these lines, *see* Caroline Forell, "What's Wrong with Faculty-Student Sex: The Law School Context," 47 *Journal of Legal Education* 47 (1997).

5. Regina Barreca, "Contraband Appetites," in *The Erotics of Instruction* 2 (Regina Barreca and Deborah Denenholz Morse, eds., 1997).

6. *Meritor Savings Bank v. Vinson*, 477 U.S. 57, 68 (1986).

7. T. S. Eliot, *The Wasteland* 231–242 (1922).

8. Sylvia Law, "Good Intentions Are Not Enough: An Agenda for Law School Deans," 77 *Iowa Law Review* 79, 85 (1991).

9. Policies of Tufts and Indiana Universities (on file with author).

10. William Kerrigan, "New Rules About Sex on Campus," *Harpers*, Sept. 1993, at 35–36. Law professor Sherry Young has thrown down a supporting gauntlet and agrees that the "new feminists" (they seem to be the same as Naomi Wolf's "victim feminists") "would like to prohibit as much heterosexual sex as they can get away with." Sherry Young, "Getting to Yes: The Case Against Banning Consensual Relationships in Higher Education," 4 *American University Journal of Gender and Law*, 269, 298 (1996).

11. Kerrigan, *supra* n. 10 at 35–36.

12. Jane Gallop, *Feminist Accused of Sexual Harassment* 38–39 (1997).

13. *Id.* at 38–39.

14. Young, *supra* note 10, at 270.

15. Gallop, *supra* note 12, at 12. "Screwing these guys definitely did not keep me from taking myself seriously as a student. . . . Seducing them made me feel kind of cocky and that allowed me to presume I had something to say worth saying." *Id.* at 42. For a dissection of Gallop's position on the benefits of student-faculty sex, *see* Carol Sanger, "The Erotics of Torts," 96 *Michigan Law Review* 1852 (1998).

16. Jane Gallop, *Around 1981: Academic Feminist Literary Theory* (1992).

17. Young, *supra* note 10, at 270.

18. 716 F.2d 1167 (7th Cir. 1983).

19. *Id.* at 1169.

20. *Id.* at 1171.

21. *Id.* at 1172.

22. *Id.*

23. 715 F. Supp. 862 (N.D. Ill. E.D. 1989).

24. *Id.* at 864.

25. *Id.* at 868. *See also Perez v. MCI World Com Communications*, 154 F. Supp. 2d 932, 942 (N.D. Tex. 2001) ("[T]he mere fact that two co-workers had an 'affair gone wrong' does not in itself turn sex-neutral harassment into harassment based on sex").

26. *Id.* at 869. *See also Succar v. Dade County School Board*, 60 F. Supp. 2d 1309 (S.D. Fla. 1999) (case presents "the classic setting of a love affair gone awry"; harassment by co-worker resulted from "hurt feelings and bruised ego," not the plaintiff's sex).

27. 955 F. Supp. 526 (D. Md. 1997).

28. Wives play prominently in the firing and transferring of former lovers; *see also Kahn v. Objective Solutions, Intl.*, 86 F. Supp. 2d 377 (S.D.N.Y. 2000) ("Kahn, who engaged in consensual sexual relations with Wolfe, her employer, was fired at the insistence of the latter's wife. Subjectively, Wolfe behaved like a cad. However, while objectively all sexual activity between the genders requires some discrimination, not all such activity gives rise to a cause of action").

29. 955 F. Supp. at 528.

30. *Id.*

31. *Id.* at 529.

32. *Id.* Using consent to determine whether behavior is or is not harassment highlights the limits of harassment law in a second set of facts. The problem here is the groping employer, the supervisor who makes a pass and is rejected, and then tries his luck with the next employee. He then leaves employee number one alone: there is no retaliation and no second request or invitation. On these facts, there is also no harassment; the aggressor accepts that his advance is unwanted. However, the employer may move on to a second employee, and perhaps a third or fourth, and just take his chances. There is no risk, in terms of harassment, to the method. But as the example shows, the focus on consent or rejection by individual employees distracts attention from the larger pattern and problem of unprofessional, disadvantaging behavior.

33. Tom Kuntz, "For Water Cooler Paramours, the Ties That (Legally) Bind," *New York Times*, Feb. 22, 1998, at 7. For a good analysis of employer policies, *see* Gary Kramer, "Limited License to Fish off the Company Pier: Toward Express Employer Policies on Supervisor-Subordinate Fraternization," 22 *Western New England Law Review* 77 (2000).

34. "Water Cooler," *supra* note 33, at 7.

35. Lynn A. Baker and Robert Emery, "When Every Relation Is Above Average," 17 *Law and Human Behavior* 439 (1993).

36. *See* Kathryn Abrams, "Subordination and Agency in Sexual Harassment," in this volume; Jane E. Larson, "Sexual Labor," in this volume.

37. Adam Rossiter, "Six-Year-Old's Sex Crime: Innocent Peck on Cheek," *New York Times*, September 27, 1996, at A14; *see also* Billie Dziech et al., " 'Consensual' or Submissive Relationships: The Second-Best Kept Secret," 6 *Duke Journal of Gender Law and Policy* 83 (1999) (suggesting that "[w]hile high visibility cases may suggest to casual observers that businesses are adopting rigorous rules against fraternization, the reality is quite the contrary. In 1995, [a study of 500 American Management Association com-

panies revealed that] only 6 percent had formal written policies addressing the questions of interoffice dating").

38. 197 A.D.2d 327 (1994).

39. "Yale Bans Sex Between Students and Faculty," *New York Times*, Nov. 15, 1997, at B2.

40. *Id.* As one federal district court noted, "That a professor would repeatedly seek out the romantic company of students, whether such attention is welcome or not, undermines the integrity of the department in which he teaches, the university which provides the forum for such behavior, and indeed the whole system of higher education." *Waters v. Metropolitan State University*, 91 F. Supp. 2d 1287, 1292–93 (Minn. 2000). In that case, the defendant had had affairs with a student, a former student, and an intern (who later became his wife). The court held that "while [the defendant] behaved badly in and following those relationships, . . . being a bad boyfriend or spouse is not legally actionable."

41. On enforcement against same-sex couples, *see Naragon v. Wharton*, 737 F.2d 1403 (5th Cir. 1984) (lesbian professor fired after suit against college by parents of student with whom professor was involved; a similar relationship between a heterosexual professor and a student had gone unchallenged). On the problems of mentoring within law firms, *see* Cynthia Fuchs Epstein, "Glass Ceilings and Open Doors," 64 *Fordham Law Review* 306, 376 (1995).

42. *University of Michigan Faculty Handbook* § 11.3, *available at* http://www.umich .edu/provost/handbook/11/11.3html; *University of Michigan Standard Practice Guide* 2–3 (1993), *available at* http://www.umich.edu/provost/handbook/spg.html#201.89.

43. *Id.* at vii.

44. Michele Aina Barale, "The Romance of Class and Queers: Academic Erotic Zones," in *Tilting the Tower* 22 (Linda Garber, ed., 1994).

45. John Glavin, "The Intimacies of Instruction," in *The Erotics of Instruction, supra* note 5, at 12, 16–17.

46. J. M. Coetzee, *Disgrace* 28 (1999).

47. As the Association of American Law Schools Statement of Good Practices explains, "Even when a professor has no professional responsibility for a student, the professor should be sensitive to the perceptions of other students that a student who has a sexual relationship with a professor may receive preferential treatment from the professor *or the professor's colleagues*" (emphasis added). AALS Executive Committee, "Statement of Good Practices by Law Professors in the Discharge of Their Ethical and Professional Responsibilities" (Nov. 17, 1989), *reprinted in* Association of American Law Schools, *1995 Handbook* 89, 91 (1995).

48. *Waters v. Metropolitan State University, supra* note 40 at 1293.

49. *Mauro v. Orville*, 259 A.D.2d 89, 92 (1999).

7

Who Says?

Legal and Psychological Constructions of Women's Resistance to Sexual Harassment

LOUISE F. FITZGERALD

[The] fact that sex-related conduct was "voluntary" in the sense that the complainant was not forced to participate against her will, is not a defense . . . the gravamen of any sexual harassment claim is that the alleged sexual advances were "unwelcome."
— *Meritor Savings Bank v. Vinson*

In 1986, the Supreme Court recognized that a woman could participate in sex against her will, without being forced, without having a knife at her throat. They said she could do it and it could still be unwelcome. Looking back, this is nothing short of miraculous. In the nearly two decades since *Meritor*, however, it has become clear that its legacy is far from completely benign. Instead of its central insight, that a woman can submit to sexual abuse without being complicitous in it, courts have taken to heart the dictum that "the gravamen of any sexual harassment complaint is that the sexual advances were unwelcome" and pursued it with vigor.

In this chapter, I argue that the way in which the law interprets *welcomeness* — in particular, the insistence that only certain acts "count" as resistance and certain behaviors "imply" consent — reflects a stubbornly androcentric view of female sexuality and men's right of access. Tenaciously maintained despite consistent empirical evidence to the contrary, this view legitimates men's ability to define reality in their own interests — to have sex when they want it and say that women want it, too, even when we say that we don't. Following a brief overview of the origin of the unwelcomeness requirement, I begin by reviewing the social science evidence demonstrating that men routinely interpret women's behavior as inviting sexual overtures despite women's assertions that they want nothing of the sort, arguing that the courts' insistence on the relevance of the victim's speech or dress not only reflects a doctrinal subtext of "implied" consent, but privileges such consent over her expressed resistance. I then review the scientific data demonstrating the numerous ways in which women resist unwanted sex-related attention at work, arguing that the law's refusal to "count" actions other than forceful assertion or complaint filing (and then only sometimes) is at variance not only with how women actually behave, but also with what is in their best interest, given the evidence demonstrating that more assertive responses are associated with deleterious outcomes of every sort.

Finally, I argue that the welcomeness inquiry is superfluous in most cases and wrongly posed in others; rather than requiring a woman to demonstrate that the man's behavior was offensive, such inquiries should focus on what he did to ascertain that he was welcome. This struggle over who gets to "say" what is unwelcome reflects the tenacity of the cultural insistence that sexual advances by any man to any woman are by definition welcome until she proves otherwise.

Unwelcomeness: An Overview

wel-come (wel kom) adj. 1. Received with pleasure and hospitality into one's company. 2. Gratifying. 3. Cordially permitted or invited, as to do or enjoy. — American Heritage Dictionary, 1982

In 1980, the Equal Employment Opportunity Commission issued guidelines for defining sexual harassment[1] and their first word was "unwelcome."[2] This seemingly obvious and innocuous descriptor has, unfortunately, turned out to be neither. It is worth noting from the outset that the critical inquiry rarely focuses on whether the conduct was *unwelcome*; rather, courts routinely scrutinize the woman's[3] behavior for clues to whether the behavior was *welcome*. Although perhaps not immediately apparent, this is clearly a distinction with a difference; interrogating unwelcomeness necessitates examining *her* perspective, whereas examining welcomeness implicates *his*.[4] Perhaps sensing this conundrum, the Eleventh Circuit attempted in *Henson v. City of Dundee* to define the concept by proposing that sexual conduct is unwelcome when (1) the target did not solicit or incite it, and (2) when it is undesirable or offensive to her.[5] With this opinion, the *Henson* court established the requirement that the unwelcomeness of any sexual conduct must be judged not only *subjectively* (the woman didn't want it) but also *objectively* (she is able to convince other people, usually men, that she didn't want it). Given this judicial history, and the world being the way it is, Chief Justice Rehnquist's subsequent assertion that sexually provocative speech or dress is obviously relevant to whether the behavior was unwelcome was probably inevitable.[6]

The logical and empirical problems with this formulation are the topics I explore in this essay. As Monnin has noted, "[T]he alleged conduct may be offensive or undesirable to the plaintiff, yet nonetheless 'welcomed' by her in the eyes of her harasser. In essence, while the complainant may subjectively find the advances offensive, ... her supervisor or coworkers may view her outward conduct as indicative of her receptiveness."[7] And therein lies, as they say, the rub.

It is my contention that this framework reflects a number of assumptions, each fallacious, some pernicious, and all of them just plain wrong. First, it assumes that observer judgments (e.g., the man's account, the supervisor's account) are both disinterested and more objective than self report (i.e., the woman's account), as if the sum of other people's subjectivities can be equated with objectivity, the "real" truth. This is not to question the importance of objective evidence in this context, but rather to emphasize that the man's self-interested emphasis on certain behavioral cues and denial of others, equally if not more salient, does not qualify as such. Not only is the man in question, that is, the accused, not a disinterested observer, but considerable empirical evidence indicates that even truly neutral male observers tend to sexualize women's behavior, reading sexual interest into situations in which it does not exist. This gendered sexual schema gives rise to the assertion that women's "real" intentions can be read from their dress or behavior, whatever they may say to the contrary. In legal phraseology, this might be termed the "doctrine of implied consent."

A second problem with the subjective/objective construction in this context is the assumption that a woman who is truly not interested in sex always behaves in a particular manner, whatever the context and whatever the cost. Decades of social science research tell us that this is not the case. Women respond to unwanted sexual conduct in a variety of ways, depending on the options that are realistically available and what is at stake (e.g., "I didn't say anything because two other women had complained and both of them got fired right after," "I couldn't quit because it was the first time in my life I ever had a job with insurance and I have two kids," or "He thought it was funny, and if I let him see that it bothered me, he just did it more; so the best thing was to just try to ignore him").[8]

Third, there is what might be called the *fungibility fallacy*. Burdening the plaintiff with proving that the man's behavior was unwelcome assumes that any woman is sexually available to any man, known or unknown — unless and until she can convince him (and the court) otherwise. This is one of the pernicious ones.

Finally, and this is also pernicious, the unwelcomeness requirement suggests that harassment is mainly about desire, not dominance or hostility — what might be called "the courtship trope." After all, it should go without saying (or, at least, without proving) that, however snug her jeans might be, the plaintiff didn't welcome her coworkers writing "Mary Jo sucks dog dicks" on the vehicles rolling off assembly lines into the public parking lot.[9] Although framed as evidence of welcomeness, the focus on the plaintiff's clothes or lifestyle often seems more intended to invoke the timeless dichotomy of good girl/bad girl, virgin/whore, painting a woman as so degraded as to be impervious to offense.[10]

To be fair, not all courts buy this;[11] in particular, a number of appellate decisions[12] have rejected such reasoning. Unfortunately, most of the damage takes place far from the rarified atmosphere of the appellate bench. Few plaintiffs can afford the costs of protracted litigation, and attorneys are often unwilling to roll the dice financially on their behalf. Critically, much of this process occurs in discovery and subsequent judicial decisions concerning what testimony is admissible. Rules limiting admissibility at trial are little comfort to a woman facing three male attorneys and the accused harasser, all poring over her gynecological records during deposition. Although some of the more egregious decisions have been overturned at the appellate level, the scarification ritual that too often characterizes discovery ensures that many give up long before that point. Indeed, one need look no further than Chief Justice Rehnquist's hostility to the civil extension of Federal Rules of Evidence 412[13] to realize that such rituals are unlikely to end anytime soon.

In the following pages, I discuss the theoretical and empirical problems with current formulations of welcomeness in the law of sexual harassment, arguing that such formulations are permeated with deeply structured assumptions about women, men, and sex — in particular, the historic distrust of women's sexuality. I conclude with a proposal that might change things.

The Doctrine of Implied Consent

Q: *And the way she flirted with you was by smiling at you and her body language. Is that correct?*
A: *Oh, yeah, smiling and we want to emphasize the body language, too. . . . Smile and kid and, uh, a couple of times she was sittin' there that I recall and I could see right down. I could see her breasts, literally . . . I mean I could look right down.*
Q. *Were you standing over her?*
A: *Probably.*
— *Defendant deposition transcript*

As Title VII[14] is currently interpreted, a woman's statement that she didn't want sex can be trumped by the judgments of others that she really *did* want it, or at least that the man was justified in thinking she wanted it, because of what she did or (more often) didn't do. In other words, she "implied" consent.[15] There are a number of problems with this formulation, not least of which is the large body of empirical data demonstrating that men tend to sexualize women's behavior and see sexual invitations where none in fact exist. Research shows that men are prone to read sexuality into objectively friendly interactions and incidental interchanges, despite women's expressed assertions to the contrary. The classic example was provided by Abbey,[16] who had male-female pairs participate in neutral conversations while being covertly observed by another male-female pair. Each participant was subsequently rated on a number of dimensions by his or her partner, as well as by the observers. Despite the mundane nature of the conversations, men rated the women as sexy, flirtatious, promiscuous, and seductive. Abbey concluded that men tend to sexualize situations in general and perceive neutral social interactions as female "seduction scenarios."

Numerous studies have since confirmed that men display a general tendency to construe women as sexually interested or available, assertions to the contrary notwithstanding. For example, the work of Stockdale,[17] Johnson et al.,[18] and Saal[19] support this proposition.[20] Whether in a social context, at school, or in the workplace, men are more likely to perceive sexual motives or intentions, describe women as promiscuous and seductive, and assume that they (we) are interested in sexual activity. Although expressions of disinterest can sometimes counter these perceptions, they often persist in the face of overt and repeated discouragement. Research further reveals that men read "implied consent" into numerous aspects of women's behavior, including the use of cosmetics,[21] alcohol,[22] or "provocative" clothing.[23] Simply being acquainted or having previously socialized significantly increases the likelihood that a woman will be held responsible if she is subsequently harassed.[24] It is this view of female sexuality that Justice Rehnquist's opinion concerning the "obvious" relevance of women's speech and dress serves to enshrine.

If all of this sounds drearily familiar, that's because it is; we have, indeed, been here before. As Susan Estrich pointed out, "Unwelcomeness has emerged as the doctrinal stepchild of the rape standards of consent and resistance, and shares virtually all their problems,"[25] and much the same parallelism appears in the research literature. As with sexual harassment, a large body of scientific evidence indicates that men in general are more tolerant of rape, less negative in their views of rapists, and more likely to attribute responsibility for rape to the victim,[26] including her clothing,[27] prior relationship to the offender,[28] the degree of her physical resistance,[29] alcohol usage, and physical attractiveness.[30] The similarity of beliefs about rape victims to those about women who have been sexually harassed has long been remarked.[31]

It is important to emphasize that men who participate in these studies are "normal" (perhaps I should say "reasonable") men. Neither deviants nor perverts, these are not necessarily men who harass women;[32] rather, men in general see sex when it isn't there and moreover insist that it is there in the face of women's assertions to the contrary. Such findings constitute the empirical subtext of the courts' vision of what is relevant, what is "obvious," and who gets to decide.

Just Say No: What Counts as Unwelcome in Sexual Harassment Litigation

If you've been sexually harassed, you ought to complain! . . . I mean, where's the gumption? — Senator Dennis DeConcini, October 1991[33]

Courts since *Barnes*[34] have held that for the plaintiff to prevail, she must demonstrate by her behavior that the perpetrator's advances were unwelcome. Unlike racial harassment, which is simply presumed to be offensive, sexual behavior is given the benefit of the doubt, theoretically because of its social utility in cases of "legitimate" romantic interest.[35] Whatever one might think of this argument, its practical implications are not necessarily perverse if women's resistance counted as evidence. Unfortunately, this is too often not the case; rather, the law constructs a narrow version of what counts as refusal, apparently viewing the situation from the perspective of the reasonable harasser and the conclusions he felt entitled to draw. The plaintiff is thus required to provide *objective* evidence that she was offended, meaning that her behavior must satisfy the man's *subjective* standards of how she would behave if she were truly uninterested in him.

This is no easy task, given that a woman's "no" is routinely interpreted as "yes," or at least "maybe." Thus, the *Barnes* court mused that "[T]he distinction between invited, uninvited-but-welcome, offensive-but-tolerated, and flatly rejected" sexual advances may be difficult to discern.[36] One is tempted to ask, "For whom?"

Despite concern that it is hard to figure out when women don't want sex, research identifies numerous ways that they resist, albeit ways the law often finds nonpersuasive. In one of the earliest studies on this topic, Livingston[37] examined the responses of 3,139 women who described harassing experiences ranging from sexual remarks and pressure for dates to attempted or completed rape. Forty-six percent of these women asserted their disinterest by asking or telling the man to stop, 12 percent avoided him, and 11 percent reported him to a higher authority, presumably a supervisor. Only 2.5 percent, however, utilized formal channels of complaint. A subsequent study[38] of nearly a thousand employed women revealed that 43 percent responded "directly" to the harasser, whereas 33 percent ignored or avoided him. Most recently, Schneider et al.[39] reported that 56.9 percent of women harassed in a private sector workplace directly told the man they didn't like what he was doing; 69.5 percent[40] sought advice or support; nearly one in three attempted to dissuade the man from pursuing them, 75 percent avoided him, and 35 percent talked to a supervisor or a union representative. Numerous other studies find similar results.[41]

Thus, fifteen years of research demonstrate that approximately one of every two targets directly resist by telling the man to stop; the great majority avoid contact with him, and a substantial number repeatedly assert that they are unavailable or uninterested. Even those who respond less directly are clearly unencouraging — ignoring the man, walking away, etc. It's difficult to understand how even the most optimistic of men could interpret such behavior as "welcoming."

Nonetheless, in *Trautvetter v. Quick*, the plaintiff was found to have "welcomed" the advances she repeatedly refused over a period of weeks before finally submitting.[42] The court in *Kouri v. Liberian Services* opined that the plaintiff was "hopelessly indirect" in her efforts to convince her supervisor that she was happily married, delivered an "attenuated message," and "never made any realistic effort to cut it off."[43] Finally, the court in *Dockter v. Rudolf Wolff Futures, Inc.* agreed that the plaintiff had indeed rejected her boss's sexual overtures, but opined, "her initial rejections were neither unpleasant nor unambiguous, and gave [him] no reason to believe his moves were unwelcome."[44] Really? By whose standards?

The response the law apparently finds most compelling is the one that woman make least often; making a formal complaint appears to be the legal sine qua non of an "appropriate" response. Although acknowledging that such a complaint is not a necessary element of a sexual harassment claim, the EEOC suggests that "when there is some indication of welcomeness . . . the charging party's claim will be considerably strengthened if she made a contemporaneous complaint or protest,"[45] and research shows that having filed such a complaint is a strong predictor of success in court.[46]

Despite received wisdom that reporting offensive behavior is normative, expected, and expectable, very few women actually do this,[47] and outcomes are generally not favorable for those who do. In one study of several thousand college students and employed women,[48] only 3 percent of those harassed reported the offender. Asked why not, they replied that they didn't know where or how to do so or (and this was much more common) they were afraid — afraid of not being believed, of being blamed, of making the situation worse.[49] Unfortunately, such fears are often well grounded. Eleven percent of those in the first Merit Systems study who complained about harassment said that it made things worse,[50] and Livingston[51] found that reporting was significantly correlated with higher levels of emotional distress. Although this finding could be taken to imply that those who were distressed were more likely to report, this is not necessarily the case; Hesson-McInnis and Fitzgerald[52] found that more assertive responses, including reporting, were associated with worse consequences of every sort — job-related, psychological, and health-related — even after the seriousness of the harassment itself was taken into account. Stockdale[53] reports similar findings.

Most recently, Bergman and her colleagues[54] examined the impact of reporting harassment in a sample of more than 6,000 female military personnel, confirming that complaints of harassment not only had no positive impact but actually tended to make things worse, even after accounting for the impact of the harassment itself and that of a tolerant organizational climate.[55]

In short, women don't report because they're afraid to report — and these fears appear to be well founded. Even the minority who do report and *say* that it makes things better (presumably in the sense that the harassment stopped) are more damaged by their experience than those who don't.[56] I guess that's the difference between objective and subjective evidence.

Damaged Goods: Character as Evidence of Welcomeness

The District court reasoned that a person who would appear nude in a national magazine could not be offended by the behavior which took place at the McGregor. — Burns v. McGregor Electronics Industries, Inc.[57]

The notion of welcomeness becomes particularly bizarre when applied, as it often is, to situations that have nothing to do with sex but a great deal to do with gender. When the EEOC wrote unwelcomeness into sexual harassment law and the Supreme Court gave it their imprimatur, they were apparently thinking of sex as, well, *sex* — sexual attraction, sexual desire, sexual pursuit. But sexual harassment often has little to do with attraction and pursuit, and everything to do with power, misogyny, and the crudest sort of abuse. The fact that it looks like sex, at least to some, is because men's hostility toward women is so often sexualized.

Not only are sexist and sexualized hostility[58] by far the most common forms of harassment identified in research studies,[59] but such studies also find that unwanted sexual attention, a more familiar image of sexual harassment, virtually never occurs in isolation but rather in combination with one or both of the others. Schneider et al.[60] reported that less than 5 percent in each of two separate samples of employed women reported experiencing unwanted sexual attention in isolation; in contrast, over half had experienced gender harassment (i.e., sexist or sexual hostility) either alone or in combination with sexual advances.[61]

What does it mean to welcome being called a bitch, a slut, a whore? Being asked if you've lost a pair of underpants, complete with soiled sanitary napkin?[62] Finding used condoms in your locker at work?[63] What does it mean to welcome such behavior? Can it ever be welcome? Evidently so.

Consider, for example, the case of *Reed v. Shepard*.[64] Reed, a jailer for a small county in Indiana, was handcuffed to the toilet, the drunk tank, and inside the elevator. She was targeted with lewd jokes and remarks, had her head forcefully shoved in her coworkers' laps, and had an electric cattle prod shoved between her legs. *These facts were not disputed by the defense.* The court concluded, "by any objective standard, the behavior of the male deputies and jailers . . . was . . . repulsive. But apparently not to [her] . . . [she] not only experienced this depravity with amazing resilience, but also relished reciprocating in kind . . . [t]he conclusion from the testimony must be that [she] participated freely in many of these antics and in fact instigated some of them."[65]

How did the court know this? Because, they declared, Ms. Reed had used rough language in the jail and had worn a t-shirt to work without a bra (an exhibitionistic act, they opined); in addition, she participated in "suggestive" gift giving[66] and "enjoyed" exhibiting a surgical scar on her abdomen. Reed *must* have welcomed her experiences, they reasoned, because her female co-workers were not known to be harassed. One woman testified that she had successfully deterred the men by asking them to stop. Reed, on the other hand, never complained about her coworkers; she testified that she felt she *had* to participate to be accepted in her workgroup. "It was important for me to be a police officer . . . and if that was the only way that I could be accepted, I would just put up with it and keep my mouth shut,"[67] noting further, "One thing you don't do as a police offer, you don't snitch out another . . . officer. You could get hurt."[68]

Without the full record of the trial, of course, it is impossible to determine whether what the court saw as "asking for it" was really survival; but it isn't really all that difficult to understand how a woman might see such behavior as necessary, particularly in the macho environment of law enforcement. Even absent this framework, it is difficult to understand the court's conclusion that going braless to work signaled that Reed welcomed having a cattle prod shoved between her legs. Despite the court's assertions, it doesn't appear that her behavior was "in kind" — she didn't handcuff her coworkers to the toilet, nor shove their heads into her crotch. As one commentator has remarked in an analysis of a similar case, "The courts concluded that the plaintiffs consented because they engaged in acts similar to the ones about which they complained. But the plaintiffs' actions were *not* the acts about which they complained; to suggest they are is to focus attention on the plaintiffs' conduct, . . . leaving unexamined [the men's] responsibility for their acts."

Conclusion

"Anything other than 'yes' must be interpreted to mean 'no' " . . . unless the defendant "can show by objective evidence that the target affirmatively and freely solicited or consented to his advances." — Radford[69]

As structured by the Supreme Court in *Meritor*,[70] the gravamen of any sexual harassment claim is whether the alleged sexual advances were unwelcome. Unlike cases of racial and religious harassment, in which offensive behavior is *assumed* to be unwelcome, the court has placed welcomeness at the heart of the sexual harassment inquiry and burdened the plaintiff with proving she neither invited nor welcomed the conduct of which she is complaining. And, despite the direction to consider the "totality of the circumstances," courts too often focus mainly on the woman's behavior, interpreting it in a particular way and ignoring other, equally or more likely, meanings.

Especially problematic is the pattern of putting women in a double, or even triple, bind. In the ultimate irony, one court went so far as to equate speaking out with silence. In *Ukarish v. Magnesium Elektron*, the D.C. Circuit concluded that *aside from complaining to her supervisor and keeping a diary detailing her abuse*, the plaintiff "appeared to accept [working conditions] and joined in [them] as one of the boys and *did not complain* to anyone."[71] If this logic means anything, it means that as long as the welcomeness inquiry remains central to Title VII claims, women's behavior will continue to be scrutinized and found wanting.

So, what to do? The history of rape law—indeed, of rape itself—tells us that any consent inquiry[72] is one to which women's answers will never be judged satisfactory. I suggest, then, that we ask someone else. Specifically, I propose that it is reasonable to suggest that certain acts be considered harassing and unwelcome *per se:* that is, conduct that conveys not sexual interest but, rather, sexual hostility or aversion. Examples would include calling women by degraded names for female body parts; epithets, slurs, taunts, and gestures,[73] the display or distribution of obscene or pornographic materials,[74] and other threatening, intimidating, and hostile acts.[75] As with racial harassment, to which it bears perhaps the closest resemblance, *such behavior should be presumed to be unwelcome;* the appropriate inquiry thus becomes (1) whether the behavior actually occurred, and (2) whether it rises to the level of seriousness or pervasiveness necessary to trigger the standard.

With respect to unwanted sexual attention, the issue is somewhat more complicated, as consensual sexual relationships do of course occur in the workplace. Thus, at least as the law is currently structured, welcomeness is a legitimate area of inquiry and proof. With due respect to the *Meritor* Court, however, it is not possible to infer it primarily by citing the responses that a woman *doesn't* make. Victims react in a variety of ways for a variety of reasons; in particular, the choice not to file a complaint appears to have to do mainly with a rational fear of retaliation and cannot be taken to imply that the situation was either welcome or trivial. There is simply no single behavior that will serve as a universal litmus test for determining whether sexual attention was unwelcome.

True welcomeness, on the other hand, (i.e., enthusiasm, desire, reciprocity) is generally unmistakable. Thus, I propose that the burden be shifted—that the man be required to demonstrate how he knew he was welcome. If this appears an improbable scenario, think how improbable the situation is now— when *any* advance, by *any* man, to *any* woman is *by* definition welcome unless she can prove otherwise. This is, I submit, a very odd assumption. It would seem far more reasonable to suggest the opposite: that sexual attention in the workplace be *presumed* unwelcome, unless the man can determine otherwise. Thus, the burden falls on the defendant to demonstrate how he knew he was welcome. Shifting the burden of communication in this manner focuses the inquiry where it belongs — on his behavior, rather than hers.[76]

The ground we are contesting here is tenaciously defended,[77] which should tell us that we are going in the right direction. If we doubt what is at stake, we have only to recall the words of Humpty Dumpty, that famous epistemologist of *Alice in Wonderland*: "Words mean what I say they mean . . . no more, and no less."[78] Challenged by Alice, an uppity woman, as to whether words could mean so many different things, he replied, "The question is 'Who is to be master?' That's all."[79]

Notes

Note to Epigraph: *Meritor Savings Bank v. Vinson*, 477 U.S. 57 (1986).

1. Equal Employment Opportunity Commission, *Fair Employment Practices, Labor Relations Reporter* (BNA 1980).

2. "Unwelcome sexual advances, requests for sexual favors, and other verbal or physical conduct of a sexual nature constitute sexual harassment." *Id.*

3. A leading text on sexual harassment law states, "A court may consider the complainant's sexually provocative speech or dress, participation in sexual horseplay and use of foul language at work, friendly association with the alleged harasser, and failure to report alleged incidents of harassment to superiors." Barbara Lindemann and David D. Kadue, *Sexual Harassment in Employment Law* 171–72 (1992).

4. I follow the usual convention in referring to the target as "she" and the offender as "he" while recognizing that this is not universally the case.

5. *Henson v. City of Dundee*, 682 F.2d 897, 903 (11th Cir. 1982).

6. "[I]t does not follow that a complainant's sexually provocative speech or dress is irrelevant as a matter of law in determining whether he or she found particular sexual advances unwelcome. To the contrary, such evidence is obviously relevant." *Meritor Savings Bank v. Vinson*, 477 U.S. at 69.

7. P. N. Monnin, "Proving Welcomeness: The Admissibility of Evidence of Sexual History in Sexual Harassment Claims Under the 1994 Amendment to Federal Rules of Evidence," 48 *Vanderbilt Law Review* 1155, 1165 (1995).

8. All examples not cited to published cases are drawn from my experience as an expert witness and consultant in sexual harassment litigation. Cases citations are not given (and names are altered) to protect the privacy of the plaintiffs. In the present example, each plaintiff was attempting to explain what she did and didn't do to convey that the man's behavior was unwelcome; the first two repeatedly told the man to leave them alone, but neither filed a complaint nor quit the job. The third, a waitress who was repeatedly groped by the restaurant owner under the guise of "inspecting her uniform," attempted to avoid him by changing her shift.

9. *Id.*

10. It is also regularly offered as evidence that she is impervious to any damage as well, *see, e.g., Jenson v. Eveleth Taconinite Co.*, 824 F. Supp. 847 (D. Minn. 1993), but that's a tale for another day.

11. *See, e.g., Kotcher v. Rosa & Sullivan Appliance*, 53 F.E.P. Cases 1148, 1150 (N.D.N.Y. 1990) (when supervisor pretended to masturbate and ejaculate behind complainant's back, actions were of "such a degrading nature that no ordinary person would welcome them").

12. Probably the most well known is the Eighth Circuit's reversal of the District Court's ruling in *Burns vs. McGregor Electronics Industries, Inc.*, 955 F.2d 559 (8th Cir. 1992).

13. Chief Justice Rehnquist's opposition to the 1994 civil prong amendment to Rule 412 included refusing to sanction the amendment as provided under the Rules Enabling Act. Congress passed the amendment over his objection.

14. Parallel state laws give rise to the same problem.

15. An earlier version of this section appeared in Louise Fitzgerald et al., "Why Didn't She Just Report Him? The Psychological and Legal Implications of Women's Responses to Sexual Harassment," 51 *Journal of Social Issues* 117 (1995).

16. Antonia Abbey, "Sex Differences in Attributions for Friendly Behavior: Do Males Misperceive Females' Friendliness?" 42 *Journal of Personality and Social Psychology* 830 (1982).

17. Margaret S. Stockdale, "The Direct and Moderating Influences of Sexual-Harassment Pervasiveness, Coping Strategies, and Gender on Work-Related Outcomes," 22 *Psychology of Women Quarterly* 521 (1998).

18. Catherine B. Johnson et al., "Persistence of Men's Misperceptions of Friendly Cues Across a Variety of Interpersonal Encounters," 15 *Psychology of Women Quarterly* 463 (1991).

19. Frank E. Saal, "Friendly or Sexy? It May Depend on Whom You Ask," 13 *Psychology of Women Quarterly* 263 (1989).

20. I am not arguing an essentialist position. Women are not immune to such beliefs; however, they are much less likely to hold them than men. The gender differences are reliable and substantial.

21. Jane E. Workman and Kim K. P. Johnson, "The Role of Cosmetics in Attributions About Sexual Harassment," 24 *Sex Roles* 759 (1991).

22. James D. Johnson et al., "Perceptual Ambiguity, Gender, and Target Intoxication: Assessing the Effects of Factors That Moderate Perceptions of Sexual Harassment," 27 *Journal of Applied Social Psychology* 1209 (1997).

23. Kim K. P. Johnson and Jane E. Workman, "Clothing and Attributions Concerning Sexual Harassment," 21 *Home Economics Research Journal* 160 (1992).

24. Johnson et al., *supra* note 22; Timothy Reilly et al., "The Factorial Survey Technique: An Approach to Defining Sexual Harassment on Campus," 38 *Journal of Social Issues* 99 (1982).

25. Susan Estrich, "Sex at Work," 43 *Stanford Law Review* 813, 827 (1991).

26. Irina Anderson and Geoffrey Beattie, "Gender Differences in Attributional Reasoning About Rape During Actual Conversation," 22 *Issues in Criminological and Legal Psychology* 3 (1995); Sandra L. Caron and D. Bruce Carter, "The Relationships Among

Sex Role Orientation, Egalitarianism, Attitudes Toward Sexuality, and Attitudes Toward Violence Against Women," 137 *Journal of Social Psychology* 568 (1997); James D. Johnson et al., "Differential Male and Female Responses to Inadmissible Sexual History Information Regarding a Rape Victim," 16 *Basic and Applied Social Psychology* 503 (1995).

27. Jane E. Workman and Robin Orr, "Clothing, Sex of Subject, and Rape Myth Acceptance as Factors Affecting Attributions About an Incident of Acquaintance Rape," 14 *Clothing and Textiles Research Journal* 276 (1996).

28. Mark A. Barnett et al., "Factors Affecting Reactions to a Rape Victim," 126 *Journal of Psychology* 609 (1992); Susan T. Bell et al., "Understanding Attributions of Blame in Stranger Rape and Date Rape Situations: An Examination of Gender, Race, Identification, and Students' Social Perceptions of Rape Victims," 24 *Journal of Applied Social Psychology*, 1719 (1994); R. Lance Shotland and Lynne Goodstein, "Sexual Precedence Reduces the Perceived Legitimacy of Sexual Refusal: An Examination of Attributions Concerning Date Rape and Consensual Sex," 18 *Personality and Social Psychology Bulletin* 756 (1992); R. Lance Shotland and Lynne Goodstein, "Just Because She Doesn't Want to Doesn't Mean It's Rape: An Experimentally Based Causal Model of the Perception of Rape in a Dating Situation," 46 *Social Psychology Quarterly* 220 (1983); Richard L. Wiener and Stephen Vodanvich, "The Evaluation of Culpability for Rape: A Model of Legal Decision Making," 120 *Journal of Psychology* 489 (1986); Cynthia E. Willis and Lawrence Wrightsman, "Effects of Victim Gaze Behavior and Prior Relationship on Rape Culpability Attributions," 10 *Journal of Interpersonal Violence* 367 (1995).

29. Sheila R. Deitz et al., "Attribution of Responsibility for Rape: The Influence of Observer Empathy, Victim Resistance, and Victim Attractiveness," 10 *Sex Roles* 261 (1984); Judith E. Krulewitz and Elaine Payne, "Attributions About Rape: Effects of Rapist Force, Observer Sex and Sex Role Attitudes," 8 *Journal of Applied Social Psychology* 291 (1978); Travis Langley et al., "How Behavioral Cues in a Date Rape Scenario Influence Judgments Regarding Victim and Perpetrator," 4 *Forensic Reports* 355 (1991).

30. Dietz et al., *supra* note 29; Sheila Deitz and Lynne Byrnes, "Attribution of Responsibility for Sexual Assault: The Influence of Observer Empathy and Defendant Occupation and Attractiveness," 108 *Journal of Psychology* 17 (1981); Johnson et al., *supra* note 22 at 1209; Bill Thornton and Richard M. Ryckman, "The Influence of a Rape Victim's Physical Attractiveness on Observers' Attributions of Responsibility," 36 *Human Relations* 549 (1983).

31. See, e.g., Mary P. Koss et al., *No Safe Haven: Male Violence Against Women at Home, at Work, and in the Community* (1994); Kathryn Quina and Nancy L. Carlson, *Rape, Incest, and Sexual Harassment: A Guide for Helping Survivors* (1989).

32. There is considerable data that men who endorse what are known in the social science literature as "rape myths" are more likely to also indicate that they would force a woman to have sex if they knew that no one would ever know; and, men who can be identified as having a tendency to sexually harass, *see* John B. Pryor, "Sexual Harassment Proclivities in Men," 17 *Sex Roles*, 269 (1987), have been shown to respond sexually to cues about power, *see* John A. Bargh et al., "Attractiveness of the Underling: An Automatic Power Sex Association and Its Consequences for Sexual Harassment and Aggression," 68 *Journal of Personality and Social Psycology* 768 (1995). However, such beliefs

are also widespread among men *without* these tendencies, that is, men in general. See Kim Lonsway and Louise F. Fitzgerald, "Attitudinal Antecedents of Rape Myths Acceptance: A Theoretical and Empirical Reexamination," 68 *Journal of Personality and Social Psychology* 704 (1995).

33. This comment, made in a news conference during the confirmation hearings of Justice Clarence Thomas, was subsequently quoted by Anthony Lewis on the Op-Ed page of the *New York Times* on October 11, 1991.

34. *Barnes v. Costle*, 561 F.2d 983 (D.C. Cir. 1977).

35. Lindemann and Kadue note that sexual advances, although potentially offensive, may reflect a friendly or romantic interest and often have social utility, while acknowledging in a footnote that "Some commentators question whether any social utility could outweigh the disadvantages to women." *See supra* note 3 at 135.

36. The EEOC expresses a similar view.

37. Joy A. Livingston, "Responses to Sexual Harassment on the Job: Legal, Organizational and Individual Actions," 38 *Journal of Social Issues* 5 (1982).

38. James E. Gruber and Michael D. Smith, "Women's Responses to Sexual Harassment: A Multivariate Analysis," 17 *Basic and Applied Social Psychology* 543 (1995).

39. Kim T. Schneider et al., "Job-Related and Psychological Effects of Sexual Harassment in the Workplace: Empirical Evidence from Two Organizations," 82 *Journal of Applied Psychology* 401 (1997).

40. Percentages total to more than 100 because the participants were allowed to indicate all the responses they made. Although not always apparent from the way data are reported, harassing situations are rarely one-time events; rather, they unfold over time. In response, women make numerous efforts to manage the situation, efforts that generally escalate as the man becomes more persistent.

41. Barbara A. Gutek and Mary P. Koss, "Changed Women and Changed Organizations: Consequences of and Coping with Sexual Harassment," 42 *Journal of Vocational Behavior* 28 (1993); Koss et al., *supra* note 31.

42. *Trautvetter v. Quick*, 916 F.2d 1140, 1150 (7th Cir. 1990).

43. *Kouri v. Liberian Services*, 1991 WL 50003, 6 (E.D. Va. 1991).

44. *Docktor v. Rudolf Wolff Futures*, 684 F. Supp. 532, 533 (N.D. Ill. 1988).

45. Equal Employment Opportunity Commission, *Fair Employment Practices, Labor Relations Reporter* (BNA 1990).

46. *See* David E. Terpstra and Douglas D. Baker, "Outcomes of Sexual Harassment Charges," 31 *Academy of Management Journal* 185 (1988); K. M. York, "A Policy Capturing Analysis of Federal District and Appellate Court Sexual Harassment Cases," 5 *Employee Responsibilities and Rights Journal* 173 (1992). Even formal complaints are no panacea, however. In a recent case in which I was involved, the defendant argued that the intercourse he physically forced on the plaintiff was consensual, despite the fact that she had complained that same day to both his supervisor and the police. The jury agreed. Although jury decisions can't be laid at the feet of the courts, it is the legal requirement that the plaintiff bear the burden of proving she didn't want sex when the defendant says she did that allow them to occur.

47. Julie Woodzicka and Marianne LaFrance recently demonstrated that women research participants who actually experienced harassing behavior in a laboratory situation reacted considerably less assertively than a comparable group asked to imagine what they

would do in such a situation. They note that the results indicate that women operate on the assumption that they will be angry and confrontational in response to harassment, but that in actuality targets were generally nonconfrontational. Those who did object did so politely and respectfully. Julie A. Woodzicka and Marianne LaFrance, "Real Versus Imagined Gender Harassment," 57 *Journal of Social Issues* 15 (2001).

48. Louise F. Fitzgerald et al., "The Incidence and Extent of Sexual Harassment in Higher Education and the Workplace," 32 *Journal of Vocational Behavior* 152 (1988).

49. Many were also reluctant to cause trouble for the man or his family.

50. U.S. Merit Systems Protection Board, *Sexual Harassment of Federal Workers: Is It a Problem?* (1981).

51. Livingston, *supra* note 37.

52. Matthew Hesson-McInnis and Louise F. Fitzgerald, "Sexual Harassment: A Preliminary Test of an Integrated Model," 27 *Journal of Applied Social Psychology* 877 (1997).

53. Stockdale, *supra* note 17.

54. Mindy E. Bergman et al., "The (Un)resonableness of Reporting: Antecedents and Consequences of Reporting Sexual Harassment," 87 *Journal of Applied Psychology* 230 (2002).

55. I am not arguing that women should never be expected to report sexual harassment, only that it is not reasonable automatically to infer welcomeness when they don't.

56. Hesson-McInnis and Fitzgerald, *supra* note 52.

57. *Burns v. McGregor Electronics Industries, Inc.*, 955 F.2d 559 (8th Cir. 1992).

58. Social science research has identified 3 broad categories of offensive, sex-related workplace behaviors: *gender harassment, unwanted sexual attention,* and *sexual coercion.* See Michelle J. Gelfand et al., "The Latent Structure of Sexual Harassment: A Cross-Cultural Confirmatory Analysis," 47 *Journal of Vocational Behavior* 164 (1995). Gender harassment, by far the most common, has nothing to do with attempting to establish a sexual relationship; rather, it consists of crude, offensive, and degrading behavior directed at women simply because they are women. The behaviors described in *Robinson v. Jacksonville Shipyards*, 760 F. Supp. 1486 (M.D. Fla. 1991), are a case in point. Research in the U.S. military suggests that this set of behaviors, what social scientists had previously labeled gender harassment, can be further distinguished as either sexist hostility (e.g., comments such as "If we fired all the women, we'd be able to get something down around here" or "No woman's going to drive a de-icer while I'm in charge") or sexual hostility (e.g., "She walks like she's been ass-fucked"; referring to a plant department consisting only of women as "cunt corner"). Unwanted sexual attention is just that, and sexual coercion refers to attempts to manipulate women into sexual cooperation by means of subtle or direct threats to their jobs or a related benefit. Although broader than their legal counterparts, each of these categories maps onto Title VII law; sexual coercion is the behavioral counterpart of the *quid pro quo* claim, whereas gender harassment and unwanted sexual attention are the behavioral components of a hostile environment.

59. Louise F. Fitzgerald et al., "Measuring Sexual Harassment in the Military: The SEQ-DoD," 11 *Military Psychology* 243 (1999); Louise F. Fitzgerald et al., "Measuring Sexual Harassment: Theoretical and Psychometric Advances," 17 *Basic and Applied Social Psychology* 425 (1995); Fitzgerald et al., *supra* note 48; Schneider et al., *supra* note 39.

60. Schneider et al., *supra* note 39.

61. The discussion of "welcomeness" is generally carried on very much in the abstract. In point of fact, much of what passes in legal discourse for "sexual advances" is really nothing of the sort, unless one counts comments such as "Get any this weekend?" "Your man able to satisfy you?" or even "On your knees, bitch." The reality of what women encounter in the workplace is rendered invisible by the sanitized constructions with which it is described. Indeed, a defendant human resources director once testified that he routinely rephrased complainants' descriptions of their experiences so as not to offend managers and others who reviewed them.

62. *Morris v. American National Can Corp.*, 730 F. Supp. 1489 (E.D. Mo. 1989).

63. *Jenson v. Eveleth Taconite Co.*, 824 F. Supp. 847 (D. Minn. 1993).

64. *Reed v. Shepard*, 929 F.2d 484 (7th Cir. 1991).

65. *Id.* at 487.

66. Compare *Showalter v. Allison Reed Group, Inc.*, 767 F. Supp. 1205 (D.R.I. 1991), in which the court found that male employees' suggestive gift giving was not relevant to whether the women had been sexually harassed.

67. *Reed*, 939 F.2d at 492.

68. *Id.*

69. M. F. Radford, "By Invitation Only: The Proof of Welcomeness in Sexual Harassment Cases," 72 *North Carolina Law Review* 499 (1994).

70. *Meritor Savings Bank, supra* note 6, at 57.

71. *Ukarish v. Magnesium Elektron*, 1983 WL 593 (D.N.J. 1983).

72. The technical distinctions between the legal concepts of consent and welcomeness need not concern us here.

73. *Rabidue v. Osceola Refining Co.*, 584 F. Supp. 419 (E.D. Mich. 1984).

74. *Robinson v. Jacksonville Shipyards Inc.*, 760 F. Supp. 1486 (M.D. Fla. 1991).

75. *Jenson v. Eveleth Taconite Co.*, 824 F. Supp. 847 (D. Minn. 1993); *Reed v. Shepard*, 929 F. Supp. 484 (7th Cir. 1991).

76. Suggestions that the communication burden be shifted from the plaintiff can be found in the legal literature for well over a decade, *see, e.g.,* Estrich, *supra* note 25; Radford, *supra* note 69; M. J. Shaney, "Perceptions of Harm: The Consent Defense in Sexual Harassment Cases," 71 *Iowa Law Review* 1109 (1986); J. S. Weiner, "Understanding Unwelcomeness in Sexual Harassment Law: Its History and a Proposal for Reform," 72 *Notre Dame Law Review* 621 (1983), with no appreciable effect.

77. Chief Justice Rehnquist's determined resistance to the civil extension of Fed. R. Evid. 412 is perhaps the best recent example.

78. Lewis Carroll, *Alice in Wonderland and Through the Looking Glass* (Grosset and Dunlap 1999) (1872).

79. *Id.*

8

Subordination and Agency in Sexual Harassment Law

KATHRYN ABRAMS

In February 1998, Jeffrey Toobin published an article in the *New Yorker*[1] that challenged the direction of sexual harassment doctrine. Toobin argued that feminists — led by Catharine MacKinnon — had gone wrong by arguing that "all sex is harassment and all harassment is sex." Not only did apparently innocent sexual relationships come under scrutiny through this equation, but salient forms of harassment tended to be neglected in the focus on sex. To make the latter point, Toobin highlighted the work of Vicki Schultz.[2] Schultz stresses the continuity of sexual harassment with other forms of employment discrimination and argues that many debilitating forms of harassment — from equipment sabotage to refusals to mentor — are eclipsed when legal actors look primarily for sexualized harassment, rather than for efforts to preserve valued jobs as bastions of male competency.

Toobin's article is disturbing not only in its reductive characterization of MacKinnon's view of sexual harassment, but because it describes Schultz as an antidote to if not an adversary of MacKinnon. Schultz herself appeared to have had something more inclusive in mind when she stated: "It is time for a reconceptualization of sex-based harassment — and harassment law — along more comprehensive lines. It is time to focus on gender along with sexuality, on the monopolization of work competence, along with sexual abuse."[3] While Toobin's juxtaposition may be partly a journalistic trope[4] — the old lion and the young lion of sexual harassment law battling for primacy before the neo-Gothic spires of Yale Law School — it reflects a strategy that has been prevalent among critics of feminist jurisprudence. The personal dimension of this strategy is to present feminists with even partly divergent positions as committed antagonists. The more significant, intellectual dimension is to limit feminists to a single description of the wrong of gender oppression and to a single value or norm in seeking to ameliorate it. The paradigmatic version of this strategy was the argument of workplace traditionalists in the 1970s and 1980s: women who sought access to traditionally male jobs as well as maternity leave "couldn't have it both ways." This critique demanded a unitary structure to feminist arguments, even if acknowledging sameness *and* difference was the most effective path to equality, or the most accurate description of women's patterns in the workplace.

Limiting feminism to articulation of one kind of dynamic or the vindication of one normative value is not, however, simply an opponent's strategy. It is also a problem to which feminists have contributed, often with the best of intentions. Some feminist theorists have seen one problem, or one value, as so crucial that it makes little sense to talk about others. Other feminists have pursued a single norm or focus in their work for more strategic reasons. They have assumed, quite plausibly, that a single value was all the courts or the public could assimilate: feminism had to be "high concept," or analytically straightforward, if it was going to penetrate an often resistant popular consciousness. Or feminists have analyzed particular areas by reference to one value because they believe that that value has been neglected in previous analysis. Toobin's essay provides a useful reminder that single-norm feminism cannot be considered a safe harbor. This strategy can also be used to limit our efforts and to play one feminist off against another. Strategic considerations may now join substantive considerations to point toward a different kind of feminist account: women's oppression reflects an extraordinarily complex set of dynamics, and feminists who seek to vindicate women's equality may be required to vindicate more than one value or norm at a time.

In this essay, I will endorse a vision of feminism that advances more than one norm, and I will explain how it might be implemented in the area of sexual harassment. The norms or values I will discuss are those on which I have focused in my recent work: the norm of antisubordination — developed paradigmatically in the work of Catharine MacKinnon — and the norm of agency. By "agency" I refer to a constellation of ideas that have increasingly come to the fore in feminist theorizing and argumentation.[5] The term refers, in some contexts, to the capacity for self-definition or self-direction, a capacity that has often been comprehended within the term "autonomy" in classical liberal analysis.[6] But the term *agency* also refers to conceptions and capacities that are not so easily contained within a liberal frame. Within constructivist analytic frameworks that characterize human subjects as socially formed or produced, agency may reflect purposive resistance against structurally imposed constraints,[7] or possibilities for movement that are created by the intersection of various strands of social influence, or by the potentially enabling character of power as it circulates.[8] Because sexuality has often been a site of constraint, or a site at which constrained, abjected, conflicted, or self-defeating forms of subjectivity have been produced—both through sexualized domination and through the normalization of a narrow range of sexual practices—*sexual* agency is often a particular focus of this analysis.

Feminism and Agency

Why should feminists care about agency? Forms of agency that are resonant with liberalism are, admittedly, valorized in our political culture. But to understand why these norms, and the more constructivist understandings of agency with which they are increasingly intertwined, should be viewed as aspirational *by feminists*, who may feel that they have already articulated goals more directly connected with improving women's condition, requires more careful consideration. Why, for example, does agency merit attention alongside a value as central to feminist analysis as antisubordination?[9]

First, agency reflects an aspect of what is lost through women's oppression that is not fully captured by the more relational concept of subordination. Some of the harm of oppression consists in the ways that women are dominated by men, the ways that they are confined to devalued positions within a range of hierarchies. But another, equally important part of the harm consists in the effects such domination and confinement produce on women's ability to make choices for themselves. They may be impeded, both externally and internally, in choosing who they are going to become, or in expressing their sexuality or gender in ways that depart from conventional norms.[10] To insist on women's agency is to call attention to this harm of women's oppression.

Second, focusing on agency helps us glimpse the ambivalence—and the potential for change—that exists within women's subordinated condition. Women subject to subordination, as I argue above, can come to see themselves through the lenses provided by powerful men and powerful institutions. Yet the notion of agency helps us to identify the space between influence, or even construction, and determination. A woman may perceive the relentless tattoo of sexual objectification or normalization, yet also experience dissonant glimpses of herself as a sexual subject. She may be burdened by a pervasive sense of professional constraint, yet find in herself an affinity for something beyond those bounds, and a capacity to seek out those who can help her get there. Whether this impulse arises from some gap in the structures of oppression, or from an intersection of structures or discourses that is both constraining and enabling, women often manifest both self-constraint and some limited forms of self-deliverance.

Focusing on agency thus has the descriptive value of giving us a more nuanced picture of women's present lives.[11] It has the political value of reminding women of what they have done — even under appalling constraints — and what they might do if these constraints were eased. Women who realize that they are capable of pleasure, of plans, of resistance — even in fleeting moments — understand the stakes of their liberation and are better able to attempt what it requires.[12] Finally, a focus on agency has the normative value of helping to direct the process of feminist legal change. Feminists can assess or shape doctrinal initiatives in relation to the goal not simply of ending women's subordination, but also of vindicating their capacity for self-definition and self-direction. They can marshal the social imagery of law to present women as injured yet potentially resilient, capable of playing a role in the achievement of equality.

Subordination, Agency, and Sexual Harassment

Sexual harassment, as analyzed by MacKinnon and others, is a practice that enacts the subordination of women in the workplace. It can exploit women sexually in a context in which economic constraint shapes the character of their response; it can curtail their professional opportunity by importing forms of sex-based devaluation that pervade the larger society into the workplace.[13] In this sense, legal regulation of sexual harassment has been widely understood to address features of the work environment that contribute to women's subordination. What might it mean to approach the legal regulation of sexual harassment with an eye not only to ending women's subordination but to highlighting and fostering women's agency,[14] sexual and otherwise?[15]

To bring the norm of agency into the legal framework requires that we ask at least two questions. First, are there attributes of agency that women manifest in the workplace that we should be particularly concerned with fostering or protecting? A worker makes a variety of choices in the workplace through which she expresses who she understands herself to be, or affects who she is capable of becoming. Many of these are professional choices: about the kind of work she wants to do, the kind of tasks she will undertake within a particular work area, whom she wants to mentor her, and more. The ability to express or develop herself in these ways can be radically curtailed by sexual harassment, in both its sexualized and nonsexualized forms.[16] Those concerned with agency, in this sense, could address it the same way they address subordination: through stricter regulation of workplace harassment.

However, there are other choices that workers make that are not directly related to the performance of their professional tasks, but are also not entirely separable from the selves workers bring to the workplace. These choices include various aspects of personal self-presentation, such as the ways that they express gender or sexuality. Some feminists, such as Susan Estrich, have argued that expressions of sexuality are distinct from, and in a sense exogenous to, the goals of any given workplace. To curtail such expression, in the hopes of reducing sexually coercive behavior, is a tradeoff Estrich endorses.[17] Yet not all feminists, particularly those concerned with women's agency, would agree. While the expression of sexuality may be peripheral to the purposes of the workplace, it may not be so easy to disentangle from the other personal attributes of those who work there. This particularly true when "expressions of sexuality" refer not simply to expressions of sexual interest in another person, but also to expressions or performances that manifest a conception of one's sexuality or gender, or seek to problematize assumptions about sexuality or gender held by others. These conceptions may be expressed in one's dress, posture, gaze, use of touch, tone of voice, preferred subjects of conversation or forms of humor, and more. The inclination — or even the ability — to mute the sexual or gender-related aspects of one's persona in an employment setting may be great in some people, and virtually nonexistent in others: it is one of the myriad ways in which people vary sexually, and politically. It seems likely that many would feel constrained or even baffled by an injunction to "check their sexualities," or any other features of their gender identity, "at the door."[18] Moreover, an injunction of this sort would bear more heavily on those men and women whose sexuality, or gender, is perceived as nonnormative, for their expressions would be more readily identified and stigmatized.[19] But this constraint might also bear heavily on women as a group: injunctions against sexual expression by women have been a longstanding part of gender socialization; consequently, women's exploration of the meanings of gender and sexuality — explorations that may not be readily contained in one's private or nonwork life — may be distinctively illuminating, resistant, or even liberatory.[20]

Proscription of all sexual expression in the workplace is therefore not an adequate answer for those feminists who are concerned with women's agency. We must constitute the workplace as a setting in which workers need not disentangle attributes of sex and gender from other personal characteristics, and where workers exploring a range of sex and gender identities can manifest them without fear of antagonism or constraint. Because protecting such manifestations may require less rigorous regulation of, for example, sexual talk in the workplace, than an approach grounded solely on antisubordination norms, these expressive or performative goals may exhibit some tension with the goal of eliminating sexual subordination in the workplace. Whether this tension is, to some degree, irresolvable is an interesting, and potentially fruitful, theoretical question that I do not address here.[21] My approach is more practical. If we, as feminist theorists and advocates, are to propose and seek to implement particular elements of a sexual harassment doctrine, it would be best if that doctrine could reflect the range of normative goals that we hold, even if some of those goals *at their outer limits* press in different directions. The challenge is to identify points of tension, as well as points of mutual reinforcement, and to effect pragmatic compromises where necessary.

The second question that a concern with agency entails is a more direct question of application. We must ask how the elements of the current sexual harassment claim[22] facilitate or undermine this goal, and how might they be modified so as better to promote it. In making this assessment, we should bear in mind that the law can serve social or political goals through both its proscriptive and its constructive functions. The proscriptive function concerns the decisional aspects of legal doctrine: what kinds of actions does legal doctrine proscribe? what kinds of attributes or circumstances does it render more or less predictive of legal victory? The constructive function reflects the fact that law, like a range of other social and linguistic practices, contributes to popular images of particular kinds of acts and particular groups of people. The way that sexual harassment law might contribute to women's agency both proscriptively and constructively was illustrated by the 1993 landmark case of *Harris v. Forklift Systems*.[23]

In this case, the Supreme Court rejected an emerging doctrinal requirement that sexual harassment plaintiffs demonstrate "serious psychological injury" in order to recover. Decisionally, this requirement would have erected an additional hurdle for plaintiffs seeking recovery, one that required expert testimony or potentially stigmatizing evidence of disability. It also would have served, in a broader social sense, to define what it means to be a victim of sexual harassment: it means being psychologically damaged or compromised. By rejecting this requirement, the Supreme Court proscribed a broader range of conduct, including even that harassment that does not lead to serious psychological injury; it permitted recovery to a broader range of plaintiffs, including those like plaintiff Theresa Harris, who remained sufficiently uncompromised to complain to her coercive boss and threaten to quit if the conduct continued. On a constructive level, the Court projected the image of a victim of sexual harassment — perhaps a victim of sexualized injury more generally — as a woman who is not entirely compromised by her mistreatment, who is capable of acts of self-protection and self-assertion, even in the midst of oppressive treatment.[24]

Doctrinal Modification: The Case of Unwelcomeness

To begin to explore how sexual harassment doctrine might serve the goal of agency, as well as of antisubordination, I will focus on the element of unwelcomeness. Unwelcomeness, one of the five doctrinal elements of the sexual harassment claim, is not the only place we can explore the relation between sexual harassment regulation and agency. This relation can be affected by the "pervasiveness" element, as I demonstrated above; it might also be addressed through the requirement that harassment be "on the basis of sex."[25] But unwelcomeness has been one of the elements of the sexual harassment claim in which the actions of the target have come under closest scrutiny. This scrutiny has often operated to deny the agency of those women claiming sexual harassment. Courts adjudicating this element have censured women for expressing their gender or sexuality in nonconforming ways: women who are not traditionally feminine, who manifest what might conventionally be perceived as sexuality in their self-presentation, or who tolerate any degree of sexual play in the workplace, are often said to have welcomed the conduct of which they later complain.[26] The question is how adjudication of this element might be modified to reflect what feminists concerned with agency want in the workplace, and what we consider women to be, or to be capable of becoming.

The first question, at least in theory, is whether we want to require a showing of unwelcomeness at all. The assumption behind the test was that it was necessary to distinguish sexual harassment from sexual conduct in the workplace that was acceptable. This assumption, in a workplace that seeks to value and foster women's agency, is not necessarily a problem. However, most decisionmakers at the time this element was framed sought to distinguish harassment from what was described as "courtship" behavior. Many employers and decisionmakers understood harassment simply to be courtship behavior that was not desired or reciprocated by the recipient.[27] At the very least, courtship behavior was assumed to be sufficiently dominant among sexual behaviors occuring in the workplace that a court must find — indeed, the plaintiff must bear the burden of proving — that the conduct alleged to be harassing was not this kind of behavior. Neither of these latter assumptions would seem to be valid, in light of what we have learned about sexual harassment over the past two decades.

The assumption that harassment can be considered, paradigmatically, to be unwanted courtship has been problematized by a range of different feminist analyses. These analyses vary in their characterizations of sexual harassment, but all reach the conclusion that sexual desire is only occasionally involved in harassing behavior and is incidental to its central dynamic — be it reinforcing sex-differentiated power relations,[28] policing the boundaries of normative gender formation,[29] or establishing the workplace as a zone of masculine competency[30] or masculine control.[31] Additionally, while courtship behavior undoubtedly occurs in some workplaces, workplace behavior reflecting sexual desire, sexual identity or other sexuality- or gender-related attributes is so hugely varied, that it makes little empirical sense to treat courtship behavior as a norm that must be disproved in every case.

In fact, given the heterogeneity of harassing behavior, it may make little sense to subject all of it to the same unwelcomeness test. It would be analytically more precise — and more responsive to the varying experiences of plaintiffs — to tailor the showing that separates acceptable from unacceptable sexual behavior to the nature of the harassment that is being alleged. One important category of harassing behavior includes physical violence, sexual assault, sexualized and nonsexualized derogation, equipment sabotage, and disciplining of gender nonconformity by any of the above practices. Behaviors within this category constitute coercive, insulting conduct that would not be welcomed by anyone. Their restriction will compromise the agency only of those whose sex or gender identity demands the abuse or derogation of others, on the basis of their sex or gender identities. For these reasons, conduct within this category should not be subject to an unwelcomeness test. Triers of fact should proceed directly to the remaining questions of "related[ness] to sex," pervasiveness, and employer liability.

A second category, consisting of requests for sexual contact, is more ambivalent. Such requests may be made in a context where they are coercive and constitute either quid pro quo or hostile environment sexual harassment. However, they may also be made in settings that are more indicative of noncoercive sexual interest, or sexual jocularity or play not intended to culminate in sexual contact at all. Thus we may not want to brand such requests as categorically inappropriate, by obviating a showing aimed at distinction. Yet it is not clear in this context that "unwelcomeness" provides the appropriate ground for separating the acceptable from the unacceptable. The question here is not so much whether the woman welcomed the request, as Drucilla Cornell and others have suggested, but how the request was made.[32] Was the full context such that the request seemed to be aimed at a mutually agreeable encounter or were the language and setting such that the request appeared to be aimed at something more unilateral or coercive?[33] With this understanding in mind, the plaintiff should be required to show that the defendant's approach had a unilateral or coercive character.[34]

A third category of harassing behavior, to which an unwelcomeness test seems more appropriate, is nonderogating sexualized talk.[35] A pure subordination approach might brand this form of activity in the workplace categorically undesirable as well. But I suspect nonderogating sexualized talk is not something we want to proscribe, or even treat as presumptively harassing, in a workplace where workers' sexual personae are valued as a central part of who they are. While a subordination approach might assess sexualized talk by some objective standard, an approach that is also concerned with agency — and is therefore prepared to acknowledge the plural and various character of sexualized talk — might focus on whether such talk was agreeable to the particular claimant.

It seems unlikely, however, that the Court will be willing to differentiate the showings required for different kinds of harassment. The harassment cases of the past few terms have revealed a Court that is satisfied to identify sexual harassment in a flexible, "common sense"[36] manner — except, interestingly, when it comes to the element of employer liability.[37] The unwelcomeness test is likely to remain with us, and to be applied to all varieties of sexual harassment. The question then becomes: what kind of showings should be taken to establish unwelcomeness under an approach that seeks to foster agency as well as to fight subordination?

First, the norm of agency should guide the showings that are taken to establish unwelcomeness on the part of plaintiffs. Theorists of gender subordination, such as Catharine MacKinnon, have explained why contemporaneous objection to the harassing party should not be required.[38] Women accurately perceive themselves to be in a precarious position in the workplace, and they often need their jobs to support themselves or their families. But theorists have not always explained what kind of a showing should be required of plaintiffs who seek to prove unwelcomeness. Some courts have simply allowed plaintiffs to assert the unwelcomeness of the conduct at trial, making the finding of unwelcomeness a function of the credibility of the plaintiff's testimony. While this approach has what I refered to earlier as the "proscriptive" virtue of permitting plaintiffs to win a larger number of cases without demonstrating uncommon heroics, it has a drawback in the "constitutive" realm: it may suggest to legal decisionmakers, or to the public, that women are unresistant or passive in the face of harassing conduct. This approach to proof of unwelcomeness may also make it too easy for plaintiffs to prevail in that subset of cases where the expression or behavior is neither coercive nor derogating, but simply sexual. Both the warnings of Vicki Schultz and Ruth Colker that the sexual has begun to eclipse the discriminatory in sexual harassment cases,[39] and the concern of Janet Halley that targeting expression that is alleged simply to "offend" may favor claims of harassment brought against gender- or sexual non-conformists,[40] counsel caution in setting the bar too low in these cases.

A focus on agency could help to create a middle ground in this area. Louise Fitzgerald and others have observed that, while women often do not report unwelcome sexual harassment, they do employ certain strategies in an effort to protect themselves and their jobs: they change the subject, leave the room, avoid the harasser.[41] If the plaintiff's demonstration of such conduct is taken to show unwelcomeness, this will underscore the fact that women have strategies for self-preservation and indicating distaste—even when they're caught between the rock of a harasser and the hard place of needing a job. It will also demonstrate the varied character of women's resistance: that fact that resistance, as Susan Estrich has argued, does not always take the form of a schoolboys' fight.[42] Although judicial performance has been strikingly varied on the question of unwelcomeness, at least some courts have shown themselves to be receptive to this kind of approach. The First Circuit in *Chamberlain v. 101 Realty*[43] accepted as evidence of unwelcomeness the fact that plaintiff withdrew her hands from the defendant's grasp, changed the subject, or left his presence when he engaged in sexualized talk.[44]

The critical evidence on the issue of unwelcomeness, however, often turns out to be defendant's evidence: that plaintiff's conduct during the alleged harassment, or in the workplace in general, refutes the plaintiff's allegations of unwelcomeness. Thus, a final question is when defendant's allegations about plaintiff's conduct will be taken as defeating plaintiff's claim of unwelcomeness. What seems important here, from the standpoint of agency, is that *plaintiffs* (as with prospective defendants, above) not be penalized for sex or gender nonconformity. This goal is not entirely alien to judicial thinking about harassment, as demonstrated by the Court's willingness to find same sex harassment actionable in *Oncale v. Sundowner Offshore Services, Inc.*[45] Yet courts have often failed to recognize, or to recognize the significance of protecting sex and gender non-conformity, particularly when in comes in the unremarkable form of loud, aggressive, "vulgar," sexually explicit, or otherwise unfeminine talk or behavior among women. Though cases like *Hopkins v. Price-Waterhouse* suggest a growing judicial consciousness on this question as well, other cases, like *Reed v. Shepard*,[46] show the distance yet to be traveled. In this case, the court held that conduct, from the use of a cattle prod to the forcing of plaintiff's head into the toilet, was welcome because "Reed's preferred method of dealing with co-workers was with sexually explicit jokes, suggestions and offers."[47] Subordination analysis tells us that in a resistant workplace, some women talk in aggressive or explicitly sexual ways to fit in. Agency analysis offers the additional explanation that some women talk in aggressive or explicitly sexual ways because this expresses something about the ways they perceive themselves, or hope to challenge others to think about gender. Moreover, it reminds us that this dissonant self-perception is something we want to protect, and something that may emerge on a more frequent basis if it is not penalized in public and work-related settings. Some recent cases hold out the possibility that even this kind of analysis may be made acceptable to the courts. In *Carr v. Allison Turbine Division, General Motors Corporation,*[48] the court held that a barrage of sexualized derogation, pranks, and graffiti were unwelcome, despite the fact that the plaintiff was described as "unladylike," used vulgar language, and told dirty jokes. "[H]er words and conduct," the court held, "cannot be compared to those of the men and used to justify their conduct and exonerate their employer."[49] If courts can be persuaded that this incomparability reflects not just a difference in the magnitude of the vulgarity in question, but a difference between conduct that demeans or derogates and conduct that is simply explicitly sexual or an affront to gender norms, we may arrive at an unwelcomeness doctrine that promotes women's sex — and gender — related agency.

Pursuing more than one goal through the regulation of sexual harassment will entail complications. It will require a hard look at a range of workplace practices and a willingness to develop careful distinctions regarding sexual conduct and expression, at a time when many have become impatient about the feminist analysis of sexual conduct altogether.[50] But focusing on agency, along with anti-subordination, will help women to understand the stakes of their liberation and to identify and cultivate those qualities that will help them to bring it about.

Notes

1. Jeffrey Toobin, "The Trouble with Sex," *New Yorker*, February 9, 1998, p. 48.
2. Vicki Schultz, "Reconceptualizing Sexual Harassment," 107 *Yale Law Journal* 1683 (1998).
3. Schultz, *supra* note 2 at 1692. Although Schultz is sometimes critical of an approach that has tended to rivet legal and popular attention on sexualized conduct, her understanding seeks to integrate sexual and non-sexual forms of harassment, and she is balanced and judicious in her discussion of the drawbacks of MacKinnon's approach.
4. I thank Vicki Schultz for this insight.
5. This focus has crystallized within legal feminism in the last six or eight years. *See,*

e.g., Elizabeth Schneider, *Battered Women and Feminist Lawmaking* 76–86 (2000); Kathryn Abrams, "From Autonomy to Agency: Feminist Perspectives on Self-Direction," 40 *William & Mary Law Review* 805 (1999); Katherine Franke, "What's Wrong with Sexual Harassment?" 49 *Stanford Law Review* 691 (1997); Steven Winter, "The Power Thing," 82 *Virginia Law Review* 721 (1996); Kathryn Abrams, "Sex Wars Redux: Coercion and Agency in Feminist Jurisprudence," 95 *Columbia Law Review* 304 (1995); Martha Mahoney, "Victimization or Oppression? Women's Lives, Violence and Agency," in Martha Fineman, ed., *The Public Nature of Private Violence: The Discovery of Domestic Abuse* (1994).

6. *See, e.g.*, Joel Feinberg, "Autonomy," in John Christman ed., *The Inner Citadel: Essays on Individual Autonomy* (1989); Gerald Dworkin, "The Concept of Autonomy," in John Christman ed., *The Inner Citadel: Essay on Individual Autonomy* (1989); Diana Meyers, *Self, Society and Personal Choice* (1989) (liberal feminist revision of classical liberal view of autonomy).

7. *See, e.g.*, Abrams, "From Autonomy to Agency," *supra* note 5; Mahoney, *supra* note 5.

8. *See e.g.*, Judith Butler, "Contingent Foundations: Feminism and the Question of Postmodernism," in Judith Butler and Joan Scott, eds., *Feminists Theorize the Political* 3 (1992).

9. These questions have taken on a particular edge among feminists who have glimpsed a conflict between these norms. Some have argued that calling attention to the forms in which women's agency already exists may undermine efforts to demonstrate that women are, in fact, subordinated. While I believe tensions between the two norms are likely to arise in specific contexts, I reject the view of these norms as incompatible. Moreover, I suspect this view has been stimulated primarily by accounts that have used a concern with agency to challenge the antisubordination goal, rather than by accounts that seek to advance both norms. *See, e.g.*, Katha Pollitt, "Not Just Bad Sex," *New Yorker*, October 4, 1993, at 220 (critically reviewing Katie Roiphe, *The Morning After: Sex, Fear and Feminism on Campus* (1993)). I do not see my project as coming within this category. I retain a strong commitment to the antisubordination goal; moreover, there is also more to my concern with agency than the claim that it already exists. I argue that feminists should highlight both its emergence and its constraint under present conditions, and contend that feminists should be concerned not only with highlighting it, but with creating conditions that will support and foster it. As framed in this way, and as elaborated below, I regard antisubordination and agency as largely complementary, even mutually reinforcing, norms.

10. For a good discussion of the goal of expanding the range of choice in the way people "do their gender," *see* Franke, *supra* note 5 at 691.

11. For a fuller description of this facet of agency, *see* Abrams, "Sex Wars Redux," *supra* note 5 at 304.

12. *See* Carole Vance, "Pleasure and Danger: Toward a Politics of Sexuality," in *Pleasure and Danger: Exploring Female Sexuality* 7 (2d ed. 1992).

13. These arguments are central to MacKinnon's characterization of sexual harassment in Catharine MacKinnon, *Sexual Harassment of Working Women: A Case of Sex Discrimination* 1–25 (1979).

14. One legal theorist who approaches sexual harassment with a combination of nor-

mative goals that bear some resemblance to my own is Drucilla Cornell. *See* Drucilla Cornell, *The Imaginary Domain: Abortion, Pornography and Sexual Harassment* 167–227 (1997). In the opening to her chapter on sexual harassment, Cornell frames her central question: "how do we both endorse sexual freedom and at the same time recognized the legitimacy of feminist claims for equal citizenship?" *Id.* at 169. However, Cornell proceeds through a framework that is different than mine: she rejects MacKinnon's account of subordination and derives from the work of Rawls and Lacan the central question whether particular workplaces provide "the social bases of self-respect for all [their] workers as sexuate beings." *Id.* at 190. Moreover, it is not clear that Cornell ultimately regards (sexual) freedom and equality as distinct goals. They appear to be more closely integrated in a vision that demands for each person the conditions of self-respect (and its corollary, the prohibition on sex-based or other degradation) that are "primary goods" because they permit her to achieve personhood, including fully realized sexuate being.

15. A related question, which was only beginning to emerge at the time of the conference for which this comment was written, is whether and how we can bring feminist goals such as the antisubordination norm to an analysis of sexual harassment that is organized primarily around the norm of sexual agency. This latter form of analysis has been framed by scholars who have sought to apply the insights of queer theory to the doctrine of sexual harassment. *See, e.g.,* Franke, *supra* note 5; Janet Halley, *Sexuality Harassment* (2001) (draft on file with author). Some of these scholars, notably Halley, are explicitly skeptical about whether these two sets of norms can be reconciled or jointly pursued in a single body of doctrine. *See* Halley, *Sexuality Harassment*, at 5. This essay could be also be read as the beginnings of a response to Halley, about the possibility of integrating these norms within a coherent body of doctrine; but I would likely frame some of the following arguments differently if I were trying to integrate antisubordination goals into a doctrinal system organized around what one could term (although Halley does not) the sexual agency-related goals of queer theory, rather than trying to integrate agency goals into a doctrinal system that has been centrally animated by the antisubordination norm.

16. Vicki Schultz makes this point forcefully in "Women 'Before' the Law: Judicial Stories about Women, Work and Sex Segregation on the Job," in Judith Butler and Joan Scott, eds., *Feminists Theorize the Political* 314–24 (1992). Schultz argues that women's interest in certain kinds of work can be shaped by their experiences in particular workplaces, a point judges and advocates on both sides of the "lack of interest" controversy have missed. For example, effective mentoring and job training can cause women to take seriously kinds of work they might not previously have considered, while harassing behavior can discourage them from undertaking new training or tasks. *See also* Wendy Pollak, "Sexual Harassment: Women's Experiences v. Legal Definitions," 13 *Harvard Women's Law Journal* 35, 35–39 (1990) (describing tradeoffs made by harassed women, including author herself, in blue-collar trades).

17. Susan Estrich, "Sex at Work," 43 *Stanford Law Review* 813, 842, 860 (1991).

18. *See* Franke, *supra* note 5.

19. Gay and lesbian theorists have argued, for example, that manifestations of sexuality by individuals who depart from sexual norms are more likely to be perceived as manifestations of sexuality, while manifestations of sexuality by those whose sexuality

fits the social norm are more likely to be perceived as acceptable behavior that is not explicitly sexual (e.g., gays or lesbians who hold hands or kiss in public are often charged with "flaunting their sexuality," while heterosexuals who engage in the same conduct are not). *See* Marc Fajer, "Can Two Real Men Eat Quiche Together? Storytelling, Stereotypes and Legal Protection for Lesbians and Gay Men," 46 *University of Miami Law Review* 511, 587 (1992) ("Even where gay people participate fairly fully in non-gay community life, they understand that they must be more 'discreet' than their heterosexual counterparts").

20. For examples of feminist legal theoretical work that reflect this insight *see* Drucilla Cornell, *The Imaginary Domain* (cited at note 14); Carlin Meyer, "Sex, Sin, and Women's Liberation: Against Porn-Suppression," 72 *Texas Law Review* 1097 (1994); Susan Keller, "Viewing and Doing: Complicating Pornography's Meaning," 81 *Georgetown Law Journal* 2195 (1993).

21. Feminist theorists who have begun to address this theoretical question have differed among themselves about the irreconcilability of these goals. Cornell, *supra* note 14, suggests that they can be reconciled, through a Rawlsian and Lacanian analysis. Drucilla Cornell, *The Imaginary Domain*, at 167–230 (cited in note 14). Janet Halley, analyzing sexual harassment doctrine from the standpoint of queer theory, argues that there may be irresolvable tensions between feminist (represented importantly by MacKinnon's anti-subordination analysis) and queer approaches. *See* Halley, *supra* note 15, at 5 ("my hypothesis is that feminism and queer thinking are not going to converge. Instead I will attempt to map their non-convergence"). However, it is noteworthy that notwithstanding this provocative hypothesis, Halley's discussion of particular cases, does seek to find common ground between feminist and queer approaches, explaining what feminist gains or positions queer theory would leave intact, and what contractions of the scope of sexual harassment doctrine might make it less likely to effect the harms to nonconforming sexual performance and possibility about which queer theorists might be concerned. *See, e.g.,* Halley, *supra* note 15, at 32–36 (discussion of *Robinson v. Jacksonville Shipyards* case).

22. In using the current elements of the sexual harassment claim as a starting point, I am choosing to forgo the opportunity to reformulate the claim more systematically. Drucilla Cornell, for example, has chosen the latter route in her work on sexual harassment. *See* Cornell, *The Imaginary Domain*, at 170 (cited at note 14) (proposing new set of showings necessary to establish sexual harassment). It is my strategic judgment — particularly in the face of recent Supreme Court decisions that reaffirm and elaborate rather than alter basic elements of the claim, *see, e.g., Oncale v. Sundowner Offshore Services, Inc.*, 118 S. Ct. 988 (1998); *Harris v. Forklift Systems, Inc.*, 510 U.S. 17 (1993) — that it is more likely to be effective to propose to reinterpret or modify existing elements of the claim than to transform the elements of the claim entirely.

23. 510 U.S. 17 (1993).

24. *See* Abrams, "Sex Wars Redux," *supra* note 5, at 369–70.

25. *See* Kathryn Abrams, "The New Jurisprudence of Sexual Harassment," 83 *Cornell Law Review* 1169, 1205–25, esp. 1223 (1998).

26. Susan Estrich makes some of these arguments in her article *Sex at Work* (cited at note 17). However, her central argument is that this element has become the basis for a

"trial of the victim"—an event that perpetuates the workplace subordination of the victim in the legal context, much as a rape prosecution revictimizes the prosecuting witness. I thus see her attention to the unwelcomeness element as committed exclusively to an antisubordination goal, rather than to an effort to achieve antisubordination and agency.

It is also worth noting that courts, at least until *Harris* and perhaps afterward, have sometimes used the "pervasiveness" showing for the same purpose. A woman's conduct is generally called into question during the proof of unwelcomeness, but if that conduct demonstrates that the woman was (1) not wholly undone by the harassment alleged, but (2) didn't do anything distinct or nonconforming enough that a court could read her behavior as "welcoming" the harassment, some courts find that the woman (to judge by her behavior) couldn't have found the behavior sufficiently debilitating to alter her work environment and constitute actionable harassment. An example of this approach was the magistrate's opinion (later adopted by the district court and the court of appeals) in *Harris*. The magistrate found that Harris drank beer with the men at her workplace and sometimes engaged in rough language. Possibly because this conduct did not seem sufficiently nonconforming to signal a receptivity to the defendant's behavior, the court used it to support its conclusion that defendant's behavior had not caused "serious psychological injury" and therefore was not pervasive enough to constitute sexual harassment. *See* 1990 U.S. Dist. LEXIS 20115, 17 18 (November 27, 1990).

27. The remarkable durability of this assumption was demonstrated during the Anita Hill–Clarence Thomas hearings when sociologist Orlando Patterson argued that Hill, and her audience of feminist sympathizers, had simply misinterpreted, as harassment, Thomas's "down-home style of courtship." *See* Orlando Patterson, "Race, Gender and Liberal Fallacies," *New York Times*, October 21, 1991.

28. *See* MacKinnon, *supra* note 13.

29. *See* Franke, *supra* note 5.

30. *See* Schultz, *supra* note 2.

31. Abrams, *supra* note 25.

32. *Id.* at 1221–22. For a similar showing, embodied in a different standard, *see* Cornell, *supra* note 14 at 170–74.

33. *See* sources cited at note 28. This position has elicited strong criticism from Janet Halley, who describes this emphasis on mutuality as part of an effort to bring a "cultural feminist" lens to sexual harassment doctrine, and to impose a view of sex as valuable only when "intersubjective, caring, respectful, alert to human dignity." Halley, supra note 15 at 19–22, 21. Although Halley's view is interesting, I think it mistakes a contextually limited proposal for a broad, normative view of sexuality. My point was to suggest that mutuality—as opposed to unilaterality or coercion—might be a useful principle on which to *organize initial requests for sexual contact or intimacy, when these occur in the workplace.* This suggestion stems from my view that initiation of sexual contacts in the workplace, like sexual harassment in the workplace (as I argued in "The New Jurisprudence of Sexual Harassment" (cited in note 25), must be analyzed in ways that acknowledge the distinctive character of the workplace environment. There are several aspects of the work environment that militate against a nonmutual approach to sexual initiation. Parties in the workplace are in most cases unlikely to know each other well enough, or in

ways that permit them, to know each other's tastes in sexual initiation. More to the point, most of those in the workplace are likely to think of themselves as workers first, and, in that context, to have an expectation — not coterminous with but reinforced by the anti-discrimination mandate of Title VII — that they will be treated in a professional manner, connoting basic equality or worthiness of respect. A nonmutual sexual approach risks not only mistaking the preferences of one's addressee — a mistake which would be only a minor problem in an environment such as a bar or club. It risks making this mistake in a context where nonmutuality could be read not as an error about the interpersonally appropriate way to make a sexual approach, but as a derogation of the addressee's (presumptively equal and respect-inducing) status as a worker.

Now Halley might object to many elements of this response. She might claim that a queer perspective would problematize many or all context-based regulations of sexual initiations such as the one that I have proposed: regulations based on context are ultimately analogous to arguments that sexual nonconformists should be free to do whatever they please, but only in the well-concealed provinces of their own bedrooms. Or she might quarrel with the notion that those engaging in sexual initiation or other sexual performance should be obliged to respect, in their addressees, some presumptive, primary identity as a worker. Such hierarchizing of the mobile and diverse elements of identity might be analogized to asking a worker to "check [his] sexuality at the door." But, to my mind, these types of objections should be taken as the potential ground of difference between us, rather than the claim that I have articulated a transcontextual, moralizing view of normative sex.

34. If we understood ourselves to occupy a social world where requests for sexual contact or intimacy — notwithstanding the possibility of agency — are more often associated with coercion than with genuine interest, mutuality, or noncoercive play, we might require the *defendant* to demonstrate that his approach partook of mutuality: this is an example of an area where the two goals might exhibit some tension. It is not clear to me that this additional step is warranted, given that the expressions that might fall into this category seem to be quite various, and proof of unilateral or coercive character not prohibitively difficult to marshal.

35. In an earlier draft of this paper, I had defined this category simply as "sexualized talk." I added the adjective "nonderogating" in response to a comment by Kimberle Crenshaw that sexual talk directed at Black women in the workplace tends to be distinctively derogating or stigmatizing. *See also* Kathryn Abrams, "Title VII and the Complex Female Subject," 92 *Michigan Law Review* 2479 (1994) (verbal harassment of Black women distinctively antagonistic and derogating). The requirement that talk which is tolerated to a greater degree (by being subject to an unwelcomeness test) be nonderogating means that sexualized verbal abuse of Black women would most frequently be placed within the first category, and the nonderogating sexual language more likely to be indicative of sexual expression, exploration, or play (which, assuming Crenshaw is correct, is usually directed toward whites in the workplace) would be placed within this third category.

This distinction also tracks an important point made by scholars such as Vicki Schultz and Ruth Colker, that decisionmakers in sexual harassment cases are increasingly focusing on claims of *sexualization* to the detriment of claims of sex or gender *discrimination*.

See Schultz, *supra* note 2); Ruth Colker, "Whores, Fags, Dumb-Ass Women, Surly Blacks and Competent Heterosexual White Men: The Sexual and Racial Morality Underlying Antidiscrimination Doctrine," 7 *Yale Journal of Law and Feminism* 195, 199–200 (1995). Placing derogating talk (whether sexual or nonsexual) in a different category than nonderogating sexual talk, for purposes of demonstrating unwelcomeness, seems to be a step in the salutary direction advocated by Schultz and Colker.

Of course, this distinction is likely to spawn a range of questions about what constitutes "derogation." As a preliminary matter, I would be prepared to define as derogation that which holds up a particular individual or group (such as a group identified by gender, or race and gender, or sexual orientation and gender) for derision or stigmatization. This, of course, would be unlikely to answer all questions. But developing further refinement in making this distinction is consistent with an approach that views some forms of sexual expression in the workplace as a good thing, but much of the sexual expression that occurs in many workplaces as threatening to the equality of women and nonconforming men. Addressing the difficulties raised by this distinction is also preferable to neglecting the distinctive character of the harassment directed at women of color.

36. This language is taken directly from Justice Scalia's appeal to common sense to distinguish appropriate from inappropriate sexual behavior in *Oncale v. Sundowner Offshore Services, Inc.*, 118 S. Ct. 988, 1003 (1998).

37. *Compare Oncale v. Sundowner Offshore Services, Inc.*, 118 S. Ct. 988 (1998) (appealing to common sense and context to identify sexual harassment) and *Harris v. Forklift Systems, Inc.*, 51 U.S. 17 (1993) (taking a "totality of circumstances" approach to assessing pervasiveness of sexual harassment) *with Burlington Industries v. Ellerth*, 524 U.S. 742 (1998) and *Faragher v. City of Boca Raton*, 524 U.S. 775 (1998) (articulating elaborate multipart test for assessing employer liability in quid pro quo and hostile environment sexual harassment cases).

38. However, prompt complaint to someone in a position of authority may be understood to be required, because (1) the presence of a well-advertised complaint procedure and (2) the failure of the plaintiff to use such a procedure are the factors that are crucial in permitting defendants to assert an affirmative defense, in the employer liability portion of the case. *See Burlington Indusries v. Ellerth*, 524 U.S. 742 (1998). Interestingly, the analysis by Louise Fitzgerald, *infra* note 41, would seem to militate against imposing this requirement as well, or would at least suggest that a number of women will be required to overcome their initial reluctance to complain if they are to preclude the defendants' successful offering of an affirmative defense on this issue.

39. See note 30, *supra.*

40. See Halley, supra *note 15* at 5–6, 25–27.

41. See Louise Fitzgerald et al., "Why Didn't She Just Report Him? The Psychological and Legal Implication of Women's Responses to Sexual Harassment," *Journal of Social Issues* 3–4 (1995). *See also* Louise Fitzgerald's essay in this volume, discussing same research and proposing that it be used in the context of unwelcomeness.

42. *See* Susan Estrich, "Rape," 95 *Yale Law Journal* 1087, 1105 (1986) (dominant legal understanding of resistance tracks what "schoolboys do on the playground").

43. 915 F.2d 777, 783–84 (1st Cir. 1990). The court also took cognizance of the fact that "the employee may reasonably perceive that her recourse to more emphatic means of

communicating unwelcomeness . . . may prompt termination of her employment, especially when the sexual overtures are made by the owner of the firm." 915 F.2d at 784. *Cf. Stockett v. Tolin*, 791 F. Supp. 1536, 1543 (S.D. Fla. 1992) (finding unwelcomeness where plaintiff avoided defendant, avoided being alone in a room with defendant with closed doors, as well as on occasion pushing defendant away and asking him to stop).

44. Feminists concerned with agency would be likely to endorse reliance on such evidence in cases involving coercive or derogating expression or behavior. Were courts in fact willing to differentiate the showings that they would accept for different cases (an assumption I made earlier, but do not make in this final section of the chapter), it is a more difficult question whether feminists concerned with agency would find such evidence sufficient in cases involving noncoercive, nonderogating sexualized behavior or talk. In this context, the goal of illustrating the various and subtle forms of women's resistance might be in tension with the goal of preventing sexual harassment claims from being deployed against nonconforming manifestations of gender or sexuality in the workplace. In other words, not antisubordination and agency, but rather two different strands of a concern with agency might pull in different directions in this context. While this risk that sexual harassment claims might be deployed against gender nonconformity could potentially be managed through the "pervasiveness" requirement, it might be appropriate in the noncoercive, nonderogating category of cases—particularly those involving coworkers (to impose a requirement of more explicit objection.

45. 523 U.S. 75 (1998). Although the Supreme Court did not offer any explanation of the dynamics surrounding the harassment of Oncale, at least two of the amicus briefs offered in support of *Oncale* argued that policing or disciplining gender nonconformity is an important cause of same-sex sexual harassment, particularly among men. *See* Katherine Franke and Nan Hunter, Brief of Law Professors as *Amici Curiae* in Support of Petitioner, *Oncale v. Sundowner Offshore Services, Inc.*, No. 96–568; Catharine MacKinnon, Brief of National Organization on Male Sexual Victimization et al., as *Amici Curiae* in Support of Petitioner, *Oncale v. Sundowner Offshore Services, Inc.*, No. 96–568.

46. 939 F.2d 484 (7th Cir. 1991).

47. 939 F.2d at 491.

48. 32 F.3d 1007 (7th Cir. 1994).

49. 32 F.3d at 1010.

50. Jeffrey Toobin is not alone in taking a skeptical view of the focus on sexual conduct implicit in sexual harassment regulation. Other recent articles in the popular press have sought to portray an explosion of sexual harassment regulation, and particularly regulation aimed at policing the intimate relationships of workers. *See, e.g.,* Daphne Patai, *Heterophobia: Sexual Harassment and the Future of Feminism* (1998); Jeffrey Rosen, "In Defense of Gender-Blindness," *New Republic*, June 29, 1998, at 25; Henry Louis Gates, Jr., "Men Behaving Badly: Who Put the Sex in Sexual Harassment?" *New Yorker*, August 18, 1997, at 4.

9

Sexual Labor

JANE E. LARSON

The underlying conception of sexual harassment is a defense of women's right to participate in the public sphere of the labor market.[1] In this essay, I argue that a concern for assuring the dignity of labor for women as a collective, and not the policing of sexual boundaries between individuals, should guide the courts in defining doctrinal elements of the cause of action. I consider "sexual labor" and the definition of work, and ask what it means to get equal pay and enjoy equal working conditions. I consider how differing regimes of sexual harassment law affect women's relationship to work. I propose an alternative vision of sexual harassment law as collective bargaining by women over the conditions of their labor through the political process. Finally, and from this labor perspective, I argue for eliminating one element of the existing doctrine, the requirement of "unwelcomeness."

Sex Work

Debates over sexual harassment are, at bottom, disputes about the level of sexualization of the workplace that a society will accept as normal "background noise"—that is, neither an unreasonable imposition nor an expression of hostility.[2] "Unwelcomeness" is the doctrinal place where lines are drawn between acceptable and unacceptable levels of workplace sexualization. For women who work, this level sets the price they must pay to have a job.[3]

In her 1983 book, *The Managed Heart*, sociologist Arlie Russell Hochschild defines "emotional labor" as work that "requires one to induce or suppress feeling in order to sustain the outward countenance that produces the proper state of mind in others."[4] Hochschild illustrates emotional labor's demands through the example of the flight attendant. Hired for their grace and charm, flight attendants must make passengers feel content so that they will choose to fly on the employer's airline in the future. In the face of passenger fatigue, boredom, discomfort, and abuse, the attendant must smile and reassure.[5]

The measure of skill in such emotional labor, Hochschild observes, is to make it appear effortless and sincere, not a task the employee is performing but an innate quality she possesses. Hochschild observes further that asymmetrical norms govern the claims that employers and customers make on male and female workers in the realm of "emotional labor." Women are more likely to be employed in jobs that require emotional labor, and at the same time emotional labor is often not recognized as work when performed by women, being seen instead as the natural expression of femininity.[6] But if emotional labor requires no special effort, then it need not be compensated; as Maureen Arrigo succinctly puts it, "employees as a general rule are paid not for who they 'are,' but for what they 'do.' "[7]

There is a parallel of sexual labor that women in a sexualized workplace must perform. Fending off solicitations, ignoring personal remarks, not seeing the pictures or hearing the words, making light, acting demure or flirtatious or crude, talking back, or playing along — these are all forms of sexual labor. Yet they are usually not recognized as work, being seen instead as the natural expression of an innate condition of femaleness.

Thus even if male and female employees are paid the same, if the women must accept less amenable working conditions, be exposed to greater risk of insult and injury, and perform uncompensated sexual and emotional labor, they are effectively being paid less than the men around them who are not affected by this workplace sexualization. This creates a sex-based disparity in wages and working conditions, and the measure of that disparity in important part is the legal requirement of "unwelcomeness."

How "Unwelcomeness" Works in the Workplace

Following the Supreme Court decision of *Meritor v. Vinson* (1986), the courts have used a multipart test for proving hostile environment sexual harassment. The plaintiff must demonstrate that: (1) she is a member of the protected class; (2) she was subjected to unwelcome sexual harassment in the form of requests of sexual favors or other verbal or physical conduct of a sexual nature; (3) the harassment was based on her sex; and (4) the harassment unreasonably interfered with her work performance and created an intimidating, hostile or offensive work environment.[8] Unwelcomeness is core and not incidental to the claim: "The gravamen of any sexual harassment claim is that the alleged sexual advances were unwelcome."[9]

The "unwelcomeness" requirement means that employers are not necessarily liable for harassing acts that are objectively objectionable — that is, so offensive, severe, and pervasive as to undermine working conditions in the eyes of any ordinary person. Having shown this, the plaintiff must prove in addition that she did not accept what an ordinary person would reject.[10] The defendant who cannot deny that the plaintiff was badly treated nonetheless may defeat a discrimination claim by introducing evidence bearing on her dress and manner, sexual history, and other sexual conduct outside of work, with the goal of proving that the plaintiff wanted or liked the bad treatment.[11]

The existing structure of "unwelcomeness" proof thus establishes that sexual targeting and abuse of a subordinate or coworker is not necessarily unacceptable workplace conduct. Even conduct that an ordinary person would find objectionable is still lawful so long as the individual target does not find it unwelcome.

In the case law, we find that the woman in a male-dominated workplace who "goes along to get along"[12] finds her efforts to be one of the guys turned against her to show that she welcomed the conduct she now complains of.[13] "By any objective standard," observed the Seventh Circuit, "the behavior of the male deputies and jailers towards [plaintiff] Reed . . . was, to say the least, repulsive."[14] (Coworkers had grabbed Reed's crotch, persistently made crude jokes and invitations, and on several occasions handcuffed or physically imprisoned her.) "But apparently not to Reed," the court concluded, and so dismissed her sexual harassment claim.[15] The woman who tries a different tactic and seeks to deflect or avoid rather than confront her harasser finds that her soft response fails to communicate a hard enough "no." Although the plaintiff in a clerical position repeatedly but politely fended off her supervisor's advances from the moment she began a new job, the Seventh Circuit concluded her rejections were "neither unpleasant nor unambiguous," and so did not give the supervisor reason to know that his moves were unwelcome.[16]

It follows that if prevailing norms of acceptable conduct don't always apply in the workplace, then every dog gets at least one bite at each potential target. Each woman worker must be "tested" for her acceptance level. How else is the harasser supposed to know she doesn't really want it? Once he asks, so long as he "takes no as no," according to Gloria Steinem in her effort to distinguish Bill Clinton from Clarence Thomas and Bob Packwood, the "key concept [of] respect for women's will" is maintained.[17]

The "unwelcomeness" doctrine sets up a workplace dynamic antithetical to the purposes of Title VII. It focuses exclusively on the experience and interests of the individual target, and not the workplace environment generally. And it focuses on the one-shot sexual encounter (the asking and answering), and not the repeat-round employment relationship.

By focusing on the preferences of the target, the unwelcomeness rule hides the extent to which the working conditions of women as a collective are structured by the sexualization of the workplace that any individual woman's negotiation of welcomeness or unwelcomeness permits. Any workplace can be sexualized to the greatest extent permitted by the most accepting or weak worker. If the least resistant sister sets the sexual dignity level for the workplace, it is like having the most starving worker set the minimum wage. Other workers can bargain up from there, but their opening position is weakened.

Blithe images like Steinem's of a one-shot transaction redeemed by respect for consent — "he proposed, she disposed, and he went away" — further distort the true dynamic of the workplace environment. Taking "no as no" draws a good enough boundary in a sexually charged exchange between adults in a social setting like a bar or a party. But power circulates differently in workplaces, and different interests are at stake. Workplaces are characterized by shared physical space, the necessity for continuing effective interaction with coworkers and superiors, and a high cost of exit — in short, repeat encounters.

Carol Rose illustrates the dynamic of repeat encounters by considering how it structures male-female negotiations over the distribution of domestic burdens.[18] In a shared household, women begin from a position perceived as weaker because they are expected to carry a disproportionate burden of housework. As a result, when they try to negotiate a better deal, their male partners challenge them at every turn. (This relates back to Hochschild's point about the asymmetrical norms that govern the claims we feel free to make on male and female workers for uncompensated labor.)[19] Rose uses the example of the husband who without argument shares the cooking chores with his camping buddies, but puts up a relentless fight when asked to pitch in within the household he shares with his wife. He just does not expect her to demand a fair deal. Challenged at every turn, the women will tire of fighting for things the men get without a fight. Failing to fight, the women will be perceived as weaker still, and offered still worse bargains.[20] The broader point is that when bargainers of differential power meet for repeat rounds, their initial position of inequality is intensified, creating a downward spiral of worsening offers for the weaker player.

In bargaining over sex, whether at work or not, the initial expectation of female weakness can be established based solely on the disparity across numbers of physical size and strength between women and men.[21] But the expectation of female weakness also may be grounded in the fact that as a social group women are poorer and less well-positioned, and men richer, more powerful, and the beneficiaries of ancient and enduring assumptions that they belong on top. Finally, the expectation of relative female weakness may be reinforced by the presence of individual women in the workplace who are more willing than others to cooperate with the sexualization agenda, or less inclined to confront harassers directly, creating expectations that affect the bargaining position of all the women there.

In the specific context of workplace sexual bargaining, the unwelcomeness rule accelerates the downward spiral. If the existing rule means you cannot know until you ask, the law creates a workplace culture in which the female workers are defined as available at least for asking. Some women may welcome sexual opportunity at work. Other women, faced with repeated solicitations, may just get tired of saying "no" and managing the discomfort; after a while they just give in. Having gained the upper hand once, the rational stronger player will offer the weaker — or someone just like her (members of the relevant group are easy to identify) — an even worse deal the second time around.

Unreasonableness as Against Unwelcomeness

If we treat sexual harassment as a question of worker rights rather than an issue of sexuality, we must ask whether the presumptions about acceptable workplace sexualization created by the existing "unwelcomeness" rule accords with the understandings and preferences of working women and men. If the answer is yes, then the existing law is appropriate: The burden should be on the employee who wants less sex to make her atypical preference known, and the plaintiff should therefore carry the burden of proving unwelcomeness, as she currently does. But if the ordinary worker prefers some sexual restraint, then perhaps unwelcomeness should be only an affirmative defense and not the plaintiff's burden.[22]

I would suggest, however, that the unwelcomeness inquiry be eliminated altogether.[23] This would allow the sexual harassment claim to be proved by evidence that the conduct complained of was both objectionable and an inter-

ference with working conditions as measured by a standard of objective reasonableness. If a worker of ordinary sensibilities would perceive the sexual
conduct complained of as humiliating, degrading, abusive, severe, and pervasive (substantive standards the law already requires to prove that the conduct
complained of was more than merely annoying), the law should find the conduct sexually harassing, whether the target welcomed it or not.[24] The objective
standard proves the harassment has actually changed the terms and conditions
of employment, and this is all Title VII requires.[25] It should not matter whether
the employee minds does or does not mind being treated differently from a
worker of a different sex.[26]

Either alternative to the current unwelcomeness doctrine — allowing unwelcomeness only as a defense, or eliminating it altogether — presumes, perhaps conclusively, that women do not welcome workplace sexual treatment
that workers in general would judge to be abusive, degrading, humiliating,
coercive, or deeply undignified. It also sidesteps the uncertainty created under
existing law about whether unwelcomeness is measured by an objective or
subjective standard.[27]

Collective and Individual Interests

As a measure of the conditions of women's labor, these alternatives to
the existing "unwelcomeness" requirement work like a union contract, raising
the base contract price for all workers by the power of the collective and
preventing the strong from making private bargains with the weakest in order
to drive down the market price. Groups with common interests may act collectively to negotiate norms, ideologies, or laws in order to advance their position. This can happen through a regulated structure of private bargaining,
such as that established by the labor laws, or through collective participation
in cultural or political contests. Sexual harassment should be viewed in this
light: Using their political power, women have pressured judges and lawmakers to set some outer bounds on the amount of sexual labor they must
perform as the price for their right to work.[28]

This vision of sexual harassment law as a collectively-bargained-for labor
contract offers a new perspective on the tension between individual and collective interests intrinsic in the question of unwelcomeness. In the same way that
the power of unions is undermined by mechanisms such as "right to work"
laws that allow any individual worker to bail out of the collective, the potency
of the sexual harassment guarantee is undermined by legal standards that
elevate individual experiences or subjective measures.

As a civil rights measure, sexual harassment must center the collective rather than the individual interest as its touchstone. The purpose of Title VII is to eliminate discrimination in the terms, conditions, and privileges of work, and thus to open the labor market to women. Its purpose is not to provide tort-like protection for the invasion of individual rights of sexual integrity.[29] Accordingly, the legal test for sex-based harassment must advance the collective interests of women as a laboring class, even if they sometimes conflict with the preferences of individual women as desiring sexual subjects.[30] Such is the price of collective action in the context of labor relations, and the same hardnosed claim must be made in the context of sexual harassment. An objective standard of unwelcomeness in sexual harassment doctrine assures security and dignity of labor to women as a working class.

Notes

I am grateful to Linda Hirshman for co-ownership of these ideas, and to the organizers and participants of the Yale Symposium at which this essay was first presented. Finally, to Catharine MacKinnon, who deserved this honor in her own country and house.

1. Within the history of the United States, demands to participate in the wage labor market have been an expression of the broader demand for sex equality and female emancipation. The Declaration of Sentiments at Seneca Falls claimed the right to profitable employment and to one's wages. See "Declaration of Sentiments and Resolutions, Seneca Falls" (1848), reprinted in *Feminism: The Essential Historical Writings* 76 (Miriam Schneir, ed., 1972). *See also Bradwell v. Illinois*, 83 U.S. (16 Wall.) 130 (1872) (right of women to enter the professions). The right to work has been recognized within international law as a human right. *See* Universal Declaration of Human Rights, Art. 23: "[e]veryone has the right to work, to free choice of employment." U.N.G.A. Res. 217 (1948). These sentiments were codified in the International Covenant on Economic, Social and Cultural Rights, Art. 7, 993 U.N.T.S. 3 (1966), entered into force January 3, 1976.

2. Because sex work is not the job description (and might be judged criminal or exploitative if it was), workplace sexualization is like workplace socialization — not what people are being paid for, but part of what comes from interacting with other human beings in a social setting like the workplace. What society — and law — accepts as a tolerable level of workplace sexualization is a location of political struggle, and sexual harassment law is one arena.

3. Not all, but much sexualization in public places — at work, on the streets, at school, in the media — is directed at females. The evidence for this fact is indisputable; the explanation, however, is greatly debated. I regularly use the female pronoun in this essay, but this is not to deny that boys and men are subject to sexual harassment.

4. Arlie Russell Hochschild, *The Managed Heart: The Commercialization of Human Feeling* 7 (1983).

5. *See id.* at 8.

6. *See id.* at 174–81.

7. Maureen J. Arrigo, "Hierarchy Maintained: Status and Gender Issues in Legal Writing Programs," 70 *Temple Law Review* 117, 162 (1997).

8. *See Meritor Savings Bank, FSB, v. Vinson*, 477 U.S. at 63, 68 (1986). The plaintiff also must establish respondeat superior liability on the part of the employer. *Id.*

9. *Id.*

10. *See Harris v. Forklift Systems, Inc.*, 510 U.S. 17, 21–22 (1993) ("Conduct that is not severe or pervasive enough to create an objectively hostile or abusive work environment — an environment that a reasonable person would find hostile or abusive — is beyond Title VII's purview. Likewise, if the victim does not subjectively perceive the environment to be abusive, the conduct has not actually altered the conditions of the victim's employment, and there is no Title VII violation").

11. In *Meritor* the Supreme Court held that evidence regarding the plaintiff's clothing, demeanor, and language in the workplace was relevant to the question of unwelcomeness. *See Meritor, supra* note 9, at 69. See also Susan Estrich, "Sex at Work," 43 *Stanford Law Review* 813, 828 (1991) (unwelcomeness inquiry focuses decisionmakers on the victim's conduct as opposed to that of the defendant).

12. *See* Beth A. Quinn, "The Paradox of Complaining: Law, Humor, and Harassment in the Everyday Work World," 25 *Law and Social Inquiry* 1151, 1173 (2000).

13. *See, e.g., Reed v. Shepard*, 939 F.2d 484, 487 (7th Cir. 1991) (plaintiff who participated in sexual banter and jokes failed to demonstrate unwelcomeness); *Weinsheimer v. Rockwell International Corp.*, 754 F. Supp. 1559, 1561 (M.D. Fla. 1990) (same).

14. *Reed, supra* note 13, at 486.

15. *Id.*

16. *Dockter v. Rudolf Wolff Futures, Inc.*, 913 F.2d 456, 459 (7th Cir. 1990). Although the appeals court found the evidence demonstrated a "hostile environment," plaintiff's response to repeated sexual advances and touching from her boss did not communicate unwelcomeness. *Id.* at 458–60.

17. Personal conversation between Gloria Steinem and Katha Pollitt, *quoted in* Katha Pollitt, "Free Willy," *Nation*, Feb. 16, 1998, at 9. For an expansion of the point, see Gloria Steinem, "Feminists and the Clinton Question," *New York Times*, Mar. 22, 1998, at 4:15.

18. Carol M. Rose, "Women and Property: Gaining and Losing Ground," 78 *Virginia Law Review* 421 (1992).

19. Rose is careful to emphasize that the bargaining outcome will be the same whether women are in fact more weak or cooperative than the men with whom they negotiate, or simply are perceived to be so. *See id.*

20. *See id.*

21. Some women are larger and stronger than some men, but across numbers women are smaller and weaker than men. Where force is a permitted tactic, this physical disparity across numbers allows males as a class to dominate females as a class, and has done so in history. *See* Gerda Lerner, *The Creation of Patriarchy* (1986) (male appropriation by force of female sexual and reproductive capacity is the foundation of patriarchy, and also of slavery, private property and class).

22. Gillian Hadfield, " 'Rational Women': A Test for Sexual Harassment," 83 *California Law Review* 1151, 1185–86, would retain unwelcomeness as an affirmative defense.

23. Susan Estrich and Camille Hebert, among others, suggest abandoning the unwelcomeness element altogether. *See* Estrich *supra* note 11, at 826–47; Camille Hebert,

"Sexual Harassment is Gender Harassment," 43 *University of Kansas Law Review* 565, 571 (1995).

24. The "worker of ordinary sensibilities" is the "reasonable person" adopted by the Supreme Court in *Harris* as the objective measure of a workplace's hostility or abusiveness — without any of the special pleading required by the *Harris* standard to show that the plaintiff is in fact one of those reasonable creatures. *See Harris, supra* note 10, at 21–22.

25. "The critical issue, Title VII's text indicates, is whether members of one sex are exposed to disadvantageous terms or conditions to which members of the other sex are not exposed." *Harris, supra* note 10, at 25 (Ginsburg, J., concurring).

26. This is contrary to the Supreme Court's majority position in *Harris* that "if the victim does not subjectively perceive the environment to be abusive, the conduct has not actually altered the conditions of the victim's employment, and there is no Title VII violation." *Id.*

27. In *Meritor, supra* note 8, for example, the Court stated that consent is not a defense, but goes on to deem evidence of plaintiff's provocativeness relevant to a consideration of "the context in which the alleged incidents occurred." *Id.* at 69. Why it is relevant is not explained. In *Harris, supra* note 10, the Court held that the test for whether a work environment was abusive was whether a reasonable person would find it so, but also whether the plaintiff perceived it to be so. *Id.* at 21–22. This left open the issue of welcomeness and the relevance of evidence that might indicate the plaintiff was receptive to an objectively sexually hostile workplace.

28. This analysis is expanded in Linda R. Hirshman and Jane E. Larson, *Hard Bargains: The Politics of Sex* (1998).

29. These are fundamental interests to be pursued in other areas of law, as my own work argues. *See* Jane E. Larson, "Women Understand So Little, They Call My Good Nature 'Deceit': A Feminist Rethinking of Seduction," 93 *Columbia Law Review* 374 (1993).

30. Katherine Franke, for example, is concerned that abandoning the unwelcomeness requirement will undermine women's agency by casting doubt on their ability to consent to or object to sexual advances in the workplace. *See* Katherine M. Franke, "What's Wrong with Sexual Harassment?" 49 *Stanford Law Review* 691, 746–47 (1997).

Unwelcome Sex
Toward a Harm-Based Analysis

ROBIN WEST

The legal transformation of the same worldly phenomenon — unwelcome sexual behavior foisted by relatively powerful men upon relatively less powerful girls and women, in workplaces, in schools, and in the military — from an unnamed, pervasive, natural, and hence invisible quality of public life, to the source of private injuries which might but most likely would not sustain a tort action, to a clear cut deprivation of civil and constitutional rights, has been a breathtaking feminist triumph of the last quarter of the twentieth century. But the speed of that transformation has not been without costs. One of the costs may be that the sheer rapidity of that transformation — from unregulated natural fact, to possible tort, to civil and constitutional right violation — has obscured the nature of the harm that unwanted sex visits upon the woman or girl who suffers it. If sexual harassment is a violation of civil rights because it is a form of discrimination, then it appears that the harm lies in the discrimination. Alternatively, if sexual harassment subordinates women, then the harm lies in the substantive inequality that results from it. Either analysis establishes a fit between the worldly phenomenon of harassment and the legal idea of discrimination, but neither rests on nor seemingly requires an elucidation of the actual harm — the nature of the burden unfairly imposed, or the way in which harassment entails inequality. We do not have, and until recently have not felt the need to produce, multiple, conflicting, cumulative, rich, nuanced, and disseminated descriptive accounts of the harms to which this conduct leads.

This descriptive impoverishment has hampered the development of doctrine and slowed progress toward ending the harassment itself, in a number of ways. First, it burdens the efforts of plaintiffs in hostile environment cases who have suffered "psychological damage only" from winning their lawsuits — we have not generated a stock of knowledge against which jurors or judges can draw in recognizing such damage when they see it. Second, the same descriptive impoverishment also burdens and confuses our attempts to respond to evidentiary and doctrinal challenges. "Unwelcomeness" is surely central to the harm of harassment, but how do we respond when courts and juries arguably interpret a woman's sexual self-presentation as "welcoming," even in the face of shockingly hostile and predatory sexual advances? We need to collectively decide how to best address problems posed by fact finders' false beliefs and resulting biases, such as their tendency to read sexual desire and receptivity — and hence a "welcoming" attitude — into women's self presentations, but we cannot do that coherently without a sense of what is and isn't essential to the cause of action, as opposed to what is evidence of it. Third, and I think of greatest consequence, this descriptive impoverishment has left the doctrine itself vulnerable. Without a coherent and convincing account of the harm at its core, both the meaning and application of this still new legal entitlement are up for grabs, and the outcome of this battle for the soul of sexual harassment law which we are now witnessing may not be at all congenial with the feminist impulse that was originally at its heart.

These comments are a partial attempt to fill that gap. In the first part, I want to present one account of the psychic and political harm occasioned by sexual harassment, wherever it happens, and as it is traditionally understood and defined — unwelcome sexual behavior within the context of unequal relationships of power.[1] In the second part, I will contrast the harm of sexual harassment with the harm which may or may not follow from a very different kind of contested sexual interaction in schools — harms arguably caused by consensual *and welcome* (whether or not wise) sexual relationships between professors or teachers and graduate students, professional students, undergraduates, and high school or middle school students. I want to make clear in this section why these consensual and welcome relationships are not and should not be regarded as sexual harassment even if they involve people with hugely unequal power, rank, or prestige: namely, they do not involve the psychic and political harms to personhood which I will argue are central to harassment. I also want to insist, however, that it is imperative that we attend carefully to the quite different sorts of harms they may often cause.

Unwelcome Sex

Unwelcome sex — including consensual but unwelcome sexual intercourse in the home and in marriage, unwelcome sexual attention and behaviors in schools and at work, and unwelcome sexual hassling on the street — is a unique but foundational harm to a person's psychic integrity, or put differently, a unique harm to *personhood*, particularly as personhood is understood, constructed, reflected, and expected in a liberal society. The person anticipated by and rewarded by liberal legal norms and institutions is a person whose actions and choices more or less reflect his *preferences*, and whose preferences, in turn, more or less reflect his own assessments of the pains or pleasures to be had from various projected choices, and whose calculus of lived pains and pleasures, finally, more or less accurately reflect both his felt desires and his objective interests. Such an individual's choices and acts can reliably be viewed as proxies for his well-being — his choices reflect his preferences, which in turn are grounded in his pains and pleasures, which in turn spring from his desire, and which if fulfilled will promote his objective well-being and his subjective satisfaction and happiness. It is because of this faith in the cohesive unity of the fulfillment of individual desire, the promotion of individual well-being, the experience of pain and pleasure, the formation of preferences, and the individual's chosen actions that liberalism so thoroughly relies upon individual choice as the vehicle for measuring and bringing about improvements in public welfare. The subject who is the beneficiary of liberalism's most fundamental projects is characterized by what we might call a triple "hedonic unity" — a unity between that person's true interest and his experienced pains, pleasures and desires, a unity between his experienced pleasures and pains, and his preferences, and finally a unity between those preferences and his acts and choices.

The woman or girl who endures unwanted sexual intercourse, or unwanted sexual attention, or the unwanted sexualization of her workplace or school is a woman or girl for whom this hedonic unity has been fractured, and fractured in a particular way, as a result of which she does indeed become — as Andrea Dworkin has stated — a vagabond, or more prosaically, profoundly dysfunctional. The woman or girl who endures unwanted intercourse, or unwanted sexual attention, or the unwelcome sexualization of her workplace or school, is and is perceived to be a person who does not act, choose, or prefer so as to resist pain: her acts are hedonically severed from, rather than accurate measures of, her calculus of her physical, bodily pains and pleasures. Her actions and choices, in these unequal relationships, may indeed reflect her preferences — her preferences, after all, may be to endure whatever she needs to endure to keep the job, or to avoid future abuse, or to maintain the connection with a teacher, or to keep herself and her children economically secure — but her preferences do not reflect her most basic and fundamental experiences of her own physical, bodily pains and pleasures. Unwelcome sexual intercourse or harassment that women consensually endure is a source of pain rather than pleasure, but our actions and preferences do not reflect that subjective fact. Indeed, the sexually harassed woman in the workplace, or in the school, or in the family, is in the midst of a series of hedonic perversions: rather than resist pain and the source of it, she absorbs it into her body, both figuratively and literally. Rather than form her preferences, make her choices, and then take action on the basis of her own physical or sexual pleasures, she chooses and acts — even if the choice is to do nothing — in a way that promotes the harasser's, rather than her own, hedonic well-being. The pain she actually experiences takes the form of what is widely touted as pleasure, and for various reasons she may react with seeming pleasure to what she is experiencing as painful.

For the woman who lives in this vortex of hedonic perversion, the severance or fragmentation of hedonic experience (the experience of pleasure and pain) from preference, choice, and act (our being in the world) might be or become pervasive, and then foundational, and then, particularly in a world in which such injuries are not meaningfully regulated or deterred, normative. The fragmentation of hedonic experience is pervasive whenever harassing work, school, marriage, or intimate life is the pervasive environment of our lives: for the women, not so few, who endure unwelcome sexual harassment at work, are sexually hassled on the street, and then come home to unwelcome sexual intercourse, endured for whatever reason, these perversions are pervasive. It is foundational to whatever degree sexual desire and sexual choices, and the connection between those choices and those desires, defines our understanding of and concept of the connection between our body and our place in the world. We often, of course, men as well as women, sacrifice our own pleasures, or endure pains, in order to achieve greater ends, whether those ends be prudential, noble, moral, or foolish. But the woman who endures unwelcome sexual intercourse or harassment endures physical pain in her own body for no greater end than the sexual or sadistic pleasure of others, and for no greater reason than necessity, and in the process enacts and promotes a contemptuous disregard of her own body's wisdom — a literal as well as metaphorical alienation of her body and its pains and pleasures over to the instrumental and inconsequential ends of others. That endurance, finally, becomes normative when the fragmentation it implies becomes a way of being not only sexually but in other areas of life as well — when the sexualized woman simply becomes

someone who by definition reacts to the imposition or threat of pain by absorbing it into her body rather than by resisting it; whose calculus of pains and
pleasures to which she refers when acting is routinely the pains and pleasures
of someone else and never herself; and who reacts as a matter of habit to what
she is experiencing as pain as though it were trivial. The fragmentation of self
occasioned by sexual harassment and unwelcome sex has become "normative" when that fragmentation not only affects but virtually defines the woman's presence, actions, and being, in all worlds of commerce, learning, and
intimacy, not only the sexual.

Now it may well be that the individual constructed by and anticipated by and
assumed by liberalism is not a particularly attractive or even morally defensible
self — he is egoistic to the point of narcissism, uncaring, and seemingly oblivious to the constraints of justice on his actions. We can debate that until the
cows come home. Regardless, there is a world of difference between a thoughtful and conscience-driven rejection, both in theory and in life, of the norms of
liberal individualism as a stunted ideal, and the experience and reality of being
excluded from participation in those norms by virtue of psychic injury. A
woman who engages in or endures or tolerates unwanted, unwelcome, undesired, and unpleasurable sex sustains multiple derivative injuries, in addition
to the central psychic harm of the fragmented self, all consequent to the dominance of liberalism and liberal individualism in daily modern life. First, her
competency in the worlds of commerce and bargain is compromised: she may
go through life and through the day making bargains and those bargains may
even promote welfare, but the welfare they promote will not be hers. It is not
possible to be a profit maximizer when one is, is perceived as, and is treated as, a
creature whose raison d'être is the absorption of physical pain for the pleasure
of another. It is indeed impossible to do your job when you've been sexualized
in the workplace: job performance is no longer why you are *there*. Second, a
woman's *autonomy* in a world that so treasures and values autonomy is threatened: such a woman is, after all, demonstrably constrained to act in a way that
harms her and bestows meaningful benefits on virtually no one. She is and is
perceived to be, for that very reason, profoundly unfree. Third, her *integrity* is
undermined: she speaks, chooses, and acts in a manner consistently untrue to
her self. Her self identity is compromised. And finally her agency — that quality
of life which perhaps more than any other singular feature so defines the
distinctively liberal understanding of the self-in-the-world — her power to have
an impact upon the world in accordance with her own inner life force — is
destroyed. A woman whose purpose is to absorb pain for another's pleasure is
not an agent: she is not forming and reforming the world by virtue of her agency
and her presence in it. She is, rather, an object in the world, not an actor upon it.

Put differently, or more functionally, unwelcome sex *in all forms* makes it impossible for the woman who endures it to participate in the forms of self, personhood, and identity anticipated by and expected by liberal society. She becomes the antiliberal: the woman who receives and absorbs unwanted sex and sexual behaviors simply *is* the person whose bodily, physical observed choices and behaviors have no relation to her felt pains and pleasures, her desires, her subjective selfhood, or her well-being. Her pleasures, desires, subjective selfhood, and ultimately her well-being no longer count. She is the person for whom the unity of the subjective experience of life, the formation of desire, the expression of desire, and the act in the world — again, a unity central to liberal conceptions of the self for almost two centuries now — is undermined, precluded, or shattered. Her being-in-the-world is that of an instrument for others rather than that of an agent, and her physical presence is the presence of an object rather than a subject. Her acting, choosing, preferring self is for the hedonic satisfactions of others rather than for herself.

The unwelcome and pervasive sexualization of workplaces and schools is thus the public reinforcement of a harm that pervades and often defines women's private and intimate lives as well. Unwelcome sexual intercourse — intercourse wanted by men but not by women — is for many women virtually a structural feature of heterosexual dating and married life. It receives uninterrupted cultural sanction, and more than occasional explicit legal protection. The understanding that unwelcome, undesired, unwanted, unpleasurable and even physically painful sexual intercourse, so long as it is desired by a man and consented to by his female partner, is a positively good thing, is central to our understanding of marriage, of the family, of intimate heterosexual life, and for all of those reasons, of women's expected and presumed and assumed nonliberal and antiliberal identity. It is a part of the air that women and not men breathe. This constrained and enforced identity as one who willingly engages in sex that is not wanted, welcomed, or enjoyed, is precisely the identity that sexual harassment in workplaces and schools enforces: public space and public life, in effect, provide no relief. The harm of unwanted sex, then, is central to the disrespect and disregard and spirit murder we suffer on the job and in school, as well as to the inabilities, disabilities, and inequalities in various spheres of public life, including the political and civic, as well as the economic, which that disregard engenders.

The harms caused by the sufferance of unwanted sex and unwanted and unwelcome sexual attention at home or school are accordingly different, and profoundly so, from the harms caused by the sufferance of rape — sex which is of course also unwelcome, but is nonconsensual and forced as well. The harms of rape are also not widely understood, or at least, not as widely understood as they ought to be—the invasiveness and forced intimacy of rape, coupled with its often invisible violence, is its most gendered and consequently most mysterious and misread dimension. But nevertheless, at least comparatively, the harm a rape causes, once the occurrence of a rape is conceded, are visible and intelligible, particularly from a liberal perspective: rape, like all crimes of violence and force, entails a severance of the connection between act and will, or between preference and choice, that is traumatic, injurious, and often life-threatening. The harms occasioned by the endurance of unwelcome sexual attention and intercourse, by contrast, are widely and normally sustained by women and girls at home, in school, and in workplaces, and are so pervasive as to define a sex rather than distinguish particular victims. The damage is so widespread and the harm so utterly internalized that it still comes as a shock to contemplate the illegality of the conduct that gives rise to it. But the harm itself, it is important to emphasize, is quite different. Rape traumatizes and endangers and violates the acting, choosing, preferring, deciding, protecting self—it is the choice and power and autonomy and freedom to not engage in sex when one prefers and chooses not to that is destroyed. Unwanted sex, by contrast, undermines not the autonomy of the choosing self but the integrity and self-regard of the hedonic experiencing self—the expectation that our preferences and hence our choices and actions coherently reflect our own physical pleasures, desires, revulsions, and pains. It is not the preferring, acting, choosing self that is destroyed, but rather the integrity and coherence of the pained, repulsed, pleased, or desirous self that is undermined. Unwanted sex in any form—harassment, hassling, unwanted intercourse—is ultimately an attack on the integrity of desire.

One mark of women's eventual equality, as is now often noted, will be the end of rape. But another mark, and indeed a necessary one if the first is to be meaningful, will be the end of unwanted sex: a world in which women do not endure unwanted sexual intercourse, behavior, conduct, advances, or interactions in the family, in marriage, in the workplace, in the military, or in school. That will be a profoundly more equal world, and a more pleasurable one to boot. The sheer recognition of the distinctive harms of consensual but unwelcome sexuality, and of its pervasiveness in women's but not men's lives, and of its consequence for women's well-being, is a big first step. Currently, a hegemonic ethic erects consent as a marker of gains in well-being, political sensibility weds the fulfillment of at least male desire to preference, economic ideology presents consensual bargains as superior in all ways, pareto and otherwise, to regulation, and a dominant culture celebrates the commodification of our sexual lives as a form of postmodern, hip, liberated capitalistic chic. Our fragile ability to *see* rather than be blinded by the harmfulness of the consensual but unwelcome sexualization of women's lives in homes, marriages, schools, and workplaces, and more specifically our ability to see the harms done by these consensual but unwanted sexual arrangements against the blinding hegemonic and ideological forces, is evidence of a social and societal transformation of evolutionary, and not just revolutionary, proportions.

Consensual and Welcome Sex

What, if anything, follows from this account of the harmfulness of unwelcome sex to the status of consensual but fully *welcome* sexual relations between teachers and students in schools, or between persons of different rank in the military? Let me start with some preliminary and logical implications. First, consensual and welcome sexual relations between teacher and students or military personnel of unequal rank do not carry with them the harms peculiar to unwelcome harassment. The student or private may be having a lousy and unpleasant affair. The affair may, in retrospect, have been clearly exploitative. It may not, as I will discuss momentarily, have been in the student or private's best long-term interest, all things considered, to have engaged in it. It may even be bad for women that she engaged in it, and reflective of harms sustained by women that she wanted to. But nevertheless, if welcome, such sex does not carry at least what I've argued above to be the distinctive harms of unwelcomeness: if she was acting on desire, she did not suffer the severance of act and pleasure and pain — of choice and bodily integrity — peculiar to unwelcome harassment. If she was acting on her own desire, she did not absorb pain to further the pleasure of another. She did not alienate her hedonic and sexual self. She acted, in short, as an agent, rather than having been acted upon as object. Again, if such relationships are harmful, they must be harmful for reasons other than these — if welcome, they simply are not harmful by virtue of unwelcomeness.

However, it does not follow from this straightforward implication that these relationships are *harmless*, or even less, that they are something we ought to celebrate. All that follows is that if they are harmful, they are harmful for reasons other than those I have outlined above. It does not mean they are harmless. I stress this, because it is a pervasive and damaging mistake to infer the goodness of welcome sex from the harmfulness of unwelcome sex — just as, for that matter, it is a pervasive and damaging mistake to infer the goodness of consensual sex from the harmfulness of rape. Sometimes, after all, as even an ardent a liberal as John Stuart Mill well understood, our pleasures, pains, and desires do not in fact serve our interests or well-being, (just as our preferences may not reflect our pleasures and pains and desires). If so, and if the disservice is sufficiently severe, there may be a plausible case for paternalistic intervention. Such may be the case here: it may be that even welcome sexual relationships between students and teachers are so perversely skewed by the power imbalance between them that they almost invariably fail to serve the interest of the weaker party, even if she is a willing and happy participant. A number of schools and universities, including apparently Yale University, have so decided. Nothing I have said here directly informs that issue one way or the other.

Nevertheless, some pragmatic lessons are in order. Minimally, what follows, I think, from a clear elucidation of the harm of unwelcome sex is the pragmatic importance of distinguishing sharply between the problem of unwelcome sex and the problem, if it is one, of consensual and welcome sex between people with unequal power. Unwelcome sex, whether at home or in the public spheres of work, school, or military life, is a pervasive harm, and the perception of it as a harm is a great advance, but it is a harm which by virtue of its pervasiveness is elusive, and an advance which by virtue of its boldness is fragile. That fragile understanding is threatened by the lack of clarity that might come from unholy alliances. For surely, as the public debate over the Paula Jones, Monica Lewinsky, and Bill Clinton scandals has amply demonstrated, other reasons, and distinctly nonfeminist reasons, exist for condemning consensual sex — *whether welcome or not* — in the workplace, in schools, and in the military. For moralists and social conservatives, such sex, again whether welcome or not, is sinful because it is outside of marriage, and is for that reason alone harmful not only to the individuals affected but also to the institution of the family and the institution of marriage. Patriarchists as well have reason to worry about nonmarital school and workplace sex. Whether such sex is welcome or unwelcome, sex outside of marriage threatens the monopoly power of male sexuality within marriage. If unwelcome, it does so by ceding to other men sexual access and prerogative, or, if welcome to the woman, it threatens male marital prerogative simply by providing an outlet for the expression of true rather than constructed desire. Academic administrators, military commanders, and other institutional instrumentalists have good bureaucratic reason to worry about school, military, and workplace sex: sex is institutionally dysfunctional. A well-run, tightly administered, smoothly oiled school or military base is better off without it. Sex up and down the ranks in schools, workplaces, or the military is an affront to discipline, order, uniformity, and conformity.

These bureaucratic, patriarchal, or moralistic reasons for condemning nonmarital sex, of course, are utterly unlike the reasons for prohibiting unwanted sex that I tried to outline above. Among many other differences, the harm of unwanted sex as described above is a harm experienced by women in intimate and married life as well as in public life, while the harm of consensual non-marital sex that concern social conservatives and patriarchists is the harm to the power of patriarchal institutions to mandate the sufferance of unwelcome sex within marriage and to regulate or ban the enjoyment of welcome sex outside of it. Politically, those worried over the pervasiveness of sex outside of marriage seek to maintain hegemonic commitment to the value of marital sex, whether wanted or unwanted, and the value of institutional discipline outside of it. From a socially conservative or moralistic (or, for that matter, institutionally instrumental) perspective, the "welcomeness" or "unwelcomeness" of the sexual conduct—central to feminist understandings of the harm—is utterly and profoundly beside the point: unwelcomeness does not make marital sex any less of a good, and welcomeness does not make nonmarital sex any less of a harm. The two forces do overlap politically in their condemnation of unwanted sex outside of marriage. Feminists condemn such sex because it is unwanted and harmful to women, and social conservatives, and patriarchs and bureaucrats, condemn it, not because it is unwelcome or harmful to women, but because it is nonmarital, and accordingly harmful to both private and public patriarchal institutions. But the overlap is just that—an overlap. It does not reflect any submerged but fundamental shared interests between vulnerable women and the military establishment, or between girls and school administrators. Even less does it reflect a meaningful convergence of feminist and patriarchal or bureaucratic views on the ways in which we should conceive of or construct our shared and public, or individuating and private, social worlds.

Now, these institutional, patriarchal, and moralistic reasons for condemning sex in schools or in the military or in the workplace may be good or bad, as reasons go: whether you credit them or not depends largely on whether and how much you value marital sexual monopoly, biblical conceptions of virtue, well-run schools, pedagogical authority, and military discipline. But whether they are good or bad reasons, they have distinctive advantages in the court of public opinion over whatever feminist reasons there may be for understanding the harms of unwelcome school or workplace sex, to say nothing of feminist reasons for suspicion regarding welcome sex in such fora: they are well understood, even by those who deny their seriousness, and they are widely, although obviously by no means universally, embraced by a large and nonliberal consensus of institutionalists, patriarchs, and moralists. For precisely that reason, wherever consensual and nonmarital sex is challenged as harmful, there is a tremendously high risk that the claim will be heard as asserting the existence of these social and moral harms—harms to family, marriage, church, school, state, political authority, or the economy — rather than as asserting the existence of political and psychic harms to women. And for precisely that reason, we need to worry that whenever consensual, nonmarital sex is claimed as harmful, the distinctively feminist understanding that the harm is a harm to women and of a political and psychic nature, will simply drop off the map of public understanding. Again, all I am trying to do here is make a minimal prudential point: feminists should be clear that, whatever might be our worries or reservations about the "unwelcomeness" requirement as an evidentiary matter, it is unwelcome sexual conduct that lies at the heart of sexual harassment, and it is therefore unwelcome sexual conduct, not welcome and desired sex at school or in the workplace, that is the target of sexual harassment law.

Should we, though, expand harassment law to include even welcome sexual relations between persons of disparate power in schools and in the military? These relations are, after all, often exploitative, regardless of whether or not they are targeted for other reasons by social conservatives. That is true enough, but here again, I think, minimally a word of caution is in order. Surely, if feminists, acting in alliance with school administrators or the military brass, and for whatever reason, also target consensual *and welcome* sexual relations between unequals in schools or the military, the risk or probability of widespread confusion between feminist and conservative understandings of the targeted harm becomes a virtual certainty. Unwelcomeness, again, is of utterly no importance to the social conservative case against nonmarital sex — from a conservative perspective, "unwelcomeness" does not render marital sex harmful, and welcomeness does not reduce the harm of nonmarital sex. Furthermore, the social conservative case against nonmarital sex of either a welcome or unwelcome sort is deeply understood in this culture. The feminist case is not. By targeting *exactly* the same behavior — welcome sex outside of marriage — whether or not it is done in the name of protecting women and girls against relationships which in retrospect seem to have been exploitative, the harm targeted by such a regulation may be misunderstood as the harm of nonmarital sex quite generally, and the traditional debate between conservatives and liberals on the wisdom of regulating against it will be off and running. Feminist understandings of the quite clear harms of unwelcome sex (to say nothing of the far more subtle harms of welcome sex) will be drowned out. Again, the public and media response to the Lewinsky and Jones scandals surely bears this out.

So far, let me stress, I have raised only prudential reasons against regulating or prohibiting welcome sex in schools or in the military between unequals. These prudential reasons, to my mind, are determinative: we should not go down this path, because the attempt to do so on women's behalf will be quickly co-opted. Let me end by distinguishing, and distancing myself from, a second argument against regulating welcome consensual sex on campuses, which has been raised by a growing number of either liberal or postmodern pro-sex commentators (and others) over the last few years.[2] The argument, in essence, is something like the following: The welcome sexual relationship within which an identity might be forged is worthy of celebration and protection rather than condemnation, for precisely the same reasons that we ought rightly to condemn unwanted sex. Welcome and desired sex in these fora as well as in any other is expressive of precisely the hedonic unity of desire, pleasure, and preference so threatened by unwelcome sex. If sexual desire — welcome, warm, and enjoyed, whether or not accompanied by romantic love — can triumph in the bureaucratized and militarized and authoritarian and hierarchical and masculine worlds of orders, directives, uniformity, and spiritual death, then surely such sexual desire, with or without love, ought to be embraced. Enjoyed and wanted sexual relationships — including most emphatically those between persons with different amounts of power — might after all embolden rather than disempower, might connect rather than alienate, might demystify rather than obfuscate, might facilitate rather than retard learning and competency, might nurture rather than undermine healthy self-regard, and for all of these reasons might be expressive of liberalism in its best light: the healthy and anarchic and physical and liberating impulse within the liberal tradition, rather than the profit-maximizing and commodifying and alienating. These affairs and the impulses and desire they express, after all, when genuine, evidence above all else our deepest desire to know and be known — a desire which when not perverted is central to a questing and curious spirit. They bring women into the liberal celebration of selfhood and ego and the unity of desire and action. They express a healthy self-regard and rebellious and liberal or postmodern challenge to those who would undermine that self-regard, not in the name of patriarchal sexual monopoly, but rather in the name of bureaucratic capitalism, or fetishistic and soul-deadening false pedagogical idols. If nothing else, they constitute a hedonistic excess which might be politically astute, if the oppression of sexual exploration and pleasure is central to some systematic and orchestrated campaign of subordination.

This is a tremendously appealing — even seductive — suggestion, and it is one in which those of us who have participated in such relationships as either teachers or students might take considerable comfort. Nevertheless, even if we acknowledge the possibility of such affairs, and even if we value them when they occur and treasure our memory of them if we think we have enjoyed them, we ought to be wary of celebrating all such relationships on these grounds. It is not at all clear that the experiences of women and girls within unequal sexual relationships in schools have any even remote connection to the celebration of selfhood and affirmation of self-esteem claimed on their behalf. First, at least with respect to high school and middle school girls, a growing body of empirical observation seems to show the obvious, and that is that there is simply no such Bacchanalian celebration of selfhood going on: for teenage girls the line between welcome, enjoyed consensual sex and unwelcome sex is utterly and literally fictional.[3] Teenage girls cite every reason imaginable for having or pursuing or initiating a sexual relationship with peers or with older men, from peer pressure to overt coercion to low self-regard and simple confusion — *except for* the pleasure to be had from them, or the fulfillment of desire to be sought, or the satisfaction of sexual urges. The same may well be true of teenage undergraduate students as well.

Whether or not there is value in consensual and welcome sexual relationships between teachers and truly adult students, however, is a harder and open question. I do not think we have even begun to answer it. To answer it, we need to know not only how those relationships are experienced, but where they lead. Do they lead to stable marriages or long-term relationships, happy productive lives, decent mothering, healthy intimacy, defensible life plans? Do they form the bases of good and flourishing intimate lives? They may, but they may not: they may lead, more often than not, to flattened self-esteem, abruptly curtailed careers, a jolting redefinition of oneself away from principal actor to helping partner, and ultimately, to an appendage-like life-of-mind-numbing and spirit-deadening boredom. If so, then even if they are enjoyed, they may be enjoyed not for the celebration and affirmation of life their postmodern defenders claim, but for reasons that reflect and go to the heart of our collective injury in a society that sexualizes us: they may be enjoyed precisely because they redefine the self as an adored and worshiped sexual creature, rather than a stumbling, bumbling, erring student, in need of paper topics, grades, and recommendations; because of the limits they impose upon our risk-taking rather than the vistas they open; because of the certainty and stillness they inspire in our aspirations, rather than the life and movement they engender within and around us. If so, in my view, they are in no one's long-term interest, and certainly not the weaker woman's. These relationships may very well, in fact, represent a severance of objective interest and well-being from subjective desire and pleasure that is at least as profound as the severance of desire and pleasure from objective choice and act manifested by sexual harassment and suffered by harassed women, or the severance of act and choice suffered by victims of rape. These are, I think, hard and important questions. They are also, though, questions that we cannot answer by any route other than a careful examination of the quality of our lives. We certainly cannot answer them by logical inference: again, we should no more infer that welcome consensual sexual relations in schools are all-things-considered good, and good for you, from the fact that they are *welcome* than we should infer that sex is welcome from the fact that it is consensual. Welcome sex might be desired and enjoyed but nevertheless harmful because injurious to interest, just as unwelcome sex might be fully consensual but nevertheless harmful because undesired. If it is welcome, then it is not going to carry with it the harms of unwelcome sex. But that does not mean it is harmless. It may carry with it different harms.

How, then, should a school regulate against this backdrop of uncertainty? That is, simply, a difficult question raising familiar issues of paternalism and false consciousness — questions not raised, it ought be emphasized, by prohibitions against and regulation of sexual harassment. The difficulty of the question should not deter us from trying to answer it, but it does suggest that schools should tread cautiously. Women do, after all, differ from each other, and have strikingly different ambitions, plans, and strengths. We have different levels of sexual desire or intensity, differing degrees of devotion to our intimate partners and children, differing aptitudes for and commitment to career rather than domestic goals and ambitions. Our interests are different, and regulating or legislating against desires on the basis of presumed interest is tricky business, here as elsewhere.

All things considered, I think we probably ought not do it. But we should be clear, I think, on the reason for caution. It is not, to my mind, because we have decided that such relationships are *good*. Their goodness no more follows from their welcomeness than does the goodness of unwelcome sex follow from its consensuality. Rather, we ought not regulate against these consensual and welcome relationships not because they are prima facie good, but for the straightforward and traditionally liberal reason that it is hard to say whether and when they are harmful, and for the pragmatic and feminist reason that trying to do so will overshadow, and may obliterate, our still fragile understanding of the harms threatened by unwelcome sexual conduct on the job, in homes, and in schools — conduct that no woman *wants* to tolerate, that does considerable and demonstrable harm, and that no one in liberal society ought to be forced to endure. Sexual harassment, traditionally understood, is the name we have given that harm. We can and should use the state as a partner in ridding our work and school worlds of it. We should not obscure the goal by conjoining it with a campaign against desire, a campaign that is more likely than not to be obscured and then co-opted by conservative and institutional commitments to the prevailing and still largely patriarchal orderings of family, academic, and military life.

Notes

1. *See* Catharine MacKinnon, *Sexual Harassment of Working Women: A Case of Sex Discrimination* 7 (1979).

2. *See* Jane Gallop, *Feminist Accused of Sexual Harassment* (1997); Duncan Kennedy, *Sexy Dressing* (1996).

3. *See* Sharon Thompson, *Going All the Way: Teenage Girls' Tales of Sex, Romance, and Pregnancy* (1995).

PART **III**

Same-Sex Harassment

Theories of Harassment "Because of Sex"

WILLIAM N. ESKRIDGE, JR.

Where does Title VII "draw the line" between impermissible workplace sexual harassment and permissible, even if squalid, misconduct? The statute tells employers they cannot "discriminate against any individual with respect to his compensation, terms, conditions, or privileges of employment because of such individual's race, color, religion, sex, or national origin."[1] This text does not clearly tell the Equal Employment Opportunity Commission (EEOC) or the courts where to draw the line, owing in part to the ambiguity of the word *sex*, in part to the lack of a clear policy underlying the prohibition, and in part to the importance of context in drawing such lines. Each of sex's different meanings can entail more than one underlying policy of Title VII, and the application of any one definition or any one policy is influenced by the interpreter's factual and normative understandings. Given these multiplicities, the statutory analysis is mobile, uncertain, and therefore manipulable.

Table 11.1 illustrates some ways employees can be "harassed" in the workplace, as popularly understood or as felt by the employees. Scenario 1, where a male supervisor sexually gropes and threatens a female employee, strikes most people as the classic case of harassment, yet the early cases held that Scenario 1 did not violate the statute. Trial judges reasoned that any harm to the employee was "because of" her attractiveness, or her uncooperative attitude, not "because of sex."[2] Appellate judges have analyzed the situation more

Table 11.1 Scenarios of Workplace Harassment

Scenario 1.	Mechelle, a female employee, is groped and threatened with rape by her supervisor Sidney, who explains that he wants sex with her.
Scenario 2.	Michael, a male employee, is groped and threatened with rape by his supervisor Sidney, who explains that he wants sex with Michael.
Scenario 3.	Mechelle, a female employee, is denigrated by her supervisor, Sidney, as not "aggressive" enough to do her job, which is "man's work" anyway.
Scenario 4.	Michael, a male employee, is denigrated by his supervisor, Sidney, as a "sissy boy" not "aggressive" enough to do "man's work."
Scenario 5.	Michael, a male employee, is taunted by coworkers as a "faggot" and is mock-raped. Michael complains to the supervisor, Sidney, who laughs it off.
Scenario 6.	Mechelle, a male-to-female transsexual employee, is taunted by co-workers and is mock-raped. Mechelle complains to the supervisor, Sidney, who refuses to listen. "You're too weird," he says.

Note: These scenarios are variations of *Meritor Savings Bank v. Vinson*, 477 U.S. 57 (1986). An important difference is this: Mechelle Vinson, the real-life complainant, was sexually assaulted and not just groped and threatened. All six scenarios assume that the employer is found legally responsible for the conduct of the supervisor, in accord with *Burlington Indus., Inc. v. Ellerth*, 524 U.S. 742 (1998), and *Faragher v. City of Boca Raton*, 524 U.S. 775 (1998).

liberally, and the early cases have been decisively overruled and rejected by the Supreme Court.[3]

The early judges were neither illogical nor crazy, and the sponsor of the sex discrimination amendment to Title VII, Representative Howard Worth Smith of Virginia, might have agreed with their dispositions. But the original logic or policy of Title VII, if any there ever was, has been overtaken by developments in the workplace and the greater legal and political voices of women. The illegality of Scenario 1 is now settled, but the other scenarios still present difficult issues for the EEOC and the courts. An ultimate goal of sex discrimination jurisprudence is to bring coherence to employer obligations, but an intermediate goal might be just to understand the theoretical choices.

That is my purpose: to explore some of the potential voices in Title VII, as they relate to the semantic and policy choices offered by the statute. Like most other statutes, Title VII's evolution will be driven not by the dictionary or the original legislative history, but by the pragmatics of the nation's shifting political consensuses on issues presented by women, gay men and lesbians, and transgendered people in the workplace.

The Multivocality of "Sex"

Title VII does not define *sex*, except to say that it includes pregnancy.[4] The Supreme Court typically looks to standard dictionaries of the era to discern statutory meaning of undefined terms. The 1961 edition of *Webster's* defines the word *sex* to mean as many as three things:[5]

"[o]ne of the two divisions of organisms formed on the distinction of male and
   female," or *sex as biological dimorphism;*
"[t]he sphere of behavior dominated by the relations between male and female," or *sex as gender* (man = masculine, woman = feminine);
"the whole sphere of behavior related even indirectly to the sexual functions
   and embracing all affectionate and pleasure-seeking conduct," or *sex as
   sexuality.*

Which of these is the statutory meaning(s) of sex?

The answer to that question might make a difference to sex harassment law. For example, if sex means nothing more than biological dimorphism, Scenarios 1 and 2 are easier to characterize as sex discrimination than Scenarios 3–6, because it is easier to prove that biological women are being treated differently than biological men. While the complainants in Scenarios 1 and 2 can persuasively argue they would not have been harassed if they had been a man or a woman, respectively, the same is less apparent for the complainants in Scenarios 3–6. In Scenarios 3–4, the employer could argue that Sidney valued aggressive workers of either sex and, therefore, was not differentiating on the basis of biological dimorphism. So, too, for Scenario 5 the employer could say that discrimination, if any, was because of Michael's perceived sexual orientation, and not his sex. From the employer's point of view, the actions in Scenario 6 were not occasioned by Mechelle's biology, but by her effort to change or hide her "real" biological sex. For Scenarios 5–6, however, Michael and Mechelle could respond that the employer would have treated a woman's complaints of mock rape more seriously.

If, instead, sex means gender, Scenarios 3–4 are more likely to be considered cases of sex discrimination, because the supervisor in both cases might be viewed as differentiating based upon traditional ideas about gender. Scenario 3 becomes a particularly compelling case, if the employer is understood to insist that there are categories of work that are intrinsically masculine. Given traditional gender notions of man as sexually aggressive and woman as sexually receptive, Scenario 1 remains an easy case if sex means gender, although Scenario 2 becomes more ambiguous for the same reason. Scenario 5 might be brought within the statute if the decisionmaker accepts the strong historical and psychological link between stigmatization of homosexual orientation and departure from traditional gender role.[6] Even Scenario 6 could fit within the statute if sex means gender: the bad treatment seems inspired by Mechelle's insistence not only that her biological sex does not match her gender identity, but that the former must be changed in order to conform.

If sex means sexuality, Scenarios 1–2 remain core violations and Scenarios 3–4 less so, just as they were under a reading of sex as biological dimorphism. Pursuant to an understanding of sex as sexuality, Scenario 5 also becomes a core violation, because Michael is being harassed because of his sexual orientation, and perhaps also because of sexual fears his coworkers have about themselves. Scenario 6 is a possible violation, dependent on whether prejudice against transsexuals can be characterized as based on sexuality as well as gender. Under a sex as sexuality reading of Title VII, the fact that the offending conduct is sexual in nature for Scenarios 1–2 and 5–6 may add something to the cogency of those claims. In contrast, the employer might distinguish Scenarios 1–2 from 5–6 on the ground that "genuine" lustful male-female sexual advances (1–2) are different from conduct that is merely "hazing" or expressions of disgust (5–6). Such a strategy could exclude claims on behalf of gay and transgendered people.

Table 11.2 maps the various regulatory permutations of the various definitions of *sex*.

Unfortunately, Table 11.2 and the exercise it encapsulates are incomplete, because (1) the dictionary terms are themselves contestable; (2) further context creates complexities for the analysis; and, most important, (3) the application of any of the different definitions of sex discrimination requires an appreciation of the statutory purpose or policy.

As an illustration, consider how these problems complicate the analysis of Scenario 2, where a male employee is harassed by a male supervisor. This scenario can be brought within the statute on the ground that the supervisor would not have assaulted someone of the "opposite sex." But what if Sidney were bisexual and harassed both women and men in the office? Even if Sidney were attracted only to men, what if Michael were a biological woman passing as a man? Or a female-to-male transsexual? Are all of these variations discrimination "because of" the employee's biological "sex"? (Scenario 6 offers further play along these lines.) One might still say that the discrimination is because of the employee's sexuality, but that term is just as intractable as sex. Sidney might claim that he is just hazing Michael, engaging in a locker-room domination game with a subordinate employee. When does hazing become sexual? When is it ever not sexual? So perhaps Scenario 2 falls outside the

Table 11.2 Regulatory Implications of Different Meanings of "Sex":
Does Harassing Conduct Constitute Statutory Sex Discrimination?

	Biology	Gender	Sexuality
Scenario 1	Yes	Yes	Yes
Scenario 2	Yes	No?	Yes
Scenario 3	No?	Yes	No
Scenario 4	No	Yes	No
Scenario 5	No?	Yes?	Yes?
Scenario 6	No?	Yes?	Yes?

statutory prohibition, as the analysis of sexuality as gender originally suggested. But gender offers explanations that bring the conduct within the statute. For example, if Sidney claims he was just hazing Michael, he might be engaging in ritual boys-culture behavior that seeks to "feminize" male subordinates. Within that understanding, Sidney may in fact have been harassing Michael because of (and to reinforce) his gender.

One can analyze Scenarios 3–6 in a similar way: the answers provided in Table 2 become increasingly tentative once the complexities of biological sex, gender, and sexuality are contemplated. The complexities multiply if Title VII's deployment of sex involves more than one of the possible definitions. How can the lawyer or agency official or judge mediate these ambiguities? Another way to analyze these scenarios is to consider the statutory purposes or goals. What purposes or policies does Title VII entail?

Multiple Statutory Theories

Title VII does not announce its statutory goal(s), and its legislative history overwhelmingly emphasizes the remediation of job discrimination against people of color. Its sex discrimination provision was added as a "killer amendment" by Representative Smith, who was both a foe of the civil rights bill and a fan of the long-debated Equal Rights Amendment.[7] There was very little serious legislative debate about the sex discrimination provision. Moreover, Congress amended Title VII in 1972, 1978, and 1991. The 1978 amendment extended the statute to include pregnancy-based discrimination.[8] The 1991 amendment overrode a series of conservative judicial constructions of Title VII but, significantly, left intact the case law recognizing sexual harassment as a claim for relief.[9] It is not a straightforward exercise to aggregate the different legislative assumptions at the different points in time. As with the definition of sex, therefore, the policies animating the evolving statute are complex and constructed over time rather than simple and received at the statute's birth.

Consider possible statutory policies at a high level of abstraction. Title VII's prohibition of sex discrimination might emphasize either *liberal, weberian* policies, *feminist, antisubordination* policies, or both. Ironically, both liberal and feminist policies are antipatriarchal. Liberal thinker Max Weber saw patriarchy in organizational terms, whereby economic and social structure was personalized around the father or master, characteristic of feudal culture. Modern culture, in contrast, seeks to organize production around objective, meritocratic rules, rather than subjective, personalized practices.[10] Weberian rules are more suitable for the modern world than patriarchal practices because they are more efficient and better fit individual talents with their most productive use. From this perspective, the evil of sexual harassment is that it violates the merit principle and disrupts the workplace.

In partial contrast, early feminist writers Lin Farley, Carroll Brodsky, and Catharine MacKinnon viewed patriarchy as the physical as well as psychic subordination of women. They emphasized the ways in which workplace harassment keeps women subordinate — segregating them in "women's work," keeping their salaries low, and impeding their advancement — and thereby reinforces a patriarchy of female subordination to male power.[11] MacKinnon and subsequent feminist writers have pressed the argument that Title VII's goal is to overturn the systematic subordination of women in the workplace.

Liberal motives probably dominated the birth and early history of Title VII, but feminist ones were more prominent in the 1978 and 1991 amendments. Hence, both kinds of policy thought are potentially relevant to the statute's application. Moreover, there is no single liberal or feminist theory regarding Title VII. The two theoretical stances are themselves multifarious. At least six variations can be imagined, most well-represented in the academic literature. Each variation would press sexual harassment law in somewhat different directions.

1. *Free Market (Chicago School).*[12] A Chicago-style libertarian philosophy finds workplace departures from the meritocratic ideal to be lamentable but posits that such departures will be disciplined by the presumptively well-functioning free market: firms tolerating stereotype-based decisionmaking and disruptive harassment on the job will lose valuable employees to more civilized firms and, hence, will tend to fail. State intervention is probably not necessary to solve weberian problems, according to this school of thought. Indeed, state regulation in the form of Title VII adds administrative and transactions costs, as well as institutional costs of forcing greater sex integration on

firms that operate most efficiently with sex-segregated forces. Because such free marketeers believe Title VII should be repealed, nothing should be a violation under their approach. Absent a repeal of Title VII, Chicago-style theorists, some of whom are now judges, might urge that the statute be construed narrowly.[13]

2. *Formal Equality.*[14] Drawing from procedural theories of civil rights law, formal equality theory emphasizes the policy that similarly situated employees should be treated similarly, along the criterion of "sex." Most adherents of formal equality theory treat sex as biological and, therefore, only insist that women and men be treated the same in the workplace. Scenarios 1–2 are the core statutory violations, to the extent that Mechelle and Michael would not have been sexually assaulted "but for" their being a woman and a man, respectively. Scenarios 3–4 would not be considered violations, so long as the employer applied aggressiveness criteria to both men and women; there would, however, be a violation under Scenario 3 if the comments are read to reflect sex-segregated job decisions. Scenario 5 is unclear: Michael is not entitled to relief if the employer treats gay employees different from straight ones, but ought to get relief if the employer would have treated a woman's mock-rape complaint more seriously than a man's. Note how definitional ambiguities centrally reemerge in this kind of theory: if formal equality theory defines sex to include gender and sexuality, as many gay and feminist theorists argue it should,[15] then Scenarios 3–6 are transformed from ambiguous cases to clearer violations of the statutory commandment.

3. *Institutional Rationality.*[16] Perhaps closest to the weberian spirit, an institutional rationality approach would defend Title VII because it seeks to root out irrational prejudice from the workplace and to assure that decisions are based upon merit rather than upon factually unsound gender stereotypes or raw emotions such as prejudice or sexual attraction. Put bluntly, institutionalist theory seeks to degender and desexualize the workplace. Scenarios 1–2 most transparently violate that goal. Scenarios 3–4 are ambiguous in this way: even if the supervisor's comments about man's work and sissy boys are off-base, the conduct in those scenarios might not be serious enough to justify regulatory intervention if in fact Mechelle and Michael are not as aggressive as other employees and aggressiveness is important to the task at hand; an institutionalist perspective might defer to the employer as to those issues. Scenarios 5–6 are unclear for a different reason: there are institutionalist disruptions on both sides; the supervisor is allowing destabilizing gender and sexuality wars to go on, but the complaining employees themselves might be said to have sexualized the institution, and the weberian judge might be reluctant to guarantee perceived "troublemakers" job security.

4. *Sexuality.*[17] Although cognizant of arguments from markets, formal equality, and institutional function, feminist theories focus on subordination, especially of women. Sexuality-based theory posits that the main engine of misogyny is the way in which intercourse has been constructed so that the man is the aggressor and is on top, the woman is passive and is beneath the man. Gender role (man/boss, woman/helper) tracks this pattern in the workplace, and the goal of Title VII must be to derail this hierarchy. Hence, sexual harassment is illegal because it enforces sexual subordination by reinforcing traditional gender roles. Under an ambitious version of this theory, such as that propounded by Professor MacKinnon, all six scenarios are core violations of the statute, because all six replicate the pattern of male subordination of the feminine or the female.[18] Critics claim that a sexuality-based theory of women's subordination renders Scenarios 3–4 less central to the statute, not because sexuality feminism considers these practices benign, but because its focus on sexuality as the engine of patriarchy has in practice deflected attention from the ways that old-fashioned gender stereotypes remain powerful as well.[19]

5. *Gender Role.*[20] Other feminists start with gender stereotypes, rather than male-aggressive sexuality, as the main engine of workplace patriarchy. The key problem which Title VII ought to address is the continuing sex segregation of work, in which traditional men's work (the prestige jobs) remains male and traditional women's work (the lower-level jobs) remains female. As to that problem, unwelcome sexual touching is no more important than sexist assumptions about "men's work" and "women's work." Thus, for gender role theory, Scenarios 3–4 are just as important violations as Scenarios 1–2, and sexual harassment theory has erred in obsessing about Scenarios 1–2 to the frequent obliteration of Scenarios 3–4. Scenario 5 is also an important violation because gender role theory (like most versions of sexuality theory) accepts the argument that homophobia is a weapon of sexism.[21]

6. *Benign Variation.*[22] Virtually all feminist theories and most liberal theories view biology-based (man/woman) variation as benign and therefore are suspicious of employer rules or practices that treat women and men differently. Most such theories also treat gender (masculine/feminine) variation as benign and therefore are suspicious of employer rules or practices that treat macho women and effeminate men differently. Some feminist theories take the next normative step and argue that all gender variation and most sexual variation are benign; they are suspicious of employer rules or practices that treat cross-dressers, gays and bisexuals, and transgendered people differently from other women and men. Not only would benign variation theory treat all six scenarios (except maybe Scenario 2, where the complainant is not a gender or

Table 11.3 Regulatory Implications of Various Sex Discrimination Theories: Does Harassing Conduct Constitute Statutory Sex Discrimination?

	Liberal Theories			Feminist Theories		
	Free Market	Formal Equality	Institutional Equality	Sexuality	Gender Role	Benign Variation
Scenario 1	No?	Yes	Yes	Yes	Yes	Yes
Scenario 2	No?	Yes	Yes	Yes	Yes?	Yes?
Scenario 3	No	No?	No?	Yes?	Yes	Yes
Scenario 4	No	No	No	Yes?	Yes	Yes
Scenario 5	No	Unclear	Unclear	Yes	Yes	Yes
Scenario 6	No	No?	Unclear	Yes	Yes	Yes

sexual nonconformist) as violations of Title VII, but such theory would consider Scenario 6, the hard or unsympathetic case under the other theories, as a core violation of the statute, which should be construed to protect gender as well as sexual nonconformity.

Let us pause to collect our thoughts about the different liberal and feminist theories as they relate to the six sexual harassment scenarios posted at the beginning of this chapter. Table 11.3 arrays the various theoretical stances, with notation of ambiguities. Table 11.3 must be read guardedly, for reasons already emphasized. All of the theories are fuzzy as to certain scenarios, and some results for any of the theories could change under new factual assumptions. Nonetheless, Table 11.3 suggests some surprising as well as unsurprising conclusions.

Not surprisingly, Scenario 1 is a clear violation under five of the six theories (and possibly all six); this is the core violation of the statutory command. Also as one would expect, the feminist theories are much more likely to find liability for sex-based harassment, especially in Scenarios 3–6, than liberal theories. Less expected is that the feminist theories are much more supportive of liability even when the complainant is a man, as in Scenarios 4–5. Most surprising (to me) were provisional observations that both liberal and feminist theories were open to liability for employer toleration of coworker assaults on gay and transgendered people, the conduct described in Scenarios 5–6. Early case law was dismissive of such claims, perhaps in part because judges viewed "homosexuals" and cross-dressers as deranged individuals. A more factually based understanding of lesbians, gay men, bisexuals, and transgendered people as capable human beings promises to open the minds of libertarian as well as feminist decisionmakers to arguments that workplace harassment of these people violates both weberian as well as feminist precepts.

The Law and Politics of Sex-Based Harassment

Given the textual and policy indeterminacies of Title VII, theory is critical, but not all theories are created equal. The role of normative theory for the evolution of Title VII law depends less on the brilliance of the theory and more on the theory's political constituency. Free market theory seems to have astonishingly little constituency, even among corporate leaders, and drops out of the analysis. Weberian theory of institutional rationality has a strong constituency among employers, especially the big megacompanies that influence policy by lobbying the agency, legislature, and, through amicus briefs, the courts. Given its moorings in traditional equal protection jurisprudence and the rule of law, formal equality theory has a strong constituency among judges, who of course decide the cases. The Supreme Court is attracted to this theory but remains attentive also to the political equilibrium reflected in agency and legislative views and to the personal views of the Justices. Two of the Justices are women, one of whom has herself been a leading feminist thinker and the foremost proponent of the application of formal equality norms to women and sex. Other Justices have shown an intellectual interest in feminist theory. Feminist theory's biggest constituency is the people in this country who are women working outside the home, gay people, and other kinds of gender-benders. To the extent that feminist theory has been propelled by the sexuality-as-patriarchy idea, that theory has a powerful constituency as well. The gender role theory and, to a lesser extent, benign variation theory are now making their own claims to reflect women's workplace experiences and, thereby, to represent this important constituency. For cultural reasons, these theories have not displaced or supplemented sexuality theory, which strongly appeals to the country's ambivalence about the power of sexuality and its aversion to public performances of sexuality.

In short, the dominant intellectual debate draws from theories of formal equality, institutional rationality, and sexuality as patriarchy. Therefore, Scenarios 1–2, clear violations under all three theories, remain the core of sex harassment law, essentially because they involve sexual misconduct anathema to both the weberian workplace and the feminist utopia. Scenarios 3–4 are less likely violations, because they do not sexualize the workplace and have a more indirect connection to women's subordination. Homophobia still makes many liberals and feminists nervous, and fear of other people's homophobia makes officials and judges fearful and often timid; these phenomena render Scenarios

4–6 less likely situations for violations under current political conditions. The sexual violence entailed in Scenarios 5–6, however, makes those cases likely violations under some circumstances.

This thought experiment also suggests frontier issues that Title VII decision-makers will have to confront in the next decade. Apart from the extremely important issues of employer responsibility for supervisor or employee misconduct, examined elsewhere in this book and in recent Supreme Court decisions, cutting-edge issues for Title VII sex harassment liability include the following: (1) Can gendered slurs, such as those in Scenarios 3–4, constitute the sole basis for liability? Is some kind of sexualized statement or conduct necessary? (2) Do slurs, assaults, and taunts regarding sexual or gender orientation constitute actionable harassment? Gay supervisors can create liability by harassing employees of the same sex. Can homophobic supervisors create liability by harassing gay employees? Can a gay man make out a case that the employer would not tolerate harassment against women that it allows against men? Can a lesbian make out a case that antilesbian assaults are a historical way that men have terrorized all women, not just lesbians? (3) Under what circumstances, if any, do cross-dressers and other transgendered people have claims for sex harassment?

In answering these questions, the Supreme Court will be guided not only by theory, by political equilibria pertaining to issues of gender and sexuality, and by the Justices' personal views about proper workplace policy, but also by other evolutive considerations: agency positions, the Court's own precedents, and overall shifts in social power.[23] The Court pays careful attention to the "informed judgment" of the EEOC, which has expertise in implementing the statutory scheme, creates reliance among the regulated population, and is well-informed politically.[24] In the *Oncale* case, where the Court held that same-sex harassment could be actionable, the EEOC developed a range of situations where Scenario 2 should result in liability, and the Court or lower courts will probably move in that direction. The EEOC has informally taken the position that nonsexual but gender-based harassment is actionable, as in Scenario 3, but the agency's official guidelines do not address that kind of harassment.[25] The EEOC silence is deafening on issues of gender and sexual variation presented in Scenarios 4–6. EEOC silence, ambivalence, and certainly hostility would discourage the Court from breaking new ground as to these scenarios. The EEOC's stance is not static, however. New factual or legal developments, or the fresh political priorities of a new presidential administration, could press the EEOC in either protective or deregulatory directions. Any thoughtful and well-documented policy pressed by the agency would be one the courts would take seriously and to which most judges would defer.

For rule of law, political, and efficiency reasons, the Court adheres closely to its statutory precedents and may be willing to extend related constitutional precedents to inform statutory cases. For example, the Court ruled in *Price Waterhouse v. Hopkins*[26] that an employer violated Title VII when it denied a job promotion to a woman substantially because the other managers considered her too "mannish." If the Court feels impelled to extend this precedent to issues of sex harassment, Scenarios 3–4 become more likely candidates for liability. (The Court's constitutional equal protection precedents, which focus on discrimination inspired by outmoded gender stereotypes, might also be read to support liability in Scenarios 3–4.) Even lower court precedent can be influential. Federal appellate courts have, thus far, tended to hold that Title VII does not protect gay or transgendered workers from harassment because of their sexual or gender variation. Normally, the Supreme Court would defer to such lower court consensus, unless the Justices believe it runs against their decisions in *Hopkins* and *Oncale*. That depends on how broadly the Justices read those recent precedents, which, in turn, depends on who is on the Court. Hence, future appointments to the Court may influence the resolution of Scenarios 5–6.

Finally, shifts in social power influence the evolution of statutory law. The best example of that phenomenon is Title VII itself, which in a generation has been transformed from a toothless symbol to an aggressive instrument against sex harassment in the workplace. No one thinks that dramatic shift occurred as a matter of logic alone. The importance of women's voices does not predetermine judicial resolution of sex harassment issues, especially where women's interests are clouded by theoretical and popular disagreement. Complementing women's political power is the increased salience of openly lesbian, gay, and bisexual employees and managers. If gay people could be dismissed as psychopathic criminals by the Warren and Burger Courts, they can no longer be so dismissed by the Rehnquist Court. Gay voices emphasize theories of gender equality and benign variation and, accordingly, seek to press Title VII beyond Scenarios 1 and 2, toward liability in Scenarios 3–5 (but with an astonishing reticence, thus far, about Scenario 6).[27] If the Supreme Court is cleverer than it was in *Bowers v. Hardwick*,[28] it will avoid definitive resolutions of these issues until the polity and the Justices have a chance to absorb some of the lessons of gay experiences and theories.

Notes

1. Civil Rights Act of 1964, § 703(a)(1), 42 U.S.C. § 2000e-2(a)(1).

2. E.g., *Miller v. Bank of America*, 418 F. Supp. 233, 236 (N.D. Cal. 1976), rev'd on other grounds, 600 F.2d 211 (9th Cir. 1979); *Barnes v. Train*, 13 FEP Cases 123, 124 (D.D.C. 1974), rev'd sub nom. *Barnes v. Costle*, 561 F.2d 983 (D.C. Cir. 1977). *See* Lisa

A. Granik, "Running in Hermeneutical Circles: Challenging/Embedding Social Hierarchies Through Litigation" (Yale J.S.D. diss. 1997).

3. *Meritor Savings Bank v. Vinson*, 477 U.S. 57, 65 (1986), following EEOC, Guidelines on Discrimination Because of Sex, 29 C.F.R. ch. XIV, § 1604.11(a).

4. Civil Rights Act of 1964, § 703(k), 42 U.S.C. § 2000e(k) (as amended by the Pregnancy Discrimination Act of 1978, *see* note 8 below).

5. *Webster's New International Dictionary of the English Language* 2296 (2d unabridged ed. 1961).

6. *See* William N. Eskridge, Jr., "Law and the Construction of the Closet: American Regulation of Same-Sex Intimacy, 1880–1946," 82 *Iowa L. Rev.* 1007 (1997); Francisco Valdes, "Queers, Sissies, Dykes, and Tomboys: Deconstructing the Conflation of Sex, Gender, and Sexual Orientation in Euro-American Law and Society," 83 *Calif. L. Rev.* 1 (1995).

7. *See* Cynthia E. Harrison, "Prelude to Feminism: Women's Organizations, the Federal Government, and the Rise of the Women's Movement 1942 to 1968," at 472–473 (Ph.D. diss., Columbia Univ.), discussed in Katharine M. Franke, "The Central Mistake of Sex Discrimination Law: The Disaggregation of Sex from Gender," 144 *U. Pa. L. Rev.* 1, 23–25 (1995).

8. Pregnancy Discrimination Act of 1978, Pub. L. No. 95–555, 92 Stat. 2076, codified at 42 U.S.C. § 2000e(k); *see Newport News Shipping & Dry Dock Co. v. EEOC*, 462 U.S. 669 (1983) (liberal interpretation of 1978 amendment).

9. *See Faragher v. City of Boca Raton*, 524 U.S. 775, 792 and 804 n.4 (1998) (1991 amendments essentially ratified the broad construction of sex discrimination to include sexual harassment).

10. *See* 3 Max Weber, *Economy and Society: An Outline of Interpretive Sociology* 998–1002 (Guenther Roth and Claus Wittich eds., 1968). For applications of Weber's ideas to workplace discrimination, *see* Rosemary Pringle, *Secretaries Talk* (1988); Rosabeth Moss Kanter, *Men and Women of the Corporation* (1977).

11. *See* Carroll M. Brodsky, *The Harassed Worker* (1976); Lin Farley, *Sexual Shakedown: The Sexual Harassment of Women on the Job* (1978); Catharine A. MacKinnon, *Sexual Harassment of Working Women: A Case of Sex Discrimination* (1979).

12. *See* Richard Epstein, *Forbidden Grounds: The Case Against Employment Discrimination Laws* (1992); Richard Posner, "The Efficiency and Efficacy of Title VII," 136 *U. Pa. L. Rev.* 513 (1987).

13. For an example of narrow construction, *see Jansen v. Packaging Corp. of Am.*, 123 F.3d 490, 515 (7th Cir. 1997) (en banc) (Posner, C. J., dissenting). Compare *id.* at 552 (Easterbrook, J., concurring). *Jansen* was affirmed, and the approaches proffered by both Posner and Easterbrook rejected, by the Supreme Court in *Ellerth*, 524 U.S. 742 (1998).

14. *See Price Waterhouse v. Hopkins*, 490 U.S. 228, 262 (1989) (O'Connor, J., concurring); *Harris v. Forklift Sys., Inc.*, 510 U.S. 17, 25 (1993) (Ginsburg, J., concurring); *Oncale v. Sundowner Offshore Servs., Inc.*, 523 U.S. 73 (1998) (Scalia, J.) (suggesting this approach). On the civil rights model underlying this theory, see Paul Brest, "In Defense of the Antidiscrimination Principle," 90 *Harv. L. Rev.* 1 (1976).

15. *See* Andrew Koppelman, "Why Discrimination Against Lesbians and Gay Men Is Sex Discrimination," 69 *N.Y.U. L. Rev.* 197 (1994); Sylvia Law, "Homosexuality and the

Social Meaning of Gender," 1988 *Wis. L. Rev.* 187, as well as sources in note 6 above. I develop the implications of this argument in William N. Eskridge, Jr., *Gaylaw: Challenging the Apartheid of the Closet* 218–31 (1999).

16. *See Burlington Industries, Inc., v. Ellerth*, 524 U.S. 742 (1998) (Kennedy, J., for the Court); *Faragher*, 524 U.S. 775 (Souter, J., for the Court). Intellectual roots of institutionalist theory are in Henry M. Hart, Jr., and Albert M. Sacks, *The Legal Process* (William N. Eskridge, Jr., and Philip P. Frickey eds. 1994 [tent. ed. 1958]). Five Justices of the current Supreme Court, including Kennedy and Souter, took the Legal Process course from either Hart or Sacks when they were in law school.

17. *See* MacKinnon, *Sexual Harassment;* Susan Estrich, "Sex at Work," 43 *Stan. L. Rev.* 813 (1991); Miranda Oshige, "What's Sex Got to Do with It?" 47 *Stan. L. Rev.* 565 (1995) (student note).

18. See the *amicus* brief Professor MacKinnon filed in *Oncale*, 523 U.S. 73, emphasizing the theoretical as well as practical reasons for broad application of Title VII to same-sex workplace harassment, including the alleged "hazing" behavior in that case.

19. *See* Vicki Schultz, "Reconceptualizing Sexual Harassment," 107 *Yale L.J.* 1683 (1998).

20. *See* Mary Anne Case, "Disaggregating Gender from Sex and Sexual Orientation: The Effeminate Man in the Law and Feminist Jurisprudence," 105 *Yale L.J.* 1 (1995); Schultz, "Reconceptualizing Sexual Harassment"; Camille Hébert, "Sexual Harassment Is Gender Harassment," 43 *U. Kan. L. Rev.* 565 (1995).

21. See the sources in notes 6 and 15 above.

22. *See* Katharine M. Franke, "What's Wrong with Sexual Harassment?" 49 *Stan. L. Rev.* 691 (1997); Samuel A. Marcosson, "Harassment on the Basis of Sexual Orientation: A Claim of Sex Discrimination Under Title VII," 81 *Geo. L.J.* 1 (1992); *Cf.* Gayle Rubin, *Thinking Sex: Note for a Radical Theory of the Politics of Sexuality* (1984), excerpted in William N. Eskridge, Jr., and Nan Hunter, *Sexuality, Gender, and Law* 250–259 (1997).

23. *See* William N. Eskridge, Jr., *Dynamic Statutory Interpretation* chs. 2–3, 5 (1994) (evolutionary factors in statutory interpretation over time).

24. *Vinson*, 477 U.S. at 65, quoting *General Elec. Co. v. Gilbert*, 429 U.S. 125, 141–42 (1976). *See also Faragher*, 524 U.S. at 806 (EEOC construction important background for developing rules governing employer liability for the harassing acts of supervisors).

25. *See* Franke, "Sexual Harassment," 709–710 and nn.78–79, 89.

26. 490 U.S. 228 (1989).

27. In an unprincipled move, the proposed Employment Nondiscrimination Act of 1996 (and subsequent bills), which would have prohibited employer discrimination because of sexual orientation, excluded transgendered orientation from its protections. *See* Eskridge and Hunter, *Sexuality, Gender, and the Law* 948–958, 1102–1146, for discriminations against transgendered people.

28. 478 U.S. 186 (1986). The Court in *Hardwick* treated gay people's assertion of their right to privacy in consensual sexual relations to be "at best, facetious" and gave the serious arguments in that case the back of its collective hand. Such a dismissive treatment of human rights claims has brought more trouble to the Court than to lesbians and gay men. *See* Eskridge, *Gaylaw*, ch. 4, for analysis of *Hardwick* and its critical reception.

What's Wrong with Sexual Harassment

KATHERINE M. FRANKE

The Problem

What exactly is wrong with sexual harassment? In the United States today, it goes without saying that workplace sexual misconduct is a form of sex discrimination. How has this come to go without saying? Is there something we should be saying about it that illuminates it's *a priori* sexism? The time has come to ask these questions anew, some twenty years after the publication of Catharine MacKinnon's groundbreaking book in which she first articulated how sexual harassment institutionalized the sexual subordination of women to men in the workplace. Since 1979, as courts have come to embrace a cause of action for sexual harassment under Title VII of the Civil Rights Act of 1964, legal scholars have provided rich and nuanced accounts of what I have called the *what*[1] and what Kathryn Abrams has called the *how*[2] of sexual harassment. Yet until recently, the *why* of sexual harassment has remained underexamined by courts and commentators alike. It is to this issue — why should sexual harassment be considered a form of sex discrimination? — that both legal scholars and the Supreme Court have turned their attention of late.

Unfortunately, now as in 1979, a number of foundational questions remain unaddressed in the jurisprudence that has evolved in response to this "fact" of our working lives. First, what does it say about our legal conception of gender-based subordination that we treat sexual harassment as a form of sex discrimination? Second, why should we treat sexual harassment differently from, say, racial or ethnic harassment, or other forms of seemingly "nonsexual" sex discrimination, for that matter? The answer to both of these questions turns, in significant part, on the fact that the conduct in question is sexual in nature. Yet, why does offensive conduct gain this entirely special status once it is recognized as sexual? In other words, what is the significance of the sexual nature of the conduct to our understanding of it as sex discrimination?

The task of feminists in the 1970s and early 1980s was to illuminate how gender-based structural inequality was accomplished through sex. Sex is not just a drive or a feeling, they argued, it is power. Having persuaded courts that gender-based power is at stake when men solicit sex from women in the workplace, we are now paying the price of having oversimplified the message in order to make it comprehensible to a legal audience. In this chapter I will briefly describe how, during the first twenty years, the judiciary has answered the question: What's wrong with sexual harassment? I will then propose a new direction for sexual harassment law specifically and sex discrimination law more generally, that corrects for the short cuts and mistakes that the courts have made in developing an overly formalistic approach to an extremely complex workplace dynamic that affects women and men in all strata of the wage/labor market.

Twenty Years of Sexual Harassment Jurisprudence

Initially, courts dismissed the claims of sexual harassment plaintiffs as trivial complaints about inharmonious working relationships, gripes about the personal proclivities of male workers that were unrelated to employers' responsibility, or whining about what was the inevitable sexual attractions that result from men and women working together. Yet, in the mid- to late 1970s courts began to be more receptive to the notion that there was a connection between unwanted sexual advances and sex discrimination. We inherit today what has been an evolution in juridical reasoning about why sexual harassment violates laws prohibiting sex discrimination in the workplace.

The central judicial conception of the discriminatory nature of sexual harassment is grounded in notions of formal equality: Men and women are not to be treated differently in the workplace *because of their* sex. Thus, courts have asked: Is the complained of harassment something that would not have taken place *but for* the victim's sex? In other words, would he have sexually harassed her if she had been a man? This formal principle of equality enables a court to isolate those practices that are sex-based discrimination from those that are not.

Employed in sexual harassment cases from the very beginning, the *but for* formulation of the wrong of sex discrimination quickly became an unstated premise underlying all sexual harassment litigation. So much so that the Supreme Court summarily concluded in 1986 that "[w]ithout question, when a supervisor sexually harasses a subordinate because of the subordinate's sex, that supervisor 'discriminate[s]' on the basis of sex."[3] Yet the Supreme Court offered no explanation for why this conclusion could be asserted "without question." For the Supreme Court as well as lower courts, this short cut was animated by the belief that men sexually harass women as an expression of their (hetero)sexuality: "When someone sexually harasses an individual of the opposite gender, a presumption arises that the harassment is 'because of' the victim's gender. This presumption is grounded on the reality that sexual conduct directed by a man, for example, toward a woman is usually undertaken because the target is female and the same conduct would not have been directed toward another male."[4]

After a period of time courts began to ignore the "because of sex" element of the plaintiff's case when female plaintiffs alleged that men had engaged in unwelcome, explicitly sexual conduct. If the conduct was sexual, it went without saying that it was discriminatory, and the court simply moved on to employer liability. "Sexual harassment can take different forms, both sexual and non-sexual. 'The intent to discriminate on the basis of sex in cases involving sexual propositions, innuendo, pornographic materials, or sexual derogatory language is implicit, and thus should be recognized as a matter of course. A more fact intensive analysis will be necessary where the actions are not sexual by their very nature.' "[5]

It may be that it is legitimate to draw such an inference, or even presumption, in cases where a man is charged with sexually harassing a woman — but drawing this inference based upon our intuition that this is what the conduct *means* must take place within the context of a theory of *why* sexual harassment is, or can be, a form of sex discrimination. The inferences we draw in these central cases are an efficient application of what principle of discrimination?

This very question could no longer be ignored once the courts had to determine whether to extend these principles of sex equality to same-sex sexual harassment. Offensive conduct of a sexual nature, removed from the different-sex context and located in a same-sex context, presented a challenge to the notion that it was the sexual nature of the conduct that rendered it sex discrimination. By the late 1990s, federal courts began to see more and more same-sex sexual harassment cases, where men, primarily,[6] complained of being sexually harassed by other men. The anxiety and confusion expressed in the court's opinions in these cases reflected some of the flaws underlying the resolution of previous different-sex cases, as well as the paucity of Supreme Court guidance illuminating the underlying nature of the sexual harassment cause of action. What could go without saying in the different-sex cases — if the conduct was sexual, it must have been "because of sex" — was an awkward proxy for a theory of discrimination in the same-sex cases.

Many courts outwardly struggled with the question of whether, and if so, why the sexual harassment of a man by another man was the same kind of harm as that which Congress sought to prohibit when it proscribed sex discrimination in Title VII. In order to answer whether there was any sexism in same-sex harassment, courts had to be clearer about the discriminatory wrong at stake in different-sex cases. What were they to do when an implicit heterosexual presumption was destroyed? If the courts took a "boys will be boys" view of this conduct, didn't it risk reversion to the pre-1975 view that sexual harassment was just private obnoxious behavior, not discrimination?

In 1998, the United States Supreme Court addressed the problem of same-sex sexual harassment for the first time, and in doing so was forced to articulate its conception of the wrong of sexual harassment with more specificity than it had in the past. In *Oncale v. Sundowner Offshore Services*,[7] the Court held that in some circumstances the sexual harassment of a man by other men can be a form of sex discrimination. Unfortunately, rather than forging a principled path out of the thicket of previously muddled sexual harassment jurisprudence, the Supreme Court compounded the errors perpetrated by lower courts.

In *Oncale*, as in its other sex discrimination cases, the Court framed the problem as one of equal treatment. To this end, they relied on the views Justice Ruth Bader Ginsburg had expressed in a 1993 sexual harassment case: "The critical issue, Title VII's text indicates, is whether members of one sex are exposed to disadvantageous terms or conditions of employment to which members of the other sex are not exposed."[8] This case demonstrates the degree to which the Supreme Court's sex discrimination thinking is influenced by Justice Ginsburg — a former women's rights attorney who is deeply committed to a conception of sex discrimination grounded in formal equality.

Thus, the guiding principle reinforced by the Court's *Oncale* decision is a "but for" conception of the wrong of sexual harassment. Indeed, the Court's primary example of discriminatory sexual harassment is sexual conduct that is motivated by desire — whether heterosexual or homosexual. But they said more: not all unwelcome expressions of desire amount to sex discrimination. Concerned that Title VII not be transformed into "a general civility code," the

Court insisted that the statute does not reach the "genuine but innocuous differences in the ways men and women routinely interact with members of the same sex and of the opposite sex."[9] So, boys must be left some room to be boys. And, of course, so must girls.

This opinion seems to indicate that the Supreme Court, including Justice Ginsburg, was asleep or simply not interested when feminists and the greater public alike explored the gendered nature of sex in our culture over the last twenty years. Left completely ignored in the Supreme Court's sexual harassment jurisprudence are notions of structural inequality and the relationship between gender-based power and sex. The rule that emerges from the *Oncale* decision, and that must guide the lower courts when they resolve similar cases, is whether the male plaintiff was treated differently than a woman would have been had she been in his position. But his was an all-male workplace—there were no women to whose experiences we could compare that of Mr. Oncale. The only viable avenue left to Oncale was to prove that his attackers were gay, and that they went after him because they desired him, and not women.

Well, what's wrong with that? First, it figures the locus of the wrong on the harasser's subjective motivation: "Why did he/they do it?" Yet one of the great strengths of Title VII generally, and sexual harassment jurisprudence specifically, is that it applies to conduct that has either the purpose or the *effect* of discriminating on the basis of sex. Over time, Title VII has proven to be an effective weapon in combating social attitudes about the relative interests and abilities of men and women that are not necessarily grounded in animus so much as outmoded myths and stereotypes. Thus a male boss who interjects sexual comments and behavior into his working relationship with a female colleague may be guilty of sexual harassment whether he naively meant to flatter or invidiously hoped to "get off" on her presence in the workplace. *But for* causation undermines this significant strength of the statute by shifting our attention back to the purpose rather than the effect of such conduct.

Second, to regard sexual harassment as a form of sex discrimination because the harasser would not have undertaken the conduct "but for" the sex of the victim is to understand the harasser to have engaged in sexual harassment primarily because he finds the target physically attractive, would like to have sex with her or him, and/or derives libidinous pleasure from sexualizing their otherwise professional relationship. Interestingly enough, on this view, the harasser's sexual orientation, either assumed or proven, plays a central role in determining whether the offending sexual conduct was "because of sex." In fact, in these cases "but for" causation collapses into sexual orientation. Under this view, a harasser only sexually harasses members of the class of people that he or she sexually desires. As such, "because of sex," primarily means "because of the harasser's sexual orientation," and only secondarily means "because of the victim's sex."

What, then, is wrong with understanding sexual harassment as an expression of sexual desire? A great deal. First, as a logical matter, this reasoning works only in a world populated exclusively by Kinsey Ones and Kinsey Sixes, that is, people who are exclusively heterosexual or exclusively homosexual in their attractions, desires, and sexual behavior.

Yet it would be both a theoretical and a descriptive mistake to characterize offensive workplace sexual conduct primarily as the expression of sexual desire. While most, although certainly not all, people differentiate between men and women in their choice of sexual partners, what the courts have done is build a theory of discrimination on this contingent empirical foundation of differentiation. Rather, sexual harassment is better understood as the expression, in sexual terms, of power, privilege, or dominance. Something more has to be said about sex in order to understand its unwelcome expression as inherently discriminatory in nature. What makes it sex discrimination, as opposed to the actions of "a philanderer, a terrible person, and a cheapskate,"[10] or a racist for that matter, is not the fact that the conduct is sexual, but that the sexual conduct is being used to enforce or perpetuate gender norms and stereotypes.

While the courts are clearly working from an outdated and inaccurate description of the complexity of human sexuality, the use of these old chestnuts in sexual harassment jurisprudence is particularly dangerous for their insistence that all sexual behavior is always, already, and exclusively about sexual desire. To understand sexual harassment primarily in terms of misplaced sexual desire is wrong for many of the same reasons that it is a mistake to understand rape as primarily a crime of passion or lust.[11] Psychologist John Pryor has closely studied the factors, dynamics, and proclivities that make a man likely to sexually harass ("LSH") women with whom he works or studies. Among other things, according to the methodology set forth by Neil Malamuth, Pryor found that LSH men also tested likely to rape ("LR").[12] Furthermore, like LR men, LSH men demonstrated attitudes and belief structures that included acceptance of interpersonal violence, the desire to dominate women,[13] high authoritarianism, and difficulty assuming other people's perspectives, that is, they had difficulty being empathetic. Finally, Pryor's findings indicated that LSH men believed deeply in sex-role stereotypes and endorsed stereotypic views of male sex-role norms. In summary, building on the rape studies, Pryor confirmed the notion that men engage in offensive sexual conduct in the workplace primarily as a way to exercise or express power, not desire.

While cognitive psychological studies indicate that the equation of sexual harassment with sexual desire represents a descriptive error, it may reflect a racial bias as well. Theorists such as Kimberlé Crenshaw have argued that the claim that rape is fundamentally an expression of male sexuality employed toward the end of controlling female sexuality "eclipse[s] the use of rape as a weapon of racial terror."[14]

Several observations are in order regarding the impact that the *Oncale* decision has had on subsequent sexual harassment jurisprudence. Tragically, the Court's reasoning has reinforced the lower courts' inclination to make sex matter too much and for the wrong reasons. I suppose we should have anticipated this misplaced emphasis on sexual desire in sexual harassment jurisprudence. Having pointed for years at sex and demanded, "Look at this! This is sexism in action!" we are now in the tragic position of ending up with a judiciary that sees sexism only if there is sex. Ruth Colker[15] and Vicki Schultz[16] have amply demonstrated how courts have come to overemphasize the role of sexual conduct in workplace sex-based harassment, such that it has become more and more difficult to make out a harassment case in the absence of explicitly sexual conduct.

Increasingly, in post-*Oncale* decisions where the plaintiff alleges that she suffered a combination of explicitly sexual and nonsexual, yet gender-based harassing behavior, courts ignore the nonsexual harassment in determining whether the plaintiff was discriminated against on the basis of her sex: "general harassment, if not sexual is not actionable,"[17] declared a recent court. That same Kansas court determined that a female plaintiff had submitted *no* evidence of gender-based harassing conduct, since all she alleged, in the court's view, was gender-neutral behavior: "interrupting her, giving her a poor evaluation, opening her mail, going through her desk, advising her he could do anything he wanted."[18] Someone please call the Carol Gilligan Hot-Line! This increasing inclination to recognize harassment as sex discrimination only where the conduct is explicitly sexual is further evidenced by the number of courts that separate out the sexual and the nonsexual conduct and examine them separately. By decontextualizing the nonsexual conduct, courts make it more easily understood as mere personality conflict or "simple belligerence."[19] With the sexual conduct eclipsing the other nonsexual harassment, courts seem less inclined to draw an inference that the nonsexual conduct is gender-based.[20]

Worse yet, if the complained of conduct was sexual but did not evince sexual desire on the part of the harasser, some courts have been quick to dismiss the conduct as beyond the scope of Title VII. For instance, Laura Schmitz, a receptionist, was told by her boss that her attire undermined office productivity because "any 'hot-blooded male' in the office could be aroused," and that "he would never let his wife leave the house dressed as [she] was." After recounting this and other ways in which Schmitz's male superiors portrayed her as a loose woman, the court made clear, however, that they "never asked Schmitz for a date, never expressed any sexual interest in her, and never touched her." For this reason, the court concluded that "[plaintiff] fails to satisfy the first prong [because of sex] because she cannot show that she was subjected to sexual advances or requests for sexual favors."[21]

Next, *Oncale*'s admonition that Title VII does not impose a civility code on the workplace has had the effect of kicking open the door to a new "horseplay" defense to sexual harassment claims. Since *Oncale* was decided, all of the following conduct has been dismissed as "mere" teasing or horseplay that reflects the genuine but innocuous differences in the ways men and women routinely interact with members of the opposite sex: male workers bringing a novelty item called a "condom tree" to work, calling female coworkers nicknames like "Bumper" and "Bullets" (referring to her breasts), a male supervisor caressing a female employee's hand while playing cat and mouse with her timecard, running a hand under a female worker's skirt and up her thigh, and calling a woman babe, doll, good-looking, honey, playing with her hair while she was talking to customers.[22] "A slip of the tongue here and there is absolutely protected by the law, for excessive litigation imposes an unnecessary drain upon business, thereby leading to artificially depressed wages and inflated prices. *Moreover, in our pluralist society, no employee can expect the rough and tumble professional world to completely accommodate his or her private sense of decency, civility, and morality.*"[23]

One of the more interesting nomenclatorial exercises that courts have undertaken of late is the parsing of words and expressions such as "bitch," "blow me," "kiss my ass," and "fuck you" or "fuck me," to determine whether or not they manifest actual sexual interest or gender-based animus as opposed to "mere" anger or frustration—after all, discrimination turns in the balance. Here, as with the "but for" construction of "because of sex," courts are primarily concerned with discerning the speaker's intent in order to determine the true meaning of these common expressions. Since, one court reasoned, "ass" refers to a portion of the human anatomy shared by both sexes, there is nothing discriminatory about a man yelling at a female coworker on a construction site: "Get your ass back in the truck!"[24] When a male firefighter shouts "blow me" to a female coworker, there is no reason to conclude that this "innocuous" comment was a sexual come-on, and it therefore provides no evidence of sex discrimination.[25] Since sexual harassment is about misplaced desire, where there is no desire there can be no discrimination.

Finally, given the Supreme Court's insistence in conflating discrimination and desire, lower courts are evolving an approach to same-sex harassment whereby sexual harassment is becoming a status crime for gay men. That is to say, lower courts are so inclined to see *any* expression of sexuality by a gay man as an expression of desire, that little need be shown about the discriminatory nature of a gay man's behavior other than that it was plausibly sexual in nature. Thus we have the federal courts at once developing a jurisprudence of (hetero)sexual harassment that increasingly erases the genderedness of inter-sexual sexual behavior, while carving out a rule of (homo)sexual harassment that overdetermines gay male behavior as necessarily bespeaking desire, and therefore ineluctably amounting to discrimination because of sex. In both cases, desire figures too much and for the wrong reasons in this second genera-tion of sexual harassment jurisprudence.

The Next Wave

Given that the lower courts cleared and the Supreme Court has now paved a jurisprudential path that oversignifies sex as desire and underappreci-ates the interrelation between sex, gender, and discrimination, how might we reroute the jurisprudence of sex equality? To begin with, rather than asking whether the harassing conduct amounts to desire, the courts should be asking a different question: What is the sex doing? Most people who consider sexual harassment to violate proscriptions against sex discrimination do so for the reason that they consider sexual harassment to work a kind of sex-based inequality. This must be right. But why is it so? The key, in my view, is to understand what sexual harassment does, that is, the ways in which unwelcome and offensive conduct of a sexual nature produce or reflect sex inequality that can be fully understood only by reference to gender norms and orthodoxies.

In many cases, particularly cases between people of different sexes, sexual harassment violates a norm against sex discrimination because it reflects, per-petuates, and enforces a notion of women as sex objects, rather than compe-tent coworkers, while at the same time reinforcing the notion of the male harasser as a sexual subject, who has the power to subordinate a female coworker through sexual means by sexualizing her. It actually "puts women in their place." In this sense, sexual harassment is the tool by which subordinat-ing gender stereotypes — femininity figured as sexual vulnerability and avail-ability, masculinity figured as sexual aggressiveness and conquest — are actu-ally inscribed on men and women in the workplace. Thus, in some cases, sexual harassment can be understood as an instance of gender-based stereo-typing that reproduces and reinforces larger cultural systems of gender-based subordination in the sense that all things feminine are regarded as inferior to all things masculine. This account of the equality component of sexual harassment theory differs from other subordination accounts to the extent that I urge a refocus away from subordination based upon sex differences, and toward subordination based on gender orthodoxies and stereotypes.

But to understand sexual harassment merely as a breach of the equality commitments of Title VII is not only to elide the full potential of Title VII, but also to provide too jaundiced an account of the relationship between gender stereotypes and discrimination. Again, I will ask, "What does the sexual conduct do?" In many cases, it is used as a means by which to punish men and women alike who transgress workplace and larger cultural gender expectations. So, for instance, the sexual harassment of the first women to work in shipyards, steel mills, surgery suites, or other male-dominated sectors of the wage/labor market can be understood to violate equality norms in the workplace — men use sex as a means of preserving workplace power for themselves. But the conduct must also be understood to both affect and reflect notions of gender-based autonomy or agency. These women were doing men's work, that is, masculine work, and the harassment was the punishment they received for refusing to comply with workplace norms that *gender* certain work as properly and proprietarily men's work. The fact that the harassment was sexual in nature is not central to understanding it as a violation of Title VII. Sexual harassment often reflects this type of intersexual gender policing.

Which brings us to many forms of same-sex sexual harassment — intrasexual gender policing. Where men use offensive sexual conduct as a means by which to enforce particular orthodoxies of masculinity in men — clearly Title VII has been violated, just as it was when Ann Hopkins was denied partnership at Price Waterhouse because she wasn't feminine enough.[26] Thus, intrasexual and intersexual workplace policies and practices, sexual or not, that have the purpose or effect of reinforcing or perpetuating an orthodoxy that masculinity is the proper and natural expression of male agency or that femininity is the proper and natural expression of female agency clearly violate Title VII, not so much for reasons of sex-based subordination, but for reasons of gender-based autonomy or agency. To the extent that offensive sexual conduct is used as the tool by which these gender orthodoxies are enforced in the workplace by men against other men, or women against other women, that amounts to discrimination on the basis of sex.

For some time, feminists have resisted the demand that we choose between sameness and difference theories of sex discrimination. These theories must be nuanced enough to accommodate both sameness and difference in different contexts for different reasons. So too, our sexual harassment jurisprudence should accommodate both equality and autonomy conceptions of the norm against sex-based discrimination. Typically equality and autonomy are viewed as being in tension with one another — but that is not the case here. Rather, each is incomplete without the other. To understand Title VII in this way requires that we position gender-based norms and stereotypes at the center of such a theory. Thus, instances of same-sex sexual harassment, just as instances of different-sex sexual harassment, violate Title VII where the conduct of a sexual nature serves to reinforce or perpetuate sexually subordinating gender norms — typically that women are inferior to men. So too, Title VII must include a proscription against the enforcement of gender orthodoxies, by sexual or other means. In either case, the fundamental question to be asked is "what is the sexual harassment doing?" In most different-sex cases this is an easy question to answer, as the conduct complained of so clearly reproduces and perpetuates larger cultural norms of women as both subordinate and sexually vulnerable to men. Thus, appropriate inferences and presumptions of discrimination may and should be drawn in most different-sex cases. In same-sex cases, however, important questions must be asked with respect to the ways in which unwelcome sexual conduct may be a tool in the enforcement or policing of gender norms and rules. Thus, if an Ann Hopkins-type woman is harassed, sexually or otherwise, by the female actors on *Baywatch*, she must be able to state a claim under Title VII — even though this conduct does not take place between people whose relationship is framed by structural sexual inequality and may not be motivated by desire.

In the end, the wrong of sexual harassment must consist of something more than that the conduct would not have occurred "but for" the sex of the target, that the conduct was sexual in nature, or that it was something men do to women. The "something more" I suggest is that we regard sexual harassment as a tool or instrument of gender regulation. It is a practice, grounded and undertaken in the service of hetero-patriarchal norms. These norms, regulatory, constitutive, and punitive in nature, produce gendered subjects: feminine women as sex objects and masculine men as sex subjects. On this account, sexual harassment is sex discrimination precisely because its use and effect police hetero-patriarchal gender norms in the workplace.

To successfully conceptualize same-sex sexual harassment as a form of sex discrimination requires, to my mind, that we understand sexual harassment to be a multivalent form of discrimination that includes notions of institutionalized gendered subordination as well as notions of gender-based autonomy or agency. It is these twin concerns — that of equality and autonomy — that must be accounted for in a sophisticated theory of the wrong of sexual harassment as a form of sex discrimination — whether between persons of different or same sexes.

Notes

1. Katherine Franke, "What's Wrong with Sexual Harassment?" 49 *Stanford Law Review* 691, 771–72 (1997).

2. Kathryn Abrams, "The New Jurisprudence of Sexual Harassment," 83 *Cornell Law Review* 1169, 1170 (1998).

3. *Meritor Savings Bank v. Vinson*, 477 U.S. 57, 64 (1986).

4. *Hopkins v. Baltimore Gas & Electric Co.*, 77 F.3d 745, 752 (4th Cir.), *cert. denied*, 117 S. Ct. 70 (1996).

5. *Anderson v. Deluxe Homes of PA, Inc.*, 131 F. Supp. 2d 637, 644 (M.D. Pa. 2001), *quoting, Andrews v. City of Philadelphia*, 895 F.2d 1469, 1482 n.3 (3d Cir. 1990).

6. Some women have accused other women of sexual harassment, but these cases are relatively few when compared with the number of cases in which men objected to the treatment they received from other men.

7. 118 S. Ct. 998 (1998).

8. *Harris v. Forklift Systems, Inc.*, 510 U.S. 17, 25 (1993) (Ginsburg, J., concurring).

9. 118 S. Ct. 998, 1002–03 (1998).

10. Susan Estrich, "Sex at Work," 43 *Stanford Law Review* 813, 819 (1991).

11. The notion that rape is a crime of lust persists today even in the highest echelons of law enforcement, notwithstanding longstanding critiques debunking such a notion. The Hate Crime Statistics Act (HCSA) mandates that the Attorney General collect data about crimes that manifest evidence of prejudice based on race, religion, sexual orientation, or ethnicity. Pub. L. No. 101–275, 104 Stat. 140 (1990), codified at 28 U.S.C. § 534(b)(1). In 1995, Senator Paul Simon's office asked the FBI whether it would support the addition of gender to the HCSA. The FBI responded: "The inclusion of gender bias to the Hate Crime Statistics Act is not recommended at this time for several reasons, including the following: 1. A gender bias motivation would be very difficult to determine, e.g., is the crime of rape motivated by lust or hate? Police officers would have to explore the psyche of the offender to determine if hate was a motivating factor." Letter from C. David Evans, Acting Assistant Director, Criminal Justice Information Services Division, U.S. Department of Justice, Federal Bureau of Investigation, to Honorable Paul Simon 4 (July 5, 1995).

12. John B. Pryor, "Sexual Harassment Proclivities in Men," 17 *Sex Roles* 269 (1987).

13. John B. Pryor et al., "A Social Psychological Model for Predicting Sexual Harassment," 51 *Journal of Social Issues*, 1 (1995).

14. Kimberlé Crenshaw, "Demarginalizing the Intersection of Race and Sex: A Black Feminist Critique of Antidiscrimination Doctrine, Feminist Theory and Antiracist Politics," 1989 *Chicago Legal Forum* 139.

15. Ruth Colker, "Whores, Fags, Dumb-Ass Women, Surly Blacks, and Competent Heterosexual White Men: The Sexual and Racial Morality Underlying Anti-Discrimination Doctrine," 7 *Yale Journal of Law and Feminism* 195 (1995).

16. Vicki Schultz, "Reconceptualizing Sexual Harassment," 107 *Yale Law Journal* 1683 (1998).

17. *Unrein v. Payless Shoe Source, Inc.*, 51 F. Supp. 2d 1195, No. 97-4158-RDR, 1999 WL 455455, at *9 (D. Kan. June 3, 1999).

18. *Id.*

19. *Morris v. Oldham County Fiscal Court*, 201 F.3d 784, 791 (6th Cir. 2000).

20. *See* for example, *id.* at 796–99 (Clay, J., dissenting in part); *Duggins v. Steak 'N Shake*, 2001 WL 92166, *6 (6th Cir. 2001).

21. *Schmitz v. ING Securities, Futures & Options, Inc.*, 191 F.3d 456, No. 98–3007, 1999 WL 528024, at *3 (7th Cir., July 20, 1999).

22. *Pascouau v. Martin Marietta Corp.*, 185 F.3d 874, No. 98–1099, 1999 WL 495621, at *1 (10th Cir. July 14, 1999); *Thomas v. Henderson*, 44 F. Supp. 2d 915, No. 98–71533, 1999 WL 252648, at *8 (E.D. Mich., Apr. 27, 1999); *Webb v. Cardiothoracic Surgery Associates of North Texas*, 139 F.3d 532 (5th Cir. 1998); *Maddin v. GTE of Florida, Inc.*, 33 F. Supp. 2d 1027, 1032 (M.D. Fla. 1999).

23. *Dinkins v. Charoen Pokphand USA, Inc.*, 133 F. Supp. 2d 1237, 1250 (M.D. Ala. 2001) (italics supplied).

24. *Gross v. Burggraf Construction Co.*, 53 F.3d 1531 (10th Cir. 1995).

25. *Sechrist v. Wyandotte County/Kansas City*, No. CIV.A. 98–2219-KHV, 1999 WL 450947, at *5 n.4 (D. Kan., June 22, 1999).

26. Ann Hopkins was denied partnership at Price Waterhouse due to the fact that she wasn't feminine enough in the eyes of the male partners who voted on her candidacy. They said she was "macho," needed "a course at charm school," and "should 'walk more femininely, talk more femininely, dress more femininely, wear make-up, have her hair styled, and wear jewelry.'" *Price Waterhouse v. Hopkins*, 490 U.S. 228, 235 (1989) (quoting defendant's exhibits and district court opinion, 618 F. Supp. 1109, 1117 (D.D.C. 1985)). The Supreme Court found that this conduct amounted to gender discrimination because "an employer who acts on the basis of a belief that a woman cannot be aggressive, or that she must not be, has acted on the basis of gender." *Id.* at 250.

I3

Sexuality Harassment

JANET HALLEY

The Supreme Court has held that same-sex sex harassment may be sex discrimination within the ambit of Title VII. Its opinion in *Oncale v. Sundowner Offshore Services*[1] tells us that same-sex harassing conduct that meets other criteria in the doctrinal scheme is conclusively sex discrimination when it is motivated by erotic attraction. Thus the Court indicates that same-sex erotic overtures at work can be sex discrimination, and invites lower courts to test for erotic content by inquiring into the sexual orientation of the individual defendant. Where the defendant in a same-sex sex harassment case is not homosexual, the Court tells us, the "social context" will indicate whether harassing conduct is sex-based and thus sex discriminatory. The purportedly clarifying example is the (presumptively heterosexual) coach of a professional football team. This person does not engage in actionable harassment when he "smacks" a player on the butt out on the field (the Court seems not to notice its own salacious double entendre), but he may if he commits the same act upon a secretary (male or female) back in the office. Apparently we know that the former act does not constitute sex discrimination; while the latter, if objectively severe, makes the office a hostile environment for members of the secretary's sex. If this strikes you as a bit mysterious, do not be concerned. Justice Scalia closes with an assurance that courts and juries will use *common sense* to distinguish "simple teasing and roughhousing among members of the same sex" from actionable sex discrimination.

Common sense is precisely what I am afraid judges and juries *will* use. After all, homophobia and homosexual panic are common sense. To be sure, a gay-friendly analysis has to welcome the Court's decision that same-sex sex harassment is actionable sex discrimination: without it, federal antidiscrimination law would have explicitly declared open season on gay men and lesbians, leaving us unprotected from sexual interference that can threaten our very ability to work and learn. But with it, federal antidiscrimination law may *implicitly* declare open season on gay men and lesbians, leaving us unprotected from lawsuits that threaten our very ability to work and learn. Moreover, insights provided by the same-sex context precipitate concerns across the board. I ask here whether sex harassment enforcement has become sexuality harassment — a mechanism of social control that pro-gay and feminist thought, alike, should find alarming.

The Male-Female Model on Male-Female Sexual Harassment

In the book that did more than anything else to inaugurate sex harassment law — *Sexual Harassment of Working Women*, published in 1979 — Catharine A. MacKinnon proposed that women's sexual injury is sex discrimination. Here is the male-female model of sex harassment as MacKinnon stated it in her book:

> Analysis of sexuality must not be severed and abstracted from analysis of gender. What the current interpretations of rape [as an exercise of power, not of sexuality] fail to grasp . . . is the argument most conducive to conceiving sexual harassment as sex discrimination: a crime of sex *is* a crime of power. Sexual harassment (and rape) have everything to do with sexuality. Gender *is* a power division and sexuality is one sphere of its expression. One thing wrong with sexual harassment (and with rape) is that it eroticizes women's subordination. It acts out and deepens the powerlessness of women as a gender, *as women.*[2]

Sex appears here both as the difference between men and women (I will call this sex1, to indicate bodily dimorphism, the purportedly stable difference between male and female bodies) and as erotic appeal, genital eroticism, and everything that makes "fucking" a central focus of attention (I will call this sex2). Sexuality is the structural rather than interpersonal dimension of sex2; when she used the term in this paragraph, it appears that MacKinnon was not thinking about sexual orientation at all.

The crucial term, however, is gender. Rape and sex harassment are homologous crimes of sex1 because they use sex2 to generate gender. Gender renders men as men (that is, superordinate) and women as women (that is,

subordinate). Women *as women* are powerless. Their *gender* is this subordination. More than that: gender renders this ranking what men and women *are;* it
produces rather than reflects sex1.[3] This is the most radical element of Mac-
Kinnon's theory of sex2. The reality of sex1, and the consciousness in which
that reality seems real, natural, and inevitable, are *effects* of power. Sex hierarchy is ontologically and epistemologically "nearly perfect":[4] by producing
both its own reality and our every mode of apprehending that reality (with the
sole exception of feminist method as MacKinnon defines it), it almost completely occupies the horizon of possibility.

I will call this the male-female model. It is a neat, tight system. Purportedly
operating on the ground of sex1 but actually producing it, men use sex2 to
make themselves superordinate, and that is their gender, and to make women
subordinate, and that is our gender. They win; we lose.

Of course, this is not inevitable; rather, it is a historical catastrophe. Almost
luckily, rape and sex harassment are especially concentrated forms of sex2.
Just like myriad other rituals of heterosexual interaction, but with particular
force and clarity, rape and sex harassment give men and women gender (that
is, makes them men and women), which, for MacKinnon, means their relative
place in a male-female hierarchy. And here is where MacKinnon places her
Archimedes' lever. According to *Sexual Harassment of Working Women*, the
laws of rape and of sex harassment, when they provide a remedy for the injury
of sex2 *based on a woman's claim to women's point of view*, provide ways of
exposing this terrible mistake, interrupting the ontological and epistemological seamlessness of sex2 and enlisting the energies of the state in the project of
justice.

Now the claim of any one woman to "women's point of view" is necessarily
problematic. Some women disagree with other women who claim sexual injury, and some women disagree that sexual injury is a manifestation of wom-
en's sexual subordination. In two important theoretical articles published in
the feminist journal *Signs* in 1982 and 1983, MacKinnon recognized this
problem and acknowledged that it challenges her idea that a woman claiming
sexual injury speaks of women's experience from women's point of view.
Boldly, she refused to explain the problem away on grounds of false consciousness or of the verity of any biological woman's experience, attributing the
paired objections to the object-subject polarity that feminism detects at the
heart of male power.[5] The dilemma is not feminism's fault; it arises from the
historical capture of objectivity for, and as, the male point of view, and the
resulting object*ification* of women, the rendering of their powerlessness *as*
their subjectivity. Thus "true feminism," "feminism unmodified," MacKinnon
argued, must be radical: "Women's situation offers no outside to stand on or

gaze at, no inside to escape to, too much urgency to wait, no place else to go, and nothing to use but the twisted tools that have been shoved down our throats. If feminism is revolutionary, this is why."[6]

Hence the centrality of *method* in the *Signs* articles: feminism does not *have* the truth of women. Rather, it seeks an unprecedented disruption in the conceptual and social order by untying women's experience from the truth-feeling, objectivity-subjectivity dyad: "The project is to uncover and claim as valid the experience of women, the major content of which is the devaluation of women's experience."[7] "The pursuit of consciousness becomes a form of political practice."[8] And within that political practice, the radical project is "the claim of feminism *to* women's perspective, not from it."[9]

The 1982 *Signs* article derailed this radicalism, however, when it invoked women's experience as the source of authority for the claim that sexuality is a form of power generating male superordination and female subordination. The slip occurs in stages. MacKinnon was at first frank that her own interpretive inductions led to the claim: "*I think* that feminism fundamentally identifies sexuality as the primary social sphere of male power. The centrality of sexuality emerges . . . from *feminist practice* on diverse issues, including abortion, birth control, sterilization abuse."[10] How did feminist practice — much of it by practitioners who would have resisted MacKinnon's assessment of sexual injury and of sexuality — provide this insight? "If the literature on sex roles and the investigations of particular issues are read in light of each other, each element of the female *gender* stereotype is revealed as, in fact, *sexual*."[11] Past passive verbs; a bad sign for agency and plein air interpretation. But pay no attention to the man behind the curtain, for he is about to emerge as women asserting their experience of sexuality as subordination: "*Women experience* the sexual events these issues codify as a cohesive whole. . . . The defining theme of that whole is the male pursuit of control over women's sexuality."[12] MacKinnon's interpretive insight has become the meaning of feminist practice across the board and, ultimately, the substantive centrality of sexual subordination to women's experience of gender (and thus sex1). Sexuality is sex discrimination. Q.E.D.

In the 1983 *Signs* article the sexual subordination idea had become so central to MacKinnon's reasoning that it could be induced and deduced in the same gesture: male dominance provides the substantive, social, context for construing the meaning of particular sexual encounters to women — and the meaning of particular sexual encounters to women reveals that male dominance is their substantive, social context. This circularity may explain the remarkable grammatical stability of "the meaning" of sexual encounters from women's point of view. "[T]he injury of rape lies in the meaning of the act to its victims"[13] — that is, surely, all women — and we know what that is: "The law distinguishes rape from intercourse by the woman's lack of consent coupled with a man's (usually) knowing disregard of it. A feminist distinction between rape and intercourse, to hazard a beginning approach, lies instead in the *meaning* of the act from women's point of view. What is wrong with rape is that it is an act of the subordination of women to men."[14] Note the exclusive article ("*the* meaning"): MacKinnon concludes that the subordination of women to men is structural. And note the rhetorical posture MacKinnon assumes, of hearing "the meaning" emerge "*from*" "*women's* point of view": she warrants her finding by its real authorship in the collectivity of women. (Note that the formulation is no longer "to" but "from" women's point of view — precisely what had been disavowed the year before.) MacKinnon's 1983 confidence in these inferences was so strong that she could affirm that particular women, interpreting particular sexual encounters, always have access to this meaning: "the only difference between assault and (what is socially considered) non-injury is *the meaning* of the encounter *to the woman*."[15]

For all the fixity of the male-female model as women's point of view, in 1983 MacKinnon was unready to suggest that, because "the woman" knows "the meaning," the rules governing rape (her primary example in the second *Signs* article) should be altered to affirm her experience and disaffirm his. This reticence arises in part from a bold conclusion that the state, its law, and the rule of law are male. MacKinnon "propose[d] that the state is male in the feminist sense" not only because it pursued and protected men's interests in sexual control over women by adopting particular rules (which presumably could be rewritten), but because, "[f]ormally, the state is male in that objectivity is its norm." The very "rule form . . . institutionalizes the objective stance as jurisprudence," which, in liberalism, is "the law of law."[16] Asking the law, rather than women, to speak the meaning of sexuality from women's point of view would be a hopelessly contradictory undertaking. And so rewriting the rules of rape adjudication to make women's subjective experience decisive would merely reinscribe the terms of male dominance into the feminist project:

> [E]ven though the rape law oscillates between subjective tests and more objective standards invoking social reasonableness, it uniformly presumes a single underlying reality, not a reality split by divergent meanings, such as those inequality produces. . . . One-sidedly erasing women's violation or dissolving the presumptions into the subjectivity *of either side* are alternatives dictated by the terms of the object-subject split respectively. These are alternatives that will only retrace that split until its terms are confronted as gendered to the ground.[17]

As the *Signs* articles repeatedly affirm, women's subjective experience, no less than men's, is part of the epistemological dilemma posed by male dominance. To move "toward a feminist jurisprudence," for the MacKinnon of 1983, was to critique that dilemma as an opening for a feminist consciousness currently unattainable in its terms. And so, just after affirming, in the passage quoted above, that "What is wrong with rape is that it is an act of the subordination of women to men," MacKinnon turned from law and rape, to the system of meaning in which they are embedded: "the issue is not so much what rape 'is' as the way its social conception is shaped to interpret particular encounters."[18]

It seems quite fitting, then, that the second *Signs* article ends in the mode of critique. The last section warns that "making and enforcing certain acts as illegal reinforces a structure of subordination," catalogues the dilemmas posed for her feminist project by liberal and left jurisprudence, insists in its last line that "[j]ustice" would require something quite "new" — and avoids any effort to reconcile the idea of a charge of rape or cause of action for sex harassment by a particular woman with the problematic relationship that may obtain between her understanding and "women's point of view."[19]

In a 1989 volume collecting and revising much of her earlier work, including the *Signs* articles, MacKinnon seeks a synthesis between her early theoretical work and two decades of her feminist law reform activism. By then she was ready to draw conclusions about law that seemed out of reach in the *Signs* articles. Consider this revision of the passage on rape quoted just above:

> [W]hen an accused wrongly but sincerely believes that a woman he sexually forced consented, he may have a defense of mistaken belief in consent or fail to satisfy the mental requirement of knowingly proceeding against her will. Sometimes his knowing disregard is measured by what a reasonable man would disregard. This is considered an objective test. Sometimes the disregard need not be reasonable so long as it is sincere. This is considered a subjective test. A feminist inquiry into the distinction between rape and intercourse, by contrast, would inquire into the meaning of the act from women's point of view, which is neither. What is wrong with rape in this view is that it is an act of subordination of women to men. It expresses and reinforces women's inequality to men. Rape with legal impunity makes women second-class citizens.[20]

The changes are subtle but substantial. MacKinnon is no longer seeking to establish a feminist distinction; instead she now aims to frame the question for "feminist inquiry." And while she doesn't suggest that she wants *courts* to ask this question, her 1983 reticence to do so has been revised away. She addresses "the act" now as a particular, not a general one; there is a particular accused; and we will understand his act critically if not legally by inquiring into "the meaning of the act from women's point of view." Moreover, that point of view is no longer dangerously merged into the subjectivity that male dominance has assigned women: in a remarkable shift, to inquire after it is to *avoid* the twin falsities of objective and subjective tests. The truth of rape's wrong is the same—"it is an act of subordination of women to men"—but MacKinnon now replaces her 1983 invitation to critique with a denunciation of "[r]ape with legal impunity." Legal punishment of rape apprehended from women's point of view would be a *feminist* project.

Once again she insists that the male point of view is not only male super-ordination but also the objectivity of the law, its neutrality, and the very substance of its idea of equality.[21] But now she also insists that, confronting this impenetrable system from within it, there can be "feminist law": "Abstract rights authoritize [*sic*] the male experience of the world. Substantive rights for women would not. Their authority would be the currently unthinkable: nondominant authority, the authority of excluded truth, the voice of silence."[22] An individual woman who suffers sex harassment at work thereby exemplifies, in her sexual injury, women's gender. As long as her legal cause of action for sex harassment performs the perspective produced by women's point of view, it will allow her to interrupt the ontological seamlessness joining male superordination with the law, enabling her to make not only her injury but the injury of all women visible, audible, and interruptible.

The idea that the legal claim of one woman flawlessly reveals the injury that male superordination and female subordination inflict on all women seems quite foreign to the radicalism and the critical stance of MacKinnon's *Signs* articles, but nevertheless pervades her practice of legal remediation. The MacKinnon-Dworkin antipornography ordinance would have allowed an individual woman to obtain an injunction against "trafficking" in "pornography" "as a woman acting against the subordination of women." Though MacKinnon and others frequently argued that enforcement would not be arbitrary or boundless because plaintiffs would have to "prove injury,"[23] that is precisely what women complainants seeking to enjoin "trafficking" in pornography were *not* required to do. Instead, one woman could act for all women, without any showing of actual harm to herself or anyone else, and enjoin the production, sale, exhibition, and distribution of a wide array of "pornography," even against defendants—even against *women* defendants—who thought in good faith that the materials were not subordinating to women.[24] Similarly, MacKinnon would remove any requirement that an individual woman prove that her employer fired her with actual illegal intent; "[s]tatistical proofs of disparity would be conclusive"[25] because harm to an individual woman is the 100 percent pure distillate of the harm suffered by all women. Clearly the private lawsuit is an opportunity to remedy the injury sex2 imposes on all women.

Feminist critics of MacKinnon's theory of gender, and of her prescription for using law to undo gender, have objected to this reification of all women in the body and speech of the one who happens to file a claim.[26] In the following pages I will attempt to articulate gay-positive, queer-affirmative, and sex2-positive feminist reasons to extend their critique.

The Male-Female Model on Male-Male Sexual Harassment

Almost twenty years after publishing *Sexual Harassment of Working Women*, MacKinnon wrote a brief in the *Oncale* case for a group of amici committed to stopping violence by and against men.[27] It shows how MacKinnon's male-female model works when it incorporates three new elements of sex harassment: men's subordination *of a man*, male-male *sex2*, and thus *sexuality* reconstrued as the social dimension not of male-female sex2 but of sex2 more generally.

The facts alleged by Joseph Oncale are disturbing. Working on an oil rig in an all-male workforce, he was repeatedly threatened and assaulted by his supervisor and two coworkers. They threatened to rape him; twice they held him down while placing their penises up against his body; once they grabbed him in the shower and did something (one cannot be sure quite what) with a piece of soap. His complaints were ignored, and he quit under protest.

In the male-female model as the MacKinnon Brief elaborates it, Oncale suffered sex discrimination because he was injured *as a man*. He and other male victims of male sexual aggression are "victimized through their masculinity, violated in their minds and bodies as individual members of their gender."[28] This happens because they are given not only the *worse* gender, but the *wrong* one: "They are feminized: made to serve the function and play the role customarily assigned to women as men's social inferiors. . . . For a man to be sexually attacked, by placing him in a woman's role, demeans his masculinity; he loses it, so to speak. This cannot be done to a woman. What he loses, he loses through gender, as a man."[29]

This formulation endorses a rigid, monolithic association of men with male gender with superordination, and of women with female gender and subordination. This endorsement is even normative to the extent that it maintains MacKinnon's project of articulating "the authority of excluded truth, the voice of silence." Adopting the perspective of male victims of male sexual violence requires us to recognize that they are persecuted by other men because they fail to represent dominant masculinity seamlessly. Here the Brief seems to detach sex1 from gender, to recognize a liberatory project of loosening the stringencies of masculinity. But the Brief's articulation of the wrong suffered by Oncale also requires us to acknowledge that his primary, definitional injury is the loss of masculine superordination. How can this be a compensable loss in a feminist theory of injury?

The answer lies in the totalism of the male-female model.[30] Like *Sexual Harassment of Working Women*, the MacKinnon Brief formulates the male-female model not as natural — it is, au contraire, a historical contingency which the law can resist[31] — but as exhaustive of all possibilities for arranging sex1, sex2, gender, and sexuality. This is unequivocally clear for women: a woman has no masculinity to lose. Men, however, can endure gender downward mobility. Though the Brief is careful to flag the socially constructed quality of male gender, it is equally insistent that a man who loses masculinity is necessarily feminized: *there is nowhere else for him to go*. Thus men who lose their masculinity do so in "their gender, as gender is socially defined,"[32] but there is nothing socially negotiable about their fate "as men": because of the harassment they "*are* feminized."[33] Similarly, the Brief posits that the attacks on Oncale "violat[ed] (what is conventionally considered) his manhood."[34] This would be a nice recognition of the social negotiability of that outcome except for the parentheses, which give us the option of reading the violation as real: the attacks "violat[ed] . . . his manhood." Whether it is conventional or not, his manhood is all Joseph Oncale has got that is properly his. Take it away, and he is wronged.

The MacKinnon Brief reveals the structural ambitions of the male-female model again when it insists that homoeroticism and homosexuality have no independence of its terms. The male-female model *subsumes* same-sex-ness, rendering antigay discrimination both irrelevant to, and fundamentally the same as, sex discrimination. It is irrelevant because a homosexual harassing a person of his or her own sex is acting *just like* a heterosexual harassing a member of "the opposite sex,"[35] and because victims of sex harassment are victims whether they are straight or gay.[36] Harassment is harassment no matter who does it to whom; it always reproduces the paradigm of male-female harassment, and thus we need not take into account anything distinctive about the same-sex-ness of the parties. But at the same time homosexuality is really fundamentally male-female gender all over again. The sex of one's sexual object choice is a "powerful constituent" of one's gender, and antigay discrimination fundamentally disadvantages people for deviating from gender expectations.[37] As MacKinnon wrote on her own behalf in 1989, "Since sexuality largely defines gender, discrimination based on sexuality *is* discrimination based on gender."[38]

The Brief thus maintains the structural reach of the male-female model by simultaneously evacuating sexual orientation of any distinct components and flooding it with gender understood as male superordination and female subordination. This is, I think, a big mistake.

The Brief itself sounds three warning notes. First, consider the fourteen amici on whose behalf MacKinnon wrote the Brief. Most are men's anti-violence groups, variously committed to stopping male violence against men or against men and women, to rehabilitating male abusers and to intervening on behalf of men who have suffered sexual violence; Men Against Pornography is of course among them. In the appendix they all repeat the male-female model like a mantra — with one exception, the New York City Gay and Lesbian Anti-Violence Project, the only explicitly gay organization on the Brief, which doesn't even allude to it.[39] Why would a pro-gay stance cause this group to differ in this way from every other amicus on the brief?

The MacKinnon Brief's second warning note sounds when it argues that the homosexual orientation of the "perpetrator" (not the "defendant") may be relevant because it would make a male-male harassment case homologous to a male-female case. This would be a good thing for the plaintiff, the Brief acknowledges, because the court would then be in a position to say that the defendant would not have selected a woman as his target.[40] This is a quick and easy route to a legal finding of sex discrimination, one that the Supreme Court explicitly opened up in its decision in *Oncale*. Gay rights organizations have fought to foreclose this route ever since circuit courts first opened it, however, because it is also a quick and easy route to homophobia via the inference that because the defendant is homosexual, he probably has done this bad sexual thing.[41] In a male-male case the inference is even richer, borrowing as it does from the male-female model: because the defendant is a male homosexual, he is a sexual dominator.

The Brief warns that courts may be institutionally unable to make findings of parties' sexual orientations, and counsels courts to prevent "homophobic attacks."[42] But it entirely misses the commonsense status of the virulent inference from defendant's homosexuality to his character as a sexual wrongdoer. Indeed, the Brief virtually invites the Supreme Court to indulge in it by dropping an entirely unnecessary footnote quoting from Joseph Oncale's deposition testimony: "I feel that they made homosexual advances toward me," Oncale opined, according to the Brief, "I feel they are homosexuals."[43]

This is the third warning note, and it sounds like the last gasp of a small yellow bird. Neither lower-court opinion in *Oncale*, and none of the briefs submitted to the Supreme Court, brought this detail in the record to the Justices' attention. And the Justices did not ask for it: the questions they certified for their review made no mention of homosexuality. *Oncale* made its way up the appellate ladder as an "Animal House" case:[44] the plaintiff's allegations of cruel, repeated, and unwelcome sexual assaults were persistently read as male-male homosocial high jinks gone awry — in Justice Scalia's terms, "simple teasing or roughhousing among members of the same sex" that is aberrational only in that it has become "objectively" severe.[45] Alternatively, of course, Oncale's deposition testimony could support a reading of the scene as homosexual predation. It is difficult to escape the conclusion that the MacKinnon Brief aimed to induce the Court to adopt just such a reading.

But there is another way to imagine the case, and none of the facts published in the various court decisions in the case preclude it. Please note that, in developing this alternative reading, I am not saying anything about the human being Joseph Oncale, or making any truth claims about what actually happened on the oil rig. Instead, I am going to put his allegation of unwantedness aside, as a mere allegation, and then devise a narrative that connects the remaining dots. And since that heuristic produces the equivalent of a court's knowledge of a same-sex sex harassment case of this type up to and beyond summary judgment, the pattern I draw will become a prediction about an alarming class of cases that will make it to trial under *Oncale*.

In this version it was Oncale, as well as or possibly not his coworkers, who were homophobic. We can imagine that a plaintiff with these facts willingly engaged in erotic conduct of precisely the kinds described in Oncale's complaint, or engaged in some of that conduct and fantasized the rest, or, indeed, fantasized all of it — and then was struck with a profound desire to refuse the homosexual potential those experiences revealed in him.

Here is where I think the problem with the male-female model emerges for analysis. It is just so complete and so settled. Men are over there with masculinity and superordination; women are over here with femininity and subordination. Sex2 and sexuality are never good; they are always tools by which women are assigned subordination and men either assign or suffer it. Sexual orientation both matters and doesn't matter precisely and only to the extent it confirms this mapping. Everything is accounted for; there is nothing left over. Oncale transparently represents all men injured by this totalized gender system because the system frames all options for understanding his injury.

But Joseph Oncale's hesitant sense that his attackers "are homosexuals" is volatile in a way that interrupts this neat pattern. Does his "feeling" about his attackers tell us that they are homosexuals or that he might be? That they attacked him on the oil rig or that he attacked them by invoking the remarkable powers of the federal court to restore his social position as heterosexual? Merely asking the question indicates that some same-sex sex harassment cases are going to be profoundly misread if we assume that sex, gender, sexual orientation, and sexual power have social meaning, and should have legal meaning, inasmuch as they are fixed to particular persons by a male-female distinction.

Against the Male-Female Model

Title VII operating to regulate sexual interactions in the workplace is extremely porous to existing antigay attitudes, and can become another form of antigay regulation. When Justice Scalia complacently dedicated the reach of hostile environment liability in same-sex cases to the "common sense" of judges and juries, he opened Title VII to just such a homophobic project. After all, the very same Justice, less than two years before, had written an enraged dissent in *Romer v. Evans* asserting that it was completely reasonable for the voters of Colorado to regard homosexuals as "socially harmful."[46] If and when the possibilities implicit in his position are realized, Title VII will take us beyond sex harassment to sexuality harassment.

How is feminism going to react to this possibility?

In the concluding pages of this essay I'd like to be as clear as I can, as briefly as I can, about the scope and depth of the challenge. I'll proceed by comparing the law-reform tendencies of feminisms that trace women's subordination to sexuality, with three alternative ways of understanding the relations among sex1, sex2, gender, sexuality, and social power: gay-identity, queer, and sex2-affirmative feminist analytics.

Some thumbnail definitions of these projects are in order before I return to sex harassment law. Women's-subordination feminism posits that women are subordinated to men. Some women's subordination feminisms claim that this is a structural feature of human life (MacKinnon; cultural feminism in its "patriarchy" mode), while others think that subordination is more episodic (historicist Marxist feminism; cultural feminism in its "social meanings" mode). Some object to women's subordination as an unjust effect of power (MacKinnon); others detect in it an error in values (cultural feminism). And whereas some locate the primary or paradigm site of women's subordination in the market-family complex (Marxist and socialist feminisms), others locate it in sexuality (MacKinnon, cultural feminism focused on sexuality rather than maternity). I will call the latter sexual subordination feminism.

The gay-identity and queer projects differ from each other in ways substantially parallel to the divergence between sexual subordination feminism and sex2-affirmative feminism. Each seeks the welfare of a different kind of sexual subject. A gay identity approach posits that some people are homosexual and that the stigma attached to this kind of person should be removed. It is receptive to claims that homosexuality is biologically caused, and often asserts that lesbians and gay men are very different. By contrast, a queer approach regards the homosexual-heterosexual distinction with skepticism and even resentment, building arguments that it is historically contingent and is itself oppressive. It regards gender with the same skepticism, and so does not celebrate strong identity differentiations between gay men and lesbians or between men and women generally. A gay-identity approach fosters specifically gay culture and gay ghettos, and engages in loyalty projects like "outing" and the denunciation of homosexuals who "convert" to heterosexuality. Conversely, a queer approach thinks it is fine to be "queer in the streets, straight in the sheets"; encourages contingent and alterable sexual identification along dimensions other than the sex of one's sexual object choice, such as the object's gender or particular sexual acts; and takes within its purview not only same-sex love that does not express itself in sexual acts, but also cross-sex love that does.

Thus a gay-identity analytic thinks that there *are* homosexuals just as women's-subordination feminisms think that there *are* women; they object to the social subordination of these discrete constituencies; and they at least tend to, if not need to, maintain the discreteness of the identities on whose behalf they labor in order to present themselves as coherent. Queer thought, by contrast, is anti-identitarian. It dissociates male bodies, masculinity, and superordination from each other, rendering sexuality a domain in which sex1, gender, and power are highly mobile. The masculinity of women — Judith Butler's reflections on the lesbian phallus; Judith Halberstam's on female masculinity — and the appetitive sexual abjection of men — Richard Rambuss's machinehead and Leo Bersani's homos[47] — could not be noticed in the vocabulary of the male-female model and would be decried as morally defective by cultural feminism. Queer thinking *agrees* with MacKinnon and cultural feminism that sexuality is shot through with power, but it is convinced that the result is only episodically and certainly not structurally domination. Perhaps one way to encapsulate this understanding of power is to consider Michel Foucault's lexical choice: he persistently used the French word *pouvoir* so that he could conceptualize power as the capacity to create effects and eschewed the word *puissance*, which would have carried the sense of subordinating force.[48]

Sex2-affirmative feminism shares all of that with the queer project, but adds one more element: it insists that the people currently designated "women" have a vital interest in gaining access to all the power that characterizes sexuality. The term "sex positive" has misled many bystanders to suppose that this strand of feminism thinks sex2 is or should be all good, all positive, all happy. Not so.

That is more properly the idea of cultural feminism. Instead, sex2-affirmative feminism seeks *for women* a full-face encounter with (to track Carole S. Vance's brilliant title) the pleasure and the danger of sexuality.[49]

Sexual subordination feminism, and especially the male-female model, underwrite the regulation of sexuality through sex harassment law. The gay-identity, queer, and sex2-affirmative feminist projects cannot applaud all the results. I am working on a book, also to be entitled *Sexuality Harassment*, which will lay out the differences and argue for policy choices, within feminism and outside it, that render sex harassment law more responsive to these left constituencies and motives. Here it must suffice to give a rapid sketch of some key points.

I'll start with homosexual panic—the terror that some people feel when they think that someone of their own sex finds them sexually attractive. Homosexual panic can be extremely dysphoric. Some people might even say that having a homosexual panic experience at work was unwelcome and sufficiently severe to alter the conditions of their employment and create an abusive working environment. Under *Oncale*, they can sue for that. And since juries might well think that a single same-sex erotic overture was more "severe" than a single cross-sex one, these suits could place gay men and lesbians in the workplace (especially the "known" ones) under tighter surveillance than their obviously heterosexual counterparts.

Both gay identity and queer thinking are thus in tension with feminist projects that seek a copious definition of a "hostile work environment." From a gay identity perspective, *Oncale* should be read as a direct, disproportionate threat to the constituent group. And there is more to it than that if we move in a queer direction. The idea there is to regard homosexual panic with the utmost suspicion. It's not just that the experience appears silly; it's deemed to be *in bad faith*. The idea is that no one would *panic* over the possibility of a homosexual engagement unless he or she both didn't *and did* want it. Homosexual panic, when it produces an attack on a gay man or lesbian, is thought to be a way of punishing someone else for desires that are properly one's own. A queer approach would question whether the homosexual panic plaintiff is making credible assertions about what the supposed perpetrator did to initiate his or her dysphoria, and whether the plaintiff's reaction is objectively reasonable. It would want the doctrinal machinery applied at these points to be skeptical, resistant to the plaintiff.

And so a queer approach dissents from feminist efforts to make these bits of the doctrinal machinery more plaintiff-friendly. For instance, it would be worried about a recent change in the Rules of Evidence, sought and hailed by feminists, barring admission of evidence of plaintiff's sexual history in civil cases involving "sexual assault." (Sexual assault includes any unwanted sexual touching, so a lot of sex harassment cases are governed by this new rule.)[50] This exclusion would make it difficult to undermine the credibility of a homosexual-panic complainant. And rethink from this perspective feminist efforts to tailor the reasonableness inquiry to match the "perspective" or "social knowledge" attributed to the plaintiff's demography. Both gay identity and queer projects would worry, for example, about the Ninth Circuit's holding that the socially sensitive judgments in cases involving women's complaints about the behavior of men are subject to a "reasonable *woman*" test.[51] What's next? Are we going to refer these elements in male-male cases to the "reasonable (thus presumably the heterosexual) man"? I hope not. The queer and sex2-affirmative feminist trajectories across these bits of doctrinal turf seem to be on a collision course with sexual-subordination feminism.

And there is even more to the problem than that. Unlike a gay-identity approach, a queer approach tends to minimize rather than maximize the differences between same-sex eroticism and cross-sex eroticism. There are many reasons for this, but I would suggest that the chief one is a sense that gender and power circulate far more complexly and with far more contingency than is thought in most women's-subordination feminisms. The phenomenon of lesbians wearing dildos (big news fifteen years ago) leads to heterosexual women wearing dildos (not news yet, but it's happening). What's the difference, asks queer theory? Or take a footnote from Jessica Benjamin's book *The Bonds of Love*. There she tells us that "A woman who had once been involved in a sadomasochistic relationship complained of her partner that 'he was bumbling, he never hurt me where or how *I wanted* to be hurt.' Indeed," Benjamin continues, "a good sadist is hard to find: he has to intuit his victim's hidden desires, protect *the illusion* of oneness and mastery that stem from *his knowing what she wants*."[52] Feminism focused on the badness of women's sexual pain at the hands of men, and committed to the idea that women's sexual subordination is the core reason for women's social subordination, has trouble liking a sentence like that. But queer thinking and sex2-affirmative feminism have no problem with it; indeed they exult over how it rearranges conventional associations of the feminine with subordination and the masculine with power.

This tendency in queer and sex2-affirmative feminist thinking creates a deep tension between them and what may be *the* central goal of women's-subordination feminist law reform in the area of sexuality. If the queer project reacts with so much skepticism to claims of same-sex sexual injury, and if the reason for that lies not only in its understanding of the historical fate of same-sex love but in its understanding of the complexities and ambivalences of eroticism, then the queer and sex2-affirmative feminist projects undermine our reasons for believing women who assert that they are sexually injured by men. If same-sex sexual injury can be phantasmatic, and based as much on desire as its opposite, why not also its cross-sex counterpart? Indeed, sex2-affirmative feminism might even say that we insult women by attributing to them such milquetoast psyches that they can be imagined incapable of fomenting powerful phantasmatic cathexes and desires. And so we have queer and sex2-affirmative feminist projects of asking whether, when a woman claims that a male coworker or supervisor or teacher injures her by desiring her sexually, we should believe her, or think her claim of injury is reasonable. And here we are near the heart of the sexual-subordination feminist sexual regulatory project, which has been to change things so that women are believed when they claim sexual injury.

Finally, a certain antinomianism persistently characterizes the queer and sex2-affirmative feminist undertakings. They are *liberation* projects, and so regard the state as a fickle source of succor. Take Michael Warner's brilliant, angry denunciation of gay centrists' efforts to secure recognition of same-sex marriage.[53] His position is not that the effort is sure to produce unmanageable backlash, or that marriage is an intrinsically patriarchal institution, but that the state's management of a distinction between married and unmarried sexual relationships is both rigid and normative, and that normativity about sexual relationships should neither be rigid nor come from the state. He would be happy to see the discrimination against homosexuals now carried out through marriage law resolved not by access to marriage, but by erasure of it. Closing that particular swimming pool would be fine with him. Legal feminists have forgotten — indeed, they have done much to bury — a long tradition of second-wave feminist activism premised on the view that the state hurts women more than it helps them when it frames rape as a more profound injury than generic assault. As Pamela Haag documents, these feminists sought to maximize women's sexual stamina by learning and teaching self-defense and by defetishizing rape.[54] This historical legacy indicates that current sex2-affirmative feminism only *appears* to have emerged as a reaction to the regulatory excesses of sexual-subordination feminism; instead, it is an indigenous form of American feminism of longstanding vitality. And it is, as Haag demonstrates, antinomian.

So, gay-identity thinking, queer theory, and sex2-positive feminism — both as theories and as constituencies — want to reshape the way we think about sex harassment regulation. Let us note, moreover, that many *women* have been important developers of these theories and stakeholders in the corresponding constituencies. At the very least they seek to challenge the authority of sexual-subordination feminism to speak for women, or to describe women's point of view, on the question of sexual injury. More broadly, all of these analytics and constituencies seek a new understanding of the tradeoffs we make when we seek to punish and deter the sex- and sexuality-based injuries which — they readily admit — men sometimes do inflict on women. Maximizing the regulatory reach of the state — and let's remember, of *management* — into workplace sexuality may do much to address those injuries; but it also brings costs which sexual-subordination feminism cannot register as such. One solution, proposed by Vicki Schultz in an important paper,[55] is to return to the socialist feminist idea that it is in the market — not, or not primarily, in sexuality — that we should locate the energies that produce women's subordinations. Her work allows us to imagine refocusing sex harassment regulation to emphasize women's equal participation in the workforce obtained in the most sexually liberating, rather than the most sexually regulatory, terms possible. Perhaps it is time to break even more eggs than Schultz does. But certainly it is time to rethink the way we assess feminist law reform achievements — that is, the way we describe and manage our relationships to the feminist state.

Notes

1. 523 U.S. 75 (1998).

2. Catharine A. MacKinnon, *Sexual Harassment of Working Women: A Case of Sex Discrimination* 220–21 (1979).

3. "Sexuality, then, is a form of power. Gender, as socially constructed, embodies it, not the reverse. Women and men are divided by gender, made into the sexes as we know them, by the social requirements of heterosexuality, which institutionalizes male sexual dominance and female sexual submission. If this is true, sexuality is the linchpin of gender inequality." Catharine MacKinnon, "Feminism, Marxism, Method and the State: An Agenda for Theory," 7:3 *Signs* 515, 533 (1982).

4. Catharine MacKinnon, "Feminism, Marxism, Method and the State: Toward Feminist Jurisprudence," 8:4 *Signs* 635, 638 (1983).

5. *Id.* at 637–38 n.5.

6. *Id.* at 638–39.

7. *Id.* at 638.

8. MacKinnon, *supra* note 3, at 543.

9. *Id.* at 536.

10. *Id.* at 529 (emphasis supplied).

11. *Id.* at 530.

12. *Id.* at 532.

13. MacKinnon, *supra* note 4, at 652.

14. *Id.* at 651–52 (emphasis in original).

15. *Id.* (emphasis added).

16. *Id.* at 644–45.

17. *Id.* at 652, 654–55 (emphasis added).

18. *Id.* at 652.

19. *Id.* at 655–58.

20. MacKinnon, *Toward a Feminist Theory of the State* 181–82 (1989).

21. *Id.* at 155–70.

22. *Id.* at 248–49.

23. For example: "In 1982, Andrea Dworkin and I advanced our equality approach to pornography through our ordinance allowing civil suits for sex discrimination *by those who can prove harm through pornography*." MacKinnon and Ronald Dworkin, "Pornography: An Exchange," *New York Review of Books*, March 3, 1994, 47–48; rpt. in Drucilla Cornell, *Feminism and Pornography* 121–29, at 121 (2000).

24. I relied on the ordinance as reprinted in *American Booksellers Ass'n v. Hudnut*, 598 F.2d 323 (7th Cir. 1985), *aff'g on other grounds* 598 F. Supp. 1316 (S.D. Ind. 1984), *aff'd* 106 S. Ct. 1172 (1986) (mem.) and *In Harm's Way: The Pornography Civil Rights Hearings*, 438–57 (Andrea Dworkin and Catharine MacKinnon eds., 1997). *See also* MacKinnon, "Pornography, Civil Rights, and Speech," 20 *Harv. C.R.-C.L. L. Rev.* 1, 60 (1985) ("The hearings establish the harm. The definition sets the standard"); and MacKinnon, "The Roar on the Other Side of Silence," in *In Harm's Way*, 3–24, for a general defense of the assertion that the hearings were conclusive on this point.

25. MacKinnon, *supra* note 20, at 248.

26. *See, e.g.,* Wendy Brown, *States of Injury: Power and Freedom in Late Modernity* 131 (1995).

27. Brief of National Organization on Male Victimization, Inc. et al., *Oncale v. Sundowner Offshore Services, Inc.*, 523 U.S. 75 (1998) (No. 96-568), *reported at* 8 U.C.L.A. *Women's Law Journal* 9 (1997) [hereinafter MacKinnon Brief].

28. *Id.* at 7.

29. *Id.* at 10.

30. In 1982 MacKinnon described male power as "total on the one side and a delusion on the other." MacKinnon, *supra* note 3, at 542.

31. MacKinnon Brief, *supra* note 27, at 11.

32. *Id.* at 7.

33. *Id.* at 10 (emphasis added).

34. *Id.* at 25.

35. *Id.* at 1, 24.

36. *Id.* at 25.

37. *Id.* at 26–27.

38. MacKinnon, *supra* note 20, at 248 (emphasis added).

39. MacKinnon Brief, *supra* note 27, appendix, at 8–9.

40. *Id.* at 24.

41. See, for example, the amicus brief filed in *Oncale* by Lambda Legal Defense and Education Fund and the ACLU on behalf of themselves and a number of women's, gay-rights, free-speech, and lesbian legal advocacy organizations: Brief of Lambda Legal Defense and Education Fund et al., *Oncale v. Sundowner Offshore Services, Inc.*, 523 U.S. 75 (1998) (No. 96–568).

42. MacKinnon Brief, *supra* note 27, at 24.

43. *Id.* at 23 n.7.

44. I am borrowing this nifty term from Katherine M. Franke, "What's Wrong with Sexual Harassment?" 49 *Stanford Law Review* 691, 768 (1997).

45. *Oncale*, 523 U.S. at 82, 81.

46. *Romer v. Evans*, 517 U.S. 620, 645 (1996) (Scalia, J., dissenting).

47. Judith Butler, "The Lesbian Phallus and the Morphological Imaginary," in Butler, *Bodies That Matter* 93 (1993); Judith Halberstam, *Female Masculinity* (1998); Richard Rambuss, "Machinehead," 42 *Camera Obscura* 96 (1999); Leo Bersani, *Homos* (1995).

48. Thanks to Alan Hyde for the observation.

49. Carole S. Vance, *Pleasure and Danger: Exploring Female Sexuality* (1984).

50. Federal Rules of Evidence 412 (1995); *see also* Jane Harris Aiken, "Sexual Character Evidence in Civil Actions: Refining the Propensity Rule," 1997 *Wisconsin Law Review* 1221 (1997).

51. *Ellison v. Brady*, 924 F.2d 872, 875–76 (1990).

52. Jessica Benjamin, *The Bonds of Love: Psychoanalysis, Feminism, and The Problem of Domination* (1998), 64n (emphases added).

53. Michael Warner, *The Trouble with Normal* (1999), chapter 2, "What's Wrong with Normal?" 41–80, and chapter 3, "Beyond Gay Marriage," 81–148.

54. Pamela Haag, " 'Putting Your Body on the Line': The Question of Violence, Victims, and the Legacy of Second-Wave Feminism," 8.2 *differences* 23 (Summer 1996) 35–44.

55. Vicki Schultz, "Reconceptualizing Sexual Harassment," 107 *Yale Law Journal* 1683 (1998).

14

Discriminating Pleasures

MARC SPINDELMAN

The Supreme Court's announcement in *Oncale v. Sundowner Offshore Services, Inc.*,[1] that same-sex sexual harassment can be actionable sex discrimination under federal antidiscrimination law, changes the social context against which it was decided. No longer, for instance, are men guaranteed all the protections male supremacy has traditionally offered them when they sexually subordinate other men. In refusing to desexualize same-sex sexual violence or render it legally invisible, *Oncale* disrupts the conventional social meanings that that violence has had. After *Oncale*, one cannot be certain how "boys will be boys," or how one is supposed to "take it like a man."

As a strike against male supremacy, *Oncale* is an important step forward for sex equality rights, including the rights of lesbians and gay men. For the first time *ever*, the Supreme Court has made antigay discrimination, in the form of sexual violence at least, subject to judicial notice and action as a matter of sex equality law. Judicial decisions in *Oncale*'s wake have already begun to acknowledge this transformative potential. As Janet Halley observes: "a gay-friendly analysis has to welcome the Court's decision that same-sex sex harassment is actionable sex discrimination: without it, federal antidiscrimination law would have explicitly declared open season on gay men and lesbians, leaving us unprotected from sexual interference that can threaten our very ability to work and learn."[2]

To be sure, the time hasn't come for lesbians and gay men to let down our guard. It's always possible courts will allow themselves to be blinded by their own commitments to male supremacist norms, and so not recognize that the context-sensitive judgments *Oncale* mandates don't warrant policing same-sex sexual interactions in antigay ways. Notwithstanding this possibility, *Oncale* is cause for cautious celebration. It puts a new legal tool in the hands of those lesbians and gay men who have been sexually subordinated because of their sex.

As a case clarifying sexual harassment law, *Oncale* may help straight and gay victims of same-sex sexual harassment in the workplace, in schools, in public housing, and even in the streets. Nor is that all. As a case addressing sex inequality's structures, *Oncale* offers victims of same-sex rape, sexual assault, domestic violence, stalking, and the sex industry a new vehicle through which to lay claim to—and to name—what they've endured. We may thus finally begin to learn, through the previously silenced voices of its victims, what life under male supremacy, with its safe harbors for perpetrators of same-sex sexual violence, means *for them*: as human beings who have been harmed because of, and through, their sex. In part as a result of feminist efforts— efforts that helped produce sexual harassment law, *Oncale*, and the analysis and social movements that, in turn, produced them—the world looks better than it did before.

But just as we begin to cross the threshold *Oncale* has opened up—beyond which is fresh knowledge of power and its sexual use—"queer theory" appears in the doorway, shooing us away.

Perhaps it could have been otherwise. Acknowledging the centrality of concepts like "power," "knowledge," "domination," "oppression," and "hierarchy," and their relation to sexuality, queer theory could have aligned itself with male supremacy's critics. But, with few notable exceptions, it hasn't. Queer theory, as I begin to show here, has in significant ways aligned itself with male supremacy and its regulation of the general erotic economy that gives meaning to women's and men's sexual lives.[3]

Against the normalization of sexuality, Michel Foucault famously proposed that: "[t]he rallying point for the counterattack against the deployment of sexuality ought not to be sex-desire, but bodies and pleasures."[4] Less cryptically, while discussing the decriminalization of rape as a sexual offense, he offered: "One can always produce the theoretical discourse that amounts to saying: in any case, sexuality can in no circumstances be the object of punishment."[5] Following now standard interpretations of these thoughts, queer theory has embraced a sexual politics that, sometimes seemingly above all, eschews sexual regulation, particularly when it comes from the state, and pursues, instead, the proliferation of bodily — including sexual — pleasures.

But what does queer theory mean by "sexual regulation"? How does that meaning differ from the limitations on sexual abuse, hence on sexuality, that feminists have long opposed? What is its relation to ending sexual abuse and the role of the state in *that* — something feminists have, at times, proposed? What is the queer conception of "pleasure," and how does it relate to queer efforts to deregulate sexuality? Or to feminist efforts to end sexual violence, which some perpetrators assuredly find pleasurable?

A close reading of Janet Halley's "Sexuality Harassment" in this volume, which ventures a queer critique of sexual harassment law, offers some answers to these — and other — questions. Having examined Halley's text for what it can teach about queer commitments *against* sexual regulation and *for* sexual pleasures, I consider its position on sexual violation, highlighting some of its dangers.

The queer critique of sexual harassment law that Halley offers begins with *Oncale*. By "complacently dedicat[ing] the reach of hostile environment liability in same-sex cases to the 'common sense' of judges and juries," we're advised, *Oncale* "open[s] Title VII to . . . a homophobic project" of "antigay regulation."[6] *Oncale*, in the queer imagination, thus threatens a very scary prospect: "The Supreme Court [having] held that same-sex sex harassment may be sex discrimination within the ambit of Title VII," sexual harassment law is poised to become — if it hasn't already — a doctrine of sexuality regulation, a dangerous, oppressive "mechanism" of sexual "surveillance" and "social control."

Queer theory isn't only concerned that sexual harassment law may regulate sexual acts that cause sexual harm. It's also concerned with sexual harassment law's regulation of desire. Understood as different aspects of queer opposition to sexual regulation, what might appear an unfortunate (perhaps Freudian) slip turns out to have deeper shades of meaning: the observation that queer theory wishes (and wishes us) to ask "whether, when a woman claims that a male coworker or supervisor or teacher injures her *by desiring her sexually*, we should believe her, or think her claim of injury is reasonable[,]" serves as one way, more or less, to recapitulate the complaint that, "Title VII operat[es] to *regulate sexual interactions* in the workplace[.]"

Once "sexual regulation" is defined in these expansive and doctrinally inexact terms, queer theory sees the occasion for such regulation woven throughout sexual harassment law. Like others before, queer theory contends that different elements of sexual harassment claims — what's legally "unwelcome," "severe," even "unreasonable," for example — are all forms of "sexual regulation" susceptible of homophobic interpretation by judges and juries.

Halley adds to this the new argument that sexual harassment suits themselves (and not just their elements) may become a legitimate vehicle for homophobic expression, a tool for "sexuality harassment," especially after *Oncale*. As well, she proposes that bringing a sexual harassment suit can itself *be* a homophobic sexual act, bound up with, and perhaps even motivated by, the same sexual dynamics that are usually the target of sexual harassment prohibitions.

It would, of course, be worrisome if homophobic plaintiffs, wrongly claiming sexual harassment that never occurred, were permitted to sue. She predicts just such an "alarming class of cases" will arise under *Oncale*, but cites not one example. Indeed, so far as is discernible from Halley's text, not a single case over the more than twenty years of reported sexual harassment decisions with which *Oncale* is consistent, and criticized by Halley as consistent, has. Not after *Oncale* either.

To deliver on her prediction, Halley serves up a fantasy reconstruction of the "disturbing" facts of *Oncale*. This is how we are to imagine Joseph Oncale's sexual violation: "In this version, it was Oncale, as well as or possibly not his coworkers, who were homophobic. We can imagine that a plaintiff with these facts willingly engaged in erotic conduct of precisely the kinds described in Oncale's complaint, or engaged in some of that conduct and fantasized the rest, or, indeed, fantasized all of it — and then was struck with a profound desire to refuse the homosexual potential those experiences revealed in him."[7] Later, referring to Oncale's deposition testimony — where he says about his harassers, "I feel that they made homosexual advances toward me. I feel they are homosexuals"[8] — we are asked: "Does [Oncale's] 'feeling' about his attackers tell us that they are homosexuals or that he might be? That they attacked him on the oil rig or that he attacked them by invoking the remarkable powers of the federal court to restore his social position as heterosexual?"[9]

These questions are provocative. But Oncale's "feeling" about his attackers' sexual orientation tells us nothing about whether he was — or wasn't — sexually harassed. Whether he is or isn't gay doesn't either.

All the same, Halley bids us to suppose that Oncale is a typical closet case: both homophobic and gay. If we do, would that mean he wasn't sexually harassed because of his sex? That he wasn't sexually harassed at all? What if Oncale's supervisor had made good on his multiple threats to rape Oncale, or if Oncale's supervisor and one of his coworkers had carried through on their attempted gang rape of Oncale in that shower stall? Would the rape not have been sex-based if Oncale had been an openly gay man? Would it not (or no longer) have been rape? If not, what would we have called it: Fantasy? Just sex? Are gay men unrapable because they're gay? Does the closet make its occupant unharassable? Following Halley's reconstruction of *Oncale*, are we to pretend that gay men who fantasize about rape are self-hating or homo-phobic — or both — when they *are* sexually violated *and complain*?

I think not. But as important, neither current law nor an understanding of sexuality as unjustly structured by male dominance finds such questions about same-sex cases "profoundly" difficult to read.[10] Indeed, these two perspectives (which, since Oncale won, converge) present a single answer to these ques-tions, and a response to Halley's wonder about what Oncale's "feeling" re-veals: No one's right not to be sexually harassed turns on the sexual identity, conscious or otherwise, of the perpetrator or the victim.[11] Whether harassing acts are sexual or sex-based doesn't — and shouldn't — depend on whether the perpetrators of sexual harassment or its victims "were" or "are" or "could be" gay, whether self-identified or self-denied.

Having catalogued the homophobic perils of sexual harassment law she sees, Halley sets out to show how "[s]exual subordination feminism, and especially [radical feminism], underwrite the regulation of sexuality through sex harass-ment law."[12] Largely between the lines, Halley hints that sexual harassment law's homophobic possibilities expose it as the province of radical feminist theorizing. One version of this argument, certainly, bursts forth in the observa-tion that "[i]t is difficult to escape the conclusion that [the *amicus* brief Cathar-ine MacKinnon filed in *Oncale*] aimed to induce the Court to adopt . . . a reading" of what happened to Oncale as a "scene" of "homosexual predation."

The march toward this conclusion effectively begins with a gloss on an argument found in MacKinnon's *Oncale* brief.[13] According to Halley, the brief maintains that "the homosexual orientation of [a] 'perpetrator' [of sexual harassment] . . . may be relevant because it would make a male-male harass-ment case homologous to a male-female case. This would be a good thing for the plaintiff, the Brief acknowledges, because the court would then be in a position to say that the defendant would not have selected a woman as his target."[14] Her partial response to this is that:

> This is a quick and easy route to a legal finding of sex discrimination, one that the Supreme Court explicitly opened up in its decision in *Oncale*. Gay rights organizations have fought to foreclose this route ever since circuit courts first opened it, however, because it is also a quick and easy route to homophobia via the inference that because the defendant is homosexual, he probably has done this bad sexual thing. In a male-male case the inference is even richer, borrowing as it does from [MacKinnon's sex equality] model: because the defendant is a male homosexual, he is a sexual dominator.[15]

There's something to this point. One needn't struggle to imagine that — or how — a putative harasser's actual or presumed homosexuality in a same-sex harassment case could lead to an inference that he has (probably) engaged in inappropriate sexual conduct. The gay man's sexual "proclivities" — the male supremacist (*not* radical feminist) belief that he is invariably indiscriminate in his sexual interest in other men and will have sex with any man if only given the chance — are mythic. "As if," Guy Hocquenghem writes, "the homosexual never chose his object and any male were good enough for him."[16]

The widespread circulation of this male supremacist myth sheds light on the reasons lesbian and gay rights organizations, along with many feminists, have maintained that sexual orientation is irrelevant to the determination whether sexual harassment in any given case is legally actionable sex discrimination.[17] As MacKinnon's *Oncale* brief, rejecting the male supremacist vision of gay men as indiscriminate sexual predators, explains: "Sexual orientation on its face disposes of nothing. Gay men do not initiate unwanted sex to all men any more than lesbian women welcome sexual attention from all women. Needless to say, from knowing a person is [lesbian or] gay, one cannot deduce that [she or he] sexually harassed another person,"[18] or, for that matter, that she or he was sexually harassed.

Proposing that sexual orientation doesn't or shouldn't determine sexual harassment liability, of course, doesn't mean that lesbians and gay men won't be liable for sexual harassment if and when they commit it. But so far as I'm aware, nobody has seriously argued we should not be — or not, perhaps, until now. Lesbian and gay rights organizations, and others, seem to agree with MacKinnon's *Oncale* brief, that "[a]lthough care must be taken that [protecting lesbians and gay men from sexual harassment doesn't] create an opening for homophobic attacks, [holding lesbians and gay men up to sex equality obligations] merely applies the same standard to everyone."[19] In terms of equality of citizenship, of rights *and responsibilities*, this is only common sense.

Halley curiously suggests otherwise. After telling us, for instance, that MacKinnon's *Oncale* brief "warns that courts may be institutionally unable to make findings of parties' sexual orientations, and counsels courts to prevent 'homophobic attacks,' " she insists that the brief "entirely misses the common-sense status of the virulent inference from defendant's homosexuality to his character as a sexual wrongdoer."[20]

Inadequacies in the description of MacKinnon's brief aside, this doesn't follow. In general terms, the brief propounds a feminist case against male supremacy, including its position that homosexuals are, characterologically, sexual wrongdoers. It expressly argues that: "Gay men do not initiate unwanted sex to all men any more than lesbian women welcome sexual attention from all women. Needless to say, from knowing a person is gay, one cannot deduce that they sexually harassed another person." So far from "entirely miss[ing] the commonsense status of the virulent inference from defendant's homosexuality to his character as a sexual wrongdoer," the brief doesn't miss it at all. It tackles the status of this inference directly, and denounces it explicitly.

Of course, this doesn't preclude a homophobic interpretation of *Oncale*. One can generate such an interpretation by appealing directly to the energies of homophobia as a substantive source of interpretation,[21] or, more circuitously, for example, by demanding that *Oncale*'s author, Justice Antonin Scalia, though speaking for a unanimous Court, had homophobic designs that control what *Oncale* means.[22] But none of this is to say — and Halley never does — that *Oncale* recommends, much less compels, its own homophobic interpretation. As she acknowledges in different ways, her antigay interpretation of *Oncale* is normative, not descriptive.[23] She fears that, with *Oncale*, "federal antidiscrimination law may implicitly declare open season on gay men and lesbians[.]"[24] Presumably, homophobic interpretations of sexual harassment law could follow. But what does that mean? That we should allow an inequality like the inequality homophobia promotes to determine sex equality rights?

A similar issue, recall, arose around matters of race, with the possibility that sexual harassment charges could be unjustly levied against men of color. The answer was to fight the racism within society and law, not succumb to it by eliminating the sex equality tool. We aren't told why homophobia requires a different conclusion now. But that's what we need to know. Racism, after all, can operate as sexual discrimination.

These considerations position us to consider the smoking gun submitted as evidence for the conclusion that the brief "virtually invites the Supreme Court"[25] to read what happened to Oncale homophobically, as an incident of homosexual predation — an invitation that the Court, through Justice Scalia, apparently declined: a footnote in MacKinnon's brief, quoting Oncale's deposition testimony. About his harassers, again, Oncale said: "I feel that they made homosexual advances toward me. I feel they are homosexuals."

In order to conclude that homophobic intentions animated this footnote in MacKinnon's *Oncale* brief, one has, at a minimum, to downplay the brief's unequivocally argued commitment to sex equality rights for lesbians and gay men, and that of the fourteen groups that signed and filed it. But the brief affirms that collective commitment early on: "Other legal requisites being met, if acts are sexual and hurt one sex, they are sex-based, regardless of the gender and sexual orientation of the parties."[26]

Supporting this argument, the brief exposes the social reality that "[t]he sexual orientation of the parties inevitably arises in, and is implicated in ruling on, same-sex harassment."[27] The brief mentions this social fact in order to criticize it: "The sexual orientation of the parties is, however, properly irrelevant to the legal sufficiency of sexual harassment claims."[28] "[N]either the rights of victims nor the liability of perpetrators of sexual harassment should turn on their sexual orientation."[29]

MacKinnon's brief repeatedly highlights its position that sexual harassment law shouldn't be allowed to embody male supremacy's heterosexual assumptions. The brief, for instance, both reveals and condemns the thinking animating the "denial that interactions among men can have a sexual component,"[30] and the suspension of that denial when one of the men involved is (or is suspected of being) gay.

Moreover, the brief indicates that its critique of male dominance in the same-sex harassment context would be incomplete without explaining how such dominance causes discrimination against lesbians and gay men. Accordingly, the brief provides an independent account of why discrimination against lesbians and gay men is sex discrimination in violation of sex equality law. Prominently among the briefs in the case and in important ways uniquely, it argues that its analysis compels the conclusion that gay rights *are* sex equality rights, a conclusion Halley, apparently, rejects as "a big mistake"[31] but never fully and persuasively engages. Exactly how the brief, given its argument squarely to the contrary, issues a pro–gay rights homophobic invitation is never explained.

So, what function does that footnote in MacKinnon's brief, quoting Oncale's deposition testimony on his "feeling" about his attackers, serve? Its purpose is to emphasize the brief's *opposition* to homophobia. The footnote appears in the course of the brief's reminder that some courts, improperly, had allowed male dominance to guide their understanding of what could be counted as actionable sex discrimination in same-sex harassment cases.[32] Read in this context—the context in which it actually appears—the footnote illustrates the understanding of same-sex harassment cases the brief repudiates: that Oncale's attackers, like other perpetrators of same-sex harassment, "must be" gay because the harassment at issue was *sexual.*

But there's more. Had it not mentioned Oncale's remark, MacKinnon's brief would have failed to acknowledge an unsympathetic fact about the plaintiff on whose behalf it was filed. It would have thus left the remark undisavowed by those lesbian and gay rights advocates supporting his side in the case. As well, given the brief's express argument for lesbian and gay rights, it would have been deceptive for the brief to be silent about this aspect of the record.

One can only imagine what later commentators would have said had the brief left such a homophobic statement lurking in the record — and in the mouth of the plaintiff whose legal position it supported — without mention.

Properly understood, then, it's hard to see how anyone could argue that the footnote — or, more generally, MacKinnon's *Oncale* brief — "invites"[33] the Supreme Court to indulge "the virulent inference from defendant's homosexuality to his character as a sexual wrongdoer," "virtually" or not. Equally baffling is why "[i]t is difficult to escape the conclusion that [MacKinnon's brief] aimed to induce the Court to adopt" a homophobic reading of Oncale's troubles. This is exactly what the brief *does not do*.

Like her other work, Halley's "Sexuality Harassment" teaches us about the art and ethics of interpretation. But we should remember that the texts she reads are the *effects* of interpretive choices she makes, but not their cause. What, though, *does* cause her readings?

A queer commitment to oppose "sexual regulation" could. Marshalling the forces of homophobia — an ideology of sexual regulation — *against* sexual harassment law may make it possible to portray sexual harassment law and radical feminist theorizing in the area as dangerous, related forms of sexual control. But it's homophobia — not sexual harassment law *or* radical feminist theory — that's ultimately the real danger Halley's analysis identifies,[34] raising the question: How can homophobia provide any normative grounds for argument within a queer project when it is something queer theory professes to oppose? Might it be that homophobia is not only a powerful source of sexual subordination, but of sexual pleasure, as well? Might success in challenging sexual harassment law as a form of sexual regulation help clear the space for queer pleasures to inhabit?

Halley's "Sexuality Harassment" doesn't expressly talk much about pleasure nor yet pleasure's virtues.[35] But it does provide a number of sketches of the way queer pleasures are arranged.[36] What may be the crispest diagram emerges in the course of the explanation why queer theory "tends to minimize . . . the differences between same-sex eroticism and cross-sex eroticism."[37] The "chief" reason for this, it is suggested, is the queer "sense that gender and power circulate far more complexly and with far more contingency than is thought in most women's-subordination feminisms." Cited with approval in support of this point is "[t]he phenomenon of lesbians wearing dildos," claimed to "lead[] to heterosexual women wearing dildos[.]" Soon after that comes a rehearsal of the lament that "a good sadist is hard to find: he has to intuit his victim's hidden desires, protect the illusion of oneness and mastery that stem from *his* knowing what *she* wants." These examples nicely illustrate the deeply hierarchical structure of those sexual pleasures queer theory "exult[s]" for the way — or so we're told — they "rearrange[] conventional associations of the feminine with subordination and the masculine with power."[38]

Having defined queer pleasures in terms of sexual hierarchy, Halley can comment: "[f]eminism focused on the badness of women's sexual pain at the hands of men, and committed to the idea that women's sexual subordination is the core reason for women's social subordination, has trouble liking" discriminating pleasures like these. Feminist rejection of such *nostalgie de la boue* is, evidently, a mistake in the queer view, because it fails to recognize that such pleasures — to repeat — "rearrange[] conventional associations of the feminine with subordination and the masculine with power."

One wonders how. How, for instance, does some women "being" masochists who will their own sexual subordination rearrange *any* of the conventional associations between gender and hierarchy? How does a woman who sexually subordinates a man by buggering him orally or anally — or both — with a strap-on dildo disrupt the "conventional association" between either "the masculine" and dominance or "the feminine" and subordination? Are penises, strap-on or not, not gendered? Is "fucking"? Are women, because they're sexed female, entirely excluded from male sexual subject positions? Can women, because they're gendered female, ever fully occupy them? What about the person dominated by a penis? Are we to believe that, socially speaking, men cannot be sexually subordinated because they're sexed as men? How about women sexually dominating men like men more typically do women? How any of these possibilities would "rearrange" rather than reinforce gender hierarchy is, at best, obscure. All that's "rearranged" — when that — is the biological sex of the participants.

Though ready to endorse the pleasures of sexual hierarchy and to assert that they can discombobulate gender norms, Halley's analysis overlooks how those pleasures are conditioned and flooded with social meaning by male supremacy. And that one can't simply rewrite the social meanings of such sexual acts without acknowledging the pervasive social reality of sexual inequality.

Indeed, the pleasures of sexual hierarchy may depend in important ways — ways queer theory hasn't so far adequately theorized — on the continuing vitality of the social meanings of sexual acts that, on the level of social meaning, queer theory proposes it can, *ipse dixit*, "rearrange." What's sexy about a woman acting like a man by fucking a man thus being treated like a woman, if not its seeming violation of male supremacy's definition of sex-appropriate gender roles in sex? Taking up a gender role that's "inappropriate" for one's sex may be sexy, even feel subversive. But it does nothing to rewrite gender roles or dissociate them from gender. At most, perhaps, doing so may give further proof (if any were needed) that gender roles aren't biological, but rather, as Foucault and MacKinnon recognized long ago, the product of social relations.

A more basic point, however, must be made. By stressing that women, including lesbians, can be sexually dominant, and that men, presumably including gay men, can be sexually dominated, Halley's normative enthusiasm for the pleasures of sexual hierarchy risks making it seem that the sexual subordination forced upon members of these groups is the product of our own unwillingness to pursue the hierarchical pleasures we should. From this it's a small step to claiming that our social subordination is a matter of our own choosing, too. After all, if our position in sexual hierarchy helps to determine our position in social hierarchy — and who has shown that they're entirely separate? — what does queer faith in existing mobilities within sexuality imply? That we've had meaningful — dare one say, "unoppressed"? — choices about our position in both sexual *and social* hierarchy? Had we only made different sexual choices, lesbians and gay men could have been socially dominant instead? Is gender inequality a mass, collective sexual fantasy?

Hierarchy seems pervasively to frame the options for the normative queer understanding of the social world. So it's no surprise that queer theory would align itself (or has) with "sex[-]affirmative feminism," and its "insist[ence] that . . . 'women' have a vital interest in gaining access to all the power that characterizes sexuality,"[39] as sexuality is presently defined. To radical feminists, however, these objectives look nothing remotely like "liberation projects." Without a critique of hierarchy, they perpetuate it, animated by the *un*liberating and *un*imaginative aspiration of giving queers "access to all the power that [presently] characterizes sexuality," meaning, "all the power" of male dominance, hence (ever-greater) access to being on top and enjoying all the pleasures and dangers of sex discrimination.

These aren't the only ways queer approval of hierarchical pleasures leads analysts like Halley astray. Consider, for example, the confident, critical description of radical feminism as MacKinnon is said to have articulated it. Halley calls it a "neat," "tight," "fix[ed]," "rigid," "monolithic," "exhaustive," "total," and "totalized" theory of sexuality. In radical feminism, according to her, "[e]*verything* is accounted for; there is *nothing* left over." Similarly, she claims radical feminism holds that "[s]ex[] and sexuality are *never* good; they are *always* tools by which women are assigned subordination and men either assign or suffer it." Indeed, her summary of "the problem" with radical feminist theory is that it's, well, just "so settled" and "so complete."

We've heard this all before. Radical feminism, however, sharply conflicts with Halley's interpretation of it, though she (like others) discusses the conflicts not at all. We do learn that radical feminists believe gender is socially constructed, a "historical contingency,"[40] in her words. But we don't learn that sexuality, in radical feminism, isn't "an overarching preexisting general theory that is appealed to in order to understand or explain, but a constantly provisional analysis in the process of being made by the social realities that produce(d) it."[41] Nor do we discover from Halley's text, except perhaps very obliquely,[42] that radical feminism is not — *yes, not* — a critique of sexuality in its every form. Within radical feminism's theory of sexuality abides that oppositional sexuality built of equality, mutuality, and respect, which can exist on the social level and, though maybe only in "truly rare and contrapuntal glimpses,"[43] sometimes already does.

Interpreting radical feminist theory through the normative queer lens of hierarchical pleasures may make it appear that radical feminism, with its radical sexual egalitarianism, is "nearly perfect,"[44] "almost completely occupies the horizon of [sexual] possibility," or worse. Then again, maybe it's simply the extent of the hegemony of male dominance over sexuality that creates this impression. Whatever the reason, a queer reading of radical feminism seems inclined either not to notice or to dismiss radical feminism's contingency and principled limits, along with its visionary dimensions. But it's distorted to caricature without them.

A similar point can be made about the skepticism we're urged to adopt toward claims of sexual violation. The argument is deceptively simple: skepticism toward claims of same-sex sexual injury propels us toward skepticism toward claims of sexual injury across the board. The moment of transition from same-sex to cross-sex cases arrives interrogatorily: "If same-sex sexual injury can be phantasmatic, and based as much on desire as its opposite, why not also its cross-sex counterpart?" This question is the analytic bridge built to the queer project of "asking whether, when a woman claims that [she has been sexually injured], we should believe her, or think her claim of injury is reasonable." On this logic, recalling Halley's reconstruction of the facts of *Oncale*, the reason to be skeptical of women who say men harmed them sexually is the same as the reason to be skeptical of (homophobic) men who say that they have been sexually injured by other men: they may *profess* that they didn't want it, but actually — they did. The basic point is developed when we're formally presented with the call for queer "skepticism to claims of same-sex sexual injury," predicated in the analysis on a queer understanding of "the historical fate of same-sex love" and "of the complexities and ambivalences of eroticism[.]"

Now, one might be at least slightly skeptical of some same-sex cases, based on a claimant's homophobia or homosexual panic. Claims comprised of antigay motives constitute antigay sexual violence, hence an abuse of sex equality law. Under some circumstances, and considering the history of same-sex love and the "complexities and ambivalences of eroticism," we might thus decide to ask whether a homophobic claimant's allegations of sexual harm reflect same-sex sexual desires denied. If they do, the homophobic allegations could be treated as being "in bad faith."

But, in an unreconstructed Freudianism, Halley advocates skepticism not of some, but of *all* claims of same-sex sexual harm. In one relevant sense, of course, we already view all claims of same-sex injury — indeed, all claims of sexual injury — skeptically: they require proof. The only issue *Oncale* resolved was whether victims of same-sex sexual abuse would be *permitted to prove their claims in fact*, as cross-sex claimants already were. Halley's skepticism, by contrast, is total, extending beyond factual proof. If it was sexual, why should we believe the victim didn't want it?

But why should we assume that all same-sex injury claims are (to use her excellent term) homologous to claims brought by homophobic or homosexual panic claimants? Without justifying this assumption, the queer reasons for skepticism of homophobic claimants can't properly be used to underwrite skepticism of nonhomophobic claims. No such explanation, however, is provided.

Perhaps with an antisubordination theory of sexual injury in mind, it is supposed that that all claims of same-sex injury are homophobic insofar as they make sexual subordination a — or *the* — cognizable legal harm. This could be so if "homophobia" were to be defined to include (any) opposition to same-sex sexual inequality — a definition queer theory might well embrace if it wanted to hold that same-sex sexuality is *always* normatively good when hierarchical in form. Under these circumstances, queer theory could maintain that any claim for same-sex sexual injury will be homophobic, even if none of the parties "is" lesbian or gay. Why? The definition of sexual harm *as* sexual subordination in every one of these cases would render the claim of sexual harm homophobic *per se*.

Halley's approval of the sexual pleasures of hierarchy, her interpretation of radical feminism, including her misreading of MacKinnon's *Oncale* brief, and her imaginative reconstruction of *Oncale*'s facts, to give some examples, appear to move in these very directions. But "homophobia" defined to include opposition to sexual hierarchy would seem to make it homophobic to treat "homophobia" as a wrong of sexual subordination. Indeed, such a definition might even compel the conclusion that to be for sex equality, including sex equality rights for lesbians and gay men, is to be antigay. Since Halley doesn't expressly define "homophobia" in just these terms, this queer definition —

with all it implies — may or may not be hers. Lacking it, however, the basis for saying that queer theory "undermine[s] our reasons for believing women who assert they [have been or] are sexually injured by men"[45] is questionable.

Even if it defined homophobia in such a peculiar fashion, queer theory would have some difficult questions to answer. To mention a few: Doesn't queer skepticism in all same-sex cases hold the credibility of victims of homophobic violence captive to the bad faith of its actual or would-be perpetrators? Doesn't queer skepticism in same-sex cases, as applied to lesbians and gay men, perpetuate antigay stereotypes about lesbian women's and gay men's capacity for truth telling, especially in matters sexual? Isn't that heteronormative? Isn't there room in queer theory to recognize that lesbians and gay men may know — and be able truthfully to tell — the difference between sexual pleasure and sexual harm?

These questions spawn others which some feminists might also wish to ask: Given that the reasons offered for queer skepticism are reasons for not protecting perpetrators of homophobic violence, why aren't they also already reasons for believing those whom such violence harms? Believing victims of sexual harm, more generally? Can queer theory argue for unmodified skepticism toward same-sex sexual injury claims and completely avoid cooperation with male supremacy? We needn't answer these questions to notice that Halley doesn't consider that the reasons she gives don't fully support queer skepticism toward claims of same-sex sexual violation. Nor does she consider that those reasons may undermine such broad skepticism, with its patently antigay implications, or that the case for queer skepticism is thus radically incomplete.

Feminists could have predicted the justificatory gap between the queer argument for same-sex skepticism and the reasons given on its behalf. Feminists committed to believing those who claim sexual injury (for all the reasons we do) are likely to see queer (or any other) skepticism to claims of sexual injury, same-sex or cross-sex, as a product of "sex panic": panic over the possibility of meaningful sex equality for women, lesbian and not, and gay men, which is to say, panic over the elimination of male dominance, and with it, the sexualization of hierarchy *per se*.

But it's also possible to read the discrepancy in queer thinking as a reflection of unstated ambivalence toward the very skepticism it's proposed we should endorse: an ambivalence that may be produced by a queer commitment to promote the proliferation of hierarchical sexual pleasures. Skepticism of cases of same-sex sexual harm may have the potential to create further space for, and to unleash, the sexual pleasures that sex equality law might otherwise "police." At the same time, however, queer skepticism has the potential to create the space for, and to unleash, the sexual displeasures sex equality law might otherwise *prevent*. Given its scope, how could same-sex skepticism *not* be expected to produce displeasure? Disbelieving those who claim same-sex sexual injury may decrease the likelihood that homophobic plaintiffs could prevail at law, hence that their abuse will ever be publicly visible. To do so, however, would strip lesbian and gay victims of sexual injury (among others) of the benefits of sex equality protections available now by law.

It's precisely because queer skepticism in same-sex sexual injury cases may lead to the production not only of pleasures, but also displeasures, that a queer commitment to pleasures could — and should — cause ambivalence about skepticism to the range of same-sex sexual injury claims. If pleasure matters to queer theorists, displeasure should, too. Queer ambivalence about a rule of skepticism toward claims of sexual harm thus ought to increase, the wider the reach of such a skeptical rule. As queer skepticism expands — from homophobic cases to all same-sex cases, to cross-sex cases, too — the stronger the currents of pleasure may flow. But likewise the stronger the pull of displeasure's undertow.

Ambivalence may also help explain why, although Halley's analysis reads as a call to erase, or to roll back, existing sexual harassment rules, her conclusion loses its radical steam, failing expressly to call for any actual modification to the current sexual harassment regime. Instead, we're told, it "seek[s] a new understanding of the tradeoffs we make when we seek to punish and deter the sex-[based] and sexuality-based injuries which — [it] readily admit[s] — men *sometimes* do inflict on women."[46]

And yet one senses there's something more Halley wishes to say. With an approving nod, we're presented with Vicki Schultz's "solution," to deemphasize the sexual dimensions of the injury that sexual harassment law addresses. Schultz's proposal, Halley writes, "allows us to imagine refocusing sex harassment regulation to emphasize women's equal participation in the workforce obtained in the most sexually liberating, rather than the most sexually regulatory, terms possible." (Unmentioned is the fact that sex discrimination law already prohibits the gender harassment Schultz seeks to cover, if not always as fully as we might like.) In an enigmatic phrase, Halley adds: "Perhaps it is time to break even more eggs than Schultz does."

Halley's conclusion thus seems conflicted: unprepared to occupy the terrain that the queer critique of sexual harassment law and theory has endeavored to clear, but equally unprepared to abandon it. A queer commitment to the production of pleasures could produce precisely this position. For reasons suggested a moment ago, the erasure, or the rollback, of sexual harassment law may well protect and release a considerable degree of pleasure — for perpetrators most of all. But such a proposal would also protect and release a considerable degree of displeasure — especially for victims. A queer commitment to the sexual pleasures of hierarchy, produced under conditions of male dominance, seems (enough) to precipitate this conflicted conclusion.

The definition of sexual injury hasn't much concerned queer theory, viewed from the vantage point of a feminism interested in stopping sexual violence. Queer theory — whether through its silence, it disagreement with sexual regulation (particularly by the state), its talk of pleasure (long a colony of gender privilege), or its refusal to confront male supremacy as such — has all too often seemed to deny that opposition to the entire matrix of sexual violence is a legitimate cause for concern and action. But despite all this, feminists have long suspected — or at least I have — that queer theorists couldn't seriously deny the existence and pervasiveness of sexual violation: of women by men, men by men, women by women, and sometimes, by women of men.

Halley shows that queer theory isn't utterly insensitive to these concerns. Within it, she tells us, there's room for recognizing the utility of feminist projects that "seek to punish and deter sex-[based] and sexuality-based injuries."[48] And to "admit" that men "sometimes" do inflict these injuries on women. After this grand gesture, however, we are not told under exactly what conditions queer theory does (or will) recognize that sexual harm has been done. But we can venture an informed guess. Within its own project, queer theory has offered some ideas about one form of sexual violence — homophobia — that might serve as the basis for queer thinking about other forms of sexual harm. Halley's analysis, for instance, can be read to posit that what's wrong with homophobic violence is that it's the product of sexual desires denied and projected outward, hence is "thought to be a way of punishing someone else for desires that are properly one's own." Substantively, it looks like this is why queer theory says homophobic violence — epitomized by the person who has an experience of homosexual panic and attacks a lesbian or gay man as a result — is "deemed to be in bad faith."

On its own, this queer understanding of the wrong of homophobic violence might not be terrifically worrisome, even though it locates the origin of the harm of sexual violation where male supremacy locates it: in the head of its perpetrators, rather than in the meaning and impact of the acts in the lives of its victims. But as the fountainhead of a general definition of sexual injury, the queer understanding of homophobia is dangerously volatile, even regressive. Should it become the legal understanding of sexual injury, law could become a set of psychological immunities for perpetrators of sexual violence to deploy, spreading skepticism of claims of sexual injury across the board.

Drawing on the queer understanding of the wrongfulness of homophobia, male perpetrators of sexual violence against women, for example, might offer that they shouldn't be held legally accountable for committing the acts of which they stand accused. Invoking queer theory, couldn't these perpetrators maintain that, in raping women, they demonstrate their own desires to have sex with (maybe be sexually dominated by) other men? If so, couldn't they contend that holding them legally liable for the manifestation of their closet fantasies is to regulate same-sex desires? Is legal accountability under these circumstances homophobic? "Sexuality harassment"? Should there thus be no liability here at all? No liability unless or because perpetrators didn't act "in bad faith" — with, that is, the "right" wrong state of mind?

Alternatively, couldn't sexual perpetrators invoke queer theory to argue that, in pressing charges, those claiming to be victims of sexual violence show *their* secret willingness to engage in precisely the sort of sexual "play" they now seek to describe, legally, as "harm"? With queer theory, couldn't these perpetrators propose that suits for sexual injury can themselves be a form of sexual violence (*pace* Cover), that engaging in sexual violence is a way of "punishing someone else for desires that are properly one's own,"[49] and so conclude that complaints of sexual injury should give rise to skepticism that "the victim" has actually suffered harm? If that, why not flat-out disbelief?

In these and other ways, the queer understanding of homophobia threatens to breathe life back into the *ancien* (read: male supremacist) *régime*. Underscoring the seriousness of this threat is queer theory's commonly maintained silence about existing, but underdiscussed, forms of same-sex sexual harm, including same-sex domestic violence, stalking, prostitution, and rape. Male supremacy, for years, legislated a certain silence around these acts, rendering them, until recently, ineffable in life and in law. It implied that gay men, *qua* gay, tacitly consented to acts of sexual violence or even that they actually desired them. A queer understanding of sexual injury, built on the queer vision of the wrong of homophobia, could make it that much more difficult than it's recently started to become, to hold perpetrators of these crimes legally accountable for committing them. But it hasn't.

Perhaps as a hedge against the unsavory possibilities its psychologized understanding of homophobia opens up, queer theory hasn't called for the eradication of sex equality law — *yet*. As we've seen, what it seeks, instead, is a socalled "new understanding of the tradeoffs we make when we seek to punish and deter . . . sex-[based] and sexuality-based injuries."[50] But this call for a "new" accounting of sex equality rules poses some deep problems for queer theory. Among them, that there's nothing "new" about treating sexual injury as a harm that takes place in perpetrators' heads or doubting the truthfulness of those who maintain they've been sexually harmed. Nor is the impulse to regard sex equality law, including sexual harassment law, as a form of surplus repression.

But the problems run even deeper than that. To be blunt, the calculation that queer theory seems to call on us to make — How much sexual violence should we tolerate to have sex with pleasure? — makes no sense. How can queer theory (or anyone else) say how much sexual abuse we should accept for the absence of abuse? Much less say so under the sign of "liberation"?

One of radical feminism's many lessons is that we don't have to tolerate *any* sexual violence in the name of good sex — or anything else. Notwithstanding widespread stories to the contrary, radical feminism opposes and seeks to end the definition of good sex and sexual violence, including sexual harassment and rape, as the same thing.

And so the time has come for us to ask at last: Having assailed feminist successes of recent years, including *Oncale*, will queer theory underwrite male supremacy's definitions of sex and sexual injury? Victims and survivors of sexual violence deserve to know.

For B.K.

Notes

Given this chapter's discussion of the brief Catharine MacKinnon wrote and filed on behalf of a coalition of grassroots organizations working against sexual violence in *Oncale v. Sundowner Offshore Services, Inc.*, 523 U.S. 75 (1998), *see* Brief of National Organization on Male Sexual Victimization, Inc., et al., at 23 n.7, *Oncale v. Sundowner Offshore Services, Inc.*, 523 U.S. 75 (1998) (No. 96–568), it bears mention that I also worked on this brief. An extended and more comprehensively annotated version of this chapter is in progress.

1. 523 U.S. 75 (1998).

2. Janet Halley, "Sexuality Harassment," this volume. This may illuminate Halley's signature on the Law Professors' Brief in *Oncale*. Brief of Law Professors as Amici Curiae in Support of Petitioner, at 32, *Oncale v. Sundowner Offshore Services, Inc.*, 523 U.S. 75 (1998) (No. 96–568).

3. I realize that "queer theory" is diverse; what follows is engagement with one important set of impulses within it.

4. Michel Foucault, *The History of Sexuality*, Volume I: *An Introduction* 157 (Robert Hurley trans., 1990).

5. Michel Foucault, *Politics, Philosophy, Culture: Interviews and Other Writings, 1977–1984* 200 (Lawrence D. Kritzman ed., 1988).

6. For quotations in this and the next five paragraphs (unless otherwise clear from context), see Halley, this volume (some emphasis added).

7. *Id.* at 192.

8. *See* Brief of National Organization on Male Sexual Victimization, Inc., et al., at

23 n. 7, *Oncale v. Sundowner Offshore Services, Inc.*, 523 U.S. 75 (1998) (No. 96–568) ["MacKinnon"].

9. Halley, this volume, at 192.

10. *Id.*

11. Curiously, Halley, recognizing this point, doesn't treat it as a reply to her questions about what Oncale's "feeling" reveals.

12. For quotations in this paragraph, see Halley, this volume.

13. Halley emphasizes the N.Y.C. Gay and Lesbian Anti-Violence Project's statement, which appears in MacKinnon's brief. Halley's related argument depends on it being "the only explicitly gay organization on the Brief[.]" *Id.* at 191. It wasn't. *See* MacKinnon, at A-6.

14. Halley, this volume, at 191 (note omitted). *But see* MacKinnon, at 23–24.

15. Halley, this volume, at 191 (note omitted).

16. Guy Hocquenghem, *Homosexual Desire* 55 (Daniella Dangoor trans., 3d ed. 1993). *Accord* MacKinnon, at 24.

17. *See, e.g.,* Brief of Lambda Legal Defense and Education Fund et al., at 13, *Oncale v. Sundowner Offshore Services, Inc.*, 523 U.S. 75 (1998) (No. 96–568) ["Lambda"]; MacKinnon, at 4, 12–14, 23–28.

18. *Id.* at 24.

19. *Id.* (footnote omitted). *See, e.g., Lambda*, at 18, 24–28.

20. Halley, this volume, at 191 (note omitted).

21. *See id.* at 183, 195.

22. *See id* at 193.

23. *See id* at 183, 189, 195.

24. *See id* at 183 (emphasis removed).

25. *Id.* at 191.

26. MacKinnon, at 4.

27. *Id.* at 23 (note omitted).

28. *Id.*

29. *Id.*

30. *Id.* at 11.

31. Halley, this volume, at 191.

32. MacKinnon, at 23–28.

33. For quotations in this paragraph, see Halley, this volume.

34. The same holds true for Halley's criticism of Federal Rule of Evidence 412 (1995), and her concern about a victim-centered standard of legal reasonableness in sexual injury cases. Halley, this volume, at 195–196.

35. The one express mention of "pleasure" in Halley's text comes when she "track[s] Carole S. Vance's brilliant title," saying that "sex[]-affirmative feminism seeks *for women* a full-face encounter with . . . the pleasure and the danger of sexuality." *Id.* at 195 (emphasis in original).

36. Halley's discussion of *Oncale*'s facts, *id.* 192, and of "the masculinity of women . . . and the appetitive sexual abjection of men," *id.* at 194, are to similar effect.

37. For quotations in this paragraph and the next one, see *id.* (some internal quotations removed and emphasis modified).

38. *Id.* at 196. Unclear is whether the "same-sex love that does[n't] express itself in sexual acts," *id.* at 195, within the queer purview, is sexual.

39. For quotations in this paragraph and the next one, see *id.* (some emphasis added).

40. *Id.* at 190.

41. Catharine A. MacKinnon, "Points Against Postmodernism," 75 *Chi.-Kent L. Rev.* 687, 695 (2000).

42. *See infra* text accompanying note 44.

43. Catharine A. MacKinnon, *Toward a Feminist Theory of the State* 153 (1989).

44. For quotations in this paragraph and the next two, see Halley, this volume (some emphasis removed).

45. *Id.* at 197.

46. For quotations in this paragraph and the next one, see *id.* (some emphasis added).

47. For quotations in this paragraph, see *id.* (some emphasis removed).

48. For quotations in this paragraph, see *id.*

49. *Id.* at 195.

50. *Id.*

15

Gay Male Liberation Post Oncale
Since When Is Sexualized Violence
Our Path to Liberation?

CHRISTOPHER N. KENDALL

Introduction: Identifying that "Moment in Sexism
Where Male Supremacy and Homophobia Converge"

In August 1991, Joseph Oncale began work as a roustabout on an oil rig for Sundowner Offshore Services. Shortly after Oncale started employment, his supervisor, John Lyons, approached him and stated, "You know you got a cute little ass boy" and threatened to "fuck him from behind." Remarks of this sort soon became a constant in the life of Joseph Oncale: "If I don't get you now, I'll get you later. I'm going to get you. You're going to give it to me."

John Lyons and two of Oncale's coworkers came close to "getting" Joseph Oncale but they didn't have to "get" him physically (that is, rape him) in order to get their message across. On one occasion, Oncale was grabbed from behind, pulled down onto his knees and held immobile while Lyons unzipped his own pants, pulled out his penis and placed it on the back of Oncale's head. A day later, Oncale was again forced to the ground while Lyons placed his penis on Oncale's arm. That same night, Lyons and another man attempted to rape Oncale while he was showering. He was, to quote Oncale, lifted off the ground by his knees while, "John Lyons grabs the bar of soap and rubbed it between the cheeks of my ass and tells me, you know, they're fixing to fuck me."

Joseph Oncale managed to escape from this assault and subsequently asked

John Lyons' superior to be removed from the oil rig. Before he could leave, however, he was again approached by Lyons, who stated, "You told your Daddy, huh? Well, it ain't going to do you no good because I'm going to fuck you anyway." Joseph Oncale left his job in November 1991 for fear of being raped, and to this day suffers "severe panic attacks and other episodes of long-term post-traumatic stress." Shortly after leaving the oil rig, "he became dizzy, numb in his hands, and had a rapid heartbeat, which symptoms he continues to attempt to control and treat with medication and counselling."[1]

It has been almost twenty years since Catharine MacKinnon first argued for the elimination of those socially imposed gender hierarchies that daily result in the types of workplace harms that arise from and further ensure social inequality. MacKinnon's book *Sexual Harassment of Working Women* has done much to educate the judiciary and public about the role and meaning of gender and sexuality in the lives of men and women. Having said that, it is clear upon rereading this work, even twenty years after its publication, that there remains much to be learned from the work as a whole and the vision of equality its author demands.

One quotation strikes me as particularly relevant in this regard. Discussing the role of homophobia in propping up the inequalities central to the sex discrimination she challenges, MacKinnon writes, within the context of gay male sexual harassment: "It would be strange, if efficient, if a landmark sexual harassment case were decided in a homosexual context, simultaneously recognizing that sexual harassment and employment deprivation in a same-sex context can be sex discrimination. But stranger things have happened than a simultaneous legal precedent for gays and for women sexually harassed by men — for reasons deriving from that moment in sexism where male supremacy and homophobia converge."[2]

Within her overall theory about the role of systemic gender polarity in maintaining the conditions which ensure workplace inequality, MacKinnon's foregrounding of the role of homophobia as a "weapon of sexism"[3] has received little if any attention from the judiciary. Legal commentators too have all but ignored her analysis in this regard, while nonetheless writing extensively on what they claim to be her views on this very subject. In sum, harassment within a same-sex context has rarely received the kind of equality analysis called for by MacKinnon and those who share her views on the place of male dominance in the subordination of gay men and lesbian women. That is, until now.

In December 1997, the U.S. Supreme Court was asked to determine whether Joseph Oncale could sue for sexual harassment by his male superiors as sex discrimination under Title VII. On March 4, 1998, the Court held that he could, explaining that Oncale's case should be remanded for further proceedings consistent with the Court's opinion that men who are taunted or abused by other men on the basis of gender are entitled to compensation for damages resulting from the sex discrimination to which they have been subjected.[4] It is clear then that Catharine MacKinnon's hypothetical has arrived and that Joseph Oncale and others victimized by their coworkers will be allowed their day in court, should they want it. It is also clear that the Court accepts her argument that sexual harassment must be looked at within the broader context of systemic sexual inequality.

As far as I'm aware, Joseph Oncale is not gay. Nor are the men who sexually harassed him and threatened to rape him. Nor are the men who witnessed this abuse but who failed to intervene. The question I want to ask in this chapter, however, is, would it matter if they were? This might seem an odd question given the extreme violence to which Joseph Oncale was subjected. How, after all, could the sexual orientation of any of these men be relevant to the type of abuse that ultimately occurred? Unfortunately, the question is not as strange or uncommon as one might have hoped.

What happened to Joseph Oncale could be and sometimes is any page on any gay male pornography spread. I am not suggesting that the men who wanted to rape Oncale used or had even seen gay porn. That isn't really the point. What I am saying however, is that the gay male defense of pornography, now widespread in our community, risks making a game of the inequality and violence directed at Joseph Oncale and that this has far-reaching consequences for society as a whole. Specifically, I want to argue that, in doing so, gay men do little more than prop up the types of sex inequalities that allowed it to happen in the first place and which daily result in the homophobic and sexist abuse of all those who are subordinated in the name of male supremacy. The question I want to ask today is: can we as a community built on a historical struggle for sexual equality expect to achieve it if we do little more than sexualize and trivialize the very power structures and imbalances which are the source of our inequality? I think not, and I rather suspect Joseph Oncale would agree.

What I propose to do in this essay is to outline just what a victory for Joseph Oncale along the lines suggested by Catharine MacKinnon's sex equality analysis means for gay men. I will limit my analysis to gay men because of what I see as a concerted effort on the part of many in the gay male community to justify the types of sexual abuse and inequality that harmed Joseph Oncale and which are just as harmful when used by and/or against gay men.[5] This is

perhaps best reflected in the almost universal celebration of gay male pornography as liberating, progressive, and empowering — a rights strategy I will
briefly critique in this chapter.

What I want to argue is that insofar as same-sex sexual harassment is concerned, the sexual orientation of the parties harassing or being harassed is in
many ways irrelevant. The end result is the same: that is, the continued sexualization of gender inequality and the power imbalances that are central to both
homophobia and sexism. I want to argue that so long as Joseph Oncale as a
straight man is subjected to ridicule and abuse along the lines of gender, gay
men stand to lose their struggle for equality. What happened to Joseph Oncale
is every bit as entrenched in homophobia as a bat over the heads of two gay
men daring to hold hands while walking down the street. Both create and
depend on a gendered hierarchy and both are central to male dominance. Both
reject equality and promote hierarchy, penalize mutuality and applaud conformity, ridicule compassion and celebrate contempt. As such, both are central to
sexual inequality and very much an issue of sex discrimination. As such, gay
men would do well to applaud any court decision which recognizes the need to
eradicate the social stereotypes that harmed Oncale and which harm us.

Joseph Oncale ultimately settled his civil action out of court. I want to
argue, however, that if Joseph Oncale had won at trial — and there is little
reason to believe that he would not have won, given the Supreme Court's
ruling in this case — gay men and all women would also win. But I want to go
one step further and argue that if Joseph Oncale had won on the basis that it is
sex discrimination for men to force other men to engage in a sexualized relationship that has little if anything to do with reciprocity, socially the Supreme
Court's decision will prove a shallow victory if we assume that the pain experienced by this man is somehow turned on its head within the context of gay
male interactions simply because we as a community have decided to rename
the abuse suffered "sex," hence liberation. It is my firm belief that gay men
today risk doing just this — a point no better illustrated than in the pornographic sexualization of inequality now evident in the production, distribution, and defense of gay male pornography.

Men on Men: Why Biological Sameness
Failed to Protect Joseph Oncale

To understand why what happened to Joseph Oncale is sex discrimination one needs to know a little bit about woman-hating and malestream culture. John Stoltenberg explains that "the system of male supremacy requires
gender polarity — with real men as different from real women as they can be,

and with real men's superiority to women expressed in public and in private in every way imaginable."[6] What happened to Joseph Oncale epitomizes why, as Stoltenberg so rightly argues, sexual "difference" is, for men, so vitally important. Indeed, what happened to Oncale epitomizes what happens in a society in which gender differences manifest themselves sexually. By subordinating him through sexual violence and harassment, by creating a hierarchy between him and those who did all they could do to prove they were "real" men, Joseph Oncale's attackers ensured that their victim was, at a very basic level, stripped of male status and power, ridiculed as one to be used by those with it, and ultimately forced to assume the position of one without power. Joseph Oncale was in effect rendered inferior for not being "man enough" to be the aggressor — that is, one for whom social empowerment is assured as a result of gender male privilege manifesting itself in sexual conquest. What happened to Joseph Oncale epitomizes what it means to be "male" as socially defined in our society. Indeed, the facts of *Oncale* are male supremacy in action. They tell us that men they have two options: be violent and aggressive, hence masculine and in control, or be the person upon whom that power is exercised sexually. The result for society is an imposed system of gender inequality in which "male" is top and "female" is bottom — a system in which men should and must, if they want to maintain the privilege that attaches to those who are male, reject any form of sexual expression that is nonhierarchical, nonabusive, nonalienating, read equal.

Biologically, Joseph Oncale is a man. As such, he has the option socially of benefiting from gender male privilege. What we need to keep in mind, however, is that to those who abused him, Oncale was little more than an inferior — an unequal through which to valorize their masculinity while stripping Oncale of his. To Oncale's attackers and others like them, biology is in many ways insignificant. What matters is the ability to reassert again and again who is in charge and to prove it by buying into a system in which those with power are those who practice and assert male dominance on those who cannot or who choose not to. What Joseph Oncale's ordeal tells us is that power does not depend on the biological capabilities of those who exert it — i.e., that it does not depend on an essentialized notion of sex. Harassment in a non-same-sex setting is harmful not simply because it involves a biological male violating a biological female, as the essentialist reading would have it, but because, as MacKinnon's feminist reading has it, it involves sexually abusive behavior by those socially permitted to do it and socially defined by doing it. Similarly, within the context of same-sex harassment, the mere absence of biological "opposites" does little to undermine the very real harms resulting from an abusive power play in which "male" equals masculine, equals dominant. The forced coupling of two biological males does nothing to undermine (indeed, it only reinforces) those sexual and social power inequalities divided along gender lines if those behaviors central to the preservation of gender hierarchy (cruelty, violence, aggression, homophobia, sexism, racism, and ultimately compulsory heterosexuality through which heterosexual male dominance is preserved) are not themselves removed from the presentation of sexuality as power-based.

What happened to Joseph Oncale happened because we live in a society which continues to insist on attaching benefit to male sexual aggression and the inequalities that result from it. For women and men made socially inferior on the basis of gender, the acting out of sexual violence built on male/female polarity is but one more extremely forceful and effective tool with which to preserve that gender hierarchy necessary for social inequality. It is clear then that what happened to Joseph Oncale epitomizes all that *is* sex discrimination.

If It Can Happen to Him, It Can Most Definitely Happen to Us: The Role of Sex Discrimination in the Lives of Gay Men

But what of gay men? What does what happened to Joseph Oncale say to us about gender inequality and its role in our lives? If we accept that what happened to Joseph Oncale would not have happened if we lived in a society in which men were not obsessed with proving their gender adequacy and superiority, then it goes almost without saying that the violence to which some gay men are subject on an almost daily basis would not occur were the attitudes and stereotypes which resulted in Joseph Oncale being harassed eradicated. To subscribe to masculinity, as did those who attacked Joseph Oncale, and to benefit from the social, economic, and sexual privilege offered "real" men, one must also support and promote compulsory heterosexuality — an ideology and political institution which embodies those socially defined sets of behaviors and characteristics that ensure heterosexual male dominance and which result in sexual inequality.

The hostility directed at gay men finds its source in the power structure that resulted in Joseph Oncale being sexually harassed, ridiculed, subordinated, and abused. The male power structure that harmed him is the same one directed at preserving compulsory heterosexuality — that construct which, in turn, harms us. To talk of sex discrimination is to talk of gender and the inequalities that arise within a society in which gender differences are polarized and hierarchical — a society in which those who are "male" get privilege and those who are not, do not. I refer here not to gender as biologically determined but rather gender differences as socially constructed and as defined by specific behaviors which ultimately result in the gender categories "male" and "female." As MacKinnon explains: "Gender is an inequality, a social and political concept, a social status based on who is permitted to do what to whom. Male is a social and political concept, not a biological attribute, having nothing whatever to do with inherence, pre-existence, nature, essence, inevitability, or body as such."[7]

It is this social definition of male and female, with defining and rigidly enforced characteristics for each, which ultimately results in gender inequality. In order to reap the benefits awarded to those who are "male" in our society, one must worship and be all that is masculine—that is, a socially constructed set of behaviors and ideas which ultimately define who belongs to the male gender class and which determine who gets and maintains the power commensurate with male gender privilege. Under this system, "masculinity is seen as the authentic and natural exercise of male agency and femininity as the authentic and natural exercise of female agency."[8] To subscribe to masculinity, and to benefit from the privilege afforded "real" men, however, one must *also* support compulsory heterosexuality—an ideology and political institution which embodies those socially defined sets of behaviors and characteristics that ensure heterosexual male dominance and which result in sexual inequality.[9]

In this sense then, gender (a system of social hierarchy) and sexuality (through which the desire for gender is constantly reproduced) become inseparable. As MacKinnon again notes, within a system of gender polarity in which male equals dominance, female submission, "the ruling norms of sexual attraction and expression are fused with gender identity and formation and affirmation, such that sexuality equals heterosexuality equals the sexuality of (male) dominance and (female) submission. . . . Sexuality becomes, in this view, social and relational, constructing and constructed of power."[10] Heterosexuality must thus be enforced, made compulsory because it is deemed necessary to ensure the survival of both masculinity and femininity, defined as male over female, through which male dominance over women is ensured. Lesbians and gay men challenge this requirement because they deny the inevitability of heterosexuality. As Act-Up member Robert Goss notes: "[g]ay and lesbian sexual identities form a counter-practice that deconstructs the rigid definition of masculinity and femininity and social constructions based on these definitions. They transgress many dualistic strategies that support heterosexist sexual identities. . . . Gay and lesbian power arrangements [thus] challenge the unequal production and distribution of heterosocial power in our society."[11] Thus, sexuality constructs men as superior to women, ensuring that gender remains hierarchical, ensuring that heterosexuality remains the norm through which gender inequality is maintained, requiring that those who challenge those norms through which gender remains polarized are penalized for non-conformity. As MacKinnon notes: "Sexuality then is a form of power. Gender, as socially constructed, embodies it, not the reverse. Women and men are divided by gender, made into the sexes as we know them, by the social requirements of its dominant form, heterosexuality, which institutionalizes male sexual dominance and female sexual submission. If this is true, sexuality is the linchpin of sexual inequality."[12]

Once we see the extent to which heterosexuality, made compulsory, ensures the maintenance of gender as a system of dominance and submission, of sexual hierarchy, we can begin to see the extent to which anti-gay stereotypes play into and undergird sex inequality.[13] Together, sexuality and gender form the basis of institutionalized sexism. Sexuality, as constructed, represents the normative ideology of male superiority over women and the hostility directed at lesbians and gay men finds its source in this power structure, aimed as it is at preserving compulsory heterosexuality.

Lesbian activist Suzanne Pharr argues that homophobia works to maintain gender roles because it silences those men whose sexual identity and behavior will, it is believed, "bring down the entire system of male dominance and compulsory heterosexuality."[14] This has led her to refer to homophobia as a "weapon of sexism," responsible for propping up those gendered stereotypes that are central to sexism and all patriarchal inequalities.[15] In a system built on sexual hierarchy, nothing is more threatening to those who benefit from it than the notion that there can be love and justice between equals, that inequality need not be. Gay men, to the extent that they choose to build same-sex relationships, monogamous or otherwise, based on mutuality, reciprocity and respect — relationships which reject hierarchical gender roles and the sexually abusive relationships that result from gender polarization — are seen as a threat to male supremacy because they challenge the social constructions assigned to the definitions "male" and "female." Homophobia — which can be seen as a reaction to the actual or perceived violation of gender norms — is but one way to ensure that men do not violate those gender roles central to male power. For gay men, this results in silence, for fear of being identified, and ultimately results in invisibility. And this is exactly what homophobia is about: ensuring that gay men, to the extent that they do not conform, to the extent that they fail to partake in a system of sex inequality, are prevented from making public that which their enemies find so politically and socially subversive.

There are numerous examples of the extent to which heterosexual male privilege relies upon and ultimately insists upon the preservation of gender inequality. One obvious example, however, is the extent to which it is used to preserve "that bastion of patriarchal power, the nuclear family."[16] Patriarchy is the "manifestation and institutionalization of male dominance over women and children in the family and the extension of male dominance over women in society in general."[17] Lesbian and gay male relationships have the potential to reject hierarchical concepts of gender. They therefore challenge the notion that social traits, such as dominance and subordination, masculinity and femininity, equal and unequal are needed. Because they do so, they are seen as challenging patriarchy and the male supremacy derived from it and are consequently punished for "not participating fully in [the] daily maintenance of women's oppression."[18]

It goes without saying that much time and effort, often manifesting itself through violence and hostility, has been directed at silencing the public expression of any lesbian and gay male discourse and reality which challenges patriarchal privilege.[19] Indeed, so pervasive is antilesbian and gay male discrimination in our society that the consequences for any who dare to speak and challenge socially imposed definitions of "normal" are far from appealing or empowering.

For lesbians and gay men, the hostility directed at us ultimately ensures the suppression of lesbian and gay male public expression and visibility — a suppression deemed necessary for the maintenance of systemic inequality, linked to heterosexual privilege. As Jeffrey Byrne notes, "because of the vicious circle of labeling and silencing to which lesbians and gay men are subjected, the personal costs of coming out in a still largely heterosexist and often violently homophobic society serve to ensure the continued invisibility of lesbians and gay men."[20] And it is this invisibility which is at the heart of homophobia — a socially imposed muzzle aimed at silencing those whose very existence threatens to subvert gender male privilege.[21] As Pharr explains, "misogyny gets transferred to gay men with a vengeance and is increased by the fear that their sexual identity will bring down the entire system of male dominance and compulsory heterosexuality."[22] Homophobia, which finds expression in gay bashing, employment discrimination, and familial and social ostracization, reminds all men that if they "break ranks with males through bonding and affection outside the arenas of war and sport" they will be "perceived as not being 'real men', that is, as being identified with women, the weaker sex that must be dominated and that over the years has been the subject of male hatred and abuse."[23]

Returning to Joseph Oncale, it should be clear from the above that what happened to him would not have happened in a society in which men did not feel the need to sexually enforce their perceived right to dominate on the basis of gender superiority. Joseph Oncale was a victim of sexism because those who harassed him did so in the belief, socially sanctioned, that their masculinity entitled them to subordinate a gendered inferior. For gay men, it should be clear that if we can do something to stop what happened to Joseph Oncale, that is if we can move toward a society in which inequality achieved through sexual violence need not be, then a great deal can probably also be done to eliminate the abuses to which we, as gay men, are also subjected. For it is clear that without sex discrimination, there would not appear to be much need for homophobia. Without those gender hierarchies which are at the core of sex discrimination, there would be no need to penalize those men and women who do not conform to the notion that sexuality must be hierarchical — men and women whose very existence threatens the power imbalances so crucial to maintaining sexual inequality.

But this, of course, begs the question: what if gay men themselves partake in the role play that allowed *Oncale* to happen in the first place? It is clear from the above that gay male sexual relationships have the potential to undermine gender norms. But what if this potential *isn't* realized? That is, what if gay men refuse to challenge the patriarchal definitions of "male" and "female" through which those who subscribe to compulsory heterosexuality find privilege? To effectively challenge such definitions, gay men must, as Frye explains, "be the traitor to masculinity that the straight man has always thought he was."[24] But what happens when gay men refuse to be this traitor and opt instead to sexualize, play with, and ultimately trivialize inequality? That is, what happens if, as a community, we adopt and promote a model of behavior that does little to ensure that those who are the victims of unwanted sexual advances have the right to say no and the right to seek recourse when this assertion is ignored?

Gay Male Pornography: Objectifying Joseph Oncale, Dehumanizing All of Us

Lest you think the above questions are irrelevant within the context of what happened to Joseph Oncale, I would ask that you consider the following quotation taken from an article in *Manscape*, a magazine which promises its readers the very best in gay male erotic entertainment. It is a quotation that is neither extreme nor atypical in this sense: "I pushed him lower so my big dick was against his chest; I pushed his meaty pecs together. They wrapped around my dick perfectly as I started tit-fucking him like a chick. His hard, humpy pecs gripped my meat like a vice. Of all the things I did to him that night I think he hated that the most. It made him feel like a girl. I sighed, 'Oh, my bitch got such pretty titties! They was made for tittie fuckin, made to serve a man's dick.' "[25] What we see from the above is that, as in much written or pictorial gay male pornographic presentations, the physically more powerful, ostensibly straight male is glorified. It, like much gay male pornography, encourages those who use it to become more valued, more "male," less "female." It encourages them to do what they can do: "change status."[26] According to the gender roles it constructs, some are entitled to sexually abuse and control while others (i.e., those who are descriptively less "male," and thus socially less relevant and equal) are not entitled to the respect, compassion, and human dignity that only true equality can provide. What it provides is a sexualized identity politic which relies on the inequality found between those with power and those without it; between those who are dominant and those who are submissive; between those who are top and those who are bottom; between straight men and gay men; between men and women. It asks simply that gay men become the real men they should have been all along. It fails to tell them, however, that to the extent that gay men do so, homophobia is victorious and sexism remains in place. Gay male pornography reinforces a system in which, as Catharine MacKinnon explains, "a victim, usually female, always feminized" is actualized.[27] The result is the promotion of those gender power inequalities that reject a nonassimilated gay male sexuality and ensure that homophobia and sex discrimination remain intact.[28]

This point is clarified by an examination of those pornographic materials recently defended by gay rights advocates before the Supreme Court of Canada in the recent case of *Little Sisters Book and Art Emporium*.[29] In that case, the Court was asked to determine if gay male and lesbian pornography violates Canada's anti-pornography laws. Little Sisters Book Store, and those intervening on their behalf, argued that it could not. Specifically, it was argued by pro-pornography advocates that same-sex pornography was liberating, central to the formation of positive lesbian and gay male identities, and life affirming. The Court ultimately rejected these arguments, finding instead that lesbian and gay male pornography, like heterosexual pornography, violates the sex equality interests of all Canadians. Despite this ruling, many gay men continue to protest, arguing, in effect, that gay male pornography *equals* gay male identity. These arguments, once examined within the context of what I have said above, are troubling, and an analysis of some of the materials defended in that case reveals why.

In many of the materials that are part of the record in *Little Sisters*, and defended by Little Sisters Bookstore and their supporters, we get materials that sexualize racist stereotypes and degrade members of racial minorities for the purpose of sexual arousal. Gay Asian men, for example, are presented as smaller and more feminine than their Caucasian counterparts and thus as willing to be sexually subordinated by a more dominant, more stereotypical white male. While degrading to Asian gay men, the materials also justify through sex the attitudes and inequalities that make racism and sexism a powerful and interconnected reality. The white male is one who seeks out an inferior Asian other; the young Asian is presented as ready and willing to serve his sexual needs and fantasies. The white male is superior; the Asian male inferior. In a similar vein, the reader is offered materials in which African-American men are presented as violent sexual predators who care only to emasculate white men through rape or in which the same men are presented as sexually desiring to be the slaves of white men needing to reaffirm a masculinity threatened by the African-American male. The result affronts all persons seeking equality and makes that equality less likely.

In the name of identity, Little Sisters also offered materials, defended as different from straight pornography, hence harmless in the gay community's special world, in which gay men sexualize incest and sex with children, reinforcing the stereotype that gay men "recruit" by preying sexually on boys. In them, gay men are purported to reveal their "initiations" into sexuality as children through graphically presented sexual assaults by fathers, uncles, and older siblings, with these assaults in turn presented as pleasurable for both the abuser and the child involved. From these and other materials, we are told to glorify masculinity and men who meet a hypermasculine, muscular ideal. The result is such that men who are more stereotypically feminine are degraded as "queer" and "faggots" and are subjected to degrading and dehumanizing epithets usually used against women, such as "bitch," "cunt," and "whore." These men are in turn presented as enjoying this degradation.

In these and other gay male pornographic materials, violence by one man against another man or men is presented as sexual for the persons involved and for the consumer of these materials. For example, in the magazine *Entertainment for a Master*, one of the exhibits Little Sisters defended in the case, reciprocal battery, pain and abuse are promoted as a form of equality: "Then I struck out at him. The leather was longer than a belt would have been. It allowed me to use it on the whole of both his cheeks. It left one broad stripe of red across the white expanse of muscle. He reared up. No amount of preparation would have steeled him so well that he wouldn't scream at the shock of the whipping. When, he moved, he jerked the rawhide holding his balls to Glen and the chains that joined the nipple, forcing his lover to experience a jolt of pain himself."[30] Similarly, the magazine *Dungeon Master — The Male S/M Publication*, which would also have been freely imported if Little Sisters had its way,[31] presents men torturing other men in sexually explicit ways with hot wax, heat, and fire, while sexualizing this abuse as sexually arousing for the abusers, the persons injured, and, again, for the consumer. Likewise, the magazine *Mr. S/M 65* presents photographs of men being defecated on and who derive pleasure from eating and drinking excrement. The film *Headlights and Hard Bodies*, in turn, includes footage of men sexually using other men who are being pulled by neck chains, hit and whipped while tied to poles, penetrated by large objects and/or subjected to clamping, biting, and pulling of their nipples and genitals. The men presented as "slaves" are shown in considerable pain but finding sexual enjoyment from the abuse inflicted on them by others. Those released from bondage kiss the man or men who beat them and thank them for putting them in their place with whips and verbal degradation. *Mach* magazine, in turn, glorifies sexually explicit torture in a military setting, while detailing the kidnapping, torture, and sexual mutilation of prisoners of war. In a photograph in the same magazine, two young men are shown confined to a cage. One, face down and bent over, is being slapped by an older man in a Nazi military uniform. Another is chained and hung in stirrups with a hand shoved down his throat.

The question that needs to be asked is: what does the above say and do socially when gay men accept and promote it in the name of sexual freedom? It has been argued that the dynamics presented in gay porn are not harmful in the way in which similar dynamics would be in an opposite sex setting because the sexuality portrayed actually goes a long way in subverting the gender divisions evident in society at large — the same gender divisions that form the basis of the abuse inflicted on Joseph Oncale and to which many women are subjected on an almost daily basis. This argument is most often worded as follows: the harms of gendered power inequalities are undermined in gay pornography because the men in gay pornography and gay men generally have the "option" of participating in a role reversal not normally afforded women — that is, they can "take turns" being top and bottom, thus further challenging the idea that gender roles are fixed or immutable and thereby questioning the assumption that men must always be on top.[32]

What arguments of this sort overlook is the fact that although roles can be reversed, there are still clearly defined roles — roles which support a "which of you does what to whom" mentality. There is always a top and there is always a bottom, carefully articulated so as to differentiate between those with and those without power. What proponents of gay porn are really advocating is that we participate in a mutuality of reciprocal abuse. In other words, we are expected to find strength in and be empowered by a model of equality which liberates by stressing that while I might at one level be expected to assume the status of a subservient "bottom" at the hands of a descriptively more masculine "top," any resulting disempowerment is rendered nonharmful because I also have the option of becoming that top if I so desire. Frankly, I desire neither. I want to neither control nor be controlled. I neither want to dehumanize nor be dehumanized. I neither want to overpower nor be over-powered. What I want is *real* equality, something not offered in gay male pornography. For what this focus on role reversal as a means of undermining gender inequality overlooks is the fact that the pleasure to be found in gay pornography is the pleasure of controlling and dominating others. Hierarchy remains central to the act. The "mutuality" is to be found in shared degrada-tion and reciprocal sexualized inequality.

Some will argue that they find validation in the pornographic representation of dominance and submission because it reaffirms that they can be sexually penetrated and should not feel ashamed of the pleasure found in anal inter-course.[33] I would probably be more willing to accept this argument if the pleasure promised did not require that the person penetrated (in the context of all pornography, dominated) assume the status of someone being punished for their failure or inability to be a gendered equal. To those men who find valida-tion in the pornographic sexualization of submission, I want to ask what it says about being gay generally that our chosen identity must be realized at the hands of a masculine, ostensibly straight male? Why, specifically, must sexual pleasure and the empowerment allegedly promised by it be found only in the form of submission presented as atonement for, or the inevitable consequence of, perceived gendered inadequacy? Are we now to believe that our sexual identities depend on fixating on the abuse suffered at the hands of someone else's more conforming masculinity? And for those who choose instead to abuse, I ask what it means for their liberation and mine that power is found only in the ability to emulate those sexual/social behaviors that, once ac-cepted, ensure that sexual power is afforded only those who reject equality and who in so doing reinforce the very foundations of compulsory heterosex-uality and the harm, including homophobic harm, that results from it?

The "pleasure" which pro-pornography advocates argue is found in role reversal is a pleasure which relies on sexualized hierarchy. It is a pleasure defined by power and by those who already have it. While some might find pleasure from being dominated, from being verbally and physically abused and ridiculed (and again one must ask why), it is worth noting that not all of us are quite so eager to participate in any process of shared dehumanization. By promoting its distribution, by defending its message, however, and by masking the abuse presented as an issue of free will, gay men do little to offer protection to those of us for whom implied consent is anything but consensual. As Sey-mour Kleinberg notes, "to play with powerlessness is to deny it, and worse, to immune oneself from sympathy for those who are truly helpless prisoners."[34]

I also query whether the pleasure allegedly found in being the bottom to a masculine top and the ability/willingness to take turns being that bottom (the pornographers' skewed version of reciprocity) is in fact as readily promoted in gay pornography as advocates would have us believe.[35] For while we all acknowledge that there is always a bottom in gay pornography, the real power promised by gay pornography, the real focus of all that is deemed to be sexually stimulating, is found in the hands of those who are presented on top and who, as such, assume the status of real men. And while this top might assume the role of a submissive bottom at times, the fact remains that when he does so, he becomes descriptively less relevant, less powerful, less "male." He is stripped of the power derived from eroticized masculinity and instead assumes the role of someone whose manhood is lessened. Hence, while gay men have the option of being both top and bottom, the fact remains that there is always a top and *he* is very much the focus and the idealized masculine norm. In this sense, it is the role, not the individual, that is the unit of analysis. As the "top," the gay male is given liberty to refer to those beneath him as "girlie," "slut" — read "female" socially defined. In essence, because he is overtly masculinized, he ensures that those beneath him are in turn feminized. Because gay male pornography focuses on the party who ultimately penetrates, and because in gay male pornography the characteristics of the more aggressive, more masculine, more male penetrator are always valorized, this offers much support to the argument that in order to "fuck" you need to be superior and that in order to be "fucked" you need to be sexually accessible and socially inferior.

To understand just how central the messages in gay male pornography are in maintaining the sexual norms that allowed Joseph Oncale to be victimized one needs to look at their effect socially on those gay men who accept its message. In addition to the harms caused to the young men used to produce it,[36] gay male pornography has a much larger systemic effect and one which is now more apparent than ever before — that is, a gay male culture and community obsessed with manliness and a sexuality defined by power and the right to overpower. Whether it be within the confines of the gay bar, the gym, the bathhouses, or cruising parks, or even on the street, gay male identity today is concerned less with compassion and commitment to others than with self-gratification and the satisfaction of knowing that gay men can also reap the benefits afforded "real" men as long as they are willing and able to become these men — first and foremost, sexually. Gay men argue that they have redefined manhood by cloning their oppressors, such that it is now difficult to distinguish between straight and gay sexuality other than by biological body parts. This is not a redefinition. It is mimicry and assimilation leading to gay male invisibility. Gay men have excelled at becoming the men society has told them they should be. But it has not come without a price.

While there is much to said about gay male pornography, I want here to focus on that aspect of it which encourages gay men to "fit in," to find the validation promised in assimilation through masculine mimicry, to become what our community and its models of masculine behavior say we should be. I want to ask simply whether this commitment to hypermasculinity does anything to ensure gay male liberation? More important, I want to ask whether this is what gay men have in mind when they talk of subversion — the type of subversion that was supposed to help Joseph Oncale. The answer it seems to me is self-evident.

Masculine mimicry does not map our road to justice. Rather, it ensures only that those who cannot or who choose not to conform — and who, as a result, continue to be seen as a threat to heterosexual male privilege — become the victims of greater physical and emotional abuse and discrimination. Because they continue to challenge the normality of gender polarity and in the process undermine male supremacy, these "nonconformists" will remain the objects of brutal suppression. This in turn reinforces the idea that gay men can either fail to conform to male standards and be the feminized other society has always told them they are (and thus be further abused) or they can copy them. Copying them, however, will not make their effect less harmful. Gay men who choose concealment through assimilation do little more than eroticize their own oppression — making a fetish of that which ultimately muzzles them.[37] The result is a politic which ensures that masculinity remains the only gender construct allowed to speak — a politic that straight male culture has supported all along, resulting in gay male silence and heterosexual male superiority.

The desire to mimic manhood is, in a homophobic society, socially appealing. While no one should underestimate the power of homophobia and the extent to which it literally terrorizes gay men into wanting to pass as "real" men, this construct must be rejected. Becoming a man ensures only that the elimination of male gender dominance, an elimination which is necessary if liberation is in fact our objective, will be more difficult. For some, it will result in self-hate; for others, it will result in assimilation and the invisibility that comes of it. In either case, the only "victors" are those most served by homophobia and sex discrimination: those straight men who define their status by the forced invisibility of gay men and the subordination of women.

Gay male pornography does what the homophobe has done quite successfully for some time now. Specifically, it works to maintain gender roles by encouraging gay men to adopt an identity that valorizes male dominance and by stating unequivocally that those who choose not to adopt this identity have no value, no power. It embodies the very essence of sexual *in*equality by promoting all that is pro-male dominance, hence antiwoman and of necessity antigay. Gay male pornography is thus homophobic and, as such, a form of sex discrimination. It ensures that those models of sexual behavior which might undermine sex inequality are suppressed and that women and those men who *do* fail to conform remain unequal. Ultimately, this does nothing to affirm personal liberties and freedoms. It does, however, do a great deal to ensure the survival of a system of gender hierarchy that is degrading and dehumanizing and which reinforces, by sexualizing, the very power dynamics that ensure systemic inequality.

Conclusion: Rejecting That Moment in Sexism Where Male Supremacy and Gay Male Misogyny Converge

A review of what gay male pornography says about appropriate gendered behavior indicates that the harms of gender inequality, the harms that allowed what happened to Joseph Oncale to happen, are far from undermined through the sexual pairing of biological equals. Like heterosexual pornography, gay pornography glorifies those in our society who have always had power and who have always benefited from dominance and social inequality — white, able-bodied, straight men. It tells gay men that they can choose between an identity which requires that they remain that which society has told them they already are (i.e., weak, feminized) or one which requires that they become what society has told them they are not (i.e., masculinity linked with aggression) — an "option" which does nothing to undermine the gendered power dynamics which result in the often violent rejection of any gay male expression not supportive of heterosexual male power. Sexualized hierarchy may promise the gay male his masculinity, but the result is a gay male liberation that has little if anything to do with liberation and justice and which may ultimately result in considerable individual and systemic abuse and the harms that result from enforced gender polarity. Should we not then be concerned that in the name of gay male equality we are promoting a medium which asks only that we become "so fixated with gender attributes" that we forget "what it is to be human"?[38]

What happened to Joseph Oncale typifies what gay male pornography justifies in the name of sexual freedom. But freedom to do what? If, as I have argued, gay male pornography valorizes and perpetuates the inequality to which Joseph Oncale was subjected and which further ensures that sexual harassment in the workplace and elsewhere is justified and normalized, then do we not as a community have an obligation to query its role in ensuring his oppression as well as our own?

I want to make it clear here that I am not blaming gay men for what happened to Joseph Oncale. I blame a society in which harassment is justified in the name of sexual access and in which mutuality, reciprocity, and compassion for others are ridiculed and rejected. What I am saying is that what happened to Joseph Oncale can be challenged only by undertaking a radical transformation of these power dynamics and this can occur only if we nurture and promote sexual relationships which *do* question gender conformity. Gay men have a role to play in this regard but only insofar as they do not buy into the power play now called for by so many in our community.

What happened to Joseph Oncale had nothing to do with his sexual orientation. It did, sadly, have a lot to do with ours by enforcing those gender norms that ensure that the only sexual orientation to be afforded public expression is that which depends on the rejection of sexual equality. What happened to Joseph Oncale can and does happen to gay men, and the fact that we are gay when it happens to us does nothing to protect us or Joseph Oncale from harm. There is nothing homoerotic about abuse and nothing empowering about an expressive medium that encourages it. The U.S. Supreme Court's decision in Oncale effectively ensures that if a gay man is sexually harassed as Joseph Oncale was, he will have a legal claim against those who harass him. This is a point worth celebrating. To gay men I want to say, however, that turning Joseph Oncale into pornography will *not* ensure that what happened to him will not happen to us. Although gay male pornography is not the source of all our woes, when examined in light of what *Oncale* says about gender, homophobia, and sex discrimination, it is I think quite clear that harassment, just because it is sold and packaged as sex or just because it involves two men, is anything but sexually liberating or socially subversive.

Notes

1. As outlined in the court brief of the National Organisation on Male Sexual Victimization, Inc. (and thirteen others) in the case *of Joseph Oncale v. Sundowner Offshore Services, Inc., John Lyons, Danny Pippen and Brandon Johnson* (Supreme Court of the United States, October Term 1996, No. 96–568) at 2–4.

2. Catharine A. MacKinnon, *Sexual Harassment of Working Women: A Case of Sex Discrimination* (New Haven: Yale University Press, 1979) at 206.

3. *See* Suzanne Pharr, *Homophobia: A Weapon of Sexism* (Little Rock, Ark.: Chardon Press, 1988).

4. Joan Biskupic, "Court Says Law Covers Same-Sex Harassment" *Washington Post*, March 5, 1998 at A1.

5. For a similar analysis within the context of lesbian identity politics *see* Sheila Jeffreys, *Lesbian Heresy* (Melbourne: Spinifex, 1993).

6. John Stoltenberg, "You Can't Fight Homophobia and Protect the Pornographers at the Same Time: An Analysis of What Went Wrong With Hardwick" in D. Leidholt and J. Raymond, eds. *The Sexual Liberals and the Attack on Feminism* (New York: Athene, 1990).

7. Catharine MacKinnon, *Toward a Feminist Theory of the State* (Cambridge, Mass.: Harvard University Press, 1989) at 114.

8. Katharine Franke, "The Central Mistake of Sex Discrimination: The Diasaggregation of Sex from Gender" (1995) 144 *U. Pa. L. Rev.* 1 at 4.

9. *See generally* Adrienne Rich, "Compulsory Heterosexuality and Lesbian Existence" (1980) 5(4) *Signs: Journal of Women in Culture and Society* 63.

10. Catharine MacKinnon, *supra* note 7 at 131 and 151.

11. Robert Goss, *Jesus Acted Up: A Gay and Lesbian Manifesto* (New York: Harper Collins, 1993) at 1–26.

12. Catharine MacKinnon, *supra* note 7 at 118. *See also* Sheila Jeffreys, "Heterosexuality and the Desire for Gender," in Diane Richardson, ed., *Theorising Heterosexuality* (Buckingham: Open University Press, 1996) 74 at 74–77.

13. *See* Cass Sunstein, "Homosexuality and the Constitution" (1994), 70 *Ind. L.J.* 1 at 21.

14. Suzanne Pharr, *supra* note 3 at 19. Pharr is not, of course, alone in her assertion that sexism and homophobia are interconnected. Indeed, many lesbian and gay academics write of the role of gender in the lives of gay men and lesbians and the impact that this has on both sexism and heterosexism. In addition to the other authors cited throughout this chapter, *see*, in particular, Diana Majury in her insightful article, "Refashioning the Unfashionable: Claiming Lesbian Identities in the Legal Context" (1994) 7(2) *C.J.W.L.* 286; Lynne Pearlman, "Theorizing Lesbian Oppression and the Politics of Outness in the Case of *Waterman v. National Life Assurance*: A Beginning in Lesbian Human Rights/ Equality Jurisprudence" (1994) 7(2) *C.J.W.L.* 454; Andrew Koppelman, "Why Discrimination Against Lesbians and Gay Men Is Sex Discrimination" (1994) 69 *N.Y.U. L. Rev.* 197; Andrew Koppelman, "The Miscegenation Analogy: Sodomy Law as Sex Discrimination" (1988) 98 *Yale L.J.* 145; Marie Elana Peluso, "Tempering Title VII's Straight Arrow Approach: Recognizing and Protecting Gay Victim's of Employment Discrimination" (1993) 46 *Vand. L. Rev.* 1533; Francisco Valdes, "Queers, Sissies, Dykes, and Tomboys: Deconstructing the Conflation of 'Sex,' 'Gender' and 'Sexual Orientation' in Euro-American Law and Society" (1995) 83 *Cal. L. R.* 3.

15. Pharr, *supra* note 3 at 19.

16. *Ibid.* at 17.

17. Gerda Lerner, *The Creation of Patriarchy* (New York: Oxford University Press, 1986) at 239. Kathleen Gough in her essay "The Origin of the Family" in *Toward an Anthropology of Women* (New York: Monthly Review Press, 1975), lists six characteristics of male power historically enforced in family arrangements and through which male supremacy is maintained: "men's ability to deny women sexuality or to force it upon them; to command or exploit their labor to control their produce; to control or rob them of their children; to confine them physically and prevent their movement; to use them as objects in male transactions; or to withhold from them large areas of the society's knowledge and cultural attainments." These factors combined ensure and require that gender differences are maintained. They also regulate sexual relations such that heterosexuality remains compulsory, for without it, male dominance, assured through the characteristics outlined by Gough would be undermined. This is a point developed in more detail by Robert Jensen, who writes: "At their core, the sexual norms of patriarchy eroticize

domination and submission. Men in contemporary American culture are commonly trained to view sex as the acquisition of physical pleasure through the taking of women. Sex is a sphere in which men believe themselves to be naturally dominant and women naturally passive. Women are objectified, and women's sexuality is commodified; women become a thing to be fucked, fucking that can easily be purchased (for example, by paying for dinner or buying a prostitute) or taken by force if necessary. Sex is sexy because men are dominant and women are subordinate — power is eroticized. Summed up by Coveney and others (1984), the characteristics of 'normal' heterosexual male sexuality are power (the need to dominate), aggression (from the subtle to the overtly violent), penis orientation (sex is defined by penetration by a penis), separation of sex from loving emotion, objectification (sexual partners require neither respect nor sensitive understanding), fetishism (women are eroticised as body parts), and uncontrollability (men must have sex when they feel aroused)." Robert Jensen, "Getting It Up for Politics: Gay Male Sexuality and Radical Lesbian Feminism," in Sara Miles and Eric Rofes, eds., *Opposite Sex* (New York: New York University Press: 1998) at 149–50, citing the work of Lal Coveney, Margaret Jackson, Sheila Jeffreys, Leslie Kay, and Pat Mahoney, *The Sexuality Papers: Male Sexuality and the Social Control of Women* (London: Hutchinson, 1984).

18. Bruce Ryder, "Straight Talk: Male Heterosexual Privilege," (1991) 16 *Queen's L.J.* 287 at 289.

19. *See,* generally, Gail Mason and Stephen Tomsen, *Homophobic Violence* (Sydney: Hawkins Press, 1997); Gregory Herek and Kevin Berrill, eds., *Hate Crimes: Confronting Violence Against Lesbians and Gay Men* (New York: Sage, 1992); Gary Comstock, *Violence Against Lesbians and Gay Men* (New York: Columbia University Press, 1991). It is worth noting that much of the literature on antigay violence draws out the link between violence and perceived gender violations or the need to prove gender adequacy. Herek and Berrill, for example, note that the ideological link between sexuality and gender has at least three consequences: "First, gay people are stigmatized not only for their erotic behaviors but also for their perceived violation of gender norms. Second, because homosexuality is associated with deviation from something so 'natural' as masculinity or femininity, its labeling as abnormal receives further justification. Heterosexuals with deep-seated insecurities concerning their own ability to conform to cultural standards for masculinity or femininity may even perceive homosexuality as threatening their own sense of self as a man or woman. Third, a dual pattern of invisibility and hostility, denial and condemnation, is associated with gender that parallels that for cultural heterosexism. People who do not conform to gender roles — regardless of their actual sexual orientation — often are labeled as homosexual and stigmatized or attacked. Fear of such labeling leads heterosexuals and homosexuals alike to monitor their own behavior carefully to avoid any appearance of gender nonconformity." Herek and Berrill, *ibid.* at 260.

20. Jeffrey Byrne, "Affirmative Action for Lesbians and Gay Men: A Proposal for True Equality of Opportunity and Workforce Diversity" (1993) 11 *Yale Law and Pol. Rev.* 47 at 56.

21. Clearly, the need to reinforce gender roles and in the process maintain sexism is not the only reason for the social rejection of same-sex relationships. As Marc Fajer explains, however: "[a]lthough most psychological studies of homophobia suggest that the strong-

est contributing factor is belief in the importance of maintaining gender-role stereotypes, a number of studies identify other factors that may be partially responsible as well. These factors include conservative attitudes about sexual issues in general, religious beliefs, and the belief that homophiles are dangerous. Notably, however, each of these factors can be attributed in part, or at least correlated to, fear of deviation from gender-role norms." Mark Fajer, "Can Two Men Eat Quiche Together? Storytelling, Gender-Role Stereotypes and Legal Protections for Lesbians and Gay Men" (1992) 46 *Miami L. Rev.* 511 at 518.

While this chapter focuses on the extent to which antigay discrimination is an issue of sexism, I should not be seen here as implying that gender alone defines gay male identity. Indeed, to the best of my knowledge very few of the authors who have attempted to articulate the role of gender in the lives of lesbians and gay men have ever made such a claim. Rather, they have recognized that gendered and sexualized relationships are, as Debbie Epstein explains, "complexly constructed in relation to other differences, such as those of age, race, ethnicity, class and/or disability." Debbie Epstein, "Keeping Them in Their Place: Hetero/Sexist Harassment, Gender and the Enforcement of Heterosexuality," in Alison Thomas and Celia Kitzinger, eds., *Sexual Harassment: Contemporary Feminist Perspectives* (Philadelphia: Open University Press, 1997) at 158. While the authors cited above have focused their work on the role on the role of gender and sex discrimination in the lives of lesbians and gay men, they have not done so at the expense of other types of discrimination. Nonetheless, concern has been expressed by some authors that to talk of antilesbian and antigay discrimination as sex discrimination risks imposing an essentialist view on lesbian and gay identity, such that racial and class differences, for example, are ignored. *See* Cynthia Petersen, "Envisioning a Lesbian Equality Jurisprudence," in Didi Herman and Carl Stychin, eds., *Legal Inversions: Lesbians, Gay Men and the Law* (Philadelphia: Temple University Press, 1995).

To the extent that someone might say that gender is all there is, this concern is probably justified. Fortunately, few have made such a claim. Nor do I. Neither am I saying that gender inequality impacts similarly on lesbians and gay men. To argue otherwise would be to deny the considerable benefit gay men, as men, receive from buying into gender male privilege and to deny the very real concerns many lesbians have with litigation strategies which risk denying this and other differences. In this regard, *see generally* Mary Eaton, "At the Intersection of Gender and Sexual Orientation: Toward Lesbian Jurisprudence" (1994) 3 *S. Cal. Rev. L. and Women's Stud.* 183. What I am saying, however, is that within the context of a judicial decision like *Oncale* that focuses on some of the harms of gender inequality, gay men would do well to reexamine the role of gender in their own lives. To that extent, I support Fajer's claim that society's fear of possible deviations from gender-role norms does play a significant role in the regulation of gay male sexuality. Indeed, it is probably accurate to conclude that with respect to the myriad of ways in which discrimination is directed at gay men, although gender is not all there is, gender is never *not* there. As such, gay men might want to rethink their dismissal of any judicial attempt to subvert sex discrimination.

22. Pharr, *supra* note 3 at 18.

23. *Ibid.* at 19.

24. Marilyn Frye, *The Politics of Reality* (Freedom, Calif.: Crossings Press, 1983) at 146.

25. William Willcox, "That Old Time Religion" (1995) 10 (11) *Manscape* at 15–18.

26. A point made by Andrea Dworkin, with which I agree, emphasizing that while gay men are socially feminized and subordinated as such, they are not in the same position as women. Dworkin explains that "devalued males can always change status; women and girls cannot." I am not suggesting in this paper that gay men and women are equally oppressed. What I am saying, however, is that to the extent that some gay men reject socially defined "male" behavior, and express a sexuality and politic which has the potential to subvert male gender supremacy, their behavior is deemed unacceptable and is devalued as such. The gay male who does so is, as John Stoltenberg explains, "stigmatized because he is perceived to participate in the degraded status of the female." Once "smeared with female status," the gay male assumes a position inferior to those who, not feminized, reap the benefits of male-female polarity. Feminized men thus assume an inferior position in a gendered power hierarchy. *See* Andrea Dworkin, *Pornography: Men Possessing Women* (New York: Plume, 1989), and John Stoltenberg, "Gays and the Pro-Pornography Movement: Having the Hots for Sex Discrimination" in Michael Kimmel, ed., *Men Confront Pornography* (New York: Crown, 1990) at 248–50.

27. MacKinnon, *supra* note 7 at 141.

28. These arguments are discussed in more detail in C. Kendall, "Gay Male Pornography/Gay Male Community: Power Without Consent, Mimicry Without Subversion," in J. Kuypers, ed., *Men and Power* (Halifax: Fernwood Press, 1999) 86; C. Kendall, "Gay Male Pornography After *Little Sisters Book and Art Emporium*: A Call for Gay Male Cooperation in the Struggle for Sex Equality" (1997) 12 *Wis. Women's L. J.* 21; and C. Kendall, "The Harms of Gay Male Pornography: A Sex Equality Perspective Post *Little Sisters Book and Art Emporium*" (2001) 2 *Gay and Lesbian L. J.* 43–80.

29. *Little Sisters Book and Art Emporium v. Canada* (Minister of Justice) (2000) SCC 69, File No. 26858. The materials summarized in this paper were viewed by me in September 1999 at the British Columbia Court of Appeal, Civil Exhibits Division, Vancouver, British Columbia.

30. Trial exhibit, as discussed *supra* note 29. A full summation of this and the other exhibits referred to in this chapter are on file and available from the author.

31. *See Little Sisters*, *supra* note 29 at paragraphs 53 and 63.

32. *See generally* Carl Stychin, "Exploring the Limits: Feminism and the Legal Regulation of Gay Male Pornography" (1992) 16 *Vermont L. Rev.* 857.

33. *See* Michael Bronski, "Gay Publishing: Pornography," in *Culture Clash: The Making of a Gay Sensibility* (Boston: South End Press, 1984). *See also* Jeffrey Sherman, "Love Speech: The Social Utility of Pornography" (1995) 47 *Stanford L. Rev.* 661.

34. Seymour Kleinberg, *Alienated Affections: Being Gay in America* (New York: St. Martin's Press, 1980). In this regard, I would like to acknowledge and thank Philip Galanes for allowing me to read, rely on, and learn from his unpublished speech, "More Male Than Not: A Consideration of Gay Male Pornography and the Dworkin/MacKinnon Pornography Ordinance" (Los Angeles: August 1, 1990). His work and commitment to change continue to encourage me to say what must be said if equality is to be achieved.

35. A point examined in detail by Marc Simpson, *Male Impersonators: Men Perform-*

ing Masculinity (New York: Routledge, 1994) at 131–48 and Richard Dyer in "Coming to Terms" (1985) 30 *Jump Cut* at 31.

36. *See* Christopher Kendall, "Real Dominant, Real Fun: Gay Male Pornography and the Pursuit of Masculinity" (1993) 57(1) *Sask. L. Rev.* 21 at 32–37. Gay male pornography frequently places its "models" in scenarios which promote and hence are violence, cruelty, degradation, dehumanization and exploitation. While deemed merely representational, hence "fictional," the "fantasy" offered in gay male pornography uses real people—a factor most pro-porn advocates overlook. The men used in gay male pornography are frequently involved in it precisely because they are psychologically and financially at their most vulnerable. As such, they are easily exploited by an industry driven by its ability to manipulate those least likely to possess real life choices. *See* Charles Isherwood, *Wonder Bread and Ecstasy: The Life and Death of Joey Stefano* (1996). *See also* Anon, "I'm Ready for My Cum Shot Mr. De Mille: Gay Porn Is Hot, Dirty and Sometimes Sad" in *Outrage* (Sydney), August 1995 at 12–15.

37. Seymour Kleinberg, "The New Masculinity of Gay Men" in Michael Kaufman, ed., *Beyond Patriarchy: Essays by Men on Pleasure, Power and Change* (Toronto: Oxford University Press, 1987) at 123.

38. Richie McMullan, *Male Rape: Breaking the Silence* (Boston: Alyson Publications, 1990) at 27.

PART IV

Accountability

16

The Rights of Remedies
Collective Accountings for and Insuring
Against the Harms of Sexual Harassment

JUDITH RESNIK

Learning by Making Law

Twenty years of sexual harassment law has taught us a great deal about harassment, the use of sex, and gendered roles in workplaces and schools.[1] These twenty years have also taught us about law's ability to reshape discourse and actions. Celebration is appropriate to mark such success and to acknowledge that *to be* in the third decade of work on the idea and on the law of sexual harassment is, itself, an achievement.

But we also have the burden of knowing that despite the powerful insights, the scores of lawsuits and complaints, and the many regulations promulgated by governments and private entities, workplaces have not yet been transformed to understand that all persons within are equally dignified and entitled workers. Commentators have raised concerns that judges and juries impose too exacting or the wrong standards for liability, and that they fail to recognize when plaintiffs have met their burdens.[2] The massive investment of time and resources by individuals and institutions that both the lawsuits and the regulations represent has not yet shielded others from having to attempt anew (and often at great personal expense[3]) to reduce inequality in workplaces.

Moreover, the last two decades have not only been those in which the law of sexual harassment has emerged. Other developments — in the law of work, of discrimination, and of dispute resolution and in the structure of economic and political organizations — raise new challenges for those concerned about equality at work. Hostility to discrimination claims has sharpened, as has skepticism about regulation and adjudication. Workplaces are under reorganization, through downsizing, outsourcing, and globalization. With increasing frequency, employers now ask that, as a predicate to employment, workers agree to forgo resort to courts to enforce their statutory rights and to rely instead on privately based grievance procedures. Although courts once refused to enforce such waivers if entered in advance of disputes, judges now celebrate use of alternatives to litigation and uphold such contracts. In short, the remedial regimes developed thus far have not succeeded as much as had been hoped, and the availability of even those remedies may be reduced as the contexts in which they were forged change. Entry into the third decade of harassment work therefore requires revisiting the remedial structures developed during the first two decades.

Generally, litigation about harassment has been modeled after common law tort processes in which individuals are found liable for imposing harm and are ordered to pay monetary damages. The Equal Employment Opportunity Commission (EEOC) and class action suits do sometimes seek injunctions, prohibiting future misbehavior. Individuals may also obtain equitable orders for reinstatement or "front pay," money provided when reinstatement is not possible.[4] But a substantial proportion of the litigation and the commentary about harassment focuses on whether individual plaintiffs can hold other persons (coworkers, employers, and/or supervisors) responsible and obtain compensation for sexual harassment.

This essay explores the limits of the individualized model. I begin by reviewing the architecture of remedial options to show the challenges of their pursuit and to demonstrate current presumptions that the harms of harassment are, at base, injuries inflicted by individuals on each other. To the extent institutional remedies exist by way of employment policies on harassment (promoted by doctrine that permits employers to limit their own liability by having such policies), those policies typically provide for individual complaints and individualized processing of the problems raised. That conception misses both the social context that permits infliction of injury and how cultures of subordination harm participants beyond the individual(s) targeted. Further, I examine the new rules of dispute resolution that enforce agreements waiving rights of access to courts. As the mode of processing disputes about harassment shifts from the public venue of courts to privatized arbitral processes, the dispute is pressed even more into an individualized mold, to be mediated either by the disputants or through third party intervention rather than to be redressed as a social and political problem requiring structural reform of working conditions.

I object to an understanding of the sources and harms of harassment as limited to individual (and ostensibly idiosyncratic) interpersonal exchanges. I urge consideration of new and different remedies for harassment to bring into better focus the institutional character of sexual harassment. The term "sexual harassment" ought to comprehend both an affront to individuals and a structural problem for workplaces. Thus, below, I explore a range of legal rules that could help to develop an institutional and collective approach to harassment.

First, to acknowledge that harms of harassment are pervasive, undermining the integrity of all workers, any worker within a harassing environment ought to be permitted to file harassment claims. The concept of a "bystander" — someone *watching* an accident — ought not to have much place in the law of workplace harassment. Second, worker collaboration about workplace structures that foster harassment should become a priority. Instead of First Amendment claims being deployed by defendants, seeking to counter antiharassment measures, workers should consider how First Amendment and labor rights could protect their efforts to sponsor programs and protests. Similarly, rather than assume that contractual agreements to waive individual access to courts are only harmful, collective bargaining about such clauses could create remedies to supplement or to replace litigation with employer-wide programs that locate harassment as a potential part of all workplaces. Third, insurance ought to be a part of the repertoire of responses to harassment. I propose exploring the regulatory potential of various forms of insurance, both to introduce new institutional players into discussions about how to remediate harassment and to redistribute the costs of harassment to generate more incentives for its reduction. Liability insurance could be used to evaluate and price the risk of harassment. Unemployment insurance could recognize that workers should have income security when they leave hostile working conditions. Fourth, government agencies in addition to those currently chartered to deal with discrimination should be enlisted to think about harassment as a kind of workplace harm within their aegis.

All of these collective undertakings could help buffer against current trends toward privatization. Many of these suggestions would require revisions of statutes, doctrine, and practices. Remedies reflect the shape of rights. My hope is that through remedial invention, harassment law could assess how discriminatory attitudes about gender, race, and age constitute aspects of workplaces and how all workplace participants could share in the work of reconstruction.

The Successes and the Constraints of Current Remedies

Theories of remedies require theories of harm—about *who* is injured by *what* set of behaviors, imposed by individuals or entities that ought to be subjected to sanctions or required to alter practices. Upon gaining answers, the focus then shifts to *how* to remediate or to alter behavior—by paying compensation and/or by seeking to alter current practices of specific actors and organizational structures in public and private settings.

Both the remedies provided and the processes for seeking redress illuminate what kind of harm is understood to have been suffered and by whom. The choices are many: *Where* might one be required to account for injuries—in courts, administrative agencies, privately run dispute resolution programs? *Who* has the power to initiate inquiries? How is the concept of injury developed so that certain individuals are understood to be the victims or to bear the brunt of the harms and others conceived to be harm-doers, bystanders, or representatives? To *whom* must one account—judges, jurors, government-employed regulators, third-party "neutrals," coworkers? Are such processes open or closed, transparent and accessible? Do they generate records and data upon which others might build? What forms of sanctions are available—monetary damages of a variety of kinds, individualized equitable remedies, and/or structural reforms? Who really pays and in what forms of capital for the harms of harassment?

Thus far, the who, the what, the how, and the where of sexual harassment law has been shaped by traditions within United States legal culture that focus on individual claims of wrongdoing. Many kinds of civil rights cases have been assimilated into a tortlike process that understands such injuries to be akin to but distinct from general torts. For sexual harassment claims, individual complainants and occasionally small groups of individuals seek redress, first through an administrative apparatus inside a workplace or school, then in an agency, and finally in courts. By and large, defendants are identified either as individuals or as small groups of people, alleged to harass deliberately or knowingly tolerate harassing behavior.

Generally the goal is for the plaintiff to obtain monetary damages, often limited by statutory caps on liability.[5] Sometimes injunctions against future bad action are sought, but under current doctrine, individuals can seek such relief only if they can demonstrate a risk of being subjected to injuries in the future or if the case is pursued by the EEOC to vindicate independent public interests. The financing of the litigation relies heavily on statutory provisions for one-way fee shifts, obliging losers to pay the costs and fees for the attorneys employed by successful claimants.[6] Because settlements that lead to structural changes do not ensure payment of fees to attorneys as surely as do settlements and judgments resulting in monetary payments[7] and because obtaining wide-reaching relief is labor intensive, private lawyers have incentives to sue on behalf of individuals seeking damages.[8]

In addition to courts, agencies (both state and federal) respond to claims of harassment. However, given the antiregulatory gestalt that pervades contemporary United States law, administrative responses generally mimic the tort paradigm rather than invent new regulatory modes. Equal employment commissions at both state and national levels serve primarily as recipients of complaints, as an additional set of courts in which individual instances of alleged unfairness are examined through conciliation and mediation processes or adjudicatory proceedings.

To be sure, the EEOC has promulgated guidelines that have served as important markers, both aspirationally and legally, of impermissible practices as well as of appropriate remediation. Moreover, the EEOC has often provided leadership through policymaking to proffer a fulsome understanding of harassment. Further, the EEOC occasionally takes on the role of plaintiff, doing enforcement work on behalf of a group of workers injured by a pattern and practice of discrimination, or joins ongoing lawsuits as an *amicus*, urging courts to issue broad relief.

But agencies are subject to political pressures, and during the first two decades of sexual harassment law, the leaders of the EEOC have had varied approaches to its role. Limited budgets and personnel (combined, sometimes, with limited will) have resulted in a small amount of work going toward investigation and direct regulation of workplaces. Mostly, both the federal agency and its state counterparts struggle to stay abreast of the filings brought to them.

Courts are also recipients of thousands of sexual harassment complaints. Some lawyers report hostility by judges to these claims and too quick dismissals.[9] Nonetheless, the litigation around sexual harassment has produced thousands of opinions that recount interactions between individuals and that analyze the particularized instances of claimed injury — struggling over when enough misery has been shown to demonstrate objective and/or subjective statuses of subordination that result in limited work and educational opportunities. For many commentators, judge-made law has been discouraging, in that significant forms of injurious behavior are tolerated.[10] Yet these lawsuits have provided us with a thick narration of the ways in which harassment occurs and of the harms that it inflicts.

Those of us who are at workplaces and schools that have expressly committed themselves to limiting harassment owe a debt to the many individuals who have come forward with their specific injuries and who have proffered the details of their working lives for intensive scrutiny. The mountain of case law has produced sufficient evidence of pervasive harms to prompt a considerable body of rulings imposing liability on employers, supervisors, and coworkers,[11] thereby providing damages to individuals and sometimes prompting more general efforts to alter workplaces by promulgating policies that either avoid litigation or reduce institutional liability for individual wrongdoing.

A genuine shift in norms has occurred. Behavior that was commonplace two decades ago—such as male university professors openly seeking out women students and secretaries for sexual favors—has receded substantially. Through statements of policies, many employers have defined certain actions as impermissible and have, in conjunction with employees, restructured local cultures. Employment policies and actual practices now signal expectations that sex is not to be a part of workplace demands. In some workplaces, at some times, significant changes have taken place.

But I have just used the word "some" — in some workplaces, at some times — because not all share the luxury of the changes. Twenty-some years out, the wellspring of potential disputes seems unabating. Dip into any set of recent reported cases and the distressing details of "ordinary," contemporary interactions leap off the page. One such example comes from a case litigated in the 1990s and resulting in a Supreme Court decision in 2001. A woman worker in a chemical plant charged her colleagues and superiors with sexual harassment. After presiding at the trial, a district judge concluded that she had suffered "wretched indifference" resulting in her "slowly drowning in an environment that was completely unacceptable, while her employer sat by and watched."[12]

As we read set upon set of such facts, we gain new evidence of the durability of discriminatory practices and of the deep hostility that animates so many workplaces.[13] Those opposed to women joining fully in the workplace patrol the meaning of "manhood" by using harassment to limit women's access to all forms of work. Such "gender police" expend substantial amounts of time attempting to impose on others their own definitions of appropriate behavior for both women and men. The human capital lost through infliction and receipt offers painful testament to the wastefulness of subordination.

And, for every case filed and won, many cannot be brought. The barriers to litigation are multiple. "Naming," "blaming," and "claiming" are terms used by anthropologists of dispute resolution to describe the processes of identifying oneself as wrongly harmed.[14] General survey data about people who are injured—by harassment and in other ways—indicate that many people do not know how to "name" a harm inflicted, to "claim" their right to be free from it, or to "blame" individuals and institutions responsible for the injury.[15] To seek redress requires knowledge, a sense of self, determination, the ability to risk retaliation (and/or hostility from others), access to lawyers and to money. Litigation has potential for regulating and altering behavior, but reliance on a melange of individual and institutional claimants to enforce norms inevitably results in uneven patterns, with some critics arguing that "too many" or the "wrong" cases have been brought, and yet others bemoaning the underenforcement of legal norms.

New Remedial Hurdles: Globalization and Alternative Dispute Resolution

Atop these longstanding impediments, two other barriers are being erected that will add new difficulties to the pursuit of remedies. First, the political and social settings in which discrimination takes place have changed with new workplace practices. The global economy, facilitated by the breakdown in borders through technological innovation, is heralded as enabling new and more modes of work. But this "new world" has some old features: women are disproportionately represented in the low-end sector of wages and benefits.[16] Further, aspects of mobile, fast-paced, and border-free work makes the assertion of rights all the more difficult. Some work has moved offshore, far from regulatory reach. Many employers have increased their reliance on temporary workers. Claiming and proving discriminatory practices thus become harder, more risky.[17]

Second, legal rules about access to court have changed. Employers now instruct employees to sign agreements waiving rights to sue as a condition of becoming or staying a worker. If disputes arise, employees must agree to pursue remedies only through private "alternative" means. ADR is the shorthand for such alternative dispute resolution, which includes mandatory arbitration, mediation, or other non-court-based processes for employees' grievances.

Several distinct legal issues arise because of such agreements. One question is about their enforceability in general. In 1925, Congress enacted a statute, known as the Federal Arbitration Act (FAA), which recognized that agreements to arbitrate were legal contracts, enforceable in federal courts.[18] But the FAA is a complex legal text, with exceptions and an unclear reach vis-à-vis both federal and state claims. Further, enforceability can turn on the timing and the contents of agreements to arbitrate. The questions are many. Should form contracts entered *ex ante*, in advance of a dispute, be read to preclude litigation *ex post*, after a dispute has emerged? What if one of the parties has more bargaining power than the other? Should it matter if the rights sought to be litigated arise under particular federal or state statutes permitting private enforcement of rights, and specifically of discrimination claims? Should enforcement be refused if the contracting parties are an employer and an employee or an applicant for employment? Union and management? Should agreements to arbitrate prevent third parties from challenging conditions at workplaces? Limit class actions? And what about the costs of ADR? If private dispute resolution mechanisms impose user fees, should courts nonetheless enforce agreements that bar judicial remedies? What if ADR clauses are not express about how much the alternatives costs or who pays?

Judicial answers to some of these questions have changed over the decades. Initially, federal judges ruled that litigants could not waive their rights under certain federal statutes in advance of a controversy. For example, in 1953, the United States Supreme Court refused to enforce an agreement that a shareholder had entered into with a broker that would have required arbitration in lieu of litigation for an alleged breach of federal securities laws.[19] The legal question was whether the securities statute permitted waivers, an issue not expressly addressed by that legislation. The Supreme Court held that *ex ante* waivers of federal securities claims were not enforceable. The Supreme Court viewed such contracts as suspect because of unequal bargaining power. Moreover, given the important federal regulatory concerns embodied in the statutory regime, the Court found the processes of arbitration too informal to permit them to replace the regulatory opportunities provided through adjudication.

But by the middle of the 1980s, a majority of justices changed the rules. The Court returned to federal securities and consumer protection statutes and reinterpreted them to permit enforcement of *ex ante* contracts to arbitrate federal statutory rights.[20] In these decisions, the Court revisited its prior statutory interpretations, its concern about contracts between unequals, and its views of the differences between arbitration and adjudication. The Court equated the purposes of adjudication with those of arbitration, both now described as focused on dispute resolution. Arbitration, once seen as worrisomely lawless, became celebrated for its flexibility.

Some argued, however, that employment law stood apart, as unsuitable for mandatory arbitration. The 1974 decision of *Alexander v. Gardner-Denver Company* had held that labor-management contracts to arbitrate disputes did not preclude an individual from going to court to bring claims of discrimination under Title VII.[21] But by 1991, the Supreme Court ruled that an employee's agreement, in an application for employment, to arbitrate precluded a lawsuit filed under the Age Discrimination Act.[22] In 2001, the Supreme Court

held that a "dispute resolution agreement" in an employment contract prevented a worker from pursuing his claims of harassment based on sexual
orientation under a *state* law's antidiscrimination provisions.[23] In that 5–4
decision, the majority concluded that the FAA was not limited to commercial
contracts but also applied to employment disputes.[24]

A few constraints on mandatory arbitration of employee claims remain. In
1998, for example, the Court ruled that unions could not waive employees'
discrimination claims through general agreements to arbitrate. Contracts that
lack a "clear and unmistakable waiver of the covered employees' rights to a
judicial forum for federal claims of employment discrimination" do not waive
those rights. The Court specifically reserved the question of whether, were
such a waiver express in a union-management contract, it would be enforceable.[25] Subsequently, the court concluded that individual agreements not to
sue do not prevent the EEOC from seeking remedies.[26]

Other issues are open, as lower courts debate and as legislatures consider
limiting the reach of mandatory dispute resolution programs. The Supreme
Court has not yet returned to interpret Title VII itself in light of its more recent
readings of the FAA.[27] Several federal circuits have upheld *ex ante* waivers of
Title VII claims,[28] but some judges have refused to enforce a specific dispute
resolution agreement either because of failures within a given program,[29] because of the view that employers cannot, consistent with Title VII, condition
employment on *ex ante* waivers of claims,[30] or because an employee has had
insufficient notice of a waiver or has not clearly consented to it.[31] Further,
some private providers are excluding employment discrimination from mandatory dispute resolution programs. The New York Stock Exchange won
approval from the Securities and Exchange Commission to exempt employment discrimination and specifically sexual harassment claims from arbitration unless the parties agree to arbitrate *after* the dispute has arisen.[32] Some
states and localities have or are considering similar provisions, and the EEOC
has registered its opposition to "unilaterally imposed agreements mandating
binding arbitration."[33] Further, members of Congress have proposed legislation that would exempt federal civil rights statutes from "involuntary arbitration."[34]

In addition to the question of the *suitability* of arbitration for a range of
federal statutory claims, the wave of ADR contracts has also brought attention to the question of the *accessibility* of ADR.[35] Courts are now turning to a
series of issues about financing. Some programs are funded by manufacturers,
lenders, or employers, but others require significant monetary contributions
from claimants. For example, one company's "Dispute Resolution Program"

imposed half the costs of the proceeding on the complainant alleging employment discrimination.[36] Another contract requiring arbitration of consumer claims was ambiguous about both the costs of the program and how they were paid. That failure to specify and allocate ADR costs, however, did not convince a majority of the Supreme Court in 2000 to find the contract to arbitrate unenforceable *per se*. The court held that the consumer (borrowing financing for her mobile home and arguing violations of her federal truth-in-lending rights) rather than the lender bore the burden of establishing prohibitive costs.[37]

In short, the law about the intersection of dispute resolution and employment rights has some settled contours and some contested edges. But that law is not the only variable. A recitation of case law, statutes, and regulations misses the reality of many workers' lives. When presented with a contract proffered as a condition of employment, many workers are unlikely either to know the law or to seek legal advice about such agreements. Once signing such agreements, these workers may feel obliged to live by the contracts that they have entered or may find themselves ill-situated to contest legality by bringing test cases.[38] Thus, even if some waivers might not be enforceable in court, many signatories will assume their legitimacy. And, as a few courts refuse enforcement of certain kinds of contracts, employers are learning to draft agreements more likely to be enforced.

These employers are acting within a legal culture admiring of alternatives to adjudication.[39] Manufacturers, lenders, and employers are not the only ones promoting ADR. Judges, legislators, administrative agency staff, and lawyers also celebrate mediation, arbitration, and other means for resolution of discord as preferable to adjudication. Proponents of alternative dispute resolution often herald their programs as offering many means of redress, as more flexible, less expensive, and more responsive than adjudicatory processes.

Were such programs voluntary options, offered in addition to, rather than in lieu of litigation, such arguments would be plausible and, depending on the specific programs provided, persuasive. As detailed above, the hurdles to lawsuits are many, and alternative fora can, depending on structure and content, be useful.[40] But many of these programs are aimed at displacing courts, and they function expressly to close off access to courts.[41] Further, alternative processes can build in their own hurdles that discourage use. In addition to access costs, ADR processes can typically be used only by individuals. Group claims cannot be made, and neither process nor outcome is usually accessible to the public or to third parties. Further, some ADR contracts attempt to preclude signatories from participating in class litigation.[42] ADR programs prefer brokering compromises and often seek to avoid announcing norms.

Such alternatives can serve as a means of privatizing and deregulating work-place disputes.

Reshaping Understandings of "the Injured," "the Responsible," and "the Powerful"

We need to acknowledge that, even if the litigation-based traditions that have developed over the past two decades were the preferred mode of responding to sexual harassment, those avenues are functionally unavailable to many. Further, workplaces are reconfiguring, promising to be less rule-bound and therefore to make proof of injury all the more difficult. The wealth of data that lawsuits unearth and disseminate will lessen as a consequence. Reflection is required on how to shape what lawsuits remain and on other remediation possibilities.

REDEFINING INJURY

A first change is needed within the context of litigation to alter the conception of the persons injured through harassment. Much commentary, in this volume and elsewhere, has addressed the relationships among theories of gender, sex, sexual orientation, and harassment. The goal is to understand how harassment constructs gendered identities and is inflected by social meanings of what behavior is sexualized and who functions as an object of such attention.[43] But most of that discussion is focused on individual targets — women or men of different races, ethnicities, and sexual orientations and in a range of work settings. I want instead to underscore the collective and diffuse harms imposed by cultures of harassment. One way to do so is to challenge current jurisprudential constructions of the harm of sexual harassment, exemplified by rulings on who has "standing" to seek redress.

In 1998, a federal court refused to entertain a claim by "seven white men," seeking to protest the hostile environment of a police department in Richmond, Virginia, that, they alleged, demeaned workers through derogatory, racist, and sexual comments.[44] Specifically, they complained that a police supervisor "repeatedly made disparaging remarks to and about female and black members of the police force that adversely affected vital relationships and working conditions."[45] Their lawsuit, *Childress v. City of Richmond*, was rejected by the Fourth Circuit. As one member of the court explained the reasoning, "white male employees [who] allege that their white male superiors made disparaging comments about black and female coworkers" had no legally cognizable injury because they themselves were neither black nor female.[46] Although federal courts are not unanimous in their approach[47] and the

EEOC has taken a different view,[48] the Fourth's Circuit's decision in *Childress* is emblematic of several rulings that refuse claimants who identify with individuals suffering derision and who report themselves to be injured by having to participate in workplaces laden with aggressive harassment.[49]

Under the *Childress* model, the "injured" are only those who suffer the taunts and aggressive acts, and perhaps individuals understood as enough "like" the targets to fear that the harasser might turn to them or unfairly "favor" others.[50] Lost in this approach is an understanding of the structure of workplaces in which harassing behavior shapes power relationships among all individuals. Lost also is an appreciation that remedies lie precisely in the act of these "seven white men" who, through their lawsuit, rebelled against the harassers by expressing allegiance with the immediate targets. Refusing these men voice is refusing to acknowledge the disabling effects of discriminatory workplaces on all of those subjected to such conditions. In 1999, the Supreme Court recognized that men could taunt other men with sex and thus impose injury; *Oncale* is our shorthand.[51] We need also to understanding that men who taunt with sex and race injure all who work under and with them.

Those white police officers seeking redress offer another insight. They are simultaneously *harmed and responsible*. Their litigation entailed an acknowledgment of their own potential complicity and an understanding that "bystanders" is not a description that fits workplaces — cultures that are created by interactions among peers, subordinates, and managers. Institutions are deeply affected by behavior of officially less-powerful participants, as strikes by students and workers regularly demonstrate. The white male plaintiffs responded to their environment by refusing to be complicit and by acknowledging that to participate — without protest — is to assent. Through such protests can come genuine change. Law could respond by facilitating such lawsuits through doctrines such as "associational injury" (that white men have a right, infringed by harassment, to be in a diverse workplace), "third-party standing" (that white men are bringing the case on behalf of others), or through a reconception of discrimination (that white men assumed to be comfortable in a harassing atmosphere are discriminated against through gendered and raced assumptions requiring them to affiliate with such behavior).[52] I would prefer sexual harassment law to mark that, because harassment is disabling to a workplace, anyone within it can seek structural revisions. All workers need the right not to be in — and therefore a part of — a harassing workplace.

COLLECTIVE NEGOTIATIONS AND PROTESTS

Lawsuits are one — but only one — form of protest. Lawsuits locate fault in specific actors rather than showing how harms emanate more diffusely from structures of oppression. Individuals such as the white police officers ought to be able to use lawsuits as a means of affiliating with the targets of harassment but ought not to assume litigation to be their only means of doing so.

Speaking out and up against harassment is another option. Speech rights in workplaces are often raised by opponents of sexual harassment, introducing free speech as a defense to liability and as a barrier to the imposition of codes of behavior.[53] Proponents of antiharassment measures should also look to First Amendment traditions to use them affirmatively as a means of combating harassment.

What social networks and understandings would be required before strikes against harassment become commonplace? Worker organizations have long used collective action, some of it noisy and disruptive, to bring about change in the United States and elsewhere. One instance of women workers asserting power against great odds comes from the Women's Self-Employment Association (SEWA), founded by Ela Bhatt in India. There street stall workers, scrap collectors, home-based workers, and many others doing a range of subsistence work crafted a new version of a trade union that helped its members through a range of services, from health care to banking, from objecting to oppressive conditions to generating alternative work.[54] In the United States, a parallel can be seen in the "take back the night" marches, launched to mark the constraints women face because the fear of assault prevents them from moving about freely. Groups of individuals have thus created power through inventive aggregate action.

Calling for individuals and organizations to account for sexual harassment through parallel projects is possible, but only if done collectively. For example, in both the United States and Europe, survey data have been gathered that document the prevalence of harassment.[55] Workers could survey coworkers to learn of incidents of harassment and to provide aggregate information to management and unions. Collecting the data itself is a form of solidarity—a willingness to learn about facets of environments that many wish did not exist and some want to hide. Workers could also organize meetings and programs to discuss authority in workplaces, the forms of harassing and disabling behavior, and whether unions and other worker organizations are implicated.[56] Self-help remedies may enable an understanding of the many layers of power within workspaces. Success relies on collectivity. We must build on themes within the literature of sexual harassment about agency and autonomy[57] but also expand the ideas from their current focus on individual action to encompass social and political networks crossing race and gender lines. Through such collective expressions of power, some protection against retaliation might merge. The First Amendment discussion within harassment law could thus shift to explore how its premises could shelter the distribution of surveys, sit-ins, strikes, leafleting, and other forms of protest against harassment. Were the paradigm of the harassment problem to move away from singular moments of harassment (generating the "he said, she said" discourse) toward images of collective injury and responsibility (white police officers challenging their colleagues to behave differently toward nonwhites and toward gender nonconformists), we would make plain that structures of discrimination marginalize and diminish the competencies of a diverse group of workers.

Collective organizing and bargaining might also be used to generate a range of responses to employers' efforts to have workers waive their rights to sue. Workers could educate prospective employees and coworkers about the possibility of refusing to sign such agreements, about their bargaining power in certain industries, and about questions of enforceability. Further, rather than assume that all such contract clauses should be prohibited, legal rules could limit only those entered into individually by employees but permit enforcement under specified circumstances, such as if agreed upon as a part of union bargaining and/or if having certain structural features.

What might be gained if terms were bargained for collectively? Dispute resolution programs often include mini-codes of civil procedure, with provisions about statutes of limitations, discovery, sanctions, costs, and fee awards. Remedies for sexual harassment could then be broadened if, in exchange for collective waivers of litigation, new reforms were offered. For example, employees might create and the EEOC certify grievance programs. Perhaps the EEOC could participate in the bargaining over clauses and in developing model programs. Contracts might make the use of these programs optional and require that information about outcomes be distributed to workers, customers, shareholders, or other beneficiaries of a workplace's output.[58]

In other words, the preservation of individual rightseeking is neither the only nor the best means of redress. The lessons from other areas of tort law, previously understood as requiring individualized decision making and now increasingly relying on aggregate processing, are that collective procedures can increase the remedial reach, but often at the expense of stellar individual victories (and losses). For example, institutions called "claims facilities" have been created as part of group-wide settlements in many toxic tort cases. Staff at these facilities function in part like an insurance company, settling claims, in part as a provider of ADR, and sometimes akin to a court, adjudicating disputes.[59] In such group-based regimes, trade-offs between individual remediation and widespread recoveries are required. Painfully, many aggregate regimes do not redress injuries as would an individualized process.[60] But, equally painfully, individual litigation does not reach as many of the injured as do these group-wide settlements. If contractual waivers of rights to sue came through gaining rights of access to information about ADR processes, rights of collective processing, new remedies for harassment, and the ability to have lawyers paid for their assistance, then their development might help underscore collective responsibility for workplace conditions.

INSURANCE AND OTHER FORMS OF REGULATION

In addition to seeking ways to enable group-wide claiming (through lawsuits, protests, education, and collective bargaining), we should also try to change cultures of harassment by making a wider set of individuals pay for the harms. My suggestions include spreading the risk and cost through liability insurance, exploring modes of self-insurance and the provision of government security nets, and developing regulatory mechanisms in addition to the EEOC and state antidiscrimination agencies.

With the intentional tort as the paradigm, insurance against liability for harassment is theoretically unavailable. The "black letter" rule is that intentional torts cannot be insured because to do so is to sanction such action. Implicitly, with insurance comes acknowledgment that a given event—an accident or, in this case, harassment—is possible. Further, insurance can create the "moral hazard" that, by permitting the costs of injury to be shifted to a third party not directly responsible for causing the harm, more of the underlying wrongful activity will occur. Shifting monetary responsibility could also signal a diminution in moral obligation. Moreover, insurability prices the risk of a specific occurrence, and some find offensive the idea of prepayment for a promise to compensate for the infliction of intention harm.

But harassment already imposes a price on the recipients. Moreover, the last two decades of litigation about harassment have made plain that it is not only possible but also likely in certain settings. To dismiss insurance as essentially inappropriate for sexual harassment—as some commentators have done[61]— is to miss an opportunity to introduce new actors into the problem of altering workplace norms.

Some forms of liability insurance are already available, although relatively little information details what kinds of claims have been covered and paid. Insurance companies have developed a product called "employment practices liability insurance" (EPL) for a range of employment-based claims.[62] Further, about seventy firms nationwide provide sexual harassment insurance.[63] Were such insurance commonplace, how might it affect our understandings of and the incidence of harassment? Insurance is a form of regulation, in that private providers write insurance policies only after receiving information that enables them to price risk. Companies seeking insurance would have to submit to appraisal of their workplace. Insurance companies could impose higher prices on companies with records of high levels of complaints of harassment, just as insurance companies charge higher rates for insuring teenage drivers than adults.

Insurance itself is regulated, mostly by state law, requiring companies to report their pricing mechanisms to state insurance commissions, which in turn oversee rates and profits. Some information is made available to the public. Assuming that state law regimes would remain in place rather than be pre-empted by federal law,[64] insurance could be a vehicle for bringing new over-seers into workplaces, for motivating companies to lower rates by improving conditions, and for enabling public monitoring of incidence of harassment.

Of course, companies also pass the costs of insurance on either to those who benefit from their businesses or by lowering wages for workers. The costs of harassment are now imposed on individual targets, coworkers, and individuals or organizations found to have harassed or to have had insufficient internal prohibitions on harassment. Through insurance, companies would, by raising prices, shift some of those costs to those who enjoy the products of a given company's business. Or all workers could suffer because of discriminatory working conditions. Companies that mitigate the likelihood of harassment could advertise that their lower prices come from their nondiscriminatory workplaces. Consumers would thus be able to shop for less expensive products based on information about which companies pay what rates for harassment insurance. Prospective employees could likewise find better conditions and pay in companies with lower insurance costs. Broadening the set of those having to absorb the costs of harassment might create larger pools of individuals eager to lower the incidence of harassment. Thus, were the costs of insurance high enough and the product widely enough used, the expansion of an insurance market might help to alter the incentives about discrimination.

Symbolically, the availability of insurance would serve to recognize the existence of discrimination as a facet of many people's lives. In this era, in which a good deal of popular rhetoric claims that discrimination is passé—an old paradigm now replaced by a diverse and "color-blind" society[65]—the existence of insurance could serve to acknowledge that not all enjoy the freedom to work without discrimination. Practically, were insurance readily available, more companies would be in the "market" of thinking about discrimination, pricing it, and debating when to defend claims of harassment and when to try to settle them. In markets in which insurance exists, victims learn to assert their injuries, and society learns about the rate of injury and its costs. Because of required car insurance, for example, drivers, passengers, and pedestrians are taught how to file claims and not to expect to internalize the costs of accidents.

An increased use of liability insurance for harassment might already be oc-curring, driven by practices of businesses that work within contexts in which participants expect to be insured against liability. Greater use could come about through changes in legal rules, either by permitting insurance for inten-tional torts or by interpreting the standard for liability in harassment law to be based on negligence. Some commentators have argued that negligence cap-tures a good deal of the liability imposed, given that motive and intent are not much in focus in case law and that employers are held responsible if they "knew or should have known" of harassing behavior.[66] Embracing a negli-gence standard for liability in harassment would help to underscore its col-lective and structural roots, revealing that harassment stems not only from willed oppression but also from deeply imbedded customs of interaction. Cog-nitive psychologists exploring bias are increasingly concerned about "implicit bias," that all of us (of whatever genders, ethnicities, skin colors, ages, classes) are conditioned to make assumptions about other individuals based on gen-der, ethnicity, skin color, age, and class.[67] Using insurance for harassment helps to express the shared and collective responsibility for its occurrence.

A distinct question is what effect liability insurance would have on the actual litigation of harassment claims. A substantial literature analyzes the market in employment claims and debates whether and how such lawsuits help specific sets of workers.[68] Litigation is a multivariable problem; accurate prediction of the effects of changes is not possible but understanding what kinds of questions to ask is. Lessons can be drawn by considering the role insurance plays in litigation about another intentional tort, fraud. Directors and managers of companies involved in securities markets cannot get insur-ance for that intentional tort, but they do have insurance for negligence. As scholars of securities litigation have demonstrated, insurance helps to create incentives to settle cases rather than to litigate.[69] Settlements avoid the risk of a finding of intentional fraud; by agreeing to settle claims under negligence theories or without any discussion of underlying fault, defendants can obtain reimbursement from insurance for alleged wrongdoings. The settlements may not track the degree or kind of injuries imposed, but plaintiffs receive some compensation.

Were insurance to be routinely available for employers for negligent failures that result in harassment, defendants might be prompted to settle more harass-ment claims than they do currently. Would an increase in settlements be con-structive? The availability of settlements might increase the pool of lawyers willing to take on clients. Were settlement to occur earlier, the costs of its pursuit might also be lowered. Would an increase in settlements be good for harassment claimants? More claimants might be compensated, but perhaps with less careful attention to the degree of individual injury, as is the experience in some other tort-insurance compensation markets.

The discussion of liability insurance is keyed to a litigation model resting on forms of fault-finding. Other kinds of insurance, however, look toward the provision of social well-being and security and — aside from controversies about eligibility — are not so reliant on litigation. Unemployment insurance is one such example that could be an important source of protection against harassment. Work on violence against women has demonstrated how central the option of exit is to a woman's well-being. Some women cannot leave oppressive households because of physical danger. Others have no place to go. Workers subject to harassment ought also to have the ability to leave a workplace, but currently only a few states provide for the payment of unemployment insurance when a person quits work because of harassment.[70] No state of which I am aware provides such benefits for individuals such as the "seven white men" in *Childress* who do not want to work alongside harassers. Health insurance is also tied to workplaces, and hence, were workers to be free to leave work because of harassment, their stream of income, health insurance, and other forms of benefits would have to be protected.

Insurance thus functions as a means of recognition that injuries are both possible — and sometimes probable — aspects of ordinary life against which protection ought to be had. As ongoing debates about health insurance make plain, however, the contribution of insurance to public welfare varies with the degree to which the market of insurance is itself regulated and subsidized. The role of government — another source of regulation — is thus central. In the United States, the current political milieu remains at best ambivalent if not suspicious of government regulation.

But harassment law has always been predicated on moving beyond extant rules of law and cultural assumptions. Imagine that workplace safety is once again understood as a central obligation of government. Regulation of occupational safety and hazards might comprehend that, in addition to risk of injury from poorly designed or malfunctioning machines, from air in need of filtration, and from work spaces that cause back and eye strain, workers are also at risk of injury from unsafe interpersonal interactions. The EEOC could be joined by the Occupational Safety and Health Administration in efforts to make workplaces safer. Consider the other ways in which governments regulate and tax businesses — from work and building permits to licenses for professionals and for liquor — and realize the range of opportunities for laws (federal, state, local, and transnational) to intervene to damp down discriminatory practices.

These are just a few of the remedial options that can be explored, once the focus shifts away from individualized contests about specific interactions to a wider concern about the structure of workplaces. Several of my suggestions are in tension with contemporary trends, including restrictions on adjudication and hostility to government regulation, as well as legal rules on standing, preemption, and the availability of attorneys' fees. But then, so was the initial impulse to press for remedies for sexual harassment, understood only thirty years ago not as a named harm but as a feature of working life that was "just the way it was." To return to where we began, what seemed implausible then is now the framework in which we live and from which other imaginative leaps follow readily.

Notes

My thanks to Reva Siegel and Catharine MacKinnon for convening the conference and creating the book of which this essay forms a part, for their insight, energy, and commitment to helping to engender better options for all people, for their comments on this essay, and for the pleasure of sharing work and concerns. Thanks also to Dennis Curtis, Kathy Abrams, Kate Andrias, Mary L. Clark, Elizabeth Brundige, Julie Suk, Sarah Russell, and Tracey Parr for thoughtful exchanges on the topics explored here.

1. *See* Catharine MacKinnon, *Sexual Harassment of Working Women: A Case of Sex Discrimination* (1979); Catharine A. MacKinnon, "The Logic of Experience: Reflections on the Development of Sexual Harassment Law," 90 *Georgetown L. J.* 812 (2002); Reva B. Siegel, Introduction, this volume; Deborah Rhode, "Sex in Schools: Who's Minding the Adults?" this volume.

2. *See, e.g.*, Barbara Reskin, "The Proximate Causes of Employment Discrimination," 29 *Contemporary Sociology* 319 (2000); Vicki Schultz, "Reconceptualizing Sexual Harassment Law," 107 *Yale L. J.* 927 (1998); Rosa Ehrenreich, "Dignity and Discrimination: Toward a Pluralistic Understanding of Workplace Harassment," 88 *Georgetown L. J.* 1 (1999).

3. *See* Anita Hill, *Speaking Truth to Power* (1997); Pamela Price, "Eradicating Sexual Harassment in Education," this volume.

4. *Pollard v. E. I. Du Pont De Nemours & Co.*, 532 U.S. 843 (2001).

5. Title VII is the dominant vehicle for such claims. Amendments passed in 1991 provided for both compensatory and punitive damages and capped those recoveries. Monetary relief that represents equitable remedies, and specifically, front pay. *See* 42 U.S.C. § 1981a; *Pollard v. E. I. Du Pont De Nemours & Co.*, 532 U.S. 843 (2001). In addition, some plaintiffs rely on other federal and state statutes and common law torts, not subject to the caps.

Litigation for money damages poses perennial problems of how to measure losses. The literature is laden with gendered references to "soft" (emotional) injuries as contrasted with "hard" (lost wages and medical costs) injuries. The focus on "economic" injury—

often pegged to lost wages—echoes gendered opportunities in the market. Martha Chammallas, "The Architecture of Bias: Deep Structures in Tort Law," 146 *U. Pa. L. Rev.* 463 (1998). Therefore, many are aware that insufficient funds have been paid for those who have suffered injuries from a range of discriminatory practices. Yet others worry about uneven recoveries and overcompensation. *E.g.*, Cass Sunstein and Judy M. Shih, "Damages in Sexual Harassment Cases" this volume.

6. 42 U.S.C. § 2000e(5)(k); *see also* 42 U.S.C. § 1988. Payments under these statutes are calculated by multiplying hourly rates times hours to establish the "lodestar."

7. *See Buckhannon Board of Care Home, Inc. v. West Virginia Department of Health*, 532 U.S. 595 (2001). The five-person majority concluded that a litigant did not qualify as a "prevailing party" to be eligible to recover statutorily awarded fees by being a "catalyst" for change and achieving the "desired result because the lawsuit brought about a voluntary change in the defendant's conduct." Rather, a court judgment or consent decree is required. *Id.* at 1838.

8. Fee awards can be greater than backpay and benefits awards. For example, in *Pollard v. E. I. Du Pont De Nemours & Co.*, 532 U.S. 843, 845 (2001), the plaintiff obtained $107,364 in backpay and benefits, the statutorily capped $300,000 in compensatory damages, and additional "front pay." The attorneys' fees awarded were $252,997.

9. *See, e.g.*, "The Effects of Gender: The Final Report of the Ninth Circuit Gender Bias Task Force," reprinted at 67 *So. Calif. L. Rev.* 727, 883–892 (1994) (describing views of plaintiffs' attorneys that district judges did not welcome such claims and noting the comparatively high rate of reversal of district level rejections of such suits).

10. *See* Schultz, *supra* note 2. *See also* Katharine Franke, "What's Wrong with Sexual Harassment Law?" this volume.

11. *See, e.g., Faragher v. City of Baton Raton*, 524 U.S. 775 (1998); *Burlington Industries, Inc. v. Ellerth*, 524 U.S. 742 (1998). *See generally* David B. Oppenheimer, "Employer Liability for Sexual Harassment: Under What Circumstances Will a Court Hold an Employer Responsible for Harassment by a Supervisor" this volume.

12. *Pollard v. E. I. Du Pont De Nemours & Co.*, 213 F.3d 933, 937 (6th Cir. 2000), *rev'd*, 532 U.S. 843 (2001) (reversing only the holding that the cap on compensatory damages included "front pay").

13. Painful examples include *Jenson v. Eveleth Taconite Co.*, 130 F.3d 1287 (8th Cir. 1997), *cert. denied* 524 U.S. 953 (1998) *sub nom. Oglebay Norton Co. v. Jenson; Carr v. Allison Gas Turbine*, 32 F.3d 1007 (7th Cir. 1994); *Robinson v. Jacksonville Shipyards*, 760 F. Supp. 1486 (M.D. Fla. 1991). *See also* Judith Resnik, Changing the Topic, 8 *Cardozo J. Leg. Stud. and Lit.* 339 (1996) (detailing examples of the hostility and of the effort to divert discussion to topics less painful, including the relevance of First Amendment law to harassment claims).

14. *See generally* William L. F. Felstiner, Richard L. Abel, and Austin Sarat, "The Emergence and Transformation of Disputes: Naming, Blaming, and Claiming . . . ," 15 *L. and Soc.* 631 (1980–81); Austin Sarat, "Naming, Blaming, and Claiming in Popular Culture," 50 *DePaul L. Rev.* 425 (2000)

15. Julie A. Woodzicka and Marianne La France, "Real Versus Imagined Gender Harassment," 57 *J. Social Issues* 1, 15–30 (2001); Deborah R. Hensler, M. Susan Marquis, Allan F. Abrahmse, Sandra H. Berry, Patricia A. Ebener, Elizabeth Lewis, E. Allan Lind,

Robert J. MacCoun, Willard G. Manning, Jeannette A. Rogowski, and Mary E. Vaiana, *Compensation for Accidental Injuries in the United States* (1991); Donald Harris, Mavis Maclean, Hazel Genn, Sally Lloyd-Bostock, Paul Fenn, Peter Corfield, Yvonne Brittan, *Compensation and Support for Illness and Injury* (1984).

16. Saskia Sassen, "Towards a Feminist Analytics of The Global Economy," 4 *Ind. J. Global Leg. Stud.* 7 (1996); Christa Wichterich, *The Globalized Woman: Reports from the Future of Inequality* (2000).

17. Barbara Reskin, "The Proximate Causes of Discrimination: Research Agenda for the Twenty-First Century," 28 *Contemporary Sociology* 319 *Imagining Work Without Exclusionary Barriers*, 14 Yale J.L. & Feminism 313 (2002); Katherine V. W. Stone, "The New Psychological Contract: Implications of the Changing Workplace for Labor and Employment Law," 48 *UCLA L. Rev.* 519 (2001).

18. 9 U.S.C. § 1 et seq.

19. *Wilko v. Swan*, 346 U.S. 427 (1953).

20. *E.g., Rodriquez de Quijas v. Shearson/American Express, Inc.*, 490 U.S. 477 (1989); *Mitsubishi Motors Corp. v. Soler Chrysler-Plymouth, Inc.*, 473 U.S. 614 (1985).

21. 415 U.S. 36, 47 (1974). The view that this decision prohibits waivers of employment discrimination claims is expressed by Richard Posner, in "Employment Discrimination: Age Discrimination and Sexual Harassment," 19 *International Review Law and Economics* 421, 442 (2000)

22. *Gilmer v. Interstate/Johnson Lane Corp.*, 500 U.S. 20, 26 (1991). The Court ruled: "Having made the bargain to arbitrate, the party should be held to it unless Congress itself has evinced an intention to preclude a waiver of judicial remedies for the statutory rights at issue" (citation omitted).

23. *Circuit City Stores, Inc. v. Adams*, 532 U.S. 105 (2001). The five-person majority for the Court also relied on an earlier ruling (*Southland Corp. v. Keating*, 465 U.S. 1 (1984)) that the FAA applied in state courts. The 2001 decision reversed a ruling of the Ninth Circuit, which had concluded that Congress had not intended the FAA, enacted in 1925, to apply to employment contracts. The appellate court relied on the narrow construction of federal commerce clause powers at the time and the express exemption provided for interstate employees (who might have been the only employees then subject to congressional authority). *See Circuit City Stores v. Adams*, 194 F.3d 1070 (9th Cir. 1999).

24. *See generally* Katherine Van Wezel Stone, "Mandatory Arbitration of Individual Employment Rights: The Yellow Dog Contract of the 1990s," 73 *Denver U. L. Rev.* 1017 (1996).

25. *Wright v. University Maritime Service Corp.*, 525 U.S. 70, 80–82 (1998).

26. *EEOC v. Waffle House, Inc.*, 534 U.S. 279 (2002). The Fourth Circuit held that an individual who signed an employment application agreeing to arbitrate "any dispute or claim" arising from employment could not bind the EEOC to arbitrate the disability claim nor preclude the EEOC from seeking large-scale injunctive relief but that the individual contract did prevent the EEOC from pursuing backpay, reinstatement, or damages for the allegedly injured individual. Justice Stevens wrote the majority decision, reversing the Fourth Circuit and permitting the EEOC to rely on its independent authority under the statute to bring a claim. This case provides insight into business practices

that make waiver of access to court a routine feature of employment applications and of judicial interpretations that broadly construe such contracts. The dissenter in the Fourth Circuit objected that no enforceable contract to arbitrate had been entered under state law, not only because the provision was printed in a small font occupying "5/16 of an inch" on the form, but because the form was proffered at a location different from the one in which the individual was hired, and his employment was based on an oral offer and acceptance. 193 F.3d at 818 ("The majority's rule has no temporal bounds or geographical limits.")

27. The Supreme Court's decision in *Circuit City* interpreted the FAA as applying to state antidiscrimination provisions, not Title VII.

28. *See, e.g., Desiderio v. National Association of Securities Dealers*, 191 F.3d 198 (2d Cir. 1999), *cert. denied*, 531 U.S. 1069 (2001); *Seus v. John Nuveen & Co.*, 146 F.3d 175 (3d Cir. 1998), *cert. denied*, 525 U.S. 1139 (1999); *Hooters of America, Inc. v. Phillips*, 173 F.3d 933 (4th Cir. 1999); *Koveleskie v. SBC Capital Mkts., Inc.*, 167 F.3d 361 (7th Cir. 1999), *cert. denied*, 528 U.S. 811 (1999).

29. *See Rosenberg v. Merrill Lynch*, 995 F. Supp. 190, 205–11 (D. Mass.), *rev'd in part*, 170 F.3d 1, 21 (1st Cir. 1998). Judge Gertner's district court decision had held that problems of impartiality undermined the fairness of the program; the First Circuit ruled that, while arbitration could have been permissible, the form provided insufficient notice of what kinds of claims would be sent to arbitration. *See also* Employment Discrimination: How Registered Representatives Fare in Discrimination Disputes (Letter Report), GAO/HEHS-94–17 (Mar. 30, 1994) (raising concerns about the fairness of the arbitration system).

30. *Duffield v. Robertson Stephens & Co.*, 144 F.3d 1182, 1190 (9th Cir. 1998), *cert. denied*, 525 U.S. 996 (1998).

31. *See, e.g., Prudential Insurance Co. of America v. Lai*, 42 F.3d 1299 (9th Cir. 1994), *cert. denied*, 516 U.S. 812 (1995); *Rosenberg v. Merrill Lynch*, 170 F.3d 1, 21 (1st Cir. 1998).

32. Self Regulatory Organizations, National Association of Securities Dealers, Inc., *Order Approving Proposed Rule Change by the New York Stock Exchange, Inc. Related to Arbitration of Employment Discrimination Claims*, 63 Fed. Reg. 35299, 35303 (1998) (amending New York Stock Exchange Rules 347 and 600, eff. Jan. 1, 1999).

33. *EEOC Policy Statement on Mandatory Arbitration*, 915.002, 1997 Daily Labor Reports (BNA) at E-4 (July 11, 1997).

34. The Civil Rights Procedures Protection Act of 1999, 106th Cong. S. 121 (introduced Jan. 19, 1999); H.R. 872, (introduced Feb. 25, 1999).

35. That distinction was drawn by Justice Ginsburg, writing in dissent on behalf of herself and Justices Stevens, Souter, and Breyer, in *Green Tree Financial Corp.-Alabama & Green Tree Financial Corp. v. Randolph*, 531 U.S. 79 at 92–93 (2000).

36. Rule 30 (2) of the *Dispute Resolution Rules and Procedures, Circuit City Stores v. Adams*, Respondent's Brief, U.S. Sup. Ct., 99–1379, Joint Appendix, Exh. C. 2000 WL 1369473, p. 33a (Sept. 19, 2000). Arbitrators had discretion to shift that cost if the claimant prevailed to company. *Id.*, Rule 30 (4).

37. *Green Tree Financial Corp. v. Randolph*, 531 U.S. 79 (2000).

38. One of the cases cited above, *Desiderio v. National Association of Securities Deal-*

ers, 191 F.3d 198 (2d Cir. 1999), provides an exception. The plaintiff, offered a job as a broker, sought to have the contract provision requiring arbitration struck but lost in a ruling that Title VII claims could be subjected to *ex ante* mandatory arbitration requirements.

39. *See* Katherine Van Wezel Stone, "Rustic Justice: Community and Coercion Under the Federal Arbitration Act," 77 *No. Carolina L. Rev.* 931 (1999) (distinguishing a vision of arbitration based on voluntary self-regulation from the requirement that consumers arbitrate disputes).

40. *See, e.g.,* Susan Sturm, "Second Generation Employment Discrimination: A Structural Approach," 101 *Colum. L. Rev.* 458 (2001) (detailing programs at three corporations that have attempted innovative responses to discriminatory practices).

41. *See generally* Judith Resnik, "Many Doors? Closing Doors? Alternative Dispute Resolution and Adjudication," 10 *Ohio St. J. Dis. Res.* 211 (1995).

42. *See* Jean R. Sternlight, "As Mandatory Arbitration Meets the Class Action, Will the Class Action Survive?" 42 *William and Mary L. Rev.* 1 (2000).

43. *See, e.g.,* Robin West, "Unwelcome Sex: Toward a Harm-Based Analysis" this volume; Kathryn Abrams, "Subordination and Agency in Sexual Harassment Law" this volume; Janet Halley, "Sexuality Harassment" this volume.

44. *Childress v. City of Richmond,* 134 F.3d 1205 (4th Cir. 1998) (en banc), *cert. denied,* 524 U.S. 927 (1998).

45. 134 F.3d at 1207.

46. 134 F.3d at 1208 (Luttig, J., concurring in the per curium en banc decision that affirmed the district court's decision dismissing the claims).

47. *See, e.g., Leibovitz v. N.Y. City Transit Authority,* 4 F. Supp. 2d 144 (S.D.N.Y. 1988) (urging a broad conception of injury and concluding that a member of a class harassed could bring a hostile work environment claim even if she was not the target of harassment); *Clayton v. White Hall School Dist.,* 875 F.2d 676 (8th Cir. 1989) (holding that a white woman could bring a claim of hostile working environment based on alleged discrimination against a black coworker); *Carter v. Chrysler Corp.,* 173 F.3d 693, 700 (8th Cir. 1999) (concluding that, to bring such claims, a plaintiff must be a member of a "protected group").

48. The EEOC advises that victims can be anyone affected by offensive conduct. *See* EEOC Guidelines, 29 C.F.R. § 1604.11; http://www.eeoc.gov/facts/fs-sex.html (Facts About Sexual Harassment).

49. *See, e.g., Bermudez v. TRC Holdings, Inc.,* 138 F.3d 1176 (7th Cir. 1998) (refusing to permit a white female at an employment agency to bring a hostile work environment claim based on alleged prejudice of coworkers toward clients).

50. *See, e.g., Broderick v. Ruder,* 685 F. Supp. 1269 (D.D.C. 1988). The EEOC policy also notes the availability of claims of "sexual favoritism" because such working environments teach women that sex is a means of career promotion. *See* EEOC Policy/regulations, Jan. 12, 1990.

51. *Oncale v. Sundowner Offshore Services, Inc.,* 523 U.S. 75 (1998).

52. These concepts borrow from law developed in other contexts, including school and housing discrimination cases, in which courts developed the concept that members of one group have a right of association with out-group members. *See, e.g., Trafficante v. Metropolitan Life Ins.,* Col, 409 U.S. 205 (1972); *Council v. BMC Marketing Corp.,* 28 F.3d

1268, 1278 (D.C. Cir. 1994). Many decisions have recognized third-party standing, but typically when the individuals conceptualized as suffering harm directly cannot themselves bring suit. Noah Zatz offers the alternative that male workers who violate stereotypes about male hostility to female coworkers suffer gender-based discrimination. *See* Noah D. Zatz, "Beyond the Zero-Sum Game: Toward Title VII Protection for Intergroup Solidarity," 77 *Indiana L. J.* 63 (2002).

53. *See* Frederick Schauer, "The Speech-ing of Harassment" this volume; Robert Post, "Sexual Harassment and the First Amendment" this volume.

54. *See generally* Kalima Rose, *Where Women Are Leaders: The SEWA Movement in India* (1992).

55. *See* Jeanne Gregory, "Sexual Harassment: The Impact of EU Law in the Member States," in *Gender Policies in the European Union* (Mariagrazia Rosilli, ed., 2000) 175 at 182.

56. A few cases recognize the right of workers to sue unions under Title VII for creating hostile working environments through the distribution of benefits. *See, e.g., Golleher v. Aerospace District Lodge 837*, 122 F. Supp. 1053 (E.D. Mo. 2000)

57. *See* Abrams, *supra* note 43.

58. Efforts to settle a sex-discrimination case against Merrill Lynch explored giving employees the option to bring complaints to mediation but also protected access to federal courts. *See* Peter Truell, "Settlement Proposal Is Expected in Women's Suit Against Merrill," *N.Y. Times*, Jan. 28, 1998 at D1.

59. *See* Judith Resnik, Dennis E. Curtis, and Deborah R. Hensler, "Individuals Within the Aggregate: Relationships, Representation, and Fees," 71 *N.Y.U. L. Rev.* 296 (1996).

60. Worker compensation for job-related injuries is such an example, often providing schedules of damages that limit recoveries, lower the costs of pursuit of claims, and enlarge the set of individuals covered.

61. For example, at the conference from which this volume comes, George Priest argued against making insurance available.

62. Lorelie S. Masters, "Protection from the Storm: Insurance Coverage for Employment Liability," 53 *Bus. Law.* 1249 (1998).

63. Sturm, *supra* note 40, at 458 and n. 193.

64. *See generally* Sylvia A. Law, "Sex Discrimination and Insurance for Contraception," 73 *Washington L. Rev.* 363 (1998).

65. *See* Reva Siegel, "Why Equal Protection No Longer Protects: The Evolving Forms of Status-Enforcing State Action," 49 *Stan. L. Rev.* 1111 (1997).

66. *See, e.g.,* Oppenheimer, *supra* note 11.

67. A. G. Greenwald and Mahzarin Banaji, "Implicit Stereotypes and Prejudice," in 7 *The Psychology of Prejudice: The Ontario Symposium* 55 (M. P. Ann and J. M. Olson eds., 1994).

68. *See, e.g.,* Paul Oyer and Scott Schaefer, "Litigation Costs and Returns to Experience," Stanford Law and Economics Olin Working Paper #215; SRNN (April 2001); John J. Donohue and Peter Siegelman, "The Changing Nature of Employment Discrimination Litigation," 43 *Stan. L. Rev.* 983 (1991).

69. Janet Cooper Alexander, "Do the Merits Matter? A Study of Settlement in Securities Class Actions," 43 *Stan. L. Rev.* 497 (1991).

70. Diana M. Pearce and Monica L. Phillips, "When Sexual Harassment Happens: State Unemployment Insurance Coverage of Workers Who Leave Their Jobs Because of Sexual Harassment," 5 *Stan. L. and Pol'y Rev.* 74 (1994) (describing the six states and the District of Columbia that expressly provide for benefits when workers leave because of sexual harassment).

17

Employer Liability for Sexual Harassment by Supervisors

DAVID B. OPPENHEIMER

Traditionally and as a general proposition, employers are vicariously responsible for the wrongful acts of their employees, when committed at the work site. When the victim is a nonemployee such as a customer or stranger, the employer is liable under the common law doctrine of *respondeat superior*. When the victim is an employee, the employer is responsible through an insurance system known as workers' compensation, and may also be responsible under the common law tort system. Liability is generally imposed not only for torts based on negligence, but for intentional torts as well. The employer's liability, being vicarious, is imposed without regard to questions of fault.

For the most part, these principles apply to employment discrimination under Title VII of the 1964 Civil Rights Act. Thus, when a supervisor refuses to hire an applicant for employment based on the applicant's race, color, religion, sex, or national origin, or refuses to promote an existing employee, or fires that employee, the supervisor's employer is held vicariously liable. This is true regardless of whether the employer approves of such discrimination.

But in the area of sexual harassment the rules of liability are different. Applicants or employees who can describe tangible effects from the harassment, such as loss of employment or the denial of a promotion, may take advantage of the standard rule, but those bringing claims of hostile work environment sexual harassment are subject to more stringent requirements.

Until quite recently, they were required to prove that the employer itself either (1) authorized the harassment or (2) knew that it was occurring and failed to take appropriate corrective measures. This rule, variously described as "notice liability" or "negligence liability," has made it possible for supervisors to harass subordinate employees with impunity until the employees complain to the highest levels of corporate management. Two decisions of the Supreme Court handed down in 1998, *Burlington Industries, Inc. v. Ellerth*[1] and *Faragher v. City of Boca Raton*,[2] should reduce, but not eliminate, this liability loophole.

The loophole was opened in 1986 when, in *Meritor Savings Bank v. Vinson*,[3] the Supreme Court declined to decide the validity of a rule proposed by the Equal Employment Opportunity Commission in 1980, following extensive public comment. That rule imposed strict vicarious liability on employers when a supervisor created a hostile work environment. General rules of agency law, and the modern policy justifications for vicarious liability, support this rule. Because the Supreme Court avoided ruling on the EEOC rule in 1986, the courts of appeals were in disarray over the issue for more than a decade.

In revisiting the question in *Ellerth* and *Faragher*, the Supreme Court has eliminated some of the confusion and offered greater protection to millions of American workers, most of them women. Unfortunately, the Court again passed up an opportunity to adopt the EEOC rule. As a result, the question of how much more protection the new rule offers, and how much it still deviates from common law principles, remains uncertain. For workers subjected to hostile work environment sexual harassment, their right to recover for their injuries hangs in the balance.

Hypothetical No. 1: The Coffee Spill

To begin consideration of the general question of employer liability for employee misconduct, consider the following hypothetical. Assume that a patron is having breakfast at a coffee shop and the server has spilled hot coffee on her hand. The patron did not provoke it, she certainly did not consent, and the server had never done such a thing before. Nonetheless, the patron would be entitled to recover from the restaurant for her injuries. Why? Because under most circumstances the law of agency provides that a principal is responsible for the wrongful acts of its agents. When the principal is an employer, the law of agency calls it a "master," calls the employee a "servant," and provides, under a doctrine known as *respondeat superior*, that the master is liable for the torts of its servants committed within the scope of the employment.[4] Since the server's job is to pour coffee, and the injury occurred in the process of the pouring of coffee, the wrongful act occurred within the scope of employment; the employer is thus responsible.

What if the restaurant actually has a rule against pouring coffee on customers? It would still be liable. What if it had no knowledge that its server might harm a customer (or anyone else) and had acted reasonably to investigate the server's background and to protect its customers from such injuries? It would still be liable. Its vicarious liability for acts within the scope of employment is "strict" or "absolute" even though it has itself done nothing wrong.

What if it turns out that the server intentionally poured coffee on the patron, perhaps in response to a complaint that her toast was burned? In most jurisdictions, most of the time, the employer remains liable, even if it had done everything reasonable to prevent such injuries from occurring.[5] Some courts explain that the employer is liable because the wrongful act is incidental to the employee's legitimate work activities.[6] Others explain that the employer is liable because the injury was foreseeable, or a foreseeable risk of operating a coffee shop.[7] Some treat the injuries as an inherent risk of having employees.[8] Still others hold the employer responsible because it is in the best position to insure against injuries from coffee spills; they thus require the employer to spread the risk of such injuries among all its customers by including the cost of such injuries in the price of a cup of coffee.[9] Here again, the employer's liability is not premised on fault; it is vicariously liable — liable because of the wrongful act of another for whom it is responsible.

What if the coffee were spilled on the hand of a fellow employee, not a customer? In most circumstances the injured employee would be entitled to compensation from the employer or its insurance company under the workers' compensation system, a no-fault alternative to the common law tort system.[10] In many states, if the injury was deliberate the injured employee could also bring a tort action against the employee and the employer.[11]

Finally, what if instead of spilling coffee, the employee attacked a customer or co-employee with a frying pan? Even if the job did not include cooking (let alone attacking people with frying pans), the mere fact that the attack occurred on the job would often be sufficient to impose vicarious liability on the employer.[12] Here again, the responsibility is not based on the employer's own wrongdoing, it is based on a policy that favors shifting responsibility for injuries caused by employees from employees to employers.

Hypothetical No. 2: Sexual Molestation

Now let's change the nature of the tort. Assume that instead of a coffee burn, or an assault with a frying pan, the server sexually molested the patron. In many states, the employer would remain responsible.[13] Nothing in the multivolume *Restatement (Second) of Agency* suggests that she should be treated any differently than the victim of a coffee burn. But in some states the employer would not be held liable.[14] The courts in those states have what amounts to a special rule that treats the victims of sexual molestation differently than most other tort victims, depriving them of a claim for vicarious liability.

This special rule treats sexual assault as "sex" rather than "assault." That is, it gives little weight to the fact that a person (usually a woman) has been injured through the intentional wrongful act of another, instead giving primacy to the fact that the assault was "sexual." It focuses on the motives of the assailant instead of the injury to the victim. In doing so, it follows in the tracks of myriad legal rules concerning sex that treat claims by women against men with heightened suspicion and skepticism.[15]

All too often, courts hearing sexual harassment in employment cases have applied this special rule limiting liability in sexual molestation cases, instead of the general rules for compensating injury victims. Consider this actual case:[16] a young woman works as a salesperson at an appliance store. Her supervisor, the store manager, molests her in a variety of ways. He makes unwanted sexually suggestive remarks to her; he comes up from behind her at the sales counter and grabs her breasts; he presses up against her and simulates intercourse, including simulating orgasm and ejaculation; he suggests that she exchange sex for sales. She repeatedly demands that he cease and complains to other managers. He continues. On these facts, the United States Court of Appeals held that unless the employee could prove that the employer, through its very highest officials, knew of the harassment and failed to act, or provided no reasonable avenue for complaint, the employer was not responsible.

What if the store manager had not molested the employee, but had instead refused to hire her because he didn't believe women could sell appliances, or what if he hired her but then fired her based on a double standard whereby he required more sales from women than men? Under the 1964 Civil Rights Act the employer would have been responsible. What if he had refused to promote her because he was saving the assistant manager position for a man? Again, the employer would be liable. What if, instead of making her miserable through his sexual conduct at work, he'd simply fired her because she wouldn't have sex with him? Here again the employer would be responsible for his wrongful acts. In each case all twelve United States Courts of Appeals would agree that the manager's acts were sex discrimination in violation of the Civil Rights Act, and that the employer was responsible for the manager's actions. But where the supervisor harassed the employee by creating a hostile work environment, until recently most courts have held that the employer is not responsible unless it knew or should have known of the harassment and failed to act.[17]

The EEOC Guidelines on Sexual Harassment: Placing Liability Where It Belongs

In 1980, as Jimmy Carter's presidency came to an end, the United States Equal Employment Opportunity Commission (EEOC) drafted Guidelines governing employer liability for sexual harassment.[18] The Guidelines went through extensive comment and revision, and were adopted late that year. The Guidelines generally tracked the ground-breaking work of Catharine MacKinnon, celebrated in this collection of essays. The Guidelines adopted MacKinnon's distinction between quid pro quo harassment and hostile work environment harassment, and distinguished between liability for harassment by supervisors and harassment by co-employees. They provided that in cases of hostile work environment harassment by co-employees, employers would only be liable if they had notice of the harassment and failed to respond. But in all cases of sexual harassment by supervisors, whether quid pro quo or hostile work environment, the Guidelines declared that the employer would be subject to strict vicarious liability.

This distinction between supervisors and co-employees is an excellent application of the law of tort liability and agency. In the technical terms of agency law, it holds principals responsible for the wrongful acts of those agents who are acting as vice-principals, or who are abusing their authority to supervise the work of subordinate employees, or who are misusing their apparent authority to act abusively toward their subordinates. Beyond being technically correct, it follows the trend evident since the mid-twentieth century of explaining *respondeat superior* and vicarious liability on policy grounds. In policy terms, the Guidelines' position is justified by the employer's superior ability to: (1) prevent harassment from occurring, by aggressive antiharassment policies; (2) spread the cost of harassment among all employees, rather than letting it fall on the shoulders of an unfortunate few; and (3) absorb or pass on the costs of harassment as one of those foreseeable costs of running an enterprise large enough to be delegating supervisory authority to other persons. One important outcome of this policy-based loss shifting is the sharing of liability throughout all members of society, including men as well as women, rather than requiring the victims of harassment, almost all of whom are women, to bear it alone.

For these reasons, courts have imposed strict vicarious liability on employers when: an employee who was a carpenter hit a coworker in the head with his hammer;[19] four employees got drunk after work and beat up another coworker;[20] a drunken sailor opened an intake valve on his ship, causing it to sink;[21] a truck driver, angry at another driver following an accident, beat him with a wrench;[22] a restaurant manager responded to a complaint about a hamburger by beating the customer with a nightstick;[23] a counselor had sex with a client;[24] and a nurse's assistant raped a patient in a hospital.[25]

Soon after the EEOC promulgated its Guidelines, President Ronald Reagan took office. His transition team advisor on civil rights was highly critical of the new EEOC sexual harassment Guidelines, and would soon have a chance to challenge them; he complained that "the elimination of personal slights and sexual advances which contribute to an 'intimidating, hostile or offensive working environment' is a goal impossible to reach," and would lead "to a barrage of trivial complaints."[26] That advisor was later named Chair of the EEOC, and is now an Associate Justice of the United States Supreme Court, Clarence Thomas.

Meritor v. Vinson: *The Supreme Court Adopts the Doctrine of Hostile Work Environment Harassment but Not the EEOC Vicarious Liability Rule*

In 1986 the question of employer liability for hostile work environment harassment came before the Supreme Court in the case of *Meritor Savings Bank v. Vinson*.[27] The case concerned a bank manager accused of harassing his assistant. She said he repeatedly raped and otherwise molested her. He said he never touched her. Despite the fact that the only thing both sides agreed on was that there was no consensual sexual relationship, the district court inexplicably found that if the defendant had sex with the plaintiff, it was voluntary, and thus not harassment. The court of appeals reversed and returned the case to the district court to decide whether the bank manager created a hostile work environment. It further held that if the district court found harassment, it should hold the employer strictly liable in accordance with the Guidelines.[28] With its Guidelines at stake, the EEOC (under the direction of then-Chair Clarence Thomas) asked the Solicitor General to file an amicus brief in the Court.[29]

The Solicitor General's brief on behalf of the EEOC asked the Court to find that the plaintiff had not been harassed; or that if she had been harassed the employer was not responsible because the bank manager lacked authority to harass employees; and that even if he did have authority to harass her she waived her right to sue because she failed to complain to her supervisor (the bank manager who harassed her) under the bank's grievance policy. The brief is noteworthy for at least three reasons. First, it was filed in support of the employer, something the EEOC rarely did. Second, it simply ignored, and in the process disavowed, the EEOC Guidelines on employer liability. And third, it presented an argument on how agency law operates that utterly disregarded basic doctrines in the law of agency, asserting that unless the harasser had been authorized by the employer to harass his subordinates he was acting outside the scope of his authority.

The Supreme Court rejected most of the Solicitor General's argument. In the most significant portion of its opinion, it adopted MacKinnon's view that hostile work environment sexual harassment is a form of sex discrimination, and violates Title VII.[30] On the question of vicarious liability, however, the Court stated:

> This debate over the appropriate standard of employer liability has a rather abstract quality about it given the state of the record in this case. . . . We therefore decline the parties' invitation to issue a definitive rule on employer liability. . . . We do agree with the EEOC that Congress wanted courts to look to agency principles for guidance in this area. . . . For this reason, we hold that the Court of Appeals erred in concluding that employers are always automatically liable for sexual harassment by their supervisors.[31]

The sad irony of the Court's language lies in its failure to recognize that the EEOC rule was an application of agency principles. As Justice Marshall noted in his concurring opinion:

> A supervisor's responsibilities do not begin and end with the power to hire, fire, and discipline employees, or with the power to recommend such actions. Rather, a supervisor is charged with the day-to-day supervision of the work environment and with ensuring a safe, productive workplace. There is no reason why abuse of the latter authority should have different consequences than abuse of the former. In both cases it is the authority vested in the supervisor by the employer that enables him to commit the wrong: it is precisely because the supervisor is understood to be clothed with the employer's authority that he is able to impose unwelcome sexual conduct on subordinates. There is therefore no justification for a special rule, to be applied only in 'hostile environment' cases, that sexual harassment does not create employer liability until the employee suffering the discrimination notifies other supervisors. No such requirement appears in the statute, and no such requirement can coherently be drawn from the law of agency.[32]

Meritor v. Vinson *Applied: A Rejection of Agency Principles*

In the wake of the *Meritor* decision, court after court adopted a simplistic view of agency law based on the absurd principle that if a supervisor was not authorized to sexually harass his subordinates, the employer could not be held vicariously liable. A few courts imposed liability where the supervisor had what they described as apparent authority to harass, and most assessed liability if the employer had been negligent in its response to complaints of harassment, but by and large the principle of *respondeat superior* — that employers are vicariously liable for the wrongful acts of their employees — was disregarded.

For example, in *Klessens v. United States Postal Service*,[33] the plaintiff was targeted by several male coworkers for verbal sexual abuse. After three coworkers subjected her to sexual comments about their desires and/or her body, she complained to her immediate supervisor. The supervisor responded by joining in with the plaintiff's tormenters. When she then complained to her supervisor's supervisor, he too joined in, explicitly describing sexual acts that constituted additional acts of verbal sexual harassment. When she sued, the district court dismissed her case, refusing to hold her employer responsible for the harassment by her supervisor or her supervisor's supervisor under a *Meritor* agency analysis. The Court of Appeals for the First Circuit affirmed.

In *Paroline v. Unisys Corp.*,[34] a supervisor made suggestive remarks to an employee and then grabbed her and kissed her against her will. The district court granted judgment for the employer because the employee quit before the employer had a chance to prove to her it could remedy the situation. The Court of Appeals for the Fourth Circuit reversed, but held that if the employer took prompt and adequate steps following the harassment it should be excused from liability.

Even harassment by upper management was given immunity from liability. In *Steele v. Offshore Shipbuilding, Inc.*,[35] two women employees were harassed by the company's corporate vice president and general manager. He made sexual demands of the two women, made suggestive comments about their clothing, and asked them to visit him on his office couch. Despite his high position, when the women sued for sexual harassment the district court found, under *Meritor*, that the company was not responsible. The Court of Appeals for the Eleventh Circuit affirmed.

Meritor *Confronted:* Burlington Industries, Inc. v. Ellerth *and* Faragher v. City of Boca Raton

As the courts of appeals were applying, or misapplying, the agency portion of the *Meritor* decision, its demise was being written on the beach in Boca Raton, Florida, and in an office building in Chicago.

From 1985 through 1990 Beth Ann Faragher paid her way through college by working as a lifeguard for the City of Boca Raton. (She has since become a lawyer and was admitted to practice before the United States Supreme Court in 1998, on the morning her case was heard there.) She was supervised by Bill Terry, the Marine Safety Chief, and David Silverman, a lieutenant and later a captain in the lifeguard corps. The two men subjected Faragher and other women lifeguards to a barrage of sexual solicitations, abusive sexual language, misogynist name-calling, and unwanted touching. On occasion, she and the other women lifeguards complained to another manager who held the title of "training officer," but they did not complain to any officials at City Hall. The city had adopted an antiharassment policy in the wake of the *Meritor* decision, but had not distributed it to the employees working at the beach.

On these facts, the district court, in a bench trial, found for Faragher, awarding damages and attorneys' fees.[36] The Court of Appeals for the Eleventh Circuit relied on *Meritor* to reverse the district court.[37] The court held that the harassment was not within the scope of employment because the city had never authorized its supervisors to engage in sexual harassment. It rejected Faragher's arguments that the city was liable because she complained to another supervisor, and because the city was negligent in failing to discover the harassment and failing to distribute and effectuate an antiharassment policy.

In 1993, as Beth Ann Faragher's case was working its way through the district court in Florida, Kimberly Ellerth went to work for Burlington Industries as a salesperson in Chicago. One of her supervisors was a vice president in the New York office named Ted Slowik. Over the fifteen months of her employment, Slowik made repeated offensive remarks and gestures, commented on her looks (and in particular her breasts), told her she was not "loose enough" while he rubbed her knee, and warned her to "loosen up" because "you know, Kim, I could make your life very hard or very easy at Burlington."

On these facts, the district court entered summary judgment for Burlington, finding that there was no quid pro quo harassment and that the hostile work environment harassment was not reported to a high enough company official to justify *respondeat superior* liability. The court of appeals for the Seventh Circuit, *en banc*, reversed, but produced eight separate opinions with no consensus for a controlling rationale.

The Supreme Court granted hearings in both *Ellerth* and *Faragher*, using them to redefine the application of agency law in sexual harassment cases.[38] A seven-member majority adopted a middle ground, again failing to adopt the position adopted by the EEOC Guidelines in 1980, but tempering the decisions of the courts of appeals that had proven so hostile to employees. The only dissenters were Justices Thomas and Scalia, each of whom had taken strong positions against vicarious liability in *Meritor* (Justice Thomas as Chair of the EEOC, Justice Scalia as a court of appeals judge, dissenting from the circuit court's denial of further review). The majority held that in all cases involving tangible employment actions such as demotion, undesirable transfer, or firing, employers would be held strictly vicariously liable for sexual harassment of their employees. But in those cases involving no tangible action, but in which an employer's supervisor(s) had altered an employee's working conditions by creating a hostile or abusive work environment, the employer would be vicariously liable, regardless of whether it knew and whether it disapproved of the harassment, unless it could prove as an affirmative defense both (1) that it acted reasonably to prevent and remedy harassment, and (2) that the employee unreasonably failed to take advantage of any preventive or corrective opportunities it provided.[39]

Critiquing Ellerth *and* Faragher: *The Road Not Taken*

In his majority opinion in *Faragher*, Justice Souter comes to the brink of disavowing the *Meritor* Court's failure to properly apply agency law, but then cautiously steps back. He describes decisions by two of the great common law judges of the twentieth century, Justice Cardozo of New York and Justice Traynor of California,[40] applying strict vicarious liability in employment tort cases. He endorses their policy justifications for absolute employer liability. He criticizes the courts of appeals decisions denying liability in sexual harassment cases because the harassers had not been authorized to harass their subordinate employees; he lauds decisions rejecting these cases and embracing the argument that proper application of *respondeat superior* requires courts to impose vicarious liability whenever a supervisor harasses an employee, regardless of the employer's direct culpability.[41] But, explaining that the Court should not disturb a prior ruling interpreting a statute when Congress has not stepped in to correct the decision, he tries to square *Meritor* with the traditional rule, rather than abandon it.

If we accept as a given the Court's unwillingness to recognize its error in not adopting the EEOC Guidelines in *Meritor*, then, given the harsh results of decisions applying *Meritor* in the courts of appeals, the *Ellerth/Faragher* rule has much to recommend it. In cases in which a tangible employment action occurs, liability will be appropriately absolute. These are likely to be quid pro quo cases, in which strict vicarious liability was already imposed. To this extent, little has changed but the language. But at least some hostile work environment cases lead to constructive discharge. If these cases are now treated as "tangible employment action" cases, then liability analysis of these cases will move from negligence-type liability to strict liability.[42]

In the hostile work environment cases, the old rule requiring employer knowledge has been substantially weakened. Lack of knowledge is now only a defense when the employer took reasonable steps to keep informed of any harassment, and the employee unreasonably failed to take advantage of those steps to notify the employer. Any antiharassment policy that would pass muster among human resource specialists should require any supervisor learning of employee harassment complaints to report them to upper management, and should permit an employee being harassed to report the harassment to any supervisor. Had such rules been in place, the *Kotcher* holding, described in the beginning of this essay, would not have survived *Ellerth/Faragher*, nor would the *Steele* case, the *Paroline* case, or the *Klessens* case. In each of these cases, where a supervisor created or added to a hostile or abusive work environment by harassing a subordinate employee and the employee complained to other supervisors, the employer should have no viable defense.

Significantly, the Court's language should expand the ranks of employees treated as "supervisors" under Title VII, and dissuade the lower courts from treating employees with substantial supervisory responsibilities as if they were merely co-employees. A number of courts had treated mid-level and even high-level supervisors as co-employees, and thus as not responsible for maintaining a workplace free of harassment and discrimination. Explaining the distinction in *Faragher*, Justice Souter wrote, "when a person with supervisory authority discriminates in the terms and conditions of subordinates' employment, his actions necessarily draw upon his superior position over the people who report to him, or those under them, whereas an employee generally cannot check a supervisor's abusive conduct the same way she might deal with abuse from a co-worker."[43]

The opinion thus suggests that the lower courts should apply a broad view of who qualifies as a supervisor, since vicarious liability now applies whenever the harasser is "a supervisor with immediate (or successively higher) authority over the employee."[44] As Judge Barkett of the Court of Appeals for the Eleventh Circuit has explained, "as a consequence [of *Ellerth* and *Faragher*] the difference, if any, between a supervisor who is part of 'higher management' and one who is not, is no longer relevant for purposes of employer Title VII liability."[45]

Nonetheless, even viewed in its best light the defense established by the Court is troublesome; we should question why an employer should ever be excused from liability when its supervisors harass their subordinates. The new rule permits employers to shift much of the responsibility for preventing and remedying harassment to the employee. Given the inequality of power in the workplace, the responsibility appears misplaced. A rule holding employers absolutely responsible would be more likely to reduce harassment and would spread the risk of losses from harassment far more broadly.

The new rule is reminiscent of the old law of contributory negligence. That rule absolved a party committing a tort of all responsibility when the injured party was partially at fault.[46] The modern, and preferred, rule is comparative negligence.[47] Under a comparative negligence approach, the parties share financial responsibility in proportion to their fault. Had the court held that when an employer establishes an antiharassment procedure which the employee unreasonably fails to use, the employee's recovery is reduced by her comparative fault, the rule would have been far more equitable. The current "all or nothing" rule turns victims into unwilling gamblers.

Given the potential loophole created by the affirmative defense, trial judges will need to hold employers to a high standard in judging their antiharassment programs. A mere paper policy should be recognized as patently inadequate. To mount an effective policy, employers should be required to train their employees regularly in their rights and responsibilities, and to create an environment in which employees have license to complain, and supervisors are obligated to report complaints. Courts should require proof that policies have worked, and should permit employees to offer proof that the policies have been ineffective. Even with the best antiharassment programs, we should all be sobered by Louise Fitzgerald's findings, presented elsewhere in this collection of essays, that women who complain about harassment are generally worse off than those who don't complain because of the consequences they suffer.[48]

Applying Ellerth *and* Faragher: *The Road Ahead*

A number of cases decided by the courts of appeals in the year following *Ellerth* and *Faragher* suggest that they are likely to significantly broaden employer liability. But at least two new cases post a warning that American courts remain highly skeptical of claims by women alleging harassment and inappropriately sympathetic to employers. The following recent cases, from five of the twelve circuits, illustrate the potential benefits and pitfalls of the *Ellerth/Faragher* rule.

In *Gunnell v. Utah Valley State College*,[49] the plaintiff was harassed by her immediate supervisor (the director of maintenance and custodial services) and another manager (the chief of campus police). When she complained to the employer's personnel director the harassment stopped. Applying the pre-*Ellerth/Faragher* rules, the district court entered summary judgment for the employer, holding that because the harassment stopped as soon as the plaintiff complained, the employer bore no legal responsibility. The Court of Appeals for the Tenth Circuit reversed, based on *Ellerth* and *Faragher*, returning the case to the district court to determine whether the employer was vicariously liable regardless of its response to the complaint.

Similarly, in *Phillips v. Taco Bell Corp.*,[50] the employee complained of sexual harassment by her manager, and an investigation resulted in the manager being fired. The district court granted summary judgment to the employer because it took prompt remedial action. But the Court of Appeals for the Eighth Circuit reversed the district court decision. That was the old rule, the court held, but under *Ellerth* and *Faragher* the employer must also show that the employee unreasonably failed to complain. The case was returned to the district court for a determination of whether the plaintiff had acted unreasonably.[51]

In *Lissau v. Southern Food Service, Inc.*,[52] the plaintiff alleged sexual harassment by her supervisor and asserted that she was terminated because she resisted his advances. The district court entered summary judgment for the employer because the employer had no notice of the harassment. But the Fourth Circuit reversed based on *Ellerth* and *Faragher*, returning the case to the district court.

In *Smith v. First Union National Bank*,[53] another Fourth Circuit decision, the plaintiff alleged sexual harassment by her supervisor. Because she had not made a complaint under the employer's antiharassment policy, the district court entered summary judgment for the employer. The circuit court reversed and remanded for a determination of whether her failure to complain was reasonable, because her supervisor's supervisor had warned her against complaining.

In *Pacheco v. New Life Bakery, Inc.*,[54] the plaintiff alleged that she was sexually harassed by David Marson, a vice president, production manager, and 24 percent owner of New Life. Following her complaint, Marson's father, brother, and sister, co-owners in the business, investigated the complaint. Marson admitted that he grabbed and touched the plaintiff; he was ordered to desist from such behavior but not disciplined. The company decided the evidence of harassment was "inconclusive." At the conclusion of the investigation, the plaintiff was "laid off" for "lack of work," although she was then immediately replaced.[55] On this evidence the district court entered judgment for the defendant, finding that any harassment was vitiated by the immediate investigation and the cessation of any improper conduct. The Court of Appeals for the Ninth Circuit reversed the judgment, holding that the "layoff" was the kind of tangible employment action contemplated by the *Ellerth/ Faragher* rule, and that as a result the employer was strictly vicariously liable regardless of its post-complaint investigation.

By contrast, a decision by the Court of Appeals for the Fifth Circuit took a very different approach when an employee complained of hostile work environment harassment. In *Indest v. Freeman Decorating, Inc.*,[56] an employee was subjected on four occasions over a five-day period to "crude sexual comments and gestures" by her supervisor's supervisor, a vice president of the company.[57] When he made one of the remarks in the presence of a third manager, she objected, and he "profanely disparaged her."[58] She thereafter complained to a fourth manager, instigating a complaint under the company's antiharassment policy. The vice president received a verbal and written reprimand, and a seven-day suspension without pay. Because of the harassment, the employee "suffered the recurrence of an obsessive-compulsive disorder called trichotillomania (hair-pulling), anxiety, and sleeplessness, and has sought and received counseling."[59] The district court granted summary judgment to the company. The court of appeals, in divided opinions, affirmed, reasoning that either (1) the harassment was neither severe nor pervasive, and thus insufficient to create a hostile work environment, or (2) that even if there were a hostile work environment, *Ellerth* and *Faragher* had no application because the company responded with a swift and appropriate remedy, or (3) the *Ellerth/Faragher* rule was satisfied, because the employer met its affirmative defense by proving it had an appropriate policy and responded promptly to the complaint. Lost in this discussion is any recognition that *Ellerth* and *Faragher* purport to apply to all sexual harassment cases, regardless of whether the employer acts swiftly; the cases assess liability unless the employer can show not only its own reasonableness but also that the employee acted unreasonably. No argument was advanced that the employee acted unreasonably; she asked the harasser to stop, then complained to another supervisor, while at least three supervisors either harassed her or stood by watching another supervisor harass her. Yet the employee was denied any recovery for her injuries at the hands of the company's vice president.

The *Freeman Decorating* decision suggests four risks to employees pursuing harassment claims. First, despite the clear language of *Ellerth* and *Faragher*, there is a risk that courts will collapse the affirmative defense from two parts to one, permitting employers to escape liability as long as they respond appropriately when their antiharassment policy is invoked, even if the employee also acted reasonably. This would vitiate much of the new rule, and return us to the practice under *Meritor*. Second, the decision suggests that supervisors are entitled to one (or if close enough together, more than one) "free grope" before any liability for sexual harassment can attach, regardless of the consequences suffered by the harassed employee. Third, there is a risk that even when high-level managers like company vice presidents harass employees, and even when other supervisors observe harassment and stand silent, employees will be denied compensation for their injuries unless they follow the directives of the company's antiharassment procedures. Fourth, there is a risk that even harassment that (1) appears severe or pervasive, (2) was experienced by the employee as severe or pervasive, and (3) has significantly altered the employee's working conditions will be minimized and dismissed by unsympathetic judges as merely "isolated insults" rather than "actionable harassment."

This last concern is further illustrated by the divided opinions of the Court of Appeals for the Fourth Circuit in *Lissau v. Southern Food Services, Inc.*[60] The lead opinion contains a brief summary of the plaintiff's allegations, that her supervisor made "provocative statements about her appearance, . . . implied a sexual interest in her," and touched her on several occasions, "including touching her thigh when he reached down to pick up some paper on the floor."[61] From the court's description, one might easily sympathize with the district court's characterization of the alleged harassment as "not of an egregious nature."[62]

But the concurring opinion paints an entirely different picture. Judge Michael describes a campaign of harassment taking place over the course of a full year that included the plaintiff's supervisor (the district manager in charge of her office): (1) making suggestive comments about his fantasies of what her sex life might be like; (2) making frequent and continuous comments about her clothes, her legs, and her hair; (3) asking if they would "be together" and intimating they should have an affair; (4) grabbing her and hugging her passionately; (5) telling her that when he "felt her he felt like he had made love to her before"; (6) telling her frequently that she needed to have sex; (7) asking her when she'd last had sex; (8) suggesting they go to her home to have a "wild party" together; (9) putting his hand on her thigh and leaving it there until she pushed it away; (10) standing close to her in her office, having shut the door, and telling her she needed "some good sex" and to be "pounded all night long"; and (11) accusing her of having mental problems when she asked him to stop harassing her. Shortly after she complained, he fired her because he felt she was "unhappy in her job."[63]

The disconnection between the lead opinion and the concurring opinion's recitation of these facts is deeply troubling. *Southern Foods Services* illustrates a problem broader than any rule set forth in *Ellerth* and *Faragher* — that in the end, how courts apply the new rule will be highly dependent on how judges see the lives of women in the workplace. What they see will in turn depend on where they stand, where they have been, what they have experienced, and what they expect to see.

Conclusion

Despite the concerns raised by cases like *Freeman Decorating* and *Southern Food Services*, there is certainly reason to hope that in the wake of *Ellerth* and *Faragher* there will be less sexual harassment in the American workplace. Acting out of enlightened self-interest, employers are likely to be more vigilant in attempting to prevent sexual harassment. To fail to act is to invite nearly absolute vicarious liability; to act may both reduce the harassment that occurs and preserve a defense when prevention fails. The *Meritor* case gave us a decade of confusion, a wholesale abandonment of traditional agency principles, a rule that disclaimed corporate responsibility, and an army of harassed employees left without compensation. The *Ellerth* and *Faragher* cases promise that rare thing in employment discrimination law — a rule that encourages employers to take meaningful steps to prevent discrimination while increasing the possibility that victimized employees will be able to recover damages for their injuries.

Notes

1. 524 U.S. 742 (1998).
2. 524 U.S. 775 (1998).
3. 447 U.S. 57 (1986).
4. *See* Restatement (Second) of Agency (1957) Sections 2 (definitions of "master," "servant," and "independent contractor"), 219 (describing when a master is liable for the torts of its servants).
5. *Id.* at Sections 214, 520.
6. *See, e.g., Miller v. Bank of America*, 600 F.2d 211 (9th Cir. 1979) (conduct reasonably incidental to the performance of job duties is within the scope of employment); *Doe v. Samaritan Counseling Ctr.*, 791 P.2d 344, 347–48 (Ala. 1990) (same).
7. *See, e.g., Ira S. Bushey & Sons, Inc. v. United States*, 398 F.2d 167 (2d Cir. 1968) (Friendly, J.) (substituting foreseeability test for business-purpose test); *see also* J. Hoult Verkerke, "Notice Liability in Employment Discrimination Law," 81 *Virginia Law Review* 273, 311 (1995) ("The present trend is toward more expansive interpretations of the scope of employment").
8. *See, e.g., Carr v. Wm. C. Crowell Co.*, 171 P.2d 5 (Cal. 1946) (Traynor, J.); *Leonbruno v. Champlain Silk Mills*, 128 N.E. 711 (N.Y. 1920) (Cardozo, J.).
9. *See Doe v. Samaritan Counseling Ctr.*, 791 P.2d at 349 (purpose of *respondeat superior* is to "include in the costs of operation inevitable losses to third persons incident to carrying on an enterprise, and thus distribute the burden among those benefitted by the enterprise"); *Mary M. v. City of Los Angeles*, 814 P.2d 1341, 1343, 1347–49 (Cal. 1991) (listing three policy objectives of *respondeat superior* in finding county liable for rape of motorist by deputy sheriff); *see generally Perez v. Van Groningen & Sons, Inc.*, 719 P.2d 676 (Cal. 1986); William L. Prosser, *Handbook of the Law of Torts* 471 (3d ed. 1964); Maria M. Carillo, "Hostile Environment Sexual Harassment by a Supervisor Under Title VII: Reassessment of Employer Liability in Light of the Civil Rights Act of 1991," 24 *Columbia Human Rights Law Review* 41, 84–91 (1992).
10. 2 B. E. Witkin, *Summary of California Law*, § 1 (9th ed. 1987).
11. *See, e.g., Medina v. Herrera*, 927 S.W.2d 597, 600–604 (Tex. 1996) (employee may recover under workers' compensation without waiving civil action against coworker for assault).

12. *See, e.g., Rogers v. Kemper Construction Co.*, 50 Cal. App. 3d 608 (Cal. Ct. App. 1975); *Frederick v. Collins*, 378 S.W.2d 617 (Ky. Ct. App. 1964); *Fields v. Sanders*, 180 P.2d 684 (Cal. 1947); *Carr v. Wm. C. Crowell Co.*, 171 P.2d 5 (Cal. 1946).

13. *See e.g., Simmons v. United States*, 805 F.2d 1363 (9th Cir. 1986); *Lyon v. Carey*, 533 F.2d 649 (D.C. Cir. 1976); *Doe v. Samaritan Counseling Ctr.*, 791 P.2d 344 (Ala. 1990); *Samuels v. Southern Baptist Hosp.*, 594 So. 2d 571 (La. Ct. App. 1992).

14. *See generally*, Richard A. Posner, "An Economic Analysis of Sex Discrimination Laws," 56 *University of Chicago Law Review* 1311 (1989); *See, e.g., Thompson v. Everett Clinic*, 860 P.2d 1054, 1056–58 (Wash. Ct. App. 1993) (no civil action permitted against clinic for sexual assault by physician), *John R. v. Oakland Unified Sch. Dist.*, 769 P.2d 948, 955–57 (Cal. 1989) (no civil action permitted against school for sexual assault committed by school employee).

15. *See e.g.*, Susan Estrich, *Real Rape* (1987); Catharine A. MacKinnon, *Sexual Harassment of Working Women: A Case of Sex Discrimination* (1979).

16. *Kotcher v. Rosa & Sullivan Appliance Ctr., Inc.*, 957 F.2d 59 (2d Cir. 1992).

17. *See generally*, David B. Oppenheimer, "Exacerbating the Exasperating: Title VII Liability of Employers for Sexual Harassment Committed by Their Supervisors," 81 *Cornell Law Review* 66 (1995).

18. 29 C.F.R. § 1604.11 (1997).

19. *Carr v. Wm. C. Crowell Co.*, 171 P.2d 5 (Cal. 1946).

20. *Rodgers v. Kemper Constr. Co.*, 50 Cal. App. 3d 608 (Cal. Ct. App. 1975).

21. *Ira S. Bushey & Sons, Inc. v. United States*, 398 F.2d 167 (2d Cir. 1968) (action for damages for property damage).

22. *Fields v. Sanders*, 180 P.2d 684 (Cal. 1947).

23. *Dilli v. Johnson*, 107 F.2d 669 (D.C. Cir. 1939 (action for damages for assault).

24. *Doe v. Samaritan Counseling Ctr.*, 791 P.2d 344 (Ala. 1990).

25. *Samuels v. Southern Baptist Hosp.*, 594 So. 2d 571 (La. Ct. App. 1992).

26. Paul Taylor, "Thomas's View of Harassment Said to Evolve; His Record at EEOC Is Source of Dispute," *Washington Post*, Oct. 11, 1991, at A10.

27. 477 U.S. 57 (1986).

28. There is a very interesting dissent from the circuit court's denial of en banc review by three members of the D.C. Circuit, Judges Scalia, Bork, and Starr. *See* 760 F.2d 1330 (D.C. Cir. 1985).

29. Brief for the United States and the Equal Employment Opportunity Commission as Amici Curiae, at 10–13, *Meritor Sav. Bank v. Vinson*, 477 U.S. 57 (1986) (No. 84–1979).

30. *Meritor Sav. Bank v. Vinson*, 477 U.S. 57, 66 (1986).

31. *Id.* at 72.

32. *Id.* at 76–77 (Marshall, J. concurring).

33. 66 Fair Employment Practice Cases (BNA) 1630 (1st Cir. 1994).

34. 879 F.2d 100 (4th Cir. 1989), *vacated in part*, 900 F.2d 27 (4th Cir. 1990).

35. 867 F.2d 1311 (11th Cir. 1989).

36. *Faragher v. City of Boca Raton*, 864 F. Supp. 1552 (S.D. Fla. 1994).

37. *Faragher v. City of Boca Raton*, 111 F.3d 1530 (11th Cir. 1997) (en banc).

38. *Burlington Industries, Inc. v. Ellerth*, 524 U.S. 742 (1998); *Faragher v. City of Boca Raton*, 524 U.S. 775 (1998).

39. *Id., Ellerth* at 763, *Faragher* at 777 (citations omitted).

40. *See* cases cited *supra* n. 8.

41. Faragher, 524 U.S. at 793–98.

42. *See, e.g., Jones v. USA Petroleum Corp.*, 20 F. Supp 2d 1379 (S.D. Ga. 1998).

43. Faragher, 524 U.S. at 803.

44. *Id.* at 807.

45. *Coates v. Sundor Brands, Inc.*, 164 F.3d 1361, 1367 (11th Cir. 1999) (Barkett, concurring).

46. Prosser and Keeton, *The Law of Torts*, § 65 (5th ed. 1984).

47. *Id.* at § 67.

48. *See* Louise F. Fitzgerald, "Who Says? Legal and Psychological Constructions of Women's Resistance to Sexual Harassment," this volume; *see also*, Louise F. Fitzgerald, Suzanne Swan, and Karla Fischer, "Why Didn't She Just Report Him? The Psychological and Legal Implications of Women's Response to Sexual Harassment," 51 *Journal of Social Issues* 117 (1995).

49. 152 F.3d 1253 (10th Cir. 1998).

50. 156 F.3d 884 (8th Cir. 1998).

51. For a similar district court opinion, *see Corcoran v. Shoney's Colonial, Inc.*, 24 F. Supp. 2d 601 (W.D. Va. 1998).

52. 159 F.3d 177 (4th Cir. 1998).

53. 202 F.3d 234 (4th Cir. 2000).

54. 187 F.3d 1055 (9th Cir. 1999) *withdrawn*, 187 F.3d 1063 (1999) (parties settled).

55. *Id.* at 1059.

56. 164 F.3d 258 (5th Cir. 1999).

57. *Id.* at 260.

58. *Id.*

59. *Id.* at 261.

60. 159 F.3d 177 (4th Cir. 1998).

61. *Id.* at 179.

62. *Id.* at 180.

63. *Id.* at 185.

18

Sex in Schools
Who's Minding the Adults?

DEBORAH L. RHODE

The last two decades of struggle over sex in schools are a testament to partial progress. For centuries, students were sexually harassed, but the law offered neither a label nor a remedy. When I was an undergraduate, before the efforts celebrated in this volume, many of us had "a problem" with professors. But the problem was always ours, never theirs.

Over the last twenty years, much has changed, but much has remained the same. Sexual harassment now has a legal identity, complete with policies, procedures, and political infighting. But while we finally have acknowledged the problem, we are a considerable distance from solving it. Too many educators still discount both the seriousness of harassment and their own responsibility for its prevention. The challenge that remains is to increase accountability throughout the educational process.

The point of my comments is to identify the obstacles to that end and some promising responses. The obstacles arise on two levels. The first involves problems in defining the problem. We lack public consensus and adequate legal standards on key issues. How harassing must harassment be in order to hold institutions or individuals accountable? Where are the appropriate boundaries between academic freedom and abusive expression? When should student-teacher sexual relationships be impermissible?

A second level of problems involves structuring appropriate responses. Here again, we need more adequate public understanding, judicial guidance, and educational policies on fundamental issues. When should institutions be liable for harassment by students, teachers, or staff? Should standards for education and employment be comparable? How can institutions adequately prevent the harassing use of harassment procedures?

These questions implicate the most controversial concerns in harassment law. To resolve issues of accountability, it is also necessary to address a host of other contested issues involving the boundaries of sexual expression and sexual abuse. The point of this essay is not to rehearse the general discussion elsewhere in this volume, but to explore the specific challenges that arise in educational contexts. Our failure to deal adequately with sex in schools both compromises students' educational experience and legitimates sexual abuse. A society truly committed to gender equality needs to lay better foundations among its youth.

Defining the Problem

Sexual harassment in schools is a form of prohibited sex-based discrimination under Title IX of the Civil Rights Act, which covers educational programs receiving federal assistance. Many schools are also subject to analogous state statutory and common law prohibitions. Although legal standards defining impermissible conduct are still developing, most lower courts and institutions have adopted the framework endorsed by the Federal Office for Civil Rights. Its guidelines prohibit quid pro quo harassment, which involves unwelcome sexual advances or demands, and hostile environment harassment, which involves sexual conduct that is sufficiently severe, persistent, or pervasive to create an abusive educational setting, or to limit students' ability to benefit from educational programs.[1]

The prevalence of such harassment is difficult to gauge with precision. The sexes vary in their assessments of what is unwelcome or abusive behavior, and their perceptions depend partly on shifting cultural and legal standards. However, virtually all studies find significant levels of unwanted sexual conduct. In representative studies of college campuses, between 30 and 50 percent of female students report harassment by professors and 70–80 percent from peers; the incidents range from insulting comments and propositions to bribes, threats, and assaults. Research on elementary and secondary schools generally finds that between 75 and 85 percent of girls and 75 percent of boys experience harassing conduct ranging from sexual taunts to physical attacks. Over 95 percent of surveyed students observe repeated homophobic behavior.[2]

Such conduct remains common in part because many constituencies deny its significance. These denials take somewhat different form for elementary and secondary schools than for colleges and universities, but common themes emerge. Widespread assumptions are that much harassment is harmless, that victims often invite it, and that overreaction by courts and administrators is often a greater problem than the abuse they target.

ELEMENTARY AND SECONDARY EDUCATION

At the elementary and secondary level, many educators believe that abuses by teachers are rare and that peer harassment is seldom serious and largely inescapable. As one school principal put it, "children are going to bother each other, tease each other and make each other feel bad. But that is the story of man. That's part of growing up. I really think that calling it sexual harassment is too far out." A mother whose son was suspended for two days complained tearfully that the school was "robbing my boy of his childhood." His childhood included calling a classmate a dyke and shoving her face into a concrete wall.[3]

A related assumption is that victims are responsible either for provoking sexual abuse or for learning to cope with it. Parents and administrators often tell girls who complain about harassment that they "ask for it" by "inappropriate" clothing or conduct. A case in point involves the Los Angeles Spur Posse, a group of high school students who competed with each other for sexual conquests. When some of the teens faced disciplinary action and criminal prosecution for acts including harassment, molestation, and rape, many parents rose to their sons' defense. In their view, the conduct was simply part of any "red blooded American boy's" "testosterone thing." After all, "those girls were trash." Even more demurely behaved victims are told to accept the fact that the "story of man" includes the harassment of woman. As one teacher explained, people will call girls names all their lives and they "have to learn to deal with it."[4]

This willingness to trivialize harassment is encouraged by the media's fixation on trivial examples. Hard cases may make bad law, but bad cases make great press. The infrequent instances of administrative overreaction are grossly overreported. Journalists have a field day with the facts when six- or seven-year-olds are "suspended for a smooch." "Loose Lips," "Kiss and Yell," "Peck of Trouble," chortle the headlines.[5]

From these highly publicized cases, the public receives a highly distorted picture of what the problem is. Conservative critics appear correct in their descriptions of "PC paranoia": "hypersensitive," neopuritan "neurotics" seem to be swamping the system with frivolous complaints. To John Leo, the message of school harassment codes is that "chit-chat about sex can get you brought up on charges," and that the friends who might snitch to authorities should not be trusted. "Better to talk about the weather."[6]

In the equally puritanical environment that Katie Roiphe describes, baseless charges "materialize out of thin air," and even ogling will alert the feminist fanatics now patrolling school corridors. Columnist Debbie Price wonders whether we really should address restroom graffiti in federal lawsuits and turn girls "into sniveling emotional cripples?" Christina Hoff Sommers worries about the boys who are the real victims — those targeted by the "anti-male influence" of a flourishing "gender bias industry."[7]

Yet if the charge is exaggeration, critics, not complainants, are the worst offenders. Of course, borderline cases do exist, and recent changes in cultural norms have created some genuine confusion about boundaries. But the cases that now reach educational administrators and legal authorities do not involve idle chit-chat or corridor ogling. They generally feature serious repeated abuse. Girls are taunted, threatened, mauled, and raped. Gay or lesbian students and students of color are especially likely to experience physical abuse. Many victims experience fear, depression, insomnia, and loss of self-esteem; the result is lower school performance, increased absenteeism, and, in extreme cases, even suicide.[8]

Few of these victims file complaints. Contrary to popular assumptions, the most serious problem with sexual harassment enforcement involves under-reporting, not overreaction. The vast majority of students are silenced by humiliation, fear of retaliation, and skepticism about likely remedies. These concerns are well founded. Formal complaints often yield ineffectual repri-mands from administrators and severe retaliation by classmates. The much martyred six-year-old sex criminal received a one-day "in-school" suspension. He was separated from his class and missed coloring and an ice cream party. Even such minimal punishment for harassment is the exception; "boys will be boys" is still the rule.[9]

Beleaguered administrators are, of course, correct that kids can be cruel in many ways and that no sexual harassment policy is likely to transform educational institutions into Sunnybrook Farms. But we also need better strategies for increasing accountability among those who harass and those best able to prevent it.

HIGHER EDUCATION

Similar points are applicable in college and university settings. Here again, disproportionate coverage of overreaction has deflected attention from the more common problem of underenforcement. What makes news is what *is* new, so the media highlight exceptional cases with unusual facts or novel academic freedom issues. The public hears frequent accounts of the harassment charges involving a Goya portrait of a nude, sexist jokes in a fraternity newsletter, or sexist humor in faculty lectures. What remain out of sight and out of mind are the more routine cases of more serious sexual abuse.[10]

Unlike elementary and secondary schools, which generally impose appropriate prohibitions on faculty/student sexual involvement and sexually offensive classroom discussions, most higher educational institutions tolerate considerable latitude in sexual relationships and expression. While greater tolerance is clearly appropriate, given the greater maturity of students and greater role of academic freedom, the risk of abuse is also substantial. As subsequent discussion indicates, academic institutions need to strike a better balance between competing concerns. Where First Amendment values are implicated, campuses need to keep legitimate complaint mechanisms from serving illegitimate ends and silencing unpopular views. But these concerns should not obscure the equally pressing need to address exploitative relationships that do not implicate significant academic freedom issues. In commenting on the Goya incident, Katha Pollitt acknowledges that she would not defend the professor's decision to remove the portrait from the classroom. But she also points out that "this is, after all, one small classroom in a very big country. Why was its decor [such] a major news story?"[11]

As in other educational and workplace contexts, the vast majority of harassment problems in campus settings are underreported, not overregulated. The best available estimates suggest that less than 10 percent of victims file formal complaints. To most students, faculty, and staff, the personal costs of public action appear prohibitive.[12]

And with good reason. Research findings indicate that assertive responses to harassment generally have negative outcomes for victims. Formal complaints consume substantial amounts of time, energy, and occasionally money, and their payoffs include shame, ridicule, and blacklisting. Administrators and teachers who are targets of complaints typically have more power and resources than complainants. To minimize their own risks of liability, institutions generally are forced to side with the individuals who are charged with harassment, rather than with their victims. Once a case becomes public, these victims as well as their harassers are on trial and resource disparities may skew the results. A common defense strategy is to present complainants as "paranoid," "unstable," "manhating," "vixens." Such strategies, in turn, reinforce stereotypical assumptions that women's flirtatious or sycophantic behavior often is responsible for the abuse they assert. Even women who "win" in formal hearings often lose in life. The damages that they can prove do not begin to compensate for the harassing experience of a harassment proceeding.[13]

Women's reluctance to complain makes exploitative behavior less visible.

Nowhere is a selective perception more common than in debates about faculty-student sexual relationships. Only a small minority of institutions have rules banning such relationships between teachers and students under their supervision. The conventional assumption is that abusive conduct is rare, that broad prohibitions are unnecessary or unenforceable, and that many relationships end up in happy marriages. For example, opponents of categorical rules maintain:

Being sexually propositioned . . . is a normal and healthy part of life. (The real psychological and emotional tragedy probably befalls those who are not.)

It is hardly self evident that the "power imbalance" in such [relationships] favors the teacher. . . . If matters turn out badly, his career is finished.

The urge to merge is a powerful one . . . all's fair in love and war.

You can't legislate love.

[Sex with a professor can help a] female student who, for one reason or another, has unnaturally prolonged her virginity. . . . [Such relationships] can be quite beautiful and genuinely transforming.

[Consensual relationships] are none of the university's business.[14]

Some feminists raise other concerns. Literary critic Jane Gallup recognizes that women generally are at a "disadvantage" in faculty-student relationships but believes that "denying women the right to consent further infantilizes us." Law professor Sherry Young similarly maintains that "feminists should not be in the business of reducing the range of choice available to women, no matter how much they may question the wisdom of some of the choices that are made. . . . Feminists should not promote an image of women as helpless victims incapable of functioning under conditions of inequality of power."[15]

Such claims are problematic on several levels. Most students who receive sexual advances from faculty do not describe them as healthy, much less beautiful or genuinely transforming. In one representative study, almost three-quarters of those who rejected a professor's advances considered them coercive, and about half of those who had sexual relationships believed that some degree of coercion was involved. Faculty whose self-image and self-interest are at stake may underestimate the pressures that students experience. Regardless of the teacher's own intentions, students may believe that their acceptance or rejection of sexual overtures will have academic consequences. Given the power disparities involved, even relationships that appear consensual at the outset may become less so over time.[16]

Contrary to many (usually male) academics' assertions, these power differentials are not offset by students' theoretical remedies for harassment. Except in egregious cases, few students are willing to file complaints, and few institutions are willing to impose serious sanctions. Many campus codes lack adequate authorization for such sanctions, and even where the rules are clear, the evidence often is not. The result is that much exploitative conduct remains unreported, unremedied, and unacknowledged. Relationships that live happily ever after are clearly visible. Those that do not are more common but less apparent.[17]

In relationships where the professor has any advisory or supervisory authority over the student, both the fact and appearance of academic integrity are at risk. The potential for unconscious bias in evaluation, recommendations, and mentoring is inescapable. Even if the professor does not in fact offer or deliver special advantages, others may suspect favoritism. The reputation of both parties to the relationship inevitably is compromised. Neither the student, nor others whose opinions matter, can trust the objectivity of the professor's assessment.

Contrary to critics' assertions, it does not stereotype or infantilize female students to require that faculty avoid conflicts of interest. Nor does such a requirement deny either sex the right to choose a sexual partner. Rather, it simply demands that, if the "urge to merge" becomes irresistible, professors must remove themselves from evaluative authority over the students involved. Either students should transfer or faculty should make other arrangements for assessment of their work.

Part of the problem in many campus enforcement structures is that they address only those faculty-student sexual relationships that meet conventional definitions of sexual harassment. But the harms to both individuals and institutions can be significant even in the absence of an explicit quid pro quo or a pervasive hostile environment. A single unwelcome advance can inspire fears of retaliation and interfere with a student's choice of courses or mentors. A welcome advance that leads to a sexual relationship can evoke perceptions of bias and resentment among other students. Some faculty-student sexual involvement presents concerns that have less to do with harassment than with conflicts of interest and should be treated accordingly.

In short, campus enforcement strategies are both under- and overinclusive. They fail to reach much serious harassment because the costs of complaining are prohibitive. And they have been stretched to cover classroom conduct and sexual relationships that may be educationally inappropriate but that are not in any conventional sense harassing. The challenge is to craft policies that do more and less — that are more carefully tailored to address the competing values at issue.

Defining the Remedies

The central objective of harassment policies should be to minimize the need for their existence. To that end, schools should be subject to standards that encourage individual and institutional accountability. Although recent debates about those standards tend to focus on remedies, educators should not lose sight of the equally critical goals of prevention. Litigation is too expensive and intrusive to resolve the vast majority of harassment problems. The main function of liability frameworks should be to encourage educational and enforcement efforts that will prevent abusive conduct from occurring or from escalating into hostile environments.

HARASSMENT BY SCHOOL EMPLOYEES AND STUDENTS

Current case law falls far short of creating such frameworks. And the Supreme Court's 1998 decision in *Gebser v. Lago Vista Independent School District* is a step in the wrong direction. By a five-to-four vote, the Court held that schools are not liable for harassment of a student by an employee, unless officials knew of the specific misconduct and responded with "deliberate indifference." Under the majority's analysis, it does not matter if the school lacks adequate harassment policies.[18]

That decision stands in sharp contrast to other decisions governing workplace harassment from the Court's same 1998 term. In *Faragher v. Boca Raton* and *Burlington Industries v. Ellerth*, the majority held that employers could be liable for a supervisor's harassment even if they lacked specific knowledge of the abuse. However, employers could avoid such liability if they had adequate policies and procedures that the worker unreasonably failed to use. In effect, the Court has provided more protection from harassment for school employees than for students.[19]

Double standards in sexual matters are nothing new, but these are especially perverse. Students often have fewer options for avoiding an abusive situation than an adult employee, their capacities for resistance are less developed, and their values are more open to influence. Schools are powerful socializing institutions, and their failure to address harassment perpetuates the attitudes that perpetuates problems.

Moreover, the *Gebser* decision creates incentives for indifference. When ignorance is bliss, and a defense to legal judgments, why should schools establish effective complaint strategies? The less the school knows, the less its risk of liability. As Ellen Goodman noted in the *Boston Globe*, "to those of us who did not major in sexual harassment, but rather in common sense," the Court's logic seems nothing short of "bizarre."[20]

In explaining this result, Justice O'Connor's majority opinion reasoned that any stricter standard would be at odds with the overall compliance scheme of Title IX, which requires federal enforcement agencies to provide notice of any violation of nondiscrimination requirements before initiating enforcement actions. The point of this notice is to "avoid diverting education funding from beneficial uses where a recipient was unaware of discrimination in its programs and is willing to institute prompt corrective measures." However, as Justice Stevens' dissent noted, the Court's opinion creates incentives to avoid the knowledge that should trigger corrective action. Indeed, the see-no-evil hear-no-evil attitudes already in place in many education districts may now become the legal strategy of choice.[21]

A year after *Gebser*, in another five-to-four vote, the Supreme Court revisited the issue of schools' accountability for sexual harassment. In *Davis v. Monroe County Board of Education*, the majority held that a school district's "deliberate indifference to known acts of harassment" by students could give rise to liability. However, a school could be liable only where it "exercises substantial control over the harasser and the context in which the known harassment occurs," and where the conduct is so "severe, pervasive, and objectively offensive that it can be said to deprive the victims of access to the educational opportunities or benefits provided by the school." In assessing the adequacy of remedial responses, courts should not expect that administrators can entirely "purg[e] their schools of actionable peer harassment," and "should refrain from second-guessing [administrators'] disciplinary decisions.[22]

Although *Davis* clearly represents progress over the previous lower court rulings that had denied liability for peer harassment under any circumstances, it still falls short of what is necessary. Like *Gebser*, *Davis* creates an incentive for educators to avoid knowledge that might subject them to legal accountability. The problem is compounded by lower court rulings that require notice to be given to a school board member or senior supervisor with authority to ensure Title IX compliance. Given the reluctance of students to complain to anyone, such requirements often may create an unrealistic limitation on accountability where other less senior school personnel had knowledge of a problem and failed to take reasonable remedial action.[23]

A preferable approach would be to adopt the same standards appliable to employment cases. This was the approach that Justice Ginsberg proposed in her *Gebser* dissent. In essence, it would have imposed liability on school districts even if they lacked specific knowledge of harassment unless they had an effective policy for reporting and redressing such abuse that the complainant failed to use.[24]

Congress could amend Title IX to reflect either that approach or the standards developed by the Office of Civil Rights. Under OCR Guidelines adopted prior to the Court's recent decisions, a school could be liable for harassment by an "employee in a position of authority, such as teacher or administrator, whether or not it knew or should have known . . . of the harassment at issue." In the case of elementary school students, the Guidelines treat any sexual relationship with an adult school employee as nonconsensual and also create a "strong presumption" that such a relationship with a secondary student is nonconsensual. With respect to postsecondary students, the Guidelines propose a range of factors to determine whether sexual overtures were welcome, including the nature of the relationship, the degree of an employee's influence over the student, and the student's ability to consent. Consistent with this approach, campuses could also use conflict-of-interest standards to prohibit sexual relationships where faculty have supervisory authority over the student.[25]

Strict liability for such harassment reflects well-established agency law that makes institutions responsible for abuse of their authority. The rationale for that accountability is as convincing in educational contexts as in other workplace settings: employers should bear the costs of harassment because they are in the best position to spread or prevent them. As Catharine MacKinnon notes, teachers' position of trust and authority creates an inevitable possibility of abuse, for which institutions should take responsibility. Surely students, who are more vulnerable than adult employers, deserve no less protection.[26]

OCR Guidelines also authorize institutional liability for students' sexual harassment that creates a hostile environment under two circumstances: if schools lack effective harassment policies and procedures or if administrators knew or should have known of the abusive conduct and failed to take "immediate and appropriate corrective action." A negligence rather than strict liability standard is justifiable because students are not agents of a school and because peer harassment is more common and more difficult to prevent in the absence of notice than employees' misconduct. However, unlike the Court's approach in *Davis*, this standard would require school officials to take reasonable steps to investigate and respond to abusive conduct that is plainly visible, serious, and pervasive. Adult employees are not always required to make complaints of such harassment by coworkers in order to establish liability; courts use a reasonableness standard to assess the adequacy of victims' responses. No more should be expected of students, since they often justifiably fear retaliation or know that school personnel are already aware of the problem.[27]

In opposing such liability, school officials often emphasize their limited control over abusive conduct. While other employers can dismiss workers who persist in harassment, administrators believe that they have fewer options in the face of recalcitrant students or faculty who have their own due process rights. Where facts are contested or ambiguous, officials feel "caught in the middle. . . . We weren't doing the harassing. We're the entity with the deep pockets." The greater a school's responsibility to respond to severe and pervasive harassment, the greater the risk of expensive disputes over whether such harassment occurred and whether the response was adequate. As one school board attorney adds, "Schools are fighting for their financial survival, and every dollar in damages paid out in [sex harassment cases] is a dollar taken away from educational programs."[28]

Although such concerns are not without force, they overstate the costs to schools if liability is available and understate the costs to victims if it is not. Educational institutions can minimize the risks of lawsuits by either party in harassment disputes if they have appropriate policies, procedures, and training, and if they act promptly to investigate and address complaints. The vast majority of harassment victims do not seek substantial damages, and many expensive courtroom proceedings could be avoided if schools took modest corrective steps when problems first surfaced. Recent research confirms what common sense predicts: appropriate preventative and enforcement strategies reduce harassment and improve administrators' responses when complaints arise.[29]

The relatively small number of reported cases resulting in significant monetary judgments generally have involved administrators who ignored egregious abuses. Liability for such conduct often is the only way to ensure that educators take harassment seriously. Most school districts still lack adequate harassment procedures and many have implemented them only after lawsuits. While legal accountability may impose significant costs in the short run, it is also necessary to minimize them in the long run.[30]

Academic Freedom Concerns

Schools are, however, entitled to more doctrinal clarity and legal protection for sexually offensive speech that implicates significant First Amendment values. In general, the Supreme Court has permitted restrictions on expression that would substantially interfere with the "basic educational mission" or that would "impinge upon the rights of others." However, the Court also has viewed academic freedom as a "special concern of the First Amendment, which does not tolerate laws that cast a pall of orthodoxy over the classroom." The tension between schools' interests in both preventing harassment and protecting expression has provoked increasing disputes but no Supreme Court decision and few lower court rulings.[31]

This tension is complicated by educators' competing desires for bright line rules and contextual standards. To determine whether offensive speech constitutes a hostile environment that compromises the educational mission, it is necessary to consider a range of factors, including the age of the students; the content, forum, and frequency of the speech; and its relation to valid educational objectives. Whether these factors, taken together, establish a severe, pervasive, and hostile environment is a judgment on which reasonable people sometimes disagree. The subjectivity of this standard ill serves First Amendment values, which demand sufficiently clear notice of prohibited conduct to avoid chilling protected expression.[32]

How best to reconcile these competing concerns is a difficult issue calling for more extended analysis than is possible here. It is, however, possible to identify some general guidelines for the decisionmaking process.

Sex harassment claims raising significant First Amendment concerns fall along a spectrum. At one end lie complaints that clearly are without merit. These often involve speech that students consider sexist but that comes nowhere close to meeting legal definitions of harassment. Reported examples include a religion professor's classroom reference to a Talmudic story involving a sexual assault; a law professor's classroom discussion of false claims in rape cases; sexually demeaning humor in faculty lectures, fraternity programs, or student publications; a Minnesota professor's opposition to curricular proposals by women but not men; and a Scandinavian studies department's alleged insensitivity to feminist interests in literary theory. Whether the facts in these particular cases are as clear as media reports suggest is subject to dispute. For present purposes, however, the important point is not whether these were examples of frivolous claims, but rather that the risk of such claims is significant, and poses significant First Amendment concerns. Complaints about sexism should not be permitted to stifle precisely the kind of expression that academic freedom is designed to protect. Judicial and campus decisionmakers should make clear their intolerance for such harassing use of harassment procedures.[33]

A second category of harassment complaints involves classroom comments that are graphically or gratuitously sexual, but that again fall short of legal definitions of a hostile environment. Examples include obscene language; explicit discussion of pornographic material or sexual activity; and sexual references or nude illustrations that are unrelated to the subject under discussion.[34]

The danger in these cases, as Henry Louis Gates suggests, is that sexual harassment charges will become either an all-purpose prescription for "men behaving badly," or a decency code for censuring sexual content. Not all conduct that is educationally ineffective or socially unacceptable should give rise to legal liability and professional discipline.[35]

While institutional control of sexual content may be appropriate for young students, college campuses stand on a different footing. Harassment laws should not serve to replicate universities' unbecoming history of weeding out professors who offended some constituents by discussing matters like trial marriages, premarital sex, or sexual orientation. Educational communities now have other, less repressive strategies to address inappropriate or ineffective classroom techniques and to express institutional disapproval of sexist speech. Training, workshops, public meetings, open letters, course evaluations, collective protests, and disclosure of sexual content are constitutionally preferred responses to offensive expression.[36]

That is not to suggest that sexual harassment procedures are inappropriate responses to *any* speech implicating First Amendment values. Sanctions may be justifiable for expression that is truly severe, pervasive, and hostile, such as repeated comments that target particular individuals and that contribute little to the exploration of ideas. But reported cases involving classroom conduct rarely fall within this category. Clearer guidance on the scope of appropriate complaints is essential both to protect academic freedom and to preserve the legitimacy of harassment enforcement structures.

COMPLAINT STRUCTURES

Finally, and perhaps most important, educators truly committed to free inquiry as well as equal opportunity need more open and self-critical scrutiny of their efforts to combat harassment. The limited research available reveals significant dissatisfaction with current complaint processes. Common concerns involve the inadequacy of legal assistance, counseling services, and confidentiality protections available for complainants; the unnecessarily intrusive inquiry into parties' personal background or protected speech; the lack of effective remedies; and the failure to provide timely decisions with adequate procedural safeguards. Informal mediation procedures are often plagued by conflicts of interest. Administrators are caught between sometimes competing needs to provide effective remedies for complainants, to deter other abuses, and to minimize their own liability. Those tensions must be more squarely confronted, and appropriate safeguards established.[37]

We do not lack for alternative models. The last two decades have witnessed dramatic progress in the resources available to educators for addressing harassment. We are also beginning to recognize the enormous costs that it imposes. Not only does it compromise victims' educational performance and well-being, it perpetuates attitudes in students that encourage abusive conduct by adults. The challenge remaining is to create systems of accountability that will make effective harassment policies an educational priority.

Notes

1. Office for Civil Rights, Sexual Harassment Guidance: Harassment of Students by School Employees, Other Students, or Third Parties, *Federal Register* 62 (1997): 12034–01.

2. For variations in perspectives and limitations of surveys, *see* Kingsley R. Browne, "Evolutionary Perspective on Sexual Harassment: Seeking Roots in Biology Rather than Ideology," 8 *Journal of Contemporary Legal Issues* 1, 8, 27, 40 (1997). For surveys, *see* Bernice Resnick Sandler, "Student-to-Student Sexual Harassment," in Bernice R. Sandler and Robert J. Shoop, eds., *Sexual Harassment on Campus* (New York: Allyn and Bacon, 1997): 50, 56; Judith Berman Brandenberg, *Confronting Sexual Harassment* (New York: Teachers College, Columbia University Press, 1997), 12–13; Valeric E. Lee, Robert G. Croninger, Eleanor Linn, and Xianglei Chen, "The Culture of Sexual Harassment in Secondary Schools," 33 *American Educational Research Journal* 383, 397 (1996); American Association of University Women, *America's Hostile Hallways* (Washington, D.C.: American Association of University Women Educational Foundation, 1993); Judy Mann, "Where Homophobia Does the Most Harm," *Washington Post*, March 1, 2000, C15.

3. Peter Kendall, quoted in Karen Mellencamp Davis, "Reading, Writing, and Sexual Harassment: Finding a Constitutional Remedy When Schools Fail," 69 *Indiana Law Journal* 1123, 1163 (1994); Parents for Title IX Newsletter, October 1995, 1.

4. For parents and administrators, *see* Myra Sadker and David Sadker, *Failing at Fairness: How America's Schools Cheat Girls* (New York: Simon and Schuster, 1994), 9. For the Spur Posse, *see* Jill Smolowe, "Sex with a Scorecard," *Time*, April 5, 1993, 41; Emily Yoffe, "Girls That Go Too Far," *Newsweek*, July 22, 1991, 58. For the teacher's statement, *see* Tamar Lewin, "Students Seeking Damages for Sex Bias," *New York Times*, July 15, 1994, B12.

5. Deborah L. Rhode, "You Must Remember This . . .," *National Law Journal*, October 28, 1996, A21.

6. Stuart Taylor, "Real Sexual Harassment," *Legal Times*, May 6, 1996, 23 (paranoia); Katie Roiphe, *The Morning After: Sex, Fear and Feminism on Campus* (Boston: Little, Brown, 1992), 93 (hypersensitive); Lewin, "Students Seeking Damages" (quoting Gwendolyn Gregory, hypersensitive); Camille Paglia, *Vamps and Tramps* (New York: Vintage Books, 1994), 48 (neurotics); John Leo, *Two Steps Ahead Of the Thought Police* (New York: Simon and Schuster, 1994), 236.

7. Roiphe, *The Morning After*, 99; Debbie M. Price, "Victims of Their Gender?" *San Francisco Daily Journal*, 24 March 1992, 4; Christina Hoff Sommers, "The War Against Boys," *Boston Globe*, October 24, 1996, A21.

8. For abuse and retaliation, *see* AAUW, *Hostile Hallways*; Leora Tanenbaum, " 'Sluts' and Suits," *In These Times*, May 13, 1996, 23; Judy Mann, "What's Harassment? Ask a Girl," *Washington Post*, June 23, 1993, D26; Jane Gross, "Schools Are Newest Arenas for Sex-Harassment Issues," *New York Times*, March 11, 1992, B8; Stephanie B. Goldberg, "Classroom Distractions," *American Bar Association Journal*, May, 1997, 18.

9. AAUW, *Hostile Hallways*, 15–17; Brandenberg, *Confronting Sexual Harassment*, 51; Mann, "What's Harassment?" D26; Gross, "Schools Are Newest Arenas for Sex-Harassment Issues," B8; Tannenbaum, " 'Sluts' and Suits," 23. For the six-year-old's

penalties *see* Adam Nossiter, "Six Year Old's Sex Crime: Innocent Peck on Cheek," *New York Times*, September 27, 1996, A9.

10. Christina Hoff Sommers, *Who Stole Feminism?* (New York: Simon and Schuster, 1994), 270–71; Andrew Blum, "Profs Sue Schools on Suspensions," *National Law Journal*, June 6, 1994, A6, A7. For examples of serious abuses *see* sources cited in n. 8 and Ann-Marie Harris and Kenneth B. Grooms, "A New Lesson Plan for Educational Institutions: Expanded Rules Governing Liability Under Title IX of the Education Amendments of 1972 for Student and Faculty Sexual Harassment," 8 *American University Journal of Gender, Social Policy and the Law* 575, 600 (2000).

11. Katha Pollitt, "I'm OK, You're PC," *Nation*, January 26, 1996, at 10.

12. Louise F. Fitzgerald, Suzanne Swan, and Karla Fisher, "Why Didn't She Just Report Him? The Psychological and Legal Implications of Women's Responses to Sexual Harassment," 51 *Journal of Social Issues* 117 (1995). *See* Elisabeth A. Keller, "Consensual Amorous Relationships Between Faculty and Students: The Constitutional Right to Privacy," 15 *Journal of College and University Law* 21 (1988) (none of surveyed students filed complaints); Linda Brodkey and Michelle Fine, "Presence of Mind in the Absence of Body," 170 *Journal of Education* 84, 93 (1988).

13. For adverse outcomes, *see* Fitzgerald, Swan, and Fisher, "Why Didn't She Just Report Him?" 122–23; Brenda Seals, "Faculty-to-Faculty Sexual Harassment," in Sandler and Shoop, *Sexual Harassment on Campus*, 66, 77–84; Brodkey and Fine, "Presence of Mind," 93. For institutional incentives, *see* Jennie Kihnley, "Unraveling the Ivory Fabric: The Institutional Obstacles to the Handling of Sexual Harassment Complaints," 28 *Law and Social Inquiry* 69, 86 (2000). For characteristics of victims, *see id.*, 86–87; Seals, "Faculty-to-Faculty Sexual Harassment," 77; "Harassment Suit Seeks to Block Complaint Against Professor," *Employment Litigation Reporter*, June 27, 1995, 18706. For stereotypical assumptions, *see* Brown, "Evolutionary Perspective," 61; Paglia, *Vamps and Tramps*, 48. For plaintiffs' experience, *see* Deborah L. Rhode, *Speaking of Sex* (Cambridge, Mass: Harvard University Press, 1997), 103; Kihnley, "Unraveling the Fabric," at 82; Fitzgerald, Swan and Fisher, "Why Didn't She Just Report Him?" 122.

14. For the absence of prohibitions, *see* Sherry Young, "Getting to Yes: The Case Against Banning Consensual Relationships in Higher Education," 4 *American University Journal of Gender and the Law* 269, 272–73 (1996); Jerome W. D. Stokes and D. Frank Vinik, "Consensual Sexual Relations Between Faculty and Students in Higher Education," 96 *Education Law Reporter* 899 (1995). For opponents' views, *see* Edward Greer, "What's Wrong with Faculty-Student Sex? Response I," 47 *Journal of Legal Education* 437, 438 (1997) (normal and healthy); Id. (power imbalance); Dan Sabotnik, "What's Wrong with Faculty-Student Sex? Response II," 47 *Journal of Legal Education* 441, 443 (1997) (urge to merge); Dan Blatt, quoted in "University of Virginia Considers Wide Ban on Intimate Teacher-Student Ties," *New York Times*, April 14, 1993, A22 (legislate love); "Peers Denounce Professors' Sexual Views," *Washington Post*, September 26, 1993, A22 (virginity); University of Texas at Arlington faculty, quoted in Keller, "Consensual Amorous Relationships," 22 (university business).

15. Jane Gallop, "Feminism and Harassment Policy," *Academe*, September–October 1994, 16, 22. Young, "Getting to Yes," 269, 298; Margaret A. Crouch, *Thinking About Sexual Harassment* (New York: Oxford University Press, 2001), 72–74.

16. *See* surveys discussed in Caroline Forell, "What's Wrong with Faculty-Student Sex: The Law School Context," 47 *Journal of Legal Education* 1, 49, n. 11, 57, n. 39, 41 (1997). For a recent case see Deborah L. Rhode, "Professor of Desire," National Law Journal, January 27, 2003 at A17.

17. Keller, "Consensual Amorous Relationships," 22; Stokes and Vinik, "Consensual Sexual Relations," 899–906; Young, "Getting to Yes," 272–73.

18. *Gebser v. Lago Vista Independent School District*, 524 U.S. 274, 276, 294 (1998).

19. *Faragher v. Boca Raton*, 118 Sup. Ct. 2275 (1998); *Burlington Industries v. Ellerth*, 118 S. Ct. 2257 (1998).

20. Ellen Goodman, "A Mixed Grade for Court on Sexual Harassment," *Boston Globe*, July 2, 1998, A19.

21. *Gebser v. Lago Vista Independent School District*, 524 U.S. at 299, 300–301 (Stevens, J. dissenting).

22. *Davis v. Monroe County Board of Education*, 526 U.S. 629 (1999).

23. *Floyd v. Walters*, 171 F.3d 1264 (11th Cir. 1999), *cf. Canutilla Independent School District v. Leija*, 101 F.3d 393, 394–400 (5th Cir. 1996). *See* Joan E. Schaffner, "*Davis v. Monroe County Board of Education:* The Unresolved Questions," 21 *Women's Rights Law Reporter*, 79, 88–90 (2000).

24. *Gebser v. Lago Vista Independent School District*, 524 U.S. at 304 (Ginsberg, J., dissenting).

25. OCR Guidance, 12039. Whether the OCR will revise its guidelines in light of the Supreme Court's decisions in *Gebser* and *Davis* is not yet clear. *See* Heather D. Redmond, "*Davis v. Monroe County Board of Education:* Scant Protection for the Student Body," 18 *Law and Inequality Review* 393, 417 (2000).

26. *See* sources cited in David Benjamin Oppenheimer, "Exacerbating the Exasperating: Title VII Liability of Employers for Sexual Harassment Committed by Their Supervisors," 81 *Cornell Law Review* 66, 90–94 (1995). Catharine A. MacKinnon, "New Developments: Sexual Harassment Law," *Perspectives* (American Bar Association Commission on Women in the Profession Newsletter), Fall 1998, 9.

27. OCR Guidance, 12039. *See* Redmond, "*Davis v. Monroe County*," 413–14; Harris and Grooms, "A New Lesson Plan," 611.

28. Guy W. Horsley, quoted in Robin Wilson, "William and Mary Seeks to Shift Liability for Damages to Professor in Federal Sexual Harassment Case," *Chronicle of Higher Education*, June 9, 1995, A20; Alan J. Newell, quoted in Tamar Lewin, "Kissing Cases Highlight Schools' Fear of Liability for Sexual Harassment," *New York Times*, October 6, 1996, A22; Larry J. Frierson, quoted in Lewin, "Students Seeking Damages," B12.

29. Brandenberg, *Confronting Sexual Harassment*, 1–13, 49–73; Sandler, "Student-to-Student Harassment," 55; Howard Gadlin, "Mediating Sexual Harassment," in Sandler and Shoop, *Sexual Harassment*, 189.

30. Carol Shakeshaft and Audrey Cohan, "Sexual Abuse of Students by School Personnel," 76 *Phi Delta Kappan* 513–20 (March 1995).

31. For restrictions, *see Bethel School District No. 403 v. Fraser*, 478 U.S. 675 (1986); *Tinker v. Des Moines Independent Community School District*, 393 U.S. 503, 512–13 (1969). For academic freedom, *see Keyishian v. Board of Regents of the University of the State of New York*, 385 U.S. 589, 590 (1967).

306 Deborah L. Rhode

32. OCR Guidance, 12045.

33. Dirk Johnson, "A Sexual Harassment Case to Test Academic Freedom," *New York Times*, May 11, 1994, D23 (Talmud); Alan M. Dershowitz, *The Abuse Excuse* (Boston: Little, Brown, 1994), 253 (rape); Linda Seebach, "Sexual Harassment Policy Invades Free Speech Territory," *Los Angeles Daily News*, June 6, 1993 (fraternity limerick); *Iota Xi Chapter of Sigma Chi Fraternity v. George Mason University*, 993 F.2d 386 (4th Cir. 1993) (fraternity's "ugly woman contest"); Eugene Volokh, "Freedom of Speech and Workplace Harassment," 39 *UCLA Law Review*, 1796, 1802 (1992) (student parody); Michael P. McDonald, "Unfree Speech," 18 *Harvard Journal of Law and Public Policy*, 479, 481 (1995) (curricular changes); Bary R. Gross, "Salem in Minnesota," 5 *Academic Questions*, 67, 74 (1992) (Scandinavian studies department).

34. Henry H. Bauer, "The Trivialization of Sexual Harassment: Lessons From the Mandelstamn Case," 5 *Academic Questions* 52 (1992); *Dean Cohen v. San Bernardino Valley College*, 92 F.3d 958, 970 (1996) (sexually explicit discussion and profane language); *Silva v. University of New Hampshire*, 888 F. Supp. 293 (D Ntl. 1994) (sexist metaphor); Sadker and Sadker, *Failing at Fairness*, 9 (illustrations of breasts in economics lecture); Bill Boyarsky, "Harassment Policy Muzzles Free Speech," *Los Angeles Times*, November 24, 1997, B1 (speech describing oral sex); Kenneth Jost, "Questionable Conduct," *American Bar Association Journal*, November 1994, 71 (illustrations).

35. Henry Louis Gates, "Men Behaving Badly," *New Yorker*, August 18, 1997, 4.

36. Johnson, "A Sexual Harassment Case," D23. For the appropriateness of regulating indecent speech in secondary education, *see Bethel School District No. 403 v. Fraser*, 478 U.S. 675, 681 (1986).

37. Kihnley, "Unraveling the Ivory Fabric"; Gadlin, "Mediating Sexual Harassment"; Seals, "Faculty-to-Faculty Sexual Harassment."

19

Nooky Nation

On Tort Law and Other Arguments from Nature

ANN SCALES

After rereading Catharine MacKinnon's book *Feminism Unmodified* for the February 1998 conference at Yale Law School, I became a bit reluctant to participate because it seemed everything important had already been said. *It's all in there.* In 1987, MacKinnon predicted the backlash against her work, while acknowledging that its forms were unforeseeable.[1] My reluctance was dispelled however by events then emerging in Washington and Little Rock, unpredictable even by MacKinnon.

To call the conference timely would be the zenith of understatement. The year 1998 marked many milestones for sexual harassment issues, both in the law[2] and in the news. Indeed, the Yale conference coincided with some of the most dramatic developments leading up to the impeachment of President Bill Clinton. Though Paula Jones had filed her sexual harassment complaint against the President four years earlier,[3] the Monica Lewinsky story broke just weeks before the conference.[4] By the time we got to New Haven, we knew that in his civil deposition on January 17, 1998, the President had denied sexual encounters with Lewinsky and other women.[5] We knew what Lewinsky had said on the audiotapes secretly made by Linda Tripp.[6] Exactly a month before the conference, the President had firmly assured us that he "did not have sexual relations with that woman, Miss Lewinsky."[7]

The atmosphere was intense. And that was before the FBI confirmed the source of the semen on Lewinsky's blue dress,[8] before the impeachment in the House of Representatives,[9] and before the acquittal in the Senate.[10]

To see the auspiciousness of this timing, consider something else that happened after the conference. On November 13, 1998, the President settled Paula Jones' suit for $850,000,[11] even though the district court judge had granted his motion for summary judgment seven months earlier.[12] Why did he settle when he did? Conventional wisdom would suggest the goals of preventing further embarrassment, eliminating annoyance, and preserving political capital. White House advisers are said to have hoped that a settlement might avert impeachment in the House of Representatives.[13] But generally, one didn't hear it said that the President was afraid of losing the sexual harassment suit; most observers thought Paula Jones had a flimsy case.[14]

From another perspective, however, things were looking pretty good for Jones. The theory of her amended complaint (filed December 8, 1997)[15] was expansive and potentially explosive: if an employer with enormous power systematically propositions women, rewards those who say "yes," but either punishes, fails to reward, or otherwise uses his power to maintain the silence of those who say "no," isn't that quid pro quo sexual harassment?[16] Under this theory, it doesn't matter if Ms. Jones didn't suffer tangible detriments in her Arkansas state job (though I think a jury might have found that she did). What matters is that the boss treated her differently from other women, say, by not getting Vernon Jordan to serve as her personal employment agent.

I see the problems with this theory.[17] Based on the theory, however, it seems entirely possible to me that if Clinton had not settled, the Eighth Circuit might have vacated the trial court's summary judgment.[18] The case could have been remanded for (gulp!) further discovery and/or trial. In the you-ain't-seen-nothing-yet department, *either* way the Eighth Circuit ruled, *Jones v. Clinton* would have likely gone again to the Supreme Court in short order. But the President did settle, and as the *Washington Post* put it, "the mere recognition by the president that [Paula Jones's] appeal was sufficiently significant to justify his muddying the message sent by his clear district court victory is a nod, at some level, to the seriousness of her much derided claims."[19]

All that to say this: after the conference at Yale, the sexual harassment situation became very, very serious. Before the conference, however, it was all treated as a big joke. Prior to the spring of 1998, the nation was given to perceive Jones as a trailer-park-pawn-of-the-right-wing and the Lewinsky incident as an overblown instance of poor personal judgment by a person who happened to be President. And all this, the perception went, would have been small potatoes were it not for those few loonies who thought sexual harassment was something government should waste time worrying about. The media went to town on this.[20]

Just weeks before the conference, Jeffrey Toobin made such an argument in the *New Yorker*.[21] Toobin described sexual harassment law as "mired in . . . [a] murk that is threatening to engulf the White House itself."[22] Toobin claimed that sexual harassment law was "invented by accident," creating what was a jurisprudential jumble until Catharine MacKinnon came along and shaped it in her own "passionately committed," "endlessly energetic," and "relentlessly polemical" image.[23] In early 1998, a reader of the mainstream press could come to only one conclusion: that darn Catharine MacKinnon has pushed the republic to the precipice of constitutional crisis. You know the strategy. When the crunch comes, send in the Marines *and* blame the feminists.

In what turned out to be the eye of the Clinton hurricane, I could see the urgency in reiterating the necessity and singular promise of sexual harassment law. And so I eagerly participated in the 1998 conference, where my specific charge was to discuss why tort remedies are no substitute for equality-based claims of sexual harassment. Again, MacKinnon admirably addressed that problem twenty years ago.[24] Her reasons for denominating tort law as inadequate fall roughly into three categories.

First, a typical tort describes an essentially private, one-on-one, anomalous episode — a blip on the social radar, what MacKinnon called "a fall-out of order which can be confronted only probabilistically."[25] Sexual harassment, on the other hand, is comprehensible only as a group-based injury.[26] Harassment furthers the pervasively socially structured inequality of women. The group context explains why remedies for sexual harassment are not creatures of private law.

Second and relatedly, tort law tends to miss the essence of sexual harassment law: the specific nexus between inequalities in women's sexuality and in women's employment.[27] That is the central lesson of MacKinnon's book. As she put it: "When one [inequality] is sexual, the other material, the cumulative sanction is particularly potent."[28] Sexual harassment replicates itself as an *injury to work*, in an ever spiraling diminishment of women's *employment* security.

Third, tort law is damnably complicit in the social construction of femininity that has made sexual harassment law necessary. Tort law led the way in making injuries to women invisible and/or trivial and/or irrelevant to the *real* concerns of the law.[29] Recent feminist tort scholarship[30] has shown how claims for emotional injury were and are most often brought by women, how such claims have historically been associated with hysterical disorders (to which a reasonable man would not be subject),[31] and how the tort system has systematically devalued these injuries. Within this long history, women are by definition hypersensitive, and harms to women are by definition trivial.

These stereotypes are not mere nineteenth-century relics. They are everywhere in fancier models. These same notions powerfully fuel "tort reform" efforts that are so much in the news. All the recent hand-wringing about the alleged immeasurability of "nonpecuniary" losses, for example, is an echo of older skepticism about the genuineness of emotional harm and worthiness of those who suffer from it.[32] Tort law is still obsessed with "ranking" types of injuries (as in imposing high standards for proof of "intentional infliction of emotional distress") and types of damages (as in imposing statutory caps on noneconomic damages). These days, however, courts and commentators use mathematical models and economic theories that make the rankings appear neutral and rational. In fact, however, the hierarchies of value in tort law are still deeply gendered, still have disproportionate negative impacts on tort recoveries for women, and still—though more subtly—replicate the gender disparities[33] that made sex discrimination laws necessary in the first place.

By gosh, tort law is holding up *its* end of the status quo. It is mightily convenient for male supremacy that tort law keeps "emotional harms" linked to "femininity" linked to "valuelessness." Andrea Dworkin once defined femininity as "the apparent acceptance of sex on male terms with goodwill and demonstrable good faith, in the form of ritualized obsequiousness."[34] Femininity, said Dworkin, makes possible "a woman's continued existence within a system in which men control the valuation of her existence as an individual."[35] The enforcement of femininity requires all kinds of force, including economic force,[36] or, as MacKinnon put it, "masculinity is having [wealth]; femininity is not having it."[37]

The message is the same as it was in the nineteenth century: *real* torts are when locomotives jump their tracks and plow into widget factories. That is something we can sink our insurance-modeled risk-allocative teeth into. The other torts, *the girl torts*, are still, in the words of the nineteenth-century commentator, "annoying examples of despotic selfishness," which "in unconscious or half-conscious self-indulgence destroy the comfort of everyone about them."[38] That sure sounds to me like recent propaganda about how those darn feminist prudes made it so that every conceivably sexually infused gesture at work is now actionable as sexual harassment.[39]

To see what the tort model does to sexual harassment law, consider that one can rationally use the words "crucify" and "nooky" in the same sentence. One might hear, for example, "just as it is hugely disproportionate to invoke venerable tort remedies for girlish fits, we ought not *crucify* a guy for trying to get a little *nooky!*" Similarly, Jeffrey Toobin tried to contrast the majesty of law with the triviality of sexual harassment when he reported training sessions for masons in New Haven. In these sessions, masons are allegedly taught the "five-second rule," according to which male workers ought not look at a female coworker for more than five seconds because it might be against the law.[40] Just cop a peek and you're headed for the pokey. Girls are so much trouble!

Welcome to the vicious cycle. Tort law teaches, on the one hand, that female frailty is induced by female existence in the private sphere, where we have too much free time for self-indulgent development of neurosis.[41] On the other hand, that same frailty is a reason for keeping women out of the public sphere, or at least for keeping economic independence and decision-making authority out of our shaky little hands. The media assault on sexual harassment law partakes of the same naturalism. Toobin's piece, for example, consistently treats "human sexuality" as something that unquestionably just happens in any and all contexts, and "consensual" sex as unproblematically cool.[42]

The antidote for this vicious cycle is to maintain our focus on equality as the soul of sexual harassment law, to insist upon recognition of the nexus between economic and sexual inequalities *imposed* upon women, and mercilessly to interrogate any alternatives to equality-based sexual harassment solutions that claim authority from either nature or neutrality. In short, we've got to stay away from tort-type approaches.

Practically, there is seldom any advantage to using tort law as a remedy for sexual harassment. Before passage of the Civil Rights Act of 1991,[43] it was commonplace to append state tort claims to federal or state employment discrimination claims, as vehicles for obtaining non-wage-based compensatory damages and punitive damages, and, in some situations, jury trials. The favorites were intentional infliction of emotional distress and wrongful discharge. Since 1991, state tort claims are usually necessary only when the compensatory damages and punitive damages claimed exceed the caps in the federal statute, or, more commonly, when plaintiffs and their lawyers have missed the statutory deadlines for filing administrative claims as required by Title VII and most state employment discrimination statutes.[44]

There is also an immensely practical reason for *avoiding* tort law (and tortlike thinking) in sexual harassment cases: the confusion with workers' compensation remedies. Every state has a workers' compensation scheme; every scheme has an exclusivity provision; all of these schemes and exclusivity provisions are somewhat different from each other; all of them are constantly litigated. Basically, however, workers' compensation statutes are no-fault schemes, intended to provide relatively modest but relatively speedy compensation to persons injured on the job from expected industrial risks. The law of sexual harassment, on the other hand, requires a showing of injury to equality rights. Sexual harassment law is not a claim upon an incomplete insurance system for injured workers. Nor is it a system to protect the special sensitivities of women, nor even (unless such damages are part of a given case) a claim that requires a plaintiff to have been physically or mentally injured at all. Let us not forget what are perhaps the *happiest* words ever written by Justice O'Connor: "Title VII comes into play before the harassing conduct leads to a nervous breakdown."[45]

The distinctions between workers' compensation and sexual harassment law are not so hard to grasp.[46] Nonetheless, in most states, plaintiffs who plead tort claims instead of or in addition to civil rights claims can expect a defense based on workers' compensation exclusivity provisions.[47] Further, state courts are all over the map about the existence, number, and nature of connections and preclusions resulting from the unhappy presence in the same lawsuit of the different legal theories.[48]

Inconvenience and confusion of purpose, however, are not the greatest dangers here. The worse possibility is that a sexually harassed plaintiff would get so little for her injuries.[49] She would get almost nothing after the recent and hugely successful workers' compensation "reform" efforts. Fueled by hysteria over the "insurance crisis," and accompanied by the constant drumbeat of law and economics scholarship, most states have substantially reduced benefits for injured workers.[50] Not surprisingly, among the largest reductions are in benefits for mental stress.[51] That means tiny payments, as the alert reader will recall, to *girls*.[52]

Thus, tort law is inadequate, largely superfluous, really confusing, and affirmatively destructive to equality-based sexual harassment law. A theoretical overlay (with potential practical hazard) urges the point. There was a time when I could say without fear of contradiction that the purpose of tort law was to provide compensation for personal injuries inflicted either intentionally or inadvertently. Since then, however, law and economics ideologies have successfully insinuated themselves into tort litigation and discourse, causing existential distress within tort law about *why it is there*.

Professor George Priest made remarks at the 1998 conference that exemplified the primary point of this essay — how tort law and theory can undermine the promise of sexual harassment law.[53] Specifically, Priest introduced the topic — sure to become a hot one — of whether sexual harassment ought be an insurable risk for employers. Keep in mind that Priest is an architect[54] and visible proponent[55] of the "insurance theory" of compensation. The insurance theory is part of the law and economics movement which deploys, in variations from mild to wild, a means-ends analysis of legal phenomena with market efficiency almost always as the normative measurement of both means and ends. In this vast literature, economics is the engine that drives common law rules and remedies, particularly in the area of tort law. The most prominent law and economics analysts do not, often unfortunately, confine themselves to tort issues.[56]

The insurance theory of compensation stands in opposition to the traditional "make whole" justification for tort remedies. With the basic notion that payments to injured persons should be a function of what types of insurance choices hypothetical individuals would make in hypothetical markets,[57] the insurance theory in effect concludes that insurability should define both tort liability and damages. Whether or not this theory makes a lot of sense in tort law (which I would not concede), it should have no applicability in current sex equality law. For example, in the legislative history of the Civil Rights Act of 1991 (enlarging remedies for sex discrimination), Congress put great weight on the "make whole" justification for compensation, after hearing extensive testimony on what discrimination really does to real women.[58]

With the stage thus set, consider what Priest said at the 1998 conference. He urged that tort principles are incommensurate with sexual harassment law. True enough. Surprisingly to some, he opined that sexual harassment law did not go far enough and that employer liability should be expanded (and the audience could be heard to murmur, "go, George, go"). I am not sure, however, that everyone heard him say that sexual harassment ought therefore *not* be an insurable risk.

We really need for sexual harassment to be insurable for at least two reasons. First, a successful sexual harassment claimant should get her money without being squeezed more than she has been already by the wringers of trial. If an employer cannot acquire or enforce insurance for such a judgment, she could have to endure round after round of further litigation at her own expense, while the discriminator pulls out all the stops to protect the business.

Second, the power of insurance companies is likely to force compliance with the law,[59] and to do so *preventatively* and *not overbroadly*. People in the field are profoundly aware that, indeed, the ounce of prevention is worth the pound of cure. Happily, insurance companies have trade organizations and armies of well-paid risk managers and attorneys that can draft adequate sexual harassment policies and procedures (as part, one hopes, of larger antidiscrimination plans) for their insureds. They can force their insureds to adopt and conform to those policies. Though I am ordinarily not cozy with the insurance industry, I would rather let it take on a big chunk of prevention work than to leave it up to individual employers or institutions.

For those reasons, I believe it is worth taking a little time to respond to Priest's assertion that employers ought not be able to insure against sexual harassment claims. His assertion was largely a function of the "moral hazard" theory, according to which someone other than a consumer of goods or services actually pays for those goods or services. The hazard is that the consumer's behavior changes because of the third-party payer: that the consumer, with no purse constraints, will be oblivious to the actual costs imposed by its conduct. In the insurance context, insureds will theoretically take fewer precautions to prevent insurable harms, and may even be stimulated to engage in risky and/or illegal conduct. So, according to this theory, insurance coverage for sexual harassment claims would encourage employers to let sexual harassment run rampant in the workplace.[60]

Given that sex inequality is itself a whopping moral hazard[61] — plenty encouraged by every institution of male supremacist culture — I hesitate to exacerbate things by advocating insurability for sexual harassment claims. Fortunately, however, the moral hazard argument for such insurance doesn't usually stand up under closer scrutiny. An employer that owns any assets must realistically purchase liability insurance. To purchase insurance at a reasonable cost, one must be insur*able:* both the availability and cost of insurance are functions of the insurance applicant's past conduct and potential for prevention of the risk sought to be covered.[62] Being sued for denying economic equality (usually accompanied by lurid press coverage) is just not good for business. And litigation itself, even when financed and handled by an insurer under its duty to defend, can be hugely disruptive to an employer's business.

Even if some employers are less conscientious in preventing discrimination because they are insured, which I am not alone in doubting,[63] the moral hazard theory already represents a balancing of public policies. On one hand is the policy against encouraging bad behaviors, and on the other is the policy in favor of providing compensation to victims of those behaviors. If the contest is between creating a highly speculative "moral" effect and getting timely compensation into the hands of real victims of sexual harassment, that's an easy choice for me.

In spite of tort doctrine ghosts hovering in the shroud of law and economics theory, the market is responding to the revolutionary facts that sexual harassment was finally legally "discovered" and that women aren't going to take it anymore. One of the hottest new insurance products out there is employment-related practices liability (EPL) insurance,[64] specifically designed to cover liability for discrimination and other employment disputes. The specificity of this coverage is an important step in getting sexual harassment out of the tort law swamp. EPL policy definitions typically track legal definitions; coverage for sexual harassment flows from a legal finding of liability, rather than depending on tort distinctions such as intentional versus negligent conduct.[65]

Of course EPL policies are not magic bullets. When the EPL coverage litigation gets going, insurers will probably assert all conceivable contractual and extracontractual defenses to coverage, including moral hazard and other public policy claims.[66] Put another way, the insurance industry delightedly engages in aggressive marketing of EPL policies, loves collecting employers' premiums, but really hates to write big checks. When insurance companies surprise nobody by acting like insurance companies, those of us who care about sexual harassment should be prepared to rebut all those tired tort-law arguments and to demonstrate the real social costs of sex inequality.

I would like to make one more general, perhaps even metaphysical point. I once said to Catharine MacKinnon that the power of her work resided in that she had "exposed the contingency of gravity while exploiting its force." This comment was provoked by an analogy attributed to Andrea Dworkin by MacKinnon years before, regarding their antipornography work. The opposition to their work, Dworkin is said to have said, enjoyed a pretense of inevitability, like the laws of nature — like gravity.[67]

So it often seems in the project of eliminating sexual harassment. As Dworkin points out, lawyers and particularly law teachers are a big part of the problem. Let's face it: we think too much within the law, as if the law were the end of some story, instead of a stack of snapshots taken of ongoing social struggles. We get stuck in legal distinctions as if they were not merely contingent marks on an abstract of real life. We often squelch liberatory impulses when we "problematize" legal doctrine for publishers and tenure committees. We get domesticated. We have problems telling it like it is. The cause of clarity suffers, while real harms to real women sit there like an elephant on the kitchen table. We can do better.

We now know that gravity is contingent, at least in space, and who knows, maybe even in time. In my experience, gravity is surely more relentless on some days than on others. The point is that zero-gravity (or gravity with any coefficient) is imaginable, is replicable, and is exploitable, as per the purpose of John Glenn's second journey into space.[68] Similarly, law and sexuality are both extraordinarily powerful forces; both appear at moments to be inevitable, but both in fact are changing all the time.

We honor the courageous women — such as Pamela Price, Mechelle Vinson, and Lois Robinson — and now the men such as Joseph Oncale who pushed the envelope on the alleged inevitability of sexual oppression in the workplace. Each of these people — to borrow a phrase from Dworkin[69] — had to inhabit a subjectivity outside the laws of gravity, even to name the harm to themselves. And *then*, amazingly, they asserted their own access to the force of law, their ownership of their own sexualities, and their right, damn it, to make a living. Thus was gravity reinvented. And equality supplied the pull.

Notes

Thanks to Laura Spitz for her research, editing, and support.

1. Catherine A. MacKinnon, "Sexual Harassment: Its First Decade in Court," in *Feminism Unmodified* 103, 104–5 (1987): "With sexism, there is always a risk that our demand for self-determination will be taken as a demand for paternal protection and will therefore strengthen male power rather than undermine it. It is never too soon to worry about this, but it may be too soon to know whether the law against sexual harassment will be taken away from us or turn into nothing or turn ugly in our hands."

2. In 1998, the United States Supreme Court decided twice as many (four) sexual harassment cases as it ever had before. The opinions of most relevance to this essay, addressed more fully by David Oppenheimer in this volume, established an affirmative defense to employer liability for supervisor harassment of employees. *Burlington Industries, Inc. v. Ellerth*, 118 S. Ct. 2257, 2270 (1998); *Faragher v. City of Boca Raton*, 118 S. Ct. 2275, 2293–94 (1998). In 1998, the Court also set a (much too high) standard for school district liability for teacher-student harassment, *Gebser v. Lago Vista Independent School District*, 118 S. Ct. 1989 (1998), and underscored that standard the next year in a case involving student-student harassment. *Davis v. Monroe County Board of Education*, 119 S. Ct. 1661 (1999). In 1998 the Court also decided *Oncale v. Sundowner Offshore Services*, 118 S. Ct. 998 (1998). In holding that same-sex harassment was actionable without regard to the sexual orientation of the perpetrators, *Oncale* represents, in my view, the most promising judicial pronouncement on sexual harassment to date.

3. *Jones v. Clinton*, Civil Action No. LR-C-94-290 (E.D. Ark. 1994). The progress of the case was held up largely by President Clinton's claim of executive immunity from civil suit, rejected unanimously by the United States Supreme Court. *Clinton v. Jones*, 117 S. Ct. 1636 (1997).

4. Susan Schmidt, Peter Baker and Tony Jones, "Clinton Accused of Urging Aide to Lie; Starr Probes Whether President Told Woman to Deny Alleged Affair to Jones's Lawyers," *Washington Post* A1 (January 21, 1998).

5. *Id*. We learned much more about the President's deposition, and the statements of many of the "other women," just after the Yale conference. Peter Baker, "Clinton Deposition Focused on Lewinsky," *Washington Post* A1 (March 5, 1998).

6. Kathy Sawyer and Susan Schmidt, "On Tapes, Lewinsky Describes Trysts with Clinton," *Washington Post* A18 (January 25, 1998).

7. John F. Harris and Dan Balz, "Clinton More Forcefully Denies Having Had Affair or Urging Lies," *Washington Post* A1 (January 27, 1998).

8. That confirmation was made public the day the House of Representatives released the Starr Report. Charles R. Babcock, "The DNA Test," *Washington Post* A22 (September 22, 1998).

9. On December 19, 1998, the House approved two articles of impeachment. Peter

Baker and Juliet Eilperin, "Clinton Impeached; House Approves Articles Charging Per-jury, Obstruction; Mostly Partisan Vote Shifts Drama to Senate," *Washington Post* A1 (December 20, 1998).

10. The President was acquitted of the charges on February 12, 1999. Peter Baker and Helen Dewar, "Clinton Acquitted; Two Impeachment Articles Fail to Win Senate Major-ity; Five Republicans Join Democrats in Voting Down Both Charges," *Washington Post* A1 (February 13, 1999).

11. The November 13 settlement is noted in *Jones v. Clinton,* 36 F. Supp. 2d 1118, 1123 (E.D. Ark. 1999) (holding President in contempt for lying in his January 17, 1998, deposition). On joint motion of the parties, the Eighth Circuit dismissed the case on December 2, 1998. *Jones v. Clinton,* 161 F.3d 528 (8th Cir. 1998). Ms. Jones' lawyers got most of the money. "Jones to Get $200,000 from Clinton Settlement," *Washington Post* A12 (March 5, 1999).

12. *Jones v. Clinton,* 990 F. Supp. 657 (E.D. Ark. 1998) (granting summary judgment).

13. Peter Baker, "Clinton Payment Ends Jones Suit," *Washington Post* A1 (January 13, 1999).

14. *See* Judy Mann, "The Presidency and Press in Peril," *Washington Post* E3 (February 27, 1998).

15. *Jones v. Clinton,* Civil Action No. LR-C-94-290 (E.D. Ark. 1997).

16. *See id.* at paragraphs 43, 60–62, 68. As it was this "new" quid pro quo theory that might have shaken the foundations of the republic, I won't address Paula Jones' hostile work environment harassment claim except to say this to those who thought, in this case, "there was no harm in asking." Note the following allegations in the Amended Com-plaint, *id.:* (1) in the hotel room, he exposed himself *after* he had first approached her and she had refused his advances, para. 18–21; (2) also in the hotel room, he referred twice to her superior, who was a Clinton appointee, para. 17, 24–25, 31; (3) as she left the room, Clinton said, "[y]ou are smart. Let's keep this between ourselves," para. 24; (4) there were four subsequent encounters with Clinton or (the second defendant) State Trooper Danny Ferguson that were sexualized and/or threatening, para. 35–38; and (5) she was there-after treated badly by some supervisors and transferred to a position with no likelihood of advancement, para. 39. This is not a flimsy or frivolous story. In granting the motion for summary judgment, the district court seemed to be ruling on the weight of these allega-tions, trivializing them all the way, 990 F. Supp. at 671–77, which might have been enough for the Eighth Circuit to reverse her order regarding the hostile work environ-ment claim. *See Rorie v. United Parcel Service, Inc.,* 151 F.3d 757, 762 (8th Cir. 1998) (reversing summary judgment in hostile environment claim): "[W]e cannot say that a supervisor who pats a female on the back, brushes up against her, and tells her she smells good does not constitute sexual harassment as a matter of law." *See also* Moira McAn-drew, "How the Supreme Court's Reiteration of Sexual Harassment Standards Affirmed in Faragher and Ellerth Would Have Led to Jones' Survival in Jones v. Clinton," 47 *Cleveland State Law Review* 231 (1999).

17. For an extended discussion of those problems, *see* Robert W. Gordon, "Impru-dence and Partisanship: Starr's OIC and the Clinton-Lewinsky Affair," 68 *Fordham Law Review* 639, 654–66 (1999). The President was impeached in part for perjury in the Jones case, that is, for lying about his relationship with Monica Lewinsky. In his sweeping

excoriation of the conduct of Kenneth Starr's office, Gordon concludes that the perjury allegations were baseless. The crime of perjury requires that false statements be "material"; the Lewinsky matter, Gordon argues, could have no effect on the outcome of the Jones case. *Id.* In my view, however, Gordon assumes too readily that the district judge fully understood the new theory of Jones's amended complaint. Explaining her decision to prohibit further discovery and admissibility at trial of Lewinsky evidence, the judge seems fundamentally to confuse its purpose. Judge Wright stated that, even assuming the comparative evidence would show "that he conditioned job benefits on sexual favors and attempted to conceal an alleged sexual relationship," the evidence "was still nothing more than Rule 404(b) evidence, i.e., evidence of other alleged wrongful acts, and . . . not therefore essential to the core issues in this case." *Jones v. Clinton*, 993 F. Supp. 1217, 1220 (E.D. Ark. 1998).

18. For example, in the response to the President's motion for summary judgment, Jones filed 700 pages of affidavits and deposition testimonies from various witnesses, including women who claimed to have had sex with Clinton, and Arkansas state troopers who claimed to have shadowed his movements. These testimonies allege that Clinton and/or his agents used both threats and promises of reward to silence both women who had sexual encounters with him and those who knew of such encounters. Eric Pooley, "Kiss but Don't Tell," *Time* 40 (March 23, 1998). Even if not all of those accounts were admissible or credible, they would seem to raise a pile of genuine issues of material fact.

19. Editorial, "The Paula Jones Settlement," *Washington Post* C6 (November 15, 1998).

20. Many of these outbursts are collected in Deborah Zalesne, "Sexual Harassment Law: Has It Gone Too Far, or Has the Media?" 8 *Temple Policy and Civil Rights Law Review* 351, 367 (1999): "The media has us convinced that feminism is holding the workplace hostage, that employees are recklessly bringing false claims, and that employers are overreacting to their fear of liability by enforcing overbroad policies in ways that lead to absurd results." The 1998 conference at Yale sent at least one commentator into orbit. Robyn E. Blumner, "Stretching the Meaning of Sexual Harassment," *St. Petersburg Times* 1D (March 8, 1998). Describing the conference as "chilling," Blumner goes so far as to accuse Catharine MacKinnon of harboring a secret agenda of pushing the law "to where there's no turning back." "What this comes down to is a group of militant feminists who have declared war on men and their sexual desires. . . . *It's hard to say where the madness will end.*" *Id.* (emphasis added).

21. Jeffrey Toobin, "The Trouble with Sex," *New Yorker* 48 (February 9, 1998).

22. *Id.*

23. *Id.* at 49–50.

24. Catherine A. MacKinnon, *Sexual Harassment of Working Women: A Case of Sex Discrimination* 164–73 (1979).

25. *Id.* at 172.

26. *Id.*

27. *Id.* at 171.

28. *Id.* at 1.

29. Again in MacKinnon's words, tort law "provided civil redress for sexual invasions at a time social morality was less ambiguous in defining a woman's sexuality as intrinsic

to her virtue, and her virtue as partially constitutive of her value, hence as capable of compensable damage." *Id.* at 164.

30. A generative piece in this scholarship is Martha Chamallas and Linda Kerber, "Women, Mothers, and the Law of Fright: A History," 88 *Michigan Law Review* 814 (1990).

31. Dean Prosser, in his first edition, noted the "distinctly masculine astonishment" that women would ever suffer such injuries. Quoted in Chamallas and Kerber, *supra* note 30 at 833.

32. *See* Lucinda Finley, "Female Trouble: The Implications of Tort Reform for Women," 64 *Tennessee Law Review* 847, 861 (1997); Martha Chamallas, "The Architecture of Bias: Deep Structures in Tort Law," 146 *University of Pennsylvania Law Review* 463, 507–8 (1998).

33. *Id.* at 488–521.

34. Andrea Dworkin, *Right-Wing Women* 80 (1982).

35. *Id.* at 81.

36. *Id.* at 82.

37. Catherine A. MacKinnon, *Toward a Feminist Theory of the State* 131 (1989).

38. S. W. Mitchell, *Lectures on the Diseases of the Nervous System, Especially in Women* 266 (2d ed. 1885), quoted in Chamallas and Kerber, *supra* note 31 at 825.

39. Toobin, *supra* note 21 at 48 (describing sexual harassment as "a legal area that come to be invoked almost automatically whenever a case involves a sexual intrigue (real or imagined, consummated or thwarted) between two people at different levels of a chain of workplace command").

40. *Id.* at 55 (reporting conversation with Vicki Schultz). While I have no doubt that some "training" exercises are excessive (such being the nature of backlash), the attribution of this anecdote to Vicki Schultz out of the full context of her work exemplifies the classic strategy of pitting feminist against feminist. In reality, Schultz's work elaborates MacKinnon's original insight that sexual harassment concerns the nexus between women's economic and sexual vulnerabilities. *See* Vicki Schultz, "Reconceptualizing Sexual Harassment," 107 *Yale Law Journal* 1683 (1998); Vicki Schultz, "Talking About Harassment," 9 *Journal of Law and Policy* 417 (2001).

41. Chamallas and Kerber, *supra* note 30 at 848.

42. Toobin, *supra* note 21.

43. 42 U.S.C. § 1981A.

44. *See Phifer v. Herbert*, 115 N.M. 135, 848 P.2d 5 (Ct. App. 1993) (failure to meet deadline for administrative complaint did not bar claim for sexual harassment in tort form). Compare the confusing situation in Texas. *Vincent v. West Texas State University*, 895 S.W.2d 469 (Tex. Ct. App. 1995) (tort claim after reporting of sexual harassment barred by failure to meet civil rights administrative deadline); *Perez v. Living Centers-Devcon, Inc.*, 963 S.W.2d 870 (Tex. Ct. App. 1998) (tort claims arising from sexually harassing behavior not barred by failure to meet administrative deadline).

45. *Harris v. Forklift Systems, Inc.*, 114 S. Ct. 367, 370 (1993).

46. For articles on the distinctions, confusions, and intentional obfuscations *see* Comment, "The Sexual Harassment Claim Quandary: Workers' Compensation as an Inadequate and Unavailable Remedy: *Cox v. Chino Mines/Phelps Dodge*," 24 *New Mexico*

Law Review 565 (1994); Ruth C. Vance, "Workers' Compensation and Sexual Harassment in the Workplace: A Remedy for Employees, or a Shield for Employers?" 11 *Hofstra Labor Law Journal* 141 (1993); Darryll M. Halcomb Lewis, "Sexual Harassment Under Workers' Compensation Law," 44 *Labor Law Journal* 297 (1993).

47. *See Green v. Wyman-Gordon Co.*, 664 N.E.2d 808 (Mass. 1996) (sexual harassment as "recast" version of tort claims preempted by workers' compensation statute); contra *Byrd v. Richardson-Greenshields Securities, Inc.*, 552 So. 2d 1099 (Fla. 1989) (plaintiff's tort claims arising from sexually harassing behavior not barred by workers' compensation exclusivity provision in light of governmental commitment to eliminating sex discrimination). Courts regularly dismiss workers' compensation defenses when sexually harassed plaintiffs do not include tort claims among civil rights claims. *Folan v. State/Department of Children, Youth, and Families*, 723 A.2d 287 (R.I. 1999); *Byers v. Labor and Industry Review Commission*, 561 N.W.2d 678, 682 (Wis. 1997) (sexual harassment complainants under state human rights code act as private attorneys general to enforce the rights of the public and to implement a public policy the legislature considered to be of major importance).

48. *See Anderson v. Save-A-Lot, Ltd.*, 989 S.W.2d 277, 282–87 (Tenn. 1999) (describing variations among jurisdictions); articles cited *supra* at note 46.

49. "Except for the convenience of employers and the flimsy benefit the victims of sexual harassment might achieve by quicker, but much smaller awards, it is difficult to conjure a reason for workers' compensation courts handling sexual-harassment cases." Lewis, *supra* note 46, at 306, quoted in *Anderson*, 989 S.W.2d at 287.

50. These developments are described and their justifications soundly thrashed in Martha T. McCluskey, "The Illusion of Efficiency in Workers' Compensation 'Reform'," 50 *Rutgers University Law Review* 657 (1998).

51. *Id.* at 783–86, 804–08.

52. These workers' compensation changes go whole hog for the hierarchies of injuries and damages, demonstrated to be sex discriminatory. Chamallas, *supra* note 32.

53. An audiotape of Priest's February 28, 1998, remarks is on file with the author.

54. Most cited among his many articles urging tort reforms beneficial to insurance companies is George L. Priest, "The Current Insurance Crisis and Modern Tort Law," 96 *Yale Law Journal* 1521 (1987).

55. Priest has testified in favor of tort reform in many legislative settings and is a regular expert witness for insurance companies in judicial matters. *See* Common Sense Product Liability and Legal Reform Act of 1996: Hearings on S. 565 Before the Senate Committee on the Judiciary, 104th Cong. 1st Sess. (1995) (statement of Prof. George L. Priest). Priest testified in favor of that bill to limit punitive damages awards in products liability suits, and urged the Congress to go further by expanding the limits to all civil litigation, imposing limits on pain and suffering awards, modifying standards of civil liability, and eliminating joint and several liability. 141 *Cong. Rec.* S5881 (April 4, 1995). The amended bill was ultimately vetoed by President Clinton on May 2, 1996. John F. Harris, "Clinton Vetoes Product Liability Measure," *Washington Post* A14 (May 3, 1996).

56. This lack of confinement is displayed most famously in Richard A. Posner, *Sex and Reason* (1992). For example, Judge Posner suggests that strengthening sanctions for sexual harassment could deter men from initiating romantic contacts, ultimately causing

heterosexual women to suffer. *Id.* at 395. Consistently missing from the most prominent economic analyses of equality issues are the huge social facts of male dominance and the concrete harms done to women by it. See Catharine A. MacKinnon, "Pornography Left and Right" (Book Review), 30 *Harvard Civil Rights–Civil Liberties Law Review* 143, 151–64 (1995).

57. For demonstrations of the decidedly non-neutral assumptions made by proponents of the insurance theory, see Heidi Li Feldman, "Harm and Money: Against the Insurance Theory of Tort Compensation," 75 *Texas Law Review* 1567 (1997); Ellen Smith Pryor, "The Tort Law Debate, Efficiency, and the Kingdom of the Ill: A Critique of the Insurance Theory of Compensation," 79 *Virginia Law Review* 91 (1993).

58. *See* Civil Rights Act of 1991, H.R. Rep. No. 40(I) 64–73, 102nd Cong., 1st Sess. (1991) (cataloguing injuries and addressing objections to the enlargement of remedies). "Monetary damages . . . are necessary to make discrimination victims whole for the terrible injury to their careers, to their mental and emotional health, and to their self-respect and dignity. Such relief is also necessary to encourage citizens to act as private attorneys general to enforce the statute." *Id.* at 64. Congressional focus on make-whole remedies has not, however, deterred law and economics advocates. For example, in the fractured Court of Appeals opinion that gave rise to one of the Supreme Court's crucial 1998 sexual harassment cases, Judge Posner stated: "We thus cannot avoid the task of trying to create a set of agency principles that will deter sexual harassment without imposing an unreasonable burden on employers. . . . I emphasize deterring sexual harassment rather than compensating its victims because, unlike many torts — and again the clearest illustrations are torts that inflict physical injury — sexual harassment does not usually bring about a significant change in the victim's wealth. The victim may be humiliated and deeply distressed by it; rarely will she (or the very occasional he) be impoverished by it." *Jansen v. Packaging Corp. of America*, 123 F.3d 490, 510 (7th Cir. 1997) (Posner, J., concurring and dissenting) (emphasis in original), aff'd sub nom. *Burlington Industries v. Ellerth*, 118 S. Ct. 2257 (1998).

59. See Amanda D. Smith, "Supervisor Hostile Environment Sexual Harassment Claims, Liability Insurance and the Trend Toward Negligence," 31 *University of Michigan Journal of Law Reform* 263, 281–82 (1997).

60. The "moral hazard" theory is closely related to the common exclusion in liability policies for injuries arising from the insured's intentional conduct, and is the most common embodiment of the "public policy" doctrine, whereby courts sometimes refuse to enforce even the plain language of an insurance contract when to do so would violate a strong public policy. *See* Sean W. Gallagher, "The Public Policy Exclusion and Insurance for Intentional Employment Discrimination," 92 *Michigan Law Review* 1256 (1994).

61. I use the term "moral hazard" tongue-in-cheek here, as its use is an oddity in the competing theories. Law and economics work, for example, derives much of its persuasive force from the pretense that it is both amoral and apolitical. Judge Posner, for example, regards his book on sexuality as a "dispassionate scientific study," based upon a concept of "morally indifferent sex." Posner, *supra* note 56, at 85. As noted previously, of course, ignoring the political behemoth of male dominance renders most law and economics analyses of sex inequality unhelpful, at best. As MacKinnon said (comparing her approach to Posner's), "[a]n analysis of power dynamics in power terms is no more

morally based, and no less descriptive of a rational system, than an analysis of market forces in market terms." MacKinnon, Book Review, *supra* note 56 at 159.

62. James E. Scheuermann, "Employment Practices Liability Insurance: Navigating the Hazards When Exploring the Market," 29 *Brief* 64, 66 (Fall 1999).

63. For courts rejecting the moral hazard theory in discrimination contexts, *see North Bank v. Cincinnati Insurance Cos.*, 125 F.3d 983, 988 (6th Cir. 1997); *School District for the City of Royal Oak v. Continental Casualty Co.*, 912 F.2d 844, 848–49 (6th Cir. 1990), overruled on other grounds, *Salve Regina College v. Russell*, 499 U.S. 225 (1991); *Union Camp Corp. v. Continental Casualty Co.*, 452 F. Supp. 565, 567–68 (S.D. Ga. 1978); *Independent School District No. 697, Eveleth v. St. Paul Fire & Marine Insurance Co.*, 515 N.W.2d 576, 580 (Minn. 1994).

64. The number of carriers offering EPL policies is growing exponentially, while expanding coverage and reducing premiums. Francis J. Mootz III, "Insuring Employer Liability for Hostile Work Environment Claims: How Changes in Discrimination Law May Affect the Growing Market for Employment-Related Practices Liability Insurance," 21 *Western New England Law Review* 369, 388–98 (1999). In spite of the ongoing noise about an "insurance crisis," one source estimates that the cost of EPL policies has dropped 80 percent in five years. Alison Stein Waller, "And You Thought Insurance Was Dull? The New Economy Has Bred New Threats and Thus New Forms of Coverage. Do You Need Any of It?" *Business Week* F40 (April 27, 2000).

65. At least one commentator has argued that the 1998 Supreme Court decisions announcing a test for employer liability in hostile environment cases should usually serve to provide coverage under even traditional comprehensive general liability policies that exclude intentional acts. Mootz, *supra* note 64 at 413–26. That is, the new affirmative defense for employers looks like negligence: everything turns on the reasonableness of the employer's and employee's efforts to prevent or correct the harassment. *Ellerth*, 118 S. Ct. at 2270; *Faragher*, 118 S. Ct. at 2293–94.

66. *See* Scheuermann, *supra* note 52 at 64–65. To date, there is only one reported case denying coverage for a discrimination claim under an EPL policy. *Specialty Food Systems, Inc. v. Reliance Ins. Co. of Illinois*, 45 F. Supp. 2d 541 (E.D. La.), aff'd without opinion, 200 F.3d 816 (5th Cir. 1999) (age discrimination suit not covered due to untimely notice of claim).

67. Dworkin uses the gravity analogy in her introduction to the publication of the hearings on the Minneapolis pornography ordinance: "Rapists and pimps . . . seem to have the law of gravity on their side: they reify the status quo, which is what gives them credibility, legitimacy, and authority. They sound coherent. No matter what lie they tell, it passes for truth, because the hatred of women underlying the lie is an accepted hatred, a shared and unchallenged set of prejudiced assumptions. The woman who has been raped or pimped has to convince a hearer to listen because she counts. But she does not count unless she can make herself count, unless she can change the direction of gravity — turn the status quo, even momentarily, not just upside down but also inside out." Andrea Dworkin, "Suffering and Speech," in Catharine A. MacKinnon and Andrea Dworkin, eds., *In Harm's Way: The Pornography Civil Rights Hearings* 34 (1997).

68. Kathy Sawyer, "Launched into History, Again," *Washington Post* A1 (October 30, 1998). In 1962, John Glenn was the first person to orbit the earth. In January 1998,

NASA approved then seventy-seven-year-old Senator Glenn's "relentless requests for a second space flight." The Senator's winning proposal was to investigate the effects of zero gravity on changing sleep patterns and breakdown in muscle tissue, processes that occur similarly in astronauts and in earthbound senior citizens. *Id.*

69. Dworkin, *supra* note 34 at 83.

20

Damages in Sexual Harassment Cases

CASS R. SUNSTEIN AND JUDY M. SHIH

When someone has been sexually harassed, will punitive damages be deemed appropriate? If so, how much? And what is the measure of compensatory damages when much of the injury is not economic but partly dignitary, and involves a degree of suffering rather than an easily monetized injury?

We attempt to make some progress on these questions through some descriptive and empirical claims. Our basic finding is that people, including jurors, have a very hard time in mapping their judgments onto a dollar scale. Thus there is likely to be a high degree of variability and randomness. People who are similarly situated will not be treated similarly, whether plaintiffs or defendants.

This is so even if—even when—jurors' judgments about the underlying moral issues are widely shared. Thus juries that share moral judgments about the outrageousness of a defendant's conduct may well come up with very different punitive awards, and (what are agreed to be) more egregious cases may be punished less severely than less egregious cases. The same is true for compensatory damages. Juries that share judgments about the underlying facts may well come up with widely varying dollar amounts. We hope to explain this apparently contradictory statement.

More particularly, we will approach the problems raised by damages in sexual harassment cases through two routes. In the first two sections, we draw on several studies involving punitive damages and compensatory damages that are not easily monetized. Our basic conclusion is that in contexts of this kind, shared judgments may generate random awards, because jurors lack a "modulus," or standard, by which they might make sense of a dollar scale. Even if jurors agree on the appropriate evaluations of cases, different dollar awards are likely, not because of the different facts of particular cases, but because of diverse and possibly arbitrary "anchors" and "moduli," two concepts that we explain below.

The second route consists of a preliminary analysis[1] of all reported cases in which juries have awarded damages in sexual harassment cases. (Appendix 1 contains a complete list.) The basic findings are these:

1. The median awards, for both compensatory and punitive damages in cases in which such damages were awarded, are relatively low, $50,000 for both. While there are some outlier cases, there is no general reason to believe that juries are awarding obviously excessive awards, and it is reasonable to fear that some such awards are too low.

2. Compensatory damages do not appear to explain punitive awards, that is, a relatively higher compensatory award does not produce a relatively higher punitive award.

3. Many of the expected major causes of high awards—physical contact, propositioning, harassment of others besides the plaintiff—do not, in fact, appear to explain high compensatory awards or punitive awards.

4. Two factors do bear fairly consistent relationships to the size of compensatory awards. First, juries awarded comparatively higher awards in cases involving quid pro quo elements. Although quid pro quo explained very little of the total variation in award sizes, the effect was not negligible. Second, awards tended to be lower if potentially influenced by the 1991 amendment to the Civil Rights Act, which capped awards for compensatory and punitive damages under Title VII.

5. Evidence suggests that employment effects, such as firing, resignation (including constructive discharge), and negative employment effects short of termination may also explain some of the variation in the size of compensatory damage awards.

The data set is severely limited, and the sample—seventy reported cases, most if not all appealed—may be skewed. Together with other studies, however, the data set offers reason to think that outside of the context of economic injuries, both compensatory and punitive awards in sexual harassment cases are quite random, in the sense that they are not correlated with identifiable features of the particular case. More egregious harassment, such as physical contact and explicit sexual propositions, does not produce higher awards. We attribute this finding to the difficulty that people face in "mapping" their judgments onto a dollar scale—not to a belief that factors of this kind are irrelevant.

Our principal goals here are descriptive and positive, not normative. But the descriptive claims have normative implications. It is wrong to say that damage awards in sexual harassment cases are "out of control" or obviously excessive. But if the situation is as it appears, no one should be entirely pleased with it. The conspicuous difficulty that jurors have in coming up with appropriate dollar awards suggests that the legal system ought to do something to alleviate the difficulty.

In an ideal world, some kind of guideline or scale, or a translation formula based on the jury's compensatory or punitive intention, could produce substantial improvements. But there is an important wrinkle: In the distinctive context of sexual harassment cases, it might be desirable to have the kind of randomness that produces some outlier cases, in order to induce appropriate reactions from risk-averse defendants. And in the context of a newly recognized legal wrong, a degree of inconsistency and randomness might not be too high a price to pay. Our purpose is to document and to explain the inconsistency, not to say what should be done about it.

Punitive Damages: Theory and Practice

We begin with the special problem of punitive damages.

WHY PUNITIVE DAMAGES?

There are two principal theories of punitive damages. On the retributive view, punitive damages are given to express the community's sense of outrage at the moral wrong done by the defendant. In the context of sexual harassment, a judgment would therefore be made about the outrageousness of the defendant's conduct and about the harm done to the plaintiff. Especially egregious harassment—in the form, perhaps, of coerced sex or sustained bullying and humiliation—should therefore be met with punitive awards.

On the economic view, punitive damages are designed to provide optimal deterrence. On this view, the most natural justification for punitive damages is to make up for the possibility that the legal system will not detect certain violations and ensure compensation for them.[2] Punitive damages make up for the shortfall, thus producing optimal deterrence. This rationale strongly justifies punitive damages in some sexual harassment cases. It is true that sexual harassment often occurs without redress, as people suffer in silence. The award of punitive damages to the occasional, even rare plaintiff willing to bring suit is thus well justified on economic grounds.

It has also been argued that some socially illicit gains (such as the "gain" that comes from sadistic behavior) need to be deterred through punitive damages, on the theory that those gains should not "count" in the wrongdoer's calculus, and compensatory damages by themselves will not accomplish that task.[3] Of course the judgment that some hedonic gains are socially illicit is not, itself, an economic judgment. But if certain hedonic gains ought not to count, there is an especially good argument for punitive damages in sexual harassment cases, for this is unquestionably an area in which the defendant tends to enjoy his unlawful behavior. Punitive damages can thus help work against the risk that compensatory damages will not provide sufficient deterrence, insofar as the defendant receives hedonic benefits from harassing behavior.

WHY DO JURIES AWARD DIVERSE AMOUNTS?

These justifications for punitive awards suggest two basic views: punitive damages awards should reflect the degree of perceived outrage at a defendant's behavior; or punitive awards should make up for the likelihood that injured persons, including victims of sexual harassment, will not bring suit. In either case, it would be hoped that such awards would be relatively predictable.

Punitive damage awards do, however, contain a degree, and perhaps a high degree, of variability;[4] below we offer specific evidence to this effect in the context of sexual harassment. In any case it is not clear why, as a matter of general practice and actual fact, juries award the amounts that they award. Daniel Kahneman, David Schkade, and one of the present authors (Sunstein) conducted a study of about 900 jury-eligible citizens in the state of Texas, to obtain their views about punitive damages in personal injury cases.[5] Each participant was asked to evaluate punitive damage cases, by saying (a) how outrageous the defendant's conduct was, on a scale of 0 to 6; (b) how much the defendant should be punished, on the same scale; and (c) how much in the way of punitive damages the defendant should be expected to pay. There were twenty-eight total scenarios. What we learned does not answer all of the questions that need to be answered, in general and about sexual harassment in particular, but it provides some suggestive evidence.

Here, in brief, are our main findings:

1. People have a remarkably high degree of moral consensus on the degree of outrage and punishment that are appropriate for punitive damage cases, at least in the personal injury cases we offered. This moral consensus, on what might be called outrage and punitive intent, cuts across differences in gender,

race, income, age, and education. For example, our study shows that all-white, all-female, all-Hispanic, all-male, all-poor, all-wealthy, all-African-American, all-old juries, and all-young juries are likely to come to similar conclusions about how to rank cases.

2. This consensus fractures when the legal system uses dollars as the vehicle to measure moral outrage. Even when there is a consensus on punitive intent, there is no consensus about how much in the way of dollars is necessary to produce appropriate suffering in a defendant. Thus a basic source of arbitrariness with the existing system of punitive damages (and a problem not limited to the area of punitive damages) is the existence of an unbounded dollar scale.

3. Our findings of moral uniformity have one important exception, potentially bearing on sexual harassment in particular: though women and men rank cases in the same way, women rate cases as more outrageous and more deserving of punishment than men do, and this effect is amplified when the plaintiff is female. This is a modest but statistically significant finding, one to which we shall return.

4. The circumstances of the defendant matters a great deal to dollar awards. A wealthy defendant will face a larger award.

5. Harm matters as well. In our scenarios compensatory damages were held constant — $200,000 — but when the description of the injury suggested greater harm, the punitive award increased dramatically even though the jury's judgment about the outrageousness of the defendant's conduct was unaffected.

The simplest point emerging from our findings is that judgments of outrage and punitive intent are widely shared, but that dollar awards are widely variable.[6] But with shared moral judgments, what is the reason for erratic dollar awards? The most plausible answer is that judgments about appropriate dollar awards require people to engage in the well-known psychological process: "magnitude scaling without a modulus." A modulus would consist of a number — say, $100,000 — that would be said to reflect a particular level of egregiousness. Since the award of dollar amounts is unaccompanied by any modulus, jurors and even juries are at sea. The process is bound to produce a high degree of randomness, as different people select different moduli.

There is, of course, a question how much all this bears on the real world of punitive damage awards, in sexual harassment cases and elsewhere. Considerable evidence suggests that a similar problem exists there as well. Below we will show a high degree of variability in punitive awards in harassment cases, variability apparently not explicable by reference to moral judgments or underlying facts. In the general world of punitive damages, there is some predictability, to be sure, but the predictability is likely to come from the fact that jurors will seize on any available anchor, such as the plaintiff's "demand" or the compensatory award.

This increase in predictability creates serious problems of its own. There is no theory of punitive damages in accordance with which the compensatory award should have such weight in producing the punitive award. It may be, for example, that a sexually harassed person was able to achieve suitable alternative work, but if the harassment was especially egregious, a high punitive award makes sense even if the compensatory damages are relatively low.

The upshot of all this is that we have reason to think that even if people share moral judgments about the outrageousness of different sexual harassment cases, dollar amounts will have a high degree of randomness.

Compensatory Damages, Pain and Suffering, and Sexual Harassment

Sexual harassment cases often involve conventional economic damages, as when, for example, someone brings suit for back pay, or for unlawful discharge. But a large component of the compensation for sexual harassment involves pain and suffering, intentional infliction of emotional distress, and other sources of damage that are hard to quantify. Often the relevant injury is dignitary in nature; often it involves a degree of humiliation. Here is where the puzzles arise. How can such injuries be monetized?

Here and elsewhere, pain and suffering awards raise many of the same questions as punitive damages. To be sure, and importantly, such awards are nominally compensatory rather than punitive; they ask the jury to uncover a "fact" (how much was the plaintiff harmed?). But they also involve goods that are not directly traded on markets, and require a jury to turn into dollars a set of judgments that are, at the very least, hard to monetize. What is the process by which such awards are constructed? Can juries or judges make predictable or otherwise sensible judgments about dollar amounts? What are the ingredients of those judgments, whatever the instructions say? What does "compensate" mean, exactly?

Existing data, almost all of it outside the particular setting of sexual harassment (but see below), suggest that as in the context of punitive awards, compensatory judgments of this kind are highly variable and that the judgment of a particular jury is unlikely to be a good predictor of the judgments of other juries.[7] In the context of pain and suffering awards, anchors appear to be especially important, even if they carry arbitrariness of their own. Thus some jurors appear to split the difference between the figures suggested by the plaintiff and the defendant, whereas others use some (fairly random) multiple of medical expenses, and still others fasten on other aspects of the case as anchors. One study suggests that severity of injury explains only 40 percent of the variation in awards.[8] Thus it is that people with similar injuries are often awarded very different amounts of damages. Studies have found that plaintiffs with relatively small losses tend to be overcompensated and those with large losses tend to be undercompensated, and also that there is a significant degree of randomness here.

Let us investigate why there might be so much noise. Undoubtedly the effectiveness of the parties' lawyers matters a great deal; but other factors are involved. Judgments about pain and suffering require juries to make a decision about harm (with a likely ingredient, in practice, of intended punishment) and to map that judgment onto a dollar scale. In the absence of uncontroversial market measures to make the mapping reliable, the resulting verdicts are likely to be quite variable. The study we have described suggests one of the sources of the variability. A judgment about harm, perhaps made in a predictable way on a bounded numerical scale, becomes unpredictable and arbitrary when translated into an unbounded dollar scale lacking a modulus.

There is the additional problem that pain and suffering awards are made in a no-comparison condition, and hence juries may fail to provide the kinds of distinctions that would emerge if a set of cases were offered at the time of decisions. And although pain and suffering awards are essentially compensatory, there can be little doubt that such awards sometimes reflect jury judgments about the egregiousness of the defendant's behavior. Hence such judgments are likely to have a punitive component. Much further work remains to be done in disaggregating the factors that produce large or small awards for pain and suffering; we offer such a further study below.

If the psychology of noneconomic compensatory awards is similar to that of punitive damage awards, it will make sense to consider reforms. A simple reform would be to improve appellate standards for review of awards, perhaps by requiring appellate courts to engage in a comparative exercise, trying to ensure that the award at issue is not out of line with other awards. A more dramatic approach would be to move in the direction of a damage schedule to cabin the jury's judgment or by using a set of comparison cases for jury or judicial guidance. A choice among the relevant possibilities depends on judgments, first, about the importance of consistency, and second, about what might be distrusted in a jury's determination of pain and suffering awards. There are several possible problems here: the possibility that isolated juries will diverge from population-wide convictions, the difficulty faced by lay people in generating a dollar number for certain classes of injuries, or something else.

With sexual harassment in general, monetization is extremely difficult. Significant arbitrariness is entirely to be expected; similar cases may well give rise to dramatically different awards. With sexual harassment, variable awards are pervasive, and there seems to be little doubt that some plaintiffs are receiving too much and others too little. How does a jury know what amount would provide an employee, or a student, with adequate compensation for quid pro quo or hostile environment harassment? What does compensation mean, in practice? In both of these contexts, compensatory and punitive damages are likely to entangled, in the sense that juries probably do not sharply separate the one from the other. We will discuss reform proposals after outlining our findings.

Sexual Harassment Cases: A Preliminary Report

We have conducted a study of all reported jury award cases[9] in order to see what patterns are emerging.

We found seventy total cases, fifty-six involving specific awards for non-economic damages, and forty involving punitive awards. The decisions showed remarkable diversity, in both fact patterns and damage ranges. At one extreme, in *Daum v. Lorick Enterprises, Inc.*,[10] the jury awarded only $1,300 in medical expenses, meaning no noneconomic or punitive damages. The defendant company in that case had failed to investigate the reference to a criminal record on an job application and hired a convicted child molester who then tried to rape his fifteen-year-old coworker. The appellate court remanded the damage award as "arbitrary and inadequate." At the other extreme, the jury in *Kimzey v. Wal-Mart Stores, Inc.*,[11] awarded more than $50 million in punitive damages in a case involving only one plaintiff who alleged no serious sexual assault or physical touching, no quid pro quo overtones, and no retaliation for complaints. The trial and appellate court made successive reductions in the amount of the award, in the end reducing it to less than $400,000.

Here are some aspects of the cases overall. In nominal dollars, the median total award is $105,000; the median noneconomic damage award, $50,000; and the median of the nonzero punitive damage awards, also $50,000. The average awards for each of the above categories are much higher, reflecting the effect of a few extremely high awards. (A more comprehensive table of summary data appears in Appendix 2.) It is worth underlining the fact that the extremely high awards are few. Moreover, the presence of a few exceptionally large awards would not be fairly characterized as a problem if the awards were a function of identifiable characteristics of the cases, but it is hard to demonstrate a relationship between the extremely high awards and any particular set of characteristics in the cases.

Several qualifications are necessary from the outset. The data set is small; it is highly suggestive but too small to allow for reliable statistical judgments. Second, the data set may be skewed; most of these cases were appealed, and perhaps this made for an unrepresentative sample. Third, the disparities in outcomes may be explainable by reference to some variable that we have not been able to check, such as location in which the suit was brought. It is well known, for example, that Texas and Alabama are high punitive damage jurisdictions, whereas Utah is a low punitive damage jurisdiction; there are undoubtedly high and low sexual harassment damage jurisdictions too, and perhaps this explains much of the variance that we observe. (Note, however, that a variance produced by geography may be nothing to celebrate under a national civil rights statute, even if we are very enthusiastic about federalism.)

Our principal goal in exploring these cases has been to get a sense of what patterns have emerged — of whether certain factors predictably explain compensatory or punitive awards. The most surprising result was how little any of the expected factors correlated with differences in the awards. For instance, in striking contrast to general findings in federal and state law, we found no correlation between the size of compensatory and punitive awards. No matter what method, regression, or data set is used, higher compensatory awards do not produce higher punitive damages.[12] If anything, there is in fact an extremely small, statistically insignificant negative relationship between the two in these cases. Thus, compensatory awards do not appear to "anchor" punitive awards, and punitive awards cannot be said to be a positive function of compensatory awards.

In addition, few of the factors indicating the nature and severity of harassment correlated to the noneconomic compensation awards. We examined many such factors, including the presence or absence of propositions, physical contact of different types, harassment of others, adverse employment effects (such as firing or quitting), forced sex, and quid pro quo harassment. Factors that we expected to have an aggravating effect on damages included unwanted touching, visual display of either pornography or body parts, and propositions by the harasser. In fact, none of these factors consistently appeared with higher awards. Puzzlingly, some regressions even showed that more intimate physical contact, including touching of the plaintiffs' breasts or buttocks, significantly correlated with *lower* damage awards. We cannot be sure, but perhaps this finding suggests that women who are harassed are devalued — in this case literally — by virtue of that fact.[13]

The only aspect of harassment that bore a consistent relationship to higher compensatory awards was the presence of a quid pro quo element. Where the plaintiff alleged some element of quid pro quo behavior, the noneconomic awards tended to be higher. One reason for this difference may be that some, but not all, of the plaintiffs alleging quid pro quo elements filed claims for quid pro quo harassment. The jury instructions for quid pro quo claims would have differed from those for hostile work environment claims, which may have changed the jury's perception of the case. Another explanation would be that male jurors in particular might sympathize with plaintiffs who suffered a tangible economic consequence, something more common to their experience. However, the fairly consistent and sizable negative relationship between quid pro quo allegations and punitive damage awards undermines these possible explanations. Perhaps the explanation here is that quid pro quo harassment is committed by individuals, whereas punitive damages are typically awarded against companies; it is possible that jurors are sometimes reluctant to punish companies for the acts of supervisors.

A procedural difference may account for another consistent finding: lower noneconomic awards after the 1991 amendment to the Civil Rights Act. Those changes allowed noneconomic compensatory and punitive awards under Title VII. Such noneconomic damages were previously available only through state claims. Juries in some cases were asked to consider whether the actionable behavior occurred before or after the effective date as they were assessing damages under Title VII, and these cases tended to produce lower awards than other comparable cases.[14]

Some of our results suggest that employment-related factors might be significant, but these relationships are much noisier and more difficult to interpret. For instance, noneconomic awards were generally higher where the plaintiff alleged any negative employment effects, including firing, negative consequences short of firing (including unwanted transfers and retaliatory hostility from co-workers) and/or resignation. However, once we disaggregated these factors, separating employment effects into the above three components, the results were more unstable. The awards were generally lower if the plaintiff was fired, but quitting appeared sometimes positively and sometimes negatively correlated to awards. We could construct a plausible explanation for some of these results. Perhaps juries have more sympathy for plaintiffs too devastated to continue working, but less for those fired, presumably because the employers presented evidence reflecting badly on the employee. However, the inconsistency of the results in this area renders these explanations speculative, pending the collection of more data and additional analysis.

The punitive damages data also produced no reliable correlation between any relevant factor and larger (or smaller) awards. Thus the analysis indicates a high degree of randomness here as well. Compared with the noneconomic damage awards, even fewer factors produced consistently significant relationships with punitive awards. Even factors we might expect to play a particularly important role in punitive damage assessment — such as evidence that the defendant harassed others besides the plaintiff and allegations of particularly egregious touching — showed little relationship to those awards. As previously mentioned, a few of the factors demonstrating significant relationships with the awards, most notably quid pro quo, showed relationships that counteracted their apparent effect on compensatory damages.

Taken together, these findings suggest that, despite some hints of consistency, there is overall significant randomness in sexual harassment damage awards. It is possible that a larger sample of cases will reveal a more reasonable pattern of outcomes, but at least it can be said that no patterns have emerged to date.

Implications and The Future
SCHOLARSHIP AND REFORM

The discussion thus suggests a set of implications for both legal scholarship and law reform. Obviously it makes sense to engage in continuing empirical work on damage awards and their relation to facts. It is often speculated that punitive and compensatory awards in harassment cases are "out of control" or far too high; in many ways these are empirical speculations calling for empirical assessments. We know extremely little about the ingredients of high and low awards in sexual harassment cases and indeed in other areas involving damages that are hard to monetize. Lawyers could learn a great deal through some simple data collection and statistical analysis.

Moreover, it is not premature to have considerable skepticism about the capacity of juries to come up with dollar amounts for noneconomic harms or for punitive damages. Some tasks appear to be well-suited to the capacities of ordinary people, including jurors; some tasks are extremely ill-suited to those capacities. Both experimental and empirical evidence suggests that the use of an unbounded dollar scale — as a form of magnitude scaling without a "modulus," or standard by which to make sense of various points on scale — falls in the latter category. (This is not to say that it is easy to design an institution that is superior to the jury, or to produce reliable ways for making things better, though we will shortly offer some words on these questions.)

There are ample normative accounts of sexual harassment liability. But normative accounts are relatively rare about sexual harassment damages, especially with respect to noneconomic injuries and punitive awards. There is little doubt that the noneconomic injuries are often devastating, and that if adequate compensation is to be paid, a great deal of money ought to transfer hands. But how should the legal system distinguish between the more and less egregious cases? What are the factors that make one case especially egregious?

And how should those characteristics be mapped on the dollar scale, with respect to both compensation and punishment? An answer to these questions would be essential to the development of a normative theory of appropriate compensation and punishment in sexual harassment cases. Unfortunately, we have no such theory to offer here.

Ultimately a theory of that sort should be linked with institutional recommendations. For now, the simple point is that it is not easy to justify the institutions that we now have. Perhaps damage guidelines or a damage schedule would be a significant improvement. It might make sense to provide exemplar cases, guidelines, or a damage schedule, in order to cabin the jury's discretion. It might even make sense to move away from juries altogether toward another institution that could ensure a higher degree of predictability. A system of civil fines could fill the bill here.

It is possible, however, that unpredictability is not decisive in this context. Occasionally high — even excessively high — awards might be desirable as a way of giving an appropriate signal to defendants who would otherwise fail to take sexual harassment seriously. This is so especially if very high awards will, under familiar psychological mechanisms, be "available" to ordinary actors, and readily brought to mind.

CONCEPTUAL PUZZLES

Some deeper questions lie in the background. To decide on appropriate reforms, it is necessary to ask why juries are now charged with the task of making judgments about appropriate compensation in cases in which that inquiry strains their capacities. The most straightforward answer is self-consciously populist. In sexual harassment cases, perhaps no institution is likely to be especially good at uncovering the "fact" about compensation, if there is indeed any such "fact." Moreover, it is appropriate (on this view) to let the underlying decision reflect not merely facts but also the judgments of value that are held by the community as a whole.[15] Whatever fact-finding deficiencies the jury may have (as compared to, say, a specialized agency) are overcome by the value of incorporating community sentiments into the decision about appropriate compensation for injuries that are not easily monetized. On this view, compensatory judgments, at least in these contexts, are not so different from punitive judgments after all; both of them have important normative components.

Thus the simplest argument on behalf of jury judgments about compensation is that any such judgment is — perhaps inevitably and certainly appropriately — not solely compensatory. That judgment has strong evaluative dimensions, both in deciding what compensation properly includes and in imposing burdens of proof and persuasion and resolving reasonable doubts. The evaluative judgments, it might be thought, should be made by an institution with populist features and virtues. The point may well apply to judgments about compensation for sexual harassment. A populist institution, on this view, should be permitted to undertake evaluative judgments about what amount would "compensate" someone who has suffered as a result of an improper medical procedure, a lie about his private life, or an unwanted sexual imposition by an employer or teacher.

In the relevant cases, however, the problem of erratic judgments, emerging from magnitude scaling without a modulus, remains. This problem would not be severe (indeed, it would not be a problem at all) if what appeared to be erratic judgments were really a product of careful encounters with the particulars of individual cases, producing disparate outcomes that are defensible as such because they are normatively laden. But our study suggests grave reasons to doubt that this is in fact the case.

If predictability is especially important, we might want to build on earlier reforms, involving, for example, the damages schedule for workers' compensation or the social security "grid" that attempts to discipline judgments about who is disabled. On this view, an administrative or legislative body might create a kind of "sexual harassment grid" combining the basic elements of disparate cases into presumptively appropriate awards. A judge would produce a dollar award by seeing where the case at hand fits in the grid and perhaps by making adjustments if the details of the case strongly call for them. A technocratic approach of this kind could eliminate or at least greatly reduce the problem of erratic awards.[16] Whether it is desirable depends on the value of incorporating populist elements in the way that the jury system promises to do.

Elements of these various approaches can be found in reform proposals, thus far restricted to the pain and suffering context, that attempt to cabin the jury's judgment by requiring it to decide in accordance with damage schedules and to place the case at hand in the context of other cases.[17] In view of the fact that similar problems beset other areas of the law, there is good reason to consider similar reforms in the context of sexual harassment.

But this suggestion raises a special puzzle. Jury awards might be objectionable because they are *erratic*; or they might be objectionable because they are *wrong*. Our discussion here strongly supports the first point. It supports the second only to the extent that erratic judgments will, by definition, contain error. But nothing that we have said casts light on the vexing question of how to monetize the injuries from sexual harassment, either for compensation or for punishment. It is not even clear that administrators and judges have special expertise in that endeavor (whether or not they might produce uniformity). And for new and unfamiliar problems — recognized ambivalently and recently by the law — we might seek a period of trial and error, and allow a degree of randomness, before a stable social consensus has emerged. Perhaps long-recognized harms are the best places for the sort of solution recognized by workers' compensation and social security disability statutes. To these points, our only suggestion is that a high degree of unexplained variability is at least a problem for the legal system, one that ensures substantial unfairness.

There is a final wrinkle: the existence of unusually high punitive and compensatory awards in a few cases may actually be desirable as a means of deterring defendants who would otherwise be intransigent or indifferent to sexual harassment. Even here, however, there is an empirical question; perhaps defendants, actual or prospective, do not sufficiently respond to the few cases, admittedly highly publicized, in which awards are very high. To the empirical projects we have discussed here we may therefore add one more: a study of the response by employers and others to damage awards and settlements in sexual harassment cases.

Conclusion

Damage awards for sexual harassment present a special problem. The theoretical and empirical materials in related areas suggest that there is likely to be a high degree of randomness in both compensatory and punitive awards — and that the special characteristics of the case are unlikely to explain much of the variance. The problem of "scaling with a modulus" is a likely source of randomness.

The actual data, limited as it is, permit few generalizations, but they do indicate that in this context, sexual harassment awards may be especially random. Outside of the sexual harassment context, there is evidence that punitive awards can be explained largely or partly by compensatory awards; that finding is missing here. Our own study has found little correlation between any particular factor and high or low awards, either punitive or compensatory.

If dollar amounts are quite random, there is a large question about appropriate reforms. At first glance, the best approach, under ideal conditions, would be to use guidelines, exemplars, or a system of civil fines to ensure against arbitrary dollar judgments. A possible response is that in this context, extremely high outlier awards are an appropriate means of deterring risk-averse defendants. In any case there is a substantial research agenda here. First and perhaps foremost, it would be desirable to continue to track sexual harassment awards to see if clearer patterns emerge as the data set becomes larger. Second, it would be valuable to engage in experimental research, with respect to both compensatory and punitive awards, to see if there are differences of certain kinds among demographic groups (including men or women), or whether instead there are many shared judgments of facts and value amidst erratic dollars awards.

For the moment we can draw a single, general, and safe conclusion. Sexual harassment awards are not systematically excessive. But they do show a high degree of inconsistency: plaintiffs with similar injuries, and perpetrators who engaged in similar acts, are treated differently. The result pattern of outcomes shows considerable unfairness and randomness. This pattern disserves the equality-promoting aspirations of the law of sexual harassment.

Appendix 1. Cases

	Total Jury Award (nominal $/Plaintiff)	Final Award (nominal $/Plaintiff)
Baker v. Weyerhaeuser Co., 903 F.2d 1342 (10th Cir. 1990)	$90,000	$90,000
Bales v. Wal-Mart Stores, Inc., 972 F. Supp. 483 (S.D. Iowa 1997)	$28,001	$28,001
Baskerville v. Culligan International Co., 50 F.3d 428 (7th Cir. 1995)	$25,000	$0
Beardsley v. Webb, 30 F.3d 524 (4th Cir. 1994)	$84,044	$84,044
Bihun v. AT&T Information Systems, Inc., 16 Cal. Rptr. 2d 787 (Cal. Ct. App. 1993)	$1,848,000	$1,848,000
Brown v. Burlington Industries, 78 S.E.2d 232 (N.C. Ct. App. 1989)	$60,000	$60,000
Bushell v. Dean, 781 S.W.2d 652 (Tex. Ct. App. 1989)	$195,600	$195,600
Cortes v. Maxus Exploration Co., 977 F.2d 195 (5th Cir. 1992)	$147,858	$97,858
Cross v. Alabama, 49 F.3d 1490 (11th Cir. 1995)	$135,429	$135,429
Daum v. Lorick Enterprises, Inc., 413 S.E.2d 559 (N.C. Ct. App. 1992)	$1,300	NA
Davis v. City of Sioux City, 115 F.3d 1365 (8th Cir. 1997)	$102,440	NA
Davis v. Tri-State Mack Distributors, Inc., 981 F.2d 340 (8th Cir. 1992)	$82,408	$72,408

	Total Jury Award (nominal $/Plaintiff)	Final Award (nominal $/Plaintiff)
DeAngelis v. El Paso Municipal Police Officers Association, 51 F.3d 591 (5th Cir. 1995)	$60,000	$0
Delaney v. Skyline Lodge, Inc., 642 N.E. 2d 395 (Ohio Ct. App. 1994)	$52,000	$52,000
Dias v. Sky Chefs, Inc., 919 F.2d 1370 (9th Cir. 1990)	$625,000	$625,000
Dombeck v. Milwaukee Valve Co., 823 F. Supp. 1475 (W.D. Wisc. 1993), 40 F.3d 230 (7th Cir. 1994)	$100,000	NA
Eide v. Kelsey-Hayes Co., 397 N.W.2d 532 (Mich. Ct. App. 1986)	$272,000	$240,000
Farpella-Crosby v. Horizon Health Care, 97 F.3d 803 (5th Cir. 1996)	NA	$7,500
Fernot v. Crafts Inn, Inc., 895 F. Supp. 668 (D. Vt. 1995)	$435,000	$215,000
Ford v. Revlon, 734 P.2d 580 (Sup. Ct. Ariz. 1987)	$111,100	$111,100
Gares v. Willingboro Township, No. CIV. 91–4334, 1994 WL 398837 (D.N.J. June 16, 1994), 90 F.3d 720 (3d Cir. 1996)	$62,000	$62,000
Guzman v. Lowinger, 664 N.E.2d 820 (Mass. 1996)	$6,500	$6,500
Hale v. Ladd, 826 S.W.2d 244 (Ark. 1992)	$7,500	NA
Harmon v. Higgins, 426 S.E.2d 344 (W. Va. 1992)	$17,000	$0
Harris v. L&L Wings, Inc., 132 F.3d 978 (4th Cir. 1997)	$156,454	$156,454
Harrison v. Eddy Potash, Inc., 112 F.3d 1437 (10th Cir. 1997)	$142,500	NA
Harrison v. Edison Brothers Apparel Stores, Inc., 814 F. Supp. 457 (M.D.N.C. 1993)	$225,000	$0
Hathaway v. Runyon, 132 F.3d 978 (8th Cir. 1997)	$75,000	$75,000
Hoy v. Angelone, 691 A.2d 476 (Pa. Sup. Ct. 1997)	$401,000	$76,000

	Total Jury Award (nominal $/Plaintiff)	Final Award (nominal $/Plaintiff)
Huebschen v. Department of Health, 547 F. Supp. 1168 (W.D. Wisc.), 716 F.2d 1167 (7th Cir. 1983)	$196,500	NA
Hurley v. Atlantic City Police Department, 933 F. Supp. 396 (D.N.J. 1996)	$1,275,000	$875,000
Johnson v. Ramsey County, 424 N.W.2d 800 (Minn. Ct. App. 1988)	$375,000	$125,000
Jonasson v. Lutheran Child and Family Services, No. 93 C 7785, 1996 WL 327965 (N.D. Ill. June 12, 1996), 115 F.3d 436 (7th Cir. 1997)	$82,000	$70,889
Kelly-Zurian v. Wohl Shoe Co., Inc., 27 Cal. Rptr. 2d 457 (Cal. Ct. App. 1994)	$125,000	$125,000
Kimzey v. Wal-Mart Stores, Inc., 907 F. Supp. 1309 (W.D. Mo. 1995), 107 F.3d 568 (8th Cir. 1997)	$50,035,001	$385,001
King v. Kidd, 640 A.2d 656 (D.C. 1993)	$300,000	$298,000
Koester v. City of Novi, 540 N.W.2d 765 (Mich. Ct. App. 1995)	$5,000	$0
Marshall v. Nelson Electric, 766 F. Supp. 1018 (N.D. Okla. 1991)	$160,000	$0
Melsha v. Wickes Cos., Inc., 1989 WL 259991 (Minn. Dist. Ct. 1989), 459 N.W.2d 707 (Minn. Ct. App. 1990)	$134,102	$185,704
Meyers v. Chapman Printing Co., Inc., 840 S.W.2d 814 (Ky. 1992)	$100,000	$100,000
Montgomery v. Big Thunder Gold Mine, Inc., 531 N.W.2d 577 (S.D. 1995)	$25,000	NA
Morrison v. Carleton Woolen Mills, Inc., 108 F.3d 429 (1st Cir. 1997)	$150,000	NA
Nagel Manufacturing & Supply Co. v. Ulloa, 812 S.W.2d 78 (Tex. Ct. App. 1991)	$22,100	$22,100
Nicks v. Missouri, 67 F.3d 699 (8th Cir. 1995)	$74,500	$74,500
O'Connell v. Chasdi, 511 N.E.2d 349 (Sup. Ct. Mass. 1987)	$100,000	NA

	Total Jury Award (nominal $/Plaintiff)	Final Award (nominal $/Plaintiff)
Pagana-Fay v. Washington Suburban Sanitary Commission, 797 F. Supp. 462 (D. Md. 1992), 64 F.3d 658 (4th Cir. 1995)	$50,000	$0
Peery v. Hanley, 897 P.2d 1189 (Or. Ct. App. 1995)	$140,000	$140,000
Phillips v. Smalley Maintenance, 711 F.2d 1524 (11th Cir. 1983)	$25,010	$25,010
Poole v. Copland, Inc., 481 S.E.2d 88 (N.C. Ct. App. 1997)	$357,000	NA
Preston v. Income Producing Management, Inc., 871 F. Supp. 411 (D. Kan. 1994)	$33,000	$33,000
Reinhold v. Commonwealth, 947 F. Supp. 919 (E.D. Va. 1996)	$85,000	$85,000
Reynolds v. CSX Transportation, Inc., 115 F.3d 860 (11th Cir. 1997)	$334,100	$200
Sasaki v. Class, 92 F.3d 232 (4th Cir. 1996)	$276,825	NA
Sassaman v. Heart City Toyota, 879 F. Supp. 901 (N.D. Ind. 1994)	$22,000	$22,000
Smith v. Norwest Financial Wyoming, Inc., 964 F. Supp. 327 (D. Wyo. 1996), 129 F.3d 1407 (10th Cir. 1997)	$359,000	$200,000
Southeastern Security Insurance Co. v. Hotle, 473 S.E.2d 256 (Ga. Ct. App. 1996)	$65,002	$65,002
Spicer v. Beaman Bottling Co., 937 S.W.2d 884 (Tenn. 1996)	$50,000	NA
Stafford v. State, 835 F. Supp. 1136 (W.D. Mo. 1993)	$145,002	$35,701
Starrett v. Wadley, 876 F.2d 808 (10th Cir. 1989)	$75,000	NA
Stewart v. Weis Markets, 890 F. Supp. 382 (M.D. Pa. 1995)	$144,915	$10,000
Swentek v. USAir, Inc., 830 F.2d 552 (4th Cir. 1987)	$20,000	NA
Thompson v. Berta Enterprises, Inc., 864 P.2d 983 (Wash. Ct. App. 1994)	$278,000	$278,000
Todd v. Ortho Biotech, Inc., 949 F. Supp. 724 (D. Minn. 1996)	$218,000	$218,000

	Total Jury Award (nominal $/Plaintiff)	Final Award (nominal $/Plaintiff)
Troutt v. Charcoal Steak House, Inc., 835 F. Supp. 899 (W.D. Va. 1993), 37 F.3d 1495 (4th Cir. 1994)	$105,000	$75,000
Varner v. National Super Markets, Inc., 94 F.3d 1209 (8th Cir. 1996)	$30,000	$30,000
Virgo v. Riviera Beach Associates, Ltd., 30 F.3d 1350 (11th Cir. 1994)	$1,081,605	$1,081,605
Webb v. Hyman, 861 F. Supp. 1094 (D.D.C. 1994)	$300,000	$300,000
Wilson v. Safeway Stores, Inc., 52 Cal. App. 4th 267 (Cal. Ct. App. 1997)	$75,000	$75,000
Wirig v. Kinney Shoe Corp., 448 N.W.2d 526 (Minn. Ct. App. 1989)	$156,100	$43,100

Appendix 2. Sexual Harassment Awards

	Nominal $/Plaintiff	1997$[a]/Plaintiff
Average total award	$919,310	$981,292
Median total award	$105,000	$138,241
Average noneconomic damages	$100,910	$111,401
Median noneconomic damages	$50,000	$56,402
Average punitive damages	$813,575	$859,393
Median punitive damages	$15,000	$18,338
Average punitives where > $0	$1,362,738	$1,439,484
Median punitives where > $0	$50,000	$63,410

[a]Adjustments made in accordance with the broadest measure of the Consumer Price Index (CPI-U).

Notes

1. We avoid statistical detail here. *See* Judy M. Shih and Cass R. Sunstein, "What Explains Damage Awards in Sexual Harassment Cases?" (unpublished manuscript).

2. *See* A. Mitchell Polinsky and Steven Shavell, "Punitive Damages: An Economic Analysis," 111 *Harvard Law Review* 869 (1998).

3. *See id.*

4. The matter is disputed. *See* T. Eisenberg, "The Predictability of Punitive Damages," 26 *Journal of Legal Studies* 623 (1997). Eisenberg's principal evidence consists of the finding that punitive damages can often be predicted on the basis of compensatory dam-

ages. Many questions can be raised about Eisenberg's interpretation of his own data. *See* Cass R. Sunstein et al., *Punitive Damages: How Juries Decide* (Chicago: University of Chicago Press, 2002). For present purposes, the important point is that we do not find such a link in the area of sexual harassment awards.

5. *See* Cass R. Sunstein, et al., "Assessing Punitive Damages," 107 *Yale Law Journal* 2071 (1998). A follow-up study replicated this result with deliberating juries. *See* David Schkade et al., "Deliberating About Dollars: The Severity Shift," 100 *Columbia Law Review* 1139 (2000).

6. *See* Sunstein et al., *supra* note 4.

7. *See* Randall Bovbjerg et al., "Valuing Life and Limb in Tort," 83 *Northwestern University Law Review* 908 (1989); Mark Geistfeld, "Placing a Price on Pain and Suffering," 83 *California Law Review* 773 (1995).

8. Bovbjerg et al., *supra* note 7, at 923. Another study shows an additional point: judgments about pain and suffering are highly sensitive to framing effects. *See* Edward McCaffery et al., "Framing the Jury," 81 *Virginia Law Review* 1341 (1995). In particular, they are sensitive to the endowment effect — the fact that people are willing to pay less to purchase a good than they must be paid in order to get the very same good if it has been initially allocated to them. Thus losses are disvalued more than gains are valued. In the context of pain and suffering awards, the question is whether the plaintiff should be entitled to (a) the amount that he would have to be paid, before the fact, to allow the relevant pain and suffering to occur (his selling price) or instead to (b) the amount that he would be willing to pay, after the fact, to restore his health to its previous place (his "make whole" price). The useful study shows substantial differences between (a) and (b), and thus suggests that people are highly subject to framing effects in assessing appropriate awards for damages. Among one group, the "selling price" award was about double the "making whole" award. *See id.* at 1388.

9. These results reflect cases reported through February 12, 1998. The Westlaw searches typically involved the terms: "jury & award" & ("sexual"/"harass") & "employee" or "Title VII."

10. 413 S.E.2d 559 (N.C. Ct. App. 1992).

11. 907 F. Supp. 1309 (W.D. Mo. 1995), *aff'd in part, rev'd in part*, 107 F.3d 568 (8th Cir. 1997).

12. For instance, in some regressions we attempted to control for zero values, in others we excluded outliers, and in still others we adjusted for inflation. Although these variations produced divergent results, the conclusions we report reflect general consistencies across the data sets.

13. *See* Catharine MacKinnon, *Only Words* 66–67 (Cambridge: Harvard University Press, 1995).

14. The amendment also capped the maximum amount of these awards under Title VII. These numerical limitations were unlikely to anchor jury assessments, however, as most courts did not allow the juries to find out about them.

15. An underlying question, in all of these areas, involves the extent to which the damage judgment should be person-specific. Suppose, for example, that an especially sensitive plaintiff has suffered an especially severe hedonic loss as a result of libel or sexual harassment — or, by contrast, that an especially tough-skinned plaintiff has suf-

fered an unusually small hedonic loss as a result of the same conduct. Should a jury consider the extent to which the plaintiff's injury was objectively reasonable, independent of purely hedonic factors? Officially tort law incorporates a reasonable person inquiry at the level of liability, but once the defendant has been found liable, the defendant must take the plaintiff as the plaintiff experienced the injury; in other words, damages determinations are supposed to be person-specific. But we do not know if juries are willing to think in these terms, and it is also unclear that they should.

16. There is also an underlying question about the relationship between rule-bound judgment and particularistic judgment. Standards laid down in advance may leave room for erratic particularistic judgments if they are open-ended; but if they are rigid and rulelike, they may prevent the reasonable exercise of discretion to adapt to the particulars of the individual case. One issue here is how to minimize both decision costs and error costs, and in the abstract it is hard to know how much constraint on particularistic judgment will accomplish that task. For a good discussion, *see* Louis Kaplow, "Rules vs. Standards: An Economic Analysis," 43 *Duke Law Journal* 557 (1992).

17. *See* Bovbjerg et al., *supra* note 7, at 953.

PART V

Speech

The Speech-ing of Sexual Harassment

FREDERICK SCHAUER

Although a great deal of sexual harassment takes place without words, even more of it does not. Whether it be the words that are used to make the quid pro quo proposition that characterizes the classic if-you-sleep-with-me-you-will-not-get-fired form of sexual harassment, or the catcalls and other words of taunting that create the archetypal hostile environment, a vast amount of what uncontroversially counts as sexual harassment under the law takes place through the use of what would be called "speech" in the ordinary, nontechnical, nonlegal, non–First Amendment sense of that word.

For the first fifteen years of the development of the law of sexual harassment, the presence of speech in the harassing act, with only a very few exceptions, no more implicated the First Amendment's free speech clause than does the presence of speech in virtually every act of unlawful price-fixing, unlawful gambling, or unlawful securities fraud. In the past decade, however, it has become increasingly common, especially in popular and media discussion, to bring the First Amendment to bear whenever a claimed act of sexual harassment makes use of words or pictures. We now see First Amendment rhetoric marshaled to defend the very same harassing behavior that would not have generated any serious First Amendment responses ten years ago. In the past decade, but not before, sexually harassing speech that previously was not even close to being considered speech in the First Amendment sense is now taken by many people, both in and out of the courts, to implicate the First Amendment in new and previously unimagined ways.

In seeking to explain the shift by which sexually harassing speech has relatively recently become First Amendment speech, we could hypothesize that this shift represents nothing other than a natural doctrinal development, one in which the previous doctrinal error of considering sexually harassing speech to be outside the coverage of the First Amendment has finally been corrected. Under this view, the law works itself pure, and it is no surprise to see the current state of affairs moving in the right First Amendment direction. And, under this view, the previous state of affairs can be explained only by naïveté, ignorance, or the presence of pernicious forces of political correctness that keep the First Amendment away from its proper place: restricting the scope of sexual harassment law when sexual harassment, whether quid pro quo or hostile environment, takes place with the use of words — "speech" not only in ordinary language, but in the First Amendment sense as well.

The view that First Amendment scrutiny of the universe of verbal sexual harassment is the proper understanding of the task of the First Amendment, however, presupposes that there are moderately workable and well-known doctrinal or theoretical standards to determine the scope of the First Amendment's coverage. It turns out, however, that this is not the case. Although it is now obvious that the overwhelming proportion of verbal or linguistic behavior has nothing whatsoever to do with the First Amendment,[1] the boundary between the speech that implicates the First Amendment and the speech that does not is as much a matter of history, sociology, culture, and politics as it is a matter of formal constitutional doctrine or philosophical free speech theory. Once we see that neither First Amendment doctrine nor abstract free speech theory can explain why an injunction against the sale of legally obscene materials is treated as a prior restraint[2] but the licensing of speech that is central to the Securities Act of 1933 is not,[3] or why the published instructions on how to commit a contract killing are thought by some to raise First Amendment concerns[4] but the published instructions on how to (mis)use a chainsaw are not,[5] it becomes clear that we cannot ignore the role of politics, culture, economics, and numerous other social forces in determining which forms of word-based conduct inspire First Amendment rhetoric and standards and which do not.

The seeming transformation of sexual harassment from a topic about workplace abuse of power into a topic about the First Amendment provides an ideal case study for this issue, and tracing and analyzing this shift is my primary goal in this essay. For once we see that the applicability (or not) of the First Amendment is not primarily a product of formal legal doctrine, we are in a position better to understand the social forces that patrol and thus control the boundaries of the First Amendment.

The Architecture of the First Amendment

Like any legal rule, the First Amendment has both a scope of application and a prescription for what is to happen within that scope. Just as the prescriptions of the Securities Act of 1933 pertain only to certain sales of certain securities and not to all transactions of all kinds, and the regulations of the Occupational Safety and Health Administration apply to some businesses and not to others, so too do the prescriptions of the First Amendment apply only to a limited domain of behavior and not to the universe of human action.

This much is obvious, and so too is the fact that the domain of application of the First Amendment — its *coverage*[6] — is not coextensive with the forms of behavior that would count as "speech" in ordinary nontechnical English. Not only does the First Amendment cover activities that are not speech — dancing, mime, music, oil paintings, parades, protest armbands, flag waving, flag burning, and so on — but it also, and more important, does not cover numerous activities that *are* speech. To start with the most obvious examples, the speech that is necessary to make a contract, to provide a warranty, to leave one's property to one's heirs, or to consummate virtually any other sort of legal transaction does not by virtue of its speech-ness fall within the constitutional constraints of the First Amendment. To suppose that one might evade the commitments of a contract because one's *words* of acceptance of an offer are immune by virtue of the First Amendment from legal liability is simply laughable, and it is no surprise that not a single reported case has even had to consider the possibility.

Now, one response to this is to say that in all of these examples the words are *performative*,[7] producing legal consequences by virtue of their utterance — like saying "I do" at one's wedding, or a judge saying "I sentence you to ten years' imprisonment" — and thus quite separate from what the First Amendment is all about. But to accept even the exclusion of performative utterances from the scope of the First Amendment is to accept the basic point that the First Amendment does not cover all uses of words, even though the amendment itself contains no distinction between performative and other utterances. Moreover, the domain of speech that lies outside the coverage of the First Amendment is hardly limited to the performative. Numerous nonperformative propositions are similarly outside of the First Amendment's range, as with the descriptions on product labels, the representations sellers make about the securities they are selling, or the accurate information one competitor might give to another about plans for a price increase. Indeed, even the prescriptions that in First Amendment jargon might be called *advocacy* are more often than not untouched by First Amendment concerns. The First Amendment might be implicated when Clarence Brandenburg gives a speech urging his followers to commit acts of "revengeance" against Jews and African-Americans (not the labels that Brandenburg used),[8] but it is not when the leader of an organized crime syndicate urges his followers to commit acts of "revengeance" against members of a rival syndicate.[9] Indeed, the First Amendment hardly covers the full universe of *political* advocacy. When for undeniable political or ideological reasons Tom Metzger urged his followers in the White Aryan Resistance to commit acts of racial violence,[10] or when people were first urged to blow up the World Trade Center in New York,[11] the judicial response was not that these instances of advocacy satisfied the *Brandenburg v. Ohio* understanding of the clear and present danger test, but rather that neither *Brandenburg* nor any of the rest of the First Amendment apparatus was even applicable.

This last statement lies at the core of the matter. It is one thing to say that the First Amendment applies but that its high standards are satisfied. That explains what happens when a public official or a public figure makes out a case of actual malice satisfying the very high standards of *New York Times Co. v. Sullivan*,[12] and that is what happens when, even more rarely, an incitement to unlawful action carries such explicitness and such a likelihood of imminent danger that it satisfies the even higher standards of *Brandenburg*. By contrast, in all of the instances I have noted, the First Amendment's applicability has been explicitly or implicitly rejected, and consequently the regulability of the verbal act is not even measured against First Amendment standards. For a vast range of verbal, linguistic, and pictorial conduct, the First Amendment is simply not part of the picture. Indeed, although it is common for critics of some proposed constraint on linguistic acts to complain about the impermissibility of making an *exception* to the First Amendment, in truth the First Amendment is itself an exception, even if a vital one, to the principle that linguistic behavior — speech in the ordinary language sense — is subject to control according to the same standards as is any other behavior.[13] A cardinal principle of First Amendment architecture, therefore, is that the initial inquiry into whether the First Amendment and its rules, standards, tests, factors, theories, maxims, metaphors, and considerations even apply is an inquiry that is quite different from, and not dependent on, the question of whether the conduct at issue is something that the person in the street would think of as an instance of "speech."

Although it should be self-evident that looking for the presence of words, pictures, and symbols will not help much in delineating the boundaries of the First Amendment, it is far from clear what will. As a first step, we can say that the coverage of the First Amendment is delineated by the First Amendment's purposes, but the numerous posited purposes — assisting the search for truth, encouraging dissent, checking abuses of power, facilitating democratic deliberation, permitting individual self-expression, and so on[14] — remain sufficiently contested that attempts to explain the coverage of the First Amendment have produced something far short of a consensus. This is not to say that things could not be different, or that the existence of dissensus is strong evidence of the fact that there just *is* no purpose. Rather, the existing dissensus is evidence only of the proposition that lies at the center of this essay — that there is no existing First Amendment doctrinally embodied principle that provides much, if any, assistance in determining which cases are First Amendment cases and which are not. And in the absence of such an accepted doctrinal principle, the determination of the coverage or noncoverage of various forms of behavior has been a function not of doctrine but of a complex interplay of historical, political, cultural, and economic forces. As the above examples illustrate, the pervasive anomalies of First Amendment coverage strongly suggest that the determination of why some prior restraints implicate the First Amendment and others do not, why some advocacy of illegal action triggers the *Brandenburg* test and other advocacy does not, and why some speech-caused harm may generate a civil cause of action but other speech-caused harm does not has been (even if it need not inevitably be) a largely sociological rather than doctrinal matter. While determining the boundaries of the First Amendment may not be solely a matter of politics, it is nowhere near solely a matter of logic or legal principle.

Sexual Harassment as Uncovered Verbal Behavior

Against the background of recognizing the enormous universe of uncovered speech, it should come as no surprise that the presence of words has not been sufficient to embolden anyone to claim that the words that are part of a standard quid pro quo act of sexual harassment are covered by the First Amendment. Although an employer who promises a promotion in exchange for sex or a professor who offers higher grades in exchange for sex are using speech in the literal sense to make those offers, we have yet to see a claim that this speech is of the variety that the First Amendment might plausibly cover. Fearing either a Rule Eleven sanction for making a legally unsupportable claim, or fearing nothing more than judicial disbelief, those whose words have been taken to constitute unlawful acts of quid pro quo sexual harassment have yet to have the nerve to claim that those words are also covered by the First Amendment.

With respect to hostile environment sexual harassment, the history began in the same way. When the Equal Employment Opportunity Commission first promulgated its hostile environment regulations in 1980, and when the Supreme Court first endorsed the concept of hostile environment sexual harassment in 1986 in *Meritor Savings Bank v. Vinson*,[15] there was no suggestion that the First Amendment was even relevant, despite the fact that the overwhelming proportion of hostile environment cases are ones in which words or pictures are a significant part of the circumstances that create a hostile environment. Although there are many instances in which the hostile environment is created solely by pinching, groping, fondling, and various other types of unwanted touching, a survey of the kinds of events that generate hostile environment claims demonstrates that in most of them the hostile environment is created by an environment of insults, jokes, catcalls, comments, and other forms of undeniably verbal conduct. And although this verbal conduct is speech in the ordinary language sense, throughout the 1980s it appears generally to have been understood that the First Amendment was irrelevant to the issue, and that a First Amendment defense on the part of a harasser or his employer would not be taken seriously. That no one dared suggest during the hearings surrounding the nomination and Senate confirmation of Justice Clarence Thomas that his alleged behavior was nothing more than an exercise of his First Amendment rights is indicative of the fact that, throughout the 1980s, sexual harassment and freedom of speech were treated like psoriasis and the Fifth Amendment, each of independent importance but not in any apparent way related to each other. As in *Meritor* itself, the usual situation was that the First Amendment was not mentioned at all, even though some of the conduct was verbal.[16] On the rare occasions when a First Amendment defense was actually suggested in a hostile environment case, it was quickly and summarily dismissed.[17]

The Speech-ing of Sexual Harassment

Fourteen years after *Meritor*, the situation looks quite different. Hostile environment claims are now routinely met with First Amendment defenses, and indeed the entire concept of hostile environment sexual harassment is equally routinely challenged, by commentators and pundits even if less often in the courts, as an infringement of the First Amendment rights of the managers and employees whose verbal and pictorial conduct has created the hostile environment.[18] Time and again, hostile environment complaints premised on what is said to and about women in the workplace are met with the response that what is said to and about women in the workplace is an expression of a political or ideological point of view, and is consequently part of the liberty that it is the task of the First Amendment, and the larger concept of freedom of speech,[19] to protect.

If one were looking for the flash point for the shift from thinking that free speech and even verbal sexual harassment had nothing to do with each other to thinking that sexual harassment law jeopardizes the First Amendment, it would not be wrong to start with *Robinson v. Jacksonville Shipyards, Inc.*[20] In that case, the hostile environment in which Lois Robinson worked as a welder consisted in part of "[p]ictures of nude and partially nude women appear[ing] throughout the [workplace] in the form of magazines, plaques on the wall, [and] photographs torn from magazines."[21] The defendant in *Robinson* explicitly raised First Amendment defenses, the court took those defenses seriously enough to discuss them at some length in its opinion,[22] and the American Civil Liberties Union, after an acrimonious debate within its Florida chapter, filed a First Amendment-inspired amicus brief against Robinson's claim and in support of the employer.[23] Moreover, *Robinson* was the centerpiece of a number of law review articles appearing shortly thereafter, all of which took the First Amendment arguments in *Robinson* more seriously than the judge in *Robinson* did, and all of which argued that hostile environment claims in general, and not just the hostile environment claims in *Robinson*, were a direct attack on the First Amendment.[24]

But identifying *Robinson* as a turning point is only the beginning of the story. *Robinson* was undeniably important, but it is also important to understand *why Robinson* became the case that inspired the ACLU to act, the judge to take the First Amendment defenses seriously (even if in the final analysis he did not accept them), and a raft of commentators to respond.

In answering this question, we are assisted by looking at some of the cases that preceded *Robinson*. And in looking at these, we see the first suggestions of First Amendment issues in hostile environment cases — cases where part of what created the hostile environment was the use of an item that would otherwise have been thought of, in other contexts, as carrying the "aura" of the First Amendment. Whether it be the prisoner who claimed that his taunting of a member of the prison staff with a sexually explicit poem was protected by the First Amendment because the instrument of taunting was a poem,[25] or a range of cases in which pictures and magazines were at the center of the harassing scenario,[26] it is far from unreasonable to suppose that the impetus for First Amendment interest was an item that would itself have been thought to trigger First Amendment thinking.

If this is right, then it explains the salience of *Robinson*. *Robinson* not only involved the presence of words and pictures as the creators of the hostile environment in which Lois Robinson was compelled to work, but a number of those pictures were centerfold nudes from *Playboy* and other similar magazines. And if there is anything that prompts a reflexive reaction that the First Amendment is involved, it is *Playboy*. It may be hyperbole to suggest that the First Amendment would be raised as a defense if the driver of a delivery truck delivering copies of *Playboy* negligently caused an accident, or if a rolled-up copy of *Playboy* was used to commit a battery — but not much.

We see the same phenomenon in a different version in a number of other hostile environment cases. Because schools, colleges, and universities have traditionally been thought to be special First Amendment venues, and because First Amendment-inspired claims of academic freedom are often used as a defense when otherwise unexceptionable legal remedies are applied against these institutions,[27] it should come as no surprise that when otherwise routine hostile environment claims arise in the context of educational institutions, First Amendment defenses that would not be taken seriously elsewhere are treated as having greater credibility.[28] Thus, when faculty or students engage in verbal conduct that would not suggest First Amendment arguments in other workplace settings, their conduct has been held to suggest precisely those arguments when the setting is a school, college, or university.[29] Thus, a First Amendment setting such as a school, college, or university, just like a First Amendment "item" such as *Playboy*, triggers otherwise-distant First Amendment arguments and rhetoric in what would otherwise appear to be a non–First Amendment scenario.

My point, however, is not that the First Amendment is raised when some features of a setting appear, on the basis of historical associations, to make the First Amendment relevant. This is true, and of some interest, but not nearly as important as the subsequent emanations of the association. Once First Amendment items and First Amendment settings have suggested that there is a relationship between hostile environment sexual harassment law and the First Amendment, that suggestion, and that relationship, persist even in circumstances in which there is neither a First Amendment item nor a First Amendment context. In ways that were not apparent prior to *Robinson* and other cases in which First Amendment items and settings planted the idea that hostile environment sexual harassment was a First Amendment topic, after *Robinson* we saw First Amendment defenses raised, and taken seriously, even when neither familiar First Amendment items nor familiar First Amendment settings were present.[30] The important historical point is that First Amendment associations, arising in contexts in which some familiar First Amendment feature was present, then spilled over into contexts in which *no* familiar feature was present. The consequence is that situations that would have produced no First Amendment interest a decade or more ago are now seen, for virtually the first time, as raising First Amendment issues and justifying First Amendment defenses.

None of this is to deny Judith Resnik's point that shifting the terrain of argument from harassment to the First Amendment serves strategic and political purposes for those who are uncomfortable with the substance of sexual harassment law, and who recognize that First Amendment rhetoric has a special political cachet in the United States that allows free speech claims to trump equality claims when the two conflict, or are perceived to do so.[31] Nevertheless, changing the topic is likely to appear plausible only when there is a familiar First Amendment hook available initially — although, as I have tried to show, combining the desire to change the topic with the existence of a First Amendment hook will often produce a change of topic that is effective even when the hook is absent.

Harris v. Forklift Systems *and the Power of Silence*

Now that the First Amendment rabbit is out of the hat in hostile environment cases, however, it is quite hard to put it back. Even though the application of the First Amendment to standard hostile environment settings involving gender-based slurs, intimidating catcalls, omnipresent sexual jokes, suggestive comments, and aggressive and targeted posting of sexually explicit pictures appears to have no more relationship to the central concerns of the First Amendment than does verbal gambling, price-fixing, offering of securities, or making a contract, the association between the words of the hostile environment and the First Amendment has taken hold, even more in the public discourse than in the courts. And once it has taken hold, it is hard to remove it, even though, again, none of the plausible accounts of the purposes of the First Amendment appear pertinent.[32]

Once we understand the doctrinal politics of the speechification of sexual harassment, we can understand how difficult it would be to reverse that process. Nevertheless, the Supreme Court's decision in *Harris v. Forklift Systems, Inc.*[33] may well have stemmed the tide, even in unexpected ways. In this respect, the important thing about *Harris* is in what the Supreme Court did not say, and thus in what it said by saying nothing.

In *Harris*, as in most other hostile environment cases,[34] the bulk of the offending conduct was verbal, and thus linguistic, and thus speech. And given the phenomenon I have described above, and the proximity between the decision in *Robinson* and the briefing and argument in *Harris*, it should not be a surprise that the defendants raised the First Amendment as a defense in their brief,[35] and the plaintiff responded in her brief to the First Amendment defense.[36] Despite clearly knowing that the First Amendment was on the table, however, none of the Justices raised the First Amendment issue in oral argument. Much more important, however, the Court said not a word about the First Amendment in its opinion upholding Harris's claims. The First Amendment may have been relevant to the defendant, but it was plainly not relevant to the Supreme Court, the prevalence of speech in the harassing behavior notwithstanding.

Although some might argue that the Supreme Court could have made a stronger statement, or offered better analysis, by dealing with the First Amendment claim in the opinion,[37] there is another, and arguably better, view. As we know from many of our ordinary dealings, to be ignored is often more insulting than to be argued with. To be "blown off," to use the contemporary vernacular, is frequently far more dismissive and hurtful than to be engaged, even if the engaging party is engaging for the purpose of disagreeing. And if this is so in everyday life, it may be true in legal argument as well. As a consequence, one way of understanding the Supreme Court's opinion in *Harris*, and of understanding its failure even to mention the First Amendment arguments that were made, is as the Court's attempt to signal a dismissive attitude toward First Amendment arguments in cases where the connection with the First Amendment underlying concerns is as tenuous as it was in *Harris*. In an important respect, the Supreme Court "blew off" the defendant's First Amendment arguments, and it did so by saying, in as strong a way as it could, that the defendant's First Amendment arguments were so trivial that they did not even deserve a mention in the *United States Reports*. The Court, arguably, meant to insult the defendant's First Amendment arguments, and by ignoring those arguments the Court delivered the insult in the strongest way imaginable.[38]

It is perhaps too early to know whether the insult will have its intended effect. But although public commentary continues to associate the First Amendment with the application of hostile environment sexual harassment law, and although some commentators maintain that recognizing hostile environments constitutes a threat to the First Amendment,[39] it is noteworthy and important that the apparent momentum in the courts toward First Amendment annexation of hostile environment sexual harassment law, and perhaps eventually other aspects of "verbal" sexual harassment law, appears to have abated, and it is not at all unlikely that the dismissiveness of the Supreme Court in *Harris* contributed substantially to the abatement. Indeed, although commentators continue to raise free speech concerns with respect to hostile environment issues, the courts have remained as consistently dismissive of these concerns as was the Supreme Court in *Harris*.[40]

That the Supreme Court emphatically dismissed the First Amendment claims in *Harris* does not mean, of course, that it was correct to do so. One possibility, raised most prominently in the writings of Cynthia Estlund,[41] is that the workplace is for most people an important — perhaps even the most important — place in which they engage in the kind of social, cultural, ideological, and political discourse that lies both at the center of democracy and at the center of the most compelling arguments for freedom of speech. To Estlund and others, the traditional exclusion of the workplace from First Amendment norms represents a failure to appreciate the role of workplace speech in the deliberative universe. *Harris*, from this perspective, merely reinforces the marginalization of workplace from our conception of freedom of speech, reinforces a drawing-room conception of the First Amendment in which important speech takes place in overtly academic and intellectual settings, and reads out of the First Amendment what is for ordinary people perhaps the most important public forum they have.

It is important, however, to identify carefully the identity of Estlund's target. If she is arguing against those who would exclude the workplace wholesale from the universe of free speech doctrine,[42] her critique is well placed, for the view that the workplace has nothing to do with freedom of speech is undercut both by her theoretical arguments and the existing doctrine.[43] That a speech-created hostile workplace environment exists wholly outside the First Amendment is, as the Supreme Court concluded in *Harris*, a plausible position, but what makes it plausible is not that the workplace *simpliciter* exists wholly outside the First Amendment.

So if the Supreme Court was correct in *Harris*, there must be something more to the argument. And the something more seems to be a combination of two factors. First, it is less and less the case that First Amendment doctrine is unconcerned with differences among the institutional settings in which communication takes place. Although an important strand of First Amendment doctrine does intentionally ignore distinctions among institutional settings in the service of the First Amendment's inherently rule-based approach,[44] it is increasingly the case that First Amendment doctrine has become somewhat institution-specific, employing different rules, principles, categories, doctrines, and approaches in some institutions than it does in others.[45] That there is one First Amendment whose general strictures apply in the same way and with equal force to the public forum, to schools, to elections, to funding decisions, and much more is no longer a sustainable position. And if this is so, then it is far too simple to imagine that there is a domain of speech that is "entirely constitutionally protected"[46] and whose content-based control in the workplace for that reason creates major First Amendment difficulties. Content regulation is an inevitable component of all of those settings in which speech is constitutive of the enterprise, and there is little doubt that the First Amendment permits professors at state universities to give lower grades on examinations to some students than to others based on the content of their speech, allows arts funding to be based on the content of the art,[47] allows other forms of funding of speech to be based on viewpoint,[48] allows librarians to select some books and not others because of the content and even the viewpoint of those books, and in numerous other ways permits content and viewpoint to be taken into account in ways that would not be permitted for criminal regulation in the public forum. Part of the justification for the Supreme Court's flat-out rejection of the First Amendment arguments in *Harris*, therefore, is based on the fact that even if the First Amendment is relevant in the private workplace, it is a far cry from the First Amendment being relevant to the First Amendment applying public forum rules to the private workplace.

This leads, however, to the second factor explaining the outcome in *Harris*. If the workplace is neither a public forum nor a location totally devoid of First Amendment interest, then the particular form and context of harassing speech takes on considerable importance. And thus it is important to distinguish the case in which a federal regulation would hypothetically mandate control of workers who, at the workplace, criticized American foreign policy from a federal regulation mandating control of workers who would change the conditions of their coworkers' employment. The latter, much more than the former, properly characterizes the issue, and thus the actual speech with which we are concerned here looks far more transactional than propositional — in important ways closer to a contract or a warranty or an offer of securities than to a political statement in the public forum.

Now it is true that some of these transactional events are simultaneously political, social, or ideological propositions, and were this in the public forum the propositional aspects of the speech act would, as a matter of legal doctrine, dominate the transactional. Although a person's speech in the public forum can alter the conditions of someone else's participation in the public forum,[49] American legal doctrine insistently ignores the latter in order to protect the former. This preference for the propositional dimensions over the transactional (or performative) is best seen as an artifact of the public forum, however, rather than as a pervasive characteristic of the First Amendment, for the propositional dimensions, even the political propositional dimensions, of performative speech would not in any other context rescue from regulability speech whose regulation was based on its performative dimensions. Labor picketing, securities offerings, price-fixing ("How about you and I sell our goods at the same price in order to strike a blow for cooperative capitalism and a blow against Marxist-inspired government regulation" is in most contexts[50] far less of a political statement than it is a route to the federal penitentiary), and many other acts are not saved from regulability because some dimension of that act is also a political, social, cultural, or ideological proposition. Accordingly, the regulation of the way in which some workers, especially but not only supervisors, can alter the employment conditions of other workers is, outside of the domain and the institution of the public forum, much more consistent than it is inconsistent with the central themes of American First Amendment doctrine.

When seen in this way, the speech that lies at the heart of most hostile environment sexual harassment claims can also be seen as speech that is itself part of and about the job not only of the people who are affected, but also of the people who are doing the speaking. So if people can be dismissed from their jobs for making political speeches when they should be doing something else, if they can be disciplined for disclosing trade secrets to competitors, if they can be transferred for urging an otherwise unlawful strike, and if in countless other ways can be treated as people whose speech, no matter how protected it might be if made in the public forum, is part of the employment relationship when they are on the job, then it should come as no surprise that the speech of hostile environment sexual harassment, like the speech of quid pro quo sexual harassment, can consistent with existing doctrine be treated as a central and unprotected part of the job itself.[51]

The foregoing is not intended to be a full argument in favor of the Supreme Court's dismissal of the First Amendment arguments in *Harris*. It is intended, however, to show that the Supreme Court's dismissiveness of the First Amendment arguments, foreshadowed in Justice Scalia's opinion for the Court in *R.A.V. v. City of St. Paul*,[52] is consistent with an American First Amendment tradition in which it is a mistake to assume that the special rules pertaining to the public forum and otherwise public speech apply to schools, colleges, libraries, securities law, labor law, trade regulation, and a panoply of other regulatory schemes. In the final analysis, the Supreme Court's nonmention of the First Amendment claims in *Harris* was a way of showing that the rise of First Amendment arguments against hostile environment sexual harassment law was more a product of the sociological developments I have traced here than a coherent or plausible understanding of First Amendment doctrine. The

loud sound of the Court's silence as to the First Amendment in *Harris* was an
emphatic way of saying that as long as the public forum remains open and
largely unrestricted, in the workplace the ability of workers and supervisors to
adversely alter the working conditions of their coworkers and subordinates,
even with speech, is a more important dimension of the speech than is its self-
expressive dimension for individual harassers. In a larger sense, the Court
merely expressed its impatience with the implausibility of seeing every speech
act, even every propositional speech act, as raising serious First Amendment
claims. The First Amendment has always derived much of its strength from its
narrowness, for if First Amendment arguments were as widely available as the
critics of *Harris* would have them be, the likelihood that the First Amendment
would retain its current strength for core public forum political propositional
speech would be much less.[53] The Court's nonstatement in *Harris* is a statement about the fact that for First Amendment as well as gender equality
reasons hostile environment sexual harassment law is not an area in which the
First Amendment constraints are serious, but is rather an area almost entirely
unrelated to the concerns and doctrine of the First Amendment. And that is as
it should be.

Notes

I first spoke about the themes in this article in my First Amendment class at Harvard
Law School in the spring of 1997. One of the students in that class, Laura A. Rosenbury,
followed up on this class discussion with a paper from which I have benefited greatly in
writing this essay. I have also been assisted by numerous discussions with Dick Fallon.

1. *See* Frederick Schauer, "Categories and the First Amendment: A Play in Three
Acts," 31 *Vanderbilt Law Review* 265 (1982); Frederick Schauer, "Codifying the First
Amendment: *New York v. Ferber*," 1982 *Supreme Court Review* 285; Frederick Schauer,
"Speech and 'Speech' — Obscenity and 'Obscenity': An Exercise in the Interpretation of
Constitutional Language," 67 *Georgetown Law Journal* 899 (1979). *See also* Catharine
A. MacKinnon, *Only Words* (1993).

2. *Vance v. Universal Amusement Co.*, 445 U.S. 308 (1980).

3. Pursuant to section 5 of the Securities Act of 1933, an issuer may not use any
written materials, including advertisements and other factual statements, in connection
with the sale of a security unless and until those materials have been evaluated by the
Securities and Exchange Commission, a government agency, and the commission has
determined that the *content* of the materials is complete and neither false nor misleading.
In any other context, such a mechanism for official scrutiny of speech before granting
permission to publish it would be considered an archetypal prior restraint. Yet in the
securities context, this form of regulation is not measured against First Amendment
standards. *Dun & Bradstreet, Inc., v. Greenmoss Builders, Inc.*, 472 U.S. 749, 762 n.5
(1985). For rare and thus far unavailing attempts to subject the basic registration provisions of the securities laws to First Amendment scrutiny, *see* Aleta Estreicher, "Securities

Regulation and the First Amendment," 24 *Georgia Law Review* 223 (1990); Nicholas Wolfson, "The First Amendment and the SEC," 20 *Connecticut Law Review* 265 (1988).

4. *Rice v. Paladin Enterprises, Inc.*, 128 F.3d 233 (4th Cir. 1997).

5. *See* Frederick Schauer, "Mrs. Palsgraf and the First Amendment," 47 *Washington and Lee Law Review* 161 (1990).

6. On the distinction between *coverage*, the initial question of whether heightened scrutiny is applicable, and *protection*, the subsequent question of whether heightened scrutiny has been satisfied, *see* Frederick Schauer, *Free Speech: A Philosophical Enquiry* (1982); Frederick Schauer, "Can Rights Be Abused?" 31 *Philosophical Review* 225 (1981).

7. *See* J. L. Austin, *How to Do Things with Words* (J. O. Urmson and Marina Sbisà eds., 1962); J. L. Austin, "Performative Utterances," in *Philosophical Papers* 233, 233–52 (3d ed. 1979).

8. *Brandenburg v. Ohio*, 395 U.S. 444 (1969) (per curiam).

9. Clearly the best effort to struggle with these issues of the boundaries of the First Amendment's coverage is R. Kent Greenawalt, *Speech, Crime, and the Uses of Language* (1989). An earlier version is R. Kent Greenawalt, "Speech and Crime," 1980 *American Bar Foundation Research Journal* 645 (1980).

10. *Berhanu v. Metzger*, 850 P.2d 373 (Or. Ct. App. 1993). For a description of the underlying facts as presented in the Multnomah County Circuit Court (Portland, Oregon) in 1990, *see National Law Journal*, November 5, 1990; *id.*, September 26, 1994.

11. *See United States v. Salameh*, 152 F.3d 88 (2d Cir. 1998).

12. 376 U.S. 254 (1964).

13. *See* Frederick Schauer and Richard Pildes, "Electoral Exceptionalism and the First Amendment," 77 *Texas Law Review* 1803 (1999).

14. For a survey and critical analysis of the traditional free speech justifications, *see* Schauer, *Free Speech, supra* note 6.

15. 477 U.S. 59 (1986).

16. *See also Price, Waterhouse v. Hopkins*, 490 U.S. 228 (1988). In the lower courts, examples include *Tunis v. Corning Glass Works*, 747 F. Supp. 951, 955, 959 (W.D.N.Y. 1988); *Snall v. Suffolk County*, 611 F. Supp. 521, 531–32 (E.D.N.Y. 1985).

17. *See, e.g., Jordan v. Wilson*, 662 F. Supp. 528 (M.D. Ala. 1987); *Jew v. University of Iowa*, 749 F. Supp. 946 (S.D. Iowa 1990); *EEOC v. Sage Realty Co.*, 507 F. Supp. 599, 610 (S.D.N.Y. 1981); *Gilbert v. Board of Police and Fire Commissioners of Madison*, 384 N.W.2d 366 (Wis. Ct. App. 1986).

18. *See, e.g.*, Jeffrey Rosen, *The Unwanted Gaze: The Destruction of Privacy in America* 107–27 (2000); Nadine Strossen, "Regulating Workplace Sexual Harassment and Upholding the First Amendment—Avoiding a Collision," 37 *Villanova Law Review* 757 (1992).

19. Because the First Amendment in the doctrinal sense requires state action, its scope is not unlimited. But in many instances in which the First Amendment might not apply as a doctrinal matter, it is common in the United States to use the words "First Amendment" to signal what the user of the words believes to be a restriction on freedom of speech even when the restriction might not be judicially actionable.

20. 760 F. Supp. 1486 (M.D. Fla. 1991).

21. *Id.* at 1493.

22. *Id.* at 1536–39.

23. On *Robinson* as the watershed case in prompting the First Amendment defenses in hostile environment cases, *see* Judith Resnik, "Changing the Topic," 8 *Cardozo Studies in Law and Literature* 339 (1996).

24. *See* Kingsley R. Browne, "Title VII as Censorship: Hostile-Environment Harassment and the First Amendment," 52 *Ohio State Law Journal* 481 (1991). *See also* Wayne Lindsey Robbins, Jr., "When Two Liberal Values Collide in an Era of 'Political Correctness': First Amendment Protection as a Check on Speech-Based Title VII Hostile Environment Claims," 47 *Baylor Law Review* 789 (1995); Eugene Volokh, "How Harassment Law Restricts Free Speech," 47 *Rutgers Law Review* 563 (1995); Eugene Volokh, "Freedom of Speech and Workplace Harassment," 39 *UCLA Law Review* 1791 (1992). At least one prominent federal judge wondered why recognizing the First Amendment implications of hostile environment actions took as long as it did. *United States v. X-Citement Video, Inc.,* 982 F.2d 1285, 1296 n.7 (9th Cir. 1992) (Kozinski, J., dissenting). For an earlier but ignored suggestion about the relevance of the First Amendment in a range of hostile environment cases, *see* John B. Attanasio, "Equal Justice Under Chaos: The Developing Law of Sexual Harassment," 51 *University of Cincinnati Law Review* 1, 21–23 (1982).

25. *Gomes v. Fair,* 738 F.2d 517 (1st Cir. 1984).

26. *Andrews v. City of Philadelphia,* 895 F.2d 1469, 1482, 1485 (3d Cir. 1990); *Rabidue v. Osceola Refining Co.,* 584 F. Supp. 419, 433 (E.D. Mich. 1984), *affirmed,* 805 F.2d 611 (6th Cir. 1986); *Arnold v. City of Seminole,* 614 F. Supp. 853, 858 (E.D. Okla. 1985).

27. *See, e.g., University of Pennsylvania v. EEOC,* 493 U.S. 182 (1990).

28. *See generally* Mary Gray, "Academic Freedom and Nondiscrimination: Enemies or Allies?" 66 *Texas Law Review* 1591, 1594 (1988).

29. *See Korf v. Ball State University,* 726 F.2d 1222 (7th Cir. 1984); *Doe v. University of Michigan,* 721 F. Supp. 852 (E.D. Mich. 1989); *Fraser v. Bethel School District No. 403,* 755 F.2d 1356, 1370 (9th Cir. 1985).

30. *See, e.g., DeAngelis v. El Paso Municipal Police Officers Association,* 51 F.3d 591 (5th Cir. 1995); *Black v. City of Auburn,* 857 F. Supp. 1540, 1549 (M.D. Ala. 1994); *Jenson v. Eveleth Taconite Co.,* 824 F. Supp. 847, 884 n.89 (D. Minn. 1993).

31. Resnik, "Changing the Topic," *supra* note 23. On the sociological primacy of free speech claims over equality claims in much of American legal and political culture, *see* Catharine A. MacKinnon, *Feminism Unmodified* (1987); Frederick Schauer, "The Ontology of Censorship," in *Censorship and Silencing: Practices of Cultural Regulation* 147–68 (Robert Post ed., 1998); Charles R. Lawrence III, "If He Hollers Let Him Go: Regulating Racist Speech on Campus," 1990 *Duke Law Journal* 431; Mari J. Matsuda, "Public Response to Racist Speech: Considering the Victim's Story," 87 *Michigan Law Review* 2320 (1989).

32. This is not to deny that offensive workplace slurs, for example, embody a political, cultural, and ideological point of view. But so do a quid pro quo overture, a pinch, a

grope, and any other form of unwanted touching in the workplace. And once we understand that the distinction between the coverage and the noncoverage of the First Amendment does not and cannot turn on the distinction between what conduct is and is not speech in the ordinary-language sense of that word, then the fact that repeatedly calling a coworker or employee a "bitch" embodies a worldview no more makes this speech act a First Amendment issue than does the fact that groping that same coworker or employee embodies the same worldview.

33. 510 U.S. 17 (1993).

34. For another example, *see Franklin v. Gwinnett County Public Schools*, 503 U.S. 60 (1992).

35. Brief for Respondent at 31–33, *Harris v. Forklift Systems, Inc.*, 510 U.S. 17 (1993) (No. 92–1168).

36. Reply Brief for Petitioner at 10–11, *Harris v. Forklift Systems, Inc.*, 510 U.S. 17 (1993) (No. 92–1168).

37. Richard H. Fallon, Jr., "Sexual Harassment, Content Neutrality, and the First Amendment Dog That Didn't Bark," 1994 *Supreme Court Review* 1.

38. In case the message was too subtle to be understood, there was also the Court's statement a year earlier that its decision in *R.A.V. v. City of St. Paul*, 505 U.S. 377 (1992), was not to be taken to restrict the application of sexual harassment law. *Id.* at 389–90.

39. *See* the authorities cited in note 24 *supra*, and especially the contributions of Eugene Volokh.

40. For a post-*Harris* exchange, see Suzanne Sangree, "Title VII Prohibitions Against Hostile Environment Sexual Harassment and the First Amendment: No Collision in Sight," 47 *Rurgers Law Review* 461 (1995); Kingsley R. Browne, "Workplace Censorship: A Response to Professor Sangree," 47 *Rutgers Law Review* 579 (1995); Suzanne Sangree, "A Reply to Professors Volokh and Browne," 47 *Rutgers Law Review* 595 (1995).

41. *See* Cynthia Estlund, "Freedom of Expression in the Workplace and the Problem of Discriminatory Harassment," 75 *Texas Law Review* 687 (1997).

42. *See* Rodney Smolla, "Rethinking First Amendment Assumptions About Racist and Sexist Speech," 47 *Washington and Lee Law Review* 171, 207 (1990). *See also* Robert C. Post, "Racist Speech, Democracy, and the First Amendment," 32 *William and Mary Law Review* 267, 289 (1991), acknowledging some First Amendment protection for workplace speech but maintaining that in the workplace "the image of dialogue among autonomous self-governing citizens would be patently out of place."

43. See *Rankin v. McPherson*, 378 (1987); *Connick v. Myers*, 461 U.S. 138 (1983); *Givhan v. Western Line Consolidated School District*, 439 U.S. 410 (1979).

44. See Frederick Schauer, "The Second Best First Amendment," 31 *William and Mary Law Review* 1 (1989).

45. Frederick Schauer, "Principles, Institutions, and the First Amendment," 112 *Harvard Law Review* 84 (1998).

46. Eugene Volokh, "What Speech Does 'Hostile Work Environment' Harassment Law Restrict?" 85 *Georgetown Law Journal* 627, 629 (1997), as updated at *http://www.law.ucla.edu/faculty/volokh/harass/breadth.htm*.

47. *National Endowment for the Arts v. Finley*, 118 S. Ct. 2168 (1998). Indeed, even the Court's claim in *Finley* that viewpoint-based distinctions in this context are impermissible is untenable. Schauer, *supra* note 44, at 92–97.

48. *Rust v. Sullivan*, 500 U.S. 173 (1991).

49. I discuss the contours of this in Frederick Schauer, "The Ontology of Censorship," in *Censorship and Silencing: Processes of Cultural Regulation* (Robert Post ed., 1999).

50. A possible counterexample is *NAACP v. Claiborne Hardware Co.*, 458 U.S. 886 (1982), but that case is likely scant precedent for anything in light of *FTC v. Superior Court Trial Lawyers Association*, 493 U.S. 411 (1990); *Allied Tube & Conduit Corp. v. Indian Head, Inc.*, 486 U.S. 492 (1988); *International Longshoremen's Association v. Allied International, Inc.*, 456 U.S. 212 (1982).

51. On the distinction among on the job speech, off the job speech, and at the workplace but off the job speech, see Frederick Schauer, "Private Speech and the Private Forum: Givhan v. Western Line Consolidated School District," 1979 *Supreme Court Review* 217.

52. 505 U.S. 377 (1992).

53. This is of course an empirical claim about the effects of First Amendment doctrinal architecture, but it is an empirical claim I have developed at length elsewhere. Frederick Schauer, "Commercial Speech and the Architecture of the First Amendment," 56 *University of Cincinnati Law Review* 1181 (1988); Frederick Schauer, "Codifying the First Amendment: New York v. Ferber," 1982 *Supreme Court Review* 285; Frederick Schauer, "Categories and the First Amendment: A Play in Three Acts," 34 *Vanderbilt Law Review* 265 (1981).

The Collective Injury of Sexual Harassment

DOROTHY ROBERTS

Sexual harassment inflicts a collective injury. Twenty-five years ago in her groundbreaking book, *Sexual Harassment of Working Women*, Catharine MacKinnon explained that sexual harassment is a form of sex discrimination because it stems from and helps to perpetuate the inequality of women at work and in the wider society.[1] MacKinnon and other scholars have conceptualized sexual harassment to include subordinating sexual relations, as well as other conduct that promotes norms of masculinity and femininity and enforces gendered work roles.[2] The harm of sexual harassment is collective because it affects the status of all women in the workplace where it occurs, in the labor market, and in society as a whole. Although sexual harassment inflicts a personal injury on the victim, "it is a social wrong and a social injury that occurs on a personal level."[3] It is this aspect of sexual harassment — its discrimination on the basis of sex — that brings it within the purview of Title VII.

In this essay I want to reiterate the importance of recognizing sexual harassment's collective injury, especially in considering the question of whether or not harassing speech is protected by the First Amendment. I will focus on the most common claim of sexual harassment in the workplace — harassment of women by men. The harm to women is often lost in the scholarly First Amendment debate. On the one hand, arguments opposing constitutional protection of harassing speech tend to be dominated by the abstract discussion of the doctrinal boundaries of free expression.[4] On the other hand, arguments supporting constitutional protection of harassing speech promote the image of an idiosyncratic, hypersensitive woman who makes the office less fun for others.[5] This view pits the complaint of a lone woman against everyone else's right to speak freely, dwarfing the state's interest in preventing harassing speech and exaggerating the liberty interests of harassers. The major response to the First Amendment challenge to government regulation of assaultive racist speech has been to describe more elaborately the injury that this speech inflicts.[6] Understanding the harm to victims of hate speech, in turn, has led scholars to rethink how speech rules fit within a broader constitutional framework that encompasses the guarantees of both freedom of speech and equality. Now sexual harassment law is generating a similar inquiry.

An enlightening aspect of this project is the deeply rooted role of race in the history of sexual harassment law. Eliminating race and sex discrimination in the workplace are twin objectives of Title VII. Advocates and courts understood sexual harassment as sex discrimination by studying discrimination against blacks on account of their race.[7] Black women pioneered claims of sexual harassment as a violation of Title VII, and their historical experience of workplace abuse as an instrument of both race and gender subordination helped to shape sexual harassment doctrine. An examination of the racial ancestry of sexual harassment law illuminates the collective injury inflicted by sexual harassment. It also suggests that we should evaluate the competing interests at stake in the First Amendment debate in terms of a moral and legal commitment to social justice, a commitment that takes into account power struggles on the job. While this approach rejects constitutional protection of harassing workplace speech, it also cautions against characterizing the workplace as a forum that is exempt from free speech concerns.

The Nature of Sexual Harassment's Collective Injury

Women workers are personally injured by sexual harassment: they feel insulted, humiliated, and threatened by it. Many suffer psychological distress, physical assault, and interference with their work that makes it difficult if not impossible to remain on the job. Many others are fired when they complain about the abusive atmosphere or rebuff sexual propositions. Victims of workplace harassment pay a heavy price in economic, physical, and emotional terms.

Yet the harm of sexual harassment is also collective in several senses. First, sexual harassment at a job site is typically experienced by many, if not all, of the women who work there. When harassment constitutes pervasive behavior or open displays of sexist material, such as pornography plastered on the walls, it creates an atmosphere that affects everyone.[8] When harassment is directed at one worker, it can also have a negative impact on others. Because direct victims of harassment are targeted because of their sex, other women may see themselves as potential objects of hostility or actual subjects of the discriminatory message conveyed. It puts others on notice that, as women, they are being judged by a sexist standard that discounts their work competence, and they may be the next victims of abuse. Stated in Title VII's terms, sexual harassment imposes on all women on the job, as well as the individual claimant, terms and conditions of employment that are inferior to those offered to men.

Researchers at the University of Illinois recently proposed the concept of "ambient sexual harassment" to describe the indirect exposure to sexual harassment experienced by others in a victim's work group who witness, hear about, or are cognizant of the behavior.[9] Their empirical study of female employees at a public utility company and a food processing plant confirmed that ambient sexual harassment caused negative job, health, and psychological outcomes similar to those suffered by direct targets of abuse. Women who are exposed to ambient sexual harassment "report higher levels of absenteeism, intentions to quit, and are more likely to leave work early, take long breaks, and miss meetings."[10] As one of the researchers, Louise Fitzgerald, put it, sexual harassment directed at one worker pollutes the workplace like "second-hand smoke."[11]

Second, the injury of sexual harassment is collective because it helps to maintain women's subordinate position in the market and in society as a whole. Sexual harassment thrives in a racialized and gendered division of labor that segregates women into economically inferior and devalued jobs, with women of color at the very bottom.[12] Abusive male conduct helps to enforce these boundaries, which hurt all women to varying degrees. As Vicki Schultz explains, "[b]y protecting their jobs from incursion by women, or by incorporating women only on inferior terms, men sustain the impression that their work requires uniquely masculine skills," thereby "assur[ing] men a sense of identity (even superiority) as men."[13] Permeating the work environment with speech, conduct, and artifacts that represent male sexual and other prerogatives is a way of demarcating it for men only.

Because sexual harassment arises from this hierarchy, one woman's experience of abuse is never idiosyncratic. If one woman worker is being harassed on the job, it is likely that her female coworkers are being harassed as well, as are other women in the labor force. The pervasiveness of sexual harassment confirms that it inflicts a collective injury. Surveys of working women conducted during the 1970s proved that harassment was commonplace,[14] and therefore a function of gender, and enabled activists to conceptualize sexual harassment as sex discrimination. Seeing this detriment to women's collective economic status stays true to the antidiscrimination purpose of Title VII and sexual harassment law.

Charles Lawrence makes a similar point about racist speech. In arguing that racist speech and discriminatory conduct are inseparable, Lawrence suggests that we view individual racist acts as part of a totality. Because discriminatory conduct furthers the ideas of white supremacy, its impact on the societal level is greater than the sum of individual racist acts. "The racist acts of millions of individuals are mutually reinforcing and cumulative because the status quo of institutionalized white supremacy remains long after deliberate racist actions subside."[15] In a similar way, the sexual harassment perpetrated by individual harassers effects a systemic exclusion of women from full participation in the market, reinforcing women's inferior economic and social status.

Finally, sexual harassment inflicts a collective injury because it disrespects women on the basis of their group status, as women and as members of other subordinated groups. When any woman is sexually harassed it conveys a degrading message about all women. Sexual harassment treats women as a class as suitable only for inferior feminized jobs and incompetent to do masculine work. This view of women is reflected in one supervisor's declaration, "There isn't a woman alive that can make it with Yellow Pages!"[16] Thus, a common abusive technique is to treat all women employees alike even though some hold positions of higher status.[17] Female managers along with secretaries might be asked to serve coffee or photocopy documents, for example. Stereotypes based on group membership, in turn, influence social policies and attitudes that limit all group members' ability to participate equally in society. Perpetuating the belief that women workers are naturally unfit for highly respected occupations and should be subservient to men at the office or the plant generally impedes women's struggle for equality.

The Significance of Black Claimants' Perspective

Black women played a critical role in courts' recognition of sexual harassment as a form of sex discrimination.[18] How did black female claimants' racial identity illuminate the meaning of sexual harassment? Their experience of workplace abuse as a compound harm helped to clarify the seriousness of sexualized conduct by male coworkers, conduct seen previously as misguided romantic gestures. Moreover, black Americans' understanding of unequal working conditions, including the sexual exploitation of black women workers, as a collective grievance helped to place sexual harassment within the framework of employment discrimination. This experience showed, as well, that hostility directed toward women workers need not be sexual in nature to constitute discrimination.

ANALOGIZING SEXUAL HARASSMENT TO RACE DISCRIMINATION

Early Title VII challenges to sexual harassment were dismissed on grounds that sexual advances by a male boss or coworker reflected a "personal proclivity" or "an inharmonious personal relationship" between two individuals.[19] Advocates and courts turned to the law of racial discrimination for guidance in redefining employment discrimination against women and in constructing sexual harassment rules. A critical aspect of this comparison was the recognition that both types of conduct perpetrate a group-based injury. Observing that in race discrimination cases "blacks are disadvantaged cumulatively, systematically, and as a group, not just in occasional, discrete, haphazard, and isolated ways and one at a time,"[20] MacKinnon argued that courts should apply the same notion of discriminatory injury to the sexual harassment of working women.

Race discrimination provided a precedent not only for what sexual harassment was but what it looked like. The techniques used to abuse black workers informed the expansion of sexual harassment's definition from quid pro quo abuse to include hostile environment claims. Courts borrowed racial harassment analysis to determine that an atmosphere that undermines workplace equality, including verbal abuse and conduct that does not produce a tangible job detriment, could constitute sexual harassment. When the Supreme Court in *Meritor Savings Bank v. Vinson* reached this conclusion, it explicitly relied on this analogy by noting that "a requirement that a man or woman run a gauntlet of sexual abuse in return for the privilege of being allowed to work and make a living can be as demeaning and disconcerting as the harshest of racial epithets."[21]

Why had judges already understood that racially hostile environments inflict a collective harm? Perhaps it was more obvious that racial harassment is designed to maintain the longstanding domination of whites over blacks and other minorities. Racist speech, moreover, is calculated to terrorize and insult by invoking historical symbols of racial oppression and widely held group stereotypes. Burning a cross on a black homeowner's lawn intimidates by deliberately conjuring up centuries of white supremacist violence. Calling an employee "nigger" or "boy" encapsulates in a word an entire ideology and practice of degrading black people, particularly in their role as menial servants. In *Snell v. Suffolk County*,[22] white police officers harassed a Latino coworker, Officer Ramos, by dressing a Latino prisoner in a straw hat, a sheet, and a sign that read "Spic," and then calling the prisoner "Ramos's son." This abuse linked together Officer Ramos and the prisoner on the basis of their group identity and the stereotype that Latinos are prone to criminality. Consider the racial symbolism at play in *Vance v. Southern Bell Telephone and Telegraph Co.*,[23] brought by a black woman who twice arrived on the job to discover a noose hanging over her work station. By alluding to the history of white mob lynchings of blacks in the South, the stealthy harasser conveyed the double message that Vance was subservient to her white coworkers and that she risked her physical safety if she remained at the job.

The harm of racial harassment may stem from group identification. *Rogers v. EEOC*[24] centered on whether Josephine Chavez's complaint that the optometrists she worked for "segregated" their patients by race stated a Title VII cause of action. In this claim, Chavez did not object to discriminatory action directed at her; she objected to the optometrists' discrimination directed at their minority customers. Judge Goldberg, writing for the Fifth Circuit en banc, stated that "[w]hile the district court may have viewed lightly the connection between the petitioners' alleged discrimination against its patients and Mrs. Chavez's sensibilities, I think that the relationship between an employee and his working environment is of such significance as to be entitled to statutory protection."[25] To me, the harm suffered by Chavez was not a personal offense as much as a collective injury she shared with the mistreated patients. Her employers' demeaning stance toward the patients emphasized her own degraded status based on her Spanish surname and became an oppressive working condition.

BLACK WOMEN'S COMPOUND INJURY

The claims of black women workers, who were at the forefront of early sexual harassment litigation, helped to make sexual harassment's collective injury plain.[26] Black women often experience a *compound* form of workplace abuse that occurs on account of both their race and their gender.[27] Referring to a security guard as "Buffalo Butt,"[28] telling an administrative secretary that "she should stay home, go on welfare, and collect food stamps like the rest of the 'spics,'"[29] chasing a state labor department referee with a bullwhip while exclaiming, "This is my sexual fantasy for you,"[30] and calling a corrections officer "black bitch slut" and poking her rear with a fork to see if "the meat was done"[31] all target the victims' racial and sexual identity at the same time. As Kathryn Abrams observes, such epithets are "unlikely ever to be used against either black men or white women; they convey a kind of racialized sexual hostility, or sexualized racial hostility, that cannot be disaggregated into its component parts."[32] Perceiving harassment as racist as well as sexist makes it harder to dismiss it as a "romantic indiscretion" and easier to recognize it as discrimination.[33]

Workplace harassment of black women sometimes utilizes a degrading sexual construction of black women as naturally promiscuous that is both racist and sexist.[34] In numerous cases men demeaned their black female coworkers with words, pictures, and gestures that embodied this stereotype of licentious black sexuality. On her first day of work as an assistant collections manager, Maxine Munford was asked by her boss "if she would make love to a white man, and if she would slap his face if he made a pass at her."[35] After firing her for rebuffing his advances, he told her that "[i]f you would have sex with me seven days a week I might give you your job back." Helen Brooms was shown a "pornographic photograph depicting an interracial act of sodomy" by a white male coworker who "told her that the photograph showed the 'talent' of a black woman" and "stated that she was hired for the purpose indicated in the photograph."[36] The sexual accessibility of slave women still figures in the workplace abuse of black women. One harasser of a black woman coworker frequently referred to a movie about slavery and stated that "he wished slavery days would return so that he could sexually train her and she would be his bitch."[37] The gender stereotype often underlying sexual harassment—the view that women employees are "sexual fair game"—is epitomized by this mythical black woman.

BLACK WOMEN'S COLLECTIVE GRIEVANCE

The compound injury black women suffer on the job is *collective* as well as serious. Black women have a uniquely long and antagonistic experience of work in America. At a time when Victorian norms confined white women to the home, slave women were required to perform strenuous labor. After Emancipation, black women joined the wage-earning labor force in numbers that far exceeded white women. Black married women in Southern cities at the turn of the century, for example, worked outside the home five times more often than white married women.[38] Far from a benign or liberating environment, the workplace has largely been a site of degradation and danger for black women. As slaves, domestics, and menial laborers, their working life was an aspect of racial subordination and their workplace the central site of their subservience to whites.

A common feature of this subjugation was sexual exploitation. The law granted white masters unrestricted sexual access to their female slaves.[39] Freed black domestics continued to be sexually abused in the homes of their white employers. The sexual harassment of black working women, then, exploited and reinforced the racist hierarchy of the wider society. Although judges have dismissed sexual complaints on the grounds that "increased proximity breeds increased volitional sexual activity,"[40] workplace intimacy has long been the terrain of black women's subjugation.

Blacks viewed the workplace abuse of black women as a *group* grievance that was part of the struggle for liberation. Stories of slave women such as Harriet Tubman, who escaped bondage, and Harriet Jacobs, who resisted her master's sexual exploitation, are legendary.[41] After Emancipation, the mistreatment of black domestic servants at the hands of white employers became a burning community issue. Blacks saw sexual abuse as a common condition of employment of black women workers that called for collective redress. As an anonymous black domestic observed in 1912, "I believe nearly all white men take, and expect to take, undue liberties with their colored female servants."[42]

The impact of sexual exploitation of black domestic servants became evident to the entire community as many fled to northern cities in search of safer jobs. Fannie Barrier Williams, an activist in Chicago, remarked, "[i]t is a significant and shameful fact that I am constantly in receipt of letters from still unprotected women in the South begging me to find employment for their daughters . . . to save them from dishonor and degradation."[43] During this period black women's clubs, federated into the National Association of Colored Women in 1896, addressed workplace abuse by aiding and mobilizing women workers.[44] Sexual exploitation was part and parcel of white employers' general disregard for the humanity of their black employees, who were consigned to menial labor. The impossibility of disaggregating black women's race- and sex-based injuries parallels the admonition that courts should not disaggregate sexualized conduct from other gender-based mistreatment when considering women's sexual harassment claims.[45]

Blacks' collective approach to sexual harassment was mirrored by the simultaneous struggle of black workers to develop a collective understanding of all racially discriminatory employment policies. The history of black workers' union activism features a battle with the courts over the nature of Title VII's antidiscrimination mandate. While courts have individualized the meaning of and remedies for employment discrimination, black workers have sought to collectivize them.[46] Workplace indignity was part of what it meant to be a black laborer (both male and female) in a white man's world. It helped to preserve the racist ideology that put white people in charge of black workers. Employer abuse was not just an offense against individual workers; it was also an offense against the race. This collective view of racially hostile work environments reinforces the understanding of sexual harassment as a means of preserving male privilege in the market.

Collective Injury and Freedom of Speech

Recognizing the collective injury inflicted by sexual harassment bears on the constitutional status of this type of speech. Nobody suggests that an employer's threat to fire an employee if she does not have sex with him is protected by the First Amendment. But the harassing speech that creates a hostile work environment often resembles an opinion more than a threat or fighting words. In *Harris v. Forklift Systems*, for example, the discriminatory language included "We need a man as the rental manager," as well as "You're a dumb ass woman."[47] In another case, a supervisor denied the plaintiff a construction position after exclaiming, "Fucking women, I hate having fucking women in the office!"[48] Expressions of resentment about women workers' inferiority often demonstrate that other forms of mistreatment, such as denying a promotion, withholding perks, or sabotaging equipment, are sex-based. Far from needing more protection, these statements are already disregarded by most judges as evidence of sexual harassment because they are not sexual enough.[49]

Title VII proscribes harassing speech partly because of its message: it is the message that "women are not fit to work at this job," "women should be sexually available," and "men are in charge here" that creates a hostile atmosphere, interfering with women's ability to do their jobs and perpetuating a segregated workforce. By regulating workplace expression based on its disfavored message, some scholars have recently argued, Title VII violates the First Amendment's requirement of government neutrality.[50] I want to explain why the harmful impact of this message — sexual harassment's collective injury — is a reason to proscribe harassing speech rather than to protect it.

THE CONFLICT BETWEEN LIBERTY AND EQUALITY

Recognizing that Title VII prohibits discrimination does not erase the First Amendment conflict; it explains why there is a conflict. Restrictions on harmful speech create a conflict between the constitutional imperatives of freedom of speech and equality. Laws regulating racial and sexual harassment place the First Amendment's protection of harassers' speech in tension with the Fourteenth Amendment's promise of equality to women and minorities. When the state protects the free speech rights of harassers, it permits harm to women; when it protects women from harassing speech, it infringes the liberty of male workers to speak freely. But how do we resolve this clash of constitutional imperatives, when "[h]er right to be free from harassment is mirrored by his freedom to harass"?[51] We need a way of explaining why one person's interests should outweigh the other's.

The constitutional conflict is complicated by the fact that harassing speech interferes with women's liberty as well as their equality. A hostile work environment affects women's decisions about how to conduct their day, where to venture on the job, or even whether to stay at all. Sexual harassment also silences women: many victims are afraid to speak up, or feel that their views will be discredited given the employer's tolerance of the demeaning environment. Allowing sexual harassment in the workplace gives abusive employers and coworkers tremendous power to restrict the personal freedoms, including the free expression, of their victims. So, the question is not whether the government will interfere with liberty in the workplace, but with whose liberty.

How, then, can we mediate the interests at stake without privileging a priori one over the other? We need an overarching standard that explains the normative commitment that creates both constitutional protections in the first place and evaluates the speech and equality interests in relation to this commitment. Some theorists have persuasively articulated the need to place the First Amendment within a broader framework of democracy.[52] The First Amendment protects the intrinsic value of self-expression, but it is not a license for individuals to express themselves without restraint. Freedom of speech also serves the instrumental function of enabling citizens to participate equally in government, criticize elected leaders, engage in political dissent, and generally take part in "public and private forms of social power."[53] Not every regulation of expression based on its content violates the First Amendment because some speech restrictions actually further the First Amendment's democratic function.

Both equality and liberty of speech should take their meaning and importance from a commitment to social justice — the commitment to changing institutional structures to end relations of domination in ways that promote the participation of those who are currently subordinated.[54] Does this formulation unfairly privilege equality over free speech? It does not, because ensuring the free and equal participation of citizens in the social, political, and economic life of the nation is central to both values.

Without pursuing social justice, the constitutional guarantee of liberty means no more than government protection of privilege. Those who defend sexual harassment as free speech have confused liberty with privilege, and enlist the First Amendment to rationalize harassers' use of speech to preserve their privileged position in the workplace. As a student commentator astutely predicts, "if the next step in the progression of sexual harassment law is to challenge behaviors that defendants wish to preserve, rather than simply deny, the First Amendment is likely to play a more prominent role."[55] It is this conversion of liberty to privilege that creates an inescapable tension with equality, for securing positions of power inevitably obstructs the goal of creating more egalitarian social institutions. This antidemocratic effect is not apparent if sexual harassment is misunderstood as sexy talk or a personal offense. It becomes clear, however, when we see sexual harassment's collective injury to women workers. The decision whether to treat sexual harassment as illegal conduct or as free speech allocates economic and social power between men and women.

Degrading, humiliating, and intimidating speech directed against women workers obstructs the democratic process both at the job and in the broader society. This type of speech often silences women in the workplace and limits their ability to advance in their careers or even to remain on the job. By reinforcing a racialized and gendered labor market, harassing speech also maintains women's inferior economic status and constrains women's ability to participate in political struggles outside of work. Harassing speech at the workplace therefore falls outside First Amendment protection.

THE CONTEXT OF THE WORKPLACE

The analysis of the free speech issue must center on the distinctive features of the workplace, as well as the harm of sexually harassing speech. Considering the democratic function of First Amendment protection is important to determining the legality of harassing speech anywhere. Because "First Amendment doctrine is contextual,"[56] however, the evaluation of harassers' free speech claims also depends on the fact that they arise at work. A crucial feature of speech in the workplace is that it is constitutionally subject to far greater restrictions than speech in other forums, particularly public forums. Opinions about women that would be protected if expressed in a newspaper, at a town meeting, or in a classroom may be prohibited if expressed at the job. The statement "we need a man in this position" may be protected in a public debate about women's qualifications for traditionally male professions, but not as part of a campaign to drive women from a predominantly male job site. Even people who contend that pornography is protected speech should be able to tell the difference between watching *Deep Throat* at home for entertainment and showing it during a business meeting to an unsuspecting female associate.[57]

Moreover, private employers have the right to ban all kinds of speech at the workplace, including speech that is far less noxious than that covered by Title VII. The employer in *Robinson v. Jacksonville Shipyards* who violated Title VII by permitting workers to post pictures of naked women everywhere barred the same workers from reading newspapers on the job.[58] The First Amendment is implicated only when the government enforces Title VII to *compel* an employer to restrict workplace expression. Indeed, some scholars refute harassers' First Amendment claims by pointing out that employees have virtually no speech rights at all while at work.[59] I think this position is misguided for two reasons, both related to sexual harassment's collective injury.

The Purpose of Workplace Speech Regulations

First, the absolute denial of speech concerns in the workplace overlooks how speech rules regulate private relationships of power. A more accurate description of workplace speech doctrine is that employees have speech rights only in relation to broader government goals related to the workplace. Although private employers have enormous power to control their employees' speech, both the judiciary and Congress have intervened when they determine that policy concerns or statutory mandates outweigh employers' rights.[60] Courts permit government agencies to censor their employees' political speech that impedes official functions; they protect freedom of expression on matters of public concern only to enable communication necessary for civic participation.[61] Both private and public employers' interest in running an efficient office may override workers' freedom of speech.

The Supreme Court has been attentive to power imbalances in the workplace in deciding First Amendment disputes. In *NLRB v. Gissel Packing Co.*,[62] the Court upheld restrictions on employer speech during labor organizing to protect employees' rights of association from employer coercion. In distinguishing workplace speech from speech in public forums, the Court explicitly relied on the "economic dependence of the employees on their employers" and the resulting disparity in bargaining power between the two sides. While the First Amendment protects workers' speech rights where they further the broader goals of political participation and workers' right to unionize and bargain collectively, it does not protect speech that interferes with the state's interest in ridding the workplace of sex and race discrimination. The location of harassing speech is significant, but not because the workplace strips citizens of all speech rights. Rather, the context of employment makes women particularly vulnerable to injury because their livelihood is at stake, and it makes the injury collective because it concretely affects women's economic status.

Speech and Collective Action Against Harassment

Second, seeing sexual harassment as a collective injury suggests that workers may seek to engage in collective action to address it, action which requires speech protections. Sexual harassment supports a regime that depends on "women's willingness to capitulate to masculinity without asking questions, without fighting injustice, with complete servility," and that is threatened most by women joining together to topple it.[63] Just as a social justice approach recognizes that employees' freedom of speech is not absolute, so it recognizes that employers' right to restrict speech is not absolute. Prohibiting harassing speech at the workplace is constitutional because this speech inflicts the collective injury of interfering with women's liberty to pursue their vocation and of perpetuating women's unequal status. But banning worker speech might also violate the social justice mandate underlying the First and Fourteenth Amendments. Until recently, for example, federal courts and the EEOC declared that rules requiring employees to speak only English at work presumptively discriminated on the basis of national origin.[64]

In fact, workers may need speech protection to facilitate their collective efforts to transform hostile work environments. Blacks are well aware of the importance of preserving speech rights in the pursuit of social justice, for "[o]ur political tradition has looked to 'the word,' to the moral power of ideas, to change the system when neither the power of the vote nor that of the gun were available."[65] We must not forget that Title VII lawsuits are not the exclusive means for workers to contest discriminatory working conditions.

In "Employer Abuse, Worker Resistance, and the Tort of Intentional Infliction of Emotional Distress," Regina Austin explores ways to facilitate workers' collective action to challenge employer exploitation.[66] I was struck by the prominent role of workers' rebellious speech in her proposals. Austin argues that workers sometimes resist abuse by talking back: "Sassy rhetoric and a sense of style challenge the status quo and liberate the spirit. They are the sort of cultural devices that many workers employ, if not to conquer the oppressions of the workplace, then at least to create moments of resistance and autonomy from employer control."[67] Austin ends by advocating that workers broaden their "vibrant cultural resistance of the workplace" into a "highly visible social movement" that opposes all forms of supervisory harassment, including those not recognized as violations of Title VII.

When women workers are dissatisfied with conventional avenues of redress, such as union representation and Title VII litigation, they have united to contest workplace abuse. Four pioneer tradeswomen in the New York City construction industry, for example, formed Women Electricians and accepted as members any woman in Local 3 of the International Brotherhood of Electrical Workers.[68] Its immediate task was to remove the rampant pornography from job sites, a complaint the male-dominated union had ignored. For defiant workers like Women Electricians and those described by Austin, freedom to speak may be as important as the legal protection against abusive speech. But there is a critical distinction between workers' speech that promotes equality and harassing speech that destroys it.[69]

Conclusion

The collective injury inflicted by sexual harassment stems from sexual harassment's role in preserving women's inferior status in the workforce. Rules that regulate workplace speech inevitably affect power arrangements such as this. Those who defend sexual harassment using the First Amendment would have us believe that to protect workers' freedom to pursue socially beneficial projects we must protect men's freedom to demean women workers with taunts, insults, and pornography that impair their ability to do their jobs. I think we can tell the difference.

Notes

I would like to thank Sara Buehler, Stanford Law School Class of 1998, for her excellent research assistance.

1. Catharine A. MacKinnon, *Sexual Harassment of Working Women: A Case of Sex Discrimination* (1979).

2. Katherine M. Franke, "What's Wrong with Sexual Harassment?" 49 *Stanford Law Review* 691 (1997); Vicki Schultz, "Reconceptualizing Sexual Harassment," 107 *Yale Law Journal* 1683 (1998).

3. MacKinnon, *supra* note 1, at 173.

4. *See, e.g.,* Richard H. Fallon, "Sexual Harassment, Content Neutrality, and the First Amendment Dog that Didn't Bark," 1994 *Supreme Court Review* 1; Frederick Schauer's essay in this volume.

5. *See, e.g.,* Kingsley R. Browne, "Title VII as Censorship: Hostile-Environment Harassment and the First Amendment," 52 *Ohio State Law Journal* 481 (1991); Eugene Volokh, Comment, "Freedom of Speech and Workplace Harassment," 39 *UCLA Law Review* 1791 (1992).

6. *See generally Words That Wound: Critical Race Theory, Assaultive Speech, and the First Amendment* (Mari J. Matsuda et al. eds., 1993); Laura J. Lederer and Richard Delgado, *The Price We Pay: The Case Against Racist Speech, Hate Propaganda, and Pornography* (1995).

7. *See, e.g.,* MacKinnon, *supra* note 1, at 133; *Meritor Savings Bank v. Vinson,* 477 U.S. 57, 67 (1986).

8. *See Daemi v. Church's Fried Chicken, Inc.,* 931 F.2d 1379, 1385 (10th Cir. 1991) ("[E]ven a woman who was never herself the object of sexual harassment might have a Title VII claim if she were forced to work in an atmosphere where such harassment was pervasive").

9. Theresa M. Glomb et al., "Ambient Sexual Harassment: An Integrated Model of Antecedents and Consequences," 71 *Organizational Behavior and Human Decision Processes* 309 (1997).

10. *Id.* at 323.

11. Comments made at Sexual Harassment: A Symposium (Yale Law School, February 28, 1998).

12. *See* Teresa Amott and Julie Mattaei, *Race, Gender, and Work: A Multicultural*

Economic History of Women in the United States (1991); Barbara A. Gutek, *Sex and the Workplace* 22–41 (1985).

13. Schultz, *supra* note 2, at 1691.

14. Elvia R. Arriola, " 'What's the Big Deal?' Women in the New York City Construction Industry and Sexual Harassment Law, 1970–1985," 22 *Columbia Human Rights Law Review* 21, 39 (1990). *See also* Kara Swicher, "Laying Down the Law on Harassment: Court Rulings Spur Firms to Take Preventive Tack," *Washington Post,* February 6, 1994, at H1 (citing survey finding that 40 to 60 percent of women experience sexual harassment at work).

15. Charles R. Lawrence III, "If He Hollers Let Him Go: Regulating Racist Speech on Campus," in *Words that Wound, supra* note 6, at 53, 61.

16. *Stacks v. Southwestern Bell Yellow Pages, Inc.,* 27 F.3d 1316, 1318 (8th Cir. 1994).

17. Schultz, *supra* note 2, at 1711 n.130.

18. *See infra* note 26.

19. *See Corne v. Bausch & Lomb, Inc.,* 390 F. Supp. 161 (D. Ariz. 1975); *Barnes v. Train,* 13 Fair Empl. Prac. Cas. (BNA) 123, 124 (D.D.C. 1974), *reversed sub nom. Barnes v. Costle,* 561 F.2d 1983 (D.C. Cir. 1977).

20. MacKinnon, *supra* note 1, at 133.

21. *Meritor Savings Bank v. Vinson,* 477 U.S. 57, 67 (1986) (quoting *Henson v. City of Dundee,* 682 F.2d 897, 902 (11th Cir. 1982)).

22. 611 F. Supp. 521 (E.D.N.Y. 1985).

23. 863 F.2d 1503 (11th Cir. 1989).

24. 454 F.2d 234 (5th Cir. 1971), *cert. denied,* 406 U.S. 957 (1972).

25. *Id.* at 237–38.

26. Two seminal cases brought by black women are *Williams v. Saxbe,* 413 F. Supp. 654 (D.D.C. 1976), and *Barnes v. Costle,* 561 F.2d 983 (D.C. Cir. 1977). *Williams,* the first decision to hold that sexual harassment was discrimination "based on sex" within the meaning of Title VII, "marked the turning of the tide in favor of women alleging sexual harassment at work." MacKinnon, *supra* note 1, at 60.

27. *See generally* Kimberlé Crenshaw, "Demarginalizing the Intersection of Race and Sex: A Black Feminist Critique of Antidiscrimination Doctrine, Feminist Theory and Antiracist Politics," 1989 *University of Chicago Legal Forum* 139; Peggie R. Smith, "Separate Identitites: Black Women, Work, and Title VII," 14 *Harvard Women's Law Journal* 21 (1991); Judith A. Winston, "Mirror, Mirror on the Wall: Title VII, Section 1981, and Intersection of Race and Gender in the Civil Rights Act of 1990," 79 *California Law Review* 775, 797–800 (1991).

28. *Hicks v. Gates Rubber Co.,* 928 F.2d 966 (10th Cir. 1991).

29. *Torres v. Pisano,* 116 F.3d 625 (2d Cir. 1997).

30. *Braddy v. Florida Department of Labor and Employment Security,* 133 F.3d 797 (11th Cir. 1998).

31. *Stingley v. Arizona,* 796 F. Supp. 424 (D. Ariz. 1992).

32. Kathryn Abrams, "Title VII and the Complex Female Subject," 92 *Michigan Law Review* 2479, 2501 (1994).

33. Kimberlé Crenshaw, "Whose Story Is It, Anyway? Feminist and Antiracist Appropriations of Anita Hill," in *Race-ing Justice, En-gendering Power: Essays on Anita Hill,*

Clarence Thomas, and the Construction of Social Reality 402, 412 (Toni Morrison ed., 1992); Audrey J. Murrell, "Sexual Harassment and Women of Color: Issues, Challenges, and Future Directions," in *Sexual Harassment in the Workplace: Perspectives, Frontiers, and Response Strategies* 51 (Margaret S. Stockdale ed., 1997).

34. Crenshaw, *supra* note 27, at 412.

35. *Quoted in* MacKinnon, *supra* note 1, at 30. *See Munford v. James T. Barnes & Co.*, 441 F. Supp. 459 (E.D. Mich. 1977).

36. *Brooms v. Regal Tube Co.*, 881 F.2d 412, 417 (7th Cir. 1989).

37. *Continental Can v. Minnesota*, 297 N.W.2d 241, 246 (Minn. 1980).

38. Jacqueline Jones, *Labor of Love, Labor of Sorrow: Black Women, Work, and the Family from Slavery to the Present* 113 (1985).

39. Dorothy Roberts, *Killing the Black Body: Race, Reproduction, and the Meaning of Liberty* 29–31 (1997).

40. *Nichols v. Frank*, 42 F.3d 503, 510 (9th Cir. 1994).

41. Roberts, *supra* note 39, at 45–55.

42. Gerda Lerner, *Black Women in White America* 156 (1973).

43. *Quoted in* Paula Giddings, "The Last Taboo," in *Race-ing Justice, En-Gendering Power, supra* note 33, at 441, 454.

44. Amott and Matthaei, *supra* note 12, at 163–64.

45. *See* Schultz, *supra* note 2, at 1720–29.

46. *See generally* Elizabeth M. Iglesias, "Structures of Subordination: Women of Color at the Intersection of Title VII and the NLRA. Not!" 28 *Harvard Civil Rights–Civil Liberties Law Review* 395 (1993).

47. 510 U.S. 17 (1993).

48. *Heim v. Utah*, 8 F.3d 1541, 1546 (10th Cir. 1993).

49. *See* Schultz, *supra* note 2, at 1748–55.

50. *See, e.g.,* Browne, *supra* note 5; Volokh, *supra* note 5. A number of recent cases have struck down restrictions of racist speech for violating the First Amendment. *See, e.g., R.A.V. v. City of St. Paul*, 505 U.S. 377 (1992); *Iota XI Chapter of Sigma Chi Fraternity v. George Mason University*, 993 F.2d 386 (4th Cir. 1993); *Doe v. University of Michigan*, 721 F. Supp. 852 (E.D. Mich. 1989).

51. Anita Bernstein, "Treating Sexual Harassment with Respect," 111 *Harvard Law Review* 445, 468 (1997). *See also* Nancy Ehrenreich, "Pluralist Myths and Powerless Men: The Ideology of Reasonableness in Sexual Harassment Law," 99 *Yale Law Journal* 1177 (1990) (arguing that the concepts of freedom and security are inevitably relational).

52. *See, e.g.,* Alexander Meiklejohn, *Political Freedom: The Constitutional Powers of the People* (Greenwood Press ed. 1979) (1960); Cass Sunstein, *Democracy and the Problem of Free Speech* (1995); Owen M. Fiss, "Free Speech and Social Structure," 71 *Iowa Law Review* 1405 (1986).

53. J. M. Balkin, "Some Realism About Pluralism: Legal Realist Approaches to the First Amendment," 1990 *Duke Law Journal* 375, 385.

54. *See* Iglesias, *supra* note 46, at 396–97.

55. Amy Horton, Comment, "Of Supervision, Centerfolds, and Censorship: Sexual Harassment, First Amendment, and the Contours of Title VII," 46 *University of Miami Law Review* 403, 416 (1991).

56. Fallon, *supra* note 4, at 21.

57. *See* Olivia Young, "A Weapon to Weaken: Pornography in the Workplace," in Lederer and Delgado, *supra* note 6, at 18.

58. 760 F. Supp. 1486, 1494 (M.D. Fla. 1991).

59. *See, e.g.,* Mary Becker, "How Free is Speech at Work?" 29 *University of California at Davis Law Review* 815, 862 (1996) ("There is no such thing as free speech in private employment"). *But see* Cynthia L. Estlund, "Freedom of Expression in the Workplace and the Problem of Discriminatory Harassment," 75 *Texas Law Review* 687 (1997) (developing a conception of the workplace as a "satellite forum for public discourse").

60. Horton, *supra* note 55, at 431.

61. *Id.* at 428–29; Fallon, *supra* note 4, at 36.

62. 395 U.S. 575 (1969).

63. Frances K. Conley, *Walking Out on the Boys* 106 (1998).

64. *See* EEOC Guidelines on Discrimination Because of National Origin, 29 C.F.R. 1606.7(a), (b) (1997); *Gutierrez v. Municipal Court*, 838 F.2d 1031 (9th Cir. 1988).

65. Lawrence, *supra* note 15, at 56.

66. Regina Austin, "Employer Abuse, Worker Resistance, and the Tort of Intentional Infliction of Emotional Distress," 41 *Stanford Law Review* 1 (1988).

67. *Id.* at 2–3.

68. *See* Arriola, *supra* note 14, at 58.

69. I am grateful to Catharine MacKinnon for suggesting this distinction.

23

Sexual Harassment and the First Amendment

ROBERT POST

There is growing apprehension of possible tensions between the First Amendment and Title VII's prohibition of sexual harassment.[1] Often claims of sexual harassment in the workplace depend entirely upon communicative behavior, and it is uncertain how such claims ought analytically to be reconciled with a jurisprudence that protects freedom of speech.

The issue was the subject of a panel discussion at the 1998 annual meeting of the American Association of Law Schools. Eugene Volokh, a noted scholar in the area, argued that Title VII's ban on sexual harassment imposed repressive legal regulation upon expression that would otherwise plainly merit constitutional protection, like Goya's painting *Naked Maja*.[2] He concluded his remarks with the passionate plea that the constitutionality of such regulation not be determined merely by characterization, by tendentiously reclassifying as conduct that which would otherwise plainly be deemed protected speech.

Catharine MacKinnon, who was also on the panel, responded to Volokh that discriminatory acts, even if perpetrated through words and pictures, had not heretofore been deemed protected by the First Amendment. She offered the example of the sign: "Whites Only."[3] She concluded with an equally passionate plea to the effect that constitutional analysis of such discrimination not be preempted by mere characterization, by tendentiously reclassifying as protected speech what would otherwise plainly be deemed discriminatory acts.

MacKinnon argued that words and pictures that caused the harm of discrimination ought to be regulated by the law, whether the harm occurred inside or outside the workplace. In contrast, Volokh contended that indecent and pornographic speech that merited First Amendment protection outside the workplace should not lose that protection inside the workplace. Whereas MacKinnon condemned pornographic words and pictures as "discrimination on the basis of sex" in both venues,[4] and hence suggested that Judge Easterbrook's decision in *American Booksellers Association v. Hudnut*[5] striking down legal controls over nonobscene but pornographic books and movies was inconsistent with sexual harassment law, Volokh urged that such communication be safeguarded as constitutionally protected speech in both venues.

I reproduce this fascinating exchange to illustrate the importance of characterization in First Amendment jurisprudence. This jurisprudence applies to human action that is characterized as "speech."[6] But unfortunately we have only crude doctrinal and theoretical tools for determining when human action should be characterized in this way.[7] The problem is especially acute when we seek to determine the application of the First Amendment to behavior like sexual harassment that, as Fred Schauer points out in this volume,[8] have never before been subject to constitutional oversight.

In this brief essay, I shall offer a few preliminary observations about the question of constitutional characterization. I shall stake out a position that differs from the one premise upon which commentators as diverse and as eminent as Catharine MacKinnon and Eugene Volokh seem to agree: that the context of the workplace ought not to alter the constitutional characterization of speech. I shall argue, to the contrary, that the process of constitutional characterization that underlies First Amendment analysis is always deeply dependent upon social context, so that the very same communication may sometimes merit constitutional protection in one context, but not in another.

The commonly held view that identical communicative content must receive identical constitutional characterization ultimately rests on the notion that constitutional value extends to meaning, abstractly considered, rather than to the social matrix within which meaning is embedded. I have argued elsewhere that this view is fundamentally misguided.[9] Consider, for example, the sentence: "Support Bill Clinton." If written on a political sign in front of a house, the sentence would undoubtedly be seen as *speech* within the shelter of the First Amendment. But, if carved into the vinyl of a bus seat, the sentence would be deemed merely a constitutionally unprotected *act* of vandalism.[10] The content of the sentence remains unchanged, but its constitutional characterization is clearly both determinative and context-dependent. To usefully understand the debate between Volokh and MacKinnon, therefore, we must

begin to explore this influential but analytically undeveloped terrain of constitutional characterization.

Let us use the term "communication" to refer to the general processes by
which meaning is expressed and apprehended in social life. Understood in this
way, of course, communication is everywhere. The clothes I wear, my posture
at a meeting, and my choice of wine for dinner all convey meaning; they are
instances of communication. We could in fact go so far as to say that all human
action conveys intention and (therefore) meaning, and is for this reason also
communicative. In this broad sense, communication can be seen as the essence
of human sociality.

It is for this reason implausible to imagine that the First Amendment could
coherently regard all communication in the same way, because no account of
the First Amendment could possibly be broad enough to encompass all human
action. Not surprisingly, therefore, our First Amendment does not attempt to
embrace all communication.[11] In fact, the First Amendment does not even
attempt to protect all "communication" that occurs through the explicit use of
words and language.[12]

Consider, for example, the question of professional malpractice. Professional malpractice often occurs through language, both spoken and written. A
lawyer can author a negligent opinion, costing her client millions of dollars; a
doctor can offer reckless advice, endangering the life of his patient. In analyzing these questions, we do not ordinarily bring First Amendment analysis to
bear.[13] We do not say that "[t]he First Amendment recognizes no such thing as
a 'false' idea"[14] in the context of professional-client relationships, nor do we
impose severe restraints on content-based regulation of such relationships. If
we were to extend the usual panoply of First Amendment protections to the
law of professional malpractice, that law would cease to be recognizable.

This is because "the rigorous review that the First Amendment generally
demands"[15] presupposes a certain picture of social reality.[16] It imagines a
social context in which speakers and their audiences are mutually independent, so that audiences are capable autonomously of assessing the value of
speakers' communications. Paradigmatic of this independence is the relationship that the First Amendment postulates between a newspaper like the *New
York Times* and its readers.

This relationship is understood as part of a domain of public discourse in
which democratic citizens collectively use communication to determine their
common fate.[17] Because public discourse is the medium through which the
democratic enterprise of autonomous self-government is conducted, the First
Amendment postulates that within public discourse speakers and audiences

will be conceptualized as mutually independent.[18] The presumption of autonomy is seen as necessary for the democratic enterprise.[19] Traditional First Amendment doctrine embodies a fundamentally political function, for it enables the First Amendment to serve as "the guardian of our democracy."[20]

We can thus explain the failure to apply the usual "rigorous" First Amendment protection to communications between professionals and clients on the ground that we do not view such communications as within the domain of public discourse.[21] But this conclusion is inseparable from the fact that we do not deem the professional-client relationship as one of arm's-length independence, analogous to that which the First Amendment postulates between the *New York Times* and its readers.[22] To the contrary, we typically characterize clients as dependent upon the superior expertise of professionals, and we use the law to protect clients' legitimate reliance interests. This use of law is plainly incompatible with traditional First Amendment protections for public discourse, which are precisely designed to safeguard communicative exchange from legally imposed conceptions of appropriate and inappropriate deployments of communicative power.

First Amendment protections of public discourse and legal regulations of professional malpractice thus each presuppose a distinct image of the legal subject. The former imagines speakers and their audiences as autonomous and self-determining; the latter imagines clients as disempowered and dependent upon professionals. Both of these images are of course *ascriptive*. In the messy complexity of the real world, readers will in fact be more or less dependent upon the *New York Times* (and accordingly may or may not suffer the damage required by the presuppositions of the First Amendment to be legally disregarded). Clients will be more or less dependent upon professionals (and accordingly may or may not suffer the damage attributed to them by legal regulations of malpractice). In both cases, however, the complexity of the actual world will be transmuted within legal doctrine into an ideal image of social relationships so that the law can be arranged to facilitate the performance of specific social functions.

We might call this simplification "legal ascription." The process of legal ascription is well illustrated by the case of *Winter v. G. P. Putnam's Sons*,[23] in which plaintiffs alleged that they were critically injured when they hunted and cooked wild mushrooms in reliance upon the *Encyclopedia of Mushrooms*. Plaintiffs claimed that the *Encyclopedia* contained inaccurate information regarding deadly species of mushrooms, and they argued that the *Encyclopedia*'s publisher should therefore be liable under theories of strict product liability and negligence. The Ninth Circuit unanimously held that the First Amendment precluded such liability. The Court explained that any such legal control would interfere with "the unfettered exchange of ideas"[24] which the Constitution protects.

This image of an "unfettered exchange of ideas" invokes the kind of dialogue among independent persons that we ascribe to participants in public discourse. But the plaintiffs in *Winter* were precisely alleging that this independence did not apply to them. Their argument was that the law ought to recognize and protect the relationship of dependence that actually characterized their reliance upon a publication like the *Encyclopedia*, which purported accurately to compile and present factual information. Plaintiffs cited cases in which courts characterized aeronautical charts as products, rather than as speech, and in which courts therefore crafted legal rules so as to protect the dependence of pilots upon such charts, even though the charts were explicitly and essentially acts of communication.[25]

In effect, then, *Winter* rejected the plaintiffs' argument by analogizing the *Encyclopedia of Mushrooms* to the *New York Times* rather than to an aeronautical chart. Regardless of whether one believes that *Winter* reached the correct or incorrect conclusion on this question, the deeper point is that *Winter* was required to presuppose *some* image of the social relationship between the *Encyclopedia* and its audience, no matter which way it would ultimately decide the case. If *Winter* imagined that readers of the *Encyclopedia* were (or ought to be) engaged in an independent exchange of ideas, and hence autonomous participants in public discourse, it would apply, as it did, strict rules of First Amendment doctrine designed to safeguard this independence. But if it imagined that readers were (or ought to be) dependent upon the *Encyclopedia*, it would apply the doctrines of product liability law designed to protect consumers' reliance interests. Either way, *Winter* could not avoid engaging in a process of legal ascription.

Winter illustrates why the constitutional characterization of communication depends upon social context. Whether or not communication is regarded as "speech" for purposes of the First Amendment turns on the image of the legal subject that the law projects into particular social circumstances. This projection always implicitly embodies a fundamentally normative account of pertinent social relationships. Constitutional characterization is driven by this normative account.

There are no clear guidelines for this task of constitutional characterization. The text of the First Amendment will not help a court determine the proper understanding of the relationship between the *Encyclopedia of Mushrooms* and its readers. Neither will the intent of the Framers. Although we do have a strong democratic tradition that paradigmatically understands certain kinds of speech, like the *New York Times* or political debate, as within the boundaries of public discourse,[26] this tradition will not be of much assistance in a fine-grained and particular case like *Winter*. And yet, as *Winter* also illustrates, all First Amendment reasoning depends upon antecedent acts of characterization, so that the process of ascription cannot be evaded, however methodologically difficult it may be.

In recent years, the difficulties of this process have been compounded. First Amendment doctrine was originally articulated through a series of cases that involved the regulation of speech located unambiguously within the domain of public discourse. First Amendment doctrine accordingly developed to meet the functional requirements of that domain. But as the Supreme Court began to understand itself as protecting "speech" abstractly considered,[27] litigants responded by pressing claims for the constitutional protection of communication not previously understood as within public discourse.

This is the dynamic that underlies recent arguments to extend constitutional protections to communications within the workplace that are prohibited by Title VII as sexually harassing. While these arguments make the fact of constitutional characterization more visible, they also expose more sharply the formidable methodological inadequacy that envelops our understanding of such characterization. To move beyond the debate between MacKinnon and Volokh, we must engage the shapeless but fundamental issues involving the constitutional construction of social relationships.

Those who most forcefully challenge the constitutionality of Title VII harassment law have sometimes assumed that First Amendment doctrines fashioned for the protection of public discourse unproblematically apply to the workplace.[28] They have thus brought to bear standard First Amendment rules forbidding vague laws, laws regulating offensive speech, or laws discriminating on the basis of content.[29] But if the analysis of the first part of this essay is correct, these doctrines carry within them a certain picture of independent legal subjects, and the constitutionally antecedent question is whether this picture has application to the social context regulated by Title VII.

The question is complicated, because the process of constitutional characterization does not reduce to a dichotomous opposition between speech and nonspeech, between, so to speak, public discourse and aeronautical charts. The Constitution can instead assign various social functions to social relations, and it can therefore establish various First Amendment "doctrines" designed to fulfill these different functions.

The fundamental constitutional inquiry is how the Constitution ought to conceive social relationships in the workplace. This inquiry does not begin with a clean slate, for Title VII itself carries within it presuppositions about how workers ought legally to be regarded. The most precise statement of the First Amendment question, therefore, is how Title VII's characterization of the workplace ought to be evaluated by the Constitution.

In this short essay I can advance only a few preliminary thoughts. I have in other work identified three prominent and distinct ways in which American constitutional law has regarded social relationships. These may be conceived as "ideal types." Each corresponds to a particular social practice that carries within it a unique social function. Without in the least claiming that these forms of social practice are exhaustive, I suggest that they might offer a useful place to begin thinking about the relationship between Title VII and First Amendment law.

One kind of social practice that is conspicuous in our constitutional law is that of management.[30] Management arranges social relationships according to the logic of instrumental rationality. The state creates managerial domains when it establishes organizations designed to achieve specified ends. Within these domains, the state arranges resources, including persons and the speech of persons, so as to accomplish its objectives. The First Amendment has tended to accept the state's figuration of persons within managerial domains as objects whose speech can be regulated so long as it is instrumentally rational to do so.[31] Thus the speech of soldiers can be regulated so long as it is necessary for the successful functioning of the military; the speech of students within state schools can be regulated so long as it is necessary for the attainment of educational objectives; and so on.

Sexual harassment law, however, is neither defined nor applied in this instrumental way. It is true that the Supreme Court has observed that sexually harassing speech "can and often will detract from employees' job performance, discourage employees from remaining on the job, or keep them from advancing in their careers."[32] But the Court has also explicitly said that the prohibitions of Title VII are not circumscribed by such managerial considerations. At the heart of Title VII lies instead a strong commitment to a "broad rule of workplace equality"[33] that is conceptually independent of the question of whether the instrumental functioning of the workplace has been impaired.[34]

Sexual harassment law understands itself as prohibiting "a hostile or abusive work environment,"[35] which it defines in moral terms that circle around notions of "intimidation, ridicule, and insult."[36] Recognizable in this aspiration is the legal creation of a distinct social structure, which I have elsewhere called that of "community."[37] Community is a form of social organization in which the character of persons is established through socialization into common social norms. These norms reciprocally constitute both personal and communal identity. They define the forms of respect and dignity to which persons within a given community are entitled.

Violation of the respect and dignity defined by community norms is perceived as demeaning and harmful. Regarded from the perspective of community, persons are "normalized agents," because they are seen as both independent and yet disciplined by the standards that are understood to comprise normal human sociality. That is why, for example, the law of torts can hold individuals accountable to a "reasonable person" standard, even though this standard is not written down or ever made explicit. The "reasonable person" standard polices the norms of a community that the law simply assumes are socialized into the identities of all normal persons.

Those aspects of sexual harassment law that are constitutionally controversial — that do not involve explicit discrimination or outright quid pro quo arrangements — prohibit speech that is "both objectively and subjectively offensive,"[38] and that therefore injures women by violating the community norms that constitute their dignity.[39] Title VII thus imagines itself as enforcing the norms of a particular moral community, and it postulates workers as fully embedded within that moral community. Sexual harassment law imposes liability when violations of the norms of this community are so severe and asymmetrical as to constitute "*discrimin[ation] . . . because of . . . sex.*"[40]

Analytically, therefore, Title VII enforces two distinct norms, corresponding to the values of equality and of respect.[41] The norm of respect is most directly protected by the so-called "dignitary torts," which impose liability for defamation, invasion of privacy, or intentional infliction of emotional distress.[42] Some have accordingly proposed that invasions of respect within the workplace should be regulated by the dignitary torts rather than by the law of sexual harassment.[43] But this is to miss the point that sexual harassment law regulates invasions of respect that cumulatively impair equality of opportunity, which leads sexual harassment law to have a significantly different focus than the dignitary torts.

Insofar as the law of sexual harassment turns on violations of the norms that constitute respect, however, it appears to raise some of the same First Amendment concerns as do the dignitary torts. Although at one time the abusive communication regulated by these torts was classified as conduct, as "aggression and personal assault"[44] rather than as speech, this characterization was reversed by *New York Times v. Sullivan*[45] and its progeny, which sharply restricted the enforcement of these torts within public discourse. The theory of these cases was that public discourse ought to correspond to a third form of social practice, which I have elsewhere called "democracy."[46]

The function of democracy is to create a social space in which autonomous citizens can choose the nature of the moral community they wish to inhabit. Contemporary First Amendment law imagines public discourse as the site of that space. Because dignitary torts construct persons as already embedded within a particular moral community, they conceive individuals as already endowed with an identity that must be legally protected, rather than as engaged in the project of constructing new and different identities. By imposing the requirements of a particular identity, instead of maintaining a neutral and open space for the development of new identities, the dignitary torts regulate persons in ways that are inconsistent with the autonomous citizenship required by public discourse.

That is why the First Amendment has been interpreted virtually to suspend the enforcement of the dignitary torts within public discourse. The First Amendment has not, however, been interpreted completely to prohibit the enforcement of these torts. Thus, for example, although the First Amendment has been interpreted to prohibit the state from holding Larry Flynt liable for publishing an outrageous attack on Jerry Falwell's relationship to his mother in the pages of *Hustler*, it is doubtful that the state would be prevented from holding Flynt liable for privately mailing exactly the same attack to Jerry Falwell's mother.[47]

For analogous reasons, the First Amendment has not heretofore been interpreted to suspend the enforcement of the dignitary torts within the workplace.[48] That is because the workplace has constitutionally been understood as a site of community, rather than democracy. We might thus interpret those who wish to use the First Amendment to circumscribe sexual harassment law as ultimately defending the proposition that normalized agency is not, from a constitutional point of view, an entirely acceptable characterization of workers, because the American workplace should also be seen as a site of autonomous political self-construction, analogous to public discourse.[49]

There is much that can be said in favor of this position. Most persons spend large portions of their lives within the workplace, and in this country the ideal of industrial democracy has deep roots. First Amendment limits on Title VII's prohibitions on sexual harassment can thus be defended by invoking the workplace "as a kind of laboratory of diversity in which the laws of democratic engagement can be learned and practiced."[50] Although it is not plausible to imagine that speech within the workplace is flatly equivalent to public discourse, for employees are far too interdependent and vulnerable,[51] it is nevertheless possible to conceive the workplace as "a 'satellite domain' of public discourse"[52] in which constitutional law must recognize a unique and idiosyncratic balance between normalized and autonomous agency.

This suggests that the current debate over the application of the First Amendment to sexual harassment law might best be interpreted as turning on a disagreement about how the social practice of the workplace ought constitutionally to be characterized. If the workplace is viewed as a site of community, in which social norms can be fully and unproblematically enforced, harassing speech can be characterized as "abusive conduct" and regulated in ways that the First Amendment currently allows the dignitary torts to be enforced outside of the domain of public discourse. But if the workplace is viewed as an arena of political self-constitution, in which the reach of community norms is circumscribed by the value of autonomy, harassing speech should instead be seen as constitutionally protected expression, as for example it is when published in the pages of nationally distributed magazines.[53]

The issue is particularly difficult because of the very prominence of the workplace in the lives of most persons. This prominence accentuates the importance of protecting workers from oppressive regulation. But it also has other, contrary implications. As Frank Michelman has observed, democracy is "a demanding normative idea, an idea with content."[54] Democracy is itself a community norm that, like all community norms, must be reproduced by means of socialization and institutionalization.[55] That is why democratic education is necessary in order to sustain democracy.[56]

Democratic education, however, is not merely a matter of high school classes on civic government. Democratic education involves socialization into habits and manners of civility, tolerance, and equality, which might be regarded as preconditions for successful democratic deliberation and governance. The very prominence of the workplace makes it a prime location for the transmission and instauration of these norms. Thus Title VII might be seen as articulating and enforcing norms of gender equality, civility, and tolerance required by democratic citizenship itself. At the same time, however, democratic citizenship, if it is to exemplify self-governance, must allow citizens to determine for themselves the norms that define democratic citizenship. To constrain citizens to perform any particular community norms, in contexts in which they are meant autonomously to deliberate about what norms they might wish to establish, is to contradict the very premises of self-determination.

That is why democracy has the paradoxical property of suspending, in the name of autonomy, legal enforcement of the very norms necessary for the practice of democratic legitimacy.[57] Our inquiry, then, can be reframed as an exploration of the extent to which the workplace ought to be conceived as a place for the reproduction of democratic values, and the extent to which it ought to be seen as a site for the enactment of those values. Title VII *reproduces* democratic values by enforcing norms of respect and equality. But citizens *enact* democratic values by determining what they wish to become, while maintaining the space for future decisions free from the foreclosure of legal compulsion. The tension evident in the current debate over the relationship of the First Amendment to sexual harassment law is a measure of the inconsistency between these two aspirations.

Although this is not the venue in which to resolve such a profound conflict, it might nevertheless be appropriate to raise two further questions concerning the constitutional implications of using the First Amendment to protect individual autonomy within the workplace. The first concerns the relationship between constitutional values and private power. First Amendment doctrine normally imagines the state acting upon citizens by exercising direct legal control over speech. It prosecutes persons for their expression, or it makes them liable in tort, or it enjoins them. My discussion so far has followed this convention, for I have been writing as if Title VII directly regulates workers' speech. But of course this is not accurate.

Title VII imposes liability upon employers, who are then expected to meet their legal obligations by using their private power to control workers' speech.[58] Thus Title VII itself figures the workplace as a site in which workers are subject to the massive and comprehensive exercise of private power. In such circumstances, we must inquire into the meaning of constitutionally envisioning workers as either normalized agents or as autonomous citizens. In the face of such overwhelming private mastery, what difference might constitutional characterization actually make? Workers will in any event remain bound by the largely unregulated instrumental rationality of employers.

First Amendment doctrine usually ignores such imbalances of private power. So, for example, *American Booksellers Association v. Hudnut*[59] essentially held that private imbalances of sexual power were insufficient to override the First Amendment's presumption that persons within public discourse were to be regarded as autonomous. The justification for this strong presumption was that remedying such imbalances in the ways required by the Indianapolis antipornography law would impose legal controls inconsistent with the autonomy required for democratic self-constitution.[60]

Although *Hudnut*'s conclusion represents mainstream First Amendment jurisprudence, we must nevertheless distinguish between deliberate indifference to imbalances of private power within public discourse, and such indifference within the context of the workplace. Public discourse is the arena in which our collective democratic will is constructed, so the denial of autonomy amounts *pro tanto* to a denial of the scope of democratic self-determination. By contrast, not only are imbalances of private power far more salient within the workplace, but speech within the workplace has been thought to bear a much more attenuated connection to the construction of a democratic will.

Those who wish to project the constitutional value of democratic autonomy into the workplace will thus have to face the formidable intellectual task of theorizing exactly how this value ought to intersect with the exercise of private power. I suspect, for example, that when carefully examined this value may prove to have implications that go beyond workers' speech and affect the actual distribution of power in the workplace. To hold that Title VII is limited by the First Amendment may therefore be to imply that other aspects of the extensive legal regulations that permeate the workplace ought also to be limited by First Amendment concerns in ways that foster industrial democracy.

The second issue I wish to raise concerns the relationship between the constitutional value of democratic autonomy and that of equality. It should be remembered that Title VII enforces norms of civility in order to realize the legislatively more fundamental antidiscrimination norm of equality. Although the question of how this norm ought to relate to the enactment of democratic autonomy has been much discussed within recent academic literature, courts have consistently held that within public discourse the antidiscrimination norm of equality should be subordinated to the value of democratic autonomy. I have argued elsewhere that this subordination ought to be understood as ultimately founded upon a practical, rather than theoretical, judgment.[61] The considerations pertinent to this judgment, however, seem to me significantly different in the workplace than in public discourse.

First, workplace speech is by hypothesis distinct from public discourse, and it therefore presents the value of democracy in a less urgent form. The deeper and as yet unanalyzed question is, of course, exactly how the value of democracy is thought constitutionally to be present in workplace speech. But so long as some distinction exists between workplace speech and public discourse, it is clear that the constitutional value of democratic autonomy will have less constitutional force in the former.

Second, the value of equality presents stronger constitutional claims within the context of the workplace than within the context of public discourse. Constitutional protections for autonomy ultimately stem from a commitment to democratic legitimacy. Yet autonomy is only a necessary, not a sufficient, condition for such legitimacy. A stable democratic state may well also require widespread access to other fundamental social goods, most particularly those associated with work. Certainly a modern society would face a crisis of democratic confidence if the kinds of male dominance that Title VII is designed to check were effectively to exclude women from the workforce.

In the context of Title VII, therefore, equality has roots in the same constitutional value of democratic legitimacy as does democratic autonomy. Constitutional difficulties not infrequently arise because the stringent requirements of ascriptive autonomy imposed by contemporary First Amendment doctrine on public discourse may be inconsistent with competing democratic values, like those of equality. The tendency of First Amendment jurisprudence narrowly to define boundaries of public discourse, so as to confine its scope and reach, can in fact be interpreted as an effort to minimize this tension.[62]

Third, if the state were to censor public discourse in the name of equality, those censored would be excluded *pro tanto* from the process of collective democratic will-formation. Within public discourse, therefore, equality and democratic autonomy stand in a zero-sum relation, so that legislation to advance equality by censoring speech necessarily delimits democratic autonomy.[63] But because workplace speech is by hypothesis distinct from public discourse, censorship of workplace speech in the name of equality does not necessarily subtract from the process of collective democratic will-formation, and, in fact, such censorship may positively promote the underlying value of democratic legitimacy. Equality and democratic autonomy in the workplace thus do not stand in the same zero-sum relationship as they do within public discourse.

It follows from these considerations that even if the value of democratic autonomy were to be imported into the workplace, the relationship between democratic autonomy and equality must be worked through in ways that are entirely distinct from the relationship between these two values that has emerged from received First Amendment doctrine, which has developed largely within the context of public discourse.

The implication of these brief remarks is that the emerging debate about the role of the First Amendment in Title VII sexual harassment litigation holds the potential for useful and illuminating inquiry into a number of significant questions. The constitutional nature of the American workplace has long been a topic requiring more attention than it has received. The relationship of constitutional values to private power has traditionally been deeply undertheorized. And, finally, the subtle and myriad ways in which the values of autonomy and equality intertwine, reinforce, and repel each other within our constitutional jurisprudence needs far more penetrating explication than it has so far received. This essay is directed toward placing these issues at the center of what will hopefully become a constructive dialogue about the relationship between sexual harassment law and the First Amendment, a dialogue that has to date displayed a discouraging tendency to turn unproductive and formal.

Notes

I am very grateful for the constructive critiques of Richard Fallon, Catharine MacKinnon, Reva Siegel, and Eugene Volokh, which have greatly improved this chapter.

1. *See, e.g., DeAngelis v. El Paso Municipal Police Officers Association,* 51 F.3d 591 (5th Cir.), *cert. denied,* 516 U.S. 974 (1995); *Williams v. New York City Police Department,* 1997 U.S. Dist. LEXIS 13429 (S.D.N.Y. September 5, 1997). For recent articles on the subject, *see* Kingsley R. Browne, "Title VII as Censorship: Hostile-Environment Harassment and the First Amendment," 51 *Ohio State Law Journal* 481 (1991); Deborah Epstein, "Can a 'Dumb Ass Woman' Achieve Equality in the Workplace? Running the Gauntlet of Hostile Environment Harassing Speech," 84 *Georgetown Law Journal* 399 (1996); Cynthia L. Estlund, "Freedom of Speech in the Workplace and the Problem of Discriminatory Harassment," 75 *Texas Law Review* 687 (1997); Richard H. Fallon, Jr., "Sexual Harassment, Content Neutrality, and the First Amendment Dog That Didn't Bark," 1994 *Supreme Court Review* 1; Suzanne Sangree, "Title VII Prohibitions Against Hostile Environment Sexual Harassment and the First Amendment: No Collision in Sight," 47 *Rutgers Law Review* 461 (1995); Nadine Strossen, "Regulating Workplace Sexual Harassment and Upholding the First Amendment: Avoiding a Collision," 37 *Villanova Law Review* 757 (1992); Eugene Volokh, "Freedom of Speech and Workplace Harassment," 39 *UCLA Law Review* 1791 (1992). There is even a web site on the subject. *See* Eugene Volokh, *Freedom of Speech vs. Workplace Harassment Law — A Growing Conflict http://www.law.ucla.edu/faculty/volokh* (visited July 17, 2000).

2. *See* Eugene Volokh, "What Speech Does 'Hostile Work Environment' Harassment Law Restrict?" 85 *Georgetown Law Journal* 627, 642 (1997).

3. *See* Catharine A. MacKinnon, *Only Words* 12–13 (1993). *See also* Charles A. Sullivan, "Accounting for *Price Waterhouse:* Proving Disparate Treatment Under Title VII," 56 *Brooklyn Law Review* 1107, 1122 n.64 (1991).

4. *See In Harm's Way: The Pornography Civil Rights Hearings* 41 (Catharine A. MacKinnon and Andrea Dworkin eds., 1997) (testimony of Catharine A. MacKinnon). *See also* MacKinnon, supra note 3, 33; Catharine A. MacKinnon, "Pornography Left and Right," 30 *Harvard Civil Rights–Civil Liberties Law Review,* 143, 167 (1995).

5. 771 F.2d 323 (7th Cir. 1985), *affirmed,* 475 U.S. 1001 (1986).

6. Frederick Schauer, "Categories and the First Amendment: A Play in Three Acts," 34 *Vanderbilt Law Review* 265, 267 (1981); Robert Post, "Encryption Source Code and the First Amendment," 15 *Berkeley Technology Law Journal* 713, 714 (2000). First Amendment review is also triggered by government actions that serve interests which are constitutionally suspicious.

7. *See* Robert Post, "Recuperating First Amendment Doctrine," 47 *Stanford Law Review* 1249, 1250–60, 1273–77 (1995).

8. See Frederick Schauer, "The Speech-ing of Sexual Harassment," this volume.

9. *See* Post, "Recuperating," *supra* note 7.

10. For a discussion of this and other similar examples, *see id.* at 1252–54.

11. The opposite conclusion would require First Amendment supervision of virtually every restriction of human action, and that in turn would either impossibly entangle government regulation in constitutional oversight or dilute the substance of the amend-

ment so disproportionately as to make it meaningless as a restriction on government regulation. Dividing human action between "protected speech" and "unprotected behavior," even though both are equally communicative, is thus a necessary First Amendment strategy.

12. This point is illustrated by the example in text of the sentence "Support Bill Clinton" carved into a bus seat. For other examples, *see* Post, *supra* note 7, at 1251–54.

13. *See, e.g., Togstad v. Vesely, Otto, Miller & Keefe,* 291 N.W.2d 686 (Minn. 1980); *Carson v. City of Beloit,* 145 N.W.2d 112 (Wisc. 1966).

14. *Hustler Magazine v. Falwell,* 485 U.S. 46, 51 (1988).

15. *44 Liquormart, Inc. v. Rhode Island,* 517 U.S. 484, 501 (1996) (Stevens, J.).

16. *See* Robert Post, "The Constitutional Status of Commercial Speech," 48 *UCLA Law Review* 1, 46–50 (2000) [hereinafter "Commercial Speech"].

17. *See, e.g.,* Robert Post, "Equality and Autonomy in First Amendment Jurisprudence," 95 *Michigan Law Review* 1517 (1997) [hereinafter "Equality"].

18. Robert Post, "Between Democracy and Community: The Legal Constitution of Social Form," in 35 *Democratic Community: NOMOS* 163–90 (1993) [hereinafter "Democratic Community"].

19. *See* Robert Post, "Meiklejohn's Mistake: Individual Autonomy and the Reform of Public Discourse," 64 *Colorado Law Review* 1109 (1993).

20. *Brown v. Harlage,* 456 U.S. 45, 59 (1982). On the relationship between the rule that "[t]he First Amendment recognizes no such thing as a 'false' idea" and public discourse, *see* Robert Post, "The Constitutional Concept of Public Discourse: Outrageous Opinion, Democratic Deliberation, and *Hustler Magazine v. Falwell,*" 103 *Harvard Law Review* 601, 626–66 (1990) [hereinafter "Constitutional Concept"]. On the relationship between the First Amendment's disfavoring of content-based regulation and public discourse, *see* Robert C. Post, "Racist Speech, Democracy, and the First Amendment," 32 *William and Mary Law Review* 267, 290–93 (1990) [hereinafter "Racist Speech"]; Post, "Recuperating," *supra* note 7, at 1277–79.

21. *See* Robert Post, "Subsidized Speech," 106 *Yale Law Journal* 151, 174 (1996).

22. Post, "Commercial Speech," *supra* note 16, at 20–25.

23. 938 F.2d 1033 (9th Cir. 1991).

24. *Id.* at 1035.

25. *See, e.g., Brocklesby v. United States,* 767 F.2d 1288, 1294–95 (9th Cir. 1985), *cert. denied,* 474 U.S. 1101 (1986); *Saloomey v. Jeppesen & Co.,* 707 F.2d 671, 676–77 (2d Cir. 1983); *Aetna Casualty & Surety Co. v. Jeppesen & Co.,* 642 F.2d 339, 342–43 (9th Cir. 1981).

26. *See* Jürgen Habermas, *The Structural Transformation of the Public Sphere: An Inquiry into a Category of Bourgeois Society* (Thomas Burger trans., MIT Press 1991); Post, "Constitutional Concept," *supra* note 20, at 667–84.

27. *See* Post, "Recuperating," *supra* note 7.

28. *See, e.g.,* Browne, *supra* note 1.

29. For an excellent discussion of why these standards might not apply to the workplace, *see* Fallon, *supra* note 1.

30. *See* Robert Post, *Constitutional Domains: Democracy, Community, Management* 4–6 (1995) [hereinafter *Constitutional Domains*].

31. *See id.* at 199–267.

32. *Harris v. Forklift Systems, Inc.*, 510 U.S. 17, 22 (1993).

33. *Id.*

34. I am not now referring to the regulation of hate speech within public universities, which in my judgment must be analyzed on a managerial model. When state universities are not functioning as employers, but as educators, they ought to be able to restrict speech as necessary in order to achieve the goal of education. Conversely, they ought not to be able to regulate student and faculty speech in ways that are contrary to that goal. At the heart of the recent controversy over the regulation of hate speech within state universities, therefore, lies the deeper constitutional issue of the function of public higher education. *See* Post, "Racist Speech," *supra* note 20, at 317–25.

35. *Meritor Savings Bank v. Vinson*, 477 U.S. 57, 66 (1986).

36. *Id.* at 65.

37. Post, *Constitutional Domains, supra* note 30, at 3–4.

38. *Faragher v. City of Boca Raton*, 524 U.S. 775, 787 (1998).

39. Certainly there can be no sharp or logical distinction between the prohibition of quid pro quo arrangements and other aspects of sexual harassment law, if only because violations of dignity can sometimes be used as the price for refusing a quid pro quo arrangement.

40. *Oncale v. Sundowner Offshore Services, Inc.*, 523 U.S. 75, 79 (1998). Title VII does not merely impose "a general civility code," *id.*, because violations of civility are by themselves insufficient to justify liability. The violations must also amount to discrimination.

41. Title VII's enforcement of the equality norm can sometimes assume managerial aspects, *see* Robert Post, "Legal Concepts and Applied Social Research Concepts: Translation Problems," in *The Use/Nonuse/Misuse of Applied Social Research in the Courts* (J. Saks and C. H. Baron eds., 1980), but this phenomenon is largely irrelevant to the present discussion.

42. *See* Post, *Constitutional Domains, supra* note 30, at 51–67, 127–33.

43. *See, e.g.,* Jeffrey Rosen, *The Unwanted Gaze: The Destruction of Privacy in America* 94–95 (2000).

44. *Time, Inc. v. Hill*, 385 U.S. 374, 412 (1967) (Fortas, J., dissenting). *See* Post, *Constitutional Domains, supra* note 30, at 313 and n.117.

45. 376 U.S. 254 (1964).

46. *See* Post, *Constitutional Domains, supra* note 30 at 6–10. On the interrelationship between democracy, community, and management, see *id.* at 13–15.

47. *See, e.g., id.* at 170.

48. *See, e.g., Gorwara v. AEL Industries, Inc.*, 1990 W.L. 44702 (E.D. Pa. 1990), *sub. dec.* 784 F. Supp. 239 (E.D. Pa. 1992); *Bustamento v. Tucker*, 607 So.2d 532 (La. 1992); *Robinson v. Vitro Corp.*, 620 F. Supp. 1066 (Md. 1985); *Hall v. May Dep't Stores Co.*, 637 P.2d 126 (Ore. 1981); *Argarwal v. Johnson*, 603 P.2d 58 (Cal. 1979); *Contreras v. Crown Zellerbach Corp.*, 565 P.2d 1173 (Wash. 1977); *Alcorn v. Anbro Eng'g, Inc.*, 468 P.2d 1216 (Cal. 1970).

49. There are, of course, other First Amendment ways to analyze the issue, but I will not pursue them in detail in this essay. Some First Amendment scholars, for example, might ask whether speech prohibited by Title VII served the constitutional value of

"autonomy" or "individual self- realization." Yet in the context of abusive speech these concepts provide little useful guidance, because the autonomy or self-realization of the speaker must be set against that of the victim. (This normative symmetry is often over-looked, because First Amendment protection for abusive speech typically occurs within the context of public discourse, where the moral balance between speaker and victim is broken by the social function of democracy, which is understood constitutionally to trump that of community. Speech within the workplace, however, is plainly not equiv-alent to public discourse.) Sometimes those who emphasize personal autonomy also stress general issues of privacy and protection from government control. But these themes seem hardly applicable to Title VII, which applies to a workplace saturated with em-ployer control over employee behavior.

Another line of analysis might ask whether speech prohibited by Title VII serves the marketplace of ideas. The telos of the marketplace of ideas is truth, and while this has always been an excellent description of the function of the academic community, its application to other areas of social life is somewhat more problematic. Because the marketplace of ideas is a cognitively based theory, its strict application would extend constitutional protection to speech censored because of its content, but not to speech censored because of the manner of its expression. It follows that the theory would for-bid Title VII from prohibiting a workplace festooned with "civil" banners proclaiming "Women are below average workers," but it would not forbid Title VII's prohibitions against vulgar and insulting epithets and other abusive locutions. While this distinction certainly works at obvious cross-purposes with the central thrust of Title VII, it would nevertheless be constitutionally defensible so long as one were willing to contend that the discovery of truth was the central constitutional value of the workplace. I myself find this contention highly questionable.

50. Estlund, *supra* note 1, at 694.

51. Post, "Racist Speech," *supra* note 20, at 289. On constructing the boundaries of public discourse, *see* Post, "Constitutional Concept," *supra* note 20, at 667–84.

52. Estlund, *supra* note 1, at 693.

53. *See, e.g., Hustler Magazine v. Falwell*, 485 U.S. 46 (1988).

54. Frank I. Michelman, "Brennan and Democracy," 86 *California Law Review* 399, 419 (1998).

55. Robert Post, "Democracy, Popular Sovereignty, and Judicial Review," 86 *Califor-nia Law Review* 429, 441 (1998).

56. *See, e.g.,* Meira Levinson, "Liberalism, Pluralism, and Political Education: Paradox or Paradigm?" 25 *Oxford Review of Education* 39 (1999).

57. For a discussion, *see, e.g.,* Post, *Constitutional Domains, supra* note 30, at 189–96.

58. *See Burlington Industries, Inc. v. Ellerth*, 524 U.S. 742 (1998).

59. 771 F.2d 323 (7th Cir. 1985), *affirmed*, 475 U.S. 1001 (1986).

60. For a discussion, *see* Post, *supra* note 19, at 1128–33; Post, "Constitutional Con-cept," *supra* note 20, at 626–46; Post, "Equality," *supra* note 17.

61. *See* Post, "Racist Speech," *supra* note 20, at 302–17.

62. For a theoretical discussion, see Post, *supra* note 18, at 178–81.

63. Post, "Racist Speech," *supra* note 20, at 303–6.

24

The Silenced Workplace
Employer Censorship Under Title VII

KINGSLEY R. BROWNE

For the past two decades, and especially since the Supreme Court's 1986 decision in *Meritor Savings Bank v. Vinson*,[1] employers have engaged in extensive censorship of their employees' speech because of fear of liability for hostile-environment harassment.[2] To date, there has been only a little judicial recognition that requiring employers to engage in such censorship raises serious First Amendment issues.[3]

The definition of hostile-environment harassment under which employers must operate is both broad and vague. It includes "verbal or physical conduct"[4] that is "sufficiently severe or pervasive to alter the conditions of [the victim's] employment and create an abusive working environment."[5] Under this standard, courts have held that there is no requirement of intent on the part of the alleged harasser[6] or that statements be specifically directed at the plaintiff.[7] Indeed, some courts have allowed plaintiffs to rely on speech that they heard about only indirectly.[8]

Although defenders of the current system typically justify regulation by invoking the most extreme cases of obscene and abusive speech by employees,[9] harassment regulation reaches far beyond the egregious cases. Not only do obscene sexual propositions count as sexual harassment, nonobscene propositions may as well. Indeed, the Ninth Circuit has suggested that even "well-intentioned compliments" may constitute harassment.[10] Moreover, sexual material that does not constitute an advance — such as pin-ups, calendars, and sexual cartoons — may likewise be deemed harassment.[11] Sexism, like sexuality, is also regulated, so that suggestions that women do not belong in the workplace or in particular jobs may support a finding of liability,[12] as may terms of reference deemed disrespectful of women, such as "honey,"[13] "sweetie,"[14] and "babe."[15] While such expression is typically not enough by itself to justify a finding of liability, the fact that it is considered in the hostile-environment inquiry has substantial First Amendment implications.

It is the thesis of this essay that the current regulatory scheme mandates rampant employer censorship that is inconsistent with established First Amendment principles. Two aspects of harassment regulation raise especially grave First Amendment issues. First, speech is often targeted for sanctions on the basis of its viewpoint; and second, the standard for liability is so vague that employers are unsure about what they must censor and are therefore forced into overcensorship.

The First Amendment Applies to Hostile-Environment Regulation

Title VII requires employers to prevent their employees from harassing other employees. When harassment takes the form of speech, as it often does, the employer's obligation is therefore to prevent its employees from speaking. This governmentally imposed obligation to restrict speech raises serious First Amendment concerns.

Although the First Amendment restricts only governmental power to regulate speech, the necessary state action exists in the dictates of Title VII and its enforcement by the courts. Just as regulations of the Federal Railway Administration that required private railroads to test employees for drugs were subject to Fourth Amendment challenge,[16] regulations requiring private (and public) employers to regulate speech are subject to First Amendment challenge. In either case, when the employer complies with its obligations, it "does so by compulsion of sovereign authority."[17]

Elsewhere I have detailed the doctrinal argument that hostile-environment regulation cannot be justified under current law,[18] and I will not recapitulate that discussion. It is appropriate, however, to address arguments made by other contributors to this volume that the First Amendment lacks application in the workplace or at least that it does not apply in the same way that it applies outside the workplace.

Frederick Schauer has argued that regulation of workplace speech does not even plausibly raise a First Amendment issue.[19] His argument is not that the speech, because of its content, falls into some category that the Supreme Court has labeled "not speech," such as obscenity or fighting words, but rather that the workplace is not a First Amendment domain.

The notion that the First Amendment has no application in workplace harassment cases is far-fetched. In a line of cases beginning with *Pickering v. Board of Education*,[20] the Court has held that the speech of *public* employees is protected by the First Amendment.[21] Under these cases, the government has a substantial burden if it seeks to punish an employee's speech on a matter of public concern, and "[e]ven where a public employee's speech does not touch upon a matter of public concern, that speech is not 'totally beyond the protection of the First Amendment.' "[22]

The power of the government to regulate public employee speech is based upon the fact that "the government as employer . . . has far broader powers than does the government as sovereign"[23] because its "interest in achieving its goals as effectively and efficiently as possible is elevated from a relatively subordinate interest when it acts as sovereign to a significant one when it acts as employer."[24] Thus, if the First Amendment limits the government when it acts as employer, it cannot limit the government less when it acts as regulator.

Acceptance of the argument that the First Amendment provides no protection to the speech of private-sector employees would lead to the paradoxical result that the government as regulator may engage in greater speech regulation than the government as employer. As a descriptive matter, that has in fact been the consequence of the lack of attention courts have paid to the First Amendment rights of private employees; however, this result is due more to oversight than to principle. For example, in *Rankin v. McPherson*,[25] the Court held that a county constable was prohibited by the First Amendment from discharging a black employee who, after hearing of an attempt on the life of President Reagan, stated "if they go for him again, I hope they get him." In contrast, the government *as regulator* was effectively entitled to *require* punishment of a white employee for the statement that "niggers ought to be shot like [Vernon Jordan] was."[26] Similarly, vulgar criticism of racial preferences by a public employee has been held to be constitutionally protected,[27] yet criticism of racial preferences by a private employee may contribute to a hostile-environment finding.[28] It is hard to understand why the government in its regulatory capacity can compel a private employer to punish speech that a public employer acting in its capacity as an employer would be constitutionally prohibited from restricting.

Robert Post has argued that full-blown protection for speech exists only in the domain of "public discourse," a term he has defined "as encompassing the communicative processes necessary for the formation of public opinion, whether or not that opinion is directed toward specific government personnel, decision, or policies."[29] Although his definition appears to be directed toward the content of the speech, rather than its location, Post rejects the notion that much public discourse occurs in the workplace. He asserts that in the workplace "an image of dialogue among autonomous self-governing citizens would be patently out of place."[30] Yet it is not clear why this should be so. Referring to the notion that a clear split exists between work life and private life, sociologist Beth Schneider has observed: "Although this set of ideas still permeates sociological and everyday thought, it is not necessarily consistent with either individuals' opinions or the reality of their daily work or sexual lives. For generations, sociologists have found that work relationships are far from simply task-oriented, but the source of friendship and informal social ties with consequences for workers as well as their workplaces."[31] For many people, the workplace is the primary venue for discussions of social and political issues; what is on the news at night is grist for the mill the next day at work.[32] Excluding the workplace from constitutional protection deprives millions of workers of a valuable opportunity to express themselves without fear of governmentally required sanctions.

The Supreme Court has yet to weigh in on the specific question whether hostile-environment regulation violates the First Amendment, and the hints that it has given so far are ambiguous. On the one hand, in *R.A.V. v. City of St. Paul*,[33] the Court ruled that even when regulating generally unprotected speech such as "fighting words," the state may not do so in a viewpoint-discriminatory way. On the other hand, the Court in dictum encouraged some to believe that hostile-environment regulation is safe. Expressly referring to Title VII, the Court stated that "a particular content-based subcategory of a *proscribable* class of speech can be swept up incidentally within the reach of a statute directed at conduct rather than speech."[34] Arguably, the *R.A.V.* dictum would apply to harassment that is effected through such proscribable speech as obscenity and fighting words, but it gives no aid to those who would regulate other speech.

Schauer presents a novel argument that the Supreme Court has effectively decided the First Amendment issue already. He contends that the Court's failure to address the issue in *Harris v. Forklift Systems, Inc.*[35] — despite its having been discussed in some of the briefs — constitutes the strongest repudiation the Court could have issued of the applicability of the First Amendment in harassment cases.[36] According to Schauer, "[g]iven that statements usually presuppose the plausibility of their negation, a corollary is that the strongest statement of the implausibility of the negation is to make no statement at all."[37] Those disagreeing with Schauer might take solace in the plurality's observation in *Waters v. Churchill*[38] that cases should not be read "as foreclosing an argument that they never dealt with."[39]

Hostile-Environment Regulation Violates First Amendment Standards
THE REGULATION IS NOT VIEWPOINT NEUTRAL

A central principle of First Amendment doctrine is that viewpoint-based restrictions on speech are impermissible absent compelling circumstances. According to the Supreme Court, "[i]t is axiomatic that the government may not regulate speech based on its substantive content or the message it conveys" and that "[w]hen the government targets not subject matter, but particular views taken by speakers on a subject, the violation of the First Amendment is all the more blatant."[40] Courts and commentators have identified a number of viewpoint-related reasons for prohibiting expression deemed harassing. In *Robinson v. Jacksonville Shipyards, Inc.*,[41] for example, the court justified employer liability that was based in large part on the presence of sexually suggestive materials as follows:

> Pornography on an employer's wall or desk communicates a message about the way he views women, a view strikingly at odds with the way women wish to be viewed in the workplace. Depending on the material in question, it may communicate that women should be objects of sexual aggression, that they are submissive slaves to male desires, or that their most salient and desirable attributes are sexual. Any of these images may communicate to male co-workers that it is acceptable to view women in a predominantly sexual way.[42]

Thus, sexual expression may send a message that women should be viewed as sexual creatures.

Often the message that is being punished in harassment cases is not that women should be viewed sexually, but rather that they do not belong in the workplace or in particular jobs. For example, suggestions that women should not be police officers[43] or physicians[44] have been held to support hostile-environment findings. In the racial-harassment context, reference to minorities as "tokens," posters stating that "The KKK is still alive," and the wearing of "Wallace for President" buttons have also contributed to a hostile-environment finding.[45] While it is true that in some cases such expression may make it harder for women and minorities to do their job because of their reaction to it, that does not mean that regulation of the expression on that basis is viewpoint-neutral. The Supreme Court has repeatedly emphasized that the impact of speech on its audience is not a content-neutral basis for regulation.[46]

In the cases just described, and there are many more,[47] liability was imposed for statements that were deemed impermissible precisely because of their viewpoint. Statements that women's primary attributes are sexual and that they should not hold certain positions may be actionable;[48] statements expressing the opposite view would not be. Statements suggesting that blacks hired through affirmative-action plans are not qualified may be actionable;[49] statements expressing the opposite view would not be. Yet these are clearly opinions, and for the government to allow expression of one set of opinions but prohibit their opposites violates its obligation, when exercising regulatory power, to remain neutral in the marketplace of ideas.

Courts have not been reluctant to acknowledge just what they are requiring of employers. The Sixth Circuit has stated: "Title VII . . . require[s] that an employer take prompt action to prevent . . . bigots from expressing their opinions in a way that abuses or offends their co-workers. By informing people that the expression of racist or sexist attitudes in public is unacceptable, people may eventually learn that such views are undesirable in private, as well. Thus, Title VII may advance the goal of eliminating prejudices and biases in our society."[50] Thus, not only does the law require the employer to monitor employee speech for bigotry, its explicit justification is to harness the power of the government to censor speech in the Orwellian hope that changing the way people speak will change the way they think.

THE HOSTILE-ENVIRONMENT STANDARD IS HOPELESSLY VAGUE AND EFFECTIVELY MANDATES OVERCENSORSHIP BY EMPLOYERS

Some of the expression regulated by harassment rules is entitled to little First Amendment protection. Some may be obscene; some may constitute "fighting words." Such speech is freely regulable by appropriately tailored rules, at least as long as the regulation is not viewpoint based.[51] However, regulation of speech through harassment law goes far beyond these clearly regulable forms of speech, and the standard that separates the permissible from the impermissible is hopelessly vague.

The Supreme Court has repeatedly held that speech regulations must be sufficiently clear that they not create a "chilling effect" on speech, causing prudent persons to steer far wide of a line they cannot clearly see.[52] The hostile-environment standard does not satisfy this First Amendment notice requirement. Its proscription of "verbal or physical conduct of a sexual nature [that] creat[es] an intimidating, hostile, or offensive work environment"[53] gives employers little notice of what speech they must prohibit and what they may allow. As Justice Scalia observed in his concurrence in *Harris v. Forklift Systems, Inc.*, this standard lets "virtually unguided juries decide whether sex-related conduct engaged in (or permitted by) an employer is egregious enough to warrant an award of damages."[54] While such a "standardless standard" may not violate the requirements of due process when applied to nonexpressive behavior, the First Amendment requires greater specificity.

Any vague regulation of speech can create a chilling effect, as potential speakers weigh the risks of speaking. The chilling effect of harassment regulation, however, is greatly exacerbated by two features of the liability regime: employer liability and the totality-of-the-circumstances standard.

The system of holding employers, rather than harassing employees, liable substantially increases the amount of speech that is suppressed. When an individual's speech is directly punishable, the speaker's desire for self-expression counterbalances to an extent his desire to avoid punishment. The speaker may thus take a chance and test the limits of the regulation. Yet when a third party is responsible for regulating the speech and is also subject to a substantial penalty for underregulation, the incentives are far less symmetrical. The employer gains little gratification from the speech of its employees but is exposed to financial risk by it, leaving the incentives overwhelmingly on the side of restriction. Overregulation is thus relatively cheap for the employer, and underregulation is potentially very expensive.

The totality-of-the-circumstances test also heightens the incentive for overregulation. An employer cannot know whether a given expression is ultimately going to form a basis for liability without knowing what else will be said by the particular speaker and by all other coworkers. The employer must deal with speech one incident at a time, asking itself not whether the speech at issue would by itself create liability, but rather whether it might, when combined with other speech that may not yet have occurred, ultimately contribute to a hostile-environment finding.

Imagine, for example, that an employer knew that a particular expression would not be deemed "sufficiently severe or pervasive" unless it was spoken five times. A male employee makes the statement once to a female coworker, and she complains to her supervisor. Does the rational supervisor tell the male employee that he can make the statement three more times and then he must quit, or does he tell him not to say it again? The answer is obvious. Since in any ensuing litigation the employer will be faced with all speech that the plaintiff was exposed to — and the employer will be judged by the adequacy of its response — the predictable response by the employer is to silence the employee. And that is the advice that lawyers give to their clients.[55] The much-vaunted "zero tolerance" policies adopted by employers make perfect sense given the liability rules, and it is hard to fault employers for adopting them or lawyers for recommending them.

The Reaction of Employers to the Liability Regime

Most commentators who have argued against the First Amendment defense have focused on decided cases, arguing that judges and juries can distinguish between egregious and nonegregious cases. Moreover, they argue, many cases involve not just speech but often other offensive conduct such as sexual touching.[56] Thus, they contend, hostile-environment law does not result in any substantial amount of inappropriate censorship.

Judging the effects of a rule by who wins and loses in litigation is a common but misguided tendency of lawyers, who think that if the right people are winning, then the law is working properly. However, law in general, and harassment law in particular, is aimed primarily at shaping conduct outside the courtroom, and it is out there — in the workplace — that one must look to see its results.

In placing its imprimatur on the hostile-environment theory, the Supreme Court in *Meritor Savings* suggested that an effective sexual harassment policy may confer some protection on employers.[57] Since *Meritor*, lawyers have routinely counseled their clients to adopt and enforce strict harassment policies, and most employers, at least large employers, have followed this advice.

While it is true that the most visible effects of harassment law are the litigated harassment cases, these are merely the tip of the iceberg. Reported cases are a misleading indicator of the law's effects, however, involving as they often do either the breakdown of an employer's sexual harassment policy or an employer who lacks a strong interest in complying with the law. A more relevant form of data, and one that is often ignored, is the behavior of employers who seek to comply with the law. That requires an analysis of the actual enforcement of employer harassment policies.

Application of employer harassment policies is for the most part invisible to the legal system. In the vast majority of cases, employees simply comply with the instructions they have been given. When there is an arguable violation, the offending employee is counseled not to do it again and he complies with the instruction, leaving no public record of the event.

Reported cases involving application of employer sexual harassment policies are largely limited to employees having some sort of just-cause protection, since at-will employees generally have no remedy for discipline or discharge for alleged violations of such policies. There have been a few lawsuits brought by employees discharged for violating their employer's sexual harassment policies. There have also been many arbitrations pursued on behalf of unionized employees who were disciplined or discharged for violating such policies, and there have been administrative proceedings initiated by disciplined or discharged civil service employees. The employer attitude displayed in all of these reported cases is consistent with the legal advice that they receive: when it comes to avoiding sexual harassment liability, it is better to be safe than sorry, and being safe means censoring a lot of speech. Consider the following cases:

- A Miller Brewing Company executive recounted in the workplace an episode of *Seinfeld*, in which the protagonist could not recall the name of a woman he was going out with; all he could remember was that her name rhymed with a female sexual anatomical part. It turned out that the woman's name was Dolores. When a woman in the office did not understand the joke, the executive showed her a dictionary page containing the word "clitoris" (obviously, the rhyme was a bit off). The woman filed an internal sexual harassment charge, and the man was discharged.[58]
- An Arizona police officer, upon learning that he scored well on the sergeant's exam, e-mailed a friend of his, a civilian woman in the department, "Now that I am on the Sergeant's List will you sleep with me?" His friend was amused and not at all offended but unfortunately for him mentioned the message to someone who reported it to a supervisor. The officer's name was then removed from the Sergeant's List.[59]
- A computer operator brought a copy of *National Lampoon* magazine to work. It was found by a female employee who gave it to a manager. The manager decided that the pictures of scantily clad women in the magazine violated the company's sexual harassment policy, and the employee was discharged.[60]
- A leadman at an Oregon manufacturing plant along with several other male employees looked unobtrusively at a copy of *Penthouse* magazine containing pictures of local celebrity Tonya Harding. One of the employees later mentioned the magazine to a female coworker, who in turn notified management. The employee was suspended for three days.[61]
- A Hispanic woman wore an African print scarf on her head. Some black employees were offended that she would wear an African scarf and complained. She was told to remove it because it offended her co-employees, and when she refused, she was discharged for insubordination.[62]
- A superintendent of station branch operations of the United States Postal Service addressed a subordinate "on more than one occasion" as "sweet thing." He was demoted to the position of letter carrier.[63]

- A machinist foreman, while on an errand to the area in which a female apprentice was working, engaged her in a conversation in which he told her such things as that he was from the "old school" and did not believe that women had any place in the shipyards, that the apprentice program was a "joke," and that she should have gotten a "typewriter" job. Although the foreman was not her supervisor, he was demoted to a nonsupervisory machinist position.[64]
- Just before Halloween, an air traffic controller found a piece of rope in a construction area of the Indianapolis control tower and tied it in a hangman's noose and hung it over the curtain rod that cordoned off the construction area. Apparently, no one saw it, but he admitted he had done it after a second noose (which he had nothing to do with) appeared and caused a furor among black employees. Although there was no allegation that he had any racial motivation (and an arbitrator subsequently found that he clearly did not), the employee was suspended for two days.[65]
- A warehouse worker foreman in a unit that performed heavy manual labor made statements on approximately ten occasions during a four-year period "that he believed that women in general were incapable of performing work in the [warehouse] and that he would never hire a woman." Although there were no findings that he had ever engaged in any discriminatory acts, he was demoted to the position of aircraft freight loader for violation of the agency's discrimination and harassment policy.[66]

A common feature of the above cases is that the expression for which the employee was disciplined or discharged was clearly not egregious enough by itself to support a finding of employer liability for harassment, yet the expression was interpreted to be a policy violation. That fact has led some to argue that such cases cannot be characterized as an effect of harassment law; instead, they are aberrant responses — "overreaction" by paranoid employers.[67] That argument assumes that an employer should not discipline an employee until offensive speech is so severe or pervasive that it violates the law. But that is surely an unrealistic view of the situation facing the employer. The totality-of-the-circumstances standard effectively requires the employer to act before an employee's speech reaches the "severe or pervasive" threshold, not only because of uncertainty about just where the threshold lies, but also because the employer will be called upon to defend against not just that employee's speech but also the speech of all other employees. This fact has caused courts and administrative agencies to conclude that employers appropriately respond well before Title VII has been violated. As the Merit Systems Protection Board has observed, while one "isolated incident" of "sexist" harassment does not violate Title VII, "[S]uch conduct by one of its supervisory employees cannot go unchecked by the agency, lest the agency be said to condone such remarks by its employees. Furthermore, if such conduct were not to be held actionable, a course of conduct or pattern of discriminatory behavior could emerge wherein the agency as employer could ultimately be held liable under Title VII."[68] Of course, employers dealing with at-will employees need not even persuade an administrative agency or arbitrator that acting prior to reaching the legal standard for harassment is justified, since even clear overreaction to the threat of harassment liability poses little legal risk.

If the cases described above do reflect overreaction, it is largely in the sanction imposed by the employer rather than in the censorship itself. That is, while one might believe that the employers overreacted in the amount of discipline imposed, it is unlikely that any employment lawyer would think that counseling the employees not to repeat their transgressions constituted overreaction. In today's climate, no competent counsel would advise employers that they are free to allow employees to engage in "shop talk" or tell sexual, racial, and ethnic jokes as long as they are not grossly offensive; nor would competent counsel advise employers that employees should be permitted to express controversial views on racial and sexual matters. As a pamphlet issued by the Maryland Commission on Human Relations puts it, "Because the legal boundaries are so poorly marked, the best course of action is to avoid all sexually offensive conduct in the workplace."[69]

Potential Modifications That Would Reduce First Amendment Problems

Given that current hostile-environment standards cannot withstand First Amendment scrutiny, the question remains whether there are some incremental modifications in Title VII doctrine that could cure the problem or whether more dramatic measures must be taken. It appears that incremental changes would not help very much.

DIRECTLY TARGETED SPEECH

Some commentators have conceded that current harassment standards unduly restrict expression, but that the problems that I have identified can be avoided by requiring that speech be "targeted" toward a particular victim in order to be actionable.[70] Thus, a plaintiff could not rely on overheard jokes or objectionable displays that are exhibited for all to see. Such a standard would

unquestionably be an improvement over the current standard. It would eliminate liability for "harassment in the air," and it would cut down substantially
on the number of "undeserving" plaintiffs who prevail in litigation. But faith
in this revised standard reflects the outlook previously described — the view
that a law is working appropriately if the right parties are prevailing in the
litigated cases. The relevant question, however, is whether a "targeted" standard would substantially reduce the core problem of hostile-environment regulation, which is censorship by employers because of fear of liability. The
answer appears to be in the negative.

Under any sensible interpretation of a "targeted" standard, statements that
were intentionally made in the plaintiff's presence would qualify even if they
were not formally directed toward her. That is, if a woman overhears sexist
jokes or remarks and asserts that they were made because of her presence, it
would presumably be a jury question whether the statements were in fact
"targeted." Similarly, if a woman argues that suggestive pictures were posted
specifically to offend her, she may be able to get to a jury on her claim. Of
course, if the picture predated her employment in that location, such a claim
would be hard to make. However, if she complained about the first picture
after she entered the workplace and then additional pictures were posted, she
might reasonably argue that the later pictures were directed at her in retaliation for her earlier complaints.

A "targeted" standard would simply not provide the employer the tools for
distinguishing between the speech it must regulate and the speech it may allow.
Many of the cases described in the prior section could plausibly be characterized as involving "targeted" speech. While not sufficient by itself to create
liability, the speech in each of those cases could potentially be aggregated with
other speech to support a hostile-environment finding. Thus, the employer
would still experience pressure to censor the speech, and even a "targeted"
standard would still require the employer to impose viewpoint-based speech
restrictions.

INDIVIDUAL LIABILITY

No reasonably likely system of employer liability under Title VII will
substantially reduce the problem of employer overcensorship. The pressure to
overcensor is inherent in a third-party liability system that is coupled with an
inherently vague standard. The point is not that no system of employer liability will be perfect; rather, it is that no system of employer liability can avoid
the suppression of far more speech than the First Amendment can tolerate.

It may be that a better way of regulating harassment — at least harassment taking the form of speech — would be to eliminate employer liability under Title VII and rely on tort law, under which individual offending employees could be held directly liable for their actions, perhaps under the theory of intentional infliction of emotional distress.[71] Even this standard — which requires "outrageous conduct" on the part of the defendant — raises substantial First Amendment problems. In *Hustler Magazine, Inc. v. Falwell*[72] — admittedly a "public figure" case — the Supreme Court rejected the "outrageousness" standard precisely because of its lack of objective content.

Remaining First Amendment difficulties notwithstanding, an individual-liability system would eliminate some of the chief evils of the current regime. It would reduce the pressure on employers to impose draconian speech codes. No longer would the censor of the speech be someone different from the speaker, and no longer would a single party be responsible for the aggregate of speech by numerous speakers. An individual-liability system would also have the salutary effect of imposing liability on the primary malefactor. This may, in turn, create greater disincentives for individual employees to engage in egregious harassing behavior, when they know that their houses — and not just their jobs — may be on the line.

Although one might argue that the proper remedy would be simply to add an individual-liability component to Title VII,[73] there are several reasons why that would not be a good idea. First, individual liability under Title VII would be merely an adjunct to employer liability; if employers could still be liable, all the pressures for overcensorship would remain. Second, because a regime of individual liability under Title VII would presumably hold liable not just the harassers but also the supervisors who failed to take adequate steps to counteract the harassment, the pressure to overcensor would actually increase. Instead of the supervisor's risking his employer's money if he decides not to censor speech, now he would be risking his own money. Since the supervisor personally captures very little of the benefit of whatever enhanced morale might flow from declining to sanction every silly sexist statement, the situation would likely be worse than it is today.

An individual-liability tort regime would likely cause juries to view harassment cases in a more speech-protective light. Such a regime may reduce the pro-plaintiff bias of juries in sexual harassment cases, because the jury would have flesh-and-blood parties on both sides of the case, rather than having a sympathetic plaintiff on one side and a deep-pocket corporate employer on the other. Diminishing the lottery-like aspect of filing sexual harassment claims can only be a good thing. The likelihood of liability based upon offensive, but not egregious, language would be reduced, as may be the likelihood that liability would be based on any viewpoint expressed as opposed to the manner of its expression.

Some will argue that this is exactly the wrong thing to do. Employer liability places pressure on the party most able to control the workplace. While that might have been a good argument at the outset of our experiment with sexual-harassment liability, experience has shown that employer liability causes substantial overcensorship. The power to control, coupled with substantial liability for inadequate control, has led to a regime that cannot be countenanced under the First Amendment.

Eliminating employer liability would not destroy employers' incentives to prevent egregious harassment. The majority of employers will prevent the most egregious speech out of concern for efficient operation of the workplace. However, employers would probably be less hypersensitive and draw the line between what is permissible and impermissible in a different place than they are forced to draw it now.

Some take the fact that a small minority of employers tolerate truly outrageous conduct even under today's law as evidence that the law, rather than going too far, does not go far enough. Consequently, they would argue, this is no time for retrenchment. While it is true that even under today's system of employer liability some employers permit highly obnoxious behavior, that does not tell us a great deal about the incentive effects of the law, because some employers do not appear to be particularly sensitive to the governing rules.

It seems to be axiomatic for many that the continued existence of any discrimination or harassment is an argument for increasing the levels of regulation, enforcement, and sanctions. But we seem strangely selective in our insistence on a "zero tolerance" standard. Most people view murder as being worse than sexual harassment, but no one argues that the fact that the murder rate is well above zero is reflective of inadequate laws against murder or inadequate enforcement of existing laws. Why not? Probably because people understand that although murder is a bad thing, there is something in human nature that makes it inevitable. We devote substantial resources to combating crime and are pleased when crime rates go down, but each new report of a murder or robbery does not result in an outcry for more regulation. On the other hand, the assumption seems to be that phenomena such as sexual harassment and discrimination can be entirely eliminated with a little education and "attitude adjustment." Yet it is probably the case that sexual harassment, no less than any number of other forms of antisocial behavior, is a product of built-in predispositions rather than merely a lack of education.[74] If that is so, complete elimination of sexual harassment and discrimination may be no more achievable a goal than complete elimination of crime.

Conclusion

Concerns about suppression of speech by harassment law have so far been largely overshadowed by concerns about equality. Labeling speech "discriminatory" has been viewed as a sufficient basis for suppression. But if the First Amendment means anything, it means that some speech that people think is bad is beyond the reach of the law. Unfortunately, the First Amendment is too seldom viewed as a real constraint on policy choices. Rather, the analysis seems to go: "Is this a good policy? If so, then it must not violate the First Amendment." Needless to say, such an approach leads to the same results that would be reached in the absence of a First Amendment.

Proponents of speech regulation always believe that the world would be a better place without the speech they wish to censor, and they often argue that the speech they seek to censor is somehow *sui generis*, so that allowing regulation in this instance will not justify censoring other speech that they think should not be censored. But it is time to recognize that harassment regulation under the present scheme of employer liability exacts far too high a cost in suppressed expression.

Notes

1. 477 U.S. 57 (1986).

2. *See* Kingsley R. Browne, "Title VII as Censorship: Hostile-Environment Harassment and the First Amendment," 52 *Ohio State Law Journal* 481, 495–96 (1991).

3. *See, e.g., DeAngelis v. El Paso Municipal Officers Association*, 51 F.3d 591, 596 (5th Cir. 1995).

4. 29 C.F.R. § 1604.11(a)(3).

5. *Meritor Savings*, 477 U.S. at 467 (internal quotes and citation omitted).

6. *See, e.g., Ellison v. Brady*, 924 F.2d 872, 879–80 (9th Cir. 1991); *Vaughn v. Pool Offshore Co.*, 683 F.2d 922, 925 n.3 (5th Cir. 1982).

7. *See, e.g., Waltman v. International Paper Co.*, 875 F.2d 468, 477 (5th Cir. 1989).

8. *See, e.g., Schwapp v. Town of Avon*, 118 F.3d 106, 110–112 (2d Cir. 1997); *Robinson v. Jacksonville Shipyards, Inc.*, 760 F. Supp. 1486, 1526 (M.D. Fla. 1991).

9. *See, e.g.,* Deborah Epstein, "Can a 'Dumb Ass Woman' Achieve Equality in the Workplace? Running the Gauntlet of Hostile Environment Harassing Speech," 84 *Georgetown Law Journal* 399 (1996); Suzanne Sangree, "Title VII Prohibitions Against Hostile Environment Sexual Harassment and the First Amendment: No Collision in Sight," 47 *Rutgers Law Review* 461 (1995).

10. 924 F.2d 872, 880 (9th Cir. 1991).

11. *See, e.g., Andrews v. City of Philadelphia*, 895 F.2d 1469 (3d Cir. 1990); *Waltman v. International Paper Co.*, 875 F.2d 468 (5th Cir. 1989).

12. *Smith v. St. Louis University*, 109 F.3d 1261 (8th Cir. 1997); *Lipsett v. University of Puerto Rico*, 864 F.2d 881 (1st Cir. 1988).

13. *Bales v. Wal-Mart Stores*, 1998 U.S. App. LEXIS 9008 (8th Cir. 1998).

14. *Russell v. Midwest-Werner & Pfleiderer, Inc.*, 949 F. Supp. 792, 799 (D. Kan. 1996).

15. *Smith v. St. Louis University*, 109 F.3d 1261, 1263 (8th Cir. 1997).

16. *Skinner v. Railway Labor Executives Association*, 489 U.S. 602, 614–16 (1989).

17. *Id.* at 614. *See also* Kingsley R. Browne, "Workplace Censorship: A Response to Professor Sangree," 47 *Rutgers L. Rev.* 510–11 (1995).

18. Browne, *supra* note 17. *See also* Jules B. Gerard, "The First Amendment in a Hostile Environment: A Primer on Free Speech and Sexual Harassment," 68 *Notre Dame Law Review* 1003 (1993); Eugene Volokh, "Freedom of Speech and Workplace Harassment," 39 *UCLA Law Review* 1791 (1992).

19. Frederick Schauer, "Too Hard: Unconstitutional Conditions and the Chimera of Constitutional Consistency," 72 *Denver University Law Review* 989 (1995).

20. 391 U.S. 563 (1968).

21. *See also Connick v. Myers*, 461 U.S. 138 (1983).

22. *Rankin v. McPherson*, 483 U.S. 378, 386 n.7 (1987).

23. *Waters v. Churchill*, 511 U.S. 661, 671 (1994).

24. *Id.* at 675.

25. 483 U.S. 378 (1987).

26. *Moffett v. Gene B. Glick Co.*, 621 F. Supp. 244 (N.D. Ind. 1985).

27. *Department of Corrections v. State Personnel Board*, 59 Cal. App. 4th 131 (1997).

28. *Joseph v. Publix Super Markets, Inc.*, 983 F. Supp. 1431 (S.D. Fla. 1997).

29. Robert Post, "Free Speech and Religious, Racial, and Sexual Harassment: Racist Speech, Democracy, and the First Amendment," 32 *William and Mary Law Review* 267, 288 (1991).

30. *Id.* at 289.

31. Beth E. Schneider, "The Office Affair: Myth and Reality for Heterosexual and Lesbian Women Workers," 27 *Sociological Perspectives* 443, 444 (1984).

32. Geeta Sharma-Jensen, "Scandal Heats Up Workplace Banter," *Milwaukee Journal Sentinel*, February 9, 1998; Lillian Lee Kim, "Clinton Woes Provide Break from Political Correctness," *Atlanta Journal and Constitution*, February 5, 1998.

33. 505 U.S. 377 (1992).

34. *Id.* at 389 (emphasis added).

35. 510 U.S. 17 (1993).

36. Schauer, *supra* note 19, at 992.

37. *Id.*

38. 511 U.S. 661, 678 (1994).

39. The First Amendment issue was not squarely before the Court in *Harris*, where the question was "whether conduct, to be actionable as 'abusive work environment' harassment . . . must 'seriously affect [an employee's] psychological well-being.' " 510 U.S. at 20. That question focuses on the mental state of the plaintiff rather than on the conduct of the defendant.

40. *Rosenberger v. Rector and Visitors of the University of Virginia*, 515 U.S. 819, 828–29 (1995).

41. *Robinson v. Jacksonville Shipyards, Inc.*, 760 F. Supp. 1486 (M.D. Fla. 1991).

42. *Id.* at 1526 (*quoting* Kathryn Abrams, "Gender Discrimination and the Transformation of Workplace Norms," 42 *Vanderbilt Law Review* 1183, 1212 n.118 (1989)).

43. *Arnold v. City of Seminole*, 614 F. Supp. 853 (N.D. Okla. 1985).

44. *Lipsett v. University of Puerto Rico*, 864 F.2d 881 (1st Cir. 1988).

45. *United States v. City of Buffalo*, 457 F. Supp. 612, 633 (W.D.N.Y. 1978), *modified and aff'd*, 633 F.2d 643 (2d Cir. 1980).

46. *See, e.g., Reno v. American Civil Liberties Union*, 117 S. Ct. 2329, 2343 (1997); *Boos v. Barry*, 485 U.S. 312–21(1988).

47. *See* Browne, *supra* note 17; Eugene Volokh, "What Speech Does 'Hostile Environment' Law Prohibit?" 85 *Georgetown Law Journal* 627 (1995).

48. *See Lipsett v. University of Puerto Rico*, 864 F.2d 881 (1st Cir. 1988).

49. *See Joseph v. Publix Super Markets, Inc.*, 983 F. Supp. 1431 (S.D. Fla. 1997).

50. *Davis v. Monsanto*, 858 F.2d 345, 350 (6th Cir. 1988), *cert. denied*, 490 U.S. 1110 (1989).

51. *R.A.V. v. City of St. Paul*, 505 U.S. 377 (1992).

52. *See Reno v. American Civil Liberties Union*, 117 S. Ct. 2329, 2344 (1997).

53. 29 C.F.R. § 1604.11(a)(3).

54. 510 U.S. at 24 (Scalia, J., concurring).

55. *See* Beverly W. Garofalo, "Lessons from Torres: How to Avoid Liability," 12 *Corporate Counsellor* 9 (June 1997); Volokh, *supra* note 18, at 638–43.

56. Deborah Epstein, "Free Speech at Work: Verbal Harassment as Gender-Based Discriminatory (Mis)Treatment," 85 *Georgetown Law Review* 649, 653 (1997).

57. 477 U.S.57, 72–73 (1986).

58. *See* "Sexual Harassment: Jury Awards $26 Million to Executive Fired after Discussing 'Seinfeld' Episode," *Daily Lab. Rep.* (BNA) No. 137, at D-24 (July 17, 1997).

59. *Olive v. City of Scottsdale*, 969 F. Supp. 564 (D. Ariz. 1996) (court denied summary judgment to defendant on due process claim).

60. *In re RMS Technologies, Inc.*, 94 *Lab. Arb.* (BNA) 297 (1990) (arbitrator overturned).

61. *In re American Mail-Well Envelope*, 105 *Lab. Arb.* (BNA) 1209 (1995) (arbitrator ruled that three-day suspension was excessive).

62. *In re USCP-WESCO, Inc.*, 109 *Lab. Arb.* (BNA) 225) (arbitrator overturned discharge).

63. *Dubiel v. United States Postal Service*, 54 M.S.P.R. 428 (1992) (ALJ sustained charge and demotion; MSPB reduced the penalty to a thirty-day suspension).

64. *Curry v. Department of the Navy*, 13 M.S.P.R. 326 (1982) (MSPB sustained demotion).

65. *In re Federal Aviation Administration*, 109 *Lab. Arb.* (BNA) 699 (1997) (arbitrator reduced suspension to written admonishment).

66. *Holland v. Department of the Air Force*, 31 F.3d 1118 (Fed. Cir. 1994) (MSPB upheld demotion; Federal Circuit overturned, ruling that because employee had not acted on his attitudes or created a hostile environment, he had not violated any regulations).

67. Epstein, *supra* note 56, at 652; Suzanne Sangree, "A Reply to Professors Volokh and Browne," 47 *Rutgers Law Review* 595, 595 (1995).

68. *Curry v. Department of the Navy*, 13 M.S.P.R. 326 (1982). *See also Pope v. United States Postal Service*, 114 F.3d 1144, 1148 (Fed. Cir. 1997).

69. *See* Jonathan Rauch, "Offices and Gentlemen," *New Republic* (June 23, 1997), at 22.

70. *See, e.g.,* Volokh, *supra* note 18, at 1871.

71. *See* Stuart Taylor, "Real Sexual Harassment," *Legal Times*, May 6, 1996, at 23.

72. 485 U.S. 46, 55 (1988).

73. Under Title VII, most courts have held that individuals who discriminate are not individually liable. *See, e.g., Wathen v. General Electric Co.*, 115 F.3d 400, 404–6 (6th Cir. 1997).

74. Kingsley R. Browne, "An Evolutionary Perspective on Sexual Harassment: Seeking Roots in Biology Rather Than Ideology," 8 *Journal of Contemporary Legal Issues* 5 (1997).

25

Pornography as Sexual Harassment in Canada

JANINE BENEDET

Overview

The display or use of pornography in the workplace is recognized as a form of sexual harassment by provincial human rights tribunals in Canada. Although few decisions have considered this issue, tribunals have held that the presence of pornography in the workplace creates an unequal working environment for women. Grievance arbitrators under collective agreements have accepted this approach in principle, while showing greater reluctance to find harassment on the facts. Despite the debate in the United States as to whether certain kinds of sexual harassment, including workplace pornography, are protected speech under the First Amendment, there have been no serious free speech arguments in Canadian sexual harassment cases. This essay considers why this is the case, and suggests that the Supreme Court of Canada's decision in *Ross v. School District No. 15*,[1] which upheld the disciplining of a teacher for his off-duty racist speech, against his freedom of expression claim, makes the success of a similar challenge to sexual harassment laws unlikely. The fact that U.S. sexual harassment law is threatened by the First Amendment indicates that First Amendment doctrine should be reevaluated, rather than legal protections for women at work narrowed.

HUMAN RIGHTS LEGISLATION

To understand the reaction of Canadian tribunals to the use of pornography as a method of sexual harassment in the workplace, it is first necessary to understand, at least in a general way, the legal regime that governs sexual harassment in employment. While Canadian sexual harassment law is derived from, and in many respects closely parallels, its U.S. counterpart, both the definition of the wrong and its method of enforcement have followed a somewhat different path. Canadian human rights statutes have prohibited discrimination in employment on the basis of sex since the early 1970s. This protection exists in similar terms in each of the ten provinces, as well as in the federal jurisdiction.[2] These statutory rights are enforced in each jurisdiction through a provincial human rights commission and an independent administrative tribunal. The system is complaint driven: An individual makes a complaint of sex discrimination to the provincial human rights commission (a body much like the EEOC). The complaint can be made against both the employer and the individual harasser. If the commission, after an investigation, concludes that the complaint should be pursued, it refers it to a hearing before an independent human rights tribunal. The commission now has carriage of the complaint; much as in a criminal trial, the complainant is not directly a party and is typically not represented by her own counsel. The tribunal has the power to compensate the complainant for her losses, to award damages for mental anguish,[3] and to order reinstatement if the complainant has been wrongfully or constructively dismissed.

With the recognition in the United States in the 1970s that sexual harassment in employment was a form of sex discrimination,[4] it was inevitable that Canadian complainants would begin to bring their own complaints of sexual harassment in employment before human rights tribunals, relying on the prohibition on discrimination in employment on the basis of sex. The first case to accept this argument was *Cherie Bell*, decided in Ontario in 1980. In that case, two waitresses alleged that they were dismissed from their employment after refusing the sexual advances of the restaurant owner. The chair of the human rights tribunal found that sexual harassment was a type of sex discrimination within the terms of the Ontario Human Rights Code. He stated:

> But what about sexual harassment? Clearly a person who is disadvantaged because of her sex is being discriminated against in her employment when employer conduct denies her financial rewards because of her sex, or exacts some form of sexual compliance to improve or maintain her existing benefits. The evil to be remedied is the utilization of economic power or authority so as to restrict a woman's guaranteed and equal access to the work place and all of its benefits, free from extraneous pressures having to do with the mere fact

that she is a woman. Where a woman's equal access is denied or when terms and conditions differ when compared to male employees, the woman is being discriminated against.

The forms of prohibited conduct that, in my view, are discriminatory run the gamut from overt gender based activity, such as coerced intercourse to unsolicited physical contact to persistent propositions to more subtle conduct such as gender based insults and taunting, which may reasonably be perceived to create a negative psychological and emotional work environment. There is no reason why the law, which reaches into the work place so as to protect the work environment from physical or chemical pollution or extremes of temperature, ought not to protect employees as well from negative psychological and mental effects where adverse and gender directed conduct emanating from a management hierarchy may reasonably be construed to be a condition of employment.[5]

Despite these statements, the tribunal found that, on the facts, sexual harassment had not occurred. It was not until the following year that an employer was found liable for the sexual harassment of employees.[6] A number of similar decisions soon followed. These early cases made it clear that when a woman leaves her employment to avoid unwanted sexual advances, she is considered to have been constructively dismissed and therefore entitled to compensation or reinstatement.

As in the United States, the early cases in Canada were of the quid pro quo variety, but the fact situations brought before tribunals soon began to include cases closer to the hostile environment end of the spectrum. In 1982, a tribunal held for the first time that there need not be a direct causal connection between the harassment and adverse employment consequences.[7]

The Supreme Court of Canada has considered sexual harassment claims on two occasions. First, in *Robichaud v. Treasury Board*,[8] the Court confirmed that employers were liable for the discriminatory acts of their employees that occurred in the course of carrying out matters that were work- or job-related. The Court confined its decision to the question of employer liability and did not specifically address the substance of the harassment claim. Then, in 1989, the Supreme Court of Canada issued its decision in *Jansen v. Platy Enterprises Ltd.*[9] The Court overturned a decision of the Manitoba Court of Appeal that had held that sexual harassment was not a form of sex discrimination in employment, because not all of the women employees were harassed. The Court confirmed that discrimination did not have to be carried out against every member of a class in order for it to be discriminatory. It was enough that the women in question had to endure a discriminatory condition of employment on the basis of their sex.

During the 1980s, a number of jurisdictions amended their human rights legislation to proscribe sexual harassment in employment specifically. Unfortunately, the wording used in some of these provisions is narrower in scope than the jurisprudence developed by the Supreme Court of Canada under the general prohibition on sex discrimination. It appears that as part of a laudable attempt to ensure that sexual harassment was proscribed by human rights legislation, some jurisdictions in fact may have limited the existing scope of that protection.[10]

The accepted legal definition of sexual harassment in Canada shares many significant features with its U.S. counterpart. In particular, the complainant must show both that the conduct in question was unwelcome to her and that it was sufficiently severe or pervasive, described as "vexatious" in Ontario. Many Canadian jurisdictions also add the requirement that the harasser know or ought to have known that his behavior was unwelcome to the complainant. This effectively introduces a form of mens rea into the provision, one that is ill-suited to the remedial aims of antidiscrimination law and may validate, rather than challenge, male behavioral norms.

GRIEVANCE ARBITRATION

In recent years, grievance arbitration has become a forum of almost equal importance to human rights tribunals in the adjudication of claims arising from sexual harassment in unionized employment. This development results from the convergence of a number of factors. First, inordinate delays on the part of provincial human rights commissions meant that both employers and employees began to look for alternative methods of vindicating their rights. Second, more and more collective agreements incorporated antidiscrimination clauses that were grievable in an arbitral forum. Third, as more employers began to introduce and apply workplace sexual harassment policies, unionized employees who were disciplined under these policies filed grievances challenging that discipline. Finally, recent amendments to some provincial labor relations statutes make clear that arbitrators have the jurisdiction to interpret and apply the provisions of human rights statutes as they apply in the collective agreement context.[11]

Grievance arbitration can become the forum for the consideration of sexual harassment disputes either where a woman grieves her employer's failure to rectify the harassment or where the male employee disciplined for harassment challenges that discipline. Harassment cases can pit bargaining unit members against one another, placing the union in a difficult position of conflict.

Litigating sexual harassment cases through grievance arbitration has some advantages; it is typically quicker than proceeding with a human rights complaint. Yet, grievance arbitration shares the flaw of the human rights tribunal procedure that the complainant loses control of her case. Before the tribunal, her case is handled by the human rights commission; before the arbitrator, it is advanced by the union. Both the commission and the union have the authority to decide not to proceed to a hearing with the complaint.

Grievance arbitration also has some unique problems for complainants. Arbitrators sometimes lack the sophisticated and systemic understanding of inequality necessary to fairly and meaningfully adjudicate human rights or discrimination disputes. The focus of the arbitration is often on the procedural protections afforded to the alleged harasser, or the consistency of the employer's discipline procedure. This is the result of placing the issues in a context of labor relations rather than antidiscrimination.[12]

CIVIL ACTION

Unlike in the United States, in Canada victims of sexual harassment in employment are barred from bringing a civil action in the courts to seek direct redress for the discrimination.[13] Instead, victims who have left their employment are limited to claims for wrongful or constructive dismissal, arguing that their employers' failure to remedy sexual harassment forced them out of their employment. A court in these circumstances does not have the jurisdiction to award reinstatement. Damages will be limited to the amount of reasonable notice in lieu of termination that the plaintiff should have received, with the possibility, albeit remote, of punitive damages.

Sexual Harassment Claims Based on Pornography

A number of decisions of arbitrators and human rights tribunals in Canada in recent years have considered sexual harassment claims in which the conduct complained of consisted, in whole or in part, of the display of pornography in the workplace. The Canadian Human Rights Commission has included the display of pornography as a type of sexual harassment in its Guidelines. While not legally binding, the Guidelines form the basis of the commission's model sexual harassment policy, and many Canadian workplace policies contain specific prohibitions on the display of pornography.

The results of cases in which sexual harassment claims have been based on pornography have been mixed. The first was *Pond v. Canada Post Corp.*,[14] a decision of the Canadian Human Rights Tribunal. In that case, the complainant, Charlotte Pond, was employed as a postal worker in a mail-processing station. She complained about *Playboy*-type centerfolds in the work area, as well as a *Playboy* calendar. She also complained that her supervisor had a statue on his desk that depicted a Chinese woman serving wine to a Chinese man. When the statue was turned over, the genitals of the figures were visible. Pond testified that the supervisor used the statue as a catalyst for numerous comments about women's duty to serve men and Pond's sexual activities.

The employer argued that the material in question was not harassing and that it had responded adequately to Pond's concerns, making sure that the genitalia on the posters were cut out, and that the calendar was removed.[15] The employer further argued that the adjective "pornographic" was an exaggeration as applied to *Playboy* magazine.

The Tribunal held that Pond had been sexually harassed. The Tribunal noted that the burden on the complainant was to show that the conduct complained of was of a sexual nature, unwanted, and humiliating to her. The Tribunal concluded:

> Applying this broad definition of sexual harassment to the case of Charlotte Pond, to use a statue depicting the genitals to make offensive comments, namely that women are only good for serving men or for doing office work or house work, can be said to constitute sexual harassment.
>
> In addition, the presence in a workplace of posters from Playboy magazine or of posters of naked women that co-workers use as the basis of comments and jokes of a sexual nature about the size of their breasts, about their figures, etc., definitely causes embarrassment and lowers the status of women.

The Tribunal awarded the complainant $4,000 for injury to her self-respect.[16]

Three years later, the same employer was faced with another complaint of harassment involving pornography, this time in the form of a grievance under the collective agreement.[17] Once again, the complainant, Donna Perchaluk, worked in a postal station in which posters and postcards of naked women were affixed to the wall. When she complained to one of her supervisors about photos of nude women displayed on the workstation of a male coworker, Macario, the supervisor told her that he could not get Macario to take the postcards down because they did not portray full nudity, and if he asked the coworker to remove the pictures, he would have to ask other employees to take down their family photos as well. Macario received a postcard of a nude woman on a beach from another employee who was on vacation in Hawaii. The postcard said "hi" both to Macario and to the complainant, and he showed it to her. Perchaluk testified that the card was the last straw and that she left work on sick leave.

Perchaluk made other allegations of the presence of sexual objects and comments in the workplace, but the arbitrator found that they had not been proven. He accepted her evidence with regard to the posters and post-cards displayed on the wall. With respect to the Hawaii postcard incident, however, he found:

> Objectively the post card itself, in my judgment, is not inherently or intrin-sically offensive. It is simply a photograph of a reclining nude woman on a beach and the undisputed evidence is that these kinds of cards pass through Canada Post on a daily basis. It is not pornographic or obscene. I do not think that it is an illegal card (nor was that argued) and sending it would not have broken any law. It may be that it was inappropriate for Mr. Rogers to mail the card to his co-worker, Mr. Macario, to the depot rather than to Mr. Macario's home, but there is certainly insufficient evidence for me to find that doing so was a breach of some Corporation policy.
>
> The arbitrator found that there was no basis on which the Corporation could have disciplined the employee for sending the Hawaii postcard. None-theless, the arbitrator agreed that the display of the other postcards and posters in the workplace created a harassing work environment. The fact that the displayed material was not directed at the complainant was not deter-minative. The arbitrator awarded the grievor retroactive credit for her sick leave. He declined to award her any further damages.

The difference in the complainants' success in these two cases, on almost identical facts, is some indication of the difference between the handling of harassment complaints at grievance arbitration and in the human rights com-plaint process. The latter focuses more on discrimination and equality, with a corresponding recognition of the type of harm that the display of pornography can cause working women.[18] In the grievance arbitration context, the same sort of conduct is downplayed and assessed according to whether it would have broken any criminal law or company policy. In addition, the remedy given to the complainant merely recognizes that she was entitled to be sick as a result of the harassment she experienced. Such a result does very little to improve the workplace for women.

The increasing reliance on grievance arbitration as a method of vindicating these rights has also produced cases in which the prevalence of pornography in the workplace as a whole is offered as a justification for its presence in a particular case. For example, in *British Columbia and British Columbia Gov-ernment Employees' Union*,[19] two coworkers, Labinsky and Pickrell, were assembling pallets of product to be shipped from a warehouse to a retail liquor store. Labinsky placed a large piece of cardboard on top of a layer of cases on the pallet. On the piece of cardboard, he had drawn a large picture of male genitalia and the words "suck on this, you Delta sluts."[20] Pickrell allowed the cardboard to remain on the pallet and continued to stack boxes so that it was covered. It was shipped to the liquor store in Delta and unloaded by two female employees, who notified their manager. After an investigation, the employer terminated both men. They grieved their dismissals.

The same arbitrator heard both grievances at different hearings. He upheld the termination of Labinsky, who drew the picture. However, he concluded that dismissal was too severe a penalty for Pickrell, who had merely stacked the pallets, and reinstated him without pay or benefits, a suspension amounting to approximately ten months.

While the union acknowledged that the employees' conduct was deserving of discipline, it sought to mitigate their actions by relying on the fact that the warehouse as a whole was a poisoned working environment. Therefore, the employees could not be held solely culpable for acting in accordance with the standards of a workplace that the employer had not taken steps to correct. The arbitrator rejected this argument on a number of grounds. First, he noted that he had toured the warehouse and had not seen the type of environment that the union described. He also found that any sexual material that did exist was not condoned or created by the employer. The employer had acted aggressively to remove and prevent graffiti and pictures. However, he also went on to note:

> [T]here is an obvious difference between pin-ups and the material found in so called mens' magazines, and what the grievor did in this case. It may be, as was argued by the union, that the pictures and other material referred to by the union have no place in a work environment such as the liquor distribution branch warehouse and that the employer should be more vigilant in removing that kind of material if it is prominently displayed. Its existence, however, does not create the kind of poisoned work environment that the union suggests reduces the grievor's culpability for his actions in this case.

This comment has the unfortunate result of downplaying the severity and effect of the presence of commercial pornography in the workplace, as a way of distinguishing the grievor's conduct in hiding his poster in a place where it would be discovered by female employees. It is difficult to understand the distinction drawn by the arbitrator, which appears to be based in part on the fact that commercial pin-ups are common in society and are not accompanied by crude messages. It is unfortunate that the arbitrator did not simply conclude with his observation that the type of environment alleged by the union did not exist or was not condoned by the employer.

Sexual Harassment and Freedom of Expression

The first decision in the United States to base liability for sexual harassment under Title VII of the Civil Rights Act of 1964 on the display of pornography at work was *Robinson v. Jacksonville Shipyards*.[21] In that case, the employer's defense, in part, was that posting and using pornography in the workplace was protected as free speech under the First Amendment. In Canada, section 2(b) of the Canadian Charter of Rights and Freedoms, Canada's constitutional bill of rights, also extends constitutional protection to speech. It provides: "2. Everyone has the following fundamental freedoms, . . . (b) freedom of thought, belief, opinion and expression, including freedom of the press and other media of communication."[22]

The Canadian provision, which was enacted in 1982, has been interpreted quite differently than its U.S. counterpart. The Supreme Court of Canada has rejected an approach to section 2(b) that places primacy on individual self-fulfillment through speech, in favor of an approach that takes into account the equality rights of all Canadians and recognizes that, in some circumstances, "expression" can produce inequality. This has resulted in the court upholding criminal laws that target racist hate speech[23] and pornography,[24] among other areas.

This approach to freedom of expression is a reflection of a modern constitutional document that was designed not only with reference to the U.S. Bill of Rights, but also with reference to international human rights documents, which embody a balancing process that defines the rights of the individual in the context of a community. This hybridization, in turn, reflects Canadian culture, which tends to place as much emphasis on groups and group identity as on the individual and which is generally less concerned with government regulation of private behavior than is the case in the United States.[25]

In the aftermath of *Robinson v. Jacksonville Shipyards*, numerous U.S. commentators criticized the decision and argued that some or most of what is currently proscribed under Title VII is protected speech under the First Amendment.[26] The U.S. Supreme Court struggled with this distinction in dictum in *R.A.V. v. City of St. Paul*.[27] In fact, full argument on this issue was made before the Court in *Harris v. Forklift Systems*,[28] but the Court did not address the issue in its decision. At least one lower court decision after *Robinson* has held that the use of pornography at work can be constitutionally protected.[29] The argument has been rejected or avoided in a number of other cases.[30]

The tribunal in the *Cherie Bell* decision identified the potential tension between an individualist interpretation of free speech and the equality protections offered by sexual harassment law:

> The Code ought not to be seen or perceived as inhibiting free speech. If sex cannot be discussed between supervisor and employee neither can other values such as race, colour or creed, which are contained in the Code, be discussed. Thus, differences of opinion by an employee where sexual matters are discussed may not involve a violation of the Code; it is only when the language or words may be reasonably construed to form a condition of employment that the Code provides a remedy. Thus, the frequent and persistent taunting by a supervisor of an employee because of his or her colour is discriminatory activity under the Code and, similarly, the frequent and persistent taunting of an employee by a supervisor because of his or her sex is discriminatory activity under the Code.[31]

Yet despite this early recognition of a possible conflict, a freedom of expression argument has never been advanced directly in a Canadian sexual harassment case. The closest that Canadian decision-makers have come to addressing this issue is in statements like the one made by the arbitrator in *Canada Post Corp. (Perchaluk)* that the postcard sent to the complainant was not illegal and therefore not deserving of discipline.

One other decision that alludes to the possibility of a freedom of expression argument in the context of a sexual harassment claim is *Western Star Trucks and I.A.M.*[32] In that case, the grievor was disciplined for a poster he displayed during a plant election campaign for positions to the quality management committee. The grievor was not a serious candidate and had a history of running joke campaigns.

On the final day of the campaign, the grievor printed a flyer on pink paper that was entitled "Sex Sells." The flyer depicted a photograph of a woman who was nude from the waist up. Her breasts, as well as the area below the waist, were covered by signs that said "censored." There were other adjustments made to appease the "censors," for example, the woman's hands were gloved and a notation stated, "Hands can be used for erotic purposes. Disguise them."

When a manager arrived at the plant and saw the posters, he told the grievor to remove them. The grievor asked what was wrong with the posters and the manager told him that they were abusive to women. The grievor argued that he saw no problem with the poster; it was merely a joke about censorship. The grievor told his manager that the order to remove the posters violated his right to free speech. The manager told him that on company premises the employer would decide what could be posted. The grievor ultimately removed the posters. However, the next day he posted a new flyer that ridiculed the employer's order to remove the earlier poster. Its caption read: "Gee, I don't want to offend anyone." The grievor was disciplined under the company's sexual harassment policy.

The employee grieved the discipline imposed on him under the policy. At the arbitration hearing, the employer argued that there were no competing fundamental values at stake. The grievor's conduct amounted to sexual harassment and he was not exercising a right of free speech as part of a democratic process. He was not a serious candidate for the election and posted the flyers only to attract attention to himself. The union denied that the poster was sexual harassment. Its presence in the plant was fleeting, such that it had no opportunity to create a poisoned work environment. While the employer had the right to tell the grievor to remove the poster from the workplace, it did not have the right to discipline him for sexual harassment. The union, significantly, did not make a free speech argument on behalf of the grievor at the arbitration.

The arbitrator allowed the grievance and ordered that the discipline be rescinded, on the basis that human rights tribunals have generally required proof that the conduct in question is persistent or sufficiently severe to alter conditions of employment. A single incident of offensive conduct does not create a hostile work environment unless it is extremely serious. The poster was not sufficiently egregious or persistent to constitute sexual harassment.

The arbitrator in *Western Star Trucks* did not consider the employee's free speech argument. Obviously, it was not necessary to do so on the facts, since the arbitrator allowed the grievance on other grounds. It is also significant, however, that the union did not raise this as one of its arguments, despite the grievor's instinctive reaction to claim "free speech" when confronted on the plant floor.

What is important about the connection between sexual harassment in employment and freedom of expression in Canada, then, is that no one appears to be arguing that a collision between the two is imminent. There are several possible explanations for this. First, more and more sexual harassment claims are being decided in an arbitral forum, which involves the interpretation of a private bargain between the parties. The Canadian Charter of Rights and Freedoms, like the U.S. Bill of Rights, does not apply to the acts of private individuals; it applies only to government action. This does not mean, however, that it would be impossible to raise a Charter claim of freedom of expression in an arbitration. Because arbitrators have the power to interpret and apply the provisions of human rights statutes, as well as to apply the Charter, a person who grieves his discipline for sexual harassment could argue that the statutory antidiscrimination provisions on which his discipline was based violate the Charter.

While Charter claims in the arbitral forum are relatively new, this does not explain the complete absence of such an argument in Canada before any arbitral or human rights decision-making body to date. More logical, in my view, is the explanation that Canadian legal and social culture does not typically perceive the potential for free expression arguments in the act of posting pornography at work. Canadians are influenced by American culture in this respect, as is clear from the grievor in *Western Star Trucks* referring to his right to "free speech." Even the employer in that case seemed to suggest that a free expression argument should have been given more weight if the grievor was a serious candidate in the election. In general, however, Canadians are able to see incidents of sexual harassment as acts of inequality rather than speech.

The Ross *Decision*

In addition, such an argument is likely to fail, I would argue, in light of the Supreme Court of Canada's decision in *Ross v. School District No. 15*.[33] Malcolm Ross was an elementary school teacher. In his free time, Ross was an active anti-Semite who published numerous writings and appeared on local television attacking Jews and denying the existence of the Holocaust. Ross had never expressed these views at school or in the classroom. Nonetheless, his activities were well known in the community and among his students.

The parent of one student brought a complaint before the provincial human rights tribunal, arguing that his daughter's right to an education without discrimination on the basis of race or religion was compromised by Ross's presence in the classroom. His daughter was not a student of Ross; she did not even attend his school. However, she submitted evidence that she was afraid to attend sporting events and other interschool activities at Ross's school, since she had been told by other students that it was the school with "the teacher who hated Jews." There was also evidence of many anti-Semitic incidents among students throughout the district.

The tribunal ruled that Ross's continued employment in the classroom created a discriminatory learning environment for Jewish students in the district. The tribunal ordered the district to remove Ross from the classroom. If a nonteaching position for which he was qualified became available within eighteen months, he was to be awarded that position. If, however, at the end of this period no such position had materialized, he was to be discharged. The tribunal also ordered the school board to terminate Ross immediately if he published, sold, or distributed any of his previous writings or any new writings that mentioned a Jewish or Zionist conspiracy, or attacked followers of the Jewish religion.

Ross sought judicial review of the board's order as contrary to his right to freedom of religion and freedom of expression under the Charter. The New

Brunswick Court of Queen's Bench upheld the portions of the order removing Ross from the classroom. However, the court held that the portion of the order restricting Ross's writings after he had been removed from the classroom was unconstitutional. On further appeal to the New Brunswick Court of Appeal, the Court held, by a two-to-one majority, that the entire order was unconstitutional.

The New Brunswick Human Rights Commission appealed this decision to the Supreme Court of Canada. The Court unanimously held that the parts of the Board's order removing Ross from the classroom were not contrary to the *Charter*. Justice La Forest, for the Court, held that it was reasonable for the tribunal to conclude that Ross's activities outside the classroom created a discriminatory learning environment. There was evidence that Ross's activities poisoned the educational environment and created a setting in which Jewish students were forced to confront racist sentiment. Students testified to numerous incidents of taunting and intimidation of Jewish students and displays of anti-Semitic imagery. It was reasonable for the tribunal to draw an inference between the notoriety attracted by Ross's off-duty conduct and the actions of the students. The district's passivity in the face of this environment amounted to discrimination.

Justice La Forest then turned to the Charter claims. He noted that the scope of the constitutional protection for expression was very broad. It was clear that Ross's writings and statements constituted "expression." Any statement that conveys meaning falls within the broad definition of "expression," so long as it is not communicated in a physically violent manner. The Court had, in previous cases, found that hate propaganda was covered by section 2(b). The next step of the test was to consider whether the purpose or effect of the government action was to restrict the individual's freedom of expression. It was clear that the tribunal's order, while intended to remedy the discrimination, had the purpose of preventing Ross from publicly espousing his views. Therefore, section 2(b) was infringed.

Under Canadian constitutional law, however, this does not end the inquiry. The court must go on to consider whether the infringement is nonetheless justified as a reasonable limit under section 1 of the Charter, which "guarantees the rights and freedoms set out in it subject only to such reasonable limits prescribed by law as can be demonstrably justified in a free and democratic society."

The Supreme Court of Canada has developed a complex test for determining whether an infringement of a right or freedom is nonetheless "saved" by the operation of section 1 of the Charter. Justice La Forest noted that the application of the section 1 test was essentially a balancing exercise; the justification for the infringement of Ross's rights had to be considered in its social context. He agreed with the human rights commission that three contexts were relevant: the educational context, the employment context, and the anti-Semitism context. The importance of the provision of education by the state and the province's commitment to eradicating discrimination in the public school system were relevant to the constitutional analysis. In addition, it was significant that the educational services in question involved young children. Education awakens children to the values a society hopes to foster and to nurture. Young children are especially vulnerable to the messages conveyed by teachers, and less likely to distinguish between in-class and out-of-class statements. In the employment context, the province as employer had a duty to ensure that the fulfillment of public functions was undertaken in a manner that did not undermine public trust and confidence.

Finally, Justice La Forest considered the anti-Semitism context. He referred to the submission of the human rights commission in its brief that it was simply not feasible to consider the constitutional values of freedom of expression and freedom of religion, where they are relied upon to shield anti-Semitic conduct, without contemplating the centrality of that ideology to the death and destruction caused by the Holocaust. Justice La Forest noted:

> In assessing this submission, it is helpful to refer to *R. v. Edwards Books and Art Limited*, [1986] 2 S.C.R. 713 where Dickson C. J. stated, at page 779:
> "In interpreting and applying the *Charter* I believe that the Courts must be cautious to ensure that it does not simply become an instrument of better situated individuals to roll back legislation which has as its object the improvement of the condition of less advantaged persons."
> This direction is especially applicable in this appeal. The order rendered by the board was made to remedy the discrimination it found to be manifest within the public school system of New Brunswick that targeted Jews, an historically disadvantaged group that has endured persecution on the largest scale. The respondent must not be permitted to use the *Charter* as an instrument to "roll back" advances made by Jewish persons against discrimination.[34]

Finally, Justice La Forest noted that hate propaganda was not close to the core values of freedom of expression, which include the search for political, artistic, and scientific truth; the protection of individual autonomy and self-development; and the promotion of public participation in the democratic process. Where the expression in question was not close to these values, the Court could apply a lower standard of justification under section 1. Justice La Forest characterized Ross's expression in the following terms:

> Such expression silences the views of those in the target group and thereby hinders the free exchange of ideas feeding our search for political truth. Ours

is a free society built upon a foundation of diversity of views; it is also a society that seeks to accommodate this diversity to the greatest extent possible. Such accommodation reflects an adherence to the principle of equality, valuing all divergent views equally in recognizing the contribution that a wide range of beliefs may make in the search for truth. However, to give protection to views that attack and condemn the views, beliefs and practices of others is to undermine the principle that all views deserve equal protection and muzzles the voice of truth.[35]

Expression that incited contempt for Jewish people hindered the ability of that group to develop a sense of self-identity and belonging. It effectively undermined democratic values by impeding meaningful participation in social and political decision-making by Jews.

Justice La Forest held that the portions of the order that required the district to remove Ross from the classroom and assign him to a nonteaching position within eighteen months, or terminate him after that point, were a reasonable limit on Ross's expressive rights. The order was carefully tailored to accomplish its specific objective of remedying the discriminatory situation in the school district. Any punitive effect was merely incidental. Justice La Forest arrived at a different conclusion with respect to the portion of the order which required the district to immediately terminate Ross if he published any further anti-Semitic literature. The evidence simply did not support the conclusion that the residual poisoned effect of Ross's conduct would last indefinitely if he was placed in a nonteaching role. The Court severed this clause from the rest of the order and invalidated it.

Applying Ross *to Sexual Harassment Law*

The Supreme Court of Canada's decision in *Ross* has the potential to affect significantly any freedom of expression claim that might be raised in the context of sexual harassment in employment. Certainly, one would expect that the result in *Ross* would be the same if the teacher in question had published hate propaganda about women, and thereby poisoned the educational environment for female students. In addition, the Court recognized that it was within the permissible limits of the Charter to discipline an employee for the hostile environment caused by his *off-duty* speech. Clearly, if the remedial reach of human rights legislation extends to statements made outside the classroom, it extends to the creation of a discriminatory educational environment through statements made *in* the classroom.

The only significant difference between the situation in *Ross* and sexual harassment in employment through pornography is that the former occurs in an educational context involving children. Clearly, Justice La Forest put considerable weight on this factor in his reasons. Therefore, an employee seeking to raise a freedom of expression claim in response to allegations of sexual harassment could argue that *Ross* is distinguishable on this basis. Women, unlike children, are not particularly vulnerable to the views of others, to use the language of *Ross*.

Should the Supreme Court of Canada be confronted with such an argument, it should reject it for several reasons. First, it is arguable that women are vulnerable in the employment context, in that they continue to have less power and earn less money than men in the workplace. Sexual harassment through the use or display of pornography, particularly where that pornography is posted on the walls of the workplace, occurs more often in male-dominated working environments, whether blue-collar or white-collar, because the dominant heterosexual male culture affirms it. The display of pornography in a workplace is an act of domination that is carried out both on the women who work there and the women who are used to make it.

Second, a workplace that tolerates pornography produces effects that are very similar to those described by the witnesses in *Ross*. If the presence of pornography in the workplace is condoned by management, men are given implicit support for the notion that they are entitled to dominate women and to sexualize the working environment of their female coworkers. Pornography in a workplace does have an effect on the behavior of those who work there. The complainants in several of the cases discussed above testified that the presence of the pictures served as a catalyst for sexual comments or derogatory treatment. This is not to say, however, that the presence of the pornography alone is insufficient to create a sexually harassing work environment. If Ross had distributed his racist pamphlets at the school, he would have directly created a discriminatory learning environment and there would have been no need to consider the evidence of the indirect effect of his reputation on the behavior of the students.

In all other respects, the analysis should be the same as in *Ross*. The Court has already found pornography to be "expression," in that it is somehow intended to convey meaning.[36] It is likely that a court will consider that the facial purpose of a human rights tribunal's order prohibiting sexual harassment through pornography is to restrict that "expression."[37] This would produce an infringement of section 2(b), in the same way that section 2(b) was found to have been infringed in *Ross*.

Such a limit on expression, however, would clearly be justified under section 1 of the Charter according to the *Ross* analysis. Sexual harassment, like hate propaganda, lies far from the core of free expression values and is contrary to the basic principles underlying the guarantee. It curtails women's equal participation in the workforce by attacking their sense of self-worth and limits their career opportunities by barring them from certain workplaces so as to avoid being sexualized in this way.

This conclusion is supported by the Supreme Court's recognition in *Butler* that while "obscenity" — defined as sexually explicit materials that pose a risk of harm to sex equality — is expression covered by section 2(b), its distribution can be criminalized as a reasonable limit under section 1.[38] Unfortunately, *Butler* cannot be directly applied to resolve the constitutionality of sexual harassment law as applied to pornography in the workplace because the pornography at issue in the sexual harassment decisions described above, like the nude postcard and the *Playboy* calendar, does not typically meet the criminal law definition of obscenity as interpreted by the courts since *Butler*. So far, courts have resisted the characterization of nonviolent heterosexual pornography as "degrading and dehumanizing" such that it would pose a risk of harm.[39] For this reason, *Ross* is an important complement to *Butler* in supporting the argument that sexual harassment through pornography is not constitutionally protected expression.

The Supreme Court of Canada has recognized that, where the concept of "expression" or "speech" is broadly defined, offering protection to that expression in the context of a society that is attempting to remedy structural inequality requires evaluation of the content of the expression in question. This is a proposition that the U. S. Supreme Court has been increasingly unwilling to accept. This has left the U.S. Court attempting to find reasons why Title VII is not a violation of the First Amendment; the explanations offered so far are less than convincing. It is hardly surprising that the U.S. Court has largely avoided this issue.

The result in *Ross* is, in my view, correct. But what is more important is that the Supreme Court of Canada took an approach to expressive rights that permits an evaluation of speech in its social context, in that case the historical persecution of Jews. In this way, the speech itself is understood as an act of domination. The alternative approach, adopted in the United States, removes the speech in question from its social context and evaluates it only as a target of state regulation.[40] This approach, by definition, renders the speaker a persecuted minority even if his or her "speech" is nothing more than an act that perpetuates inequality. Hate propaganda matters because even though its most extreme disseminators may be publicly reviled, it works to impede the progress of racial and religious minorities in attaining full social equality. In the same way, sexual harassment in employment is important because, even though a majority of people may not practice it or condone it, it works to keep women unequal to men in the workplace — and in society more generally—through a lack of economic power. Sexual harassment, like hate propaganda, is majority speech.

The Supreme Court of Canada has done well to recognize that the potential exists for human rights instruments to be used by those with power to further roll back the gains made by disadvantaged groups. One way for members of dominant groups to do this is to exploit the expressive advantage they possess under the shelter of the constitutional protection for expression. If a court does not recognize this reality, it cannot meaningfully evaluate any claim that sexual harassment deserves constitutional protection. This characterization of the free speech claim is deliberate: If you accept what pornography does to women (in this case women at work) then proponents of the current view of the First Amendment are arguing that sexual harassment should be given constitutional protection, at least in some circumstances. Americans should consider why they are so convinced that it is impossible to design a free speech jurisprudence that does not produce this result.

Notes

1. [1996] 1 S.C.R. 826.

2. Canada Labour Code, R.S.C. 1985, c. L-2, ss. 247.1–4; Canadian Human Rights Act, R.S.C. 1985, c. H-6, s. 14(2); Human Rights Code, R.S.M. 1987, C. H-175, s. 19; Human Rights Code, R.S.O. 1990, c. H. 19, ss. 7(2), (3), 10(1); Charter of Human Rights and Freedoms, S.Q. 1975, c.6, s. 10.1, as am. by S.Q. 1982, c. 61, s. 4; Human Rights Code, R.S.N. 1990, c. H-14, ss. 12–13; Human Rights Act, R.S.N.S. 1989, c. 214, ss. 1, 5; Human Rights Code, R.S.B.C. 1996, c. 210, s. 13(1); Saskatchewan Human Rights Code, S.S. 1979, c. 24.1, s. 16; Human Rights, Citizenship and Multiculturalism Act, R.S.A. 1980, c. H-11.7, s. 7; Human Rights Act, R.S.P.E.I. 1988, c. H-12, s. 6(1); Human Rights Act, S.N.B. 1985, c. 30, s. 3(1).

3. These damages are limited. In Ontario, for example, the maximum recoverable for mental anguish is $10,000.

4. *See, e.g., Tomkins v. Public Service Electricity & Gas Co.*, 568 F.2d 1044 (3d Cir. 1977); *Barnes v. Costle*, 561 F.2d 983 (D.C. Cir. 1977); *Williams v. Saxbe*, 413 F. Supp. 654 (D.D.C. 1976).

5. *Bell v. Flaming Steer Steakhouse Tavern* (1980), 1 C.H.R.R. D./155 (Ont. Bd. Inq.).

6. *See Coutroubis v. Sklavos Printing* (1981), 2 C.H.R.R. D./457 (Ont. Bd. Inq.).

7. *See Cox v. Jagbritte* (1982), 3 C.H.R.R. D./609 (Ont. Bd. Inq.). Previous decisions, including *Cherie Bell*, had expressed agreement with such a claim; *Cox* was the first to find hostile environment harassment had in fact occurred.

8. [1987] 2 S.C.R. 84.

9. [1989] 1 S.C.R. 1252.

10. The Ontario Human Rights Code, R.S.O. 1990, c. H.19, ss. 7, 10(1) is typical. It provides: "7.(2) Harassment because of sex in workplaces—Every person who is an employee has a right to freedom from harassment in the workplace because of sex by his

or her employer or agent of the employer or by another employee. (3) Sexual solicitation by a person in position to confer benefit, etc. — Every person has a right to be free from, (a) a sexual solicitation or advance made by a person in a position to confer, grant or deny a benefit or advancement to the person where the person making the solicitation or advance knows or ought reasonably to know that it is unwelcome; or (b) a reprisal or a threat of reprisal for the rejection of a sexual solicitation or advance where the reprisal is made or threatened by a person in a position to confer, grant or deny a benefit or advancement to the person. '[H]arassment' means engaging in a course of vexatious comment or conduct that is known or ought reasonably to be known to be unwelcome; ('harcelement')."

11. *See, e.g.,* Labour Relations Act, 1995, S.O. 1995, c. 1, s. 48(12)(j).

12. In many provinces, unionized employees have, in effect, lost their opportunity to bring a claim before the human rights commission. In most cases, the commission will defer to the arbitration process and will refuse to hear the complaint until the employee has exhausted her remedies under that process. Then, if there are still outstanding issues, the tribunal may hear the claim. This is unlikely in practice, however, and most arbitrations become the sole forum for determining the claim.

13. *See Bhadauria v. Seneca College,* [1981] 2 S.C.R. 181.

14. [1994] C.H.R.D. No. 9, online: QL (CHRD).

15. The Tribunal noted that the calendar was removed in January 1989, without mentioning the fact that it would have expired by this time.

16. The maximum compensation available to a complainant under the Act at this time was $5,000. In 1998 this amount was increased to $20,000. *See* Bill S-5, S.C. 1998, c. 9.

17. *See Canadian Union of Postal Workers and Canada Post Corp.* (Perchaluk Grievance), [1997] C.L.A.D. No. 208 (Freedman).

18. *See also McLeod v. Bronzart Casting* (1997), 29 C.H.R.R. D./173 (Alberta H. Rts. Panel) (holding that the presence of newspaper and calendar posters of bikini-clad women created a discriminatory working environment).

19. (November 1, 1990), unreported (Ladner).

20. Delta was the name of the town to which the crates were being shipped.

21. 760 F. Supp. 1486 (M.D. Fla. 1991).

22. Can. Const. (Constitution Act, 1982) pt. I (Canadian Charter of Rights and Freedoms), 2.

23. *See R. v. Keegstra,* [1990] 3 S.C.R. 697.

24. *See R. v. Butler,* [1992] 1 S.C.R. 452.

25. This is reflected in the structure of the Charter itself, with its "saving" provision in s. 1, which makes all rights subject to reasonable limits, and the "notwithstanding clause" in s. 33, which permits legislatures to maintain unconstitutional legislation in certain circumstances.

26. *See, e.g.,* Kingsley R. Browne, "Title VII as Censorship: Hostile Environment Harassment and the First Amendment," 52 *Ohio State Law Journal* 481 (1991); Jules B. Gerard, "The First Amendment in the Hostile Environment: A Primer on Free Speech and Sexual Harassment,"68 *Notre Dame Law Review* 1003 (1993); Eugene Volokh, Comment, "Freedom of Speech and Workplace Harassment," 39 *UCLA Law Review* 1791 (1992).

27. 505 U.S. 377 (1992).

28. 510 U.S. 17 (1993).

29. *See Johnson v. County of Los Angeles Fire Department*, 865 F. Supp. 1430 (C.D. Cal. 1994) (looking at *Playboy* magazine in the fire station during a break).

30. *See, e.g., DeAngelis v. El Paso Municipal Police*, 51 F.3d 591 (5th Cir 1995); *Black v. City of Auburn*, 857 F. Supp. 1540 (M.D. Ala. 1994).

31. *Bell v. Flaming Steer Steakhouse Tavern* (1980), 1 C.H.R.R. D./155, at D./156 (Ont. Bd. Inq.).

32. [1997] B.C.C.A.A.A. No. 631 (Bruce), online: QL (BCCAAA).

33. [1996] 1 S.C.R. 826.

34. *Id.* at 875.

35. *Id.* at 877–78.

36. *See R. v. Butler*, [1992] 1 S.C.R. 452.

37. The Supreme Court of Canada uses the term "purpose" in freedom of expression analysis very broadly. The Court looks to the facial purpose of the law rather than to its objective or social goal; the latter type of purpose is considered at the section 1 stage.

38. *R. v. Butler*, [1992] 1 S.C.R. 452.

39. *R. v. Hawkins* (1993), 15 O.R. (3d) 549 (C.A.), leave to appeal denied, April 24, 1994 (S.C.C.).

40. *See Collin v. Smith*, 578 F.2d 1197, 1200–1201, 1210 (7th Cir. 1978), cert. denied 439 U.S. 916, 99 S. Ct. 291, 58 L.Ed.2d 264 (1978); *R.A.V. v. City of St. Paul*, 505 U.S. 377, 391, 112 S. Ct. 2538, 2548, 120 L.Ed.2d 305 (1992) and the discussion in Frederick Schauer, "Harry Kalven and the Perils of Particularism," 56 *University of Chicago Law Review* 397, 408 (1989).

26

Free Speech and Hostile Environments

JACK M. BALKIN

Does sexual harassment law conflict with the First Amendment? A number of commentators now argue that it does.[1] Generally, these objections focus on employer liability for hostile environments. Virtually no one finds fault with regulating quid pro quo sexual harassment: employers who tell employees to "sleep with me or you're fired" make threats that are not protected by the First Amendment.

Hostile environments, however, do not always involve threats. They stem from individual acts of discriminatory speech and other conduct by all the persons who inhabit a workplace, including managers, employees, and even occasionally clients and customers. A hostile environment exists when "the workplace is permeated with 'discriminatory intimidation, ridicule, and insult' that is 'sufficiently severe or pervasive to alter the conditions of the victim's employment and create an abusive working environment.' "[2] Some of this behavior may be directed at particular employees; other elements may be directed at no one in particular but may help foster an abusive environment. Even if individual acts do not constitute a hostile environment separately, they can be actionable when taken together. The test is whether the conduct, taken as a whole, would lead to an environment that the employee reasonably perceives as abusive.[3]

Employers can be liable for maintaining a hostile work environment even if management did not personally engage in any of the predicate acts. In *Burlington Industries, Inc. v. Ellerth*[4] and *Faragher v. City of Boca Raton*,[5] the Supreme Court held that employers are liable for harassment by supervisory personnel, subject to affirmative defenses when the harassment did not result in a tangible employment action like firing or demotion.[6] The degree of vicarious liability for nonsupervisory personnel (such as coworkers) is still contested, but currently most courts hold an employer liable if the employer knew or should have known of the harassment and did not take prompt corrective action.[7]

Employers who want to minimize hostile environment liability cannot merely prohibit individual instances of harassing conduct. They must also limit conduct that might, in combination with other conduct, contribute to a hostile environment. Hence employers are tempted to create prophylactic rules against all the potential components of a hostile environment. Some of these will be unwelcome physical advances, assaults, and forms of abuse. Others will be largely verbal: sexual jokes and innuendo, taunts and threats, sexually oriented cartoons, pictures, and pornography. Some of this verbal abuse may even be couched in political or factual terms; for example, coworkers might oppose affirmative action programs for women or quote scientific studies arguing that women are less competent at certain jobs. Because employers have no general interest in preserving employee speech rights unrelated to efficiency, they will impose regulations as broad as they think necessary to insulate themselves from liability.[8] The most important complaints about the constitutionality of sexual harassment law stem from these incentives to censor employee speech that might contribute to a hostile environment.

The Apparent Problem: Collateral Censorship

The concern that sexual harassment law produces employee censorship is actually an instance of a more general problem in free speech law — *collateral censorship*.[9] Collateral censorship occurs when private party A has the power to control speech by another private party B, the government threatens to hold A liable based on what B says, and A then censors B's speech to avoid liability. The offending speech may be defamatory, obscene, fraudulent, or a violation of copyright. In most situations A has greater incentives to censor B than B has to self-censor. Hence A can be expected to censor B collaterally with little regard for the value of B's speech to B or to society at large.

It is tempting but incorrect to argue that collateral censorship is never unconstitutional because there is no state action. In fact, there is state action in every case of collateral censorship, because the government has created incentives for private parties to censor each other, and expects censorship to be the result.

Even so, collateral censorship is not necessarily unconstitutional. For example, editors and publishers, driven by fear of defamation suits, may refuse to run stories by their reporters, or may severely edit them, even when the story involves core political speech, and even when the reporter insists that a story is accurate. Reporters who insist on writing what the editor or publisher forbids may be disciplined or even fired. Yet these limitations on employee speech do not violate the First Amendment. Cases like *New York Times Co. v. Sullivan*[10] and *Gertz v. Robert Welch, Inc.*[11] limit publishers' liability for defamation to prevent valuable speech from being chilled. But they do not distinguish between the rights of editors and their employees. In fact, in *Cantrell v. Forest City Publishing Co.*, the Court approved a jury charge that allowed the jury to hold the publisher liable for knowing falsehoods written by its staff writer even if the publisher was otherwise blameless.[12] Vicarious liability clearly gives a publisher strong incentives to censor employee speech, yet the Court found no constitutional problem.

In like fashion, federal securities laws require investment houses, brokerage firms, investment advisers, and even corporate officials to avoid making misleading statements about company profits, securities, and related investments. Companies are strictly regulated concerning what they may say about these matters, particularly in highly regulated procedures like proxy contests.[13] Statements made by their employees, even politically motivated statements, may subject them to liability. Thus, rational companies will often severely limit the kinds of public statements their employees may make, and discipline or terminate employees who disobey. But these rules do not violate the First Amendment because they specifically chill *employee* speech.

In both the defamation and the securities fraud cases, collateral censorship is permissible because it makes sense, given the purposes of the regulatory regime, to treat the private censor and the private speaker as the "same speaker" for purposes of First Amendment law. In both cases the private censor (the employer) has the *right to control* the content of the speaker's (the employee's) speech and is properly *responsible* for the harmful effects of that speech.

Why might it be permissible to hold one speaker liable for the harms of another? One reason is that the private censor and speaker are part of the same enterprise that produces the harm in question: they either collectively produce a single product that causes harm (a libelous publication), or their collective efforts create a harm or a risk of harm (misleading or fraudulent information about investments). Another reason is that the private censor is in the best position to avoid the harm. That might be so if the private censor is particularly good at distinguishing protected from unprotected harmful speech, can avoid harms more easily and effectively than the speaker, or has better information than the speaker.

Thus, we can identify three factors that justify treating the private censor and speaker as "the same speaker": (1) the private censor's right to control the private speaker's speech, (2) the joint or collective production of a harm or danger of harm, and (3) the private censor's superior ability to avoid the harm. Not surprisingly, these reasons resemble the traditional justifications for vicarious liability, in which courts treat employer and employee as the "same tortfeasor" for purposes of liability.[14] (They also suggest why the Court found little difficulty with holding publishers liable for reporters' speech in *Cantrell*, even though that rule clearly chills the speech of reporters.)

It is easy to see why the justifications for vicarious liability are relevant to the constitutionality of collateral censorship. If we hold the private censor responsible for the private speaker's harmful speech, it is reasonable to expect the private censor to censor. Conversely, if we don't want to encourage the private censor to censor (because we value the free flow of ideas), we should ensure that the private censor is not held responsible for the private speaker's harmful speech. Thus, collateral censorship is most acceptable from a First Amendment standpoint when vicarious liability is most acceptable, and it is least acceptable from a First Amendment standpoint when vicarious liability is least acceptable.

This reasoning also explains why collateral censorship is permissible even when the censor and speaker are not employer and employee, or part of the same business enterprise. For example, book publishers often demand that authors rewrite or even omit potentially defamatory passages as a condition of publication. No one doubts that these practices affect authors' practical ability to speak. But this collateral censorship does not violate their First Amendment rights, even when they engage in explicitly political speech. Like newspaper editors, book publishers have the right to editorial control over authors as a condition of publication and that is why they are liable for their authors' defamatory statements.

Conversely, collateral censorship is most problematic when vicarious liability makes the least sense. A good example is when liability is imposed on a distributor, a common carrier, or some other conduit that is not part of the same business enterprise as the censored speaker, lacks the right to exercise editorial control, and lacks information about the nature of the content flowing through its channels.

In fact, the one Supreme Court case that comes closest to recognizing the problem of collateral censorship seems premised on this distinction. In *Smith v. California*,[15] a state law made it a crime for bookstore owners to stock books that were later judicially determined to be obscene, even if the owner did not know of the books' contents. The Supreme Court struck down the statute, arguing that "if the bookseller is criminally liable without knowledge of the contents, . . . he will tend to restrict the books he sells to those he has inspected; and thus the State will have imposed a restriction upon the distribution of constitutionally protected as well as obscene literature."[16] Hence, "[t]he bookseller's self-censorship, compelled by the State, would be a censorship affecting the whole public, hardly less virulent for being privately administered."[17] What the Court calls "self-censorship" is actually collateral censorship.[18]

The Supreme Court thought that it was unfair to hold the bookstore owner liable because the bookstore owner lacked information about the content of each and every book. This is not simply a matter of fairness to the bookseller. Nor is it purely a concern about inefficient sorting. If our only concern were keeping harmful speech out of bookstores, we could accept a blunderbuss approach. But in the First Amendment area we should be as concerned with false positives (nonobscene books that don't get stocked) as with false negatives (obscene books that wind up on the bookstore shelves). We should be concerned about closing off means of expression to the authors on the one hand, and closing off information to audiences on the other. That is why it is a bad idea, from a First Amendment perspective, to squeeze the distributor (such as a bookstore owner or a common carrier) in the middle.

Defamation law recognizes the problem of collateral censorship through what is called the distributor's privilege. Usually someone who repeats a defamatory statement is as liable for publishing it as the original speaker (assuming the person also acts with the requisite degree of fault).[19] However, a distributor of information, like a newsstand or a bookstore, is generally not held to this standard unless the distributor knows of the publication's defamatory content.[20] The fear is that if distributors were held to be publishers, distributors might restrict the kinds of books and magazines they sold, greatly reducing the public's access to protected expression.

To receive the common law privilege, a distributor does not have to be a common carrier, which must take on all customers without oversight. Although distributors make some content-based judgments—for example, in choosing what books or magazines to stock—their editorial control is very different from and much more limited than that of the book publisher or magazine editor.

In the telecommunications industry, collateral censorship is a recurrent constitutional problem: cable companies and Internet service providers regularly act as conduits for the speech of unrelated parties. Treating them like publishers or editors would have the same sorts of effects that the Court was worried about in *Smith v. California*. Thus, in the Telecommunications Act of 1996, Congress extended a special privilege to Internet service providers whose customers post indecent, obscene, or "otherwise objectionable" matter in cyberspace, declaring that, as a matter of law, they should not be considered the publishers of such material.[21]

Hostile environment law surely produces collateral censorship. But it does not involve a distributor or conduit relationship. The employer who censors employees for fear of creating a hostile environment is more like the employer who censors employees out of fear of liability for defamation or securities fraud, and less like the Internet service provider who censors its customers, or the bookstore owner who refuses to stock certain books in order to avoid liability.

Unlike the case of the bookstore owner and the book author, the employer and employee in a hostile environment case are part of the same business enterprise. The employer has the contractual right to control the employee's speech and conduct. Perhaps more important, the law has good reasons to hold the employer accountable for the acts of its employees.

First, the employer is better able to see the larger picture about what conduct might contribute to sex discrimination. Hostile environments emerge from a combination of behaviors that not all employees may have knowledge of.

Second, the employer is better able than individual employees to prevent hostile environments from emerging, especially when they result from collective actions that no individual employee may be able or willing to prevent.

Third, precisely because the creation of a hostile environment does not stem from any single act, but from many acts taken together, it makes sense to treat the harm to equal opportunity in the workplace as a single harm. Collective action problems may reduce the incentives of individual employees to prevent hostile environments. Thus it may make even more sense to treat employer and employees as a "single speaker" engaged in a single harm than it does in the case of defamation or securities fraud.[22]

Fourth, the employer faces incentives to acquiesce in hostile environments that have no analogue in defamation or securities fraud situations. This makes the case for employer liability — and the need for incentives to police employees — even stronger. Sexual harassment is a form of sex discrimination. It helps keep jobs and employment opportunities sex-segregated according to traditional gender roles — for example, by keeping women out of higher-paying construction positions and in lower-paying secretarial positions, or by imposing obstacles to advancement for women even in integrated workforces. Employers may accept (or ignore) sex discrimination by their male employees (including sexual harassment) in order to avoid labor disruption and preserve esprit de corps and loyalty among a particular class of valuable (male) workers. In theory, employers could save money by staffing jobs with less well paid women rather than with men, but this might produce enormous labor disruptions, even with nonunionized workers. Under these conditions, acquiescence is a second-best solution for maximizing profits. Employers will accept a sex-segregated workforce with only a few token women in "male" positions (enforced by many different forms of sex discrimination, including employee harassment) as a compromise with existing male employees who want to maintain higher wages and workplace status.[23] In short, the different incentives of employers and employees may push them toward a common strategy, producing a workplace culture that distributes job opportunities by sex and enforces this result through subtle and not-so-subtle forms of discrimination and harassment.

Congress has a right to prevent this result. Title VII gives women and minorities an equal right to pursue work and an equal right to workplace opportunities. Through Title VII, Congress and the courts have imposed on all employers an obligation to guarantee their employees a workplace free from sexual discrimination and harassment, whether caused by managers or by coworkers—just as OSHA regulations require employers to guarantee a workplace free from defective health and safety conditions caused by management or by coworkers. In effect, Congress has required employers to produce a certain kind of business culture in the workplace. The Supreme Court's decisions in *Ellerth* and *Faragher* confirm this: employers are strongly encouraged to create antiharassment policies and compliance procedures.[24] The speech and behavior of individual employees is integral to the production of workplace culture, and the employer is in the best position to manage that culture, just as employers always managed business culture before the application of antidiscrimination laws.

In sum, collateral censorship is a problem only when vicarious liability for employee conduct is unjustified. Because there are abundant good reasons to hold employers liable for employees' creation of a hostile environment, the collateral censorship produced by Title VII does not offend the First Amendment.

The Real Problem: Captive Audiences

Critics can still raise other First Amendment objections, which fall into three categories. First, the courts' standard of abusive conduct is unduly vague. Second, sexual harassment doctrines are overbroad because they prohibit speech that would clearly be protected outside the workplace. Third, sexual harassment doctrines make distinctions on the basis of content and viewpoint. On closer inspection, however, none of these objections proves fatal.

The vagueness argument proves entirely too much: it applies equally to most judge-made communications torts. For example, speech is defamatory "if it tends . . . to lower [an individual] in the estimation of the community or to deter third persons from associating or dealing with him."[25] Intentional infliction of emotional distress requires words or conduct "so outrageous in character, and so extreme in degree, as to go beyond all possible bounds of decency, and to be regarded as atrocious, and utterly intolerable in a civilized community . . . [where] recitation of the facts to an average member of the community would arouse his resentment against the actor, and lead him to exclaim, 'Outrageous!' "[26] A judicial standard of sexual harassment that requires severe or pervasive intimidation, ridicule, insult, and abuse does not seem unduly vague in comparison with these torts. In fact, much of the objection to the vagueness of hostile environment doctrine seems directed at the worry that employers will collaterally censor employees. Collateral censorship will certainly occur, but it does not make hostile environment law unconstitutional, any more than it makes defamation or securities fraud law unconstitutional.

The second argument — that harassing speech would be protected outside of the workplace — is more promising. But it, too, proves unavailing. Speech that would be protected in the public square often becomes unprotected when it occurs in special social situations involving special social roles. If a White House intern sleeps with the President and falsely denies it at a press conference, her false statement is protected. However, if she repeats the same denial in an affidavit or on the witness stand, she can be prosecuted for perjury. The same words inserted into a new social context create different responsibilities and different degrees of First Amendment protection.

Sexually harassing speech that would be protected outside of the workplace becomes unprotected within it because it occurs in a relationship of economic and social dependence — the employment relation — and because it involves a form of sex discrimination that (1) materially alters the terms and conditions of employment for women, (2) reinforces the lower status of women in employment relationships, and (3) preserves gender stratification in employment markets. In short, speech used to create a hostile working environment is unprotected not because of its content, but because in the social context in which it occurs, it is a method of employment discrimination.

Employment discrimination law prevents harms to material or economic interests like salary and working conditions. But it is also concerned with the social status of women, blacks, and other minorities. It attempts to dismantle unjust forms of social stratification based on race or sex that get visited on individual employees in the workplace. Title VII protects against both material- and status-based harms because material and status elements are inextricably intertwined in the workplace, and cannot easily be separated. This should not be surprising: common sense tells us that people with large corner offices do not receive lower salaries and reduced authority as a trade-off, and people in cubicles don't get juicier work assignments as compensation. Rather, people with high status and esteem also usually enjoy better salaries and working conditions. Conversely, people lower in the hierarchy of the workplace usually enjoy less pleasant working conditions and lower compensation.

Because material benefits and social status are so deeply interconnected in the workplace, harms to people's group status that significantly impair their working conditions constitute employment discrimination under Title VII. That is why there is nothing particularly unusual or special about hostile environment liability. Hostile environment situations are just a special case of ordinary disparate treatment discrimination: they are harms to employees' group status — imposed on account of their membership in the group — that materially alter their working conditions as individuals.

Racist and misogynist speech outside the workplace can also reproduce group status distinctions and impose status harms. But the First Amendment does not generally permit recovery for harms to one's group status.[27] It allows recovery for defamation, but primarily for injury to individual reputation.[28] In the special context of the workplace, however, the First Amendment does permit people to recover for harms to group status when (and only when) these status-based harms so materially alter their working conditions that they constitute employment discrimination under Title VII. As explained in *Harris v. Forklift Systems* and *Meritor Savings Bank v. Vinson*, the plaintiff must face a workplace "permeated with 'discriminatory intimidation, ridicule, and insult' that is 'sufficiently severe or pervasive to alter the conditions of the victim's employment and create an abusive working environment'" as judged by a reasonable person.[29] Just as false speech before a jury is punishable not merely because it is false but because false speech in this setting is perjury, status-based harms in the workplace are sanctionable not merely because they are offensive but because in this setting these harms are mechanisms of employment discrimination. They are forms of disparate treatment that help sustain job segregation in the workplace.

Workers in hostile environments are surrounded by an abusive environment they cannot easily escape. First Amendment doctrines permit content-based regulation to protect "captive audiences." Simply put, a person trapped in a hostile work environment is a "captive audience" for First Amendment purposes with respect to the speech and conduct that produce the discrimination. Hostile environments do the work of job segregation by making workers captive audiences. Although courts created the captive audience doctrine for other situations, it actually makes better sense in the context of the workplace.[30]

Generally speaking, people are captive audiences when they are unavoidably and unfairly coerced into listening. According to the Supreme Court, the paradigmatic case of a captive audience involves assaultive speech directed at the home.[31] The Court's other major example has been people riding on public buses who cannot avoid looking at political advertisements.[32]

Read too broadly, captive audience doctrine would give the state enormous power to silence people based on vague notions of captivity.[33] Thus, it is not surprising that First Amendment scholars have tried to limit the doctrine to speech aimed at the home, where courts view privacy concerns as at their highest. So understood, the "captive audience" doctrine is not about captive *audiences* at all, but about the special nature of particular *places* like the home.

This view of captive audience doctrine is mistaken. It is both over- and underinclusive. People are not captive audiences simply because they are at home. They can throw away junk mailings, change the dial, activate v-chips, operate the channel blocking capabilities of cable boxes, install filtering software, or, if all else fails, disconnect the cable service, turn off the television, and stop subscribing to an Internet service provider.

Nor is the home an unalloyed example of "privacy." In the information age, we increasingly receive information in our homes rather than outside them. New technologies like the Internet redraw and even collapse the boundaries between public and private spaces. People can participate in public discourse and public deliberation on the Internet while sitting at home in their underwear. In most cases the protection of children is a much better justification for content regulation than captive audience doctrine.[34]

Conversely, limiting captive audience situations to the home misses the point of the metaphor of *captivity* — that a person must listen to speech because he or she is practically unable to leave. Children may be subject to discipline in the home, but for most adults, the place they are most subject to the discipline of others, and least free to leave, is at work. Economic coercion leaves many workers unable to avoid exposure to harassing speech. Employees are a much better example of a captive audience than the so-called paradigm case of people sitting in their homes who suddenly come across indecent speech on television.

Being "captive" is a matter of practicality rather than necessity. It is about the right not to have to flee rather than the inability to flee. The Supreme Court has suggested that people riding in buses subjected to political advertisements were a captive audience; but surely these people could have chosen other forms of transportation, albeit at greater expense and inconvenience. Even people in their homes are not physically prevented from leaving them. The point of captive audience doctrine, however, is that they should not have to be put to such a choice. The coercion brought upon them is unfair. In like fashion, minimum wage workers may have to move from job to job to avoid harassment. But the question is not whether there is another equally low-paying job available. The question is whether they should have to leave a job to avoid being sexually harassed.[35] It would undermine the central purpose of Title VII to argue that it gave workers no right to stay in a job free from sexual harassment. Moreover, as noted before, the kind of employment discrimination at issue here promotes gender segregation in job opportunities precisely by surrounding the plaintiff in a hostile environment of speech and conduct. If the plaintiff's only remedy is to leave, the mechanisms of job segregation will simply proceed unabated.

Captive audience doctrine should not focus on particular *spaces* like the home. Rather, it should regulate particular *situations* where people are particularly subject to unjust and intolerable harassment and coercion. Captive audience doctrine, like the doctrines of Fourth Amendment privacy, should protect people in coercive situations, not places.[36] "The workplace" is not a place; it is a set of social relations of power and privilege, which may or may not have a distinct geographical nexus. If a male supervisor makes an obscene phone call from his home to a female subordinate in a hotel room, this unwelcome behavior can and should contribute to a hostile work environment, even though both supervisor and subordinate are miles away from the office.

The practical necessities of earning a living and the economic coercion inherent in social relations in the workplace create captive audience situations; but this does not mean that the workplace should be treated as a First Amendment-free zone. In fact, the workplace should be an arena of special, not lessened, free speech protection. Precisely because people spend so much of their lives at work, the workplace is an important site of public discourse.[37] Much employee speech in the workplace is not, nor should it be considered, exclusively "managerial," "instrumental," or "private." We may talk more about public matters, sports, gossip, politics, and the affairs of the day at work than we do at home. The problem with existing employment law is that it gives employers too much power to control the speech of employees on every subject, not simply on matters of sex and sexuality.

One way to justify sexual harassment liability in the workplace would be to make a categorical distinction between the world of public discourse and the world of the workplace. Thus, one might argue that "there are good reasons for the law to regard persons as autonomous within the context of political deliberation, but there are equally good reasons for the law to regard persons as dependent within the workplace."[38] However, because the workplace is also an important site of public discourse, the law cannot simply insist that workers are to be regarded as dependent in all their speech interactions in the workplace. Otherwise, Congress could regulate virtually all workplace speech. Put in the language of captive audience doctrine, workers would be captive audiences for all purposes.

That is why it is important to remember that the basis of captive audience doctrine is social relations rather than geographical places. Sexual harassment helps maintain sexual stratification of the workplace using the economic dependency of workers as a powerful form of leverage. Therefore the law may regard workers as dependent and not autonomous with respect to speech that helps maintain such stratification, but not with respect to other speech.

Critics of hostile environment liability miss this point, I think, when they argue that "[h]arassment law, if viewed as an attempt to protect a captive audience, is . . . underinclusive" because it applies only to speech that "creates a hostile environment based on race, sex, religion or national origin."[39] The point is precisely that people are almost never captive audiences for every purpose, even in the workplace. They are captive audiences only with respect to certain forms of unjust coercion that use the employee's economic dependence as a springboard. Sex discrimination is one of those situations. Another is the use of economic coercion to prevent or hinder decisions about unionization, as illustrated in labor cases like *NLRB v. Gissel Packing Co.*[40]

In *Gissel* the Supreme Court upheld an NLRB order that required an employer to bargain with a union that had lost an election. The election was held to be tainted by the employer's (truthful) statements that election of a union could lead to closing of the employer's plant or, if the union called a strike, to a transfer of operations. Kingsley Browne, a critic of hostile environment liability, insists that "[t]he reasoning of *Gissel* does not support a general governmental right to regulate speech in the workplace."[41] I quite agree. *Gissel* holds that when unfair employment practices take advantage of the coercion already inherent in the employment relationship, the government may step in to regulate workplace speech in order to promote equality values and protect employees' right to bargain freely. Similarly, captive audience doctrine applies only to situations where speech and conduct together will help perpetuate job segregation or other forms of employment discrimination.

In short, we should not confuse the economic dependence of employees with their ability to participate in public discourse about the things that matter to them. Precisely because workers are economically dependent within the workplace, but engage in public discourse there, Congress might want to make them *more* autonomous within the workplace by guaranteeing them certain speech rights against their employers. This means, for example, that employee political speech that is directed to issues of public concern should be exempted as a basis for hostile environment liability as a matter of statutory construction and that Congress might even want to take positive steps to protect political speech from retribution by employers.

Clearly some political speech can contribute to sexual stratification in the workplace, at least at the margins. But it is unlikely that in most cases it is the major contributor. Working through the facts of actual cases, one is more likely to find pranks, taunts, sexual suggestions, and personal invective than political agitation as the basic technology for creating hostile environments. Because political speech is valuable, and because it contributes only marginally to sexual stratification, courts should exempt it.[42]

Some commentators have argued for a distinction between directed and nondirected speech: only speech specifically directed at a particular individual or set of individuals (such as face-to-face insults) would form the basis of hostile environment liability, while nondirected speech would be exempt. I think a better distinction is between "open" and "hidden" speech. The former is speech that openly contributes to preserving sexual stratification — that is, putting women in their place. The latter is speech relegated to private consumption by willing participants or to private conversation among willing listeners. Take the case of pornography, the classic example of nondirected speech. We should distinguish employees who keep pornography in their desk drawers out of sight from those employees who keep pornography prominently displayed around the workplace where coworkers are likely to see it. We should treat male employees who tell each other dirty jokes not intended to be overheard by female coworkers differently than employees who do so openly in order to distress and offend their female counterparts. Some speech is not intended for general consumption, particularly speech that occurs out of public view and away from other coworkers. Employees can avoid exposure to this speech with relatively little effort and the burden should be on them to do so. Thus, as a matter of statutory construction, courts should not consider "hidden" or "nonpublic" speech between willing participants as constituting a hostile environment, even if it is not overtly political in character. The same should apply to "after-hours" speech and gossip between willing participants that is not intended to be overheard by coworkers.[43]

The open/hidden distinction is superior to the directed/nondirected distinction because it is more consistent with the purposes of hostile environment liability. By itself an individual employee's comment or expression may not constitute a hostile environment, but many different acts taken together can. From the perspective of the female or black employee, the hostility of environment is experienced as a whole, not in isolated bits. It is the environment as a whole—and the felt sense that women or minorities are poorly regarded or unwelcome in the workplace—that preserves or maintains sexual or racial stratification. The open/hidden distinction imagines the cumulative effect of expression from the perspective of the victim of the hostile environment, who experiences it as a gestalt. By contrast, the directed/nondirected distinction looks at the issue of hostile environment from the perspective of the individual perpetrator, who may well not understand how his or her nondirected expression contributes to an overall feeling of unwelcomeness or second-class citizenship.

The final constitutional objection to hostile environment law is that its judge-made doctrines are content- and viewpoint-based. Once again, this proves too much: the same charge could be leveled against defamation, fraud, and most other communications torts. Juries in defamation cases are required to make content-based judgments about what kinds of statements would hold people up to shame or ridicule in the community and to assess damages based on the degree of injury to reputation. Moreover, liability for defamation necessarily depends on viewpoint. If a defendant falsely says, "Smith is a crook," she may be subject to liability, but not if she falsely says, "Smith is an honest man."

Title VII protects workers from a limited class of status-based harms in order to guarantee equality in the workplace. As in the case of defamation, if status-based harms are to be protected at all, some content-based and even viewpoint-based distinctions are inevitable. Thus, it makes perfect sense that a sign saying "Sarah is Employee of the Month" would ordinarily not give rise to liability, while a sign reading "Sarah is a dumb-ass woman"[44] might form part of a hostile environment case. Such content-based distinctions are adapted to the very reasons why employment discrimination law protects workers from status-based or dignitary injury.[45]

The Deeper Issue: Employer Control

There is some irony in libertarian complaints about employees' freedom of speech. In America the state has generally offered very little protection for employee speech. The traditional common law rule has been that employees can be fired at will absent a contractual provision to the contrary. Unless employees have sufficient bargaining power to demand "just cause" provisions in their contract, the employer can sanction or fire them for virtually any reason, including displeasure with their speech, even their political speech.[46] The common law regime is still the default rule today, and it provides employers with one of their most potent weapons for shaping the culture of the workplace and the behavior of their employees. American law stands in marked contrast with that of many other countries. In Europe, for example, employees often enjoy more substantial rights against arbitrary discharge.[47]

Thus, sexual harassment doctrines do not pose a simple conflict between some employees' liberty and other employees' equality. The question is not whether employees will have freedom of speech, but *how* employers will control employee speech — whether they will do so in response to the incentives produced by Title VII or for their own purposes.

Blaming employee censorship on Title VII diverts our attention from a larger issue: employers exercise considerable and sometimes tyrannical control over the speech and behavior of their employees. Throughout history American employers often have been deeply interested in control over the culture of the workplace. They are no less interested than the government in inculcating social norms of appropriate speech and behavior. Often they go even further, imposing elaborate dress codes and rules of social etiquette. In fact, the most important counterweights to the employer's power to shape workplace culture through hiring and firing decisions are antidiscrimination laws. Without the incentives created by sexual harassment law, employees are simply remitted to the economic and social control of employers. In other words, First Amendment challenges to sexual harassment law are a defense of employer prerogatives presented in the guise of worker liberties.

In the long run, employers will not necessarily lose much control over the workplace because of sexual harassment law. To the contrary, compliance with government regulation is often not a danger but an opportunity. Employers will use sexual harassment law as a new device for controlling their subordinates, by combining legal compliance with other bureaucratic and economic goals. Many tales of unjust compliance practices can be understood in precisely this way. The excuse of sexual harassment liability allows employers to impose ever new controls on employee behavior during an age when employees are spending more and more time at work and tend to rely more and more on the workplace to meet their partners.

When First Amendment challenges are raised to sexual harassment law, civil libertarians should not be diverted from the deeper issues of employer control and employee freedom. We can protect the First Amendment best by following the law as it is written — by awarding damages only in cases where severe or pervasive abuse materially alters employment conditions. But we should also not forget to protect employees — all employees — by working for greater speech rights against their employers than American law has seen fit to give them. For many employees, those are the speech rights that really count.

Notes

My thanks to Bruce Ackerman, Akhil Amar, Ian Ayres, Dan Kahan, Sandy Levinson, Catharine MacKinnon, Vicki Schultz, Reva Siegel, and Eugene Volokh for their comments on previous drafts. An earlier version of this essay appeared at 99 *Columbia Law Review* 2295 (1999) and appears with permission of Jack M. Balkin and the Columbia Law Review.

1. *See, e.g.,* Kingsley R. Browne, "Title VII as Censorship: Hostile-Environment Harassment and the First Amendment," 52 *Ohio State Law Journal* 481, 548 (1991); Eugene Volokh, "Freedom of Speech and Workplace Harassment," 39 *UCLA Law Review* 1791, 1846 (1992); Eugene Volokh, "How Harassment Law Restricts Free Speech," 47 *Rutgers Law Review* 563, 567 (1995); Eugene Volokh, "What Speech Does 'Hostile Work Environment' Harassment Law Restrict?" 85 *Georgetown Law Journal* 627, 647 (1997).

2. *Harris v. Forklift Systems, Inc.,* 510 U.S. 17, 21 (1993) (quoting *Meritor Savings Bank v. Vinson,* 477 U.S. 57, 65, 67 (1986)).

3. *Harris,* 510 U.S. at 21, 21–23.

4. 524 U.S. 742 (1998).

5. 524 U.S. 775 (1998).

6. *See Burlington Industries, Inc. v. Ellerth,* 524 U.S. 742, 765 (1998).

7. *See* Sexual Harassment, 29 C.F.R. § 1604.11(d) (1996). *See also Faragher v. City of Boca Raton,* 524 U.S. 775, 799–800 (1998) (collecting cases).

8. Employers are not completely free to censor employee speech, of course: they are also constrained by wrongful discharge law, union rules, and civil service regulations.

9. I borrow this term from Michael I. Meyerson, "Authors, Editors, and Uncommon Carriers: Identifying the 'Speaker' Within the New Media," 71 *Notre Dame Law Review* 79, 116, 118 (1995).

10. 376 U.S. 254, 283 (1964).

11. 418 U.S. 323, 350 (1974).

12. 419 U.S. 245, 253–54 (1974).

13. For a general discussion, *see* Burt Neuborne, "The First Amendment and Government Regulation of Capital Markets," 55 *Brooklyn Law Review* 5 (1989).

14. *See* W. Page Keeton et al., *Prosser and Keeton on the Law of Torts* 69, at 499–501 (5th ed. 1984) (describing standard justifications for vicarious liability).

15. 361 U.S. 147 (1959).

16. *Id.* at 153.

17. *Id.* at 154.

18. *See* Meyerson, *supra* note 9, at 118 n.259.

19. *See Restatement (Second) of Torts* § 578 (1977) ("Except as to those who only deliver or transmit defamation published by a third person, one who repeats or otherwise republishes defamatory matter is subject to liability as if he had originally published it").

20. *See id.* § 581 ("One who . . . delivers or transmits defamatory matter published by a third person is subject to liability if, but only if, he knows or has reason to know of its defamatory character").

21. 47 U.S.C. § 230(c)(1); *see Blumenthal v. Drudge*, 992 F. Supp. 44, 49–52 (D.D.C. 1998). In fact, the 1996 act gives Internet service providers more protection than the traditional distributor's privilege, because knowledge of defamatory content is not sufficient to subject them to liability. *See Zeran v. America Online*, 129 F.3d 327, 331–32 (4th Cir. 1997), cert. denied, 524 U.S. 937 (1998).

22. The argument for the constitutionality of collateral censorship in hostile environment cases is in some ways even stronger than in defamation and securities fraud cases because most courts currently hold the employer liable only if the employer knows or should have known of the harassment and does not take prompt corrective action. In other words, employers are not held strictly liable for employee speech (as in other vicarious liability situations) but are only liable when they fail to exercise due care in rooting out and remedying hostile environments. Hence the degree of collateral censorship should, in theory, be less in these cases.

23. I am indebted to Vicki Schultz for this argument.

24. *Ellerth*, 524 U.S. at 763–64; *Faragher*, 524 U.S. at 807.

25. *Restatement (Second) of Torts* § 559 (1977).

26. *Id.* § 46 cmt. d.

27. *See R.A.V. v. City of St. Paul*, 505 U.S. 377, 391–92 (1992); *Texas v. Johnson*, 491 U.S. 397, 414 (1989). The First Amendment may permit recovery for "fighting words," or for intentional infliction of emotional distress, *see Chaplinsky v. New Hampshire*, 315 U.S. 568, 571–72 (1942), but these categories are very limited and do not include all or even most racist or misogynist speech.

28. Compare *Gertz v. Robert Welch, Inc.*, 418 U.S. 323, 341 (1974) (discussing compelling interest in protecting individual reputation), with *Beauharnais v. Illinois*, 343 U.S. 250, 263–64 (1952) (upholding group libel statute). *Beauharnais* has never been overruled but its precedential value is generally thought doubtful, especially after *New York Times Co. v. Sullivan*, 376 U.S. 254 (1964), and *R.A.V. v. City of St. Paul*, 505 U.S. 377 (1992). *See* Laurence H. Tribe, American Constitutional Law § 12–12, at 861 n.2, § 12-17, at 921 n.9, § 12–17, at 926–27 (2d ed. 1988).

29. *Harris*, 510 U.S. at 21 (quoting *Vinson*, 477 U.S. at 65, 67).

30. *See* J. M. Balkin, "Some Realism About Pluralism: Legal Realist Approaches to the First Amendment," 1990 *Duke Law Journal* 375, 424 (1990).

31. *See, e.g., Frisby v. Schultz*, 487 U.S. 474, 487 (1988) (upholding ban on residential picketing directed at a single house); *cf. Kovacs v. Cooper*, 336 U.S. 77, 87 (1949) (upholding ban on sound trucks to protect residents).

32. *See Lehman v. City of Shaker Heights*, 418 U.S. 298, 301–4 (1974) (plurality opinion) (upholding ban of political advertising on public buses on grounds that passengers are a "captive audience").

33. *Cohen v. California*, 403 U.S. 15, 21 (1971).

34. *See* J. M. Balkin, "Media Filters, the V-Chip, and the Foundations of Broadcast Regulation," 45 *Duke Law Journal* 1131, 1137–39 (1996).

35. Vicki Schultz has described the "revolving door" phenomenon of women in low-

paying jobs who are continually forced to change jobs because of sex discrimination or harassment. *See* Vicki Schultz, "Telling Stories About Women and Work: Judicial Interpretations of Sex Segregation in the Workplace in Title VII Cases Raising the Lack of Interest Argument," 103 *Harvard Law Review* 1749, 1826, 1839 (1990). These women find themselves in a perpetual exodus from jobs that are "a dime a dozen." But the phenomenon of these forced exits is not an argument against the application of captive audience doctrine to harassment law; it is an argument for it.

36. *Cf. Katz v. United States*, 389 U.S. 347, 351 (1967) (holding that the Fourth Amendment "protects people, not places").

37. *See* Cynthia Estlund, "Freedom of Expression in the Workplace and the Problem of Discriminatory Harassment," 75 *Texas Law Review* 687, 717–18 (1997). Indeed, Kent Greenawalt argues that workers are "captive speakers," because they may have few other places to express themselves, and because "[w]hen people are working, the only place they can express themselves is within the workplace." Kent Greenawalt, *Fighting Words* 86 (1995) (emphasis omitted).

38. Robert C. Post, "The Perils of Conceptualism: A Response to Professor Fallon," 103 *Harvard Law Review* 1744, 1746 (1990).

39. Volokh, "Freedom of Speech," *supra* note 1 at 1843.

40. 395 U.S. 575 (1969).

41. Browne, *supra* note 1 at 514.

42. *Cf.* Richard H. Fallon, Jr., "Sexual Harassment, Content Neutrality, and the First Amendment Dog That Didn't Bark," 1994 *Supreme Court Review* 1, 47 (arguing for a somewhat narrower exemption for speech " 'reasonably designed or intended to contribute to reasoned debate on issues of public concern' ") (citing Harvard Law School's draft Guidelines Concerning Sexual Harassment).

43. Nevertheless, such speech might be evidence of sex discrimination, or of other speech or conduct that would constitute a hostile environment.

44. *See Harris*, 510 U.S. at 19.

45. *Cf. R.A.V. v. City of St. Paul*, 505 U.S. 377, 389 (1992) (holding that content-based discrimination within a category of unprotected speech is justified when it furthers the purpose for which the speech is unprotected). Not surprisingly, even Eugene Volokh drops his objections to content- and viewpoint-based restrictions on harassment when the harassment is directed at a particular person. *See* Volokh, "Freedom of Speech," *supra* note 1 at 1866–67.

Note, moreover, that under the logic of *R.A.V.*, one may not argue that Title VII is unconstitutionally content-based because it does not cover harassment on all subjects, but only on the basis of race, sex, national origin, and religion. Congress is permitted to decide that discrimination on those grounds is more unjust, inflicts greater or more distinctive harms on its victims, or causes greater social problems than other forms of discrimination which it has chosen not to prohibit. *See Wisconsin v. Mitchell*, 508 U.S. 476, 487–88 (1993).

46. *See* Cynthia L. Estlund, "Free Speech and Due Process in the Workplace," 71 *Indiana Law Review* 101, 116–17 (1995).

47. *See, e.g.*, Frances Raday, "Individual and Collective Dismissal—A Job Security Dichotomy," 10 *Comparative Labor Law Journal* 121 (1989).

PART VI

Extensions

27

Slavery and the Roots of Sexual Harassment

ADRIENNE D. DAVIS

In recent years, feminist scholars and activists have demonstrated the ways that U.S. slavery functioned as a system of gender supremacy. It entailed the dominance of men over women as well as whites over blacks. Adding the gender lens has shed immense light on the ways that sex, law, and power operated in the racially supremacist enslaving South. In recent years, this literature has emphasized the ways that slavery's sexual and racial subordination converged around the bodies of enslaved black women. My own contribution attempted to catalogue the legal rules that compelled black women into productive, reproductive, and sexual labor crucial to the political economy. That project characterized slavery as a "sexual political economy" to make explicit the connections between its markets, labor structure, and sexual exploitation.[1] It designated slavery a sexual economy to foreground slavery's gender hierarchies and mechanisms of subordination as well as to show how slavery offered early illustrations of the social construction and fluidity of gender and the false dichotomy between public and private relations.

Taking those insights to their logical conclusion, this essay frames enslaved women's sexual coercion through their roles as captive workers to cast the institution of slavery in a new light: as an early and particularly virulent strain of institutionalized sexual harassment. In the process, it shows how we gain better purchase on sexual harassment when we look at antecedents in U.S.

slavery. Conceiving slavery as sexual harassment sheds light on how slave law was labor law, plantations were workplaces, and enslaved women's resistance constituted gender activism. Critically, such a framework also recovers the sexual dimension of both slavery *and* sexual harassment. Casting slavery in this way hopefully yields a richer and more nuanced understanding not only of slavery, but of feminist history, theory, and contemporary activism.

Labor in Slavery's Sexual Economy

As I described elsewhere, U.S. slavery compelled enslaved black women to labor in three markets—productive, reproductive, and sexual—crucial to the political economy.[2] As an initial matter, in a world built on slave labor, enslaved women's work was central. Unlike other slave economies that enslaved women primarily as wives or concubines, U.S. slavery forced black women to perform productive labor essential to the political economy. Some enslaved women were forced to join free white women in performing productive, domestic labor for white households. But, as a general matter, slavery's markets for productive labor did not follow the gender segregation patterns of the free labor market. The overwhelming majority of enslaved women labored at tasks that in the free workforce were typically reserved for men. Slaveholders forced enslaved women to cut trees, build canals, and cart manure, as well as to plow, plant, hoe, and harvest crops. In some markets that drew heavily on enslaved men for skilled labor, slaveholders actually reserved the most arduous agricultural work for enslaved women, with a few earning the dubious honor of being rated the most valuable field hand. There was gender differentiation: enslaved men rarely did domestic labor and enslaved women were excluded from certain tasks, typically skilled labor, reserved to men. But, unlike black men, white men, and white women, all of whom labored mainly in accord with traditional gender roles, enslaved women were compelled to perform every sort of productive labor, as the political economy demanded. Significantly, forcing enslaved women to breach the sexual division of free labor did not appear to challenge the male slaveholders' own gender identity.

In addition to coercing their labor in the conventional productive markets, slavery's law and markets extracted from enslaved women reproductive and sexual labor in a form required of no one else. Enslaved women reproduced the workforce. Like other New World plantation economies, that of the United States was based on a captive black workforce. "Land and slaves became the two great vehicles through which slaveholders realized their ambitions of fortune. . . . The usefulness of land increased in proportion to the availability of black slaves."[3] But unlike its sister slave societies, the U.S. sustained its workforce through the women in it. By 1682, all of the colonies had adopted the rule of *partus sequitur ventrem* — a child inherited its status from its mother. Without regard to whether the father was free, enslaved women gave birth to enslaved children. This rule proved to be of immense economic and political significance. The South was one of the smallest importers of slaves, but had the largest slave population in the West. This demographic was inextricably tied to enslaved women's biological and social reproduction. Following the close of the (legal) international slave trade in 1808 and accompanying the rising labor demands driven by the expanding cotton market and southern frontier, a thriving domestic trade in black people emerged — supplied by black women's childbearing. In the end, "[t]he perpetuation of the institution of slavery, as nineteenth-century Southerners knew it, rested on the slave woman's reproductive capacity."[4]

Slavery also extracted sexual labor from enslaved women. Enslaved women found themselves coerced, blackmailed, induced, seduced, ordered and, of course, violently forced to have sexual relations with men. Sexual access was enforced through a variety of structural mechanisms. Most overtly, the South established markets that sold enslaved women for the explicit purpose of sex. In so-called "fancy girl" markets, principally in southern port cities, enslaved women could be bought to serve as the sexual "concubines" of one man, or to be prostituted in the more contemporary understanding of the term. According to one historian, we might understand "fancy" as referring to markets "selling the right to rape a special category of women marked out as unusually desirable."[5] Outside of these overt markets for sex, most enslaved women and girls were purchased primarily for their productive labor in the fields or plantation house, but also were expected to have sexual relations with various men (their master, his sons or male relatives, visitors, overseers, enslaved men) on the plantation as well. Whether in sex markets or "productive" ones, every sale of an enslaved woman was a sale of sexual labor — or at least of the right to compel it. Sex was part and parcel of what was expected and coerced from women in the enslaved workforce.

By the nineteenth century, the standard mechanisms to protect a woman's sexuality were the law of rape and access to patriarchal protection. However ineffective for most white women, these protections were completely unavailable to enslaved women. The criminal law of rape reflected the economic and cultural expectation of sexual access. As a general rule, law did not recognize rape as a crime when committed against enslaved women.[6] Nor did black men have the social authority to protect women in their community: "Without marriage or human rights, the female slave is a sexual vessel as well as chattel. There is no patriarchy to protect her unless the master assumes the role of her protector, that is, if she is his concubine and has his children. Her men have no power or status; they are socially dead and thus are unable to come to her aid and protection, unable to father the children they sire. There are no laws to protect her because she has no place in the law."[7]

Regardless of filial, romantic, or simply community ties, a black man could rarely protect a black woman from sexual abuse. To do so was to risk his life, and often hers. Rules of evidence and self-defense operated synthetically to criminalize any response but submission.[8] Instead, at every opportunity, the legal system endorsed the principle that slaveholders' authority over their workers included sexual control and use. Slave law delivered what the markets expected.

Once law and markets had institutionalized sexual access to enslaved women, their sexuality could be manipulated to serve any number of economic, political, and personal interests. Men might coerce sexual relations with enslaved women for sexual gratification, to garner profits, to punish work-related transgressions, or to more firmly bolster the association of white women with the cult of the pedestal.[9] Enslaved women's sexuality was made available simultaneously as an outlet for male eroticism, a market commodity, a tool of discipline, and an ideological device to justify slavery.

Thus, slavery's laws and markets collaborated to compel sexual and reproductive labor, as well as productive labor, from women in the enslaved workforce. Dictating that enslaved women gave birth to enslaved children and denying enslaved women access to either criminal rape law or patriarchal power, in effect, compelled enslaved women into reproductive and sexual labor. In fact, Jacqueline Jones points out, "[i]f work is defined as any activity that leads either directly or indirectly to the production of marketable goods, then slave women did nothing *but* work."[10] It is also important to keep in mind how race, gender, and status were simultaneously operative under slavery. Slavery's rules of race ensured that it was only *legally* black women who reproduced the workforce and who suffered in slavery's sexual markets. Of course, many enslaved people were scopically white, which actually drove the fancy market inflated prices of up to $5,000. As one historian incisively commented, "What, after all, could be more valuable than a woman of 'white' complexion who could be bought as one's private 'sex slave'?"[11] But legally, culturally, and politically, it was only "black" women who were compelled into such horrific "work."

Designating slavery a sexual political economy makes explicit the connections among its markets, labor structure, and sexual exploitation. It also directs attention toward the ways that New World slavery's geographic manifestation, the plantation, was particularly hospitable to institutionalized sexual abuse and coercion of women in the black workforce. In the South, as in the rest of New World slavery, plantations were the primary units of production. Rising prices for commodities requiring intensive labor, reduced costs of capturing and enslaving that labor, increased political stability, and improved production and distribution capabilities resulted in the plantation-based economies that characterized New World slavery. Critically, plantations were not only the primary units of economic production — they were central cultural and political units of the slave economy as well. "[The plantation] not only constituted the chief vehicle for the exercise of power in southern society but also served as the foundation of southern public beliefs and values."[12] Law and culture vested male heads of household with authority over all who lived on their plantations in both market and domestic relations. Both criminal and civil law declined to intervene in the slaveholder-enslaved relationship, except in the most egregious circumstances (which did not encompass enslaved women's sexual exploitation and abuse).[13] Moreover, the physical geography of plantations, often vast spaces, isolated from each other and denser populations, was ideal for those who sought to control the entire lives of their workforce. Plantation owners largely determined who entered and who left these vast workplaces/households, enslaved and free, black and white, female and male. Housing the workforces they enslaved, slaveholders could exercise the perpetual surveillance and scrutiny necessary to maintain racial and labor domination.

In short, the southern "plantation complex" both required and produced enslaved women's sexual and reproductive exploitation. As workplaces, plantations were the source of insatiable demand for captive labor. As households, their gender norms insisted on the sexual subservience of black, enslaved women. Finally, their physical structure provided the privacy and authority necessary to convert and coerce labor relations into sexual ones.

Slavery as Sexual Harassment

In the 1970s, feminist scholar-activists identified sexual subordination in the workplace as a primary manifestation of sex inequality: "Work is critical to women's survival and independence. Sexual harassment exemplifies and promotes employment practices which disadvantage women in work (especially occupational segregation) and sexual practices which intimately degrade and objectify women. . . . [S]exual harassment at work undercuts woman's potential for social equality in two interpenetrated ways: by using her employment position to coerce her sexually, while using her sexual position to coerce her economically."[14] Sex was part and parcel of what was expected from women as workers and had the added (or primary) effect of using the workplace to preserve gendered norms. More recent feminist elaborations of sexual harassment's injury characterize it as a "disciplinary, constitutive, and punitive regulatory practice."[15] In the end, men harass women workers because of entitlement, to achieve sexual dominance, for personal pleasure, and to discipline women as workers and as women.

All of these motivations and effects were institutionalized *and* state-sanctioned under slavery on an almost incomprehensible scale. First, sexual (and reproductive) labor is part of what was expected and extracted from them as women in an enslaved workforce. Second, conveniently, the same acts that brought economic profits and sustained the political economy also resulted in sexual domination and personal erotic gratification.[16] Third, slavery constituted a new category of labor relation: permanent, captive workers defined by race and as property, performing work essential to the means of production.[17] Sexual coercion proved a key mechanism for compelling enslaved women to labor in the three parallel markets crucial to the southern political economy. (Enslaved men may have been sexually victimized for similar purposes, a topic which is underexplored in the literature.[18] Indeed, contemporary sexual harassment theory has turned its attention to the theoretical and political dilemmas raised by same-sex harassment, which may prove insightful for trying to shed light on and comprehend the complex meanings of male sexual victimization of enslaved men.)[19] Slaveholders sexually exploited and coerced women in the enslaved workforce for profit, pleasure, and punishment — simultaneously and without contradiction.

Feminist history helps us to see women in the enslaved workforce as sexually abused and exploited. Feminist legal theory helps us to see their abuse as sexual harassment — deployed to secure sexual access as part of the labor relation and to coerce captive labor. Slavery's structural sexual abuse and coercion was directed against them not only as women, or as black women, but as *black women workers*. Consider the descriptive power of Catharine MacKinnon's powerful articulation of sexual harassment when we substitute "slaveholder" for "employer." "In these cases, we are dealing with a male who is allegedly exercising his power as [a slaveholder], his power over a woman's material survival, and his sexual prerogatives as a man, to subject a woman sexually."[20] Hence slavery maps onto — indeed in many ways provides a map *for* — these contemporary understandings of sexual harassment. Consider the following.

As stated earlier, my previous work designated slavery a sexual political economy to make explicit the connections between its markets, labor structure, and sexual exploitation. Foregrounding the interplay between slavery's political economic structure and its sexual norms also sheds light on the plantation complex as a vast workplace and one of the earliest American sites of institutionalized sexual harassment. The labor relation as defined by slavery incorporated sexual relations for purposes of pleasure, profit, punishment, and politics. The geography of plantations expedited widespread sexual exploitation for all of these purposes, granting the men who ran them sexual privacy and authority.[21] Moreover, the geography of these "workplaces" meant that enslaved women could rarely escape their sexual dynamics. Enslaved women *and* their white mistresses describe enslaved women being forced to sleep in their masters' bedrooms. There was no respite from sexual abuse at the end of the day, "at home." Plantations comprised both "home" and "work," and a master was as likely to stalk an enslaved woman in her quarters as in his bedroom. Finally, both public criminal and private plantation "justice" punished efforts to "exit" with extreme violence. Women in the enslaved workforce were, in effect, "sexual hostages."[22]

Slavery's sexual economy also divided women, making black women susceptible to sexual abuse and harassment not only from men, but from white women. Barbara Omolade has richly described the ways that slavery operated as a racialized patriarchy — one in which white men broke ranks with black men in order to dominate all women.[23] White patriarchs were also exceptionally successful in encouraging white women to break ranks with their black sisters. Slavery's sexual geography meant that enslaved women were harassed in the homes of women related to their abusers. Enraged and humiliated white wives insisted on the sale of black families fathered by their husbands, or themselves perpetrated ugly violence, at times sexual, against the women workers their husbands abused.[24] Hence, the sexual geography of the plantation complex also invited white women into sexual harassment of women in the enslaved workforce.

Finally, slavery graphically illustrates what feminists have argued since the earliest conceptions of sexual harassment: sexual subordination in the workplace is a central tool of labor, sexual, *and* racial control.[25] As Angela Davis argued at around the same time, white men claiming black women as sexual property functioned as a primary tool of repression against the entire enslaved workforce and black community more broadly.[26] White men not only wielded sexual abuse against enslaved women as individuals, but as a weapon of racial terror. Sexual authority over enslaved women was intimately bound with racial, economic, and political authority over all black workers, free and enslaved.[27] This is not a point about the "emasculation" of enslaved men, but rather about what Davis characterized as "sexual terrorism" against a workforce.[28]

In the end, while slavery's sexual harassment conforms to contemporary understandings it served interests and needs somewhat unique to slavery's distinct sexual economy. Some may worry that characterizing slavery as sexual harassment risks minimizing slavery's distinct brutal racial and gender subordination. I share their caution. Increasingly, we see history rewritten to erase embarrassing atrocities. Certainly slavery's sexual atrocities were exceptionally brutal. Sexual violence directed against black women workers was often lethal, was authorized by the state, and was part of a broader scheme of repressing a captive workforce. There is a sense in which our collective disgust, horror, and embarrassment about slavery causes us to draw a cordon noir around its sexual economy. But to exclude enslaved women from sexual harassment's history would be especially pernicious, whitewashing it, as it were. We can't let the horrifically corrupt and brutal manifestations of sexual abuse and coercion cause us to miss slavery for what it was: widespread, institutionalized, state-sanctioned sexual harassment implemented in perhaps its most corrupt form.

What do we get by conceiving enslaved women as coerced labor, plantations as some of the earliest large-scale workplaces, and slavery as sexual harassment? I would suggest three insights: one for history, one for theory, and one for contemporary activism.

Feminist History

Historians continue to contest the origins of feminism, but standard accounts locate its emergence in either the abolitionism that culminated in Seneca Falls or in the antebellum women's benevolent associations.[29] These narratives differ substantially, but both attribute the emergence of feminism to elite, literate, white women active in the early nineteenth-century public sphere. In neither account do enslaved women appear except as the objects of activism, or, if freed, as black compatriots of feminist abolitionists. Increasingly, women's history features enslaved women, but does not include them in discussions of feminism's origins.

The exclusion of enslaved women from formal feminist history takes more and less benign forms. At its most benign, it assumes that the dynamics of racial repression were so stark that they consumed the complete political consciousness of enslaved people. In this account, slavery's sexual abuse was secondary to its racial hierarchies. In its most essentialist formulation, feminism would argue that enslaved women failed to conform to the achievements of first wave white feminists: the production of public texts, organized protests, and the articulation of gender as a core axis of oppression. Neither narrative considers enslaved women as gender activists operating independently of feminism's official white foremothers or, even more radically, as their predecessors in recognizing and resisting gender subordination.[30] Conceiving slavery as sexual harassment suggests a different view of feminist history.

For generations, feminist activists have noted the difficulty of organizing women because of gender's manifestation as both subordination and privilege. In America's racially patriarchal culture, white women have often experienced gender as privilege. Even today, many women (of all races and classes) stubbornly insist that gender's privileges outweigh its price. In addition, consider again the power of geography in both enabling and masking sexual subordination. Contemporaneously with much of slavery, most nonenslaved American women worked in small-scale workplaces, often their own households. Even those white women who joined enslaved black women in working on large plantations typically had some blood tie to the patriarch of the house. When the household was the unit and site of production, sexual harassment was difficult to distinguish from other forms of sexual abuse perpetuated within families and protected by law.[31] Moreover, sexual exploitation of white women workers could be subsumed by the rhetoric — first, of paternal control over households and, later, separate spheres and gender "difference" as domesticity. The former denied its existence or attributed it to evil girls, women, and infants. The latter articulated the problem as women's abdication of the "private" domestic sphere. The solution was to remove women from the paid workforce and return them to the care and protection of men at home, again presuming paternalism. Sexual exploitation of individual women workers was condemned, but in language that continued to support gender hierarchy.

In contrast, slavery's racial supremacy may have enabled women in the enslaved workforce to recognize, politicize, and resist sexual harassment far earlier than many of their white peers. Black women in the enslaved workforce experienced sexual violence from white men unmediated by gender privilege. Nor did common gender rhetoric for mediating worker sexual abuse map onto the geography of the plantation (or enslaved women's lives). While southern planters incorporated metaphors of domesticity to describe and justify their absolute power over both their families and their slaves, the enslaved community experienced little ambiguity about the metaphor's descriptive power. By and large they were not members of the family and, even when they were, were not treated as such. From the perspective of enslaved women, paternalism failed to capture the dynamics of the plantation. Nor was anyone trying to drive them from "masculine" market work into "feminine" domestic labor. The plantation was not susceptible to separate spheres logic, nor were enslaved women's lives.[32]

Moreover, when white men laid claim to enslaved women's sexual and reproductive capacity, they did so within a larger context of racial and workforce repression. This politicized sexual abuse, removing it from the realm of "private" conflicts between individual men and women.[33] Instead, as stated above, the entire enslaved workforce experienced sexual assault as a primary mechanism of their subordination. Slave narratives — autobiographies and oral histories — are replete with stories by victims and those close to them of brutal, sometimes lethal sexual atrocities. These texts parallel formal abolitionism in making sexual abuse part of the discourse of slavery's oppression, yet depart from standard abolitionist rhetoric in important ways. In lieu of depicting enslaved women as passive victims of abuse, they record a community in rebellion against the sexual norms whites sought to impose. Enslaved women themselves mounted multiple forms of resistance, some of them more recognizable than others.[34] But, additionally, the entire community resisted the appropriation of enslaved women's bodies as sexual property. Without romanticizing or obscuring the brutality and pain of sexual abuse, these narratives suggest that the politicized context entitled individual women to the support of their communities as they experienced, resisted, and survived sexual abuse. Instead of ostracism, blame, and denial, they received advice, collaboration, and assistance. In fact, the enslaved workforce may have been one of the first in the U.S. to mount active, community resistance to widespread sexual harassment.

Contrary to arguments of some feminist theorists that other identity "clouds" the operation of gender, the racial context of slavery meant that women in the enslaved workforce were some of the first to name, politicize, publicize, and resist institutionalized sexual harassment. That they actively resisted slavery's structural gender supremacy strongly suggests that American feminist activism goes back much farther than the Seneca Falls Convention. I understand the impulse to mark moments when women gathered, issued written texts, and developed a vocabulary that called national attention to women's structural subordination. And I do not want to minimize the significance of the emergence of gender as a distinct category of analysis in history. But including slavery as part of sexual harassment history does not restrict the scope of feminism; it expands it. Confronting the fundamentally patriarchal nature of American slavery opens the possibility that, through their manifold resistance, literally thousands of black women were joining with their free white sisters in recognizing and despising gender subordination. In fact, it appears that, precisely due to the racial context of slavery's sexual economy, feminism drew some of its first activists from among the enslaved workforce. They may not have understood their oppression solely through the gender lens. Their oppression was both gendered and racialized, and they recognized it as such. But the fact that there were *two* axes to their resistance ought not erase the significance of their *antisexist* efforts.[35]

Feminist Theory

Sexual harassment was a key component of Catharine MacKinnon's dominance theory of feminism, which emphasizes sexual power as a primary mechanism of women's subordination.[36] But increasingly, feminists want to take the "sex" out of sexual harassment.[37] At the extreme end, some new frameworks characterize sexual harassment not as sexual dominance, but as economic competition.[38] In this view, men sexually harass women to preserve male-only workspaces. Hence, in the blue-collar context, men create debilitating, sometimes dangerous, hostile environments in order to force women out of relatively desirable, higher-paying jobs or jobs with greater status, flexibility, or status.[39] A less extreme critique attempts to keep the focus on dominance while shifting the emphasis of sexual harassment theory to policing gender norms or disciplinary practices. Katherine Franke puts it succinctly: men harass women to feminize them, not for sex.[40] This trend in conceptions of sexual harassment is indicative of larger trends in feminist theory. Increasingly, academic feminists are skeptical as to whether dominance adequately captures sexual harassment specifically, or sociosexual dynamics more generally. There are related efforts to redefine women's subordination as gender, rather than sexual, oppression. Implicit in some theories seeking to protect sex is that worker identities can be distinguished from gendered or sexual ones — a resurrection of public and private as oppositional and exclusive, perhaps.

Reading slavery as sexual harassment contradicts theories of sexual harassment that would segregate it from other forms of sexual violence or redefine it as economic to the exclusion of being sexual. Recall that part of the plantation complex's cultural specificity is that it functioned simultaneously as home and workplace. For enslaved women there was no respite from employer sexual abuse. Assault from a slaveholder was as likely in her home (or his) as in the fields. A theory that segregates violence according to geography — whether it happened at "home" or at "work" — defies her experience. Within the plantation complex, sexual violence constituted both sexual harassment *and* domestic violence. Relatedly, harassment often came in the form of rape, and when women were whipped and punished, it was often intensely sexualized. When an enslaved woman was raped in the field, stripped bare for whipping, sexually threatened in the fields by her slaveholder/father, or threatened with sale for refusing sex in her "master's" bed, it was all sexual and it was all economic.

Despite its historical specificity, the plantation offers a paradigm case of sexual harassment, domestic violence, rape, and incest as on a continuum of *sexual* violences.[41] Attempting, then, to disaggregate enslaved women's gendered (sexualized) identities from their worker identities results only in incoherence. Instead, comprehending sexual harassment as such is contingent on recognizing that there is not a tension between sexual desirability, contempt for women, and the denigration of women as workers.[42] Rather, they are completely consistent and mutually reinforcing — and all sexual. Despite our desire to preserve sex as the realm of the positive, part of labeling slavery a sexual economy is to remind us that we can't always conveniently segregate private, intimate relations from market, work relations, or sexual harassment from other forms of violence against women.[43] Hence, slavery puts the sex back in sexual harassment.

It also suggests the ongoing explanatory power of sexual dominance as motivating sexual harassment. White men harassed and abused black women in the enslaved workforce for any variety of reasons. Significantly, at no point was the goal of sexual coercion to force enslaved women out of the workforce or into gender-segregated work (with the exception of coerced reproduction). Having already defined gender identity (i.e., masculinity and femininity) along racial lines, elite white men appeared personally enriched, not threatened, by enslaved women's work patterns. Instead, it was to secure their submission as well as the submission of black male workers. And it had the added benefit of being erotic as defined by slavery's sexual economy.[44] In fact, efforts to leave the workplace brought punishment and repression. I am particularly empathetic to Franke's insistence that sexual harassment functions as a "disciplinary practice" to achieve "power, privilege, or dominance," and to her conscientious inclusion of new theories of gender to enrich our understanding of gender-based subordination.[45] But slavery suggests the racial and historical limits of Franke's argument. Slavery offers a fascinating early example of the fluidity and social construction of gender.[46] Enslaved women's sexuality comprised an integral part of the political economy, and as such, was regulated by that structure's material and ideological needs. Through constant manipulation, it was continuously under construction, as required by the dictates of the culture. (This is not to say that enslaved women did not resist, a point of much contention. They did, as described above.) An enslaved woman might be socially constructed as "masculine" for the purposes of productive work and brutal physical punishment, but very much a woman for the purposes of reproductive and sexual exploitation. But, while white men sexually abused them as women, they refused to impute to them the "femininity" ascribed to white women.

In short, women can be made into sexual objects without being subjected to policing along the lines of conventional gender identity. For many nondominant women, sexual harassment (and other sexual violences) continue to be imposed without the accompanying imposition of femininity. Or, "femininity" (and gender generally) has to be expanded to include an understanding of black women's sexual subordination. An analysis grounded in slavery as sexual harassment also sheds light on another mechanism of workplace sexual subordination that is at the center of much of Franke's insightful work: the ways that sexual abuse of women can be an effective way of harassing men in the workplace. Particularly when combined with other identity categories (race, class, ethnicity, religion), sexual harassment can be deployed against men without feminizing moves. When we ground sexual harassment in this expanded history, we can see more clearly how its goal is labor, racial, *and* sexual, as well as gender, control. Franke does acknowledge the racial variations of sexual harassment, but does not accordingly limit her description of perpetrator motivations or the goals of these disciplinary practices.

Barbara Omolade captures slavery's complex dynamics when she describes it as a racialized patriarchy, in which white men broke allegiances with black men, dominating both white and black women.[47] Comprehending slavery as gender supremacy suggests a different view of the relationship between sex and sexual harassment, or at least the need to refine claims. Slavery's sexual economy constituted two hundred years of racialized sexual dominance. When we look at slavery, to borrow MacKinnon's articulation of sexual harassment, "the entire structure of sexual domination, the tacit relations of deference and command, can be present in a passing glance."[48] This is not to say that enslaved women did not resist, negotiate, manipulate, and, ultimately, shape the system. As I described above, they did. But this is a primary mistake of those who oppose dominance theory: to say that men seek to dominate women, to say that patriarchy is real, is not to say that men are always completely successful. Nor is it to say that there aren't other axes of power continuously at work: slavery comprised a racialized patriarchy in which sexual abuse of enslaved women workers was part of the gender dominance by white men over white wives and the racial dominance of white men over black men. Relatedly, it is not to say that same-sex subordination isn't in play: that one way of dominating *other men* is to feminize them, including sexually. But, it is to say that enslaved women workers' sexuality was a primary site of contestation, and control and use of it was viewed as key to racial and class hierarchy. To my understanding, this seems to be in keeping with the basic tenets of dominance feminist theory. Other feminists may disagree with my conclusion, although I hope not with my characterization of slavery's brutal racialized sexual dynamics. This analysis suggests the need for contemporary feminist theories that further develop and account for slavery's distinct sexual dynamics. A theory of feminism inapplicable to or uncharacteristic of millions of enslaved women over two hundred years cannot be much of a theory for women.

Feminist Activism

One quite effective strategy among antifeminists is to whitewash feminism, erasing the presence of women of color in feminism's ranks and leadership. With specific regard to sexual harassment, advocates of ending or limiting legal relief have deployed the stereotype of the "strong" black mama, who, hand on hips, tells off employers and coworkers. They argue that white women should take lessons from their black "sisters."

Incorporating enslaved women's vigorous, systematic, and diverse resistance as part of sexual harassment history links their struggle to those of the black plaintiffs in early Title VII harassment litigation. Contradicting those who characterize feminists as white and sexual harassment as a white woman's issue, black women workers were among the first plaintiffs to bring Title VII harassment claims (against white and black men). Margaret Miller, Paulette Barnes, Diane Williams, and Maxine Munford were among the earliest women to litigate sexual harassment as prohibited sex discrimination.[49] Sandra Bundy brought an important hostile environment claim in 1981, and Mechelle Vinson was the plaintiff in the U.S. Supreme Court case affirming it as a viable cause of action under Title VII in 1986.[50] Anita Hill named it publicly in 1991, sacrificing much to do so. In 1977, Pamela Price joined her Yale classmates in arguing that the school's failure to combat sexual harassment denied their right to equal educational opportunity.[51] It took more than twenty years from the enactment of Title IX until Aurelia and LaShonda Davis, a black mother and daughter team, convinced the Supreme Court that Title IX does provide a remedy against schools for failing to curtail student-on-student sexual harassment.[52] LaShonda Davis was in the fifth grade.

Critically, it is not that black women found the sexual harassment cause of action and framework descriptive of their lives. Instead, they were instrumental and central in creating and formulating the frameworks that *described* their lives. In her discussion of the litigants with whom she worked, Catharine MacKinnon reflects:

> Black women's least advantaged position in the economy is consistent with their advanced position on the point of resistance. Of all women, they are

most vulnerable to sexual harassment, both because of the image of black women as the most sexually accessible and because they are the most economically at risk. These conditions promote black women's resistance to sexual harassment and their identification of it for what it is.[53]

It makes sense, then, that we find high percentages of black women active in bringing a legal remedy to workplaces and educational spaces, spaces long associated with racial, as well as sexual, subordination. Having fought so hard to gain access, why would black women then accept lesser status within these spaces? After years of flight, dissemblance, and physical resistance, for black women workers in particular, Title VII offered welcome legal relief.

Viewing sexual harassment through the lens of slavery also highlights severe limitations in the reach and scope of the doctrine. Sexual harassment is typically associated with women working in factories, offices, banks, and construction sites. (And LaShonda Davis has helped us, finally, to see it in schools as well.) But slavery's sexual economy calls attention to the ways women working in certain geographic configurations are particularly vulnerable to sexual abuse, especially when combined with other axes of social power(lessness), such as race, age, immigrant/document status, or imprisonment.[54] One of the defining characteristics of enslaved women's sexual exploitation was their combined lack of rights, exclusion from legal protection from sexual assault, and economic and political vulnerability. Paradoxically, Title VII continues to exclude the historical paradigm of black women's sexual harassment, domestic labor done in private, individual homes, now increasingly performed by undocumented women. Meanwhile, forced labor sweatshops, agricultural workplaces employing unpapered women, and prisons offer paradigm instances of contemporary geographies that concentrate sexually vulnerable populations of women workers. Prisons, in particular, resonate with plantations, in that women's status and sexual abuse *as workers* is often invisible.[55] In fact, prisons, like plantations, are closed geographies from which there is no exit without legal authorization. The state returns both enslaved and incarcerated women (and men) to the conditions of their subjection. Nor is the goal of harassment and abuse of incarcerated women to drive them from a workplace defined as male; rather, sex is perceived by many as, again analogously, a tool of discipline and a prerogative of power. Not surprisingly, we find women of color disproportionately represented in all four of these geographies.[56]

Recovering enslaved women as gender activists in feminist history is a powerful, political counter-blow to conservative efforts to foment racial division among feminists. In addition, it reminds us that sexual harassment activists must fight to cover women working everywhere, especially in those places where the most vulnerable — unpapered immigrants, poor women, children, and women of color — continue to labor. This should encourage us to rethink the scope of Title VII, but also to create other legal remedies that extend to modern-day equivalents of plantations, where women workers continue to be held as sexual hostages.[57]

Conclusion

The brutality of slavery's overt racial repression often causes people to miss its sexual atrocities. Not only does this obscure slavery's dynamics, but it also distorts feminist history and theory. As yet, neither feminists nor slavery scholars have confronted slavery as sexual harassment. In fact, slavery was one of the most extraordinary instances of gender supremacy in U.S. history and one of the first to institutionalize and perfect sexual harassment. Labor historians have warned against the distortions that can occur when slavery is excluded from labor history. Feminists should take heed. Understanding enslaved women as forced labor and conceiving slavery as sexual harassment sheds light on plantations as vast workplaces, slavery as early, large-scale, institutionalized sexual harassment, and enslaved women as early gender activists in naming, politicizing, and resisting sexual harassment. Such a framework also suggests directions for future research and work. First, conceiving slavery as sexual harassment gains new ground from which to view labor, racial, and sexual history. It also raises questions as to how geography, race, other axes of social power, and sexual dominance continue to influence sexual harassment's manifestations. We need to grapple more explicitly with slavery as a sexual institution.

Notes

Many thanks to Mary Anne Case, Marion Crain, Glenn George, Jill Hasday, Kevin Haynes, and Bill Marshall for helpful comments and suggestions on this essay. Kathleen Creamer provided her usual superb research assistance and editing.

1. *See* Adrienne D. Davis, " 'Don't Let Nobody Bother Yo' Principle': The Sexual Economy of American Slavery," in *Sister Circle: Black Women and Work* 103 (Sharon Harley and Black Women and Work Collective eds., 2002) (hereinafter Davis, "Principle").

2. *See* Davis, "Principle," *supra* note 1.

3. James Oakes, *The Ruling Race: A History of American Slaveholders* 73 (1982).

4. Deborah Gray White, *Ar'n't I a Woman? Female Slaves in the Plantation South* 79–80 (1985).

5. Edward E. Baptist, " 'Cuffy,' 'Fancy Maids,' and 'One-Eyed Men': Rape, Commodification, and the Domestic Slave Trade in the United States," 106 *American Historical Review* 1619, 1643 (2001); *see also* Neal Kumar Katyal, Note, "Men Who Own Women: A Thirteenth Amendment Critique of Forced Prostitution," 103 *Yale Law Journal* 791, 798 (1993).

6. *See George v. State*, 37 Miss. 316, 320 (1859). Subsequently, Mississippi amended its statutory code to extend protection from sexual assault to black girls under twelve, but only those assaulted by black men. For a more detailed discussion of Mississippi's interplay of common and statutory law, see Adrienne D. Davis, "*Loving* Against the Law: The History and Jurisprudence of Interracial Sex" (unpublished manuscript, on file with author) (hereinafter, Davis, "*Loving* Against the Law"). Thomas Morris also offers a good summary of the ways that "[r]ace, age, and status were all elements in the law of rape in the South." Thomas D. Morris, *Southern Slavery and the Law: 1619–1860*, at 305 (1996).

7. Barbara Omolade, "The Unbroken Circle: A Historical and Contemporary Study of Black Single Mothers and Their Families," 3 *Wisconsin Women's Law Journal* 239, 242 (1987); *see also* Kimberlé Crenshaw, "Demarginalizing the Intersection of Race and Sex: A Black Feminist Critique of Antidiscrimination Doctrine, Feminist Theory, and Antiracist Politics," 1989 *University of Chicago Legal Forum* 139, 158–159 [hereinafter Crenshaw, "Demarginalizing the Intersection"].

Slave husbands had no right to protect (or control) their wives' sexuality. In contrast, common law gave free (and white) husbands enormous control over their wives' sexuality: no form of marital rape was recognized as a crime and *every* form of sex outside of marriage was at least nominally criminalized. *See* Jill Elaine Hasday, "Federalism and the Family Reconstructed," 45 *U.C.L.A. Law Review* 1297, 1333–1334 (1998); *see also* Jill Elaine Hasday, "Contest and Consent: A Legal History of Marital Rape," 88 *California Law Review* 1373, 1382–1406 (2000).

8. *See* Davis, "*Loving* Against the Law," *supra* note 6.

9. Davis, "Principle," *supra* note 1, at 114–117.

10. Jacqueline Jones, *Labor of Love, Labor of Sorrow: Black Women, Work, and the Family from Slavery to the Present* 14 (1985).

11. Brenda E. Stevenson, *Life in Black and White: Family and Community in the Slave South* 180 (1996); *see also* Baptist, *supra* note 5.

12. Peter W. Bardaglio, *Reconstructing the Household: Families, Sex, and the Law in the Nineteenth-Century South* xi (1995). As one Methodist minister put it: "Every Southern plantation is *imperium in imperio*." Eugene Genovese, " 'Our Family, White and Black': Family and Household in the Southern Slaveholders' World View," in *In Joy and in Sorrow: Women, Family, and Marriage in the Victorian South, 1830–1900*, at 69, 70 (Carol Bleser ed., 1991) (quoting Reverend H. N. McTyeire, "Plantation Life — Duties and Responsibilities," *DeBow's Review*, Sept. 1860, at 30).

13. *See, e.g., State v. Mann*, 13 N.C. (2 Dev.) 263, 264 (N.C. 1824) (in reversing a criminal assault and battery conviction of a man who had hired out a slave and shot her, the North Carolina Supreme Court concluded: "The power of the master must be absolute to render the submission of the slave perfect").

14. Catharine A. MacKinnon, *Sexual Harassment of Working Women: A Case of Sex Discrimination* 7 (1979) (hereinafter MacKinnon, *Sexual Harassment of Working Women*). Similarly, Kathryn Abrams defines sexual harassment as efforts to "preserve male control and entrench masculine norms in the workplace." Kathryn Abrams, "The New Jurisprudence of Sexual Harassment," 83 *Cornell Law Review* 1169, 1172 (1998); *see also* Kathryn Abrams, "Gender Discrimination and the Transformation of Workplace

Norms," 42 *Vanderbilt Law Review* 1183 (1989); Kathryn Abrams, "Title VII and the Complex Female Subject," 92 *Michigan Law Review* 2479 (1994).

15. Katherine M. Franke, "What's Wrong with Sexual Harassment?" 49 *Stanford Law Review* 691, 696 (1997).

16. *See* Baptist, *supra* note 5.

17. *See* Laura F. Edwards, *Gendered Strife and Confusion: The Political Culture of Reconstruction* 68–70 (1997); *see also* David Brion Davis, *The Problem of Slavery in Western Culture* 60 (1966).

18. *See* sources cited in Davis, "Principle," *supra* note 1, at 125 n.60.

19. *See, e.g.,* Franke, *supra* note 15.

20. MacKinnon, *Sexual Harassment of Working Women, supra* note 14, at 92.

21. Harriet Jacobs, the heroic formerly enslaved author of a signal autobiography, documents the sexual specificity of plantations. She describes the perpetual sexual surveillance and scrutiny she endured from her master, a doctor whose primary residence was in a small town. Significantly, Jacobs dates her determination to escape her master at any cost to his decision to send her to the plantation. Jacobs offers remarkable insight into how slavery functioned as sexual harassment. Harriet Jacobs, *Incidents in the Life of a Slave Girl* 84 (1861).

22. Darlene Clark Hine, "Rape and the Inner Lives of Black Women: Thoughts on the Culture of Dissemblance," in *Hine Sight: Black Women and the Re-Construction of American History* 37, 41 (Darlene Clark Hine ed., 1994) (hereinafter Hine, "Dissemblance").

23. "The white man's division of the sexual attributes of women based on race meant that he alone could claim to be sexually free: he was free to be sexually active within a society that upheld the chastity and modesty of white women as the 'repositories of white civilization.' He was free to be irresponsible about the consequences of his sexual behavior with black women within a culture that placed a great value on the family as a sacred institution protecting women, their progeny and his property. He was free to use violence to eliminate his competition with black men for black or white women, thus breaking the customary allegiance among all patriarchs. He was also free to maintain his public hatred of racial mixing while privately expressing his desire for black women's bodies. Ultimately, white men were politically empowered to dominate all women and all black men and women; this was their sexual freedom." Barbara Omolade, "Hearts of Darkness," in *Powers of Desire: The Politics of Sexuality* 350, 352 (Ann Snitow et al. eds., 1983) (footnotes omitted); *see also* Crenshaw, "Demarginalizing the Intersection," *supra* note 7.

24. Elizabeth Fox-Genovese, *Within the Plantation Household: Black and White Women of the Old South* 325–326 (1988); *see also* Nell Irvin Painter, "Soul Murder and Slavery: Toward a Fully Loaded Cost Accounting," in *U.S. History as Women's History: Feminist Essays* 125, 132 (Linda Kerber et al. eds., 1995) ("[w]hen the household was also a work site, the influence of labor relations within families would have been magnified"); Nell Irvin Painter, "Of *Lily*, Linda Brent, and Freud: A Non-Exceptionalist Approach to Race, Class, and Gender in the Slave South," in *Half Sisters of History: Southern Women and the American Past* 93 (Catherine Clinton ed., 1994) (describing strategies of denial).

25. "[S]exual harassment can be both a sexist way to express racism and a racist way to

express sexism." MacKinnon, *Sexual Harassment of Working Women, supra* note 14, at 30. For an excellent series of essays discussing the intersection of race, sex, sexual harassment, and power, see generally *Race-ing Justice, En-gendering Power: Essays on Anita Hill, Clarence Thomas and the Construction of Social Reality* 412 (Toni Morrison ed., 1992) (hereinafter *Race-ing Justice, En-gendering Power*).

26. Angela Y. Davis, "Reflections on the Black Woman's Role in the Community of Slaves," in *The Angela Y. Davis Reader* 111, 124 (Joy James ed., 1998) (originally published in 32–4 *The Black Scholar* 3, 13 (Dec. 1971)) (hereinafter Davis, "Reflections"). Andrea Dworkin also employed this term early on to capture the circumstances of women's sexual repression. *See* Andrea Dworkin, "Pornography: The New Terrorism," 8 *New York University Review of Law and Social Change* 215 (1978–1979).

27. A germinal case on sexual authority is described in more detail in Davis, "*Loving Against the Law*," *supra* note 6. It also describes how antebellum judges and slaveholders resorted to analogies to the marital rape exclusion in defending their sexual "privacy" vis-à-vis enslaved women.

28. *See* Davis, "Reflections," *supra* note 26. bell hooks argues for a complex understanding of black men in patriarchy. She says: "To suggest that black men were dehumanized solely as a result of not being able to be patriarchs implies that the subjugation of black women was essential to the black male's development of a positive self-concept, an idea that only served to support a sexist order. Enslaved black men were stripped of the patriarchal status that had characterized their social situation in Africa but they were not stripped of their masculinity." bell hooks, *Ain't I a Woman: Black Women and Feminism* 20–21 (1981).

29. *Compare* Eleanor Flexner, *Century of Struggle: The Women's Rights Movement in the United States* (1959) *with* Barbara J. Berg, *The Remembered Gate: Origins of American Feminism: The Woman and the City, 1800–1860* (1978).

30. *See also* Robin Kelley, *Race Rebels: Culture, Politics, and the Black Working Class* (1994) (describing how labor activism and other resistance of the black working class often went unnoticed because it didn't conform to the paradigm of unionized or other formalized resistance).

31. "Physical closeness and daily contact seem to lend the appearance of individuation to relationships." MacKinnon, *Sexual Harassment of Working Women, supra* note 14, at 89.

32. "[S]ome black women have been able to grasp the essence of the situation, and with it the necessity of opposition, earlier and more firmly than other more advantaged women." MacKinnon, *Sexual Harassment of Working Women, supra* note 14, at 53. Kimberlé Crenshaw concurs: "Racism may well provide the clarity to see that sexual harassment is neither a flattering gesture nor a misguided social overture but an act of intentional discrimination that is insulting, threatening, and debilitating." Kimberlé Crenshaw, "Whose Story Is It Anyway? Feminist and Antiracist Appropriations of Anita Hill," *in Race-ing Justice, En-gendering Power, supra* note 25, at 412.

33. MacKinnon's early work took account of this history in identifying black women's leadership as sexual harassment activists and litigants. "To the extent they are sensitive to the operation of racism on an individual level, they may be less mystified that the sexual attention they receive is 'personal.' Their heritage of systematic sexual harassment under

slavery may make them less tolerant of this monetized form of the same thing. The stigmatization of all black women as prostitutes may sensitize them to the real commonality between sexual harassment and prostitution. Feeling closer to the brand of the harlot, black women may more decisively identify and reject the specter of its reality, however packaged." MacKinnon, *supra* note 14, at 53–54.

34. *See, e.g.,* Hine, "Dissemblance," *supra* note 22 (discussing how structural sexual and reproductive abuse shaped cultures of resistance in southern black women); Darlene Clark Hine, "Female Slave Resistance: The Economics of Sex," *in Hine Sight: Black Women and the Re-Construction of American History* 27, 34 (Darlene Clark Hine ed., 1994) ("when they resisted sexual exploitation through such means as sexual abstention, abortion, and infanticide, they were, at the same time, rejecting their vital economic function as breeders. . . . The female slave, through her sexual resistance, attacked the very assumptions upon which the slave order was constructed and maintained. Resistance to sexual exploitation therefore had major political and economic implications."); *see also* Leslie A. Schwalm, *A Hard Fight for We: Women's Transition from Slavery to Freedom in South Carolina* 38 (1997) ("[w]omen's encounters with the threat of rape and sexual abuse provided additional impetus for subtle, persistent resistance and occasional outbreaks of open rebellion"). Black mothers advised their daughters: "Don't let nobody bother yo' principle, 'cause dat wuz all yo' had." John Blassingame, *The Slave Community: Plantation Life in the Antebellum South* 163 (1972) (quoting Minnie Folkes, a former Virginia slave). Harriet Jacobs famously hid in her grandmother's attic for seven years, waiting an opportunity to escape *with* her children. Jacobs, *supra* note 21. Some feminist literary scholars have argued that Jacobs's embrace of Victorian feminine rhetoric in her autobiography also constituted resistance to dominant racist stereotypes about black women.

35. Black feminist theorist bell hooks made this point more generally about race and feminist politics. Speaking of late nineteenth- and twentieth-century organizations she noted: "Black women identified themselves racially calling their groups Colored Women's League, National Federation of Afro-American Women, National Association for Colored Women, and because they identified themselves by race scholars assume that their interest in the elevation of blacks as a group overshadowed their involvement with woman's effort to effect social reform. In fact, black female reform organizations were solidly rooted in the women's movement." hooks, *supra note* 26, at 163; *see also* Evelyn Brooks Higginbotham, *Righteous Discontent: The Women's Movement in the Black Baptist Church, 1880–1920* (1993). hooks also notes: "While it is true that white women have led every movement toward feminist revolution in American society, their dominance is less a sign of black female disinterest in feminist struggle than an indication that the politics of colonization and racial imperialism have made it historically impossible for black women in the United States to lead a women's movement."

36. "Gender is a . . . question of power, specifically of male supremacy and female subordination. . . . The dominance approach centers on the most sex-differential abuses of women as a gender, abuses that sex equality law in its difference garb could not confront." Catharine A. MacKinnon, *Feminism Unmodified: Discourses on Life and Law* 40 (1987); *id.* at 42–43; *see also id.* at 46–62; Catharine A. MacKinnon, *Toward a*

Feminist Theory of the State 3–80, 215–249 (1989); Catharine A. MacKinnon, "Reflections on Sex Equality Under Law," 100 *Yale Law Journal* 1281 (1991); Catharine A. MacKinnon, "Feminism, Marxism, Method and the State: An Agenda for Theory," 7 *Signs* 515 (1982); Catharine A. MacKinnon, "Feminism, Marxism, Method and the State: Toward Feminist Jurisprudence," 8 *Signs* 635 (1983).

37. Kathryn Abrams recently rendered a powerful critique of theories that reject women's sexual subordination as part and parcel of sexual harassment. "The New Jurisprudence of Sexual Harassment," 83 *Cornell Law Review* 1169 (1998).

38. *See, e.g.,* Vicki Schultz, "Reconceptualizing Sexual Harassment," 107 *Yale Law Journal* 1683, 1686–1687 (1998) ("much of the gender-based hostility and abuse that women (and some men) endure at work is neither driven by the desire for sexual relations nor even sexual in content. Indeed, many of the most prevalent forms of harassment are actions that are designed to maintain work — particularly the more highly rewarded lines of work — as bastions of masculine competence and authority").

39. MacKinnon made this point in *Sexual Harassment of Working Women. See* MacKinnon, *supra* note 14, at 9–23.

40. "[S]exual harassment is understood as a mechanism by which an orthodoxy regarding masculinity and femininity is enforced, policed, and perpetuated in the workplace." Franke, *supra* note 15, at 760; *see also* Katherine Franke, "Gender, Sex, Agency, and Discrimination: A Reply to Professor Abrams," 83 *Cornell Law Review* 1245 (1998) (hereinafter Franke, "A Reply").

41. Beverly Balos and Mary Louise Fellows make these arguments in their work, "Guilty of the Crime of Trust: Nonstranger Rape," 75 *Minnesota Law Review* 599 (1991); "A Matter of Prostitution: Becoming Respectable," 74 *New York University Law Review* 1220 (1999); *Law and Violence Against Women* 578 (1996).

42. MacKinnon, *Sexual Harassment of Working Women, supra* note 14, at 43.

43. In "'Don't Let Nobody Bother Yo' Principle'" I describe the ways that slavery offers an early challenge to public/private dichotomies that rest on distinctions between informal "family" and formal "market" relations. Davis, "Principle," *supra* note 1, at 119–120.

44. *See* Baptist, *supra* note 5, at 1621.

45. Franke, *supra* note 15, at 693, 745.

46. I describe this in Davis, "Principle," *supra* note 1, at 119.

47. *See supra* notes 7, 23.

48. MacKinnon, *Sexual Harassment of Working Women, supra* note 14, at 95.

49. These early cases are described in detail in *id.* at 59–74; *see also* Anna-Maria Marshall, "Closing the Gaps: Plaintiffs in Pivotal Sexual Harassment Cases," 23 *Law and Social Inquiry* 761, 775–782 (1998).

50. *Meritor Savings Bank v. Vinson,* 477 U.S. 57 (1986); Marshall, *supra* note 49, at 775–782.

51. *Alexander v. Yale,* 459 F. Supp. 1 (1977), *affirmed* 631 F.2d 178 (2d Cir. 1980).

52. *Davis v. Monroe County,* 526 U.S. 629 (1999), *reversing* 120 F.3d 1390 (11th Cir. 1997). Mother and daughter were named two of *Glamour* magazine's Women of the Year for 1999. "Women of the Year," *Glamour,* December 1999, at 164.

53. MacKinnon, *Sexual Harassment of Working Women, supra* note 14, at 53. In her important sociological study of "legal mobilization" through sexual harassment litigation, Anna-Maria Marshall agrees that "the complex interaction of gender, class, and race created an enormous gap between harassed women and their employers — a gap that allowed employers, sanctioned by law, to ignore the women's complaints. Yet relying on communications networks, these women mobilized the law to bridge that gap and to force employers to address their complaints." Marshall, *supra* note 49, at 765. Similarly, in an interview with Marshall, feminist activist/scholar Nadine Taub speculated: "I don't think it was an accident that many of the early cases were brought by black women because I would think that a lot of white women could be tricked into thinking that it could be worked out, whereas for black women, they knew. They'd been exploited since day one." *Id.* at 776.

54. Kimberlé Crenshaw's germinal article on intersectionality retains its tremendous explanatory power here. *See generally* Crenshaw, "Demarginalizing the Intersection," *supra* note 7; *see also* Kimberle Crenshaw, "Mapping the Margins: Intersectionality, Identity Politics, and Violence Against Women of Color," 43 *Stanford Law Review* 1241 (1991). Katherine Franke analogizes workplace to other institutional forms of sexual harassment, concluding: "Each location contributes a unique set of intersectional dynamics that render the sting of gender discipline painful and effective in different ways." Franke, "A Reply," *supra* note 40, at 1249.

55. *See, e.g.,* Angela Y. Davis, "Public Imprisonment and Private Violence: Reflections on the Hidden Punishment of Women," 24 *New England Journal on Criminal and Civil Confinement* 339 (1998); Cassandra Shaylor, " 'It's Like Living in a Black Hole': Women of Color and Solitary Confinement in the Prison Industrial Complex," 24 *New England Journal on Criminal and Civil Confinement* 385 (1998); Chris Weaver and Will Purcell, "The Prison Industrial Complex: A Modern Justification for African Enslavement?" 41 *Howard Law Journal* 349 (1998); *see also* Teresa A. Miller, "Keeping the Government's Hands Off Our Bodies: Mapping a Feminist Legal Theory Approach to Privacy in Cross-Gender Prison Searches," 4 *Buffalo Criminal Law Review* 861 (2001).

56. *See, e.g.,* Mary Romero, *Maid in the U.S.A.* (1992); Samantha C. Halem, "Slaves to Fashion: A Thirteenth Amendment Litigation Strategy to Abolish Sweatshops in the Garment Industry," 36 *San Diego Law Review* 397 (1999); Laura Ho et al., "(Dis)Assembling Rights of Women Workers Along the Global Assembly Line: Human Rights and the Garment Industry," 31 *Harvard Civil Rights–Civil Liberties Review* 383 (1996). Black women make up an even greater proportion of incarcerated women than black men do of incarcerated men. *See, e.g.,* Angela Y. Davis, "Women in Prison," *Essence,* September 2000, at 150; Dorothy E. Roberts, "Criminal Justice and Black Families: The Collateral Damage of Over-Enforcement," 34 *U.C. Davis Law Review* 1005, 1017 (2001).

57. *See, e.g.,* Victims of Trafficking and Violence Protection Act of 2000, Public Law 106–386, 114 Stat. 1464 (2000).

28

The Racism of Sexual Harassment

TANYA KATERÍ HERNÁNDEZ

Despite the fact that early on the groundbreaking book *Sexual Harassment of Working Women* observed the salience of racism to the occurrence of sexual harassment,[1] sexual harassment has by and large been viewed by courts as a transgression without color. Sexual harassers are presumed to be color blind in their selection of victims, and sexual harassment is generally viewed as a civil rights violation in which issues of race are irrelevant.[2] Yet a recent statistical analysis of the filing rates of sexual harassment charges suggests otherwise.[3]

The comprehensive study analyzes Equal Employment Opportunity Commission (EEOC) sexual harassment charge statistics, by looking at data from 1992 to 1999 along with Lexis-Nexis and Westlaw electronic reports of sexual harassment complaints from 1964 to 2000. What immediately becomes apparent in this statistical analysis of sexual harassment charges in the United States is the overrepresentation of women of color and the "underrepresentation"[4] of White women in the charging parties when compared with their demographic presence in the female labor force.[5] Although a number of factors may very well be causally connected to the disproportionate patterns in female sexual harassment filing statistics by race, primary among the likely causal factors is the powerful influence of racialized gender stereotypes. Indeed, the centrality of racialized gender stereotypes in the manifestation of sexual harassment may indicate that sexual harassment does discriminate by race.

Scholars have noted that the operation of racialized gender stereotypes conceptually distinguishes "pure" White women from "wanton" women of color. This is a distinction described by Beverly Balos and Mary Louise Fellows as the "prostitution paradigm."[6] A consideration of the Balos and Fellow's prostitution paradigm within the sexual harassment context elucidates the rationale for the seeming racial disparity in rates of sexual harassment — the policing of gender through the hierarchy of race. After an exposition of the statistical data, this essay will analyze how the prostitution paradigm, and the intersectional race and gender approach it relies upon, demonstrates the role of race in the subjugation of all women through sexual harassment.

The Statistical Racial Patterns of Sexual Harassment

In a study of 1992 EEOC sexual harassment statistics, the Center for Women in Government at the University of Albany reported that Black women complainants accounted for 14.4 percent of sexual harassment charges, women of other races (not specified) accounted for 14.7 percent of sexual harassment charges and White women accounted for 61.9 percent.[7] Although White women complainants accounted for the vast majority of EEOC sexual harassment charges, in racially comparative terms White women are underrepresented as complainants. Specifically, White women accounted for only 61.9 percent of the sexual harassment charges in 1992, even though they made up 84.8 percent of all women employed in the civilian labor force in that same year.[8] Furthermore, the data indicates an overrepresentation of women of color as complainants in comparison to their representation in the female labor force. Black women, at the time the studied statistics were gathered, made up only 11.5 percent of all women employed in the civilian labor force and yet they accounted for 14.4 percent of the sexual harassment charges.[9] Other women of color only made up 3.7 percent of women employed in the civilian labor force but accounted for 14.7 percent of the sexual harassment charges.[10] Particularly troubling is the fact that the 1992 EEOC data were not an aberration.

My own analysis of EEOC sexual harassment charge statistics from 1992 through 1999 indicates that the race-based disparity in filing charges is a pattern among women who filed EEOC charges.[11] Similarly, after surveying federal court cases from the First through Sixth Circuits containing sexual harassment allegations through summer 2000,[12] I discovered that since the inception of the sexual harassment cause of action, the same racial pattern emerged among female plaintiffs.[13]

In the United States, the amount of variation between the observed numbers of sexual harassment charges by race and the expected number of sexual harassment charges based on racial demographic percentages of the population is considerable for each year of data.[14] The Supreme Court has acknowledged that, as a general rule, for sample sizes larger than thirty, if the difference between the expected value and the observed value is greater than two or three standard deviations, then a social scientist would view the data as not being the result of pure chance.[15] The average sample size for each year of EEOC data analyzed in my study was 13,051.5, and the average sample size for each circuit of federal cases analyzed was 97.[16] The standard deviation for White women ranged from 71.5 to 84.4 and from 31.5 to 66.7 for women of color. The statistical probability of such extraordinarily large standard deviations occurring in a normal distribution is approximately zero.[17] Therefore, although a number of factors could plausibly contribute to the racial disparity in sexual harassment charge statistics, the existence of some correlation between rates of sexual harassment and race-based decision-making on the part of harassers merits closer examination. What the data suggests is that sexual harassers may target White women as victims at disproportionately lower rates than women of color. This conclusion is consistent with some of the few empirical studies to specifically focus on the influence of race on sexual harassment.[18]

Although there is no mechanism to absolutely determine whether the number of complaints of sexual harassment faithfully reflect the actual rates of sexual harassment in society,[19] the sexual harassment charge statistics suggest a general pattern of racial disparity that is highly significant given its consistency over the years.[20] The analysis of charge statistics also has the advantage of being able to draw upon data generated from one consistent definition of sexual harassment.[21] In contrast, social science researchers have observed widely varying sexual harassment statistics depending on the definition chosen by the designer of a study.[22] Furthermore, the empirical alternative of solely examining the data from successfully litigated cases suffers the weakness of grossly underestimating the societal occurrence of sexual harassment. The mechanism that pushes the majority of legal charges to settlement before litigation in court is also present in sexual harassment cases. In addition, the nature of the sexual harassment claim, with its ability to harm the reputation of the victim herself, works to artificially deflate the number of sexual harassment cases because it discourages many victims from filing meritorious charges.[23] Many of those victims who do decide to file a charge are later dissuaded from continuing to pursue their claims.[24] In fact, from 1992 to 1999, 32 to 49 percent of EEOC sexual harassment charges were administratively closed without any substantive resolution of the charge.[25] Thus, given the known difficulties of pursuing a sexual harassment claim, using EEOC charge statistics and federal court sexual harassment allegations as a rough indicator of the existing patterns of sexual harassment in society may very well underestimate rather than overestimate the actual rate of sexual harassment.

Early Explanations for the Statistical Pattern

Before 1992, descriptive evidence existed indicating that women of color were disproportionately represented among the female population of early sexual harassment complainants.[26] Catharine MacKinnon's early observations about the role of racism in sexual harassment were based on her extensive work with Black women, many of whom had been sexually harassed. At the time, MacKinnon and later Kimberlé Crenshaw theorized that the racialized nature of sexual harassment women of color experienced made it easier for them, and for Black women in particular, to conceptualize their victimization as sexual harassment, whereas White women might have experienced greater difficulty in articulating their experiences as something other than overly aggressive dating overtures.[27] Since then, political scientist Anna-Maria Marshall's study of all pivotal sexual harassment cases has begun to provide an empirical validation of the descriptive evidence.[28] Marshall has similarly theorized that Black women's "heightened consciousness around issues of race may have also made the law a more salient resource" in challenging their experiences of sexual harassment.[29]

After 1992, it became harder to rely upon that conjecture as the sole explanation for the continuing racial disparities in female sexual harassment charge statistics for several reasons. In October 1991, the publicly aired testimony of Anita Hill during the Clarence Thomas Supreme Court confirmation hearing raised public awareness about the nature of sexual harassment.[30] In addition, Congress enacted the Civil Rights Act of 1991, which allows sexual harassment plaintiffs in all states to recover compensatory and punitive damages.[31] Thereafter, the EEOC published a layperson-friendly four-page pamphlet entitled *Questions and Answers About Sexual Harassment*, which started the public campaign to bring greater awareness of the nature of sexual harassment to the public at large and to the many employers who began instituting sexual harassment policies of their own.[32]

In short, since 1991, not only are all women in the United States better informed about the existence of a sexual harassment cause of action,[33] but they are also better educated about the ways in which its manifestations give rise to a remedy at law. The view of sexual harassment as a legal claim is "now part of the national consciousness."[34] In fact, the number of sexual harassment charges increased approximately 112 percent from 1989 to 1993 (moving from 5,623 to 11,908 over the four-year period), with 1992 being the year of the greatest single increase when charges went up 53 percent.[35] Not only have the annual number of sexual harassment complaints filed with the EEOC more than doubled since 1989,[36] the EEOC reports that sexual harassment is the fastest growing area of employment discrimination.[37] Therefore, the racial disparity in sexual harassment charge statistics can no longer be correlated solely with the "benefit" women of color have in experiencing sexual harassment as a more "easily recognizable" racial hostility.

A number of empirical studies also dispute the premise that women of color are more prone to file sexual harassment charges than White women who experience the same victimization.[38] In fact, those social scientists that have discussed the role of race in sexual harassment observe that women of color may actually have a tendency to underreport instances of sexual harassment.[39] This is true despite empirical studies that suggest that women of color are disproportionately targeted as sexual harassment victims.[40] In fact, at least one study suggests that White women tend to perceive incidents of sexual harassment as more serious than women of color do[41] and classify a broader range of behaviors as sexual harassment.[42] Some psychologists theorize that because women of color are accustomed to racist and sexist behavior in the workplace, they may be less prone to immediately filing a sexual harassment complaint.[43] One study in particular found that sexual harassment victims are more likely to use internal coping methods when the harasser is outside of their racial or ethnic group[44] — of particular salience to women of color, who are primarily victimized in the workplace by White men.[45] Therefore, when a geographically diverse sample of Black working women was surveyed, the study found that Black women see Black male subordinates and supervisors as more harassing than White males with the same job status.[46] Consequently, no support was found for the hypothesis that Black women were more likely to report a White harasser than a Black harasser.[47] Similarly, another study concluded that while being employed empowers White women to challenge dominant gender role attitudes, it does not have the same effect for women of color and Black women in particular.[48] In addition, the argument that the racial disparity in charge statistics is primarily the result of the lower socioeconomic status of women of color is undermined by examining the prevalence of sexual harassment across all occupational levels,[49] and the observation that women with fewer resources tend to respond in an indirect manner rather than file formal complaints.[50] Furthermore, one study that measured sexual harassment across occupational groups still found that 16.6 percent of White women indicated they had been sexually harassed in comparison to 48.6 percent of Black women.[51] This finding is consistent with the work of sociologist James

Gruber, who asserts that occupational status does not greatly influence women's responses to sexual harassment.[52] Nor does the education level of the victim appear to have a significant impact on victim selection.[53] In contrast, Gruber states that the severity of harassment is a stronger predictor of a woman's willingness to report the incident.[54] What remains to be explored is the premise that women of color's disproportionate filing of sexual harassment complaints may be a result of enduring more severe experiences of sexual harassment, which thereby compel formal resolution.[55] But whether the racially disproportionate filing statistics can be explained as a consequence of greater severity or as a reflection of a higher rate of sexual harassment for women of color, both scenarios implicate the central importance of racial attitudes in sexual harassment victimization.

The Prostitution Paradigm Lens into Sexual Harassment

Beverly Balos and Mary Louise Fellows theorize that assumptions about prostitution underlie societal attitudes about violence against women.[56] Balos and Fellows argue that there is a "continuum of violence" against women made up by sexual harassment, domestic abuse, and rape.[57] The response to the continuum of violence is informed by what they refer to as a "prostitution paradigm."[58] In effect, the prosecution of violence against women reflects a paradigm in which a dichotomy between "respectable" and "degenerate" women is constructed, preserving legal protection only for those women who successfully demonstrate their respectability by distancing themselves from the image of prostitution.[59]

The sexual harassment context particularly illustrates the prostitution paradigm in that sexual harassers frequently equate their victims with women in prostitution and refer to prostitution in the victimization of their targets.[60] Catharine MacKinnon, the scholar who most influenced the legal understanding of sexual harassment as a form of gender discrimination,[61] stated early on that a "great many instances of sexual harassment in essence amount to solicitation for prostitution."[62] There appears to be, at least implicitly, some judicial acceptance of the prostitution paradigm. For example, courts continue to consider a plaintiff's provocative speech and dress in the assessment of whether the harassment was unwelcome conduct.[63] This legal standard condemns those women whose speech and conduct remotely resemble the stereotypical conduct of women in prostitution.

Critical to the Balos and Fellows theory is their observation that societal reliance upon racialized gender stereotypes is instrumental in the maintenance of the prostitution paradigm.[64] Women of color are stereotyped as oversexed and wanton and thus the quintessential prostitute, in contrast to the depiction of White women as inherently respectable and pure.[65] These racialized stereotypes motivate the disproportionate recruitment of prostitutes in the United States from communities of color.[66] Similarly, the globalized prostitution context reveals an intentionally disproportionate preference among sex tourists for prostitutes of color.[67]

Thus Catharine MacKinnon's early observation that Black women are the most vulnerable to sexual harassment, in part because of societal stereotypes about their sexual accessibility,[68] may be relevant in analyzing the racial disparities in sexual harassment charges by all women of color. I am not suggesting that White women are infrequently targeted for sexual harassment. In fact, White women have filed a significantly greater total number of sexual harassment claims each year than women of color.[69] What the racially disproportionate charge rates may suggest is that the social meaning of sexual harassment has a racial component. Accordingly, racialized sexual harassment is what happens to White women even if they are not cognizant of it in that way. This is true because being treated as a White woman has everything to do with how women of color are treated.[70] As Sherene Razack and Mary Louis Fellows explain, a category of "respectable" women can exist only as long as a category of "degenerate" women exists.[71] Racism facilitates the construction and maintenance of the gender manacles of respectability and degeneracy by redeploying the historical legacy of racialized gender stereotypes.[72]

This is not to suggest that all women experience sexual harassment in the same way, but rather to underscore how race has everything to do with sexual harassment generally. In other words, when White women are sexually harassed in order to maintain the workplace as a masculine domain, male peers and supervisors treat them "like colored women."[73] In short, all women are policed and subjected to the imposition of gender norms, with the threat of becoming ensnared by the prostitution paradigm.

The racialized aspect of the prostitution paradigm is particularly evident in the globalized prostitution context. For instance, sex tourist guidebooks and websites describe themselves as appealing to "the man who is attracted to women from different cultures, who wants to explore relationships with a woman who can offer a unique insight into life."[74] They also rank Asia, Brazil, Mexico, the Caribbean, and Costa Rica as the best locations to meet "good girls, bad girls, and good girls you convince to be bad girls!"[75] In fact, the globalized prostitution context is explicit in its deployment of racialized sex stereotypes and their function to police gender for all women. This is best exemplified by the article for sex tourists entitled *Why No White Women?* which purports to explain the common sex tourist preference for women of color:

> Q. Is it because white women demand more (in terms of performance) from their men during Sex? and white men cannot deliver?
>
> A: In my case, it's just that my dick is not long enough to reach them up on the pedestal they like to stand on.[76]

The racially laden prostitution paradigm that informs sex tourism and sexual harassment reveals that efforts to dismantle gender subordination must take into account the role of race. The racial disparity in the sexual harassment charge statistics underscores the importance of examining the link between race and gender in the use of sexual harassment as a "technology of sexism."[77] This is significant to all concerned about societal oppression.

Notes

1. *See* Catharine A. MacKinnon, *Sexual Harassment of Working Women: A Case of Sex Discrimination* 53 (1979) (describing Black women as "most vulnerable to sexual harassment, both because of the image of black women as the most sexually accessible and because they are the most economically at risk").

2. Sumi K. Cho, "Converging Stereotypes in Racialized Sexual Harassment: Where the Model Minority Meets Suzie Wong," 1 *Iowa J. Gender, Race and Justice* 177, 209 (1997) ("the law's current dichotomous categorization of racial discrimination and sexual harassment as separate spheres of injury is inadequate to respond to racialized sexual harassment").

3. Tanya Katerí Hernández, "Sexual Harassment and Racial Disparity: The Mutual Construction of Gender and Race," 4 *Iowa J. Gender, Race and Justice* 183 (2001).

4. My use of the term "underrepresentation" in the presentation of the racially comparative statistical data is not meant to suggest that White women should be victimized with greater frequency, but solely to depict the ways in which the sexual harassment statistics indicate significantly distinctive patterns for White and non-White women.

5. *See* Hernández, *supra* note 3, at 217–224, apps. I–V. The statistical data discussed in this essay contrasts White women and women of color as an aggregate for two reasons. First, the EEOC data collection presents statistics only for White, Black and "Other Race" women, in which Latinas, Native Americans, and Asian Pacific women are collapsed. Telephone interview with Pierrette Hickey, Director of the Charge Data System Division, EEOC Office of Communications (June 6, 2000). Beyond the pragmatic constraints of not having disaggregated data available for "Other Race" women, a comparative analysis of the ways in which racial stereotypes are used to sexualize women of color as a collective and to imbue their sexualization as an inherently interchangeable commodity supports the binary comparisons of White women with the collective of women of color. These binary comparisons are not made for the purpose of collapsing the particular experiences of various racial minority groups, but rather for the purpose of illustrating their common oppression.

6. Beverly Balos and Mary Louise Fellows, "A Matter of Prostitution: Becoming Respectable," 74 *N.Y.U. L. Rev.* 1220, 1227 (1999) (arguing that "prostitution functions as a paradigm for degeneracy" and "as a practice of inequality" in order to maintain the distinction between pure and wanton women).

7. *Cost of Sexual Harassment to Employers Up Sharply: More Employees are Bringing Charges and Receiving Compensation for Damages* (Center for Women in Government, University of Albany, Albany, N.Y.), Spring 1994 (hereinafter *Cost of Sexual Harassment*). Men of all races account for the remaining 9 percent. *Id.*

8. *See* Bureau of the Census, U.S. Department of Commerce, Statistical Abstract of the United States: 1993, at 409 (listing total female employment in 1992 at 45,381,000 and the White female employment at 38,481,000).

9. *Id.* (listing the number of Black women who were employed civilians in 1992 as 5,231 and the total number of females employed as 45,381).

10. *Compare id.* (including women of "other races" in the total number of women employed), with *Cost of Sexual Harassment, supra* note 7 (finding women of other races accounted for 14.7 percent of the sexual harassment charges).

11. *See* Hernández, *supra* note 3, at 217–222, apps. I–III.

12. This information is available on the electronic databases of Lexis-Nexis and West-law.

13. *See* Hernández, *supra* note 3, at 223–224, apps. IV–V. I chose to analyze federal sexual harassment complaints originating in the First though Sixth Circuits because those circuits encompass jurisdictions where women of color are fairly represented and are thus better indicators of racial patterns in filing statistics.

14. It is interesting to note that transnational studies of sexual harassment also suggest a racial disparity in sexual harassment victimization. *See* Azy Barak, "Cross-Cultural Perspectives on Sexual Harassment," in *Sexual Harassment: Theory, Research and Treatment* 263, 276 (William O'Donohue ed., 1997) (enumerating studies in Zimbabwe, the Netherlands, Australia, and South Africa which suggest a higher incidence of sexual harassment among women of color).

15. *See Castaneda v. Partida*, 430 U.S. 482, 497 n.17 (1977).

16. *See* Hernández, *supra* note 3, at 220, 223, apps. II, IV.

17. *See* Jay Devore and Roxy Peck, *Statistics: The Exploration and Analysis of Data* 209, 211 (3d ed. 1997) (explaining how the probability that any standard deviation which exceeds 3.89 can practically be considered zero because 99 percent of the time the variance between an expected value and an observed value is three standard deviations or less, and thus any standard deviation which exceeds that range is an extreme probability); *see also* R. A. Fisher, *Statistical Methods for Research Workers* 43 (1946) (observing that the frequency of standard deviations beyond 3.0 are exceedingly small).

18. *See, e.g.*, Constance Thomasina Bails, "Female Reactions to Sexual Harassment in the Workplace and the Impact of Race," at v (1994) (unpublished Ph.D. dissertation, Temple University) (on file with author) (concluding from a study of 208 civilian female employees at the Philadelphia Naval Shipyard that "Black females experienced more sexual harassment proportionately than their counterparts"); Lilia M. Cortina et al., "Sexual Harassment and Assault: Chilling the Climate for Women in Academia," 22 *Psychol. Women Q.* 419, 428 (1998) (demonstrating how in a study of 1,037 female

undergraduate and graduate students, Black and Latina women reported the highest incidence of sexual harassment despite sharing a common definition for sexual harassment across races).

19. Any analysis of patterns in the filing of legal complaints will contain a certain amount of uncertainty because of the inability to know whether each complaint filed is meritorious, and also how many instances of sexual harassment never resulted in a legal complaint at all. Given the inevitable potential for both overinclusion and underinclusion in estimated rates of sexual harassment, this study seeks to highlight those general patterns in the data that are so highly suggestive of racial disparity that they are both statistically and legally significant. Just as gross statistical disparities may sometimes constitute prima facie proof of a pattern or practice of discrimination, statistical disparities in the presumed rates of sexual harassment are highly probative of the role of race in the incidence of sexual harassment. *See Int'l Bd. of Teamsters v. United States,* 431 U.S. 324, 339 (1977) (detailing the value of statistics in pattern or practice discrimination suits under Title VII of the Civil Rights Act of 1964).

20. Data regarding the existence of racial disparity in the increased rates of sexual harassment complaints after the large-scale publicity of the Clarence Thomas confirmation hearing also lends greater credibility to the presumed parallel between the racial pattern in sexual harassment charges and the actual dynamics of sexual harassment victimization. From 1992 to 1999 the rate of increase in sexual harassment charges filed by women of color was 99.3 percent, while the rate of increase for White women was only 35.6 percent. *See* Hernández, *supra* note 3, at 221, app. III. In effect, the continued racial disparity in filing rates suggests that the same racial disparity may exist within the actual societal rates of sexual harassment. Moreover, the racial disparity demonstrated in the federal cases analyzed is in all likelihood a conservative depiction of the racial disparity in actual rates of sexual harassment because of my empirical decision to attribute those cases that did not specify the race of the plaintiff to the population of White women plaintiffs. I based this decision on the documented tendency that Whites have to view their Whiteness as invisible and not a race at all. *See, e.g.,* Bonnie Kae Grover, "Growing up White in America?" in *Critical White Studies: Looking Behind the Mirror* 34, 34 (Richard Delgado and Jean Stefancic eds., 1997) ("White is transparent. That's the point of being the dominant race. Sure, the whiteness is there, but you never think of it. If you're white, you never *have* to think of it"). Therefore, my count of cases involving women of color overlooks those cases in which a woman of color did not think to specify her race and those instances in which the federal judge did not view a woman of color's racial classification as salient to the sexual harassment complaint being litigated. *See* Cho *supra* note 2, at 209 (discussing the difficulty women of color have in educating judges about racialized sexual harassment). Given my conservative approach in the collection of the data, the overrepresentation of women of color in federal court case filings is especially remarkable. Furthermore, sexual harassment lawyers have observed that the difficulty judges and juries have in appreciating the permutations and harms of racialized sexual harassment leads to a predisposition for dismissing the cases on summary judgment motions. Interview with Minna J. Kotkin, Director, Brooklyn Law School Federal Litigation Clinic, in Brooklyn, N.Y. (Sept. 11, 2000). Thus, there may very well be a significant number of women-of-color plaintiffs omitted from my empirical count because of the

tendency to dismiss intersectional claims and because of the vagaries of judicial inclinations to publish their opinions with commercial electronic publishers like Lexis-Nexis and Westlaw. In short, the racial disparity is more astounding when one considers all the empirical difficulties with using the Lexis-Nexis and Westlaw universe of cases, which underappreciate the actual numbers of cases brought by women of color.

21. The EEOC defines sexual harassment generally as unwelcome sexual conduct that is explicitly or implicitly made a term or condition of employment. 29 C.F.R. § 1604.11(a)(1) (1994). Quid pro quo sexual harassment occurs when "submission to or rejection of such conduct by an individual is used as the basis for employment decisions affecting such individual." 29 C.F.R. § 1604.11(a)(2). A hostile work environment sexual harassment claim recognizes that unwelcome sexual conduct that "unreasonably interfere[s] with an individual's work performance" or creates an "intimidating, hostile, or offensive working environment" can constitute sex discrimination as well. 29 C.F.R. § 1604.11(a)(3).

22. Eric J. Sydell and Eileen S. Nelson, "Gender and Race Differences in the Perceptions of Sexual Harassment," 1 *J. C. Counseling* 99, 99 (1998) (citing two studies of workplace sexual harassment of women, with one study reporting that 21 percent of women experience this type of harassment and the other study reporting that 90 percent of women have that experience).

23. *See* Merit Systems Protection Bd., "Sexual Harassment in the Federal Workplace: Trends, Progress, and Continuing Challenges" (1995), *reprinted* in *Sexual Harassment in America: A Documentary History* 24, 24 (Laura W. Stein ed., 1999) (observing that empirical study of federal employees indicates that sexual harassment victims rarely file formal charges — only 6 percent of 1994 survey respondents who had been victimized took formal action); *see also* James E. Gruber and Michael D. Smith, "Women's Responses to Sexual Harassment: A Multivariate Analysis," 17 *Basic and Applied Soc. Psychol.* 543, 545 (1995) (discussing why women tend to have nonassertive responses to sexual harassment).

24. Patricia A. Gwartney-Gibbs and Denise H. Lach, "Sociological Explanations for Failure to Seek Sexual Harassment Remedies," 9 *Mediation Q.* 365, 372 (1992) (concluding that few women proceed to formal resolution of the sexual harassment claims they file).

25. U.S. Equal Employment Opportunity Commssion, *Sexual Harassment Charges: EEOC and FEPAs Combined: FY 1992–FY 2000*, http://www.eeoc.gov/stats/harass .html (last modified Jan. 18, 2001); *see also* U.S. Equal Employment Opportunity Commission, *Definitions of Terms*, http://www.eeoc.gov/stats/define.html (last modified Aug. 11, 1998). The EEOC has defined "administrative closure" as follows: "Charge closed for administrative reasons, which include: failure to locate charging party, charging party failed to respond to EEOC communications, charging party refused to accept full relief, closed due to the outcome of related litigation which establishes a precedent that makes further processing of the charge futile, charging party requests withdrawal of a charge without receiving benefits or having resolved the issue, no statutory jurisdiction." *Id.*

26. MacKinnon, *supra* note 1, at 53.

27. *See* MacKinnon, *supra* note 1, at 54 ("The stigmatization of all black women as prostitutes may sensitize them to the real commonality between sexual harassment and

prostitution"); Kimberlé Crenshaw, "Race, Gender, and Sexual Harassment," 65 *S. Cal. L. Rev.* 1467, 1470 (1992) ("Racism may provide the clarity to see that sexual harassment is not a flattering or misguided social overture but an intentional act of sexual discrimination that is threatening, and humiliating").

28. Anna-Maria Marshall, "Closing the Gaps: Plaintiffs in Pivotal Sexual Harassment Cases, 23 *Law and Soc. Inquiry* 761 (1998).

29. *Id.* at 776 n.24.

30. *Cost of Sexual Harassment, supra* note 7.

31. *Id.*

32. U.S. Equal Employment Opportunity Commission, "Questions and Answers About Sexual Harassment" 1 (1992). The brochure was drafted for the purpose of educating the public in a way not possible with the dense and lawyer-targeted policy guidelines of 1988 and 1990. U.S. Equal Employment Opportunity Commission, Notice N-915-035, "Policy Guidance on Current Issues of Sexual Harassment" (1988); U.S. Equal Employment Opportunity Commission, Notice N-915-050, "Policy Guidance on Current Issues of Sexual Harassment" (1990). Since 1991, resources have been produced to educate the public about the nature of sexual harassment. *See, e.g.,* Ellen Bravo and Ellen Cassedy, "The 9 to 5 Guide to Combating Sexual Harassment: Candid Advice from 9 to 5," *National Association of Working Women* (1992) (describing the problem of sexual harassment and ways to combat it, including a chapter on how to get your employer to adopt a sexual harassment policy).

33. Some federal courts recognized the cause of action as early as 1976. *See, e.g., Williams v. Saxbe,* 413 F. Supp. 654 (D.D.C. 1976) (recognizing quid pro quo sexual harassment as a violation of Title VII's proscription against sex discrimination), *rev'd on other grounds sub nom. Williams v. Bell,* 587 F.2d 1240 (D.C. Cir. 1978). Moreover, the cause of action was recognized by the Supreme Court in 1986. *See Meritor Savings Bank v. Vinson,* 477 U.S. 57 (1986) (recognizing sexual harassment in the work environment as a legal cause of action under Title VII of the Civil Rights Act).

34. Vicki Schultz, "Reconceptualizing Sexual Harassment," 107 *Yale L.J.* 1683, 1685 (1998).

35. *Cost of Sexual Harassment, supra* note 7.

36. *Compare* U.S. Equal Employment Opportunity Commission, *Sexual Harassment Charges EEOC and FEPAs Combined: FY 1992–FY 2000, available at* http://www.eeoc.gov/stats/harass.html (last modified Jan. 18, 2001) (detailing the number of annual sexual harassment charges filed with the EEOC from 1992 through 1999), *with Cost of Sexual Harassment, supra* note 7 (giving sexual harassment charge statistics from 1989 to 1992).

37. Kirstin Downey Grimsley, "Worker Bias Cases Are Rising Steadily: New Laws Boost Hopes for Monetary Awards," *Wash. Post,* May 12, 1997, at A1.

38. *See* James E. Gruber and Lars Bjorn, "Blue-Collar Blues: The Sexual Harassment of Women Autoworkers," 9 *Work and Occupations* 271 (1982) (concluding that the race of a victim does not influence the victim's response to sexual harassment); *see also* Richard C. Sorenson et al., "Solving the Chronic Problem of Sexual Harassment in the Workplace: An Empirical Study of Factors Affecting Employee Perceptions and Consequences of Sexual Harassment," 34 *Cal. W. L. Rev.* 457, 470, 475 (1998) (concluding that race did

not significantly influence women's perceptions of what constituted sexual harassment in an empirical study of 410 members of the U.S. Army).

39. *See* Jann H. Adams, "Sexual Harassment and Black Women: A Historical Perspective," in *Sexual Harassment: Theory, Research, and Treatment, supra* note 14, at 213, 214, 220–21 (describing factors that may make women of color less likely to report sexual harassment); Audrey J. Murrell, "Sexual Harassment and Women of Color: Issues, Challenges, and Future Directions," in *Sexual Harassment in the Workplace: Perspectives, Frontiers, and Response Strategies* 51, 58–59 (Margaret S. Stockdale ed., 1996) (stating that there is some evidence that Black women are less likely to report rape and less likely to quit work in response to sexual harassment); Marla R. H. Kohlman, "Locating Sexual Harassment Within Intersections of Experience in the U.S. Labor Market," at 97 (2000) (unpublished Ph.D. dissertation, University of Maryland) (on file with author) (analyzing General Social Surveys of 1994 and 1996 with conclusion that women of color are less likely to report sexual harassment than are White women).

40. *See* Barak, *supra* note 14, at 277 (describing how social stereotypes of Asian-American, Black, and Chicana women encourage sexual harassment); Darlene C. De-Four, "The Interface of Racism and Sexism on College Campuses," in *Ivory Power: Sexual Harassment on Campus* 45, 48–49 (Michele A. Paludi ed., 1990) ("The images and perceptions of women of color also increase their vulnerability to harassment"); Murrell, *supra* note 39, at 54–55 (describing how social stereotypes affect the views of perpetrators of sexual assault and may increase the chances that a woman of color is sexually harassed).

41. Mary Giselle Mangione-Lambie, "Sexual Harassment: The Effects of Perceiver Gender, Race and Rank on Attitudes and Actions" 104 (1994) (unpublished Ph.D. dissertation, California School of Professional Psychology at San Diego) (on file with author) (finding that non-White women's perceptions of the seriousness of sexual harassment was less than White women's, and in fact, almost equal to men's perceptions).

42. *See* W. Lawrence Neuman, "Gender, Race, and Age Differences in Student Definitions of Sexual Harassment," 29 *Wis. Sociologist* 63 (1992) (finding older White female college students had the broadest definitions of sexual harassment); *see also* Barak, *supra* note 16, at 283 (describing a study in which females of color had more lenient definitions of what constituted sexual harassment than White females).

43. *See* Angela M. Hargrow, "Speaking to Our Realities: From Speculation to Truth Concerning African American Women's Experiences of Sexual Harassment" 56 (1996) (unpublished Ph.D. dissertation, Ohio State University) (on file with author) (stating that African-American women "may be accustomed to racist and sexist behavior in the workplace and may feel they have to accept the harassing behaviors").

44. Kathleen M. Rospenda et al., "Doing Power: The Confluence of Gender, Race, and Class in Contrapower Sexual Harassment," 12 *Gender and Soc.* 40, 54 (1998) (citing L. M. Cortina et al., "*¿Dios míop.p.p. qué hacer?* Hispanic Women's Responses to Sexual Harassment" (May 1996), unpublished paper presented at the 1995 Annual Meeting of the Midwestern Psychological Association, Chicago); Jami Leigh Obermayer, "Women of Color and White Women's Resistance to Sexual Harassment," 1–142 (2001) (unpublished Ph.D. dissertation, American University) (on file with author) (presenting hierarchical log-linear analysis of a sample of the data collected by the Department of Defense

for its 1995 study of sexual harassment in the military and concluding that when women of color are subjected to unwanted crude sexual attention by someone of a different race, they will respond with coping and avoidance strategies rather than reporting the behavior as they would otherwise do with harassers of the same race).

45. *See* Merit Systems Protection Bd., *Sexual Harassment in the Federal Workplace: Is It a Problem?* (1981), *reprinted* in *Sexual Harassment in America: A Documentary History, supra* note 23, at 19, 21 (stating that minority women were more likely to be harassed by someone not of their race or ethnicity).

46. Hargrow, *supra* note 43, at 51–52.

47. *Id.* at 50.

48. Karen Dugger, "Social Location and Gender-Role Attitudes: A Comparison of Black and White Women," 2 *Gender and Soc.* 425, 439 (1988).

49. *See* Merit Systems Protection Bd., *supra* note 45, at 20 ("Sexual harassment is widely distributed among women and men of various backgrounds, positions and locations"); Barak, *supra* note 14, at 266 (describing prevalence of sexual harassment of female university students); Elizabeth Grauerholz, "Sexual Harassment in the Academy: The Case of Women Professors," in *Sexual Harassment in the Workplace: Perspectives, Frontiers, and Response Strategies, supra* note 39, at 29, 32–33 (detailing survey data from 210 women faculty at Purdue University which suggests that sexual harassment is relatively widespread); James E. Gruber, "An Epidemiology of Sexual Harassment: Evidence from North America and Europe," in *Sexual Harassment: Theory, Research, and Treatment, supra* note 14, at 84, 88 (concluding that there is a universality of sexual harassment experiences for women across occupational status in the United States and internationally); Elvia R. Arriola, " 'What's the Big Deal?' Women in the New York City Construction Industry and Sexual Harassment Law, 1970–1985," 22 *Colum. Hum. Rts. L. Rev.* 21 (1990) (analyzing sexual harassment in blue collar construction industry); Maria M. Dominguez, "Sex Discrimination and Sexual Harassment in Agricultural Labor," 6 *Am. U. J. Gender and L.* 231, 254–55 (1997) (describing probability samples of women farm workers who experience sexual harassment); David N. Laband and Bernard F. Lentz, "The Effects of Sexual Harassment on Job Satisfaction, Earnings, and Turnover Among Female Lawyers," 51 *Indus. and Lab. Rel. Rev.* 594, 597 (1998) (estimating from an American Bar Association survey that nearly two-thirds of female lawyers in private practice, and nearly half of those in corporate or public agency settings, reported experiencing or observing incidents of sexual harassment on the job); Maya Alexandri, Note, "The Student Summer Associate Experience with Harassing Behaviors: An Empirical Study and Proposal for Private Party Action," 19 *Women's Rts. L. Rep.* 43 (1997) (describing survey of summer associates who experienced sexual harassment).

50. Barbara Gutek and Mary P. Koss, "How Women Deal with Sexual Harassment and How Organizations Respond to Reporting," in *Sexual Harassment in the Workplace and Academia: Psychiatric Issues* 39–57 (Diane K. Shrier, M.D. ed., 1996).

51. Barak, *supra* note 14, at 277. Furthermore, the majority of working women of all races in the United States employed in private industry are employed as office and clerical workers. *See* U.S. Equal Employment Opportunity Commissionn, *Occupational Employment in Private Industry by Race/Ethnic Group/Sex and by Industry, United States,*

1998, http://www.eeoc.gov/stats/jobpat/tables-1.html (Sept. 21, 2000) (detailing the statistics which demonstrate that 25.4 percent of White women and 23.5 percent of women of color in private industry are employed as office and clerical workers).

52. Gruber and Smith, *supra* note 23, at 556; *see also* Hargrow, *supra* note 43, at 55 (concluding that job type was not highly related to rate of sexual harassment for geographically diverse study of 166 African-American working women).

53. *See* Bails, *supra* note 18, at 46 (finding "that the education of the female victims does not appear to have a significant impact on victim selection").

54. Gruber and Smith, *supra* note 23, at 552–53.

55. *See* Gruber and Bjorn, *supra* note 38, at 284–85 (observing that in a study of women who work on the assembly line in the auto industry, Black women were more severely and frequently harassed); Deborah Ann Gerrity, "Sexual Harassment's Effects on Emotional and Occupational Functioning of Female University Employees," 113 (1994) (unpublished Ph.D. dissertation, University of Maryland) (on file with author) (noting that in a study of 649 female employees of a large, public, mid-Atlantic university, African-American women were more likely to report incidents of quid pro quo harassment than White women); Barbara Ann Rosen, "Sexual Harassment of High School Females: Its Relation to Race/Ethnicity, Socioeconomic Status, and School Characteristics," 70–71 (1994) (unpublished Ph.D. dissertation, Rutgers, the State University of New Jersey) (on file with author) (describing how in a study of 361 incoming freshman at a women's college, non-Whites (excluding Asians) had a significantly higher prevalence of the most severe forms of sexual harassment).

56. Balos and Fellows, *supra* note 6, at 1280.

57. *Id.* at 1229.

58. *Id.* at 1231, 1236.

59. *Id.* at 1231. *See also* Mary Louise Fellows and Sherene Razack, "The Race to Innocence: Confronting Hierarchical Relations Among Women," 1 *Iowa J. Gender, Race and Justice* 335, 348 (1998) (articulating the respectability/degenerarcy dichotomy in relations among women).

60. Balos and Fellows, *supra* note 6, at 1235.

61. *See* Marshall, *supra* note 28, at 762, 786–87 (describing MacKinnon's involvement in this effort).

62. MacKinnon, *supra* note 1, at 159.

63. *See* Balos and Fellows, *supra* note 6, at 1232–34 (discussing cases where courts have held that provocative speech and dress are not per se inadmissible in sexual harassment cases, and that "provocatory conduct" by a wife murdered by her husband can help her husband have his murder conviction repealed).

64. *Id.* at 1269–73.

65. *Id.*

66. *See* Vednita Carter and Evelina Giobbe, "Duet: Prostitution, Racism and Feminist Discourse," 10 *Hastings Women's L.J.* 37, 45 (1999) (stating that the portrayal of Black women in pornography has fostered an environment where Black women are targeted for prostitution).

67. Julia O'Connell Davidson, *Prostitution, Power and Freedom* 37 (1998).

68. MacKinnon, *supra* note 1, at 53 (stating that Black women are most vulnerable to sexual harassment because of the idea that Black women are "sexually accessible" and because they are economically at risk).

69. *See* Hernández, *supra* note 3, at 218, app. I fig. I (detailing the mean and median figures for filing EEOC sexual harassment charges as a mean of 7,593 and a median of 7,852 for White women from 1992 to 1999, and as a mean of 4,344 and a median of 4,656 for women of color as a collective for that same timeframe).

70. *See* Martha R. Mahoney, "What Should White Women Do?" in *Critical White Studies: Looking Behind the Mirror, supra* note 20, at 642, 643 ("[R]acism is so deeply entwined and so profoundly implicated in all structures of gender oppression that it has harmed white women even as it has brought us privilege in many ways, so that we will never find freedom until we help transform all of these power relationships").

71. Fellows and Razack, *supra* note 59, at 348 (articulating the respectability/degenerarcy dichotomy in relations among women).

72. Cheryl Harris has observed: "Indeed, through the rigid construction of the virgin/whore dichotomy along racial lines, the conception of womanhood was deeply wedded to slavery and patriarchy and the conduct of all women was policed in accordance with patriarchal norms and in furtherance of white male power." Cheryl I. Harris, "Finding Sojourner's Truth: Race, Gender, and the Institution of Property," 18 *Cardozo L. Rev.* 309, 312, 314 (1996). Asian Pacific women and Latinas have also been historically positioned as lascivious "others." *See, e.g.,* Cho, *supra* note 2, at 190–95 (describing stereotypes of Asian women, including beliefs that they are exotic, masochistic and "the antidote to visions of liberated career women"); Maria L. Ontiveros, "Three Perspectives on Workplace Harassment of Women of Color," 23 *Golden Gate U. L. Rev.* 817, 819–20 (1993) (describing stereotypes of Asian women as exotic and submissive, and Latinas as "naturally sexual").

73. MacKinnon, *supra* note 1, at 30 (observing that "sexual harassment can be both a sexist way to express racism and a racist way to express sexism").

74. *Id.; see also* http://www.tsmtravel.com (travel and the single male website); http://www.ectasytour.com (Dominican Republic sex tourism website); http://www.single travel.com (international sex tourism website); and http://www.gentlemensvacation club.com (international sex tourism website).

75. Bruce Cassirer, *Travel and the Single Male: The World's Best Destinations for the Single Male* 74 (1992).

76. Julia O'Connell and Jacqueline Sanchez Taylor, "Fantasy Islands: Exploring the Demand for Sex Tourism," in *Sun, Sex and Gold: Tourism and Sex Work in the Caribbean* 37, 37 (Kamala Kempadoo ed., 1999).

77. Legal scholar Katherine Franke uses the term "technology of sexism" in part to underscore the role of sexual harassment in constructing the gender of both the harasser and the harassed by reinforcing gender stereotypes. As Franke articulates it, sexual harassers feminize their victims by treating them as sex objects rather than competent employees. In so doing, sexual harassers masculinize themselves by exercising the power to inscribe femininity on the victim. In this way, sexual harassment regulates gender. Katherine M. Franke, "What's Wrong with Sexual Harassment?" 49 *Stan. L. Rev.* 691, 693 (1997) ("Sexual harassment is a technology of sexism. It is a disciplinary practice that

inscribes, enforces, and polices the identities of both harasser and victim according to a system of gender norms that envisions women as feminine, (hetero)sexual objects, and men as masculine, (hetero)sexual subjects"). The empirical evidence of racial distinctions in the use of sexual harassment illustrates that race is strategically deployed in the regulation of gender as well.

29

Coercion in At-Will Termination of Employment and Sexual Harassment

LEA VANDERVELDE

On the occasion of celebrating the emergence of sexual harassment as a cause of action, I would like to reflect on what can be learned from this extraordinary success about the possibilities for progressive legal reform in the world of work.

Sexual harassment stands out as such a clear and significantly successful progressive reform because in the world of work, there is no general legal redress against a personally hostile workplace environment. By contrast, in Europe, where employees' interests in their jobs are afforded more legal protection, the concept of mobbing serves to provide legal redress against personally hostile workplace situations.[1] Not so in the United States.[2]

The employment relation insulates the employer from tortious action for many of the injurious circumstances that would customarily be considered tortious if occurring between neighbors or strangers. The employer is insulated against tort claims by employees by the legal nature of the relation as a contractual one. The at-will contract, a term which is an oxymoron itself, is actually a prerogative contract.[3] The at-will contract prevents most tort claims against employers under an ideology that had the victims of harassment wanted protection against harassment, they should have bargained for protection in the terms of an already unspoken contract, or that if the circumstances become too objectionable, they can always quit. In the world of work, particularly the regime of at-will termination, an employer's abuse of power is usually left without legal redress, as a privilege of employers and "part of the natural disorder of work life that cannot be changed."[4]

Consider what accounts strategically for the success and prevalence of this extraordinary legal reform in working women's (and men's) rights. Consider also the nature of embedded systemic constraints upon further progressive legal advancement. A strategic assessment of this reform's success permits us also to reset our moral compass and our expectations as to whether this reform will advance yet other instances of workplace justice.

I have a rather simple explanatory thesis of the dynamic of legal change to set forth at the outset. When progressive legal reform occurs, it seems that the likelihood of adoption of a specific legal reform is inversely related to that reform's ability to mutate to other progressive reforms. Thus, it may be the very boundedness of sexual harassment as a "sexual" form of harassment that prevents this statutory-based protection from leaching over to influence or effect additional protection against asexual forms of harassment.

Several terms in this thesis require more precise definition. A legal reform is defined as "progressive" if it expands the rights of otherwise subordinate individuals. The "subordinate" individuals to whom I refer are employees, people of color, and women. These groups are subordinate in the sense that historically they were subjected to formal legal inequality.[5] The architecture of this formal inequality stems primarily, but not exclusively, from the parallel structures of relations of private life in Blackstone's *Commentaries* — master-servant, husband-wife, father-child — as well as from the American heritage of slavery.[6]

Much of the progressive development of law has been about giving legal recognition to the grievances of subordinates so that those individuals may stand their ground, remain where they are, and defend themselves from wrongful conduct without needing to flee to protect themselves. Flight entails abandoning any reliance interest the employee has in the position, the job, all he or she may have worked for, and starting all over again.

For more than three-quarters of a century, unions created workplace forums, through grievance processing and other measures, by which employees could talk back to employers without fearing retaliation or needing to leave. Even within unionized workplaces, however, grievances were modeled after those egregious conditions shared by men,[7] and thus, harassment of a sexual nature was rarely recognized as a legitimate grievance.

Nonetheless, in the historical pattern,[8] certain human dramas keep repeating themselves. The conduct that we have come to recognize as sexual harassment long antedated modern proscriptions on discrimination against women.

Throughout the nineteenth century and much of the twentieth, sexually harassing conduct occurred and was an overwhelmingly important, life-changing
grievance for servant girls, though it received little legal recognition.[9]

A close review of the history of seduction actions teaches that law is more
responsive to defusing situations that look like (or can be modeled on) violence than it is to redressing the harms of victims.[10] In the nineteenth-century
seduction cases, the historic means by which the law dealt with circumstances
of sexual harassment, the initial focus was on averting violence between men
or the escalation of violence between the sexual assailant and the victim's male
family members. Subsequently, the focus changed from master's prerogative to
casting the situation in terms of the violence of rape and finally, and only in the
rare case, to recognizing the injustice of coercion.[11]

Coercion, either as a sustained coherent theory or as a heuristically recognizable practice, is very underdeveloped as a concept in American law. Peter
Westen discusses the need to define a baseline against which to measure coer-
cions. The relevant baseline for distinguishing threats from nonthreats for
purposes of coercion is not what the recipient's future condition will actually
otherwise be, but what the recipient expects it otherwise will be. "Coercion,"
he says, "consists of conditional promises to leave a person worse off either
than he otherwise expects to be or than he ought to be for refusing to do the
proponent's bidding."[12] What an analysis of coercion requires is the ability to
draw out of the background, the context, the assumed *ceteris paribus*, some
particular feature and to make its effects visible, to make the transparent
visible.[13] Coercion is context-dependent.

It may be that coercion receives less attention as a subject for legal intervention because it is perceived as less likely to provoke revenge or the kind of
violence that escalates out of control. Coercion is also harder for the legal
system to detect. When fact-finders (judges and juries) attempt to identify
workplace violence or rape, they know what they are looking for: overt evidence of injury and resistance, disproportionate bruises, wounds, torn clothing, blood. Instead, coercion works by camouflaging itself as choice.

At least four factors prevent the coercion model from gaining a foothold.
Coercion camouflages abuse of power (1) by coopting the victim into submitting to the superordinate's will, (2) by ascribing consent when the victim does
submit, (3) by erasing evidence of resistance, and (4) by restructuring the
victim's beliefs about what freedoms are even possible. All four of these mechanisms of camouflage can be found in various discursive engagements in both
the nineteenth-century common law seduction cases and in Title VII sexual
harassment case law.[14]

The extraordinary intractability of coercion, what makes it so bedeviling, is that it works by coopting the employee's own will. It looks like choice; it looks like the subordinate person has simply chosen the lesser of two evils, and by appearing to be a choice, it mutes the individual's ability to demonstrate outward signs of resistance, so that there are fewer indicia of "acts against type" from which coercion can be detected.

For further progressive workplace reforms to occur, however, we need to recognize asexual harassment as actionable, even if it doesn't present an immediate threat of violence, and we need a sustained theory of coercion in employment relations.

I want to address how the sexual harassment of working women fits into a larger concern about employer *harassment* of working women and men. Rather than focusing on sex, the sexual, or sexualized forms of harassment, consider all types of harassment or hazing of working people, whether sexual or nonsexual, and the relationship of harassment to work. If sexual harassment is about power, then a question ripe for the asking is, what can be learned about reforms directed at the abuse of power from this instance of "sexed" power? In this inquiry the methodology is to render the qualifiers "sexual" and "gender" dependent variables of a more general case of unnecessary systemic and structural harassment of subordinate employees by their managers or coworkers.

Harassment must, of course, be distinguished from discipline. All work requires the employee to discipline him- or herself to the tasks of the job. The employer's role in wage labor is to assign the tasks to employees and measure their performance. Managers in the modern firm devote an extraordinary amount of attention to thinking about how to motivate employees and how to structure their efforts and increase productivity by means of a variety of carrots and sticks. The manager's actions in disciplining the employee to the task can sometimes appear to the employee as harassment, and the package of carrots and sticks can seem coercive. Thus, harassment cannot be simply a question of the employee's perception that the manager's conduct or the tasks are unpleasant.

It is precisely because it is acknowledged that submitting to the discipline of work can be unpleasant to the worker that the common law tort of intentional infliction of emotional distress is rarely recognized in an employment setting.[15] The California Supreme Court has written: "Not every aggravation in normal employment life is compensable."[16] But the statement concedes too little. In fact, most courts refuse to recognize even extreme patterns of bullying as tortious and compensable, unless, of course, the employee is a protected-class employee.[17] The problem with the unfettered power accorded the employer under the at-will regime is that it fails to distinguish between requiring the employee to submit to a discipline of work and requiring the employee to submit to offensive, harassing, or coercive employer demands that may be completely unrelated and unnecessary to work discipline.

The problems of seeing, identifying, and recognizing coercion are compounded in their difficulty because all disciplinary regimes, like all legal regimes, are somewhat coercive.[18] Thus, one must identify and fish out the objectionable coercion from a sea of conduct appropriate to influence employees' task performance.

The specification of tasks and performance measurement is so essential to the theory of paid employment that there must be some way to distinguish the pattern of workplace conduct, which is wrongfully coercive and hence, truly qualifies as harassment, from the pattern of employer conduct directed at improving productivity by legitimate means.[19] The first issue is whether the manager's objectives are proper, such as enhancing productivity. The second is whether the means are legitimate incentives and disciplinary measures or whether they are discriminatory or impermissibly intrusive.

Sexual harassment seems to manage the distinction better. In the definition of sexual harassment adopted by the courts, "unwelcomeness" does the work of detecting circumstances of wrongful coercion from those that are authentically consensual. The key element of the cause of action for sexual harassment under *Meritor* is "unwelcomeness." There is an important relationship between unwelcomeness and coercion.

Is it the presence of coercion that makes sexual advances so unwelcome, or the unwelcomeness of the sexual advance that makes it coercive? Sexual advances may or may not be physically threatening. But in the workplace, sexual advances of managers in power are coercive because they have nothing to do with workplace productivity.

When sexual overtures, whether intended as harassment or not, are coupled with the workplace setting where one can be fired for any reason or no reason, the hybrid toxin has particular potency. By ignoring or rejecting the signal of an unwelcome sexual advance in the workplace, the subordinate woman must worry about what the man may do if he is rejected. It takes a tremendously mature and self-confident man to continue to work cooperatively with a woman who has declined his advances, who has spurned him.[20] The more likely scenario is that feeling snubbed by her, he would reciprocate and repudiate her. And as important, because his ego is at stake in the rejection and because he would not want even her rejection to be publicly known, he must deflect the focus of the rejection from himself and suggest that the reason for his criticism is grounded in some deficiency of hers.

This is the coercive cost to the woman of the man's unwelcome asking. This is the calculus she makes. It does not require that he articulate a quid pro quo.

Conversely, if a person is offered a desirable opportunity that they want to do anyway we call it neither coercive nor unwelcome. Coercion is the opposite of opportunity, because it is the opposite of free agency.[21]

So far, recognizing a cause of action for sexual harassment has expanded the sphere of workers' autonomy. The same end of curtailing both sexual and asexual harassment could be achieved, however, by securing to working men and women sufficient independence and autonomy that they could effectively entertain or refuse sexual overtures, that is, ignore them, brush off the harasser, or put him in his place, without peril. The vulnerability of subordinates is that they cannot refuse or reciprocate against the aggressor without hurting themselves more than they hurt the aggressor. Thus, it is not gender alone that has rendered employees vulnerable to unwelcome sexual approaches. It is also coercive circumstances of the at-will doctrine under which employers and managers enjoy virtually unlimited prerogatives to dismiss employees.

A further progressive move would be to reverse the focus and the burden of legitimation. Instead of focusing on protecting employees from misdeeds, the law could secure even greater freedom of movement and autonomy for employees by delineating limitations of power. By securing victim independence rather than proving harasser misdeed, the coercive nature of sexual as well as other forms of harassment could be neutralized. This alternative is to limit power to its proper sphere.[22] This legal strategy is the most ambitious of all. Harassment could be curtailed by limiting the exercise of unfettered power by employing firms;[23] by requiring firms to specify end-state objectives for the accomplishment of good work; or by mandating aspirational (or actual) systems of work meritocracy, just deserts, or reasonable motivational schemas.

This focus on the legitimate underpinnings of the structure of private power rather than its more graphic, provable excesses and abuses would secure the autonomy of dependent individuals to a significant extent. The advantage for dependent subordinate individuals would be their ability to limit the employing firm's power, as well as that of its managing agents, to that which was properly its own business.

For the first expanded legal strategy to succeed, we need to develop a theory of coercion. For the second further expansion to succeed, a theory of germaneness would be necessary.[24]

Within this large ideal, consider again where we stand with the first-step significance of the current legal recognition of sexual harassment. Based on my starting premise — that the likelihood of adoption of a specific legal reform is inversely related to that reform's ability to mutate to other progressive reforms — I predict that sexual activity and innuendo will (if it hasn't already) become the salient criteria for defining the limits of this legal reform. Sexual harassment's Title VII basis — in protected class antidiscrimination — almost requires this conclusion. I'm not optimistic that employment practices designed to prevent sexual harassment will be used as analogies to expand state's common law premises to prohibit other forms of personal harassment. I predict that, rather than expanding protection from sexually harassing abuse to other equally harassing, debilitating, and demeaning circumstances, judges and employers will draw the line at sex.

Employers too are likely to respond to the emergence of this cause of action by proscribing all sexual interaction between coworkers or social fraternization between supervisors and supervisees.[25] The line will be drawn here because the tort grew out of proscribed discriminatory grounds rather than the broader grounds of abuse of workplace power generally. And the line can be drawn here because Americans are comfortable with concluding that sex has no place in the workplace.[26] Neither of these premises promotes an ethos fully centered on personal autonomy.

Within the discourse of identifying the basis for legal recognition of the cause of action, selection of this regulatory strategy was supported by the proscription against discriminatory conduct. But the focus on discriminatory, "protected-class"–based harassment operates in a vacuum in which non-discriminatory harassment has no legal remedy and hence lends itself to the popular implication that discriminatory forms of harassment are more serious than other forms.

Within the feminist literature, there is considerable writing to suggest that sexual harassment is considered by some as more toxic than other forms of bullying. Why is sexual harassment so toxic?

Meritor Savings Bank v. Vinson answered the question as to why sexual harassment is so toxic, in part, by stating "because it is 'intimidating, hostile, or offensive.' "[27] But it isn't immediately clear why "sexual" (or other forms of discriminatory) harassment should be regarded as any more intimidating, hostile, or offensive than the vast range of employer conduct that occurs without legal penalty.[28] People are susceptible and vulnerable to all kinds of harassments and annoyances in the workplace. Sometimes nonsexual concentrations of attention are sufficient to drive a person to distraction. In fact, under current legal doctrine a considerable amount of employer or managerial action that is intimidating, hostile, and offensive is remediable only in the old-fashioned way: by the employee's taking the drastic step of quitting, the modern equivalent of fleeing from the offender and abandoning whatever interest they may have in the stability of their work situation. With the decline of unions, most employees have no avenue for remedying intimidating, hostile, or offensive action other than quitting. Sexual or discriminatory harassment is a grievance with a name at least, and, under Title VII, there is a forum that can be invoked.

Reading the variety of employment at-will cases leads one to the conclusion that the potential for human mendaciousness is as unbounded in some workplaces as it is in junior high school. Some workplace descriptions leave the impression that unwelcome baiting is allowed to proceed unchecked to the point of tyranny. Others leave the impression that middle-level management positions disproportionately attract individuals who wish to exercise this kind of strut, domination, and harassment of underlings. In fact, virtually every feature of an individual's body, face, habits, gait, voice, name, or background that attracts sufficient attention to depart from the norm can be decontextualized from the feelings and identity of the individual of which they are an integral part, to provide a source for isolation, goading, harassment, or humiliation, and when these unwelcome attentions are targeted at a subordinate the policing of these superficial social norms can be every bit as damaging as sexual (or discriminatory) harassment.[29] Yet in the United States—where ensuring the dignity of workers is not a recognized value protected by law, as either a property or a liberty interest, and where an individual's stake in the workplace is as tenuous as it is under at-will employment—conduct that is intimidating, hostile, or offensive does not necessarily surface as cognizable on the legal radar screen, nor does it trigger any legal intervention to correct abuses caused by private ordering.

One take on this is the misogyny point: There is no denying that harassment in sexual terms betrays an ideology of misogyny (just as race-based harassment betrays an ideology of racism.) The parallel alternative point I wish to make is that harassment of working people betrays an ideology that is antithetical to the dignity of work and its place and value in human life.

Perhaps what makes *sexual* harassment on the street or in the workplace so individually toxic is that it is backed by the latent threat of rape. In the workplace, it is a signal that the subordinate employee cannot afford to ignore; she disregards it at her peril. It eats upon her consciousness because it threatens her stable safety and security. She must assess just how sneaky and covert he may be. She must assess what he is capable of doing to her to catch her in one of the hundreds of places where they may be alone. It is the opposite of a sexual fantasy for her: It is a nightmare.

What makes *workplace* harassment so toxic is that it is backed by the latent threat of firing for no reason at all. Because most employees have no secure, independently guaranteed, legally protected relationship to the work that financially maintains them and their families (and that may even fulfill them as human beings), the corrosive effect of workplace harassment is that subordinates must respond with submission to such a signal. The social politics of the workplace can interfere with concentration and performance of work, let alone with living a satisfying private life.

I've cast this paradigm in "he" and "she" terms, but it can also take place in "she" and "she" terms. Consider the *Wagenseller* case,[30] where a hospital staff from an Arizona hospital went rafting on the Colorado River. To amuse themselves, since they were at the bottom of the canyon, they decided upon collectively revealing their bums in the buff. The nurse who refused to join in, despite pressure from her peers and her supervisor to do so, found her supervisor, who happened to be female, downrating her performance reviews, until she was eventually fired.

The case was not argued in sexual harassment terms. The overture was probably playful, intended to promote group bonding rather than sexual foreplay. Catherine Wagenseller never indicated that she feared rape by the request to undress. More likely, she simply wished to avoid the humiliation of undressing before the group. By the psychological mechanism of transference, rejection of the overture, however playful, became translated by the supervisor into a poor performance rating of the person who did not go along.[31] Rejection of her supervisor's suggestion came at a price.

What is the relationship between unwelcomeness and coercion here? It is not just that her coworkers were egging her on to do something she didn't really want to participate in; it is not merely the peer pressure. Her nonparticipation was read as rejection of their antics, and her refusal to go along eventually cost her job.

The combined effect of the at-will rule and sexually harassing behavior can be further identified and the separate effects distilled in the circumstances of the case of Teri and David Pratt.[32]

Teri Pratt began receiving frightening obscene and harassing telephone calls, which continued for eighteen months. Some of these eighty to one hundred calls demanded sex; others threatened rape. The anonymous caller knew her name, the description of her car, and where she lived at the end of a country road. Many of the calls came when her husband was out of town on work assignments. Although the state police began an investigation, they were unsuccessful in identifying the perpetrator.

So the Pratts began an investigation of their own. David Pratt took off time with pay to attempt to discover who the obscene caller was. One day the Pratts were at a company picnic when an upper-level manager, Ted Griffore, said grace over the public address system. After Griffore finished the prayer, Teri Pratt urgently rushed over to her husband. "That's the voice, that's the voice, that's the guy that's been calling us," she said. At first, David did not believe that Teri was correct. But the next week, while David was away again on a work assignment, Teri Pratt received and recorded three more obscene calls. After listening to the tapes, they concluded that Griffore, the upper-level manager at David's workplace, was indeed the caller.

David Pratt confronted the manager in his office, played the recording for him, and demanded that he admit that he was the obscene caller. While Pratt left him for a time to formulate his response, another manager spirited Griffore away out of the building to defuse the confrontation.

By demonstrating backbone and autonomy in standing up to the man who had bullied his family, Pratt took actions of independence that became a "problem" in the eyes of his employer. Someone from the company, Brown Machine, was sent to the Pratt's home soon after. Pratt was advised to take some time off until things settled down. According to Pratt, when he asked why Griffore was calling his family, the employer's intermediary told him, "Dave, you're not saved, you don't go to church."[33]

For the Pratts, one nightmare was over. The family had their telephone number changed. "We knew who it was, and we [were] no longer worried about him coming out to our place." The obscene calls stopped. The latent threat of sexual attack could be put in perspective because they knew the identity of the perpetrator; Teri Pratt could assess his level of dangerousness and since she didn't work for the company she could avoid him.

But another nightmare was still running. Pratt's assertion of his right to resist these types of threats to his family lead eventually to his being discharged. The company kept insisting upon the manager's innocence. The company suggested that Pratt spend more time going to church; they gave him a leave of absence to assist with this "personal problem of his." This fairly standard pattern of denial was coupled with ascribing the problem to the victim who complained.

The Pratts turned again to the police. The police believed that the calls were coming from Brown Machine and, after listening to the Pratts' recordings, focused their attention on Griffore. Yet, without his cooperation, the police were unable to proceed much further.

Six weeks after confronting the man who had terrorized his family, Pratt still had not been allowed to return to work. Pratt was told that Brown Machine had just cause to terminate him, but he would be given another chance to return under certain conditions. Pratt had to apologize to Griffore, or at least admit he made a mistake in his accusation, and declare in writing that he would not hold the company responsible for the obscene calls. Pratt had to drop the investigation or he would be terminated. Pratt refused. He wanted to return to work, but not under those conditions. The following day, he was fired.[34]

By December, the Pratts were having serious financial difficulties, and, in a letter to Brown Machine's president, David Pratt desperately sought his job back. Pratt met with the personnel director, who indicated that all the employees were talking about the situation. Many of the conditions were reiterated. Although Pratt still believed Griffore was the caller, he reasoned that it was best "to try and end things," especially since the harassing calls had stopped. Pratt agreed to apologize to Griffore, to the company president, and to Brown Machine, but he would not put it in writing.

At a second meeting, the company president, Mr. Sharpe, acknowledged that management had handled the situation improperly, but he did not want the company to be considered at fault. The company president had additional conditions for Pratt's return to work. He would have to apologize to Griffore and agree not to discuss the telephone calls on or off the job, and he would have to work directly for Griffore. Moreover, Pratt would have to attend church and pray with Griffore.

The president attempted to browbeat Pratt into denying that the incident ever occurred and forced him to rehearse a denial in case he was asked.[35] Sharpe forced Pratt to rehearse repeatedly, "I don't want to talk about it, I can't talk about it," which he was required to respond if he were ever asked whether Griffore was the obscene caller. If Pratt refused, he would be terminated.

At the end of the meetings, the company president made a shocking revelation: Griffore had actually confessed to making the obscene telephone calls, but the president insisted more rehearsals would be needed from Pratt before they would decide to hire him back. Pratt described his feelings: "I was feeling like I crawled, I crawled, I crawled, and I couldn't crawl any more. I mean it wasn't right."

David and Teri Pratt sued, alleging wrongful discharge, violation of Michigan's public policy, and intentional infliction of emotional distress. And they eventually prevailed,[36] but not on the straightforward grounds that would vindicate the nature of harassment to which they had been subjected.

To address the loss of his job, the Michigan court had to knit together a doctrinal hook to bring this horrible personal situation within the confines of an exception they had recognized to at-will employment, the *public* policy exception. The hook had to involve the employer's insistence that Pratt drop the police investigation, a police investigation that was by all accounts ineffectual anyway.[37] The court had to forge a connection between the internal workplace abuses within the sphere of private ordering and the external system of public reporting to the police. Without this jerry-rigged hook, the jury could not have considered the coercive effect of the loss of David Pratt's livelihood. The hook to police reporting was essential for the discharge to be deemed "wrongful" under the public policy exception.

What is so unsatisfying about this strained doctrinal approach is that it is so indirect and attenuated. By bypassing and overlooking the blatant injury to the victims as instrumental only to the public policy of their filing a police report, the doctrine appears to excuse the pernicious abuse of power. Had Pratt concluded, as a reasonable person might, that the police couldn't help him anyway, the subsequent sequence of events culminating in the loss of his job would simply have been private coercion, but not actionable under the public policy exception to the at-will rule.

In some states, even an extensive pattern of harassing phone calls is not actionable as intentional infliction of emotional distress.[38] The entire parade of indignities, psychological pressure, and coercion to which Pratt had been subjected would only have been relevant in those few states that recognize an intentional infliction of emotional distress claim, but the emotional distress claim would not allow for the significant loss to his family of his livelihood. The parade of abuses — the insistence that the victim not be vindicated when the employer knew the truth by the perpetrator's own confession, the ritual rehearsal of denial, and the indignity of being assigned to work directly under the perpetrator of the nightmare and to go to church and pray with him, all while the employer was leveraging its authority against his financial difficulties to bend Pratt to its version of the story — was not actionable under Michigan law.

In many ways the *Pratt* circumstance presents the classic posture of the early nineteenth-century seduction cases: the husband's taking the lead, and the heat, to protect his wife from sexual threats and disturbing harassment. But the harassment would have been every bit as debilitating if the anonymous phone calls had disturbed the peace of his elderly parents with anonymous nuisance calls or threatened the theft of his children's lunch money. The sexual nature of the calls may or may not have contributed to the intensity of the harassment.

The firm's willingness to coerce Pratt until, as he said, he "crawled and crawled and couldn't crawl any more" is a harassment without remedy. The coercive effect of the at-will rule is the ability of the firm to fire Pratt for failing to respond with abject servility.[39]

And yet, the latent coercive effect of the employer's at-will prerogative is generally not recognized as contributing significantly to the victim's exposure to sexual harassment. Instead, sexual harassment law focuses almost exclusively on the *sexual* aspect of the conduct, rather than the intensity of the harassment, or the inherent vulnerability of the employee to termination under the at-will rule. Sex has always been considered toxic. In American culture, as in some ways sex like nudity has always been treated sui generis.[40] And Americans have always shown almost a prurient interest in the sex lives of others.[41]

This discursive initiative is relevant to the more general question of how this exercise of sexed power influences the abuse of power deployed more generally. Could the recognition of sexual harassment contribute to a greater recognition of work dignity? Can we expand the focus of justice from employers who ban sex to employers who eliminate harassment? The toxicity of sexual harassment that is, in part, what energized the progressive reform and allowed the revolution in sexual harassment law to come about will, I fear, also limit its further expansion from the sexually specific to the more general cases of harassment.[42] In the manner in which sexual harassment is currently popularly perceived as actionable, there seems little likelihood that selecting this type of harassment from the sea of harassment and labeling it more toxic will do much for recognition of the remaining toxins.

The more general point is this: The salience of the conduct itself is what is self-limiting to the spread of legal reform—what allows the conduct to be identified against the background context presents the limits. This is not just "la plus ça change, la plus la même chose."[43] There has been change. The opening wedge of reform may not pry open further reform at all, but simply puncture the social structure of power in such a way that it is quickly and hermetically sealed to prevent further reform. It is shrink-wrapped as anomalous to other kinds of equally objectionable abuses of workplace power.

The same phenomenon has occurred in two decades of doctrinal reform of the at-will contract. The common law reforms occurring during the 1980s and 1990s have been shrink-wrapped as "exceptions" to the rule of the manager's prerogative contract rather than aggregated as cumulative reasons to reverse the rule itself and render the exercise of power to its appropriate delimited sphere. Public policy constraints on an employer's exercise of power are still conceptualized as exceptions, exceptional constraints on the exercise of the unfettered power of terminating an individual's livelihood at whim or at will. Although employers sometimes express alarm that the exceptions threaten to swallow the rule, only a single state has reversed the presumption of at-will termination.[44]

Thus, qualifying adjectives, like "sexual," accepted at the beginning of the reform effort to justify change, come back to haunt successive reform efforts.

Sexual harassment can be identified and remedied because it can be contrasted to other workplace harassment and coercion, and sex has no business in the workplace. To the degree that characteristics can be picked out of the background environment as sufficiently recognizable to alter their legal consequence, the salient elements of this reform are: (a) Some suggestion of heterosexual (more than homosexual)[45] intercourse, (b) power relation, and (c) some sexual signifier, such as disrobing, genital involvement, or touching. In every selection of elements from the backdrop, we make a more significant concession to the more widespread, but less easily separated, forms of abuse of power and brutality that as a result become seemingly more normalized.

The operational mode of thought in identifying these salient elements, these diagnostic markers, is that fact-finders can distinguish them from other forms of power and workplace harassment exactly because sex is thought to have no place in the workplace. "Disrobing or nudity, genital involvement and heterosexual sexual conduct" are not necessary to garden-variety, intimidating, hostile, demeaning, or offensive workplace treatment. This conduct can be selected out and eliminated from the managers' toolbox of prerogatives without interfering with the other incentives useful for motivating employees' productivity.

The salience of these elements was the packaging that permitted the sale of the cause of action in the first place; their shock value becomes the shrink-wrapped limitation to prevent this progressive advance from spreading out any further. These insignia come to mark the boundaries of the sexual and perhaps the sphere of bodily integrity that is the American employee's only zone of privacy in a work regime governed by the at-will regime. The subordinate subjected to other forms of hazing submits or quits.

Further secondary labor reform is unlikely if we continue on this narrow path of reform, without making the move to inductively broaden the specific to the general.[46] Nevertheless, recognition of sexual harassment is truly an advance over the state of the law in the early 1980s, when virtually no employer demand or form of harassment was legally off-limits, but it cannot address the greater problem of unremedied, vindictive harassment, of which sexual harassment is only the most publicly prominent example.

More generally, we need a unified theory of unjust workplace harassment and employment coercion. Do the firm and its representatives owe the employee less or more in terms of freedom from harassment than it would owe a stranger on the beach?[47] Presently, local culture determines legal result: The answer depends on whether you are employed in Oregon or New York.[48]

The difference is not simply a matter of degree. It is a difference in terms of the presumption attended to subordinacy, whether the law reacts in terms of protecting the subordinate's dependency or allowing the superordinate's exercise of privilege. Judges sometimes respond to dependency with empathy and sometimes with scorn. In some cases, the distinction in status perpetuates the prerogative of the persons in the hierarchically stronger position, while in other cases it curtails overreaching. This bipolar judicial reaction to employees approaching the courts with grievances has been a feature of the common law since the nineteenth century.

A theory of employment coercion needs to be tested within the constraints of the employment context, but it is consonant with employees' expectations. Most employees expect good faith from their employer and they expect that the employer won't be rash in terminating them. Most employees expect employer efforts to impel them to greater productivity, but they do not expect to be coerced about matters that are irrelevant to task performance simply because employers and managers have the power to do so.

Workplace coercion is conduct that unnecessarily pushes the employee up against the wall to obtain some illegitimate advantage. It uses a constraint that is in place in the environment like dismissal at-will for some other purpose to leverage an unjust advantage. It transgresses the boundaries between proper spheres of what should rightfully be the employee's realm of autonomy and what can legitimately be demanded by the employer.

Yet, without a unified theory of unjust workplace harassment, the rights created by sexual harassment reform result in only a workplace "no-sex" ban and secondarily, some protected sphere of bodily privacy. Not that this is not already a remarkable achievement. The boundaries of that range of privacy are sufficiently easy to mark, but they do not accord an employee an adequate "psychological" room of one's own to work and still be a free and independent person. Greater independence at the workplace would allow individuals to operate at the top of their form, without interference by, or at least undistracted by, the sexual ego or arbitrary demands of others, to their fullest capacity without unnecessary servility to unnecessarily exercised authority.[49]

Notes

1. Norbert Kollmer, *Mobbing im Arbeitsverhaeltnis* (Forkel-Verlag: Heidelberg 1997).

2. For a list of examples see the excellent article by Regina Austin, "Employer Abuse, Worker Resistance, and the Tort of Intentional Infliction of Emotional Distress," 41 *Stanford Law Review* 1 (1988).

3. Phillip Selznick, *Law, Society, and Industrial Justice* (1969) at 124–137.

4. Austin, supra note 2, at 1, 7. "If the conduct does not rise to the requisite level [to be considered 'outrageous'], it is dismissed as being among those "mere insults indignities, threats, annoyances, petty oppressions, or other trivialities to which the victim must necessarily be expected and required to be hardened." As applied to the employment

relationship, this means that every practice or pattern of emotional mistreatment except the outrageous, atrocious, and intolerable is treated as the ordinary stuff of everyday work life." *Id.* at 6–7. Footnote omitted.

5. *See* Blackstone's *Commentaries.*

6. *See Dred Scott v. Sanford,* 60 U.S. (19 How.) 393 (1857).

7. *Cf.* Lea VanderVelde, "The Gendered Origins of Specific Performance Doctrine: Binding Men's Consciences and Women's Fidelity," 101 *Yale Law Journal* 775 (1992).

8. *See* Katharine T. Bartlett, "Tradition, Change, and the Idea of Progress in Feminist Legal Thought," 1995 *Wisconsin Law Review* 303.

9. *See* Lea VanderVelde, "The Legal Ways of Seduction," 48 *Stanford Law Review* 817 (1996).

10. *Id.*

11. *Id.,* at 894–97.

12. Westen, *supra* note ?, at 587. He proposes three possible baselines: (1) defining threats in solely normative terms; (2) defining them by reference to the recipient's preferences; or (3) defining threats temporally as of the moment before which the threat was made.

13. This is true whether the theory of coercion is being called upon to recognize Theory of Coercion/exploitation, takings law, or a theory of unconstitutional conditions.

14. Thus, it is all the more remarkable that sexual harassment was recognized as it was in the *Meritor* case at all. *See Meritor Savings Bank v. Vinson,* 477 U.S. 57 (1986).

15. "In sum, where the employee suffers annoyance or upset on account of the employer's conduct but is not disabled, does not require medical care, and the employer's conduct neither contravenes a fundamental public policy nor exceeds the inherent risks of employment, the injury will simply not have resulted in any occupational impairment . . .remediable by way of civil action." *Livitsanos v. Superior Court,* 2 C. 4th 744, 17 Cal. Rptr 808 (1992).

16. *Id.*

17. *See e.g.,* the fact patterns of *Murphy v. American Home Products,* 112 Misc. 2d 507, 447 N.Y.S. 2d 218 (N.Y. Sup. 1982) on appeal, 448 N.E.2d 86 (N.Y. 1983), in which the employee was escorted from the building under guard and his belongings were dumped on the ground in front of him, and *Gantt v. Sentry Insurance,* 1 Cal. 4th 1083, 4 Cal. Rptr. 2d 874 (1992), in which the employee was falsely insinuated as being a sexual harasser himself in order to intimidate him not to testify to knowledge of other sexual harassment in the company.

18. Peter Westen has noted that "It has long been said, from Plato to H. L. A. Hart, that legal systems — indeed all laws — are coercive. Peter Westen, " 'Freedom' and 'Coercion' — Virtue Words and Vice Words," 1985 *Duke Law Journal* 541, 575–76 (1985). *See also* J. Bentham, *Of Laws in General* 54 (H. Hart ed., 1970) ("A law by which nobody is bound, a law by which nobody is coerced . . . all these phrases which come to the same thing would be so many contradictions in terms"); H. Calcine, *General Theory of Law and State* 29 (1945) ("[All the norms of a legal order are coercive norms]"); H. Leask, *The State in Theory and Practice* 53 (1935) ("[The state is an organization exercising the coercive power for social good]"); 1 M. Weber, *Economy and Society* 34 (G. Roth and C. Weitek eds., 1978) ("An order will be called . . . law if it is externally

guaranteed by the probability that physical or psychological coercion will the law by fear of legal reprisals is thereby 'coerced' into complying with the society's norm"). Hart defines "law" as a system of "coercive orders," and "coercive orders" as "orders backed by threats." Westen, *supra* (citing H. L. A. Hart, *The Concept of Law*, 19–20, 236–37 [1961]).

19. There is, of course, the much larger question of coercion in wage labor. *See generally* Robert Hale, "Bargaining, Duress, and Economic Liberty," 43 *Columbia Law Review* 603 (1943). I have limited the frame to those who are already within the employment relation. *See* David Zimmerman, "Coercive Wage Offers," 10 *Philosophy and Public Affairs*, 121, 124 (1981) (labeling a proposal coercive only if the utility of X's doing Z_1 is "considerably greater" than the utility of his not doing Z_1).

20. This doesn't presuppose that nonsupervisory men are so much more secure in their work relationships. But if a man asks and the woman rejects, the man may think it's going to be her or me. The male employee may be no more secure than the woman in his relationship to his work, but by starting the thing in motion, he has greater control over the timing of the outcome. In traditional heterosexual relations, he asks. He chose to ask; she has to deal with it.

21. Peter Westen suggests that coercion be defined as: "a constraint or promise of a constraint, Y, that X_1 knowingly brings to bear on X in order that X choose to do something, Z_1, that X would not otherwise choose to do." Westen, *supra* note 18 at 541, 567.

22. *See* Michael Walzer, *Spheres of Justice* (1983).

23. This could be implemented by mandating good faith in employment practices or by requiring just cause for discharge.

24. We can identify the immaterial in some sort of checklist, and with sexual harassment constructed as toxic because it is sexual, we have started down that path, but it will be a long path. Or we could reverse the field of focus: We could focus on what is material, what is relevant, what improves the quality and objectives of work, and with the advantage that we leave the rest to individual taste. If we could define the relation of person to work, we could indicate the extent to which sexually directed pressure was or was not a distraction and welcome or unwelcome.

This could be accomplished by something a simple and radical as recognizing an action against anyone who interferes with an individual's relation to their work. This could grow out of tortious interference law. If we required employers to define the material aspects of workplace performance, "germaneness" in Kathleen Sullivan's parallel analysis of unconstitutional conditions in public ordering (Kathleen M. Sullivan, "Unconstitutional Conditions," 102 *Harvard Law Review* 1413 [1989]), we could more easily determine the immaterial that stood in the way of employee's job satisfaction and by linking material aspects only to job security, we could grant greater degrees of personal and psychological freedom to working people. But we don't define the material, the germane to the accomplishment of task, of production, of work, or of end-product, and as a result, we create shrink-wrapped exceptions that can be narrowly proscribed.

25. Gary M. Kramer, "Limited License to Fish Off the Company Pier: Toward Express Employer Policies on Supervisor-Subordinate Fraternization," 2000 *Western New England Law Review* 77.

26. For the deeper psychological implications of sublimation as a form of social control, *see* Wilhelm Reich, *Listen, Little Man!* (1948).

27. 477 U.S. 57, 65 (1986).

28. For example: name calling, sabotaging a coworker's safety equipment, or stalking an employee in the locker room.

29. Katherine Franke has aptly explained the role of sexual harassment in policing sex role stereotypes. *See* Katherine M. Franke, "What's Wrong with Sexual Harassment?" 49 *Stanford Law Review* 691 (1997).

30. *Wagenseller v. Scottsdale Memorial Hospital*, 710 P.2d 1025 (Ariz. 1985).

31. *See Gantt v. Sentry Insurance Co.*, 1 Cal. 4th 1083, 4 Cal. Reptr. 2d 874 (1992).

32. *See Pratt v. Brown Machine Co.*, 855 F.2d 1225 (6th Cir. 1988).

33. Pratt replied, "Tim, I've been saved. Church, I'll agree, it's going to help me cope with things better, but the guy won't quit calling and the church probably won't make him quit calling."

34. Pratt was surprised that his "leave of absence" was now being considered a suspension.

35. "PRATT: But he says: suppose one of the boys says: what are they doing, keeping you quiet? He says, how are you going to respond?

"I says: I can't talk about it, I don't want to talk about it.

"He says: no, he says, that's wrong. You said can't first, he says, you got to say: I don't want to because it would be misleading to the company, and we don't want people to think that the company has done anything wrong.

"So he says: okay, what if you're out in tooling and one of the guys says: come on, Dave, tell us, was it Ted or not? What's your response?

"I said: well, I probably wouldn't say anything, I would just walk away.

"He says: no, that's an improper response. He says: you got to say this phrase, and I want you to learn it and we're going to keep rehearsing you on it. And if you slip one time, we want you to know that you're going to be immediately terminated.

"That phrase is: I don't want to talk about it, I can't talk about it.

"PRATT'S COUNSEL: Did he use that tone of voice?

"PRATT: He was loud, yes.

36. Pratt and his wife filed suit against Brown Machine, alleging wrongful discharge, "public policy tort," intentional infliction of emotional distress, and loss of consortium. The jury returned a verdict in favor of the Pratts on all claims in the amount of $152,000. The jury awarded $62,000 in economic damages for David Pratt's wrongful termination of employment; $60,000 in noneconomic damages for his termination in violation of Michigan public policy; $20,000 for intentional infliction of emotional distress; and $10,000 for Teri Pratt's loss of consortium claim in connection with her husband's emotional distress claim.

37. Michigan law requires "the location of some legislative enactment to ground a finding that a discharge is in breach of public policy." This public policy exception to the at-will doctrine is based on the principle that "some grounds for discharging an employee are so contrary to public policy as to be actionable."

38. *Russo v. White*, 241 Va. 23, 400 S.E.2d 160 (1991).

39. In support of his claim, Pratt was required to prove that Brown Machine "expressly

or impliedly required [him] to agree to compound, conceal, refuse to prosecute or refuse to give evidence in connection with an underlying criminal activity of which he had knowledge." The court continued, "If [Brown Machine] did communicate to [Pratt] that he would have to conduct himself in the manner which violated the compounding statute to continue to have a job, then [Pratt] must also prove he refused to do so, and his refusal was a determinative factor in the decision to terminate the employment relationship." The court limited Pratt's public policy claim to Brown Machine's conduct when Pratt's employment ended in September 1983; the company's refusal to rehire the plaintiff the following January was not implicated.

Pratt did not need to prove a violation of the underlying legislative enactments in order to succeed on his public policy claim. The jury could properly find on this record that Pratt's refusal to drop the investigation was the "determining factor" in his discharge; that is, that the company's legitimate reasons for firing the plaintiff were "not close to producing the adverse action."

40. Consider nuisance actions, one of the earliest nuisance actions was for keeping a bawdy house or a house of prostitution. Nuisance actions involving houses of prostitution did not lead to the promulgation of recognition of other types of nuisances. It always remained a special case of nuisance law.

41. Susan Estrich comments on toxicity of sexual activity: "[T]he 'sexual' aspect of sexual harassment and the unique meaning of such harassment in a male-female context . . . makes sexual harassment more offensive, more debilitating, and more dehumanizing to its victims than other forms of discrimination is precisely the fact that it is sexual." Susan Estrich, "Sex at Work," 43 *Stanford Law Review* 813, 819–20 (1991).

at 819–20.

Katherine Franke also recognizes the metaphor of toxicity — that for some, "the sexual aspect of sexual harassment does all the hegemonic work and has the effect and purpose of sexualizing women workers by reducing their humanity generally, and their status as workers specifically, to objects of male sexual pleasure." Franke, *supra* note 29 at 691, 715.

42. Some may say an equality analysis is what allowed sexual harassment reform to come about, but also limited its further expansion to more general reforms. Those familiar with that argument will recognize the form of the argument here.

43. Reva Siegel, "Why Equal Protection No Longer Protects: The Evolving Forms of Status-Enforcing State Action," 49 *Stanford Law Review* 1111(1997).

44. Montana is the only state that has adopted a statute requiring just cause for discharge.

45. The tersely worded Supreme Court opinion in the *Oncale* case, however, suggests that some homosexual harassment can also find cognition under sexual harassment. *See Oncale v. Sundowner Offshore Services*, 523 U.S. 75 (1998).

46. Progressive second-stage labor reform will occur, if anywhere, in the lawsuits of nurses, hospital orderlies, and other low-level health professionals. Given the contemporary contingency of American health care reorganization, the perennial cutbacks of nursing staffs and their assignments of more and more duties, the triaging of medical care, increasing geriatric population, and the expanded need for nursing care for chronic (if not catastrophic) illnesses, the workplace where one can expect further points of conflict

involving disrobing and bodily privacy are in hospitals and medical facilities. Even in the *Wagonseller* case, pressing nurse Catherine Wagonseller to disrobe could be seen as part of a culture in which health professionals routinely work with nudity. In addition, the second-stage protection of the privacy and dignity of an employee's bodily integrity could come to apply to strip searches in circumstances of suspected theft by employees. *See Bodewig v. K-Mart, Inc.*, 635 P.2d 657 (Or. App. 1981).

47. *See* Edward Tenner, *Why Things Bite Back?* 19 (1997) (paraphrasing Charles Perrow's observation that systems are either tightly or loosely coupled: "In human terms, even thousands of people on a crowded beach form a loosely coupled system. If a . . . bully kicks sand in someone's face, the limited personal space around the bathers will usually suffice to confine the problem").

48. In Oregon, the firm owes the employee something more, something resembling a duty of care, *see Hall v. May Department Stores Co.*, 292 Or. 131, 637 P.2d 126 (1981); in New York, the firm owes the employee less, *see Murphy v. American Home Products*.

49. Privacy is, in Brandeis's view, the right to be left alone to do a job, to concentrate on the job at hand rather than on something extraneous.

30

Public Rights for "Private" Wrongs
Sexual Harassment and the
Violence Against Women Act

SALLY F. GOLDFARB

"Whatever happened to privacy?" laments one commentator.[1] Another complains that "sex isn't private anymore."[2] Increasingly, the fashionable response to notorious sexual harassment cases and scandals is to deplore the fact that courts and the general public are hearing about them.[3] Sexual harassment law should be curtailed, we are told, because legal remedies for sexual exploitation are an illegitimate intrusion into a zone that should remain private.[4] According to this argument, the law has no business prying into the mix of "passion, nuance, irrationality, and lust" known as human sexuality, even when the setting is the workplace or the classroom.[5]

This line of argument, although it may appear novel to its journalistic proponents, is an obvious throwback to the view of sexual coercion in employment and education that prevailed before the appearance of Catharine MacKinnon's *Sexual Harassment of Working Women* more than two decades ago. As MacKinnon's book pointed out, sexual harassment had always been considered personal — that is, a product of intimate attraction or aberrant impulses within specific relationships, unique to the individuals involved.[6] Designating incidents of sexual harassment as personal (and therefore private) was a way of "remov[ing] the events from the social or political arena, hence from scrutiny, criticism, and regulation by legal intervention."[7] More specifically, by portraying sexual harassment as personal, courts in early cases were able to

516

conclude that the challenged actions were directed at an individual rather than an entire gender and therefore could not be a form of sex discrimination.[8]

One of the major achievements of MacKinnon's work was that it took a phenomenon that was considered personal and revealed it to be an instance of systemic discrimination against women as a class. MacKinnon defined sexual harassment as "the unwanted imposition of sexual requirements in the context of a relationship of unequal power."[9] (Then as now, the definition of sexual harassment excludes mutual, voluntary sexual interactions.)[10] By focusing her analysis on the differing power of men and women, MacKinnon showed that sexual harassment in employment and education both reflects and reinforces broader inequities between the sexes.[11] Unlike a private, individual injury, an injury predicated on the victim's membership in a disadvantaged class is a suitable subject for federal civil rights relief.[12] In MacKinnon's words, "Prohibiting sexual harassment as sex discrimination implicitly defines what has been considered private and personal as another dimension of the public order."[13]

The law and theory of sexual harassment played a crucial role in breaking down the artificial distinctions between public and private that had long blocked efforts to obtain legal relief for many forms of discrimination against women. In particular, the creation of sexual harassment as a federal civil rights violation paved the way for passage of the Violence Against Women Act, with its revolutionary federal civil rights remedy for gender-motivated violence.[14] Like the law of sexual harassment, the Violence Against Women Act had the potential to gain public recognition and public redress for harms that were traditionally viewed as private but in fact go to the heart of women's social inequality. While contemporary commentators are trying to turn back the clock on sexual harassment, recent constitutional challenges to the Violence Against Women Act have succeeded in reimposing barriers between public and private that the statute itself was designed to transcend. A brief examination of the Violence Against Women Act and its relationship to sexual harassment law will serve to illustrate how far we have come, and how far we have yet to go, in the effort to overcome centuries-old assumptions about the public and private spheres that have operated to deny women full equality under the law.

The Public-Private Dichotomy and Feminist Critiques

Long before anyone dreamed of prohibiting sexual harassment in employment, the public-private dichotomy had become deeply entrenched in American law. There are two versions of this dichotomy that are particularly relevant to feminist inquiry.

The first of these is the split between the market and the family.[15] The belief that market and family are separate and irreconcilable reached its fullest expression in the separate-spheres ideology that took hold during the nineteenth century, when a cult of domesticity arose in conjunction with the rise of industrialization and the resulting movement of work outside of the home. According to this ideology, men are naturally suited to the public world of government and commerce, whereas women (or, more accurately, white middle- and upper-class women) are destined for the private sphere of home and hearth, where they hold sway as the angel of the house, bear and rear children, and provide men with respite from the rigors of the outside world.[16] A classic expression of this world view can be found in Justice Bradley's infamous concurrence in *Bradwell v. Illinois*:[17] "[T]he civil law, as well as nature herself, has always recognized a wide difference in the respective spheres and destinies of man and woman. . . . The constitution of the family organization, which is founded in the divine ordinance, as well as in the nature of things, indicates the domestic sphere as that which properly belongs to the domain and functions of womanhood. . . . The paramount destiny and mission of woman are to fulfil the noble and benign offices of wife and mother."[18]

The law implemented the market-family dichotomy in a manner that placed women firmly in a double bind.[19] Through rules such as those denying women the franchise, excluding women from entry into the professions, and preventing married women from making contracts, the law barred women from effective participation in the public sphere. It thereby ratified and enforced the view that women belong exclusively in the private sphere. At the same time, the assumption that the law, like commerce and government generally, belongs to the public sphere dictated that the law not intrude in the private sphere of home and family. Law was therefore unavailable as a shield against wife battering, marital rape, and incest. Several nineteenth-century cases refusing redress for domestic violence employed the metaphor of a curtain concealing the home from public scrutiny.[20] In short, women were relegated to a domestic world in which the law refused to intervene.

In its classic form, then, the dichotomy between market and family actually consists of a series of opposing categories: The market is equated with the public, the male, and the presence of law; and the family is equated with the private, the female, and the absence of law. Of course, as feminist scholars have shown, this entire construct is riddled with contradictions and inaccuracies. The family and the market, far from being separate entities, are deeply interdependent. Women's paid and unpaid labor has always played an important role in the market economy.[21] Furthermore, the law has never been absent from the domestic sphere. The "private" sphere of the family has consistently been subject to legal regulation.[22] (Indeed, when the separate spheres ideology was in its ascendancy, laws regulating family relationships were actually proliferating.)[23] The very existence of a legally recognized category known as "family" presupposes legal intervention, if only because the law defines which groups fall into that category.[24]

As long as law exists, it inevitably has an effect on relationships within the family. It imposes affirmative rules, or else it refuses to do so and consequently reinforces the inequities of the status quo.[25] For example, as Reva Siegel has demonstrated, the adoption of privacy rhetoric as a rationale for not intervening in cases of domestic violence, far from being neutral, ensured that men would be able to continue dominating women and children in the family as they had done under the earlier common law right of chastisement.[26] True legal neutrality in the domestic sphere is a logical impossibility.[27] Nevertheless, the ideal of legal nonintervention in the family has been an enduring legacy of the market-family split.

The federal courts have been particularly vigorous in their attempts to keep the law out of the family and the family out of the law. The domestic-relations exception to federal diversity jurisdiction is perhaps the preeminent example of this tendency.[28] As Judith Resnik has shown, family law issues have never been entirely excluded from federal jurisdiction, but the perception of federal noninvolvement in the family is so powerful that federal and state courts alike have long assumed that family matters belong only in a state forum.[29] Resnik points out that "the dichotomy between a commercial arena . . . and the domestic scene . . . roughly parallels assumptions about state and federal jurisdictional lines."[30] The rhetoric confining family issues to state courts contains many echoes of the rhetoric confining women to the private, domestic sphere.[31] Thus, federal courts are to state courts as male is to female, market is to family, and public is to private.

There is a second version of the public-private split that has been the subject of sustained feminist critique: the split between the state and civil society.[32] The conventional liberal formulation divides the world into the public realm consisting of the state and state actors, and the private realm consisting of all nongovernmental activity. Seen through this lens, the family and the market are both components of the private sphere, in contrast to the public sphere occupied by government. This distinction has been central to the development of the state action doctrine in federal constitutional and civil rights law.[33]

On the surface, the second version of the public-private dichotomy appears to be concerned not with the relationship between men and women but rather with the relationship between the individual and the state. With its roots in the philosophy of Locke, the liberal public-private dichotomy defines us as individual bearers of private rights that must be protected from encroachment by government.[34] It follows that the Constitution is designed to protect the individual from the state, not to protect private individuals from each other.

Although not explicitly gendered, the liberal public-private dichotomy has a dramatically different impact on women than on men. Major sites of women's oppression — including the nongovernmental workplace and the home — are located in the private sphere and therefore historically have not been considered appropriate subjects for protection under federal constitutional and civil rights law.[35] Gender inequality arising from disparities in private power is invisible to a system designed to protect individuals from state interference. "For women, this has meant that civil society, the domain in which women are distinctively subordinated and deprived of power, has been placed beyond reach of legal guarantees. Women are oppressed socially, prior to law, without express state acts, often in intimate contexts."[36]

Violence against women provides a case in point. Like the split between the market and the family, the split between the state and civil society has been a major obstacle to obtaining effective legal protection against rape and domestic violence.[37] Most of the violence committed against women occurs in the context of the family and other ongoing relationships.[38] Relatively few acts of sexual assault and battering take the form of state action. Therefore, protecting individuals from overreaching by the state will do little to remedy the harm experienced by women through rape and domestic violence. This omission is especially noteworthy because violence is among the principal ways in which women's inequality is expressed and perpetuated.[39] Women are targeted for battery and sexual assault "because they are women: not individually or at random, but on the basis of sex, because of their membership in a group defined by gender."[40] Yet the absence of overt governmental involvement in these acts means that they have not traditionally been identified as sex discrimination.

Feminists have argued that notions of privacy arising from both the market-family split and the state-civil society split are responsible not only for failing to remedy women's subordination, but for reinforcing it.[41] Seen from this perspective, the "right to privacy is a right of men 'to be let alone' to oppress women one at a time."[42] Accordingly, feminist theory and activism have challenged rigid demarcations between private and public in order to obtain legal redress for discrimination against women in its many forms.[43] Both sexual harassment law and the Violence Against Women Act represent efforts to pull back the curtain concealing harms that were traditionally defined as "private," so that they could be recognized as violations of women's public right to equality.

Erosion and Endurance of the Public-Private Dichotomy

By the time *Sexual Harassment of Working Women* was published in 1979, legal reforms had significantly weakened both versions of the public-private dichotomy described above. The law no longer overtly excluded women from employment, voting, contract rights, or the various other functions in the public sphere that had previously been closed to them. The conviction that the law should not actively intervene in the family was also fading, as indicated by the emergence of state criminal and civil remedies for domestic violence.[44] The strict separation between the state and civil society, as exemplified by the state action requirement in constitutional and civil rights law, also was breaking down.[45] During the 1960s and 1970s, the Supreme Court issued a series of decisions applying nineteenth-century civil rights statutes to private actors and, in some cases, interpreting the constitutional state action requirement broadly.[46] Meanwhile, Congress was passing an assortment of new civil rights statutes prohibiting discrimination in the nongovernmental sphere,[47] which in turn were upheld as legitimate exercises of Congress's constitutional powers.[48]

However, the two versions of the public-private dichotomy remained a powerful force in American law and life twenty years ago and they remain powerful even today. The enduring influence of the market-family split is felt in the law's continued treatment of marital rape as a less serious offense than stranger rape, and in attempts to force battered women to submit their disputes to mediation.[49] Contemporary women's disproportionate caregiving responsibilities force them to spend much of their time and energy on domestic tasks, in a pattern that recalls the de jure confinement of women to the domestic sphere during the nineteenth century.[50] The division between the state and civil society continues to be a controlling principle in much of constitutional law, including doctrines like equal protection, freedom of speech, and the right of privacy.[51]

SEXUAL HARASSMENT

In seeking to have sexual harassment recognized as a type of discrimination, MacKinnon had to confront an especially persistent belief about privacy, namely, that anything to do with sexuality falls on the private side of the market-family divide. Sex is inherently private, according to this view, because it is about intimate, personal relationships and therefore properly belongs to the domestic sphere — *even when it takes place in a market setting.* MacKinnon's book exploded the notion that sexual harassment in its multifarious forms should be insulated from legal intervention simply because it arises within individual relationships. In fact, she showed that sexual harassment undercuts women's equality in the workforce precisely because it imports into the market women's traditional role in the family — that is, women are financially dependent on men and in return must remain sexually available to them.[52] She demonstrated that sexual harassment in employment entails economic as well as sexual exploitation and therefore can properly be viewed as a creature of the public, market sphere.

MacKinnon was aided in her task by the fact that Title VII of the Civil Rights Act of 1964 already prohibited nongovernmental actors from engaging in sex discrimination in employment, and Title IX of the Education Amendments of 1972 did the same for sex discrimination in federally funded education programs.[53] Thus, Congress had accepted the principle that women are entitled to equal treatment in the market settings of workplace and school, regardless of whether state action is directly involved. MacKinnon extended this victory by broadening the definition of discrimination to include inappropriate sexual behavior in those market settings, which was no small achievement.

But what about victimization that does not arise in a clearly public arena like an office, factory, or classroom? What about sexual and nonsexual violence within marriage and other intimate relationships, including violence in the most private setting of all, the home? Could federal law evolve to the point where these types of injuries would be recognized as a denial of equality? They were not recognized under the landmark civil rights statutes like 42 U.S.C. §§ 1983 and 1985(3) unless a plaintiff could show that the action was taken under color of state law or that there was a conspiracy to deprive her of a federally protected right, elements that are far from common in most rape and domestic violence cases. By the early 1990s, there was strong feminist sentiment that violence directed at women because they are women should be considered a form of sex discrimination. It remained for the Violence Against Women Act to take that step.

THE VIOLENCE AGAINST WOMEN ACT

The Violence Against Women Act (VAWA) declared for the first time that violent crimes motivated by gender are discriminatory and violate the victim's civil rights under federal law.[54] Although the legislative history of the civil rights provision focused primarily on stranger and nonstranger rape, domestic violence, and murder of women,[55] the provision covered any "crime of violence motivated by gender," as defined in the statute. The phrase "motivated by gender" was defined as an act committed "because of gender or on the basis of gender and due, at least in part, to an animus based on the victim's gender."⁵⁶ The term "crime of violence" included acts that federal or state law would consider a felony against a person, or a felony against property that presents a serious risk of physical injury to another person.⁵⁷ VAWA created a civil cause of action and permitted awards of compensatory and punitive damages, injunctive and declaratory relief, and attorney's fees.⁵⁸ The plaintiff was not required to press criminal charges or obtain a criminal conviction in order to pursue the civil rights remedy.⁵⁹

The civil rights provision in VAWA owed a great deal to sexual harassment law. The language "because of gender or on the basis of gender" was roughly modeled on Title VII, and the Senate Judiciary Committee reports repeatedly referred to Title VII, including sexual harassment case law under Title VII, as a guide to interpreting and applying the new cause of action.⁶⁰ In fact, Senator Joseph Biden, the bill's lead sponsor, defended the legislation by pointing out the inconsistency of having federal law protect women from being sexually assaulted in the workplace, but not from being sexually assaulted directly outside the workplace.⁶¹

Building on MacKinnon's work on sexual harassment, VAWA rejected the idea that federal civil rights law should not concern itself with what goes on "in private," including sexual activity. MacKinnon had analyzed the close link between "sex" as in the activity of having sex (which has traditionally been seen as private and individual) and "sex" as in the female sex (which has always been considered a public characteristic, a classification as a member of a social group).⁶² In MacKinnon's view, each of these two definitions of "sex" is essential to the other. By showing that "[w]oman's sexuality is a major medium through which gender identity and gender status are socially expressed and experienced,"⁶³ MacKinnon was able to characterize unwanted sexual activity in the workplace as a collective injury based on the victim's membership in a disadvantaged class. Similarly, supporters of VAWA emphasized that individual women are targeted for violence, including sexual violence, because of their membership in the female sex.⁶⁴ Hence, an individual act of sexual assault can properly be viewed as an instance of group-based discrimination.⁶⁵

Despite the many ways in which VAWA's civil rights remedy was a logical extension of sexual harassment law, the new statute faced fierce resistance precisely because its scope included claims that fall squarely and unequivocally in the domestic sphere, when seen through the eyes of someone who accepts the validity of the market-family split. Whereas sexual harassment cases under Title VII and Title IX are concerned with claims arising in the workplace and educational institutions, VAWA's reach extended to date rape, marital rape, and spousal battering—acts that, on the surface, appear to have nothing to do with the market.[66] While VAWA was pending in Congress, the language of the market-family split was prominent in the debate over its passage. In a particularly striking evocation of the doctrine of family privacy, the Conference of Chief Justices, which represents the state judiciary, criticized VAWA's civil rights provision on the ground that it would conflict with the marital rape exemption.[67]

Much of the opposition to the Violence Against Women Act took the form of assertions that federal courts should not interfere in the private, domestic sphere. Chief Justice Rehnquist, for example, urged Congress not to pass the Violence Against Women Act because it would create an influx of "domestic relations disputes" into the federal courts.[68] Similarly, the Conference of Chief Justices opposed the statute on the basis that domestic violence is a family law issue and family law issues belong in state court.[69] The Conference of Chief Justices was particularly concerned that women would use VAWA as a bargaining chip to extort larger settlements in divorces.[70]

Of course, the Violence Against Women Act was not a federal domestic relations law. It explicitly did not confer supplemental jurisdiction over divorce, alimony, marital property, and custody disputes.[71] VAWA's civil rights provision was an antidiscrimination law, modeled on other federal antidiscrimination laws.[72] However, it departed from previous antidiscrimination laws by addressing the fact that women, unlike men, are often discriminated against by being singled out for violence in the family and in other intimate relationships.[73]

In addition to raising arguments based on the split between market and family and corresponding assumptions about federal and state jurisdiction, the Conference of Chief Justices also invoked the split between the state and civil society. The Conference objected that VAWA's civil rights provision "appears to eliminate, or at least vitiate, the 'state action' requirement for civil rights litigation."[74] Because VAWA's scope is not limited to actions taken under color of state law, the Conference argued, it is inconsistent with existing federal civil rights laws.[75] In other words, civil rights relief can protect private individuals only from the state, not from each other. The fact that the organization representing the leading state jurists in the country relied heavily on this argument, despite the fact that the previous three decades had seen a proliferation of federal cases and statutes prohibiting discrimination by private actors,[76] demonstrates the lingering influence of the state-civil society dichotomy.

Ultimately the Violence Against Women Act gained sufficient congressional support to be enacted in 1994.[77] As a result, the federal government created a civil right to be free from gender-motivated violence — a right not limited to employment or education, and not limited to state action. But the battle over the issue of privacy did not end with the bill's passage.

After VAWA was signed into law, plaintiffs filed lawsuits alleging a variety of types of gender-motivated violence, including rape, sexual assault, nonsexual assault, sexual abuse of minors, wife-battering, and murder.[78] In a significant number of these cases, defendants raised the claim that the civil rights remedy was unconstitutional because Congress lacked constitutional authority to enact it.[79] Congress itself asserted that it had authority under both the Commerce Clause and section 5 of the Fourteenth Amendment.[80] The defendants claiming that VAWA was unconstitutional argued that violence against women is not a legitimate subject of Congress's Commerce Clause power because it does not have sufficiently close ties to the market. They also argued that violence against women is not a legitimate subject of Congress's power under section 5 of the Fourteenth Amendment because it does not have sufficiently close ties to the state. In short, these constitutional challenges simply reasserted the public-private split in both its forms. Once again, women were being told that injuries they suffer because of their membership in a class defined by their sex are too private to be eligible for federal civil rights relief.

Before the United States Supreme Court weighed in on the constitutionality of the Violence Against Women Act, there was ample reason to be optimistic that the civil rights provision would withstand constitutional challenge. Eighteen cases in the lower federal courts found that VAWA's civil rights provision was a permissible exercise of Commerce Clause power under the test established in *United States v. Lopez*.[81] These courts examined VAWA's extensive legislative history documenting the massive impact of rape and domestic violence on women's workforce participation, health care expenses, consumer spending, interstate travel, poverty, and homelessness, and they concluded that violence against women substantially affects interstate commerce. Two of these courts also held that Congress had authority to enact the civil rights provision under section 5 of the Fourteenth Amendment in order to enforce women's right to equal protection of the laws.[82] Another court declined to rule on the Fourteenth Amendment issue but stated approvingly in dicta that "the overwhelming evidence of gender-based violence adduced by the congressional committees that analyzed this problem . . . clearly established a compelling legislative interest in addressing such a widespread problem."[83]

Nevertheless, there were also signs of resistance to VAWA's message that "private" violence is a violation of public rights. In one VAWA case, the defendant argued that his "longstanding sexual relationship" with the plaintiff (which the plaintiff described as a horrific and extended campaign of sexual harassment) proved that he could not have had the requisite "animus" against women because he interacted with her "as an individual" and not "because of plaintiff's class status."[84]

Although the overwhelming majority of lower court cases that considered the constitutionality of the civil rights remedy upheld the statute, a few found it unconstitutional.[85] One of these was *Brzonkala v. Virginia Polytechnic and State University*, the case that later reached the Supreme Court as *United States v. Morrison*.[86] Despite the extensive legislative history revealing the detrimental impact of violence on women's ability to participate in the national economy, the Fourth Circuit's en banc opinion stressed the fact that violence against women is not a commercial or economic activity — unlike, in the court's view, growing wheat for personal consumption.[87] The court also emphasized that the civil rights remedy "regulate[s] purely private conduct, without any individualized showing of state action"; in so doing, it rejected the argument that VAWA was a valid exercise of Congress's power to remedy the widespread discrimination against female crime victims in the states' civil and criminal justice systems.[88] Having categorized violence against women as private under both a market-family analysis and a state-civil society analysis, the court concluded that Congress had exceeded its authority under both the Commerce Clause and the Fourteenth Amendment when it created the civil rights remedy. The Fourth Circuit's opinion revealed a preoccupation with privacy, stating repeatedly that the challenged statute was constitutionally infirm because it regulated "private" acts and "private" actors,[89] including behavior within the domestic sphere of the family.[90]

Adherence to traditional notions of privacy was not limited to opinions finding VAWA's civil rights provision unconstitutional. In *Seaton v. Seaton*, a case upholding the provision on Commerce Clause grounds and containing favorable dicta on the Fourteenth Amendment issue, the court wrote, "The framers of the Constitution did not intend for the federal courts to play host to domestic disputes and invade the well-established authority of the sovereign states. . . . [T]his court must again express its deep concern that the Act will effectively allow domestic relations litigation to permeate the federal courts. Issues related to domestic relations are better suited for the state courts."[91] In a passage reminiscent of objections voiced by the Conference of Chief Justices before VAWA was enacted, the *Seaton* opinion warned, "[T]his particular remedy created by Congress, because of its extreme overbreadth, opens the doors of the federal courts to parties seeking leverage in [divorce] settlements rather than true justice."[92] When a victory for VAWA was granted this grudgingly, it was obvious that the public-private dichotomy remained a significant threat to the statute's survival.

That threat was carried out in the Supreme Court's decision in *United States v. Morrison.*[93] By a vote of five to four, the Court struck down VAWA's civil rights remedy as an unconstitutional exercise of congressional power. Like the Fourth Circuit, the Supreme Court found that "[g]ender-motivated crimes of violence are not, in any sense of the phrase, economic activity."[94] Invoking the specter of federal intrusion into the private, domestic sphere, the Court warned that upholding VAWA would open the door to federal laws on marriage, divorce, and childrearing.[95] Although the Court conceded that Congress had made extensive findings on the links between gender-motivated violence and interstate commerce, it found that those links were indistinguishable from the indirect consequences of all violent crime.[96] Yet Congress had found that one of the primary effects of gender-based violence is to make it impossible for women to function effectively in the economic sphere,[97] an economically discriminatory impact that most other crimes do not share.

On the Fourteenth Amendment issue, the Court held that section 5 confers power on Congress to regulate only state action, not private conduct.[98] Refusing to uphold VAWA's civil rights provision as a remedial measure designed to overcome the states' systematic discrimination against female victims of violence, the Court ruled that any such measure must be provided by the states — the same states whose failure to accord women equal protection of the laws was one of the reasons why VAWA was needed in the first place.[99]

The Supreme Court thus restored the divisions between market and family and between the state and civil society that VAWA had sought to overcome. By placing women's experience of violence squarely on the private side of both dichotomies, the Court deprived victims of gender-motivated violence of access to federal civil rights protection.

Conclusion

During the last three decades of the twentieth century, feminists made enormous progress in challenging the antiquated distinctions between public and private that had made many of the greatest threats to women's equality legally invisible. We are now witnessing a backlash against that progress. The backlash is reflected in the Supreme Court's holding that Congress lacked constitutional authority to pass the Violence Against Women Act's civil rights provision because violence against women has too much to do with the family and not enough to do with the market and the state. The backlash is also visible in claims that the law should not scrutinize sexual activity, even if that activity has the effect of denying women social and political equality.

Two decades after publication of MacKinnon's groundbreaking work on sexual harassment, there is a resurgence of the view that sexual activity is private, personal, and individual and therefore cannot be a manifestation of group bias.

Critics of sexual harassment law proclaim that we should be worried about protecting women's equality, not about sex[100] — as if the two could be separated. The truth is that women are often oppressed in exactly those realms that have traditionally been considered most private: sex and the family. The creation of federal civil rights remedies for sexual harassment and violence against women were significant steps forward for women's equality under the law. One of those statutes has now been invalidated; the other remains a target of criticism. Notwithstanding their lingering appeal in some quarters, arguments based on the market-family dichotomy and the state-civil society dichotomy should not be allowed to restore the curtain that for so long shielded women's victimization from public recognition and response.

Notes

This essay was originally presented at the Sexual Harassment Symposium at Yale Law School on March 1, 1998. It has been updated to reflect subsequent judicial decisions on the Violence Against Women Act, particularly *United States v. Morrison*, 529 U.S. 598 (2000). For further discussion of the judicial response to the Violence Against Women Act, see Sally F. Goldfarb, "The Supreme Court, the Violence Against Women Act, and the Use and Abuse of Federalism," 71 *Fordham Law Review* 57 (2002); Sally F. Goldfarb, "'No Civilized System of Justice': The Fate of the Violence Against Women Act," 102 *West Virginia Law Review* 499 (2000); Sally F. Goldfarb, "Violence Against Women and the Persistence of Privacy," 61 *Ohio State Law Journal* 1 (2000).

1. Ruth Marcus, "Privacy Takes a Beating as Investigations Progress in Lewinsky, Jones Cases," *Washington Post*, February 22, 1998, at A20.

2. Richard Dooling, "Why Sex Isn't Private Anymore," *New York Times*, February 3, 1998, at A23.

3. *See, e.g.,* Wendy Kaminer, "Below the Beltway," *New York Times Book Review*, March 22, 1998, at 14; Ginger Rutland, "Just What's the Fascination with Clinton's Sex Life?" *Sacramento Bee*, April 11, 1998, at B7.

4. *See* Dooling, *supra* note 2.

5. Jeffrey Toobin, "The Trouble with Sex," *New Yorker*, February 9, 1998, at 48, 55.

6. Catharine A. MacKinnon, *Sexual Harassment of Working Women: A Case of Sex Discrimination* 27, 83–90 (1979).

7. *Id.* at 83.

8. *See id.* at 85; Catharine A. MacKinnon, *Feminism Unmodified: Discourses on Life and Law* 106–7 (1987).

9. MacKinnon, *supra* note 6, at 1.

10. *See* Catharine A. MacKinnon, "Harassment Law Under Siege," *New York Times*, March 5, 1998, at A29.

11. Because the overwhelming majority of sexual harassment cases involve a male aggressor and female victim, this chapter focuses on harassment by men of women. This is not meant to deny the existence or importance of other types of sexual harassment. *See, e.g., Oncale v. Sundowner Offshore Services*, 523 U.S. 75 (1998) (holding that same-sex harassment may violate Title VII).

12. Although legal remedies for private, individual injuries exist, they provide at best an imperfect response to sexual harassment. *See* MacKinnon, *supra* note 6, at 88, 158–74 (critiquing tort, criminal, and labor law as sources of redress for sexual harassment).

13. *Id.* at 58.

14. Violence Against Women Act of 1994, Pub. L. No. 103–322, Title IV, 108 Stat. 1902 (codified in relevant part at 42 U.S.C. § 13981 (1994)).

15. *See generally* Frances E. Olsen, "The Family and the Market: A Study of Ideology and Legal Reform," 96 *Harvard Law Review* 1497 (1983).

16. *See generally* Nancy F. Cott, *The Bonds of Womanhood* 63–100 (1977).

17. 83 U.S. (16 Wall.) 130 (1872).

18. *Id.* at 141 (Bradley, J., concurring).

19. *See generally* Nadine Taub and Elizabeth M. Schneider, "Perspectives on Women's Subordination and the Role of Law," in *The Politics of Law: A Progressive Critique* 117–39 (David Kairys ed., 1982).

20. *See, e.g., State v. Oliver*, 70 N.C. 60, 61–62 (1874) ("If no permanent injury has been inflicted, nor malice, cruelty nor dangerous violence shown by the husband, it is better to draw the curtain, shut out the public gaze, and leave the parties to forget and forgive"); *State v. Rhodes*, 61 N.C. (Phil. Law) 453, 457 (1868) ("[H]owever great are the evils of ill temper, quarrels, and even personal conflicts inflicting only temporary pain, they are not comparable with the evils which would result from raising the curtain, and exposing to public curiosity and criticism, the nursery and the bed chamber"); *State v. Black*, 60 N.C. (Win.) 262, 263 (1864) ("[U]nless some permanent injury be inflicted, or there be an excess of violence . . . the law will not invade the domestic forum, or go behind the curtain."). *See generally* Reva B. Siegel, " 'The Rule of Love': Wife Beating as Prerogative and Privacy," 105 *Yale Law Journal* 2117, 2168–69 (1996) (discussing the curtain as a metaphor for marital privacy).

21. *See* Joyce McConnell, "Beyond Metaphor: Battered Women, Involuntary Servitude and the Thirteenth Amendment," 4 *Yale Journal of Law and Feminism* 207, 243–47 (1992).

22. *See, e.g.,* Naomi R. Cahn, "Family Law, Federalism, and the Federal Courts," 79 *Iowa Law Review* 1073, 1105 n.172 (1994).

23. *See* Siegel, *supra* note 20, at 2182; Taub and Schneider, *supra* note 19, at 119.

24. *See, e.g.,* Susan Moller Okin, *Justice, Gender, and the Family* 129 (1989); Martha Minow, "Redefining Families: Who's In and Who's Out?" 62 *University of Colorado Law Review* 269 (1991).

25. *See generally* Frances E. Olsen, "The Myth of State Intervention in the Family," 18 *University of Michigan Journal of Law Reform* 835 (1985); *see also* Taub and Schneider, *supra* note 19, at 122.

26. Siegel, *supra* note 20.

27. *See generally* Olsen, *supra* note 25.

28. *See* Cahn, *supra* note 22; Judith Resnik, " 'Naturally' Without Gender: Women, Jurisdiction, and the Federal Courts," 66 *New York University Law Review* 1682, 1739–50 (1991); Siegel, *supra* note 20, at 2202–5.

29. Resnik, *supra* note 28, at 1721–29.

30. *Id.* at 1696–97.

31. *See* Cahn, *supra* note 22, at 1105.

32. *See* Olsen, *supra* note 15, at 1501–2.

33. *See, e.g.,* Civil Rights Cases, 109 U.S. 3 (1883); Robin West, *Progressive Constitutionalism* 109–14 (1994).

34. *See* Alan Freeman and Elizabeth Mensch, "The Public-Private Distinction in American Law and Life," 36 *Buffalo Law Review* 237, 239 (1987); Jennifer Nedelsky, "Reconceiving Autonomy: Sources, Thoughts and Possibilities," 1 *Yale Journal of Law and Feminism* 7, 17 (1989).

35. *See* West, *supra* note 33, at 114–21; Mary E. Becker, "The Politics of Women's Wrongs and the Bill of 'Rights': A Bicentennial Perspective," 59 *University of Chicago Law Review* 453, 507–9 (1992).

36. Catharine A. MacKinnon, *Toward a Feminist Theory of the State* 164–65 (1989).

37. Unlike much of federal constitutional and civil rights law, state criminal and tort laws do not require a showing of state action. However, conventional state remedies have proven inadequate to address violence against women effectively, due in part to pervasive gender bias against women in the state criminal and civil justice systems. *See, e.g.,* S. Rep. No. 103–138, at 42, 44–47, 49–50, 55 (1993).

38. For statistics showing the pervasiveness of violence against women in the family and in intimate relationships, *see* S. Rep. No. 101–545, at 30–44 (1990).

39. *See* West, *supra* note 33, at 116, 119–21 (discussing the role of sexual violence in women's oppression and the absence of constitutional protection).

40. *See* Catharine A. MacKinnon, "Reflections on Sex Equality Under Law," 100 *Yale Law Journal* 1281, 1301 (1991).

41. *See* West, *supra* note 33, at 120–21 ("The Constitution protects the individual against abusive and violent state conduct, but not only does it not protect women against the abuse and violence that most threatens them, it perversely protects the sphere of privacy and liberty within which the abuse and violence takes place"); Becker, *supra* note 35, at 508 ("The Fourth Amendment may have affirmatively made women worse off by giving a constitutional foundation to the notion that a 'man's home is his castle' ").

42. MacKinnon, *supra* note 36, at 194.

43. *See, e.g.,* Carole Pateman, *The Disorder of Women: Democracy, Feminism and Political Theory* 118 (1989) ("The dichotomy between the private and the public is central to almost two centuries of feminist writing and struggle; it is, ultimately, what the feminist movement is about"). The feminist challenge to traditional delineations between private and public does not necessarily entail a rejection of any boundary between the two. *See* Okin, *supra* note 24, at 127–28. In recent years, a number of feminists have examined the affirmative potential of privacy as a source of women's autonomy, a topic that is beyond the scope of the present discussion. *See, e.g.,* Anita L. Allen, *Uneasy Access: Privacy for Women in a Free Society* (1988); Linda C. McClain, "The Poverty of Privacy?" 3 *Columbia Journal of Gender and Law* 119 (1992); Elizabeth M. Schneider,

"The Violence of Privacy," 23 *Connecticut Law Review* 973 (1991); Johanna R. Shargel, *"United States v. Lanier:* Securing the Freedom to Choose," 39 *Arizona Law Review* 1115 (1997).

44. *See* Schneider, *supra* note 43, at 979–85.

45. *See* Burke Marshall, *Federalism and Civil Rights* (1964).

46. *See, e.g., Runyon v. McCrary*, 427 U.S. 160 (1976) (applying 42 U.S.C. § 1981 to private action); *Griffin v. Breckenridge*, 403 U.S. 88 (1971) (applying 42 U.S.C. § 1985(3) to private action); *Jones v. Alfred H. Mayer Co.*, 392 U.S. 409 (1968) (applying 42 U.S.C. § 1982 to private action); *Burton v. Wilmington Parking Authority*, 365 U.S. 715 (1961) (construing state action broadly). *But see, e.g., Flagg Brothers, Inc. v. Brooks*, 436 U.S. 149 (1978) (construing state action narrowly); *Moose Lodge No. 107 v. Irvis*, 407 U.S. 163 (1972) (same).

47. Examples include the Civil Rights Acts of 1964 and 1968, Title IX of the Education Amendments of 1972, and the Age Discrimination in Employment Act.

48. *See, e.g., Katzenbach v. McClung*, 379 U.S. 294 (1964); *Heart of Atlanta Motel, Inc. v. United States*, 379 U.S. 241 (1964).

49. *See* Schneider, *supra* note 43, at 976, 988–89.

50. *See* Martha Albertson Fineman, *The Illusion of Equality: The Rhetoric and Reality of Divorce Reform* 37 (1991); West, *supra* note 33, at 115–18.

51. *See* MacKinnon, *supra* note 36, at 164.

52. *See* MacKinnon, *supra* note 6, at 18, 216–17.

53. *See* Education Amendments of 1972, tit. IX, 20 U.S.C. §§ 1681 *et seq.* (1994); Civil Rights Act of 1964, tit. VII, 42 U.S.C. §§ 2000e *et seq.* (1994).

54. 42 U.S.C. § 13981(b) (1994). Aside from the civil rights remedy, VAWA contains numerous other provisions (including new federal criminal penalties) that are beyond the scope of this essay. Those other provisions were not affected by the Supreme Court's ruling on the civil rights remedy in *United States v. Morrison*, 529 U.S. 598 (2000).

55. On VAWA's legislative history, *see* generally Sally Goldfarb, "The Civil Rights Remedy of the Violence Against Women Act: Legislative History, Policy Implications and Litigation Strategy," 4 *Journal of Law and Policy* 391 (1996); Victoria F. Nourse, "Where Violence, Relationship, and Equality Meet: The Violence Against Women Act's Civil Rights Remedy," 11 *Wisconsin Women's Law Journal* 1 (1996).

56. 42 U.S.C. § 13981(d)(1).

57. *See id.* § 13981(d)(2).

58. *See id.* § 13981(c).

59. *See id.* § 13981(e)(2).

60. S. Rep. No. 103–138, at 52–53 (1993); S. Rep. No. 102–197, at 50–51 (1991).

61. *See Women and Violence: Hearing Before the Senate Committee on the Judiciary*, 101st Cong., pt. 1, at 108 (1990).

62. *See* MacKinnon, *supra* note 6, at 182.

63. *Id.*

64. *See, e.g.,* NOW Legal Defense and Education Fund, "The Violence Against Women Act of 1993: Facts on the Civil Rights Provision" 1 (April 1993) (unpublished document, on file with the author).

65. MacKinnon's analysis of sexual harassment has been criticized for focusing too

much on sexual activity and not enough on adverse employment consequences, gender role stereotyping, or acts that undermine women's competence on the job. *See, e.g.,* Katherine M. Franke, "What's Wrong with Sexual Harassment?" 49 *Stanford Law Review* 691 (1997); Vicki Schultz, "Reconceptualizing Sexual Harassment," 107 *Yale Law Journal* 1683 (1998). However, if MacKinnon had not broken the barrier that prevented sexual activity of nonstate actors from being seen as worthy of federal civil rights protection, it is highly unlikely that the far broader protection against sexual assault that was found in VAWA would have been enacted into law.

66. On the links between seemingly "private" violence against women and the market, *see infra* note 81 and accompanying text.

67. *See Crimes of Violence Motivated by Gender: Hearing Before the Subcommittee on Civil and Constitutional Rights of the House Committee on the Judiciary,* 103rd Cong. 81 (1993) (statement of Conference of Chief Justices).

68. *See* William H. Rehnquist, "Chief Justice's 1991 Year-End Report on the Federal Judiciary," *Third Branch,* January 1992, at 1, 3.

69. *See Crimes of Violence Motivated by Gender, supra* note 67, at 77–84.

70. *See id.* at 80.

71. *See* 42 U.S.C. § 13981(e)(4) (1994).

72. *See* S. Rep. No. 103–138, at 51–53, 64 (1993).

73. *See, e.g.,* Schneider, *supra* note 43, at 992 (describing the feminist analysis of domestic violence as a symptom of male domination and female subordination).

74. *Crimes of Violence Motivated by Gender, supra* note 67, at 82 (emphasis omitted).

75. *See id.* at 78.

76. *See supra* notes 45–48 and accompanying text.

77. Sexual harassment played a key role in the politics of VAWA's passage. After the 1992 elections revealed the depth of women's dissatisfaction with congressional handling of Anita Hill's sexual harassment allegations against Clarence Thomas, members of Congress were eager to enact legislation that appealed to women. *See* Goldfarb, *supra* note 55, at 396–97.

78. *See, e.g., Brzonkala v. Virginia Polytechnic Institute and State University,* 169 F.3d 820 (4th Cir. 1999) (en banc), *aff'd sub nom. United States v. Morrison,* 529 U.S. 598 (2000) (alleging gang rape by fellow students in university dormitory); *Santiago v. Alonso,* 96 F. Supp. 2d 58 (D.P.R. 2000) (alleging acts of domestic violence); *Burgess v. Cahall,* 88 F. Supp. 2d 319 (D. Del. 2000) (alleging sexual assaults and harassment by employer); *Williams v. Board of County Commissioners,* No. 98–2845-JTM, 1999 U.S. Dist. LEXIS 13532 (D. Kan. Aug. 24, 1999) (alleging rape by police officer); *Kuhn v. Kuhn,* 98-C-2395, 1999 U.S. Dist. LEXIS 11010 (N.D. Ill. July 15, 1999) (alleging physical and sexual violence by husband); *Bergeron v. Bergeron,* 48 F. Supp. 2d 628 (M.D. La. 1999) (alleging battery, assault, and attempted rape by husband); *Wright v. Wright,* No. Civ. 98–572-A (W.D. Okla. Apr. 27, 1999) (alleging physical violence by defendant against wife and daughter); *Ericson v. Syracuse University,* 45 F. Supp. 2d 344 (S.D.N.Y. 1999) (alleging sexual harassment by university tennis coach); *Culberson v. Doan,* 65 F. Supp. 2d 701 (S.D. Ohio 1999) (alleging that defendant beat and murdered girlfriend); *Doe v. Mercer,* 37 F. Supp. 2d 64 (D. Mass.), *vacated and remanded on other grounds sub nom. Doe v. Walker,* 193 F.3d 42 (1st Cir. 1999) (alleging gang rape); *Liu v.*

Striuli, 36 F. Supp. 2d 452 (D.R.I. 1999) (alleging sexual harassment and rape by university adviser); *Ziegler v. Ziegler*, 28 F. Supp. 2d 601 (E.D. Wash. 1998) (alleging assault, threats, and harassment by husband); *Griffin v. City of Opa-Locka*, No. 98-1550-Civ-Highsmith (S.D. Fla. Aug. 27, 1998) (alleging sexual harassment and sexual assault by employment supervisor); *C.R.K. v. Martin*, No. 96-1431-MLB, 1998 U.S. Dist. LEXIS 22305 (D. Kan. July 10, 1998) (alleging rape and threats of physical violence by fellow student at plaintiff's high school); *Timm v. DeLong*, 59 F. Supp. 2d 944 (D. Neb. 1998) (alleging physical and sexual abuse by husband); *Mattison v. Click Corporation of America*, No. 97-CV-2736, 1998 U.S. Dist. LEXIS 720 (E.D. Pa. Jan. 27, 1998) (alleging sexual assault, battery, and harassment by employer); *Crisonino v. New York City Housing Authority*, 985 F. Supp. 385 (S.D.N.Y. 1997) (alleging nonsexual, gender-motivated assault by employment supervisor); *Anisimov v. Lake*, 982 F. Supp. 531 (N.D. Ill. 1997) (alleging assault, harassment, and rape by employer); *Seaton v. Seaton*, 971 F. Supp. 1188 (E.D. Tenn. 1997) (alleging physical and sexual abuse by husband); *Doe v. Hartz*, 970 F. Supp. 1375 (N.D. Iowa 1997), *rev'd in part*, 134 F.3d 1339 (8th Cir. 1998) (alleging sexual abuse by priest); *Doe v. Doe*, 929 F. Supp. 608 (D. Conn. 1996) (alleging physical and mental abuse by husband).

The fact that a number of cases filed under VAWA alleged facts that might also make out a Title VII claim for sexual harassment is not surprising in light of the fact that VAWA did not require exhaustion of administrative remedies, had a far longer statute of limitations than Title VII, and permitted unlimited awards of compensatory and punitive damages. *See generally* Andrea Brenneke, "Title VII," in *Violence Against Women: Law and Litigation* 18–1 to 18–35 (David Frazee et al. eds., 1997).

79. *See* cases cited *supra* note 78.

80. *See* 42 U.S.C. § 13981(a) (1994).

81. *See United States v. Lopez*, 514 U.S. 549 (1995); *Burgess; Williams; Kuhn; Wright; Ericson; Culberson; Doe v. Mercer; Liu; Ziegler; Griffin; C.R.K.; Timm; Mattison; Crisonino; Anisimov; Seaton; Doe v. Hartz; Doe v. Doe*. *But see Brzonkala* (finding civil rights provision unconstitutional); *Santiago* (same); *Bergeron* (same). On the constitutionality of VAWA's civil rights remedy under the Commerce Clause, *see*, for example, Kerrie E. Maloney, Note, "Gender-Motivated Violence and the Commerce Clause: The Civil Rights Provision of the Violence Against Women Act After *Lopez*," 96 *Columbia Law Review* 1876 (1996); Johanna R. Shargel, Note, "In Defense of the Civil Rights Remedy of the Violence Against Women Act," 106 *Yale Law Journal* 1849 (1997).

82. *Wright; Timm*. On the constitutionality of VAWA's civil rights remedy under the Fourteenth Amendment, *see* Cass Sunstein et al., "The Constitutionality of the Violence Against Women Act," in *Violence Against Women: Law and Litigation, supra* note 78, at 6–31 to 6–36; Shargel, *supra* note 81, at 1871–83.

83. *Seaton*, 971 F. Supp. at 1190 n.1.

84. The court rejected this argument. *See Mattison* at *24. *See also McCann v. Rosquist*, 998 F. Supp. 1246, 1252–53 (D. Utah 1998) (rejecting defendant's assertion that nonconsensual touchings were "amorous" and therefore could not constitute class-based animus), *rev'd on other grounds*, 185 F.3d 1113 (8th Cir. 1999), *vacated and remanded for reconsideration in light of United States v. Morrison*, 529 U.S. 1126 (2000).

85. *See* cases cited *supra* note 81. *See also Fisher v. Grimes*, No. 98 CVD 865 (N.C.

Dist. Ct. July 22, 1999) (holding VAWA's civil rights remedy constitutional); *Young v. Johnson*, No. CV 97–90014 (Ariz. Sup. Ct. May 13, 1999) (written record of oral proceedings) (same).

86. *Brzonkala v. Virginia Polytechnic Institute and State University*, 169 F.3d 820 (4th Cir. 1999) (en banc), *aff'd sub nom. United States v. Morrison*, 529 U.S. 598 (2000).

87. *See id.* at 835 (citing, inter alia, *Wickard v. Filburn*, 317 U.S. 111 (1942)).

88. *See id.* at 862, 873–77.

89. *Id.* at 826, 853, 862, 874, 889.

90. *See id.* at 842–44.

91. *Seaton v. Seaton*, 971 F. Supp. 1188, 1190–91, 1194 (E.D. Tenn. 1997).

92. *Id.* at 1190.

93. *United States v. Morrison*, 529 U.S. 598 (2000).

94. *Id.* at 613.

95. *Id.* at 615–16.

96. *Id.* at 614–15.

97. *See S. Rep. No.* 103–138, at 54 (1993).

98. *Morrison*, 529 U.S. at 621–25.

99. *See supra* note 37. *See also* Catharine A. MacKinnon, "Disputing Male Sovereignty: On *United States v. Morrison*," 114 *Harvard Law Review* 135, 176 (2000).

100. *See* Dooling, *supra* note 2; Toobin, *supra* note 5.

Why Doesn't He Leave?
Restoring Liberty and
Equality to Battered Women

DIANE L. ROSENFELD

In 1994, I was serving as Acting Chief of the Women's Advocacy Division at the Illinois Attorney General's Office when a woman named Rhonda called me. She told me that the day after she had obtained an emergency order of protection[1] against her ex-boyfriend Steve, he followed her in his car, forced her off the road, and threatened to "rip her guts out" with a lug wrench that he held in his fist, poised in the air and aimed at her stomach. Rhonda's sixty-three-year-old father, who was with her, jumped out of the car and tried to restrain Steve. In response, Steve beat him so severely that he required a visit to an emergency room. Rhonda was terrified. Her immediate obstacle was a return to court the next day for a full hearing to extend the protection order. I agreed to accompany her to the hearing.

After the hearing, at which Steve received a month-long continuance to hire an attorney, Rhonda and I went to the cubicle of her court-assigned advocate where we discussed the need for a safety plan. Rhonda's eyes filled with tears, as she confessed that she had been sleeping in her car for the past four days. She was afraid to go to her apartment; Steve already had broken in. She also did not want to go to her father's house and risk further endangering him. Rhonda spoke of her need to hide from Steve with an air of inevitability — a fear that he would find her anyway. We all agreed she needed to go to a battered women's shelter.

At that moment the injustice of the situation suddenly became apparent to me. Why, after a woman has been beaten by her intimate partner, should she be forced to seek shelter outside of her home, while her abuser is free to roam the streets and terrorize her? Doesn't this arrangement just add insult to injury — the insult of leaving one's home to the injury of being beaten there? Why must she restrict her own freedom of movement out of realistic fear that he will stalk her and assault her again, while his freedom of movement remains relatively unfettered? How could — and should — the power of the state be used transformatively to redistribute the rights and responsibilities in this situation to reflect more fairly the conduct of the parties?

The answer, I propose, lies in the creation of batterer detention facilities to house batterers after a domestic assault. Detaining the abuser would appropriately redistribute liberty back to the woman who was victimized by the violence. Subject to a hybrid of civil commitment and criminal responsibility, the batterer would be both punished through the detention and treated through intense therapy. The woman, on the other hand, would be able to remain safely in her home and not be forced to uproot herself — and perhaps her children — in search of shelter.

The first section of this essay explores questions of citizenship, equal protection, and liberty with a focus on how a battered woman's interests are compromised under the current institutional structure and practice of the criminal justice system. In the second section, I locate batterer intervention facilities within the current legal regime surrounding domestic violence and assert that creating these facilities would be more consistent with battered women's preferences than the current structure in which they must run for their lives. I then describe how a batterer's detention facility would operate, incorporating the most current research on batterer intervention into a program with a housing component.[2] Finally, I conclude that changing the institutional structure of the criminal justice system's response to domestic violence would both change women's rights as citizens and would interrupt the pernicious and predictable cycles of family violence that plague so many of our homes.

Twenty years ago, Catharine MacKinnon analogized wife beating to sexual harassment, noting that "even acts that have been objectively illegal are systematically tolerated."[3] Expanding on this theme, Duncan Kennedy has defined a sphere he refers to as the "tolerated residuum" of abuse that exists in many heterosexual relationships.[4] This sphere includes the penumbral area of abuse that is legally prohibited but widely understood to be unpoliced. This occurs in a "legal system" that is set up "to condemn sexual abuse of women by men in the abstract but at the same time operating the system so that many,

many instances of clearly wrongful abuse are tolerated." The proposal to intervene to stop and treat abusive males is aimed specifically at changing the boundaries of the tolerated residuum, shrinking the sphere to reflect that such abuse is truly intolerable.

Prior to Catharine MacKinnon's articulation of the theory of sexual harassment, a woman whose male boss was making lewd suggestions or threatening to cut off or alter her employment usually had to accept the situation as "just life." She had no legal rights that would allow her to remain at her job and challenge the discriminatory behavior. Her choices were limited to accepting her lot or seeking employment elsewhere.

MacKinnon's theory transformed women's opportunities for participation in the workplace by giving the aggrieved party a legal right to stand her ground and work free of discrimination. The concept, theory, and practice of sexual harassment law have revolutionized the workplace by redistributing the set of entitlements with which a woman enters the market.

In a homologous fashion, it is unacceptable that women must suffer continued abuse at the hands of an intimate partner without meaningful state intervention and accept it as "just life."[5] Using sexual harassment as a model of transformative legal theory, this essay is offered in the hope that a change in the institutional arrangements surrounding domestic violence would give meaning to the promise of equal protection.

Give Me Liberty

Domestic violence implicates a battered woman's interest in both liberty and equality. A narrow focus on a battered woman's situation when the system to which she has turned for help tells her to go into hiding at a shelter elucidates her acute loss of liberty. If the lens is moved to a wider angle, the denial of equal protection of the laws comes into focus. When women are told by the criminal justice system to leave their homes and seek shelter elsewhere while men are left largely unaccountable for their own criminal behavior, the systematic preference of men's rights over women's becomes vividly apparent. This is a denial of equal protection of the laws.

When law enforcement officers respond to a domestic assault, they usually take the batterer into custody while advising the victim to seek an order of protection. At the same time, law enforcement officers will provide the victim with a list of shelters or the name of a victim advocate who will guide her to such shelters. It is at this precise moment that the meaning of the state's promise of protection is called into question and its internal contradictions are revealed. For if the state expected that the order of protection would be effective, why then does it recommend that the battered woman go into hiding for her life? A critical examination of this moment in domestic violence implicates the state's role in both denying a woman equal protection and being complicit in her loss of liberty. Not only does it condone such loss of liberty, it explicitly recommends it.

The order of protection represents the state's promise of equal protection to its citizens. For the state to recommend seeking shelter contemporaneously with issuing an order of protection is an implicit recognition that it is breaking its promise of protection as it is making it. In the context of domestic violence, liberty is a zero-sum game in which the state, by its deliberate inaction, sides with the batterer. Since the batterer's freedom is inversely related to his victim's, every act or omission by the state that preserves the batterer's freedom must be seen for what it also is — part of a systematic imposition on the liberty interests of an abused woman. Noteworthy here is the recognition that stalking laws anticipate the probability that an abuser will not be adequately restrained by the protection order, and will continue to seek out the victim. Instead of making the first state intervention as effective as possible, which the state would do if it took domestic violence seriously, it offers a series of responses that encourage the battered woman to continually seek piecemeal protection from the criminal justice system. The problem is that this response leaves her open to predictable reassault.[6]

Moreover, the state explicitly requires the battered woman to take responsibility for her own safety and for its own failure to protect her as a citizen. Battered women's shelters represent nothing less than a loss of a woman's liberty to move around freely because she, as a result of challenging the violent domination she faces at home, must now exist in hiding. She loses her freedom to go to work, to attend school, to participate in those daily activities that make up the normal texture of one's life. Through its reliance on a system that undermines the fundamental citizenship rights of an already besieged class, the state becomes complicit in not only the perpetuation of violence, but also in the maintenance of a silenced underclass. Not only are battered women implicitly told that their concerns will be ignored, but they are also denied the freedom necessary to successfully mobilize to have their rights protected.[7]

In what other crime is the blame and responsibility not only placed on the victim but also reflected institutionally? In this light, battered women's shelters can be seen as an institutionalized representation of the systematic denial of equal protection under the laws.

Indeed, the existence of battered women's shelters is an example of what

Reva Siegel calls a "status-enforcing regime" that transformed the practice of wife-beating without abolishing it, thus reinforcing male dominance.[8] The way that this regime works is by passing laws prohibiting domestic violence, while at the same time supporting structures that maintain the status quo so that the new law, while well intentioned, will not give a battered woman a right to be free from the predictable violence committed against her by her intimate partner. Rather, these laws represent just enough superficial change to quiet public outcry and fail to either address the underlying causes of the problem or to alter the power dynamics between the parties.

It is not a coincidence that the rise in the number and power of battered women's shelters grew along with the rise in the number of laws and political initiatives to fight domestic violence. Shelters now form the epicenter of response to domestic violence — they are fully integrated into government response. But laws that purport to protect while telling you to fend for yourself are not likely to provide the "equal protection" they promise. Changing the structural arrangements around domestic violence by creating facilities that reflect the state's desire and ability to hold the offender accountable would be a transformative move aimed directly at eliminating the effect of battered women's shelters as status-enforcing regimes.

While a battered woman's liberty interests will be explored in this paper, notions of equal protection are just as relevant. The legal progress women have made in the past twenty-five years has been based on equality theory rather than on liberty interests. The development of sexual harassment law represents the most significant legal gain for women to date. The right to participate in the workforce free of sexual harassment is now part of every person's entitlement. In fact, sexual harassment law took away the male entitlement to dominate women in the workplace by exploiting their sexuality. Perhaps a real response to domestic violence, as suggested in this essay, would likewise take away male entitlement to dominate them physically at home.

In the post-*Morrison* legal world in which there is no longer a federally recognized right to be free from gender-motivated violence,[9] women are, as Catharine MacKinnon puts it, sent back home to their abusers. Consider this analogy:

> One way to describe the process of change in women's legal status from chattel to citizen is as a process of leaving home. The closer to home women's injuries are addressed, the less power and fewer rights they seem to have; the further away from home the forum, the more power and rights women have gained — and with them freedom of action, resources and access to a larger world. In experiential terms, women are least equal at home, in private; they

have had the most equality in public, far from home. It is in the private, man's sovereign castle, where most women remain for a lifetime, where women are most likely to be battered and sexually assaulted, and where they have no recourse because the private, by definition, is inviolable and recourse means intervention. . . . [O]ne way to describe this dynamic is to observe that men often respect other men's terrain as sovereign in exchange for those other men's respect for their own sovereignty on their own terrain. As a result of such balances that men with power strike among themselves, represented in the shape of public institutions, men have the most freedom at home, and women gain correspondingly greater equality, hence freedom, the further away from home they go.[10]

Despite formal legal and policy changes that supposedly reflect a more enlightened view of family and gender relations, as MacKinnon notes the home remains a bastion of male domination, most noticeably where violence is involved. The abused woman is explicitly told that to stand a legitimate chance of being protected from violence she must leave her home, that she will be heard only when she speaks with her feet.

Why does the system work this way? The reluctance many male judges have to telling a man what he can and cannot do in his own home to his "own" wife strongly supports MacKinnon's point. Indeed, isn't it possible that male sovereignty depends for its existence on this very notion—that men can accept hierarchy among other men as long as they all understand themselves to be superior to women?

Battered Women's Shelters: An Institutional Analysis

Historically, battered women's shelters were a desperate attempt by women to protect other women who were experiencing abuse, mostly from violent, alcoholic husbands.[11] The battered women's movement culminated in the establishment of the first battered women's shelter in England in 1974.[12] The shelter idea spread to the United States and generated pressure to change the law to criminalize wife beating. The salient point is that when battered women's shelters were started, domestic violence was largely shielded from the eyes of the law.

Now, however, all states and the federal government have laws against domestic violence and stalking. Public officials at all levels, from local prosecutors to governors to former Attorney General Janet Reno, have decried the amount of violence against women in society, paying particular attention to domestic violence. Now that the government has asserted its political will to stop violence against women, a critical reassessment of the institutional arrangements surrounding the response to domestic violence is warranted.

In this vein, it is instructive to examine how battered women's shelters have been integrated into the state's response to domestic violence under this new legal regime that treats wife beating as criminal. While the state neither fully supports nor runs battered women's shelters, it explicitly relies upon them in its response to domestic violence. In progressive law enforcement departments, police supply information on battered women's shelters when they answer domestic violence calls.[13] At the same time, the police will usually advise the woman to seek a protective order. Underlying this seemingly redundant behavior is a realistic expectation that an order of protection will not actually provide adequate security. By referring a battered woman to a shelter, the state demonstrates that it believes both that the violence will escalate if her partner is allowed contact with her and that it is her responsibility to provide for her own safety. The same expectation that the order of protection will not adequately restrain the batterer from reassaulting his victim is reflected in stalking laws. Yet instead of seriously reforming its response, the criminal justice system routinely issues protective orders, fully aware of the likelihood that the orders will not work.

In the same way that the existence of battered women's shelters reifies the notion that the victim must seek shelter, the creation of detention facilities would instead give meaning to male responsibility for violent and abusive behavior. The current regime in which women's complaints of abuse are not treated as lethal threats forces abused women to seek other methods of assistance rather than to rely on the state for protection.

By contrast, increasing state protection from abuse would change the distribution of rights and responsibilities of people involved in domestic violence, and would make battered women more likely to call upon the state for protection.[14] It could increase the real cost and consequences to the abuser. By giving abused women an expanded range of options to deal with their situations, batterer detention facilities would represent a government response more commensurate with its promise of protection.

Whether through direct action or failure to act, the state is implicated in almost all aspects of domestic violence. Through legislation, law enforcement, judicial decision-making, and the performance of a multitude of other roles and functions, the state acts. In so doing, it takes a side — and privileges the interests of one party over the other. In a situation of domestic violence, when a woman is not safely separated from her assailant, the state's actions place her in danger of attack. The present delivery of state services in response to domestic violence is rife with state action that exacerbates and intensifies the problem, rather than addressing it effectively.

Locating Batterer Detention Facilities Within the Larger Context of Domestic Violence
CONTINUED SUPPORT FOR BATTERED WOMEN'S SERVICES

My proposal to create batterer intervention facilities and the critique of battered women's shelters as part of the facilitation of domestic violence is not to be read as an indictment of the battered women's movement or the life-saving work that battered women's advocates have done throughout the years. It is rather a critique aimed at a criminal justice system that can do a much better job of protecting its citizens from domestic abuse. Imagine for a moment the expanded range of services that battered women's advocates could provide if the batterer, rather than the battered woman, were the one detained. If the pressure to provide shelter were decreased, advocates could turn their attention to providing more long-term assistance to battered women, such as helping them find permanent new housing, new jobs, or job training so that they could advance in their careers. A battered woman would be able to evaluate her options in relative safety, while the batterer would be in detention, rather than having to run for her life and hide.

BATTERED WOMEN AND NORMATIVE PREFERENCES: WHY SHE DOESN'T LEAVE

Many of the normative assumptions made about the parties involved in domestic violence fail to address adequately the complexity of the relationship between the perpetrator and the victim. Unlike most other victim to offender relationships, in domestic violence the parties are connected emotionally and economically and often have children together. When hearing stories about domestic violence, people often ask, "Why doesn't she leave?" This question, which assumes that the woman *wants* to leave the relationship, disregards the context of intimate violence. Instead, the battered woman usually wants the violence to stop.[15] This precept should be the operating normative assumption for the creation of batterer detention facilities, as it increases the possibility that the violence *will* stop.

Focusing on the question of why she does not leave also reflects the commonly held attitude that it is the battered woman's responsibility to control (or avoid) the temper of her violent intimate partner. It reflects the deeply misogynist idea that a woman must act in a way so as not to displease her husband — a notion that underlies laws explicitly permitting a husband to beat his wife.[16]

It also assumes that there is someplace to go, and that she can go there. These presumptions have many flaws.[17] First, while battered women's shelters do exist, such shelters are only a temporary solution, and have limited space. A shelter may be unavailable when a battered woman most needs it. Even if one is available, going to it is inevitably difficult and painful. Consider how it feels for a woman who has been beaten by an intimate partner to have to then seek shelter in a strange and hidden place. She must uproot herself and her children and go into hiding. She will be cut off from familiar surroundings and her support system. She may lose contact with friends and family at the very moment when she most needs emotional support.[18] Her job may be placed in jeopardy. If she works out of her home, she may be unable to continue. Alternatively, she may justifiably fear going to work, where her abuser might find her.[19] If she has children, their school attendance will likely be disrupted. Schools are often the site of parental abduction, and battered women recognize and may simply not be willing to take this risk.

Most important, however, leaving is the most dangerous time for a woman. Battered women who are killed by their abusers have left or attempted to leave an average of at least five times.[20] It is critical to understand that because battering is about power and control, a woman leaving her abuser signifies to him a loss of control and he will predictably reassault her in an attempt to reassert control.[21] While it might seem counterintuitive, men who batter do not do it because they want the woman to leave; rather, they want her to stay, but in a subordinate position. Abused women often leave to both escape further abuse and also because they interpret the battering as a message that their batterers must hate them and want them to leave. However, it is much more complicated than that.[22] So well does the criminal justice system understand this problem that stalking laws anticipate that she will leave and that he will stalk her in exactly this manner.

Fear is often the biggest reason that women don't leave. Many abused women have been warned by their batterers that the punishment for leaving will be severe. Fear paralyzes many battered women — fear that the abuse will escalate once the abuser finds them, fear of the unknown once they leave, fear of losing custody of the children (a very common threat of batterers) and fear of abject poverty.[23] In this current environment, it is quite understandable why women don't leave if one takes a moment to consider the realities facing women in this situation.

Although frustrating to battered women's advocates, we should not be surprised that several years into the movement, people are still asking the question, "Why doesn't she leave?" The entire criminal justice system is set up to perpetuate the victim-blaming inherent in the question. Battered women's shelters reify the notion that the violence is her responsibility; invisible is the counter notion of male responsibility. In a culture that has never truly rejected the idea that a woman is responsible for her partner's violence, where the laws have codified the notion that female sexuality is an open invitation to male violence, perhaps the only surprise is that we have seen so much surface-level change in the formal response to domestic violence.

INTERRUPTING THE KNOWN CYCLES OF INTIMATE VIOLENCE

It is widely recognized that domestic violence occurs in cycles. In the tension-building phase, the man is irritable and cranky, and nothing the woman does can please him. He gradually becomes more abusive and may slap and verbally abuse his intimate partner. The next stage is the violent outbreak with acute battering. The man will "fly into a rage and become violent for no apparent reason, or state a reason that seems petty or irrational, such as his wife's cooking."[24] Reports of the violent outbreak often describe men as acting completely out of control, wild-eyed, red in the face, and foaming at the mouth. After the beating, the man is remorseful and apologetic. This is known as the "honeymoon phase." This "intermittent reinforcement" is a powerful tool to keep the woman in the relationship.[25] Many women will stay in the relationship believing in the "man they love" and hoping that his promises to change will be fulfilled.

The predictability with which domestic abuse occurs gives law enforcement a unique opportunity to intervene effectively to prevent further criminal activity. The batterer detention proposal is designed specifically to interrupt the known cycle of violence.

Integrally related to the cycles of violence in domestic abuse is what can be described as "the stalking cycle." It is predictable that when an abused woman tries to leave her abuser, he will prevent her, or attempt to prevent her from leaving through increasingly violent means. Stalking laws, which exist in every state, reflect the knowledge that the order of protection obtained by the battered woman may not be strong enough to stop the man from following her to get her back. The irony of this method of control is intriguing; the man typically beats and/or rapes the woman in an attempt to get her to stay with him. One might think from his actions that he wants her to leave, but that is not the case, as evidenced by the stalking that almost inevitably takes place after she tries to do so. Instead, stalking grows out of the abuser's feeling that "if I can't have you no one will."

The cycle of domestic violence together with the stalking cycle combine to produce an elaborate game of hide and seek in which battered women's shelters play an important role. Put simply, the abused woman hides in a battered woman's shelter,[26] and the batterer seeks her through stalking. This is far from a game, however. It is nothing less than a terroristic attempt by the batterer to regain control over the victim to resume the cycle of violence she has broken by leaving. Stalking must be treated as the lethal act that it is. Violation of a restraining order demonstrates the perpetrator's disregard for legal authority —a strong indication of his belief that his criminal behavior will not have consequences. This behavior should be read as a sign of immediate and grave danger to the battered woman, and reacted to appropriately by law enforcement. If it is not, the woman will end up like other hunted prey.[27]

Batterer Detention Facilities

In the typical cycle of domestic violence, separation is the most dangerous time for a battered woman. My proposal is aimed at safely separating the parties and defusing the volatility of the situation to prevent escalation of the violence. We are at a moment in history where our collective understanding of intimate partner violence is evolving simultaneously with an increased focus on offender management and accountability.[28]

My proposal is intended not to detract from the provision of services for battered women but to increase the range of available options in response to domestic violence.

The most current thinking on batterer intervention indicates that a constellation of services is necessary for a successful program. This includes participation from judges, prosecutors, probation officers, victim advocates, and batterer program personnel. Although a batterer detention facility does not yet exist, the information available through the various programs in place across the country is directly applicable to a program that includes a housing component. The addition of a housing component to a batterer intervention program would be fully consistent with program objectives and would augment the effectiveness of intervention by decreasing significantly the opportunity for reassault.[29]

The following subsections describe the main components of a batterer detention facility. First, the facility should be created by a local coordinated community council. It should include active judicial oversight and participation, a well-planned intake evaluation process, a work release program using electronic monitoring, state-of-the-art batterer intervention therapy, coordination with victim services, enumeration of specific responsibilities for program participants, consideration of possible funding mechanisms, and cost-benefit analysis.[30] This is only a starting point for discussion in planning a successful pilot program.

CONSTELLATION OF SERVICES:
COORDINATED COMMUNITY RESPONSE

Coordination of community services and the criminal justice system has been demonstrated to be the most effective way of addressing batterer behavior. A recent report on batterer intervention by the National Institute for Justice suggests that an integrated criminal justice response to battering should include law enforcement officers, prosecutors, judges, victim advocates, and probation officers and should promote cross-fertilization of ideas.[31] Additionally, members of the defense bar should be included in the design of batterer detention facilities, as their cooperation and involvement can troubleshoot problems that can be addressed in the planning process and facilitate their clients' participation in the program.[32] The coordinated structure will strengthen the overall delivery of services and help to ensure that the victim's safety is not neglected through miscommunication regarding the batterer's treatment.

VICTIM LIAISON

The safety of the victim is the cornerstone of the batterer detention facility proposal. Indeed, it is structured to increase the victim's range of options, as well as to redistribute the rights and responsibilities for the domestic assault. Detaining the perpetrator allows the battered woman to confront her options in relative safety. Moreover, she will be able to make these choices while staying at home, rather than being restricted by the "choice" of hiding from her abuser or going back to him.

That ultimate objective suggests that batterer detention facilities should incorporate comprehensive victim services. Victim advocates must be included in the design of the program to ensure the full consideration of victim safety concerns and the realization of victim preferences. Batterer detention facilities should also appoint a special victim liaison to communicate with victims on an ongoing basis. Victim notification is very important at certain times in the program. Currently, victims are notified when a batterer begins a program, when he is terminated for noncompliance, when he completes the program, and when there is an imminent threat to the victim's safety.[33] Notification procedures should be developed to accommodate the specific needs of victims whose abusers are in the detention program. While the victim would be informed of threats to her security, the detention program increases the extent to which the batterer's behavior is controlled and monitored. In this system, threats to her safety could and should be more immediately and effectively addressed, because he is already in a custodial setting.

The victim liaison also could perform the role of explaining safety planning and the basic features of the program. Many battered women whose abusers are in batterer intervention programs are not aware of services available to them. Victim liaisons can provide crucial information to help battered women build the support system they need, evaluate their options, improve their lives and ensure their safety. They can help the victim understand that enrollment in the batterer detention facility does not guarantee that the batterer will change. Importantly, the liaison can serve as a person for the battered woman to call when she needs support.[34]

LETHALITY ASSESSMENT PERFORMED AT INTAKE

Domestic violence cases should all be treated as potentially lethal crimes. All domestic homicides and murder-suicides have involved previous incidents of physical assaults accompanied by threats of murder. Working backward from the domestic homicide, the consistent message is that if the criminal justice system had treated the domestic assault as potentially lethal, the murder might have been prevented.

Lethality assessments should be absolutely mandatory in all domestic violence cases. Following the lethality assessment, the defendant can be held under a pretrial detention statute until he can have a hearing before a judge. Pretrial detention is constitutional under many circumstances, and most states have statutes that specifically authorize it in cases of domestic assault.[35]

The legal apparatus necessary to sustain a batterer intervention program would include a structure of incentives to make the program attractive to the batterer. The most logical of these incentives would be a resolution of the criminal complaint that does not include a finding of guilty if the batterer agrees to enter the program, completes it successfully, and fails to reassault for a given period of time.

At intake, which should take place within twenty-four hours of arrest, a specially trained batterer counselor or probation officer would explain the option of going to a batterer intervention facility and conduct the appropriate evaluation to determine eligibility.

The primary determinant of fitness for a batterer intervention facility is the performance of a lethality assessment. Conducting a lethality assessment of batterers at the intake phase can make the difference between life and death for the victim. For this reason, the evaluator should be instructed to "assume there exists a potentially lethal situation."[36] In doing so, the evaluator could and should make use of the substantial literature on assessing whether batterers are likely to kill.[37] Moreover, the lethality assessment should be conducted on an ongoing basis to monitor threatening behavior. It is critical that the lethality assessment be coordinated with victim notification services.

Evaluation criteria would include, but not be limited to, the alleged batterer's family history, his criminal record, his attitude toward control within an intimate relationship, his attitude toward and previous use of violence in intimate relationships, his history of substance and alcohol abuse, his propensity for violence outside the home, his level of contrition for the attack, his level of denial of the seriousness of the assault, whether children are involved as witnesses or as victims, and other information relevant to the batterer's propensity to commit violence against his intimate partner. The information gathered in the assessment would provide useful guidance in constructing the detention program and for coordinating safety measures with the victim's liaison.

ACTIVE JUDICIAL OVERSIGHT

Active judicial management and oversight of domestic violence cases have been shown to decrease reassault rates and to increase batterer compliance with orders of protection and attendance at court-mandated batterer intervention programs. Thus, participation by the judiciary in the operation of batterer detention facilities would be essential to their success. Ongoing judicial oversight sends the signal to both batterers and victims that their cases will be taken seriously by a criminal justice system that understands the nature of the crime and is committed to protecting victim safety.

Batterer intervention facilities should have intuitive appeal to the judiciary. They add a meaningful alternative to the current choice of jail or no-jail. Courts have too few alternatives in dealing effectively with domestic violence.[38] Judges are often uncomfortable issuing only orders of protection, knowing the probability that the order will not protect the victim. Yet, they impose jail only for the most egregious intimate partner assaults, because many judges simply feel that a prison sentence is incommensurate with the crime of domestic violence.

The creation of batterer intervention facilities as a criminal justice option is not intended to suggest that battering is not criminal. Rather, it recognizes that the common criminal sanction has not proven to be the most effective way to address domestic violence.[39] Short jail sentences without specific batterer intervention tend to have the effect of incubating violent behavior. Placing the batterer in confinement with other violent offenders offers the opportunity for male bonding over violent behavior — a problem so pronounced that batterer intervention programs take measures to confront the issue before it arises — and will likely produce an angrier batterer with stronger desire to seek revenge on his victim upon release.[40]

Moreover, jail sentences often correlate with the "honeymoon" period of the violence cycle, during which time the offender will apologize profusely from jail and claim he learned his lesson.[41] Because the dynamics and power structure of the relationship change when he is in jail — he becomes dependent on her for outside contacts and access to resources — she might be more willing to accept his apologies, as well as to pity him for being in jail. Yet, if his violent behavior in intimate situations is not addressed, he will likely repeat it when he is released.

A judiciary committed to effectively addressing domestic violence can integrate a batterer detention facility into an overall structure of sanctions for intimate partner violence. A system of graduated sanctions is the most effective way of dealing with domestic violence. Judges must be willing to issue meaningful and appropriate sentences and to respond forcefully to any violations of orders of protection.[42] Adding the option of detaining batterers in specially created facilities in no way negates the appropriateness of jail sentences in many domestic assault cases. Rather, batterer detention is intended to address effectively the criminal behavior of an entire group of batterers whose behavior is not so addressed under the current system.

WORK RELEASE

Work release would be a key component of the batterer detention facility. According to David Adams, a founder of EMERGE in Cambridge, Massachusetts, one of the country's leading batterer intervention programs, the most successful batterer programs are the ones that seek to preserve relationships, stability, jobs, and connection to community. In addition to preserving some sense of stability, the work-release option of the batterer detention facility would have several economic advantages. First, it would remove the threat of economic deprivation for the battered woman if she or her children are dependent on the batterer's income. Economic pressures are one of the most often cited reasons that battered women resist prosecution of perpetrators, especially if it means that their children may go hungry. The batterer's wages could be remitted directly to the facility, which would ensure that support payments are made. Second, judges are reluctant to incarcerate batterers when the likely result is forfeiture of employment.[43] The work-release option removes this impediment. Third, the batterer could finance participation in the program if he is allowed to keep his job.[44] This would defray some of the operating costs, as well as potentially increase the batterer's commitment to the program.

THE CORRELATIVE SAFETY PLAN: ELECTRONIC MONITORING

Batterer detention facility programs would include a "correlative safety plan," in which both the abuser and the victim are equipped with electronic monitoring devices that automatically activate whenever they are within a certain distance of each other. Rather than relying solely on the batterer's internal control mechanisms, an electronic bracelet would provide external control as well. The extra measure of security will provide the woman with an increased sense of safety knowing that he is being monitored. Such a system would dramatically increase the effectiveness of a "stay-away" order. Electronic monitoring is a method that can be used to achieve the judicial objectives embodied in a protection order.

Other available tracking devices should also be considered in planning for the victim's safety. A combination of state-of-the-art devices would likely provide the most protection.

THERAPEUTIC COMPONENT

Batterers who participate in the program would receive intense counseling and intervention therapy. Treatment modalities would be modeled after programs like EMERGE, which combines cognitive-behavioral techniques with "accountability-focused group therapy," or the Duluth curriculum, developed by the Domestic Abuse Intervention Project in the early 1980s, which situates battering within the larger context of male privilege and challenges batterers to reconceptualize gender relations in order to eliminate their violent tactics.[45] The Duluth program seeks to replace the "power and control" wheel with the "equality and nonviolence" wheel.[46]

Batterers report that the one thing that matters to them is consequences.[47] A batterer detention facility creates the possibility for consequences where none previously existed. More specifically, it would capture abusers who are in a mid-range of abusive behavior, and who previously would have only been subject to a (ineffective) restraining order. There is a large universe of batterers who could be helped by such a program.

These state-of-the-art treatment intervention models would be incorporated into and adapted specifically for the batterer detention program. Because the program is in-house, the treatment would be intensified to correlate with the batterer's physical detention. Thus, batterers could have daily sessions rather than weekly or biweekly ones. Further, batterers would receive both group and individual therapy sessions to maximize the effectiveness of the therapeutic intervention. Because the batterers would not be allowed access to their victims, different methods would be employed to measure the progress of attitudinal adjustments. The length of the detention would correlate to current treatment regimes, but may be shorter because of the increased intensity. Facilities could experiment with the program length, incorporating graduated controls for when the batterer is released. The existing literature on batterer intervention programs suggests that two months would probably be the appropriate amount of time for the in-house detention.

CAN IT WORK IN REAL LIFE?

In one sense the creation of batterer intervention facilities represents an institutional reflection of a paradigmatic shift in focus from the battered woman to the batterer. Yet in another way, it might simply be an idea whose time has come. Since I presented the ideas in this essay at the Sexual Harassment Conference at Yale Law School in 1998, I have spoken to hundreds of people about the idea. I am pleased to say that the concept has met with overwhelming support from victim's advocates, judges, law enforcement officers, academics, and other various members of the community. I have discussed the idea with representatives from different municipalities in various geographic areas.

I have encountered two concerns with the proposal, both of which can and would be addressed in designing a pilot program. The first and most serious concern was raised by a prosecutor who has worked extensively with victims. She asserted that jail is the proper place for batterers, and that any time a program is created to help batterers, it takes away from the available resources for battered women.

My response to this is twofold. First, I agree that many batterers should be in jail for their crimes against their intimate partners. However, most judges are reluctant to send them there, but would be more inclined to admit them to a program that would both detain them and offer the most effective intervention available today. The existence of the program and the added requirements of conducting a lethality assessment in itself would require judges to take much more seriously the victim's safety and the potential dangerousness of the offender. Second, resource allocation is a matter of political will and prioritizing. There is no reason that money would be taken from battered women's services to fund a batterer intervention facility. Rather, the money should be taken from prison budgets. As discussed above, allowing the batterer to participate in work-release alleviates some of the cost concerns, as he can be required to pay rent. In my opinion, lack of funding is an excuse that people use to preserve the status quo, especially in the face of a truly progressive initiative that could give women more rights. I know, based on my many years of experience in government, that budgetary measures are highly discretionary, and quite simply, where there's a political will, there's a way to get things done.[48]

The other major concern was about the right of the defendant to a fair trial. Some people thought that the program would essentially convict a defendant and sentence him without conducting a trial. As I discussed in the section on the importance of a coordinated community council, defense attorneys would be part of the planning for a pilot of the program. Many jurisdictions, including at the federal level, already have pretrial detention statutes under which a lethal defendant can be held until trial. While this program involves something less than pretrial detention, it is important to note that there is precedent for such detention. Moreover, the jurisdiction designing its batterer intervention facility can construct the program as an alternative or a deferred sentence.

Conclusion

The hope of this project is to reverse the institutionalized structure of society's response to men beating their intimate partners to produce a correlative change in the current distribution of entitlements. Quite simply, a woman should not be forced to leave her home after she has been the victim of a violent assault committed against her by her intimate partner. For the criminal justice system to consistently support this result — expecting her to leave while failing to hold the batterer accountable for his violence — perpetuates an intolerable denial of equal protection for women under the law. Moreover, to leave her in hiding and at risk of predictable future reassault denies her liberty to participate in society as a citizen.

Catharine MacKinnon is right when she points out that the Supreme Court in *Morrison* sent women back home to their abusers, where they have no rights.[49] But the Supreme Court is not our only hope. We have other viable means of fighting this battle, and it is time to work on identifying and challenging those institutional structures that keep women in their place, whether by design or effect. We must demand a public explanation from those who would defend the status quo, in which a woman can't go home again.

Notes

I wish to thank many people who have helped nurture and develop this idea, including Bernard Auchter, Mary Becker, Harvey Berkman, Bonnie Campbell, Pamela Coukos, Terry Fisher, Charles Fried, Jerry Frug, Christine Jolls, Susan Keller, Duncan Kennedy, Catharine MacKinnon, Burke Marshall, Martha Minow, Wendy Murphy, Jane DiRenzo Pigott, Laurie Robinson, William Rodriquez, Shawn Ryan, Dena Sacco, Alexa Smith, Christopher Stone, and my family. Valuable research assistance was provided by Stacey Dershewitz, Julie Mantooth, Karen Paik, Claire Prestel, Anne Robinson, Shelley Senterfitt, Shauna Shames, and Diane Welsh. This essay is dedicated to the memory of my friend Ronald V. Greer.

1. An order of protection, sometimes referred to as a stay-away order or protection from abuse order, is a common civil or criminal remedy sought by battered women to protect them against their abusers. Like other injunctions, such orders are available

immediately as emergency orders of protection. These can be issued ex parte, as in a temporary restraining order. Then the defendant is given notice and a full hearing is set for trial, usually within ten to fourteen days, depending on the jurisdiction.

2. I describe the operational aspects of batterer intervention facilities in another article entitled "Why Doesn't He Leave? The Creation of Batterer Intervention Facilities," *Domestic Violence Report*, Aug.–Sept. 1999 at 93. My thanks to Joan Zorza for suggesting the title and for her guidance in thinking about these facilities in the larger context of battered women's rights.

3. "The constituent acts of domestic battery are obvious criminal violations; they are regularly grounds for arrest and if proven, for conviction in contexts other than husband and wife. Women's attempts to gain legal redress and protection from domestic victimization are infamously ineffectual. This suggests that intimate assaults on women by men are ignored even when they are reported—even when there is an unambiguous doctrinal receptacle for the complaint." Catharine A. MacKinnon, *Sexual Harassment of Working Women: A Case of Sex Discrimination* 160 (1979) (citations omitted).

4. Duncan Kennedy, *Sexy Dressing* Etc. 126, 137 (1993). Kennedy articulates the benefits to all men in a system in which some men abuse women without consequence. He recognizes "what we might lose through more protection for women" while offering solid justifications for reduction of these illegitimate gains. Most important, he describes how the background rules on the tolerated level of abuse between partners affect them, even in situations that seem not to involve it at all. The tolerated residuum is "plausibly attributed to contestable social decisions about what abuse is and how important it is to prevent it." *Id.*

5. This particular analogy was suggested by my colleague Pamela Coukos, former public policy director of the National Coalition Against Domestic Violence, at an informal presentation of this essay on February 25, 1998. She is currently an associate at Mehri & Skalet in Washington, D.C.

6. Andrew Klein, *Re-abuse in a Population of Court-Restrained Male Batterers After Two Years: Development of a Predictive Model* 112 (1993). Klein concluded that restraining orders do not protect women from continued abuse and that almost half the men re-abused their victims within two years of the 1990 court intervention (at 63).

7. I thank Stacey Dershewitz for helping me articulate and develop these insights.

8. Reva Siegel, "Why Equal Protection No Longer Protects: The Evolving Forms of Status-Enforcing State Action," 49 *Stanford L. Rev.* 1111 at 1116. (May 1997).

9. *U.S. v. Morrison*, 120 S. Ct. 1740 (2000). In this case, the U.S. Supreme Court invalidated the civil right to be free from gender-motivated violence found in Title III of the Violence Against Women Act of 1994, Public Law No. 103-322, 108 Stat. 1941 (codified as amended at 42 U.S.C. § 13981 (1994).

10. Catharine MacKinnon, "Disputing Male Sovereignty: On *United States v. Morrison*," 114 *Harv. L. Rev.* 135, 174–175 (Nov. 2000).

11. The movement can be traced to the eighteenth century, when women began visibly agitating for legal reforms that would protect them from physically abusive husbands. By the late eighteenth century, wife beating was illegal in most states, but very few husbands were prosecuted or incarcerated. Elizabeth Pleck, *Domestic Tyranny*, ch. 10 (1987).

12. Erin Pizzey devised the idea of temporary residences for battered women. She

established a neighborhood center in England offering housing and childcare for homeless women that attracted many battered wives. Several American women visited the English shelters. The first shelter in the United States was for abused wives of alcoholic husbands in St. Paul, Minnesota, in 1974. In August 1976, there were about twenty shelters in the United States; by 1982, there were about three hundred, as well as coalitions to provide battered women with services. *Id.*

13. *See www.vaw.umn.edu/Promise/pplaw.htm* for a description of Promising Practices pertaining to law enforcement response published by the Department of Justice, Office of Justice Programs.

14. Interview with Dr. David Adams, founder of EMERGE (Batterer Intervention Program) Cambridge, Mass. (Apr. 20, 1998).

15. Barbara Hart, "Battered Women in the Criminal Justice System," in *Do Arrests and Restraining Orders Work?* 100, 101 (Buzawa and Buzawa eds., 1996).

16. The first known law of marriage was formalized by Romulus (who was credited with the founding of Rome in 753 b.c.) and required married women " 'as having no other refuge, to conform themselves entirely to the temper of their husbands and the husbands to rule their wives as necessary and inseparable possessions.' The attitudes contained in this directive, ancient though the formulation may be, sound hauntingly like the sentiments expressed by men in (current) violent relationships." Angela Browne, *When Battered Women Kill*, 164–65 (1987).

17. For an unabashed examination of this question, *see* Andrea Dworkin, "In Memory of Nicole Brown Simpson," in *Life and Death* (1997).

18. Studies show that victims facing post-traumatic stress syndrome are more likely to heal and avoid revictimization when they can stay close to their support systems. *See* Susan E. Bernstein, "Living Under Siege: Do Stalking Laws Adequately Protect Domestic Violence Victims?" 15 *Cardozo L. Rev.* 525 (1993)

19. It is common for batterers to stalk their victims at work. This has led to several companies and governmental agencies to institute workplace violence policies to protect employees in abusive situations. For example, the federal Office of Personnel Management has established a workplace violence policy.

20. N. Isaacs, L. Langford and S. Kabat, "Intimate Partner Homicides, Massachusetts 1990–1995, Peace at Home" (1997).

21. This phenomenon was termed "separation assault" by Martha Mahoney. *See* Martha Mahoney, "Legal Images of Battered Women: Redefining the Issue of Separation," 90 *Michigan L. Rev.* 1 (1991).

22. Indeed, this complication lies at the heart of gender-motivated violence. Such violence differs from other hate-based crimes because other hate crimes involve attempts to exclude those you hate, while gender-based violence is intended to put and keep women in their place. Unlike other race-based hate crimes, for example, it is impractical for men to exclude women from their lives in general. I am grateful to my former student Pam Armour for making this point.

23. *See* Bernstein, *supra* note 18 at 556.

24. Dawn Bradley Berry, *The Domestic Violence Sourcebook* 31–33 (1995).

25. "A batterer who intersperses abuse with loving acts, courtship, and gifts is unwittingly using one of the most powerful techniques for convincing the woman to stay with him." *Id.*

26. In fact, great pains are taken to ensure the confidentiality of the shelter location. This is often reflected in statutes and by tacit agreement because of the expectation that the abuser will try to find her and that she will not be safe if he does. Not all shelters are hidden, however. In Sweden, for example, battered women's shelters are found in public view. It is culturally understood that a man would be too ashamed to show his face at one of these facilities.

27. Spousal homicide studies suggest that some men may perceive "separation as an affront and actually heighten their pursuit and abuse of their partner." Edward W. Gondolf, "Patterns of Reassault in Batterer Programs," in *Violence and Victims* (1997). A recent stalking report issued by the National Institute of Justice confirms that there is a strong link between stalking and other forms of intimate partner violence: 81 percent of women who were stalked by a current or former husband or cohabiting partner were also physically assaulted by that partner and 31 percent were also sexually assaulted by that partner. *See* Patricia Tjaden and Nancy Thoennes, National Institute of Justice, *Stalking in America: Findings from the National Violence Against Women Survey* (1998).

28. Historically, we have moved beyond triage. In the late 1970s, one activist was opposed to the idea that a victim should go into hiding while her assailant was free, but she was dissuaded from questioning the need for shelter because "she received too many calls from women huddled in phone booths with their children, asking where they should go." Today, victim services for battered women are more readily available, and there is a National Domestic Violence Hotline available twenty-four hours a day with a toll-free number, 1-800-799-SAFE. It provides counseling and resource referrals for any area of the country. Although the provision of services is far from perfect, we can begin to focus on the controlling batterer behavior while continuing to take other steps to ensure victim safety.

29. Reassault rates in domestic violence hover around 32 percent, according to the most recent batterer intervention statistics. Yet, half of batterers who are in treatment programs still live with their abused partner. Living together has been found to significantly increase the risk of reassault. *See* Edward Gondolf, "Patterns of Reassault in Batterer Programs," *Violence and Victims* (December 1997). Detention facilities would correct this problem by providing a housing solution after a domestic assault. Moreover, the recidivism rate is substantial enough to warrant at least trying a new approach to stopping this predictable violence.

30. Appropriate funding will be critical to the success of a batterer detention project. I recommend a full exploration of funding possibilities, including, but not limited to, possible grants under the Violence Against Women Act, public-private partnerships, private donations, and the establishment of trust funds created through criminal penalties. A cost-benefit analysis should include preventive costs such as prosecutorial expenses saved through avoiding repeat prosecutions for severe violations and possible homicides. Moreover, it should include factors such as costs saved on hospitalization, lost wages, and increased dependency on government programs. For an extensive analysis of the costs of violence against women in this country, see generally the legislative history of the Violence Against Women Act of 1994, Public Law No. 103-322, 108 Stat. 1902 (VAWA), in which Congress concluded after four years of hearings and testimony, that violence against women has a substantial effect on interstate commerce. Based on this

finding, Congress passed the VAWA pursuant to its powers under the Commerce Clause (as well as under section 5 of the Fourteenth Amendment).

31. Kerry Healy et al., United States Department of Justice, National Institute of Justice, *Batterer Intervention: Program Approaches and Criminal Justice Strategies* (1998) (hereinafter *NIJ Report*).

32. Including defense attorneys from the inception of the project would increase the effectiveness of the program for several reasons. First, defense attorneys may be able to provide insights into any objections raised by such a program. These objections could then be addressed in the pilot planning process. Second, defense attorneys would be in a good position to advise their clients to enter the program by explaining the legal and social value of reforming the batterer's behavior. Finally, the defense bar could help discourage batterers' misuse of the criminal justice system to avoid responsibility for their criminal conduct and to harass their victims.

33. *See NIJ Report*, at 38.

34. *Id.* at 36–42.

35. *See, e.g., U.S. v. Salerno*, 481 U.S. 739 (1987); accord *Mendonza v. Commonwealth*, 673 N.E.2d 22 (Mass. 1996) in which defendant was held on evidence including threats to kill his wife, standing over her with a knife, drug addiction, a history of psychiatric hospitalizations, and assault and battery on a police officer.

36. *NIJ Report*, at 157. The Report contains an intake form from the AMEND program in Denver, Colorado. See also *www.nashville.net/police* for former Lieutenant Mark Wynn's form on lethality assessment.

37. Criteria include threats made, weapons used or threatened to be used, and when the batterer begins to act without regard to legal or social consequences. *See* Barbara Hart, Pennsylvania Coalition Against Domestic Violence, *Assessing Whether Batterers Will Kill* (1990).

38. Interview with the Honorable Shirley S. Abrahamson, Chief Justice, Wisconsin Supreme Court, May 21, 1999.

39. "Incarceration is the one sentence clearly conveying the seriousness of wife battering as a criminal offense. But, for a variety of reasons, including jail and prison overcrowding, the relative ineffectiveness of incarceration for preventing further violence, and victim reluctance to have their batterers incarcerated, judges will impose alternative sanctions." Ford, Regoli, Reichard, and Goldsmith, "Future Directions for Criminal Justice Policy on Domestic Violence" in *Do Arrests and Restraining Orders Work?* 258 (Buzawa and Buzawa eds., 1996).

40. Interview with Dr. David Adams, EMERGE (Apr. 20, 1998).

41. This is the period after the violent assault when the batterer is remorseful and promises to change. The cycles of domestic violence are explained more fully *infra*, "Interrupting the Known Cycles of Domestic Violence."

42. See *NIJ Report*, at 83. The report also makes the important point that judges should be aware of the co-occurrence of domestic violence and child abuse as well as the harm and danger to children who witness domestic violence.

43. This is not to imply that unemployed batterers would be ineligible for the program. Rather, for these men, community service arrangements could be worked out.

44. Most batterer treatment programs require the abuser to pay for the therapy. Prices

are on a sliding scale, so that poverty can be taken into consideration yet not used as an excuse to avoid therapy.

45. Central to this model is the "power and control wheel," which portrays eight abusive practices as "spokes" of male control: economic abuse; intimidation; emotional abuse; isolation; children; male privilege; coercion and threats; and minimizing, denying, and blaming. These behaviors, combined with a pattern of violence, enable batterers to control their partners.

46. The Duluth model utilizes group classes led by a trained instructor who encourages participants to confront their violent behavior and hold one another accountable. The program seeks to teach men skills to foster more egalitarian relationships and is organized accordingly around eight themes: nonviolence, nonthreatening behavior, respect, support and trust, honesty and accountability, sexual respect, partnership, and negotiation and fairness. By concentrating on the use of power and control as the nucleus of abuse, rather than the specific details of any one participant's relationship, the curriculum explores "with each abusive man the intent and source of his violence and the possibilities for change through seeking a different kind of relationship with women." Michael Paymar, *Violent No More* (1993).

47. *See id.* The book contains many anecdotal stories based on the writer's experience as a training coordinator with the Duluth Domestic Abuse Intervention Project. Batterers interviewed constantly refer to the fact that they could engage in their abusive behavior without consequences.

48. For example, former Illinois Attorney General Roland Burris created the Women's Advocacy Division during his tenure in the early 1990s. It was simply a high priority for his administration to do something about domestic and sexual violence, and he did it with no extra funding.

49. MacKinnon, *supra* note 10.

PART **VII**

Transnational Perspectives

32

Dignity, Respect, and Equality in Israel's Sexual Harassment Law

ORIT KAMIR

Sexual harassment is a universal affliction, endured and resisted by women (and men) everywhere. Since the early 1970s, U.S. feminist legal scholarship and judicial decisions have been breaking new ground, developing legal strategies designed to confront sexual harassment head-on. Although a host of social and legal issues have been resolved, others are still being investigated and debated. For example, does sexual harassment offend a fundamental social value? Should it be criminalized? Should it be treated as a tort? What should the scope of sexual harassment be? Should it be limited to the workplace or should it extend to the street? Should sexual harassment be defined in terms of human dignity? Does sexual harassment, legally speaking, infringe women's fundamental right to respect? (Do women have a right to be respected as women, and does this right imply a prohibition of sexual harassment?) How is same-sex sexual harassment to be conceptualized?

Feminist lawyers and academics around the world have been following and participating in this consequential dialogue and using insights gained there to influence perceptions and legal definitions of sexual harassment within their own legal cultures. In the following pages I introduce such developments as they have recently been formulated and successfully legislated in Israel. I illustrate how an exploration of U.S. sexual harassment law and feminist theory enabled a new conceptualization, befitting the needs, features, and circumstances of Israeli society and law. Starting with a brief analysis of some successes and limits in the development of U.S. sexual harassment doctrine, this essay will use the recent Israeli sexual harassment law to show how dialogue between U.S. and Israeli feminists brought about Israel's creative legal treatment of sexual harassment. I am convinced that just as the U.S. experience was crucial to the formulation of the new Israeli law, any development around the world can be useful for other feminist communities and their countries' legal systems. In March 1998, Israel's Knesset passed the Prevention of Sexual Harassment Law, 5758-1998,[1] prohibiting broadly defined sexually harassing behavior, in the workplace as well as in every other social setting. The new law was the product of a unique cooperation among women Knesset members, feminist activists, pro-feminist jurists at the Ministry of Justice, and feminist legal academics.[2] It was my privilege to take part in this endeavor, having proposed the theoretical framework for the new legislation. In the following pages I briefly present the theoretical, legal, and political foundations on which the new law was built. Then I lay out the major principles and articles of the new law, stressing their ideological, feminist significance.

Since 1988, Article 7 of the Israeli Equal Employment Opportunity Law, 5738-1988[3] (EEOL), has criminalized work-related harassment of an employee by an employer, based on the employee's rejection of sexual advances imposed on her by her employer or supervisor.[4] Although very narrowly defined, retaliation arising from quid pro quo sexual harassment in the workplace was thus deemed illegal. Despite this protection, years passed in which an exceedingly small handful of cases were prosecuted and only one with any meaningful judicial success.[5] Something was amiss. Therefore, in 1996, while teaching sexual harassment law at the Hebrew University, I decided to reexamine the state of sexual harassment law in the United States at that time, as well as the particulars of the Israeli legal culture, in an effort to suggest a more serviceable and effective alternative to Israel's legal treatment of sexual harassment. I concluded there was a need to start over completely and to restructure Israeli legal doctrine incorporating insights gained from a study of the U.S. experience. Having composed an analysis of U.S. and Israeli sexual harassment laws and a proposed model law, I approached the Israeli Women's Network (a feminist group), the Ministry of Justice, and Israel's Knesset Committee for the Empowerment of Women. The proposed model law and analysis were adopted by all three and served as the basis for the parliamentary formulation of the new Israeli statute.

Rethinking Aspects of Current U.S. Doctrine

More than twenty-five years of sexual harassment litigation in the United States has produced an impressive and instructive body of judicial decisions. These decisions map out the basic terrain of sexual harassment and illustrate various types of harassing behaviors and situations. Legal terms of art, such as "unwelcome sexual conduct" and "sexually hostile environment," capture women's experiences of sexual harassment and effectively translate them into concepts that both legal professionals and the public can (at least potentially) understand.

The harms of sexually harassing behavior are amply revealed in U.S. legal academic commentary. A large and ever-growing body of academic literature reveals how sexual harassment, by subjecting women to patriarchal sexual hierarchy and its sexist stereotyping, undermines women's confidence, damages their sense of autonomy, and injures their capacity to fulfill their human potential and professional capabilities. Above all, the U.S. experience with sexual harassment has established that feminist jurisprudence can help the law respond to women's experience and make a significant difference in terms of social reality.

In my exploration of legal treatment of sexual harassment in the United States, however, I encountered several drawbacks that I thought would prove problematic if incorporated into Israeli law.

First, the common-law evolution of U.S. sexual harassment law, despite its many obvious merits, may not be the most suitable vehicle to implement major (or quick) legal reform. Sexual harassment laws are designed to confront pervasive and sometimes very sophisticated mechanisms of patriarchy, challenging fundamental tenets of the existing social structure. Such sweeping legal reform may be more efficient if constructed systematically by the legislature, assisted by experts, and not incidentally, by judges deciding, ad hoc, the specific cases brought before them. Legislation would afford sexual harassment the full authoritative status of law, as well as the necessary coherence, clarity, and distinction on all legal points, which have not always been achieved in the U.S. court-made law. The Supreme Court's blunt refusal to seize the opportunity and issue a standard of employer's liability in *Meritor*[6] and its reluctance to decide whether the reasonable man standard somehow contains the reasonable woman in *Harris*[7] illustrate this point. Moreover, unfortunate decisions such as *Rabidue*[8] exemplify how, within judge-made law, a single wrong turn can cause long-term damage.[9]

A second drawback in U.S. doctrine stems from the fact that sexual harassment was legally formulated in the context of the right to equality as guaranteed in Title VII of the Civil Rights Act of 1964. While understandable and useful in the context of U.S. law, this linkage may have caused sexual harassment doctrine to focus mostly on workplace harassment. Sexual harassment of working women (and men) is undoubtedly a major issue, but it is not necessarily more significant than sexual harassment in the street, school, or family. In fact, these latter types of sexual harassment may be more prevalent and more damaging, as many women experience them very early in life when they are least able to respond effectively and preserve their self-esteem.[10] Under Israeli law, for example, the army is not considered a "workplace"; employment laws specifically exclude soldiers, while specific military laws and regulations offer proscribe unique standards and remedies for them. Most Jewish Israeli women are drafted into the army at the age of eighteen and spend at least eighteen months in that "masculine" environment, often under male supervisors. Sexual harassment in the army is an experience which deeply affects many women's identity and social behavior, yet, in Israel, is not a "workplace" issue and needs to be conceptualized and confronted on different grounds. U.S. sexual harassment doctrine has made great stride, resolving specific issues crucial to the workplace, such as employer liability. But the emphasis on the workplace may have distracted attention from other distinct areas of sexual harassment law. For example, the concept of the harasser's personal liability, crucial for the legal treatment of street harassment, has received no attention. Similarly, the unique aspects of sexual harassment in the family are still in need of conceptualization.

The third drawback of the U.S. model, also related to the link between sexual harassment and Title VII, is the prevalent definition of sexual harassment as "*discrimination* based on sex." My concern here is not with the problematic wording of Title VII, "based on sex,"[11] but with the conceptualization of sexual harassment as discrimination, that is, the exclusive association of sexual harassment with equality. From a pragmatic point of view, I worry that the judicial notion of equality, deeply embedded as it is in conservative thought, may restrict the development of sexual harassment law.

Catharine MacKinnon has forcefully argued:

> According to the approach to sex equality that has dominated politics, law, and social perception, equality is equivalence, not a distinction, and sex is a distinction. Sex, in nature, is not a bipolarity; it is a continuum. In society it is made into a bipolarity. Once this is done, to require that one be the same as those who set the standard — those which one is socially defined as different from — simply means that sex equality is conceptually designed never to be achieved. Those who most need equal treatment will be the least similar,

socially, to those whose situation sets the standard as against which one's entitlement to be equally treated is measured. Doctrinally speaking, the deepest problems of sex inequality will not find women "similarly situated" to men.[12]

The Aristotelian notion of equality, according to which "similarly situated" people deserve similar treatment, does not and cannot remedy women who suffer from sex discrimination, for the simple reason that, under patriarchy, women are not "similarly situated" to men. MacKinnon offered a radically different and highly convincing notion of equality—based on a dominance theory rather than on sameness and difference. As one commentator has observed, "MacKinnon's subordination analysis is necessary to make the logical bridge here [between any sexually harassing behavior and discrimination]. Unfortunately, her analysis is either too complicated or too radical for most judges."[13] The result has been that judges have adopted MacKinnon's conclusion, that sexual harassment constitutes discrimination, but not her dominance reasoning and rhetoric; they define sexual harassment as discrimination, but within their Aristotelian notion of equality rather than within dominance theory. This unnatural judicial combination of Aristotelian equality and the dominance-oriented conceptualization of sexual harassment as discrimination works for some of the more obvious cases, especially where heterosexual men harass only women. It does not, however, work as well for the less obvious cases where, for example, a man sexually harasses both men and women.[14]

I am convinced that in the current social reality, sexual harassment of women by men does indeed mirror and enhance the prevalent domination of and discrimination against women and is, therefore, a form of inequality. Unfortunately, I suspect that, at this stage, MacKinnon's dominance theory *is* both too radical and too complicated for most judges and laymen anywhere in the world, and that the Aristotelian notion of equality, intertwined with patriarchal ideology and reality, is still the widespread intuitive concept of equality. As a result, judicial doctrine of sexual harassment as discrimination is likely to be incoherent, unconvincing, and at times inefficient. I therefore suggested that sexual harassment not be linked solely with equality; that it might profit from the association with other social values—values less entwined with patriarchy.[15]

My fourth point is more specific and has to do with the U.S. distinction between quid pro quo and "hostile environment" sexual harassment. In *Sexual Harassment of Working Women*, MacKinnon claimed that quid pro quo sexual harassment "arises most powerfully within the context of horizontal segregation, in which women are employed in feminized jobs, such as office work, as a part of jobs vertically stratified by sex, with men holding the power to hire and fire women."[16] In pink-collar ghettos, thus, male supervisors impose their patriarchal "rights" on women not only professionally, but also sexually. Events of hostile environment, MacKinnon argued, "occur both to 'token women,' whose visibility as women is pronounced and who often present a 'challenge' to men, and to women in traditional 'women's jobs.' . . . [A] woman can put up with it or leave. . . . Most women are coerced into tolerance."[17] Hostile environment, thus, is used as a means of scaring women in traditionally male-dominated positions back to their place within patriarchy. This conceptualization was beneficial in identifying and defining typical behaviors associated with sexual harassment. It was also useful in allowing courts to first come to terms with the more blatant quid pro quo behaviors, and only then with the more subtle "hostile environment" cases. But because the legal system has recognized hostile environment sexual harassment as actionable, it is difficult to justify the categorical distinctions that judges have drawn between these two types of behaviors; quid pro quo harassment can now be easily defined as a subcategory of hostile environment. Therefore a new sexual harassment doctrine need not distinguish between quid pro quo and hostile environment.[18]

Finally, one should reconsider what I would call the "reasonable creature" standard. The conceptual difficulties inherent in the usage of the "reasonable man," the "reasonable woman" and their relatives, is familiar to anyone involved in sexual harassment law.[19] When the reasonable creature is a "person," it is more likely to be a man than a woman; when it is a "reasonable woman," the standard threatens to reinforce essentialist notions of womanhood. Furthermore, whichever standard is employed, current American legal doctrine unjustly submits the plaintiff, rather than the harasser, to the test of reasonableness.[20] And above all, in a legal field aiming to reform current societal standards, legal standards should *not* be modeled on abstractions of "average" community members, representing "average" standards and norms. Sexual harassment law is meant precisely to expose common attitudes as patriarchal; the deployment of any "reasonable" creatures to determine the definition or harm of sexual harassment defeats this purpose.[21] I therefore proposed that all reasonable creatures (as well as other fictitious creations) are evil, and no reasonable creatures are necessary in the legal treatment of sexual harassment.

Thus, from this review of the U.S. legal approach to sexual harassment, I concluded that the eradication of sexual harassment required specific legislation addressing sexual harassment in general, and not just in the workplace. I felt that the legislation should associate sexual harassment with other social values in addition to equality, that it need not make categorical distinctions between quid pro quo and hostile environment sexual harassment, and that it should not use the "reasonable creature" standard.

Israeli Legal Reality: Relevant Features

There are several features in the Israeli legal system that made plausible the passage of legislation, such as that described above. First, Israel has neither formal constitution nor a First Amendment; sexually harassing utterances can, therefore, be restricted by law more readily, without giving rise to arguments of constitutionally protected free speech. Second, the Knesset has a history of relative willingness to address women's issues through legislation. As early as 1954, the Law of Women's Work, 5714-1954,[22] provided for twelve weeks of maternity leave. The Israeli 1988 Equal Employment Opportunity Law was designed to empower women employees and to provide them with working conditions similar to those enjoyed by men. Other statutes provide for equal pay for women and men, and for women's right to retire at the same age as men. In these circumstances it seemed feasible to suggest that the Knesset address the issue of sexual harassment through legislation.

A third important feature of Israeli law is the status it affords equality, dignity, respect, and liberty. Due to the significant political influence of Jewish Orthodox parties in the Knesset and the lack of a formal constitution, equality is not a fully recognized constitutional right in Israel. In fact, the Knesset has so far refused to constitute it in legislation. As for sex equality, the 1951 law of Women's Equal Rights, 5711-1951[23] states clearly that women are equal to men in all legal matters — except for those regarding family law (a big exception). But whereas equality has not been legislated as a fundamental legal right, the combined concept of "right to human dignity, respect, honor and liberty" has recently been defined as a fundamental human right. Israel's Basic Law, *kvod haadam veheruto*,[24] enacted in 1992, is widely regarded as the country's bill of human rights, naming two central values: *herut* (liberty) and *kvod haadam* (human dignity, respect, and honor).[25] The philosophical implications of the linkage among liberty, dignity, respect, and honor deserve a separate discussion. In this context it is enough to say that this complex assembly of values has been constituted as the foundation of Israeli legal system.

Since the enactment of the Basic Law, the country's vigilant Supreme Court has assigned the right to dignity, respect, and liberty a major role in human rights law, and the Israeli public is learning to view this combined right as encompassing all human rights. Many human rights, including the right to equality, are being defined by the Supreme Court as aspects of the right to human dignity, respect, and liberty. In light of these developments, a new approach to sexual harassment law seemed feasible as well as warranted — an approach defining sexually harassing behaviors as violations of human dignity, liberty, and the basic right to respect. I should make it clear that conceptualizing sexual harassment in terms of dignity, respect, and liberty does not require its separation from notions of equality.[26] Dignity, respect, liberty, and equality need not be posed as competing or exclusionary values; on the contrary, in the context of sexual harassment law, they should rather be read as complementary.[27] Sexual harassment discriminates against women by not respecting them as women and as human beings, by violating their dignity, and by restricting their liberty to determine themselves and to lead lives free of fear and restriction. It disrespects women and violates their dignity by mirroring and perpetuating a social reality that does not treat them as equal.[28] The more commonsense notions of dignity, respect, and liberty can be useful in conveying the harm caused by sexual harassment, and in illuminating its sex-discriminatory harm.

Last but not least: because of the lack of a formal constitution, civil and criminal provisions in Israel are both easier to legislate and more readily applicable by the courts than constitutional law. Furthermore, criminal law is widely considered by Israelis as the major, if not exclusive, serious legal expression of society's fundamental values.[29] Under these circumstances, it made sense to formulate the prohibitions on sexual harassment in terms of tort and criminal laws, and not as constitutional prohibitions.[30]

Taking into consideration the lessons learned from U.S. sexual harassment law, as well as the relevant features of the Israeli legal system, I proposed model legislation, defining sexual harassment as violating the rights to human dignity, respect, freedom, and equality, and prohibiting it in all social settings. The concept was readily adopted by both the Israeli Ministry of Justice and the Knesset Committee for the Empowerment of Women. The committee, assisted by a large group of jurists, developed the proposed model into a detailed statute, which was fully legislated within a year.[31]

Israel's Prevention of Sexual Harassment Law

Israel's Prevention of Sexual Harassment Law of 1998 addresses sexual harassment in every social setting, proclaiming it a grave social phenomenon that violates fundamental social values, including human dignity and the rights to respect, freedom, and equality. The new law embodies an integrated approach: it defines sexual harassment and the resulting intimidation as both civil wrongs and criminal offenses; it further offers special remedies to employees injured by sexual harassment at work. The statute defines the prohibited sexually harassing behaviors in great detail and with precision, aiming to clarify the practical significance of the new statutory norm to the general public as well as to those charged with its enforcement. Although not employing the categorical distinction between quid pro quo and hostile environment harassments, the statutory definitions are modeled on U.S. perceptions, as developed by courts and feminist jurisprudence. The definitions do not employ the "reasonable person" standard and are drafted so as to exclude the possibility of using any such fictitious character in the definition of sexual harassment (and particularly in assessing the victim and her behavior). Sexual harassment is defined per se, but specific reference is made to employment-related sexual harassment and to sexual harassment containing a blatant abuse of authority. Let me explicate in greater detail the statute's most significant articles.

Article 1, titled "Purpose," manifests the law's objective: "to prohibit sexual harassment in order to protect human dignity, [and the rights to respect,] liberty and privacy, and to promote equality between the sexes."[32] The official explanatory notes[33] stress this ideological point, condemning sexual harassment as being "a widespread social phenomenon injuring many, and women in particular." The notes state that sexual harassment, *inter alia*, humiliates its victims, degrades them, and invades their privacy; it undermines the victim's right to self-determination, autonomy, and control over the person and sexuality; it constitutes discrimination. The explanatory notes specifically emphasize that "sexual harassment aimed at women humiliates them with respect to their gender or sexuality and places obstacles in their way of integrating into the realm of careers and into other aspects of life as equal participants, thus denying them equality." The statute therefore explicitly combines the U.S. approach, which defines sexual harassment as an infringement of the right to equality, with the definition of sexual harassment as an injury to human dignity and an infringement of the right to respect in general, and of women's right to respect in particular. The explanatory notes declare that the set of values set out in article 1 "shall guide the courts when required to construe the provisions of the proposed law." The courts are thus instructed to interpret the law as part of the legal protection afforded by the Israeli legal system to promote human dignity and the right to respect, but also to draw from U.S. judicial experience and legal academic scholarship in treating sexual harassment as an issue of equality and discrimination, particularly sex discrimination.

Article 3, which lies at the core of the statute, contains detailed definitions of eight types of "sexual harassment." Due to its importance, I will quote it in full:

3. (a) Each of the following acts constitutes sexual harassment:

(1) blackmail by way of threats, as defined in section 428 of the Penal Law, where the act demanded to be performed by the person is of a sexual character;

(2) indecent acts, as defined in sections 348 and 349 of the Penal Law;

(3) repeated propositions of a sexual character to a person, where that person has shown to the harasser that he is not interested in the said propositions;

(4) repeated references directed towards a person which focus on his sexuality, where that person has shown to the harasser that he is not interested in the said references;

(5) an intimidating[34] or humiliating reference directed towards a person concerning his sex[, gender,][35] or sexuality, including his sexual tendencies;

(6) propositions or references as described in subsections (3) or (4), directed towards one of those enumerated in subsections (a) to (c), in such circumstances as specified in such subsections, even where the person harassed has not shown the harasser that he is not interested in the said propositions or references:

(a) a minor or a helpless person, where a relationship of authority, dependence, education or treatment is being exploited;

(b) a patient undergoing mental or medical treatment, where a relationship of authority between the patient and the person treating him is exploited;

(c) an employee in the labor relations sphere and a person in service, within the framework of such service, where a position of authority in a work relationship or in service is being exploited.

(b) Prejudicial treatment[36] is any harmful act, the source of which is sexual harassment or a complaint or court action filed in relation to sexual harassment.

(Article 2, the "definitions" section, determines that a "reference means reference in writing, orally, by way of visual or vocal medium, including computer or computer material, or by conduct.")

Article 3 establishes three categories of sexually harassing behaviors, the first of which includes mostly "criminal" behaviors. As is apparent from article 3, some of the modes of conduct defined as sexual harassment are already prohibited by provisions of the Israeli Penal Law of 5737-1977.[37] Such modes of conduct have nevertheless been defined as types of sexual harassment for two reasons. First, in order to supply a full and clear definition of the new norm prohibiting sexual harassment, such a definition should refer to any conduct amounting to sexual harassment, even if such conduct is already classified as part of another legal category, and is prohibited as offending another protected social value.[38] The second reason is that unlike the Penal Law, which delineates only criminal offenses, the new statute also condemns the modes of conduct prohibited by it not only as criminal offense but also as tortious wrongs and labor law violations. Defining the criminal offenses of "indecent acts" and sexual blackmail by way of threats as sexual harassment enables the victim of such acts to file a tortious action against the perpetrator, and/or to sue the employer for intimidation and/or injury resulting from such acts, if the sexual harassment occurred within the workplace.

Sexually harassing behaviors that are also prohibited by the Penal Law are categorically prohibited by the Prevention of Sexual Harassment Law, regardless of whether the harassed person voiced objection or refusal. The new law states that sexual harassment amounting to "blackmail by way of threats" or to "indecent acts" as defined by the Penal Law are acts to which an individual cannot legally consent. Sexual degradation and humiliation (defined as sexual harassment in article 3(a)(5) of the statute) are not prohibited, per se, by the Israeli Penal Law. Nevertheless, the severity of such acts imposes a duty on all persons to realize that they are prohibited, thus the new law does not require that the harassed person indicate to the harasser that sexual degradation or humiliation are undesirable her (or him). Let me emphasize that degradation and humiliation are defined in the statute as referring to the victim's *gender, sexuality,* or *sexual tendencies*. A person may not, therefore, be degraded regarding his or her "masculinity" or "femininity," however defined, owing to any sexual activity or due to a sexual tendency attributed to him or her (regardless of the "veracity" of such attribution). Impudent sexist remarks addressed to a woman may degrade her as a woman and constitute sexual harassment; pornographic pictures may, under certain circumstances, and most certainly if targeting a certain person, constitute a degrading or humiliating reference addressed to a person with respect to his gender or sexuality (article 3[a][5]); a reference attaching degrading meanings to the sexuality attributed to a person may amount to sexual harassment, whether the sexuality thus attributed is heterosexual, homosexual, or bisexual. "Gay-bashing," as such, is actionable sexual harassment under Israeli law.

The second category of conduct that article 3(a) defines as sexual harassment includes behaviors allowed, even socially desired, when performed with mutual consent: "repeated propositions of a sexual character" and "repeated references directed towards a person, which focus on his sexuality." Such conduct may be perceived as neutral or as having positive social value, and is definitely not negative in itself. It becomes sexual harassment only when it is undesirable to the person at whom such behavior is aimed. Therefore, in order for such conduct to constitute sexual harassment, one must communicate to the person making the proposals a lack of interest in the behavior. The official explanatory notes emphasize that "the law does not purport to enforce a moral code or to intervene in voluntary social relations, but to prevent people from forcing themselves on others, who are not interested in such contact, especially when such coercion takes place while abusing an authoritative position."

Regarding this second category, let me further clarify that the phrase "references which focus on a person's sexuality" (in clause 3[a][4]) replaced the phrase "references to a person as a sexual object" which appeared in an earlier draft of the law. The final version, which is the broader of the two, declares that a recurring reference to certain aspects of a person's appearance, his or her attractiveness, his or her sexual behavior (actual or imagined) or the sexual interest inspired in the speaker (or in others) — may all be acceptable, desirable, and even complimentary in certain contexts, and undesirable, harassing, and threatening in others. In order for such conduct to be actionable sexual harassment the person at whom it is aimed must communicate her dissatisfaction to the perpetrator.

As for a person's duty to show that she is not interested in the conduct she may be experiencing as harassing: the statute pronounces (in article 2) that the harassed person must show his or her position "by words or by conduct, provided that there is no reasonable doubt as to the meaning of such conduct." The harassed person is, therefore, encouraged to be active in the expression of his or her position with respect to the conduct in question. It is, however, sufficient that such position, if not verbally expressed, be expressed in a manner that is reasonable under the circumstances of the case; the victim is not required to cause the perpetrator to actually comprehend the message expressed. The perpetrator may be impervious to the messages relayed to him by the victim, and the latter is not required to employ unreasonable measures in order to affect the perpetrator. Let me stress that the criterion of reasonableness is only applied to the *doubt* whether the harasser could/should have understood the victim's rejection; it is not an invocation of judicial use of the fictitious "reasonable *person*" as a model character. If the court does choose to call on the comprehension abilities of the "reasonable person," it will be to measure the *harasser's, and not the victim's* comprehension.[39]

The third category of prohibited conduct includes sexual harassment characterized by an extremely disadvantageous balance of powers between the harasser and his victim. Subparagraph 6 of article 3(a) states that a minor, a "helpless person,"[40] a patient, or an employee, when sexually propositioned or addressed within an authoritative relationship, is not required to express any position toward the sexual proposals or references. Even in the absence of any such expression, such acts may be deemed sexually harassing. This approach accounts for the inherent weakness of such harassed individuals in relation to their harassers, a weakness which may deny them the possibility of expressing (or even experiencing) free will regarding the sexual advances. In these situations, the person in the authoritative position is required to develop the necessary sensitivity and respect to identify which conducts may be grasped by his subordinates as sexually harassing, and to refrain from them. Let me point out that this category does not necessarily disparage the claim that *any* sexual harassment of a woman by a man, in any social context, involves an abuse of hierarchical power. It merely awards special treatment to sexual harassment in which hierarchy plays a particularly blatant role.

Article 3(b) defines intimidation ("prejudicial treatment") related to sexual harassment as "any harmful act, the source of which is sexual harassment or a complaint or court action filed in relation to sexual harassment." Harmful conduct following an objection to sexual harassment is, therefore, actionable. Furthermore, intimidation may occur when the harassed person submits to the harassment (and cooperates in the sexual relationship required of her), or even prior to any refusal or submission to the advances. Intimidation may accompany the harassment, such as when it is used to apply pressure against the harassed individual in order to cause her to submit to the harassment. Intimidation may also be inflicted on a person not sexually harassed, for example someone who assists a harassed person to confront harassment by filing a complaint or an action against it. Such intimidation is also actionable under article 3(b).

Under article 6, all types of sexual harassment defined in article 3 constitute civil wrongs. All of them (except blackmail by way of threats and indecent acts, already prohibited by the Israeli Penal Law) are also defined in article 5 of the law as criminal offenses. The criminal sanction set out in article 5 is two years' imprisonment for sexual harassment, three years for related intimidation, and four years for both sexual harassment and related intimidation. Article 5 further prohibits publication of a victim's name. It also prohibits an examination of her sexual history and provides for a hearing of the victim's testimony without the defendant's presence.

Article 6(b) contains a unique provision, unprecedented in Israeli law: in a civil action for sexual harassment or related intimidation, the court may assess punitive damages against the harasser and award them to the victim. Such damages may not exceed an amount equivalent to $15,000 (linked to the consumer price index). The explanatory notes to the legislation set out the rationale behind this provision:

> The receipt of compensation for such wrongs usually entails the proof of
> damage caused to the claimant. In a sexual harassment context, the damage is
> often inflicted on the harassed person's dignity, self-confidence and his rights
> to respect and to a reasonable quality of life within the work and any other

environment. Since these injuries are inherent to the nature of the harassing behavior, the proof of conduct embodies the proof of damage. It is therefore suggested that the claimant not be burdened with the need to prove any damage as a prerequisite for the adjudication of compensation. In order to balance the harassed person's protection with the defendant's rights, it is suggested that a ceiling be set for the compensation adjudicated without proof of damage.

This article proclaims that a harassed person need not wait for an emotional breakdown or for any other "quantifiable" injury in order to sue for sexual harassment and demand its termination. It further guides the court not to impose on victims any burdens of proof which might deter them from filing actions. Thus, a claimant is not to be required to prove a position, a good reputation, or special life circumstances that make her particular dignity or right to respect worth a certain amount. On the contrary, the article declares that sexual harassment injures "esteemed" and "ordinary" persons alike, whether or not such injury is assessable by any professional tools (psychological or other). Any incident of sexual harassment, injuring the harassed person's dignity and her rights to respect, equality, freedom, and privacy, causes her damage by the mere infringement of basic rights; the victim need not prove any additional injuries. The article further refers to "strong" harassed persons who were not devastated by the harassment, whether emotionally or financially. The law reflects the idea that such persons are worthy of protection and support, since the harassment itself infringes on their dignity, right to respect, and joy of life, even though their stamina prevented the harasser from inflicting tangible injuries on them. A harassed person proving damages beyond the infringement of his or her human rights *per se* (such as loss of earning capacity) may, of course, claim more than the $15,000 ceiling.

Article 6(c) sets the prescription period for a civil action filed due to sexual harassment or intimidation at three years.

Articles 7–9 and 11 create and regulate employers' responsibility and liability for sexual harassment in the labor relations sphere.[41] The statute determines a clear, general provision regarding employers' liability which applies to all employers, to all types of harassment and to anyone (employee or client)[42] harassed by any of the employer's employees (or by a person appointed on behalf of the employer, not being his or her employee under the labor law). Most significantly, employers' liability for sexual harassment in the labor relations sphere is civil and not criminal, and only comes into play when an employer fails to meet the requirements explicitly imposed on him by law. The liability provision (article 7[a]) reads as follows: "An employer has a duty to take such steps as are reasonable in the circumstances, so as to prevent sexual harassment or adverse[43] treatment in the labor relations sphere, on the part of his employee or on the part of a person in charge on the employer's behalf, even where such a person is not his employee; an employer is also obliged to deal with cases of sexual harassment and adverse treatment . . . efficiently."

Article 7(b) further establishes that, in addition to complying with the other requirements of the law, an employer employing twenty-five or more employees must formulate and publish regulations containing the law's essential provisions concerning sexual harassment and intimidation in the workplace. The regulations must also specify the ways of submitting sexual harassment or intimidation complaints to the employer and the employer's procedure for handling them.[44] The employer's failure to meet these requirements is a prerequisite for imposing employer liability for sexual harassment.

Articles 9 and 11 clarify that these provisions apply to the state and the civil service, to the Israeli Defense Forces (IDF), the Israeli police force, and the prison service as well as to anyone employing a worker employed by a personnel agency.[45] Owing to the special interest in sexual harassment in the workplace, let me expand on the provisions regulating employer liability.

The law's employer liability provisions provide that, having control over acts committed by their employees, employers must do everything in their power to prevent their employees from harassing any person (whether another employee *or any other person*) in the labor relations sphere. In order to prevent sexual harassment, employers must make it clear that complaints of sexual harassment committed by their employees may by addressed to them, and that if such complaints are filed, they will be handled with the utmost effectiveness. At this point, article 7(a)(2) requires an employer to "deal *efficiently* with a case of sexual harassment or adverse treatment [i.e., intimidation] which has come to his notice, and to do *everything within his power* to *prevent the recurrence of the said acts* and to *rectify the harm* caused to the complainant as a result of harassment or adverse treatment [intimidation]" (emphasis added). It should be noted that, according to the wording of the article, employers must attend to harassment or intimidation even if no complaint is filed, provided only that they become aware of the harassment or intimidation in one way or another. The "remedy of the injury" means reinstating the condition of the injured party, to the extent possible, to her condition prior to the harassment or the intimidation, or indemnifying her for expenses incurred as a result of the harassment or the intimidation (such as expenses incurred in psychotherapy). Furthermore, "efficient" treatment, aimed at preventing the recurrence of harassment or the continued injury inflicted on a harassed employee or client, may call for removing the harasser from his duties or transferring him elsewhere, without imposing the price of terminating the harassment on its victim.

Additionally, a major employer, such as the civil service, the IDF, or a university, must publish regulations clarifying to its employees, and to anyone coming into work-related contact with them, that sexual harassment by employees within the work environment is prohibited and setting forth the procedure for complaint. These actions are intended to elucidate the applicable norm and to convey the message that sexual harassment is treated seriously by the employer.[46]

It should be emphasized that the employer's responsibility for sexual harassment committed by his employee is in addition to the perpetrator's personal liability and does not exempt a harassing employee from personal legal liability for his misconduct.

An employer who has established complaint procedures (and a major employer who has further published clear regulations) and has effectively handled a given occurrence of sexual harassment bears no legal liability for that occurrence. This approach is designed to encourage employers to handle complaints of sexual harassment with the utmost efficiency, as such action protects them against legal liability for employee-inflicted harassment.

Article 10 confers on the Labor Court the sole jurisdiction for civil actions regarding sexual harassment or related intimidation of an employee at work. This sole jurisdiction applies whether the action is filed against the employer, against a person appointed by the employer, or against another employee; whether based on the personal responsibility of the employer, of the appointed person, or of the employee being sued; or on the liability of the employer as such (i.e., under article 7). The underlying assumption is that the Labor Court is the most competent judicial authority in the sphere of employment relations and the most sympathetic to the distress of employees. This is also the employees' cheapest and most accessible tribunal. The statute determines that the provisions of articles 10, 10A, 12 and 13 of the Israeli EEOL apply to such a proceeding, that is, that the court is empowered to issue injunctions; the plaintiff or the complainant may request that the hearing be held *in camera;* an employees' organization may file an action also without an individual plaintiff, and the court may allow a women's organization (or another relevant nongovernmental organization) to voice its position.[47]

The new Prevention of Sexual Harassment Law, which came into effect in September 1998, offers new ways of confronting the phenomenon of sexual harassment. In drafting the statute we tried to voice women's experiences, our perceptions, and insights gained through feminist jurisprudence. Our hope was that this legislation would mark the beginning of a new era in the awareness of this social disease among the Israeli public. I am delighted to report that in the intervening time remarkable changes have started taking place. Thanks to massive media coverage of the new legislation and the first complaints under it, women, employers, and the Israeli public at large have become aware of the social problem and the relevant legal duties, remedies, and sanctions. The term "sexual harassment" has become widely familiar and meaningful. Many employers around the country have adopted behavior codes, as required by law, also providing employees with relevant information and legal training. Women have begun to file complaints within workplaces, in universities, with the army authorities, and with the police. Lawyers have begun to take professional interest in the subject, and police officers are trained to identify sexual harassment and handle complaints. A complaint filed by a young secretary against a prominent minister eventually led to his resignation from political life and triggered much public interest and debate concerning sexual harassment and the law.[48] These encouraging first steps indicate that the Israeli public, and women in particular, have begun to breathe life into the law in an attempt to challenge and change social reality.

Notes

This essay, as well as the model law, which has become Israel's Prevention of Sexual Harassment Law, are dedicated, with deep gratitude and admiration, to Catharine MacKinnon, who taught me to think about sexual harassment and supported me throughout the legislation process. I am grateful to my friends Marc Spindelman and Rebecca Johnson for the helpful comments and conversation.

1. SH 166 (SH= Sefer Hachukim, i.e., Book of (Israel's) Statues).

2. In the Knesset, MK Yael Dayan of the Labor Party, Chairperson of the Knesset Committee for the Empowerment of Women, was the major force behind the advancement of the new legislation; MKs Tamar Gujanski of the Israeli Communist Party and Anat Maor of Meretz played a major role as well. In the Ministry of Justice the project was embraced, defended, and advanced by Gloria Wiseman, Head of the Criminal Division, and Dan Ornstein, Head of the Labor Division; in the Ministry of Labor, it was advanced by Michael Atlan, legal adviser. Rachel Benziman, legal adviser to the Israeli Women's Network, represented feminist activism. Ruth Ben Israel, expert in labor law, represented the Law Faculty of the Tel Aviv University, and I was at the time a member of the Law Faculty of the Hebrew University in Jerusalem.

3. SH 38.

4. This reference to sexual harassment (in article 7 of the EEOL) was initiated by the legal department of the Israeli Women's Network; it was highly influenced by U.S. law and jurisprudence, particularly by MacKinnon's writings.

5. The first and only Supreme Court decision regarding sexual harassment in civil

service was *not* brought under the EEOL; writing it, the Justices referred to the new legislation which was already drafted. The decision came out a day before the new law was legislated, i.e., in 1998.

6. *Meritor Savings Bank, FSB v. Vinson,* 447 U.S. 57 (1986). It took twelve years before the Supreme Court was willing to address the issue in *Burlington Industries, Inc. v. Ellerth,* 118 S. Ct. 2257 (1998) and *Faragher v. City of Boca Raton,* 118 S. Ct. 2275 (1998).

7. *Harris v. Forklift Systems, Inc.,* 510 U.S. 17 (1993).

8. *Rabidue v. Osceola Refining Co.,* 805 F.2d 611 (6th Cir. 1986).

9. For criticism of the *Rabidue* decision *see* Glenn George, "The Back Door: Legitimizing Sexual Harassment Claims," 73 *Boston University Law Review* 1, 18–19 (1993); Mary Joe Shaney, "Perceptions of Harm: the Consent Defense in Sexual Harassment Cases," 71 *Iowa Law Review* 1093, 1122–1123 (1986); Ann Juliano, "Did She Ask for It? The 'Unwelcome' Requirement in Sexual Harassment Cases," 77 *Cornell Law Review* 1558, 1579–1587 (1992); Sara Needleman Kline, "Sexual Harassment, Wrongful Discharge, and Employer Liability: The Employer's Dilemma," 43 *American University Law Review* 191, footnote 55 (1993); Susan Collins, "*Harris v. Forklift Systems:* A Modest Clarification of the Inquiry in Hostile Environment Sexual Harassment Cases," *Wis. Law Review* 1515, 1522–1525 (1994); Susan Estrich, "Sex at Work," 43 *Stanford Law Review* 813, 843–847 (1991); Wendy Pollack, "Sexual Harassment: Women's Experience vs. Legal Definitions," 13 *Harvard Women's Law Journal* 35, 62–69 (1990); Nicolle R. Lipper, "Sexual Harassment in the Workplace: A Comparative Study of Great Britain and the United States," 13 *Comp. Lab. L.* 293, 322–323 (1992); Beverley Earle and Gerald A. Medak, "An International Perspective on Sexual Harassment Law," 12 *Law and Ineq. J.* 43, 56 (1993).

10. For an analysis of sexual harassment on the street see Cynthia Grant Bowman, "Street Harassment and the Informal Ghettoization of Women," 106 *Harvard Law Review* 517 (1993).

11. This issue was explored by Katherine M. Franke in "What's Wrong with Sexual Harassment?" 49 *Stanford Law Review* 691 (1997).

12. "Difference and Dominance: On Sex Discrimination" in Catharine MacKinnon, *Feminism Unmodified* (1987) 33, 33–44.

13. Franke, *supra* note 11, 729.

14. MacKinnon, *supra* note 12, 107.

15. A similar suggestion, on different grounds, was developed by Anita Bernstein in "Treating Sexual Harassment with Respect," 111 *Harvard Law Review* 445 (1998).

16. Catharine MacKinnon, *Sexual Harassment of Working Women: A Case of Sex Discrimination* (1979) 32.

17. *Ibid.,* 40.

18. The Canadian approach to sexual harassment is a good example of a different treatment of this issue. *See Janzen v. Platy Enterprises Ltd.* (1989), 59 D.L.R. (4th) 352, [1989] 1 S.C.R. 1252.

19. For the latest treatment of the subject, and references to previous writing, *see* Bernstein, *supra* note 15.

20. *Ibid.,* 506.

21. From this perspective, the "respectful person" suggested by Bernstein (*supra* note 16) is just as problematic.

22. SH 154.

23. SH 248.

24. SH for the year 5752, p. 150.

25. The official translation of the title is "Basic Law: Human Dignity and Liberty," but a more accurate translation of the Hebrew *kavod* (and therefore also of the phrase *kvod ha-adam*) should mention dignity, respect, honor (and even glory). In the context of this discussion I focus on dignity and respect and do not explore the implications of their association with honor and glory. For further discussion of the relationship between honor, glory, dignity and respect *see* Orit Kamir, "Honor and Dignity Cultures: The Case of kavod and kvod ha-adam in Israeli Society and Law," in *The Concept of Human Dignity in Human Rights Discourse* (David Kretzmer and Eckart Klein eds., 2002).

26. I am grateful to Catharine MacKinnon, Rachel Benziman, and Frances Radai, who helped me work out this point while preparing the model legislation.

27. For an interesting analysis of respect, liberty, and equality *see* Robin West, "Toward a First Amendment Jurisprudence of Respect: A Comment on George Fletcher's Constitutional Identity," 14 *Cardozo Law Review* 759 (1993).

28. This point, as well as the reformulation of the rights to freedom and privacy in this context, obviously needs more theoretical explication, which is beyond the scope of this essay. I hope to pursue these issues in greater detail elsewhere.

29. I share in Israeli legal academia's concern at the tendency to overuse the criminal law and assign it social functions which should have been performed through constitutional and administrative law. Nevertheless, given that such is the current state of affairs, it must be pragmatically acknowledged when proposing new legislation.

30. On the status of sexual harassment as a tort "in all but name" in the U.S. legal system, *see* Bernstein, *supra* note 15, 510. For a detailed suggestion for the criminalization of sexual harassment in the United States *see* Carrie N. Baker, "Sexual Extortion: Criminalizing *Quid Pro Quo* Sexual Harassment," 13 *Law and Inquiry Journal* 213. For a discussion of "melioristic law reforms" that attempt to change both criminal and tort laws *see* Anita Bernstein, "Better Living Through Crime and Tort," 76 *Boston University Law Review* 169 (1996).

31. The bill passed its first hearing in August 1997, and the second and third hearings on March 10, 1998, in honor of International Women's Day.

32. *See supra* note 24.

33. The official explanatory notes are drafted by the Ministry of Justice and are attached to the draft law for the first call in the Knesset. The notes serve courts as guidelines for interpretation.

34. This is clearly a mistake in the official translation; the accurate translation would be "degrading."

35. The Hebrew *min* means both "sex" and "gender"; the explicit intention was to refer to both.

36. A better translation would be "intimidation"; in my discussion I use that term, as "prejudicial treatment" seems unclear.

37. SH 226.

38. After deliberating the issue of rape, the Knesset Committee for the Empowerment of Women decided that although rape constitutes sexual harassment of the most severe kind, it already receives sufficient legal treatment and public attention, and need not be included in the scope of the new law.

39. I see a significant difference between (1) measuring the reasonableness of a conduct and that of the "person" performing it (the one judges specific behavior, the other, character and personality); and (2) examining the reasonableness of the perpetrator's conduct and that of the victim's response. Personally, I would have replaced reasonableness with a different criteria altogether, but examining the perpetrator's conduct is the least evil option.

40. This category is defined elsewhere in Israeli law.

41. This expression is defined broadly as "the workplace, another place where an activity on behalf of the employer takes place, in the course of employment or where, in any place whatsoever, a position of authority in a work relationship is being exploited." A vacation organized by the employer, a trip to a place where work-related activity takes place, or "social" relations in which a person in an authoritative position harasses an employee subordinate to him or her, even after work hours, are all deemed as being "in a labor relations sphere." A salesperson selling from door to door is also acting "in a labor relations sphere."

42. By "client" I mean any person coming into contact with any of the employer's employees within a working relationship.

43. The phrase should have been "prejudicial treatment," or, as I prefer to translate it, "intimidation."

44. Article 8 determines that the failure to publish such regulations is punishable by a fine, with an additional fine being imposed for every week in which the offense continues.

45. Soldiers, inmates, and persons under arrest may all sue the army, the prison service, or the police force for sexual harassment committed against them by soldiers, policemen, or wardens.

46. An institution such as a university must, according to the employer liability clauses, publish regulations prohibiting the harassment of employees, students, and any other person by any university employee belonging to the academic or administrative staff. The responsibility of the institution does not extend only to the employees thereof, but also to any person harassed by an employee of the institution within his or her work at the institution. Furthermore, the provisions of article 7(G), adopted by the legislature as a reservation to the proposed law, specifically requires that educational institutions take reasonable measures in order to prevent sexual harassment among students, as well as the sexual harassment of any person by students. Educational institutions must refer in their regulations to harassment of this kind and handle complaints of harassment committed by students. This provision, not approved by the committee, is, in my view, far-fetched.

47. Article 15 of the Prevention of Sexual Harassment Law replaces article 7 of the EEOL. The new article 7 prohibits employers or anyone appointed on their behalf from causing harm to employees in connection with (1) sexual harassment or (2) a complaint or action filed concerning a harm caused by sexual harassment, or (3) assistance rendered to another employee regarding a complaint or an action against such a harm. (I believe that an error occurred in the letter of the law, reading, in Article 7(a)(2) and (3) "in respect

of harmful conduct" rather than "in respect of sexual harassment or harmful conduct.") The prohibition of harm under the provisions of the new article 7 of the EEOL corresponds to the prohibition of "intimidation" ("prejudicial/adverse treatment") contained in the Prevention of Sexual Harassment Law but is broader in scope; a harm is already constituted after *an isolated occasion* of sexual harassment of the types defined in articles 3(a)(3) and 3(a)(4) of the Prevention of Sexual Harassment Law (whereas "intimidation" is constituted only after recurrent incidents of such behavior). In other words, under the EEOL, the definition of sexual harassment is broader than in other contexts. Moreover, the provisions of article 9(b) of the EEOL were amended by the Prevention of Sexual Harassment Law. This amendment provides that, when an employee proves that she was sexually harassed, it is the employer who must prove that he has not engaged in harmful conduct.

48. The minister, Itzhak Morechai, was not convicted of sexual harassment, but the complaint filed under the law led to his conviction of other sexual offenses, committed before the law came into effect. The legal decision, given in March 2001, invoked great public interest.

33

Dignity or Equality?

Responses to Workplace Harassment
in European, German, and U.S. Law

SUSANNE BAER

The legal reactions to the social problem of sexual harassment in Europe, particularly in the European Union and in Germany, have been based on dignity as the fundamental right of men and women that has been violated in such cases. German and European law conceptualize law against sexual harassment differently from the United States, where jurisprudence is based on a specific interpretation of the right to equality. In the year 2000, European law moved in the direction of a focus on equality, rather than dignity. New directives based on article 13 of the European Treaty define workplace harassment as discrimination.[1] However, a query remains: At first glance, this difference raises the question of "dignity or equality?" in a comparative effort to find the better solution. Yet in a comparative analysis of sexual harassment law across legal codes and cultures, there is more to ask. The very question of "dignity or equality?" indicates a problem in both traditional and more recent legal philosophy. Ultimately, a reformulation of this question might offer a more useful approach to sexual harassment law in general.

In the tradition of liberal philosophy, dignity and equality have been distinguished. Dignity, as part of liberty, has been interpreted as a principle and a right categorically distinct from equality, which has been seen as a principle and a right based on symmetrical comparison. In law this not only leads to a distinction between liberty interests and equality rights but results in a hierarchical relation between the two. Liberty reigns across the spectrum of liberal constitutions.[2] Equality, in contrast, is treated as a secondary, for some even antiliberal concern. Rights are put in a scheme of conflict. Where this scheme is applied, it is necessary to find a response to the question of "dignity or equality?"

In some countries and some areas of the law, however, this conflict scheme has been replaced by a scheme of interrelatedness. The latter conception might also be based on insufficiently theorized considerations in the tradition of liberal philosophy. In this case, dignity and equality are interpreted as interrelated principles that inform one another and lead to a more coherent and encompassing look at constitutions. In combining individual interest with a social concern, these interrelated principles contribute to a more democratic constitutionalism. Then the hierarchy between liberty interests and equality rights is replaced by an interrelated interpretation of all rights relevant in a given case. From this point of view, "dignity or equality?" is no longer the question, but liberty is interpreted in light of equality just as equality is considered part of liberty rights.

Here, I would like to demonstrate the difference that results from such an interrelated interpretation. The choice of one of these two conceptual schemes is neither purely theoretical nor simply doctrinal. It informs doctrine in European,[3] German, and U.S. sexual harassment law,[4] where the traditional scheme of conflict — rather than interrelation — has been applied more or less consistently. In addition, the choice of schemes informs large segments of legal philosophy. The conflict scheme forms the basis of liberal legal thinking and is favored by some recent legal theorists, including some who write from a feminist perspective.[5] In the attempt to withdraw from the asymmetrical, substantive, antihierarchical equality approach that, particularly in North America, has been based on Catharine MacKinnon's work,[6] as well as in a rejection of MacKinnon's view of gender as sexualized hierarchy,[7] some theorists shift the focus of legal responses to discrimination away from equality and to some version of dignity, agency, or self-respect. As I will show, such theories continue to subscribe to a scheme of conflict rather than aim at a scheme of interrelatedness.

My remarks on regulations and theoretical arguments point not only to the difference produced by the choice of scheme. I will also attempt to demonstrate the inadequacy of the conflict scheme when dealing with discrimination. This will be done from a comparative point of view that treats the U.S. approach to sexual harassment and the substantive theory of equality developed in U.S. feminist legal theory as one set of rules, and the European and German approaches as another. In conclusion, the alternative scheme of interrelatedness offers the more systematic approach to law against sex discrimination in the form of harassment at work, to fundamental rights, and to the constitutional foundations of democracy as a whole.

Traditions in Philosophy: Positions in the Law

In liberal philosophy, and within a tradition of legal theory, dignity and equality have been seen as rights to be distinguished, or even as conflicting. To name but one example, Immanuel Kant called liberty the only natural right, and named equality as a secondary right, almost derivative.[8] Such liberal philosophy informs law and legal politics. In most liberal jurisdictions, equality and dignity, with dignity either as a right of its own or as a feature of liberty, are treated separately, as distinct from each other, and differently as well. For example German constitutional lawyers have applied (and are still taught to apply) a three-step test to dignity and liberty rights, and a structurally different, comparative test to equality.[9] The difference in tests leads to a difference in results, in that the three-tier liberty test adheres to a stricter scrutiny in jurisprudence, while the comparative-equality test gives way to broader legislative or administrative discretion. This suggests further that problems within equality jurisprudence like the longstanding disregard of discrimination are based on problematic, ultimately Aristotelian, symmetrical interpretations of equality as such.[10] In addition, problems of the law's disregard of discrimination might in fact be attributed to the scheme of conflict that situates dignity and equality as rights apart.

Such traditions and the jurisprudence that is built upon it, however, are not monolithic. For example, Cicero added equality to the Aristotelian concept of citizenship, which for Aristotle was fully compatible with the exclusion of slaves and women.[11] John Locke also emphasized the importance of equality that he derived from a notion of rationality then grounded in God's equal creation.[12] Liberal philosopher Immanuel Kant, as much as he is known to privilege liberty, also interpreted dignity as a feature of both equality and liberty.[13] Contemporary liberal thinkers, such as Jürgen Habermas[14] and Axel Honneth,[15] also tend to conceptualize liberalism on the basis of equal respect, easily translatable into dignity and equality thought together rather than apart. And some feminist philosophers, like Austrian Herta Nagl-Docekal,[16] fully integrate both rights into a coherent scheme. Thus, although some liberal philosophy tended to view dignity and equality as separate, a scheme of interrelatedness can be found here as well.

Newer Developments in Legal Theory

In legal theory, particularly in theory developed from a feminist perspective, equality as a right against discrimination has been interpreted as a constitutional guarantee of equal liberties for all. Thus dignity has served as a part — albeit often implicitly — of an interpretation of equality as an asymmetrical right against subordination. Recently, such approaches have increasingly come under attack. In particular, the strong, asymmetrical, substantive version of equality, also known as the antisubordination, antihierarchy, or simply and originally the "inequality interpretation" of the right to equality,[17] has been heavily criticized.

A somewhat traditional critique is based on an understanding of law as a preserver of the status quo rather than an engine of change. In German constitutional law, this conservative understanding of law has been explicitly rejected by the Federal Constitutional Court.[18] In a decision on the right of married persons to keep their last names, the Court stated that unequal treatment may not be justified by referring to the traditional structure of a situation, such as marriage. "The constitutional provision would lose its function to implement gender equality for the future, if social realities were to be simply accepted."[19] One cannot tell from the German wording of the decision whether the Court considers the situation to be dissimilar, as in traditional equality analyses, or to be unequal, as demanded in substantive interpretations of equality. However, the doctrinal arguments and the discussion of equality in later cases suggest that a substantive interpretation gains hold in the German court's jurisprudence.[20]

Another critique of the equality approach has been articulated in a comparative study of sexual harassment law. Thus Robert Husbands refers to a dignity-based approach which he describes as "broader" than equality.[21] Yet it remains unclear how much "broader" law can legitimately be. For many, sexual harassment law already covers too much behavior, particularly in the form of speech. Usually, "broader" implies less definition and specificity, but such an understanding then leaves us with traditional gender-neutral blindness, and the potential ineffectiveness of such laws. For some, a law is "broader" if it is not directed at discrimination that primarily hurts women. But sexual harassment law covers men too if they are discriminated against and thus harmed based on their gender. The argument against such law does not only miss a point but is polemic rather than legal in nature.

A more interesting and sophisticated version of a dignity-based approach is articulated by American legal theorist Drucilla Cornell. According to Cornell, an adoption of MacKinnon's equality standard "inevitably implicates a woman's systematic subordination to men."[22] Cornell thus refers to the "feminist" or "postmodern" dilemma that might be avoided only with great difficulty in law. The dilemma results from the tension between a legal statement of gender hierarchy which perpetuates that hierarchy on the level of language and thus, within the symbolic order, and is yet intended to combat it.[23] Cornell thus criticizes sexual harassment law for its invasion into the "imaginary domain," the sphere of symbolic existence of men and women. To avoid the invasion, Cornell proposes an approach based on the Rawlsian concepts of self-respect, freedom, and personhood. This approach would offer a "legal guarantee of the social bases of self-respect."[24] This "primary good" should, according to Cornell, become the comparative standard by which to judge unequal power relations.[25] The right to self-respect in this view would be violated when "sexual shame" is enforced by "reducing individuals to projected stereotypes or objectified fantasies of their 'sex.' "[26]

Ultimately, however, Cornell's argument for replacing equality with respect and a right to an imaginary domain is not fully convincing. First, it is possible and exigent to distinguish between the language of the law and the particular functions, forms, and structures of legal discourse, and the symbolic constructions in other discourses. It is misleading and ultimately disables the effectiveness of any law if legal terms are confounded with terminology used in other contexts. This is not to say that a critique of the closed nature of legal discourse is not needed and valid. Yet it remains important to note the difference between a discriminatory statement and a law that names what to do against it.

Second, to invoke the right to an imaginary domain and against "sexual shame" does not constitute an adequate replacement for an equality analysis. Cornell's description of the right to respect[27] closely resembles the descriptions used in German constitutional doctrine of violations of the right to dignity. It contains the well-known elements of gender neutrality, individuality, and free will. But it is precisely in reference to these elements that traditional legal philosophy, traditional interpretations of equality, and the corresponding anti-discrimination laws have proven inadequate in combating discrimination. Laws based on gender-neutrality tend to hide the realities of gender hierarchies, individuality has been shown to hide the established claims to privilege of men as members of a group defined by its gender, and free will has been recognized as a legal fiction that often, as in labor law, legitimizes exploitation.[28] In sum, law based on such a scheme of individual human beings is incapable of grasping the complex realities in which we live.[29]

Translations of Theory into Doctrine

Recent accounts of law against sexual harassment in particular and against sex discrimination in general that shift away from a substantive interpretation of equality are not purely theoretical. They can be easily translated into what many constitutions in the world, including article 1 of the German Basic Law (*Grundgesetz*) calls dignity.[30] Therefore, the trends in recent legal theory described above are yet another example of an application of the scheme of conflict. In these approaches, dignity and equality are kept apart.

In particular, an argument like that formulated by Drucilla Cornell is not isolated today. Efforts have been made to conceptualize the harm done in gender relations in gender-neutral terms. Attempts to define harm as not group-related seem to fit the individualistic liberal model of the legal subject better than feminist or critical race theory approaches, which situate the harm of discrimination within a social, and thus both individual *and* group-related, context. In theory, references to agency, unwantedness, consensual relationships, self-determination, and, ultimately, liberty indicate such a trend. In law, references to dignity replace laws against inequalities and discrimination. Before I discuss doctrine, a remark on the motivation for such turns in theory seems appropriate.

REASONS TO TURN BACK

Replacements of equality law with more dignity-oriented analyses are attractive for various reasons. After all, there is a stigma attached to "quotas," affirmative action, "special" laws for women or historically disadvantaged groups, and other equality strategies from the 1950s until today. To avoid the stigma, it seems politically and strategically promising to appeal to a generally applicable, widely accepted norm.[31]

In addition, the turn from equality to dignity can easily be situated within a theoretically attractive focus on constructions and destructions of the self. A dignity-oriented analysis of sex discrimination refers to a universal and ultimately to a moral category.[32] It promises a neutral and objective way to define injustice, while apparently leaving enough space for individual differences. Thus, dignity seems to avoid eclipsing the individuality of the person, as constructivists point out, in the assumption of structural inequality.[33] The dignity-centered approach also seems to evade the dilemma between the necessity to restate gender-based victimization by naming and attempting to create law against it.[34]

Finally, an analysis of discrimination based on dignity rather than equality might be more suitable to anyone who draws on experiences not primarily shaped by inequality. More precisely, dominant interpreters of the law and dominant theorists tend not to be defined in terms that indicate subordination. Heterosexuality, whiteness, the Judao-Christian tradition, and something that may be called a "male focus" are still setting the standards in law and philosophy. With this in mind, it seems more than likely that persistent inequality will not serve as the primary source of interpretation and understanding. Rather, the denial of respect, or the deprivation of dignity, is an experience accessible even to people who belong to socially dominant groups. Furthermore, a focus on dignity does not endanger a privilege one wants to preserve.[35]

However, and particularly from the perspective of those not privileged, not dignified, and not yet equal, it can be shown that the price for these gains of a shift in theory is too high to pay. The theoretical turn, motivated by strategic and philosophical considerations, has dangerous consequences in doctrine, and in life.

REALITIES TO CONSIDER: ASPECTS OF COMPARATIVE ANALYSES

In the case of sexual harassment of working women, the similarity of social realities of the problem throughout the world warrants a direct comparison of legal responses. In their specificity, the cultural significance and discourses surrounding words and acts that constitute harassment surely differ. On the whole, however, experiences seem to be the same. Yet legal responses are quite dissimilar. Laws against sexual harassment in Europe and in the United States differ in ways that exemplify the difference between dignity- and equality-based approaches to sex discrimination. And just like the theoretical turns toward dignity, the legal responses are based on the scheme of conflict between dignity and equality, rather than on a scheme of interrelatedness.

In European and German law, sexual harassment in the workplace has been conceptualized as a violation of individual dignity.[36] Culturally, this makes a lot of sense. If you ask about the nature of the harm done by sexual harassment, Germans would tend to refer to dignity as the right of women that has been violated in such cases. This correlates to a European understanding of harm, and particularly to the understanding of harm developed in Europe after 1945, where human dignity became the referent for harm of the worst kind. Although laws corresponding to Nazi ideology referred to dignity, when it was mentioned at all, as a racially divisive concept that was exclusively attributed to Aryans, and while the fascist interpretation of equality thus attributed rights to people based on their difference as defined in racial terms, postwar law and postwar German constitutionalism in particular defined dignity as the primary right of any individual regardless of their differing capabilities or characteristics.[37] Today, dignity has become the universal standard for gross violations of individual rights. In comparison, when asked what right is violated by harassment, people in the United States tend to refer to equality. To many individuals, it indicates an unequal status that women are sexually harassed at work, and it seems to violate a right to equal opportunities in making one's living. This correlates to the understanding of harm established by the U.S. civil rights movement where equality was used in litigation for the right against violence, harassment, and unequal access to public facilities. In the United States, equality seems to provide the standard for violations of rights.

In addition to the cultural aspects that shape different understandings of harassment, the constitutional frameworks in which laws are situated in Europe and the United States also vary.[38] Here, cultural difference becomes a doctrinal one. In the German Constitution, or Basic Law, dignity is the first, basic, and, to most, fundamental individual right. In Europe this is part of the constitutional consensus since many member states of the European Union inscribed a right to dignity into their constitutions,[39] and the newly proclaimed European Charter of Fundamental Rights also sets out with a right to dignity.[40] In Germany the basic right to universal human dignity is understood as an explicit answer to the Holocaust—the "never again" in constitutional law—and is adjudicated as a prohibition of inhumane and degrading treatment. Although there are also strong legal responses to the Holocaust in equality law, the violations of individuality as such are the primary concern in the German constitutional tradition.[41] This can be understood as a rejection of fascist group-based ideology and the attempt to reinstall respect for any individual regardless of where and to whom they belong. Degrading treatment, then, as German constitutional lawyers would put it, is prohibited if it turns people into objects, stigmatizes them, or deprives them of fundamental liberties.[42] Here, we find some similarities between German constitutional interpretation and the theoretical developments around understandings of discrimination described above.

In comparison, the U.S. Constitution does not mention dignity. One effect of this absence might be the construction of so many cases as problems of the First Amendment.[43] Since dignity can be interpreted as a feature of liberty, this makes sense. On the other hand, when we consider the right to equality, important aspects of dignity are missing. In the United States, as many scholars have eloquently demonstrated,[44] equality is predominantly interpreted as a symmetrical and rather formal right, not as a substantive, antihierarchical provision. Then, dignity is not even implicitly part of equality jurisprudence, just as liberty is not seen as correlating with equality. It can thus be said that American jurisprudence implicitly applies the scheme of conflict rather than the scheme of interrelatedness.

In the German Constitution, the guarantee of human dignity is not only explicit but it also a universal, gender-neutral, and individualistic provision. Since dignity is at the top of the list of German basic rights, the *Grundrechte*, it is available as a *tertium comparationis* for equality, as a standard by which to measure the substance of unequal treatment. Here, the German Constitution opens a door to an interrelated approach to dignity, liberty, and equality. Dignity offers a way to interpret equality asymmetrically, different from jurisprudence in the United States. However, when we consider the German law against sexual harassment, this door has not yet been fully opened. While constitutionally interrelatedness seems to be the way to go, the legislature and the courts still apply a scheme of conflict, at least when it comes to sex discrimination. This is particularly problematic because it contradicts the constitutional revisions after German unification, which turned the right to sex equality from a right against unfair distinctions into one against gender-based disadvantage, and thus moved from symmetry and formalism to a more substantive understanding of equal rights.[45] A strong equality provision applies, however, only when a problem is conceptualized as an inequality. If sexual harassment or any other form of sex discrimination is not seen as an inequality, strong equality provisions will not work for women in that case. Here the scheme of conflict prevails on the level of epistemology. In doctrine, this has problematic consequences.

DOCTRINAL DETAILS

In Germany, unlike in the United States, sexual harassment has not been defined as an inequality in the law. Here, dominant cultural understandings became legislation, because as in the European Commission, women in Germany fought for the equality analysis and lost to an at least primarily dignity-based approach to law against harassment at work.[46] This legislative decision for dignity based on the scheme of conflict that excludes equality reasoning results in significant doctrinal problems. Some are known from the legal developments in the United States. While there is no binding legislative definition of sexual harassment in the United States, case law offers analogies to all the features European legislation spells out. However, case law defines harassment as an inequality. In addition, although not legally binding, the EEOC describes sexual harassment as a prevailing problem of discrimination in the workplace.[47] In interpreting Title VII of the Civil Rights Act, the courts in the United States indicate that quid pro quo or hostile environment harassment violates the guarantee of equal rights. The situation in Europe is different.

Worldwide, law against sexual harassment exhibits some specific doctrinal features: the definition of the problem, the relevance of the actor's subjectivity, the definition of harm, the relevance of the subjective experience of the person who has been harassed, the assessment of responsibility for harm done, the defenses allowed, the sanctions, and the procedures in which those are assessed. German law[48] defines sexual harassment as intentional, definitely of a sexual nature, and at least in part recognizably rejected — or proven unwelcome — activity that violates the dignity of individuals at work. The standard by which to measure the nature of ambiguous acts and then assess the harm is that of gender-neutral, individual dignity. Dignity is not defined but referred to, thus invoking the constitutional interpretation described above. A closer look at some of these elements of the German law, and of the European regulation,[49] reveals the problems that arise from that. This reveals the assumption that law against sexual harassment is better conceptualized based on the scheme of interrelatedness between dignity and equality, than on the scheme of conflict, and in this case, on dignity alone.[50]

First, German law defines sexual harassment as intentional behavior. Thus, the acting individual's subjectivity is relevant. Here, German law follows the path of dignity, since it is the intended degradation that counts as a violation of this individual right. In contrast, an equality approach to sex discrimination would not attribute such significance to the acting individual's intent. As we know from feminist research on sex discrimination, discriminatory behavior is deeply ingrained, systemic, and normalized, and therefore often not intentional in the legal sense. In addition, equality demands a reasoning that is oriented toward effects rather than intent, toward harm done rather than thoughts, and thus toward insignificance of an acting individual's mindset. This has been acknowledged by the European Court of Justice which, in a case on discrimination based on the pregnancy of job applicants, stated that for sex discrimination law to work a discriminatory act should imply the liability of the acting individual without any requirement of intent.[51] In conclusion, if law against sexual harassment were understood as law against discrimination, the intent requirement in German law would clearly violate this European standard. But since German law is designed to protect the dignity of workers, it is at least as difficult to prove this point. Even the European dignity-based recommendation against harassment recognizes as harassment only those acts that the actor knew or should have known to be harmful to the victim. This, too, is not seen as violating the Court's requirements in sex discrimination law because in the case of harassment dignity is the primary focus.

Second, German law requires harassment to be of a sexual nature. The law seems to intend the exclusion of sexuality from the workplace, thus reinforcing a traditional distinction between the public (ideologically defined as nonsexual) and the private (defined as the space of intimacy). It is unclear what exactly "sexual" means, however, or where exactly to draw the distinction. Because much harassment of working women refers to their gender but not all harassment explicitly sexualizes them, this would be important to know. In addition, and without further explanation of the nature of "sexual" behavior, legal regulation of sexual expression tends to become a device to establish moralistic imperatives of prudence rather than combat discrimination. For example, in German dignity jurisprudence, peep shows are seen as violations of a constitutional right while other forms of prostitution are legal.[52] In German criminal law, some pornography is legal, some not. The courts and the legislators thus define various aspects of sexuality as either good or bad rather than look for systematic responses to discrimination. In the decision regarding peep shows, the right to dignity was used as a right against an uninhibited male sex drive rather than to protect women from exploitation when it occurs.[53] Again, the dignity-based approach leads exactly in that direction, while the equality approach tends to work another way.

Similarly, the European Commission defined sexual harassment as "unwanted behavior of a sexual nature or other behavior based on sex, which violates the dignity of working women and men. This may include unwanted physical, verbal or non-verbal behavior."[54] According to the emphasis on the sexual nature of discriminatory behavior, the primary concern of European law is, as in Germany, sexuality. Harassment, then, is only a problem when sexuality is implicitly or explicitly at play. In the courts, and without a feminist analysis of sexuality and its meaning in the construction of gender, this turns sexual harassment into a moral sin rather than acknowledging it as a problem situated within a sexualized gender hierarchy. Regarding the approach taken by the European Commission, it is noteworthy that the definition of harassment emphasizes not only sexuality but also links sexual behavior as a moral sin with dignity as the right in question. The European Commission rejected an explicit recognition that harassment has to do with gender — an idea present in the North American equality approach to sexual harassment law.[55] Thus, the Commission picked a dignity approach consciously, conceived it in the scheme of conflict, as distinguished from equality, and, by creating a moralistic definition of harassment, immediately revealed its problems.

Third, German law recognizes harassment only if women object to it. The definition in article 2, section 2, number 2 requires that sexual acts or invitations to them, sexual touching, sexual remarks, and pornography at work have to be recognizably rejected — or proven unwelcome — to count as sexual harassment in the legal sense. This requirement is based on various problematic assumptions. It assumes that women in the hierarchies of the workplace and of gender are capable of saying no; it assumes that harm occurs only after such rejection; and it assumes that if rejection were not required, women would sue men for no reason.[56] With the rejection requirement, the disabling effect of harassment that consists, in part, of the silencing of the harassed, is not recognized. Furthermore the law says that women have to "recognizably" reject. This tends to privilege the perpetrator's perspective, since courts tend to ask whether he was the one who recognized a "no" as such. If the harasser does not see the unwelcomeness of his behavior, we face the structural problem known from rape law where the mental state of the rapist defines what happened.[57] It also portrays the harassed person as a powerful subject modeled according to an epistemologically male norm. Again, the problem of a rejection requirement in a legal definition of sexual harassment can be attributed to the approach taken and the scheme applied.

Doctrinal details reveal that, in sum, the dignity-based approach that informs German and European law tends to individualize behavior,[58] privilege a perpetrator's perspective, conceptualize human beings as autonomous subjects without a consideration of the social hierarchies at work, and ignores the function of sexuality in gender discrimination. A systematically equality-based approach, in contrast, would recognize the harm of discrimination in its social context, accept sexualization as a means of sex discrimination, and use objective yet victim-sensitive standards rather than follow the perpetrator's point of view.[59]

Taken together, these three elements render the European and the German law against sexual harassment at work quite inadequate to address the problem. Underlying the problems of the doctrinal details is the perspective, as the normatively shaped point of view, from which discrimination can be judged.[60] Many acts of harassment are ambiguous in nature. They are justified by harassers as well-meant and not harmful while the harassed individuals experience harm. As such, in the courtroom, harassment is most often an excellent case of a conflict of perspectives.[61] Then, if law is based on dignity, as in Germany, or, with Cornell, on self-respect, the harm and the activity causing it are individualized, the perpetrator's perspective privileged, and the social interaction judged from a moralistic point of view.[62] Structurally, German law defines harassment as a crime rather than a social phenomenon within a structure of sex-based disadvantage. As an alternative, an equality-based approach to sex discrimination law recognizes sexual harassment as a violation of a right against sexualized hierarchy, as an interaction situated in a discriminatory context producing harm, and requiring the law to stop whatever a perpetrator thought he was doing. Structurally, that kind of law does not define harassment as a crime but as damaging behavior. Then a potentially harassing activity is judged from a socially adequate, relational, equality-focused, power-sensitive point of view.

Conclusion

In Europe and in Germany, law against sexual harassment at work is based on dignity as the right in question, while U.S. law developed from an analysis of harassment as discrimination and thus as a violation of the right to sex equality at work. As liberal philosophy tends to posit these two approaches in a scheme of conflict, the doctrinal differences produced by these

approaches merit some attention. Three important features of sexual harassment law in Europe reveal that a dignity-based approach tends to address only
inadequately the problem of discrimination. The same is true for theoretical
attempts to conceptualize sex discrimination in gender-neutral, dignity-like
terms.

On the other hand, an equality-based approach tends to open the door to a
more adequate assessment of the problem at hand. However, with a move
from the scheme of conflict to a scheme of interrelatedness, equality will serve
the need to work as a normative standard in cases of discrimination only if
equality itself is conceptualized as a substantive right against hierarchy. Such a
combination of dignity and equality, with dignity as a point of reference for an
equality analysis, can be found in German constitutional law and in some
insufficiently acknowledged parts of the liberal tradition of legal philosophy.

A comparative account of sexual harassment law reveals the similarities, the
differences, and the advantages and disadvantages of a dignity-based and an
equality-based law against discrimination.[63] It also reveals that cultural understandings translate themselves into the law, and that differing legal, and particularly constitutional, traditions tend to shape even the small doctrinal reactions to the social world. Yet some conclusions drawn from the comparison
can be generalized.[64] For sex discrimination law to work, some features have
to be attained. The structure of sex discrimination law must not follow the
path of criminal and tort law provisions but work along a civil rights model.
An intent requirement contradicts everything we know about the nature of
discrimination. Sexuality is an important factor of sex discrimination, but
sexual nature is not sufficient to define how this works. Women at work are to
be recognized as subjects, fully capable of knowing what they want, and yet it
is inadequate to require anyone to fight back in a situation of sexual harassment. Therefore, rejection requirements are inadequate as well.

In the United States, law against sexual harassment has been fought for by
women who saw themselves as targets of discrimination, violated not only in
their rights to bodily and psychological integrity, but in their rights as women
(or, for some men, as gay men), and because of their gender. As a common-law
culture, the U.S. system favors a version of legal development in which doctrine is shaped in the courts. In Europe and in Germany, law against sexual
harassment has developed differently. It has been legislated by governing
bodies, the Commission in Europe, and a branch of the federal government in
Germany. The legislation was a response to demands from women in workers'
unions and the women's movements, who, in the European context, were
women working in the European institutions themselves. In Germany, legislation resulted in response to such demands as well, but was primarily a reaction
to the legally binding European demand to draft legislation according to the

Commission's imperative. The European laws have been fought for by women as well, but in the legislative process, feminist demands are more likely to be watered down to gender-neutral declarations. In legislative bodies, it is usually not the women who experienced harassment who argue for a law against it, while in courts, it is exactly these women who shape the understanding of harassment in law. Legislation might settle a matter more securely, but case law is often shaped much closer to realities.

Finally, if we go back to the philosophical starting point, we must address the question of the relation between dignity and equality, and what a choice between the scheme of conflict and a scheme of interrelatedness might mean in the real world of civil rights. The traditional scheme of conflict has proven to be an inadequate response to discrimination, and it is inadequate in both its solely dignity-based version, as in the German and European case, as it would be inadequate in a solely traditional equality-based approach, in which equality is a symmetrical and rather formal right to equal treatment. Alternatively, a scheme of interrelatedness between dignity and equality might be applied to legally address sex discrimination.[65] Then equality is an asymmetrical, substantive right against in this case sexualized hierarchies, and dignity is the normative point of reference which guarantees equal respect for every individual. This approach requires the law to recognize human beings as socially situated subjects. It asks the law to respond to the tension between an attribution of autonomy that can be derived from the right to individual dignity of human beings, and the social inequalities such human beings experience in the world, which are introduced by way of reference to the right to equality. With this approach, the law can recognize the systematic rather than arbitrary or intentional character of sex discrimination. A call for autonomy, for agency, or for an individual domain alone is inadequate to grasp what discrimination means, and what it feels like. Rather, a call for equal respect, for dignified equality, might serve as a guideline for those who want to combat it. Sexual harassment law, then, looked at from a comparative perspective, seems to be at its best when grounded in this interrelated approach. The question is not "dignity or equality?" but what features the law has to offer to guarantee individual dignity on an equal basis for all.

Notes

I am grateful to Uta Stiegler and Ulrich C. Baer for reading draft versions, and to Catharine MacKinnon for extensive critique.

1. Directive 2000/43/EC of the Council (June 29, 2000) of implementing the principle of equal treatment between persons irrespective of racial or ethnic origin; Directive 2000/78/EC of the Council (November 27, 2000) establishing a general framework for equal treatment in employment and occupation, to be found at *www.europa.eu.int/eurlex/en/index.html*.

2. Younger constitutions do not necessarily follow that tradition. For example, the Republic of South Africa emphasizes equality as an asymmetrical right against oppression.

3. *See generally* Amy G. Mazur, "The Interplay: The Formation of Sexual Harassment Legislation in France and EU Policy Initiatives," in *Sexual Politics and the European Union* 35 (Amy Elman ed., 1996). *See also* Jean Gregory, "Sexual Harassment: Making the Best Use of European Law," 2 *European Journal of Women's Studies* 421 (1995). Note that Swedish law does not explicitly address harassment. *See* Amy R. Elman, "Feminism and Legislative Redress: Sexual Harassment in Sweden and the United States," 16 *Women and Politics* 1 (1996). On Great Britain, *see* "Sexual Harassment at the Workplace: Implementing Policies, the Union Role and Legal Aspects," *IRS Employment Trends* 5 (1992). For a different perspective from Britain, *see* Colin Bourn, "Harassed by Discrimination Law?" 142 *New Law Journal* 1059 (1992).

4. For the elaborate version of the argument with an analysis of German labor, tort, and criminal law on sexual violence, and a discussion of equality theories in this context, see Susanne Baer, *Würde oder Gleichheit? Zur angemessenen grundrechtlichen Konzeption von Recht gegen Diskriminierung am Beispiel sexueller Belästigung am Arbeitsplatz in der Bundesrepublik Deutschland und den USA* (1995).

5. The most prominent example in feminist legal theory is Drucilla Cornell, *The Imaginary Domain: Abortion, Pornography, and Sexual Harassment* 168 (1995). The force of tradition is perfectly caught in the title of an article by Mary E. Becker, "Prince Charming: Abstract Equality," 8 *Supreme Court Review* 201 (1987).

6. The first outline may be found in Catharine MacKinnon's *Sexual Harassment of Working Women: A Case of Sex Discrimination* (1979), and a theoretical foundation in MacKinnon's *Toward a Feminist Theory of the State* (1989). *See also* Christine Littleton, *Alternative Theories of Sexual Equality* (1984); Martha Minow, "Equalities," 88 *Journal of Philosophy* 633 (1991).

7. Much criticism is directed against the "rigidity" of MacKinnon's understanding of gender. One way of understanding it is based on a radically constructivist approach, according to which gender is conceptualized as a constructed phenomenon rather than as an experienced reality. Then, MacKinnon's deconstruction of gender, particularly in *Toward a Feminist Theory of the State, supra* note 6, at chapter 7, can be understood as critique of an invention transformed into law, not as a rejection of peoples choices, a suggestion of widespread false consciousness, or a simple reductionism to essentialist models. I discuss this in relation to the critique articulated by Judith Butler in *Excitable Speech: A Politics of the Performative* (1997). *See* Susanne Baer, "Inexcitable Speech: Zum Rechtsverständnis postmoderner feministischer Positionen am Beispiel Judith Butler," in *Kritische Differenzen—geteilte Perspektiven* 229 (Antje Hornscheidt et al. eds., 1998).

8. Immanuel Kant, "Die Rechtsordnung als denknotwendige Bedingung allgemeiner Freiheit und Gleichheit," *in Werke*, Band 6, at 229–31, 237–38 (Akademie Ausgabe 7, 1906). The derivative nature of equality is engraved in the European Convention of Human Rights and Freedoms, where article 14 is only applied in conjunction with an article protecting liberty interests.

9. For a more thorough discussion, see Susanne Baer, "Equality: The Jurisprudence of the German Constitutional Court," 5 *Columbia Journal of European Law* 249 (1999).

10. The Aristotelian interpretation of equality holds that persons or situations of a similar nature, or "similarly situated," require similar, or equal treatment, while dissimilarities require or at least legitimize inequality. For further discussion, *see* Catharine A. MacKinnon, "Reflections on Sex Equality Under Law," 100 *Yale Law Journal* 1281 (1991).

11. Marcus Tullius Cicero, "Naturrecht als universale Teilhabe am ewigen Weltgesetz," in *Der Staat*, at 25, 80 (1964). German legal philosopher Norbert Hoerster relates that to the concept of human dignity in *Klassische Texte der Staatsphilosophie* 24 (Norbert Hoerster ed., 1976).

12. John Locke, Second Treatise of Government, 4 (Mark Goldie, ed., 1993) (1690).

13. For example, this can be seen in Kant's discussion of the third legal principle, the right of the citizen called *sibisufficientia*. *See* Kant, *supra* note 8.

14. *See* Jürgen Habermas, *Die Einbeziehung des Anderen: Studien zur politischen Theorie* (1996), and his discussion of John Rawls in chapters 2 and 3.

15. *See* Axel Honneth, *Kampf um Anerkennung* (1994), where he refers to traces of a tradition of social philosophy in Marx, Sorel, and Sartre, and describes intersubjective conditions of personal integrity, which include the rights to respect and solidarity. *Id.* at 209. These rights can be interpreted as dignity and equality. See also the discussion by John Gardner, "Liberals and Unlawful Discrimination," 9 *Oxford Journal of Legal Studies* 1 (1989); and Virginia Held, "Liberty and Equality from a Feminist Perspective," in *Enlightenment, Rights and Revolution: Essays on Legal and Social History* 69 (Neil MacCormick and Zenon Bankowski eds., 1989).

16. Herta Nagl-Docekal, "Gleichbehandlung und Anerkennung von Differenz: Kontroversielle Themen feministischer politischer Philosophie," in *Differenz und Lebensqualität* 9, 18–20 (Herta Nagl-Docekal and Herlinde Pauer-Studer eds., 1996).

17. *See* MacKinnon, *Sexual Harassment of Working Women, supra* note 6. I understand the work of Cass Sunstein and Deborah Rhode as slightly different versions of equality thinking. For the German discussion, *see* Baer, *supra* note 4; and Susanne Baer, "A Different Approach to Jurisprudence? Feminisms in German Legal Science, Legal Cultures, and the Ambivalence of Law," 3 *Cardozo Women's Law Journal* 251 (1996).

18. The first statement can be found in a decision on pension law from 1981, Entscheidungen des Bundesverfassungsgerichts (BVerfGE) (Federal Constitutional Court), 57, 335 (345) (FRG). It should be noted that many constitutional scholars tended or still tend to ignore the potential of this doctrine. For extensive analyses, *see* Ute Sacksofsky, *Das Grundrecht auf Gleichberechtigung* (2d ed. 1996).

19. BVerfGE 84, 9 (18–19).

20. This is particularly true in the night shift decision from 1992, BverfGE 85, 191. *See also* the decision on discrimination in access to paid work from 1993, BVerfGE 89, 276.

21. Robert Husbands, "Sexual Harassment Law in Employment: An International Perspective," 131 *International Labour Review* 535, 558 (1992).

22. Cornell, *supra* note 5.

23. The most often cited description of the dilemma may be the one by Audre Lorde, "A Master's Tool Will Never Dismantle the Master's House," in her collection of essays *Sister Outsider* (1984).

24. Cornell, *supra* note 5, at 227.

598   Susanne Baer

25. *Id.* at 206.

26. *Id.* at 170.

27. *Id.* at 227.

28. In reactions to law against racist discrimination, including harassment at work, many claimed that freedom of contract, a right the constitution protects as part of free will under article 2, sec. 1, Basic Law, covers acts of subordination. For details of the German discussion see Susanne Baer, "Ende der Privatautonomie oder grundrechtlich fundierte Rechtsetzung?" 35 *Zeitschrift für Rechtspolitik* 290 (2002).

29. For a wonderful discussion of the nature of the subject in law see the collection of essays in *Sexing the Subject of Law* (Ngaire Naffine and Rosemary J. Owens eds., 1997); and Nicola Lacey, *Unspeakable Subjects* part I (1998).

30. In India, law against sex discrimination has sometimes been based on modesty, a concept closely related to dignity in its individualistic emphasis. *See* Martha Nussbaum's essay in this volume.

31. Cornell, *supra* note 5, at 194 ("unilateral imposition"). In Europe, the discussion focuses on gender-mainstreaming, often understood and sometimes abused as a replacement for equality strategies. As embodied in article 3, section 2 of the Treaty of the European Community, gender-mainstreaming is the structural device to turn equality into practice.

32. *See* John Rawls, *A Theory of Justice* (1971). For a similar approach and an impressive defense of universality based on a Kantian idea of the subject, see Renata Salecl, *The Spoils of Freedom* (1994).

33. Cornell, *supra* note 5, at 225 (referring to Judith Butler).

34. *See generally* Martha Minow, *Making All the Difference: Inclusion, Exclusion and American Law* (1990); Susanne Baer, "Dilemmata im Recht und Gleichheit als Hierarchisierungsverbot: Der Abschied von Thelma und Louise," 28 *Kriminologisches Journal* 242 (1996).

35. It may be interesting to note that in the Republic of South Africa, in which men share a history of racial oppression with women and in which racial oppression was often sexualized, law offers a strong guarantee of equal rights as well as a strong protection for individual dignity. This indicates a scheme of interrelatedness between the two, rather than the traditional scheme of conflict. However, as reports on the diminishing impact of women on politics point out, ongoing gender hierarchy supports a trend to emphasize dignity rather than equality.

36. On newer developments, *see* note 1.

37. The discussion around the meaning of dignity among constitutional scholars was, however, for a long time imprinted by this history. In the 1950s and 1960s, some argued that dignity should be gained individually and thus not attributed to anyone just because he or she was human. The courts decided from the beginning that dignity serves as a right against degrading treatment of anyone as a less valuable human being. For further discussion, *see* Baer, *supra* note 4, at 217–19.

38. For a discussion of jurisprudence from around the world see my chapter on dignity, self-determination, and privacy in Norman Dorsen, Michel Rosenfeld, Andras Sajo, and Susanne Baer, *Comparative Constitutionalism* (forthcoming, 2003).

39. Belg. Const. art. 23; Greece Const. art. 2; Italy Const. arts. 2, 41; Port. Const. art.

1; Spain Const. art. 10; Swed. Const. art. 2. *See* Peter Häberle, "Die Menschenwüde als Grundlage der staatlichen Gemeinschaft" in 1 *Handbuch des Staatsrechts* 20 n.1 (Josef Isensee and Paul Kirchhof eds., 1998).

40. The charter was drafted under heavy German influence, partly since Roman Herzog, a German constitutional scholar, presided over the drafting convention. The whole process and results may be found on the Internet at www.consilium.eu.int (visited July 1, 2001). On the significance of the charter, see Susanne Baer, "Grundrechtecharta ante portas," 33 *Zeitschrift für Rechtspolitik* 361 (2000).

41. Article 3, section 3 of the Grundgesetz reads: "No one may be prejudiced or favored because of his or her sex, parentage, race, language, homeland and origin, faith, religious or political opinion. No one may be disadvantaged because of his or her disability."

42. *See generally Grundgesetz-Kommentar* art. 1 (Ingo v. Münch and Philip Kunig eds., 4th ed. 1996).

43. In comparison, First Amendment jurisprudence tends to cover many incidents which could be argued under other constitutional provisions, if a more detailed scheme of individual rights were at hand. For example, the famous Skokie controversy may be discussed not only as a free expression problem, but as a potential violation of the dignity of Holocaust survivors, or, for that matter, as a violation of their right to live as equals, treated with equal respect, in a community. *See Skokie v. Nationalist Socialist Party of America*, 366 N.E.2d 347 (1977); *Collin v. Smith*, 578 F.2d 1197 (7th Cir.), *aff'g* 477 F. Supp. 676 (N.D. Ill. 1978). However, the pure presence of a right to dignity within a constitution cannot tell us the story of its practical effect. For example, the constitutional right to dignity in India is more often used to broaden the powers of the federation rather than to protect individuals from harm.

44. For the most far-reaching interpretation, see MacKinnon, *supra* note 10.

45. Article 3, section 2 of the Grundgesetz was amended in 1994. Before that, it stated: "Women and men are equal." The new second sentence reads: "The state shall promote the social implementation of equality of women and men and shall work toward the removal of existing detriments."

46. *See* Evelyn Collins, "European Union Sexual Harassment Policy," in *Sexual Politics and the European Union* 23 (Amy Elman ed., 1996). Husbands ignores the fundamental difference when he lists the EC recommendation under equal opportunities laws, since the Commission wanted dignity for both men and women. *See* Husbands, *supra* note 21, at 546. For EC law, see Commission Recommendation 92/131/EEC of November 27, 1991, on the Protection of the Dignity of Women and Men at Work, art. 3, 1992 O.J. (L 049) (hereinafter Commission Recommendation on the Protection of the Dignity of Women and Men at Work) ("Whereas unwanted conduct of a sexual nature, or other conduct based on sex affecting the dignity of women and men at work, including the conduct of superiors and colleagues, is unacceptable and may, in certain circumstances, be contrary to the principle of equal treatment within the meaning of Articles 3, 4 and 5 of Council Directive 76/207/EEC of 9 February 1976 on the implementation of the principle of equal treatment for men and women as regards access to employment, vocational training and promotion, and working conditions").

47. 29 C.F.R. § 1604.11(a) (1992).

48. My translation of the Federal Law for the Protection of Employees (*Beschäftig-tenschutzgesetz*). More equality oriented approaches can be found in laws of the German Länder, e.g., Hessen and Berlin. A brief annotated collection of these laws can be found in *Frauengleichstellungsgesetze des Bundes und der Länder: Kommentar für die Praxis* (Dagmar Schiek et al. eds., 1996).

49. One further element is responsibility. In German law, employers are rarely held responsible, while in U.S. law (and even more so in Canada and Belgium) this is more often the case, and there is greater employer responsibility for preventive measures and complaint and sanction systems. Other elements are defenses and sanctions: in German law, we find labor-law-type reactions of employer reprimanding harasser, including the danger of paternalism. Other legal systems in which sexual harassment is framed as a violation of contracts of employment, of duties rather than rights, include those of Belgium, Italy, Portugal, and Switzerland. *Cf.* Husbands, *supra* note 21, at 547. Another important element of harassment law is procedure; German law does not install special agents, although we do find, in some affirmative action plans, a designated employee to handle complaints. On Belgium, *see id.* at 555. On newer developments, see note 1.

50. *See also* the reference to dignity in Canadian equality jurisprudence. *E.g., Miron v. Trudel* [1995] D.L.R. 693 (Can.).

51. Case C-177/88, 1990 E.C.R. I-3941 (Dekker).

52. Entscheidungen des Bundesverwaltungsgerichts (Federal Administrative Court) (BVerwGE) 64, 274 (Peep-Show I); BVerfGE 84, 314 (Peep-Show II). Constitutional scholars criticized these decisions for imposing values rather than adjudicating rights.

53. The same happens in criminal law, where criminalized "sexual" behavior is what turns men on, not what harms women. For further discussion, *see* Baer, *supra* note 4, at 252.

54. Commission Recommendation on the Protection of the Dignity of Women and Men at Work, *supra* note 46, art. 3.

55. *See* Victoria A. Carter, "Working on Dignity: EC Initiatives on Sexual Harassment in the Workplace," 12 *Northwestern Journal of International Law and Business* 431 (1992); Anthony B. Haller, "Sexual Harassment: An Import from America?" 4 *Business Law Review* 229 (1983). In France, law acknowledges harassment as an abuse of authority; since it ignores gender hierarchy, harassment among coworkers is not actionable.

56. In the hearings, a conservative member of Parliament stated that there are women who would like to be harassed, but are not, and who want to gain attention with an unfounded complaint. *Focus*, November 8, 1993, at 53 (citing a member of the Bundestag von Stetten) ("Kein Herz fuer Machos").

57. For further discussion of German criminal law provisions on rape, *see* Baer, *supra* note 4, at 119–46; on the rights of victims, *see* Alexandra Goy, "The Victim-Plaintiff in Criminal Trials and Civil Law Responses to Sexual Violence," 3 *Cardozo Women's Law Journal* 335 (1996).

58. The correlation between dignity, characterized as honor, and individualization has first been discussed by 2 Alexis de Toqueville, *Democracy in America*, bk. 3, ch. 18 (Phillips Bradley ed., 1945).

59. For a discussion of the standards for "unwelcomeness" in U.S. law, and for a

critique of the "reasonable woman standard," which may be more adequately conceptualized as the "reasoning woman perspective," *see* Baer, *supra* note 4, at 159–79.

60. *See* Cornell, *supra* note 5, at 175; Baer, *supra* note 4, at 159.

61. Cornell, *supra* note 5, at 199.

62. *Id.* at 186, 202 (referring to "a conception of sexual shame").

63. From a comparative perspective, I should point out that U.S. law, despite its equality approach, features some extremely problematic aspects as well. One is the defense of
sexual harassment based on the right to freedom of speech. Regarding sexual harassment,
freedom of speech is not an issue in Europe. This might be a time-lag of sensitivity, but it
may also demonstrate a willingness to combat violations of personal freedom and equality in any form, including speech. As with every other constitutionally guaranteed right,
freedom of speech is limited by rights of others. The example of pornography is a case in
point. For further discussion, *see* Susanne Baer, "Violence: Dilemmas of Democracy and
Law," in *Freedom of Speech and Incitement against Democracy* 63 (David Kretzmer and
Francine Kershman Hazan eds., 2000). In sum, harassment cannot be justified by referring to free speech. For similar conclusions, *see* Cornell, *supra* note 5, at 187.

64. The difference between the dignity-based and equality-based approaches is also
evident in the case of pornography. In Germany, as in many other legal systems, pornography is regulated as obscenity, which is legitimated with references to the protection
of morals and dignity. In fact, pornography is available. The legal response ignores the
harm of gender discrimination and sexual violence, and criminalizes sexualities outside
the heterosexual norm, particularly sexual expression by gays and lesbians. Despite the
fact that solidarity with gays and lesbians should not be abused to legitimize sexual
violence, an equality-based approach to pornography would focus on harm, rather than
the preservation of a specific kind of sexual morality. It situates pornography in a context
of inequality, not in a context of bad taste.

65. This is the case in Israel. *See* Orit Kamir's essay in this volume.

34

French and American Lawyers
Define Sexual Harassment

ABIGAIL C. SAGUY

The concept of "sexual harassment," first articulated by American feminists in the mid-1970s, has since moved well beyond the small feminist and legal circles where it was born, becoming a household name, not only in the United States but in other nations as well. How has the concept of sexual harassment traveled across national boundaries? How have the distinct legal and cultural traditions of other countries shaped the meaning of "sexual harassment" abroad? This essay addresses these issues, in the case of France, drawing on a cross-national sociological study of how sexual harassment has been defined in the United States and France.[1]

This essay describes sexual harassment law in action, drawing primarily from twenty in-depth interviews, conducted in 1996 and 1997, with ten French and ten American lawyers who have worked in the area of sexual harassment. The argument is further informed by an additional forty in-depth interviews, conducted between 1995 and 2000, with French and American activists, public figures, human resource personnel, and union activists; legal analysis of statutes and jurisprudence in the two countries; content analysis of more than six hundred articles published in the American and French popular press from 1975 to 2000; and twenty-three brief telephone interviews conducted during the summer of 1997 with the human resource or personnel departments in French corporate workplaces.[2]

As major industrialized democracies where sexual harassment is a documented social problem,[3] France and the United States are sufficiently similar to warrant comparison. These countries are rendered even more comparable by virtue of the fact that both have high rates of female employment and independent women's movements, two of the main structural factors thought to foster strong sexual harassment laws.[4] Yet, these two nations have quite different political, legal, and cultural traditions, which, I will show, influence how sexual harassment is conceptualized.

National Laws

American feminist activists could have taken several legal avenues to address sexual harassment, including tort law, criminal law, and labor law.[5] However, the U.S. courts eventually accepted the argument proposed by Catharine MacKinnon and others that sexual harassment is a form of sex discrimination in employment, under Title VII of the 1964 Civil Rights Act, which makes it illegal to discriminate on the basis of race, color, religion, sex, or national origin.[6] Under Title VII, employers are held liable for condoning, tolerating, or doing too little to prevent discrimination, including sexual harassment, in the workplace.[7] The former can be ordered to pay compensatory and (since 1991) punitive damages to plaintiffs who win their lawsuits.[8]

Although American jurisprudence on this issue is still in a state of flux, there are two classes of sexual harassment recognized by the courts: quid pro quo and condition of employment.[9] In the quid pro quo or sexual coercion type, employees are given an ultimatum: either submit to sexual demands or lose their jobs, job benefits, or chances of promotion.[10] In the condition of employment or hostile environment type, the boss does not threaten an employee with loss of employment or benefits. Instead, an employee may be the object of unwanted sexual attention by a boss or coworker, who makes insistent and invasive demands for sex or emotional intimacy despite a series of rejections.[11] Alternatively, sexual objects like pornography, sexual jokes, or sexist insults can be used to humiliate someone because that person is of a different gender (usually female).[12]

The basic principles of American sexual harassment jurisprudence were in place in the early 1990s, when French Parliament began discussing sexual harassment bills, during Penal Code reform. With the support of the Office of Women's Rights and the European Union, French feminist organizations, including notably the Association Européenne Contre les Violences Faites aux Femmes aux Travail (AVFT; European Association Against Violence Toward Women at Work) and the Union des Femmes Françaises (UFF; Union of French Women), pushed for a sexual harassment law. Unlike the law that ultimately passed, the AVFT proposal, the UFF proposal, and the formal recommendation on sexual harassment issued by the European Commission (EC) in November 1991[13] targeted hostile environment as well as quid pro quo forms of harassment. Each of these bills also addressed harassment among peers as well as across hierarchical lines.

During French Parliamentary debates, however, the legal definition of sexual harassment was limited to the quid pro quo form of sexual harassment. The Penal Code statute, which was passed in 1992 and went into effect in 1994, qualifies sexual harassment as:

> The act of harassing another by using orders, threats, constraint, or serious pressure in the goal of obtaining sexual favors, by someone abusing the authority conferred by his position, is punished by [a maximum of] one year of imprisonment and [a maximum] fine of 100,000F [$14,000].[14]

Under French penal law, harassers — rather than their employers — are condemned for sexual harassment, because they individually abused their official authority to demand "sexual favors" from a person under their command. Unlike in the U.S. penal system, it is possible to request civil damages from the accused within the context of a French penal trial, although French courts typically accord victims of sexual harassment no more than 20,000F ($3,000). In the French Penal Code, sexual harassment is limited to verbal pressures for sexual relations. If any physical groping is involved, the misdemeanor is classified as sexual battery, which carries a heavier sentence of a maximum of five years in prison and a maximum fine of 500,000F (Article 222–27). According to AVFT activists who follow these cases, the more typical sentence for sexual battery combined with sexual harassment is no more than two to three months behind bars. In the same year that they added a sexual harassment statute to the Penal Code, French lawmakers unanimously passed a second law, modifying the Labor Code, which was designed specifically to outlaw employment retaliation linked to sexual harassment at work.[15] This statute, which was passed and went into effect in 1992, states:

> No employee can be penalized or dismissed for having submitted or refusing to submit to acts of harassment of an employer, his agent, or any person who, abusing the authority conferred by their position, gave orders, made threats, imposed constraints, or exercised pressure of any nature on this employee, in the goal of obtaining sexual favors for his own benefit or for the benefit of a third party.
>
> No employee can be sanctioned or fired for having witnessed acts defined in the preceding paragraph or for having recounted them.
>
> All contrary decisions or acts are automatically legally void (*nul de plein droit*).[16]

Under this statute, employees who suffer retaliation can claim reinstatement or, if they prefer, monetary compensation for lost salaries and moral suffering. The *nullité* provision, laid out in the statute's third paragraph, is reserved for serious offenses and should translate into the equivalent of at least one full year's salary in compensatory damages, but this clause is often disregarded in sexual harassment cases, yielding smaller awards.[17] Two subsequent statutes allow but do not require employers to discipline sexual harassment in the workplace and require employers to include sexual harassment in the company's internal regulations and post the latter in the firm and in places of recruitment.[18] As others have pointed out, these are very weak provisions for employer liability.[19]

The reasons why French sexual harassment law ended up so different from American sexual harassment law is a question I discuss at some length elsewhere.[20] It is worth noting here, however, that while proponents of sexual harassment legislation drew on North American and European feminist legal analysis and jurisprudence to strengthen their platform both intellectually and politically, their opponents used anti-American rhetoric to discredit the bill as an import that would replicate "American excesses" of litigiousness, Puritanism, and the battle of the sexes in France. During parliamentary debate, French lawmakers explicitly cited "American excesses" as justification for employing "a more restrictive but more realistic definition" of sexual harassment in French law.[21] French sexual harassment laws were thus born in a political context that was both extremely international and very local.

Group-Based Injury or Individual Harm?

Laws are formalized rules that serve to define the boundaries of acceptable behavior and to assign publicly sanctioned and enforced punishment for those who fail to respect those limits. By categorizing behavior in particular ways and not others, laws also provide a cognitive structure for understanding social behavior. For instance, by legally defining sexual harassment as a subset of employment discrimination under Title VII, the U.S. courts have affirmed MacKinnon's arguments that sexual harassment is a group-defined injury in employment.[22] This legal categorization privileges a "discrimination frame" of sexual harassment, in which the victim's gender and her/his experience of employment consequences are primary.[23]

In early French legal formulations of sexual harassment, a discrimination frame was also important. The AVFT's sexual harassment bill pointed out that sexual harassment is "based on sex" and can compromise "equality in employment" and "working conditions"—important aspects of a discrimination frame.[24] The EC, which, under the equality clause in the Treaty of Rome, can only make suggestions to nation-states in the economic domain, also stressed the implications of sexual harassment on gender equality in employment. Early French parliamentary bills placed the sexual harassment penal statute under the category of discrimination in employment. This may seem like a legal oxymoron to an American audience, where discrimination is a civil, not penal, offense. However, during the time these bills were being debated, employment discrimination was addressed in the Penal Code, in Section I of Chapter V: Harm to Human Dignity. French discrimination law was also different from its American counterpart in that it recognized intentional discrimination but not "indirect discrimination," or practices that have a disparate impact on a particular group without being explicitly discriminatory.[25] Discrimination law in France was weakly enforced, and high standards of proof of discriminatory intent made it difficult to prove.

Because American and French discrimination law are so dissimilar, French sexual harassment law would have been extremely different from American sexual harassment law, even if the penal statute had remained in the section on discrimination. However, after review by the National Assembly and the French Senate, the National Assembly's Commission of Laws moved the sexual harassment bill out of the section on discrimination into the rubric "Sexual violence other than rape," according to the logic that "the misdemeanor of sexual harassment does not appear to be discriminatory because it exists regardless of the sex of the victim or of the author of the misdemeanor. In reality, it is much closer in nature to sexual violence."[26] The section on sexual violence is found in Chapter II: Harm to the Physical or Psychic Integrity of a Person, of Title II: Harms to Human Beings (*des atteintes à la personne humaine*), in Book II of the Penal Code: Crimes and Misdemeanors Against Persons. Sexual harassment is thus legally categorized primarily as a deviant individual attack that is physically, psychologically, or morally harmful and violates the victim's free will, rather than as a form of group-based discrimination.[27]

Discrimination and Interpersonal
Violence Frames in Interviews

Consistent with their respective national laws, the American and French lawyers interviewed were more likely to conceptualize sexual harassment as discrimination and interpersonal violence, respectively. The American lawyers thus emphasized the negative impact sexual harassment has on a person's working conditions: "The conduct or behavior you're complaining about has to interfere with your ability to do the work." They also stressed the discriminatory basis of the behavior, saying that sexual harassment is driven by "stereotypical ideas of what the role of a woman is." Finally, the American lawyers interviewed condemned nonsexual and sexual forms of gender harassment equally: "[If a boss insults all female and only female employees], then it's sexual harassment, because he is making this distinction based on sex."

In contrast, the French lawyers interviewed echoed the interpersonal violence frame of French law. As one French feminist lawyer put it: "I consider sexual harassment to be an individual attack, but sexism is an attack on the group." Another French lawyer explained: "Sexual violence (*agression sexuel*) is something that must be penalized, in order to preserve people's moral and physical integrity based on the fact that it is totally unacceptable for a person to be forced to do something she does not want to do."

According to this perspective, in which sexual harassment is an intentional attack on a particular individual, the concept of "hostile environment" makes little sense. This is illustrated by the following French lawyer's response to a vignette that described a scene in which a female truck-driver complained about the display of pornographic posters in a break room: "For it to be sexual harassment, you would have to show that the posters were put up after her arrival. If they were there before she arrived, you cannot say that they are directed at her and therefore, you cannot say that there was sexual harassment." Unlike their American counterparts, the French lawyers interviewed typically shrugged off sexist behavior that did not involve physical violence or coercion as "societal," "human," or otherwise outside of the law. Included among such behavior were bosses who disparage female and only female employees.

While not legally dominant, the discrimination frame continues to be developed by some French social actors, notably the AVFT, which is part of larger international feminist networks.[28] Some French lawyers affiliated with the AVFT or other feminist groups also used elements of a discriminatory frame to discuss sexual harassment: "It is rare that women are at the head of a corporation. If the guy were to tell his version in the firm, everyone would laugh at her, and she would be more vulnerable in the end than the man." By affirming that women are not only different but also socially unequal, this lawyer recognized the basic premise of the equality discrimination approach.

Sexuality as Bad Business

While the American lawyers interviewed framed sexual harassment as a form of sex-based discrimination in employment, in advising employers, they discouraged a wide range of sexual behavior at work, regardless of whether or not it was discriminatory. According to them, it is inadvisable to allow dating at work, especially across levels of hierarchical authority: "[I] advise supervisors that [dating at work] is not something that's favorably looked upon, because of the problems that can arise from it. And if [they] arise, the supervisors [are] not only placing the employer in jeopardy from a lawsuit, but they're placing their job in jeopardy."

Often, unlike American courts, American but not French respondents used what I call a "business frame" to claim that sexuality is inappropriate in the workplace and antithetical to productivity. The following comment expressed a general sentiment among American lawyers: "I don't think it would be a bad thing [to get flirtation out of the workplace]. I'd love to see that. We want to create an environment where anyone who comes into work can do the best kind of work possible. In most instances, that [means] removing all the nonsense that's going on around them and the harassment so that they can focus on their work." Condemning sexual relations in the workplace or among people who work together because such relations are "bad for business" or "unprofessional" represents a different rationale than condemning sexual behavior because it contributes to gender inequality in employment. Yet this rationale seemed to coexist with a discrimination frame in the minds of American lawyers and employers, even if it has no founding in U.S. law.

Legal Climate

The interviews suggest that French and American lawyers operate in very different legal climates, in regards to sexual harassment. In the United States, successful plaintiffs may receive significant compensatory and punitive damages from their employer.[29] The fear of lawsuits, which may be inflated by the media and the human resource profession,[30] encourages firms to take sexual harassment claims seriously. In the words of one American defense lawyer: "It might be to protect them from liability, but most of the employers that I deal with are very concerned about sexual harassment issues and are willing to take the action that they need to take. Whether it's training, you know, having the policies in place. And when they get complaints, taking them seriously."

According to many lawyers, firms in the United States are quick to dismiss or otherwise sanction people accused of sexual harassment, even when the case would be questionable in court. As one female lawyer said bitterly: "I had [as a client] an employee, who made . . . a very off-color remark. The woman was very offended by it. She went to her superiors, and my guy was disciplined with the loss of his job. Now, he obviously made a comment that was out of line, but it was an isolated incident. He subsequently apologized for it; he went to training to get [his] consciousness raised. In my mind, you don't deserve to get fired for a mistake of that magnitude when you have a long-term relationship with your employer."

The American defense lawyers I interviewed play it safe by frowning on any behavior over which their client could potentially be sued. During the interviews, I presented respondents with a series of vignettes that described different sorts of workplace behavior. I then asked them if the behavior described was sexual harassment or not and why. Some of the vignettes, like the following one, described behavior that would be "borderline," according to American sexual harassment laws. Nonetheless, the American lawyers said they would be concerned about the behavior:

> A.S.: A male boss has been dating one of his female employees. He breaks up with her and begins dating another employee. His ex-girlfriend is upset, humiliated, and angry. During work hours, she calls her rival a slut and a whore and suggests that she only has her job because the boss wants to use her sexually. Her coworkers laugh at these comments, creating a very uncomfortable situation for the boss's new girlfriend.
>
> RESPONSE: I haven't seen that, but I think she might be able to prove a case of hostile environment. I mean, it's the behavior of calling her a slut, and calling her names that are associated with that type of behavior could get [there] . . . especially if coworkers are jumping on the bandwagon, and they're creating an environment so hostile that she's having difficulty working in it. As a management lawyer I would argue it's not sexual harassment/hostile environment. That's not what [the law] was designed to prevent. But, I think it could get there.
>
> A.S.: So, you'd advise management to do something about the situation?
>
> RESPONSE: Absolutely. In all these cases, I advise them do to something about it. . . . There's always a court that might be willing to extend [the definition of sexual harassment].

American employees are increasingly likely to consult lawyers about potential sexual harassment claims. American lawyers interviewed said that only 5 to 10 percent of the numerous sexual harassment complaints they receive are legitimate or actionable. According to an American lawyer doing mostly plaintiff work, some people "think that they are gonna win the lottery and try to turn something into something that's much bigger than it is. [Others] genuinely feel that they have been harmed, but the harassment hasn't necessarily risen to the level that is actionable or that I think I can do something for them legally." Among behavior that American lawyers said did not rise to the level of actionable sexual harassment include men who address female employees as "girl" or "honey" or abusive bosses who insult all workers, regardless of their sex. Lawyers also spoke of situations in which people were untruthful to "get someone that they weren't particularly fond of."

In contrast and independent of sexual harassment law, punitive damages are not part of the French legal system, and compensatory damages are typically low, especially for moral or psychological harm. The French lawyers interviewed reasoned that the high costs and low benefits of sexual harassment lawsuits in France discourage victims of even egregious sexual harassment and battery from pressing charges. Without the specter of expensive lawsuits, they said, employers do not address the problem. Indeed, all twenty-three representatives of French branches of large multinational corporations I surveyed during the summer of 1997 reported that sexual harassment was not a major concern in their company at the time. Though the labor law *requires* all French employers to include sexual harassment in their international regulations, according to the survey, only seven of the twenty-three firms — six of which were French branches of American companies — did so. Even these relatively progressive firms said that they had no particular programs or initiatives in place. According to discussions with members of the AVFT as late as October 2002 this has changed very little since the survey was conducted.

The fact that sexual harassment is a penal offense in France carries a powerful symbolic message that sexual harassment is a serious infraction. However, this viewpoint is out of step with common French assumptions about the gravity (or lack thereof) of sexual harassment. According to the French lawyers interviewed, many people do not think sexual harassment is serious enough to warrant prison time, which makes them reluctant to appeal to the sexual harassment penal statute. According to one: "Because you have to choose between penal court or nothing, you chose nothing because penal court is too serious in people's lives. Here, [many forms of sexual harassment are] not considered serious enough to risk being condemned before a penal court." Several French lawyers said they would like to see employers develop internal grievance procedures, as an intermediary solution for dealing with, say, sexist jokes or the display of pornography. However, because employer liability is so limited in France, employers have few incentives to do so.

American and French lawyers interviewed painted contrasting pictures of the legitimacy of sexual harassment law in each country. American respondents expressed enthusiasm to be working in such a thriving area of law: "It's just a fascinating area of law, and the case law is actually evolving right now. It's an exciting area to be in. I enjoy it."

In stark contrast, French respondents emphasized the obstacles facing lawyers in this field in their country. They said that they have no financial incentives for representing sexual harassment plaintiffs or advising employers. Moreover, they said their colleagues denigrate them for representing sexual harassment plaintiffs. A feminist female lawyer affiliated with the AVFT explained: "When you are the AVFT's lawyer, you feel a bit as if you were representing the SPA, la Société Protectrice des Animaux (the Association for the Protection of Animals). Everyone laughs. It's morally trying. I do it because of conviction." Another lawyer who works with the AVFT said: "You rarely hear a lawyer accused of having a particular interest in bad checks because he works on this type of case. On the other hand, a lawyer interested in sexual harassment is said to be personally obsessed with sex." These respondents said that most of their colleagues consider sexual harassment litigation to be a fad or a pretext used by employees who will not take responsibility for bad job performance.

Paradoxically, and unlike the situation in France where labor law is more adequate, American employees may increasingly appeal to Title VII because it is the only legal avenue they can use to contest employment decisions. In the words of one American lawyer: "A lot of people feel harassed, period. It might not be sexual: they don't feel they're treated correctly by their employer, [but] if it's not based on their sex, if it's not based on their race, there's nothing they can do." According to another: "People are losing their jobs, being demoted, and they want to ascribe it to something. So, they'll try and make it sexual harassment, they'll try and make it racial discrimination, they'll try and make it anything they can to see if they have a way out." In stark contrast, according to members of the AVFT, French lawyers are reluctant to invoke the relatively recent sexual harassment laws, preferring instead to use more traditional claims like wrongful discharge. The French lawyers I interviewed said that sexual harassment cases are particularly difficult to win. Moreover, they said that, even when they do prevail, judges often rule according to another statute like wrongful discharge.[31] This effectively stymies the evolution of sexual harassment jurisprudence. Starting in 1999 and 2000, the AVFT found it had greater success in court when its own employees (trained as lawyers), rather than external lawyers, began representing plaintiffs. They attributed their success to their familiarity with the specific women's situations, their feminist analyses, and their willingness to depart from traditional French legal argument.

Cultural Climate

The meaning that sexual harassment has in the United States and in France is shaped by societal attitudes and practices, particularly regarding sexism, attitudes toward money, and the use of formal versus informal negotiation. The interviews suggest that public denunciation of sexism is stronger in the United States than in France. According to one American lawyer, times have changed in the United States, although there are still those who are behind the times: "I think that some men just don't get it yet: that that's not appropriate anymore. That you don't just go and put your arm around somebody." In the words of another American attorney: "[Expectations that women should have to sleep their way to the top are] gone, that's absolutely gone, and no one should have to do that."

While American lawyers readily condemned a wide range of behavior, such as men expecting women to serve tea or calling female workers "girls," as sexist, some of the French lawyers showed little appreciation for the gravity of sexism. A male French lawyer with high status in the French legal establishment explained that, in his mind, sexist comments were simply not comparable to racist or anti-Semitic remarks:

> RESPONSE: In France, we have a fundamental liberty: freedom of expression. As long as one is expressing an opinion, one has the right to express it. I understand that [a sexist joke or comment] can annoy, distress, or shock a young woman, but, after all, one has the right to think this way, right or wrong, as long as the words are not racist [or] anti-Semitic which are forbidden.
> A.S.: Sexist comments are different from racist comments?
> RESPONSE: Ah! For me, it's very different. It is not at all the same cultural notion. [Anti-Semitism] is an ideology that is completely unacceptable as such. And then there is a text, a legal text that reprimands it; the legislature has taken a stand, because of the whole history behind anti-Semitism. I cannot see how one could assimilate a sexist comment with anti-Semitism for the simple reason, it seems to me, that it is natural (*le droit naturel*) that man is made one way and woman another. There was Adam and Eve and they have the right to discuss what is in their eyes sexuality, with all that that implies. In contrast, anti-Semitism, is an ideological approach that goes against nature.

This respondent begins by arguing that sexist comments are protected under legal principles of freedom of expression but undermines his own argument by pointing to the substantial restrictions that French law puts on freedom of expression, as in the case of racism or anti-Semitism. The discussion about anti-Semitism reveals the true issue at stake here: for this respondent, unlike racial difference, sexism, which is conflated with sexuality, is natural and real.

The above view was extreme for my sample, which included many female and feminist French lawyers. Those that condemned sexism, however, said that they were in the minority in modern France. One female French lawyer, affiliated with the AVFT, said that women who denounce sexist behavior, like misogynist jokes or comments, are considered: "in need of a good fuck [*mal-baisées*]. [French people] don't consider such things to be a sexist attack. They consider it very French. It's awful but I don't think I'll see that [change] in my lifetime." Another female French lawyer said: "[Men] think that a woman is always lucky when a guy [notices and comments on her]. That shows that she is considered beautiful, desirable, that you like her, you'd like to do her. That should honor her." In other words, it is not just that French law does not address much sexist behavior and sexual objectification of women. To many French men and women, such behavior is culturally acceptable and even desirable.

The interviews further suggest that different national attitudes and behavior concerning money influenced how French and American respondents approached sexual harassment. Since the passage of the Civil Rights Act of 1991, U.S. courts assign monetary compensation for moral or psychological suffering. In France, this is not the case, and the concept is offensive to many. As the following lawyer explained: "There is a kind of prudery, or reserve, or denial, call it what you will, about money. When we go to court, it's not about a financial request. It's about an attack on public order or on an individual. Therefore, there is this feeling that you have to know how to avoid this individual attack. And the best way might be by not dramatizing a situation, which will make someone more violent." The general uneasiness that French people feel with monetary equivalence for moral suffering is supported by previous research that shows that the French, compared to Americans, do *not* perceive the economic market to be an essentially fair arbiter of human worth and interpersonal disputes.[32] This approach to money, however, does not explain judges' reluctance in applying heavy penal sentences for sexual harassment, nor the fact that so few sexual harassment victims press penal charges. To understand this, the second part of the respondent's comment is key. In saying that sexual harassment victims should be able to avoid or minimize the gravity of what they suffer, this respondent reveals the extent to which sexual harassment is still trivialized in France. This was made strikingly clear in a 1992 French survey, conducted by Ipsos-*Le Point*, which found that 47 percent of female and 45 percent of male respondents did not think it would be sexual harassment if a woman seeking a promotion was asked by her supervisor to go away with him to "discuss it," and 20 percent of female respondents and 24 percent of male respondents did not consider it sexual harassment if a male employer asked a female candidate if she would be ready to undress before him.[33]

Another argument French lawyers gave for their mistrust of far-reaching sexual harassment laws was that they, and French people as a society, preferred informal interpersonal negotiation to law and formal grievance procedures when dealing with social sexual relations. According to a feminist female lawyer: "Sometimes a well-delivered slap in the face of an adversary might have an even greater effect than a court hearing." Plenty of Americans, though none of my respondents, also take this view, often with trivializing and blame-the-victim implications. However, in France this argument is often part of a critique of what is perceived to be the highly formalized nature of social relations in the United States. As one female French lawyer put it: "Everything [in the United States] seems codified. I'm a bit for freedom of desire, its expression. I say to myself, its crazy this notion of codifying social relationships. I need more freedom."

The United States is thus painted as a country in which individual freedom is sacrificed to excessive laws. So-called American excesses, greatly exaggerated by the French media, are thus used to stymie French sexual harassment jurisprudence by trivializing the problems these American laws address and discouraging people and their potential lawyers from filing complaints. According to one penal lawyer who works with the AVFT, anti-American rhetoric even paralyzes French judges: "The judges think first of the excesses in the United States, [which constitute] the pole of repulsion for the French judge. That is, [they reason:] 'See the excesses in the United States?' Therefore, to not fall into the same excesses, they do nothing at all, a type of institutional block and denial." Ironically, in a general desire to resist American influence, French lawyers and judges give the United States an enormous amount of symbolic power by *opposing* so strongly what they perceive to be the American model.[34]

Conclusion

The concept of "sexual harassment" provides a new perspective on behavior that is all too old. Originally articulated in the United States, this term has since been translated across the globe becoming, for instance, *harcèlement sexuel* in France and *seku hara* in Japan. This linguistic evolution is closely linked to legislative changes in the United States and abroad, as laws have been enacted and jurisprudence developed to combat sexual harassment. From a distance, it seems that the same idea and legislation is spreading across the globe. However, closer examination reveals that the concept and law of sexual harassment is actually transformed in its transnational translations.

There are several lessons that can be drawn from the French case that are particularly relevant in the current American context. Some observers, including Supreme Court Justices Thomas and Scalia,[35] have argued that, by holding employers liable for hostile environment sexual harassment, U.S. courts put too much of a burden on employers to control workplace behavior that is already inconsistent with their interests. The French case, however, demonstrates the dangers of the alternative scenario: when employers' liability is seriously limited, the former are unlikely to take any preventive or remedial action that can help victims of sexual harassment. Those who blame the American system of monetary awards for spurring too much litigation (and enriching lawyers) should learn from the French case that, when there are no incentives for lawyers to represent sexual harassment victims, they are less likely to do so. Finally, this study suggests that American ideas about sexual harassment have made an imprint on the rest of the world but not in the way many assume. In the case of France, social actors continue to largely reject, rather than adopt, the American model, or, more accurately, a perceived and distorted image of "American excesses" of litigiousness, Puritanism, and man-hating feminists. In so doing, French actors have actually given the United States huge symbolic influence, while simultaneously contesting its authority.

Notes

This research, and the larger project of which it is a part, benefited from generous support from the National Science Foundation, the French government, the Robert Wood Johnson Foundation, the Department of Sociology at Princeton University, the Council for European Studies, and the Woodrow Wilson Foundation. Support was also provided by the following Princeton University-based research grants: the program in French Studies, the Center of International Studies, the Compton Fund, the Council on Regional Studies, and the Center of Domestic and Comparative Policy Studies. I owe many thanks to the interview respondents for their time and patience and to the Association Européenne Contre les Violences Faites aux Femmes aux Travail (AVFT; European Association Against Violence Toward Women at Work) for their invaluable assistance and support. Thanks to Naim Antaki, Joanne Augustin, Jennifer Boittin, Dana Deaton, Juliette Dellecker, Michelle Coyne, Anne Fonteneau, and Yvette Ho for transcribing the interviews. Thanks to Paul DiMaggio, Ben Guttman, Catharine MacKinnon, John Skrentny, Charles W. Smith, and Viviana Zelizer for comments on previous drafts of this essay.

1. *See* Abigail C. Saguy, *What Is Sexual Harassment? From Capitol Hill to the Sorbonne* (2003).

2. Details about the methodology are available upon request from the author and are also described in *id.*

3. U.S. Merit Systems Protection Board, *Sexual Harassment in the Federal Workforce: Is It a Problem?* (1981); Louis Harris, *Le Harcèlement sexuel: Enquête des français: perceptions, opinions et évaluation du phénomène* (1991).

4. Jane Aeberhard-Hodges, "Sexual Harassment in Employment: Recent Judicial and Arbitral Trends," 135 *International Labour Review* 499 (1996); Robert Husbands, "Sexual Harassment Law in Employment: An International Perspective" 131 *International Labour Review* 535 (1992); Catharine MacKinnon, *Sexual Harassment of Working*

Women: A Case of Sex Discrimination (1979). The female share of employment was 46.3 percent in the second quarter of 2000 in the United States and 45.1 percent in 1999 in France. *See* OECD Quarterly Labour Force Statistics, No. 3, (2000).

5. *See* MacKinnon, *supra* note 4, at 158 for a discussion of the promises and short-comings of these approaches.

6. Title VII of the Civil Rights Act of 1964, 42 U.S.C. § 2000e to 2000e-17 (1994).

7. *Faragher v. City of Boca Raton*, 524 U.S. 775 (1998); *Burlington Industries v. Ellerth*, 524 U.S. 742 (1998).

8. Civil Rights Act of 1991, 42 U.S.C. § 1981a (1994).

9. *See* MacKinnon, *supra* note 4.

10. *Barnes v. Costle*, 561 F.2d 983 (D.C. Cir. 1977).

11. *Ellison v. Brady*, 924 F.2d 872 (9th Cir. 1991).

12. *Robinson v. Jacksonville Shipyards*, 760 F. Supp. 1486 (M.D. Fla. 1991).

13. 92/131/EEC.

14. *Code Pénal* [*C. Pén.*] art. 222–33 (Fr.). "Serious pressure" was added in 1997. *See* Charles Jolibois, "Rapport," 265 *Sénat: Session Ordinaire de 1997–1998*, 32 (1998). This statute was modified to apply to coworkers as well as to professional hierarchical superiors with the passage of Law 2002–73on January 17, 2002 (Journal Officiel, "Loi no. 2002–73 du 17 janvier 2002 de modernisation sociale" 15 *Journal Officiel* 1008 [2002]). For a discussion of why this law was passed and its implications see Saguy, *supra* note 1, "Epilogue: Plus ça change, plus c'est la même chose." To date, only those con-victed of sexual harassment and sexual battery have been put behind bars (for a few months only).

15. Françoise Dekeuwer-Defossez, "Le harcèlement sexuel en droit français: Discrimi-nation ou atteinte à la liberté?" 13 *La Semaine Juridique* 137 (1993).

16. *Code de Travail* [*C. Trav.*] art. L. 122–46 (Fr.).

17. Catherine Le Magueresse, "Sur la nullité des mesures prises à l'encontre d'une salariée victime de harcèlement sexuel," 5 *Droit Social* 437 (1998).

18. *C. Trav.* art. L. 122–47 (Fr.); *C. Trav.* art. L. 122–48 (Fr.).

19. Mirielle Benneytout et al., "Harcèlement sexuel: Une réforme restrictive qui n'est pas sans danger," 599 *Semaine Sociale Lamy* 3 (1992); Margot Felgentrager, "Droit et harcèlement sexuel," 3 *Pratiques Psychologiques* 45 (1996).

20. Abigail C. Saguy, "Employment Discrimination or Sexual Violence? Defining Sex-ual Harassment in American and French Law," 34 *Law and Society Review* 1091 (2000).

21. Journal Officiel, "Seconde Session Ordinaire de 1991–1992," 350 *Journal Officiel* 32 (1992).

22. *See* MacKinnon, *supra* note 4, at 172.

23. I borrow the concept of frame from social movement research. *See* William A. Gamson, *Talking Politics* (1992); David Snow and Robert D. Benford, "Ideology, Frame Resonance and Participant Mobilization" 1 *International Social Movement Research* 197 (1988); Sidney Tarrow, "Mentalities, Political Cultures, and Collective Action Frames: Constructing Meanings Through Action," in *Frontiers in Social Movement The-ory* 174 (Aldon D. Morris and Carol McClurg Mueller eds., 1992). The way social movement theorists use the term is quite different from Goffman's original concept of "frame." *See* Erving Goffman, *Frame Analysis: An Essay on the Organization of Ex-*

perience (1974); Nathalie Heinich, "Pour introduire la cadre-analyse," 535 *Critique* 936 (1991).

24. AVFT, "Proposition d'Amendement de L'AVFT," 10 *Cette violence dont nous ne voulons plus* 59 (1990).

25. *Griggs v. Duke Power Co.*, 401 U.S. 424 (1971). Law 2001–1066, passed on November 16, 2001, introduced the concept of indirect discrimination to French law (Journal Officiel, "Loi no. 2001–1066 du 16 novembre 2001 relative à la lutte contre les discriminations," 267 *Journal Officiel* 18311 [2001]). It is too soon to tell what the concrete effect of this will be on French jurisprudence.

26. Sylvie Cromer, "Histoire d'une loi: La pénalisation du harcèlement sexuel dans le nouveau Code pénal," 1 *Projets féministes* 108 (1992).

27. *See* Dekeuwer-Defossez, *supra* note 15, at 137.

28. *See* AVFT, *De l'abus de pouvoir sexuel: Le harcèlement sexuel au travail* (1990); Abigail C. Saguy, "Sexual Harassment in France and the United States: Activists and Public Figures Defend their Definitions," in *Rethinking Comparative Cultural Sociology: Polities and Repertoires of Evaluation in France and the U.S.* 56 (Michèle Lamont and Laurent Thévenot eds., 2000).

29. *See* Cass Sunstein with Judy Shih, "Damages in Sexual Harassment Case," this volume.

30. Lauren Edelman et al., "Professional Construction of Law: The Inflated Threat of Wrongful Discharge," 26 *Law and Society Review* 47 (1992); Erin Kelly and Frank Dobbin, "Civil Rights Law at Work: Sex Discrimination and the Rise of Maternity Leave Policies," 105 *American Journal of Sociology* 455 (1999).

31. CA Paris, September 18, 1996. SA Frans Maas c./Mme. Ch. L'H, cited in Le Magueresse, *supra* note 17.

32. *See* Michèle Lamont and Laurent Thévenot eds., *Rethinking Comparative Cultural Sociology: Polities and Repertoires of Evaluation in France and the U.S.* (2000); Marie-France Toinet et al., *Le Libéralisme à l'Américaine: L'Etat et le marché* (1989).

33. N = 1,000. *Le Point*, "Médiations," 1010 *Le Point* 63 (1992).

34. Thanks to Eric Oliver for pointing out this irony to me.

35. *Burlington*, 524 U.S. 742, 770.

35

Sexual Harassment in Japan

YUKIKO TSUNODA

The history of Japanese sexual harassment laws is a very short one. Indeed, the *Fukuoka* case,[1] the landmark Japanese court decision in the concept of sexual harassment was introduced to the Japanese legal community and to Japanese society as a whole, was decided in 1992.[2] During the intervening years there have been numerous developments in Japan's sexual harassment law, culminating in inadequate revision to the Equal Employment Opportunity Law which took effect in April 1999.[3]

This essay will give the reader an overview of Japanese sexual harassment law and, to this end, will focus on three points. First, the essay will describe the historical and social context in which the *Fukuoka* case was brought. Next, the essay will describe the impact that the *Fukuoka* case has had on the subsequent development of Japanese sexual harassment law. Finally, the essay will summarize the current state of Japanese sexual harassment law and the steps that still need to be taken.

The Historical and Social Context of the Fukuoka Case

Japanese society traditionally has not recognized the concept of sexual harassment, even as women began to enter the workforce around the turn of the century.[4] For example, notwithstanding the pervasiveness of sexual harassment behaviors in Japanese society and workplaces, the Japanese legal system has traditionally denied relief to the victims of such behaviors.[5]

Things changed little through the 1960s and 1970s.[6] In fact, although there were several cases in those decades involving sexual harassment, the plaintiffs in those cases were the harassers themselves who, after being terminated for raping female employees, sued their former employers for wrongful discharge.[7] Moreover, although those courts generally acknowledged that the female employees had been raped, the courts nonetheless did not acknowledge that their rights had been violated.[8] In short, as late as the 1980s, no lawyers were advocating for the rights of the female employees, who were arguably the true victims.

This state of affairs changed considerably in the mid-1980s when the Japanese women's movement began to focus on the right to sexual autonomy in the workplace.[9] Japanese working women had gradually begun to identify the fundamental obstacles to developing equality in the workplace.[10] Indeed, things had changed such that by 1989 the *Fukuoka* case could not only be brought, but won. Several factors caused this change. First, by the middle of 1980s, groups of women had begun to recognize the injustices in the workplace and to try to correct these injustices. Another factor was the arrival in Japan of the idea, articulated in a pamphlet published in the United States, that change be effected through the legal system.[11] That pamphlet, along with the 1986 U.S. Supreme Court decision in *Meritor Savings Bank v. Vinson*,[12] which several Japanese law journals synopsized,[13] inspired me and my colleagues to formulate a plan to correct workplace injustices and effect change by working within existing laws such as the Japanese Civil Code. The lack of an effective Japanese sexual harassment statute severely reduced any plaintiff's chances of success, and working within the Civil Code required one to prosecute what amounted to a tort claim.[14] Without a sex discrimination law and sexual harassment statute, the claims would have to be brought as tort claims, although because the Japanese Constitution guarantees sex equality, they were torts of sex discrimination. It was in this legal context that the *Fukuoka* case was brought.

The *Fukuoka Case*

The plaintiff was at the time a thirty-one-year-old unmarried woman. The defendants were her immediate supervisor, a chief editor, and the employer, a publishing company. On numerous occasions, both inside and outside her workplace and directly related to her job, the chief editor had spread rumors about her sexual activity, including a rumor that she had had an affair with one of the company's major clients. The chief editor then had stated that her presence might damage the company's good reputation. The plaintiff finally asked her employer's president and chief executive to stop the chief editor's actions. They refused to credit her testimony, however, and so did not take any action against the chief editor. In fact, the executives felt that the problems were personal disputes between the employees that did not concern the employer. The executives then insisted that if the employees could not resolve their problems among themselves, the plaintiff should resign.

Physically and emotionally devastated, the plaintiff left the company. After hearing her story, we decided to take her as a client and to prosecute her claims. One year after leaving her employer, she filed a lawsuit against the defendants. We had three objectives in bringing the *Fukuoka* case. One was to vindicate the rights of the plaintiff and to make the defendants liable for the plaintiff's injuries. The second was to establish sexual harassment as a distinct legal theory within the scope of a tort claim so that it would be easier to bring and win similar cases in the future. The third was to establish the notion of employer liability for sexual harassment in the workplace.

The plaintiff claimed that she was sexually harassed because she was a woman and, therefore, that her constitutionally guaranteed rights had been violated, for the Japanese Constitution prohibits any discrimination based solely on sex.[15] We argued that her case should be considered sexual harassment and that sexual harassment was sex discrimination under the Constitution. To persuade the court, we needed a new concept, because her case might easily have been dismissed as a normal incident in the workplace according to then-existing notions. The plaintiff also relied on the Civil Code's general tort remedies by arguing that the editor had violated two of the plaintiff's constitutionally guaranteed fundamental human rights. One was her right to sexual self-determination.[16] The second was her right to work.[17] The plaintiff's theory, therefore, was that the defendants had violated her rights by sexually harassing her in the workplace, by sexually insulting her, and by forcing her to quit. After a thirty-two-month trial, the court's all-male panel of judges ruled that the chief editor was liable not just for a general tort, but also for the newly created tort of sexual harassment. The court also awarded the plaintiff damages in the amount of 1.65 million yen ($13,095).[18] Just as significant, however, was the fact that the court for the first time rendered an opinion on employer liability, finding that the employer was liable for the editor's sexual harassment and for the unlawful acts of its president and chief executive. The court further stated that employers are responsible for taking the measures required to ensure that their employees' personal rights are not violated. The court then held that the president and the chief executive had neglected to take the measures necessary to maintain a nonhostile work environment and that they had, by compelling the plaintiff to resign, engaged in sexual harassment.[19]

Thus, all three objectives in bringing the *Fukuoka* case were met. Not only were the plaintiff's rights vindicated and sexual harassment established as a distinct legal theory, but the notion of employer liability for sexual harassment in the workplace was also established.

The Impact of the Fukuoka Case

The *Fukuoka* case has changed the Japanese public's attitude toward sexual harassment behaviors. Indeed, it was in the course of reporting the *Fukuoka* case that a popular magazine coined the term *sekuhara* and made it a part of the Japanese lexicon.[20] The usage of the term quickly spread throughout Japanese society. The case itself made headlines throughout Japan. In fact, many publications, both legal and nonlegal, soon began to discuss the issue of sexual harassment. Even before the *Fukuoka* case, the Labor and Economic Department of the Tokyo Municipal Government already had published leaflets giving advice on how to deal with sexual harassment.[21] In 1994, the department set up a committee consisting of a legal scholar, a journalist, and a female lawyer to study how to prevent sexual harassment, and the same year issued a manual for preventing sexual harassment.[22] The manual defines both the quid pro quo and hostile environment forms of sexual harassment, refers to the *Fukuoka* case and the guidelines of the United States Equal Employment Opportunity Commission, and proposes methods by which to prevent sexual harassment for employers, trade unions, and employees.[23] It advises employers to create policies against sexual harassment and grievance procedures.[24] Last, a Tokyo-based bar association has since 1989 maintained a counseling hotline for the victims of sexual harassment, and published a similar guidebook.[25]

Although the public still seems somewhat reluctant to impute liability to the employer and tends to think that sexual harassment is a problem exclusively caused by harassers,[26] the *Fukuoka* case established the concept of employer liability, and so companies have been alerted to the need to take preventive measures in order to avoid lawsuits.[27] Moreover, now that sexual harassment behavior has been identified and become a legal issue, women workers have realized that they have a tool to address the situations that long have silenced them.[28]

As a result of this change in attitude, many women decided to fight against sexual harassment. In several of the larger Japanese cities, women workers created their own unions, because existing unions were mainly organized by male full-time workers, and even unions with many female members generally did not like to address sexual harassment.[29] The existing unions ignored not only sexual harassment issues but also sexual harassment incidents, so women's trade unions and other women's organizations became engines to fight against sexual harassment.[30] Victims also became less hesitant about confronting their harassers and employers. These confrontations often lead to out-of-court settlements, the number of which exploded in the nine years following the *Fukuoka* case.[31] When settlements could not be reached, victims did not hesitate to bring lawsuits against their harassers and employers. In more than nine years following the *Fukuoka* case, there were approximately more than one hundred court cases of sexual harassment nationwide, a remarkable number in a nation like Japan that disfavors civil litigation.[32]

The public, however, is still reluctant to impute liability to employers. In fact, in more than half of the court cases, plaintiffs have sued only the harassers.[33] That is, the victims more often than not have declined to sue their employers. It is extremely difficult under the Japanese social and legal regimes for employees to fight against their employers, especially for those employees who still want to remain with their employers.[34] Under the Japanese legal system, injunctive relief is theoretically possible. However, I have heard of only one injunctive order case in the late 1980s, which was not published. The reason why injunctive relief is rarely sought is that it is very difficult for the victims to take legal actions against the company while they are holding their jobs. In addition, there is still in Japanese society a certain stigma associated with being a civil litigant. Thus, although it has been more than a decade since the *Fukuoka* case, the courts have not fully developed the law of employer liability, for they simply have not had many opportunities to do so.

Moreover, in the few instances in which the courts have addressed employer liability, the courts have declined to issue standards on just what the employer should have done. For example, in 1997 the Tokyo High Court dealt with employer liability in the *Yokohama* case.[35] In that case, the appellant had previously sued the harasser, her immediate supervisor, and the company for which both parties were working. The appellant claimed, inter alia, that the company should be liable for the actions of her harasser.[36]

The court ultimately held that the company was liable for the harasser's activities, finding that he had harassed the appellant while carrying out the company's business. On the other hand, the court denied the appellant's argument that the company committed the tort of not maintaining a proper working environment by not transferring her harasser. The court's reasoning was that the company did not have a sufficient basis for believing that such a transfer was necessary, for it found that the parties offered different stories to the company and that the company could not have been required to transfer the harasser on the basis of such information.

Finally, the court in the *Yokohama* case neglected to articulate the standards that the company should have established for resolving employment-related issues. The predictable result, of course, is that companies have had little incentive to change their internal procedures and corporate cultures. Thus, while it is certainly offensive when a 1997 survey of Japan's companies by the Labor Ministry finds that only 5 percent of the respondents have sexual harassment policies in writing,[37] it is by no means surprising.

The State of the Law Today and the Steps That Are Still Necessary

Shortly after the *Fukuoka* case was filed in 1989, a groundswell of support for including sexual harassment provisions in the Equal Employment Opportunity Law (EEOL) emerged.[38] In 1997, primarily in response to the efforts of dedicated women's groups, employee representatives, and labor law experts, Japan adopted a revision to the EEOL.[39] The revised EEOL requires employers to take dutiful care to prevent sexual harassment, although there are no sanctions for failing to do so.[40] This nonetheless represents substantial progress, because the employer-representative members of the advisory committee to the Labor Minister had traditionally insisted that the availability of a Civil Code-based tort claim was sufficient protection for sexual harassment victims.[41]

Under the revised EEOL, Labor Ministry officials give guidance to those employers who do not take necessary preventive measures against both quid pro quo and hostile environment sexual harassment.[42] As noted previously, there is no penalty for failing to follow such guidance. But the lack of a legal sanction is not in itself the biggest flaw of the revised EEOL, for even if victims are still, as before, forced to look to the Civil Code, a court is likely to be receptive to their claims if the victims can show that their employer has failed to satisfy the guidelines.[43] Rather, the biggest flaw of the revised EEOL is that it limits its definition of the "workplace" to actual business premises and attendance at mandatory functions. This is especially problematic in Japanese society, for many instances of sexual harassment occur at work-related functions where attendance, although not explicitly mandatory, is nonetheless expected.[44] This limitation is especially galling in light of the fact that several court cases have already recognized that sexual harassment can occur outside the workplace and after business hours. For example, in 1998, the Chiba District Court held that the harasser and his company were liable for sexual harassment that occurred in a motel which, if decided under the revised EEOL's definition of the "workplace," would not have been considered to be the workplace.[45] In that case, the plaintiff was invited to join a dinner with her boss, the harasser, and his friend. After the dinner, the boss offered her a ride home, which she accepted. However, her boss instead drove her to a motel and raped her there.

The Japanese government must expand the revised EEOL's definition of the "workplace," and its unwillingness to do so might reflect its lack of understanding of just how indispensable such an expansion is to establish employer liability for sexual harassment that occurs at work and on related occasions.

In addition, there is some question as to whether lawsuits are the appropriate means for sexual harassment victims to recover damages. First, tort law generally limits relief to monetary compensation, and the size of the award is usually very small.[46] Indeed, as noted previously, the damages awarded by the court in the *Fukuoka* case were far less than the actual damages suffered by the victim. Also, plaintiffs in many cases seek only emotional damages, and Japanese courts have traditionally estimated emotional damages done to human dignity lower than damages done to real property.[47] Finally, Japanese civil law does not recognize the concept of punitive damages.[48] In fact, the Supreme Court ruled in 1997 that an award of punitive damages granted by a U.S. court was not enforceable in Japan.[49] This is because Japanese law sees punitive damages as a criminal penalty that does not belong in the realm of civil law.[50] Because employers who lose civil sexual harassment cases are assured of not having to pay punitive damages, it seems likely that many employers will not seriously consider the results of such lawsuits. This in turn gives employers little incentive to take preventive measures.

Nonetheless, lawyers representing victims of sexual harassment are persuading courts to award all damages. This has led to some positive changes. For example, in the *Chiba* case mentioned above, the court awarded the full amount of damages claimed by the plaintiff, which were 3 million yen for emotional damages and 300,000 yen for legal fees. In 1997, the Kumamoto District Court awarded 3 million yen to a sexual harassment victim who had been raped by her harasser, although she had originally asked for 5 million yen for her emotional damages.[51]

Nevertheless, sexual harassment victims have had mixed results in bringing their cases. In fact, there appears to be a common pattern to those cases in which the plaintiffs lost, and that is that the courts in those cases apparently did not feel that the plaintiff was a "real victim."

For example, in the Yokohama District Court in 1995 (the *Yokohama* case),[52] the plaintiff had had her hair and shoulders touched frequently by her immediate supervisor, the defendant. One day before lunch time, when only the two of them were in the office, he forcibly hugged her, kissed her, and touched her breasts, hips, and genital area. She tried to resist him by crossing her arms over her breasts, trying to push away his hands, and saying, "No, no, you might miss your lunch," but he continued to touch her. When he stopped, he said that he felt very satisfied and was pleased that she had not cried out. The next day she told her colleagues about the incident. Although her supervisor apologized to her, he nonetheless denied any wrongdoing, whereupon she reported him to his supervisor. After being orally reprimanded by his supervisor, he retaliated by refusing to assign her work. She felt extremely uncomfortable to be in the same place as the harasser and soon left the company. The court said that because the alleged sexual assault was very similar to criminal behavior, she could have resisted him more strongly, immediately screamed for help, and could easily have escaped through the unlocked door. The court also said that it did not believe her story, because she seemed to have managed the situation very rationally. In her testimony, she said that she had quickly examined her situation and had concluded that she was not sure of successfully escaping from him and was afraid of inciting him to more violence by shouting or crying out. In response to her explanation, the Court said that it surely would be unreasonable and unexpected for a woman in her situation to manage as she had. It concluded that it could not believe her story and ruled in favor of her supervisor.

That court apparently expected her to behave in the way it imagined a "real victim" would behave. The Akita District Court in 1997 relied on similar reasoning to find against a sexual harassment victim.[53] The antiquated concept of a "real victim" is a part of the so-called rape myth — yet the court still believed in this outdated notion. Since then, Japanese women have been acting to defeat these outdated notions of victims of sexual violence. In the *Yokohama* case, on appeal to the Tokyo High Court, the appellant submitted the expert opinion of a feminist counselor for victims of sexual violence that the appellant had acted reasonably when she was sexually harassed by presenting findings about how the victims of sexual violence in the United States act.[54] The High Court then reversed the decision with respect to the unreasonableness of the behavior of the appellant and held that she had been sexually harassed. This decision gave Japanese women hope that judges could change their views on victims of sexual violence. In 1998, the Akita Branch of Sendai High Court reversed the decision of the Akita District Court and stated that there was no simple rule of the "real victim."[55]

Conclusion

Ever since becoming aware of the concept of sexual harassment, Japanese working women have worked studiously to educate people and change society's attitude toward sexual harassment. Anti-sexual-harassment movements led by such women have united many and have helped to create Japan's laws against sexual harassment. Also, in recent years, a movement to recognize victim's rights has emerged in Japan. This movement has encouraged the victims of sexual harassment to speak out and society as a whole to listen to their voices. One result of this movement has been the establishment, in 1997, of the National Campus Sexual Harassment Network by students and employees in universities and colleges throughout Japan. Several universities and colleges have taken the next step toward establishing equality in the workplace and society as a whole by creating anti-sexual-harassment policies and grievance procedures.[56]

After the revised EEOL was enacted, relatively big companies and local governments have created anti-sexual-harassment policies and grievance procedures; yet many women work in small companies without any such policies and under very poor and unstable conditions. Therefore, the progress mentioned in this essay benefits them little. In addition to this, sexual harassment lawsuits could not effectively target the root cause of the problem: sex discrimination in the workplace and a society as a whole. By taking place within Civil Code, the effect of our sexual harassment litigation is limited, making even more necessary the sex discrimination law that we have long wanted.

Notes

1. The accepted format for citing sexual harassment case authority in Japan does not reference the names of the parties, in order to protect the identities of plaintiffs. Instead, citations generally reference the name of the city in which the court hearing the case was located. The *Fukuoka* case was heard in the Fukuoka District Court in Fukuoka City, hence its name.

2. *See* Judgment of April 16, 1992, Fukuoka Chiho Saibansho, Heisei Gannen (1989) (Wa) No. 1872, Songai Baisho Seikyu Jiken (Japan), 1426 HANJI 49. For a detailed discussion of this decision, see Hiroko Hayashi, "Sexual Harassment in the Workplace and Equal Employment Legislation," 69 *St. John's Law Review* 37 (1995). Hayashi also submitted a legal opinion in the *Fukuoka* case as an expert witness for the plaintiff.

3. *See* Danjo Koyo Kikai Kinto Ho, Law No. 45 of 1985. Japan originally enacted this law in 1985 in order to satisfy the requirements of the United Nations Convention on the Elimination of All Forms of Discrimination Against Women. Since its enactment, it has been widely criticized by working women and labor scholars for the inadequate remedies available under it. Moreover, this law, unlike Title VII of the Civil Rights Acts of 1964 in the United States, addresses only women workers, and so it is not a true sex discrimination law.

4. *See* Michiko Nakajima, "In Sekusharuharasumento No Houritsumondai [Legal Questions on Sexual Harassment]," 956 *Jurisuto* 12, 17 (1990); *see also* Wakizo Hosoi, *Joko Aishi [A Tragic History of Women Factory Workers]* 258–268 (1988). The textile industry was one of the prominent industries during Japan's period of industrialization, and was in large part staffed by women workers. This book chronicles the horrible working conditions of women in these factories in 1920s.

5. *See* Hosoi, *supra* note 4, at 258–68.

6. *See* Nakajima, *supra* note 4, at 15–16.

7. The plaintiffs in those cases generally lost. For example, in the *Nagano Dentetsu* case of 1970, the Nagano District Court ruled that the employer's discharge of the plaintiff was legal. *See* Judgement of March 24, 1970, Nagano Chiho Saibansho, Showa Yonjuunen (1965) (Wa) No.177. Kaiko Muko Kakunin Jiken (Japan) 600 HANJI 111. That court reasoned that the plaintiff's conduct toward a female employee severely damaged the defendant, Nagano Dentetsu, its good reputation, and caused financial harm to the defendant. *See id.*

8. *See, e.g.,* Judgment of March, 24, 1970, Nagano Chiho Saibansho, Showa Yonjuunen (1965) (Wa) No. 177. Kaiko Muko Kakunin Jiken (Japan) 600 HANJI 111; *see also* Michiko Nakajima, "Josei no Hatarakukenri to Sekusharuharasumento [Women's Rights To Work and Sexual Harassment]," *in Onna 6500 nin no Shogen [6500 Women's Testimonies]* 170 (1991) at 15–16.

9. *See* Nakajima, supra note 8, at 170. In the mid-1980s women workers and activists were demanding that the Japanese government issue a sex discrimination law, when the United Nations asked Japan to ratify the Convention on the Elimination of All Forms of Discrimination Against Women. After the government issued the original EEOL, which was far from a sex discrimination law, many women felt that they had failed. Some of them sought a new agenda that would help to eradicate sex discrimination in the workplace. They started to work with groups, such as a rape crisis center, that were dealing with sexual autonomy and found that there was a link between sex discrimination in the workplace and sexual autonomy in women's lives.

10. *See* Masako Oowaki, et al., Josho in Hataraku Onnatachi no Saiban [Epilogue to Court Cases of Working Women] (1996).

11. The original title of this pamphlet was *Stopping Sexual Harassment: A Handbook* published by the Project for Education and Research in Detroit in 1980, and it advocates effecting change through the United States Title VII of the Civil Rights Act of 1964. Although Japanese law does not have an analogue to Title VII, a women's group called Hatarakukoto To Sei Sabetsu Wo Kangaeru Santama No Kai [Considering Working and Sex Discrimination] nonetheless translated it into Japanese and disseminated it through women's groups nationwide in 1988. This group later conducted the first nationwide research on sexual harassment in 1989. The findings were published in 1991 and submitted to the Fukuoka District Court as a supporting document for the plaintiff of the first case. It helped the judges to understand that sexual harassment was a problem that was faced not only by the plaintiff but also by many Japanese working women.

12. 477 U.S. 57 (1986).

13. *See* Akira Okuyama, "Amerika ni Miru Rodokankyo to Seisabetsu-Seiteki Iyagarase (Sexual Harassment) to Kominkenho dai Nanahen (Title VII) [Working Environment

and Sex Discrimination in the U.S. — Sexual Harassment and Title VII]," 523 *Hanta* 18 (1984); Akira Okuyama, "Amerika no Hataraku Josei to Seitekiiyagarase (Sexual Harassment) [Working Women and Sexual Harassment in America]," 23 *Seijyo Hogaku* 1 (1987); Taisuke Kamata, "Seiteki Iyagarase Koui to Kominkenho Dai Nanahen-Bei Saikosai *Vinson* Hanketsu no Igi [Sexual Harassment and Title VII: The Importance of the *Vinson* Decision in the U.S. Supreme Court]," 75 *Hogaku Kyoshitsu* 87 (1986).

14. *See* Minpo [Civil Code], arts. 709, 715. Article 709 provides that any person who intentionally or with fault infringes upon another person's rights shall be liable for damages. Article 715 provides, among other things, that a person who employs another person to carry out an undertaking is liable for damages done to a third person by the employee in the course of the undertaking.

15. Article 14 of the Japanese Constitution mandates equal treatment under the law for all people and prohibits discrimination in political, economic, or social relations that is based on race, creed, sex, social status, or family origin.

16. Article 13 of the Japanese Constitution provides that all of the people shall be respected as individuals and that the supreme consideration in legislation and in other governmental affairs is the preservation of their right to life, liberty, and the pursuit of happiness, to the extent that such preservation does not interfere with the public welfare. We argued that the right to sexual self-determination should be included in Article 13.

17. Under Article 27 of the Japanese Constitution, all people have the right and the obligation to work.

18. The plaintiff claimed 3 million yen for her emotional damages and 670,000 yen for legal costs, while the court awarded the plaintiff 1.5 million yen for her emotional damages and 150,000 yen for her legal costs. The court awarded only half of the claimed damages because it held that the plaintiff was partly responsible for being harassed by acting very aggressively and assertively against the chief editor and by herself spreading at least one of the rumors. The court also awarded legal costs in accordance with the court's own internal rules regarding such awards, which are usually 10 percent of the awarded damages.

19. The court, however, did not articulate the form that appropriate measures should be taken, for it noted that the company resolved the problems between the plaintiff and the chief editor in an inadequate way and stated the basic principle that employers should not violate employees' personal rights. Thus, legal scholars criticized the court's decision as ambiguous.

20. *Seku* is a contraction of the Japanese pronunciation of "sexual," and *hara* is the same with respect to "harassment." This is a common way to create a new Japanese term from English.

21. *See* Masaomi Kaneko, "Rodogyosei No Genba Kara Mita Honsaiban Hanketsu [The Fukuoka Case and Its Judgment from the Viewpoint of Labor Administration]," in *Shokuba No "Joshiki" Ga Kawaru [The "Common Sense" of the Workplace Is Changing]* 125, 128–132 (Shokuba Deno Seiteki Iyagarase To Tatakau Saiban O Shiensurukai ed., 1992). In this article, Kaneko noted that the Labor and Economic Department of the Tokyo Municipal Government started a consulting service for workers with respect to sexual harassment in 1989. In addition, the Tokyo Municipal Government's Committee on Women's Issues made recommendations to prevent sexual harassment. In March

1992, shortly before the *Fukuoka* case decision, the assembly of the Tokyo Municipal Government discussed the necessity of issuing guidelines to prevent sexual harassment. According to Kaneko, the *Fukuoka* case resulted in these activities.

22. *Sekusharu Harasumento Boshi No Tameni [How to Prevent Sexual Harassment]* (Tokyoto Rodo Keizaikyoku ed., 1994).

23. *See id.* at 17–45.

24. *See id.* at 17–36.

25. *Sekusharu Harasumento Houritsu Sodan Guidebook [A Guidebook to Legal Consulting on Sexual Harassment]* (Daini Tokyo Bengoshikai ed., 1994).

26. *See* Akira Okuyama, "Zaigai Nihon Kigyo to Sekusharu Harasumento Mondai [Japanese Companies in Overseas and Sexual Harassment]," 1097 *Jurisuto* 56, 60 and n.14. Okuyama points out that in Japan, people generally still think of sexual harassment in the workplace as a personal problem between male and female workers and, therefore, that solely the harasser should be responsible for it. In note 14, Okuyama cites a poll jointly conducted by *Asahishinbun* (a major Japanese newspaper) and Harris in the U.S. about sexual harassment in which 70 percent of Japanese respondents considered sexual harassment as a personal problem and only 18 percent of the Japanese respondents considered it as a problem that should be treated by companies.

27. *See Sekusharu Harasumento [Sexual Harassment]* (Nikkeiren Kohobu ed., 1990). The Nikkeiren is a large organization to which major Japanese companies have membership. This book discusses sexual harassment law in the United States, how to create better understanding regarding sexual harassment, and also includes the anti-sexual-harassment policies of Japanese companies which have U.S. parent companies such as AT&T, Xerox, and Baxter.

See also Sekuhara Shokku [Sexual Harassment Shock] (Kyoei Kasai Kaijyo Hoken Sogo Kaisha ed., 1991). Kyoei Kasai Kaijyo Hoken Sogo Kaisha is an insurance company which offered training on how to manage sexual harassment in the workplace, mainly to Japanese companies in the United States. This book gave information about sexual harassment to companies in Japan from legal and risk management perspectives.

28. *See Hashirinagara Kangaeta Sannen, in Shokuba No "Joshiki" Ga Kawaru [The "Common Sense" of the Workplace Is Changing]* 143, 143–51 (Shokuba Deno Seiteki Iyagarase To Tatakau Saiban Wo Shiensurukai ed., 1992); *see also* Kanagawa Kenritsu Josei Senta [Women's Center in Kanagawa Prefecture], *Sekusharu Harasumento Chosa Kenkyu Hokokusho [The Report on Study and Research on Sexual Harassment]* 1–11 (1998).

29. According to the *Rodo Kumiai Kihon Chosa* [The Basic Research on Labor Unions] in 1993 conducted by the Labor Ministry, the percentage of female unionized workers was 17.6 percent, whereas that of male unionized workers was 28.1 percent. Female workers concentrated in small companies and retailers or other service sectors in which workers have not traditionally been well unionized. In addition, 30 percent of female workers were part-time workers, a category that is traditionally even less unionized than full-time workers. *See* Maki Oomori, *Gendai Nihon No Josei Rodo [Women Labor in Contemporary Japan]* 104–26 (1990). Oomori discussed the relationship between female workers and labor unions and notes that since female workers have traditionally comprised only a very small percentage of union membership—both in general

membership and leadership positions — female workers have been reluctant to join these organizations. Oomori also writes that traditional labor unions composed largely of male workers should reexamine their activities and strive to include women in their agendas.

30. For example, the supporting groups for the *Fukuoka* case included women's trade unions from areas other than Fukuoka, such as the Onna No Yunion (Women's Union) in Yokohama, Kanagawa prefecture. That union is not especially large but is fairly powerful for, in addition to its telephone hotline counseling services, it successfully negotiated sexual harassment and other cases for employees with their employers.

31. The exact number of the out-of-court settlements is uncertain because, to the best of my knowledge, no one keeps such statistics. Nonetheless, according to my personal conversations with attorneys who handle sexual harassment matters, many cases are settled in this way.

32. *See* Hideo Mizutani, "Nihon Ni Okeru Sekusharu Harasumento no Genjo To Doko [The Present Issue of Sexual Harassment and Trend of Courts Decisions on Sexual Harassment in Japan]," 51.5 *Houritsu no Hiroba* 8, 10 (1998).

33. *See id.* Mizutani reviewed twenty-three Japanese court decisions from 1990 to 1997. The plaintiffs sued both the harassers and their employers in only ten of those cases, and of these ten plaintiffs, only two remained with their companies after they filed their cases.

34. From my experience as a practitioner, one of the difficult decisions facing a plaintiff contemplating filing a sexual harassment case is whether to sue her employer. This is because a plaintiff generally desires to avoid being ostracized within her company, so in cases where the plaintiff needs employee colleagues to appear before the court as witnesses, the plaintiff is generally hesitant to sue her employer along with the actual harasser.

35. *See* Judgment of November 20, 1997, Tokyo Koto Saibansho, Heisei Nananen (Ne) No. 7414, Songai Baisho Seikyu Jiken (Japan), 728 Rohan 12. The appellant, who was the plaintiff in the trial court and who filed immediately after the rendering of the *Fukuoka* case, appealed from the Yokohama District Court.

36. *See id.*

37. *See* Shokuba Ni Okeru Sexual Harassment Ni Kansuru Chosa Kenkyukai [Research and Study Advisory Committee of the Ministry of Labor], *Shokuba Ni Okeru Sexual Harassment Ni Kansuru Chosa Kenkyukai Hokoku [Research and Study on Sexual Harassment in the Workplace]* (1997). The purpose of the committee's research was to formulate guidelines for the prevention of sexual harassment and include these in the next revision of the Equal Employment Opportunity Law.

38. For example, the Committee on Women's Rights in the Japan Federation of Bar Associations examined the Equal Employment Opportunity Law shortly after its enactment and rendered its comments in March 1991. (In the early 1990s, the Japan Federation of Bar Associations recommended that the Labor Ministry amend the EEOL.) *See Danjo Koyo Kikai Kintoho No Sekogo No Minaoshi Ni Kansuru Ikensho [Recommendations on Reexamination on the Equal Employment Opportunity Law After Its Enactment]* (Nihon Bengoshi Rengoukai ed., 1991).

39. *See* Danjo Koyo Kinto Ho (Equal Employment Opportunity Law), Law No. 92 of 1997 [hereinafter Revised EEOL].

40. Article 21 of the Revised EEOL provides that employers must take dutiful care to protect women workers from sexual conduct which may disadvantage them in labor conditions or may damage their working environment. It also requires the Labor Ministry to issue guidelines for said prevention. Nonetheless, although the Revised EEOL defines and proscribes both quid pro quo and hostile environment sexual harassment, it, in a crucial oversight, does not define the term "sexual harassment" itself.

41. *See* Working Group of the Advisory Committee to the Minister of Labor, Fujin Shounen Mondai Shingikai Fujinbukai Ni Okeru Shingijokyo Ni Tsuite [Report Submitted by a Working Group on Women's Issues to the Committee on Women and Minors] (July 16, 1996).

42. *See* Revised EEOL, art. 25.

43. To date, no court has heard this issue because the Revised EEOL became effective in April 1999. Nonetheless, when the author discussed the possibility of filing a lawsuit based on Article 21 of the Revised EEOL as a tort claim with Professor Mutsuko Asakura and Michiko Nakajima, a lawyer who specializes in the issues of women workers, we agreed that plaintiffs will have a better chance of success if they show that their employers have failed to meet the guidelines promulgated by the labor ministry.

44. *See* Masaomi Kaneko, "Jichitaishokuba to Sekusharu Harasumento [Sexual Harassment in the Workplace of Local Governments]," 51.5 *Horitsu no Hiroba* 27, 34–35 (1998). Kaneko notes that sexual harassment situations most commonly occur at after-hours drinking events where business people negotiate and network and where attendance by female support staff employees is expected, if not mandatory. This way of conducting business is in fact deeply rooted in the traditions of Japanese business society.

45. *See* Judgment of March 26, 1998, Chiba Chiho Saibansho, Heisei Hachinen (Wa) No. 1057, Songai Baisho Seikyu Jiken (Japan) (unpublished decision).

46. *See* Mizutani, *supra* note 32, at 16.

47. *See* Yasuhiro Hashimoto, 1.3002 *Saiban Ni Miru Kingakusantei Jireisyu* [*Court Decisions on Estimating Money*] (1988). Hashimoto analyzed awards for emotional damages and found that the upper end for such awards was approximately 1.6 million yen, while the vast majority were between 50,000 yen and 500,000 yen.

48. *See* Judgment of July 11, 1997, Saiko Saibansho, Heisei Gonen (o) No. 1762, Shikko Hanketsu Seikyu Jiken (Japan) 90 HANJI 1624.

49. *See id.*

50. *See id.*

51. *See* Judgment of June 25, 1997, Kumamoto Chiho Saibansho, Heisei Hachinen (Wa) No. 1178, Songai Baisho Seikyu Jiken (Japan), 1638 HANJI 135. Judgment of May 24, 1999, Sendai District Court, Heisei Jyunen (1998) (wa) No. 333, Songaibaisho Jiken (Japan), 1013 HANTA 182. It awarded the plaintiff 7.5 million yen and this case was appealed by the both parties and Sendai High Court increased this amount to 9 million yen.

52. *See* Judgment of March 24, 1995, Yokohama Chiho Saibansho, Heisei Yonen (Wa) No. 2024, Songai Baisho Seikyu Jiken (Japan) 670 ROHAN 20. The appellate court decision for this case is Judgment of November 20, 1997, Tokyo Koto Saibansho, Heisei Nananen (Ne) No. 7414, Songai Baisho Seikyu Jiken (Japan), 728 Rohan 12, cited *supra* note 35.

53. *See* Judgment of January 28, 1997, Akita Chiho Saibansho, Heisei Gonen (Wa) No. 516, Songai Baisho Seikyu Jiken (Japan), 1629 HANJI 121.

54. *See* Judgment of November 20, 1997.

55. Judgment of December 10, 1998, Akita Branch of Sendai High Court, Heisei Kyunen (1997) (Ne) No. 21, Songaibaisho Jiken (Japan), 1681 HANJI 112. It awarded the appellant (plaintiff) 1.8 million yen.

56. Those policies and grievance procedures have encouraged victims to take action against sexual harassment. As a result, harassers—mostly faculty members—have been reprimanded. When the internal mechanism fails to resolve the problem, a victim or harasser brings a lawsuit. Court cases of campus sexual harassment have increased recently. The media usually report them; therefore, the public has been informed of and educated about this issue.

36

The Modesty of Mrs. Bajaj
India's Problematic Route
to Sexual Harassment Law

MARTHA C. NUSSBAUM

Modesty "Outraged"

On July 18, 1988, Mrs. Rupan Deol Bajaj, Special Secretary for Finance in the Indian Administrative Service, Punjab cadre, went with her husband, also a senior IAS officer, to an official dinner party at the home of their colleague Shri S. L. Kapur, the Commissioner of Finance.[1] Among the guests was Mr. Kanwar Pal Singh Gill, Punjab's Chief of Police, whom many regard as a national hero for his leading role in crushing the Sikh separatist insurgency.[2] The party took place on a lawn behind the house. According to Indian middle-class tradition, the women (called "ladies" by the Court) were sitting apart from the men in a semicircle, and the men faced them in another semicircle.

Around 10:00 p.m., Mr. Gill crossed over to the women's side, taking a vacant chair about five seats away from Mrs. Bajaj, who was talking to two other women. As Mrs. Bajaj later described the incident in her police report:

> After about 10 minutes Shri K. P. S. Gill got up from his seat and came and stood directly in front of me, standing straight but so close that his legs were about four inches from my knees. He made an action with the crook of his finger asking me to stand and said, "You get up. You come along with me." I strongly objected to his behavior and told him, "Mr. Gill. How dare you! You are behaving in an obnoxious manner, go away from here." Whereupon he

repeated his words like a command and said, "You get up! Get up immediately and come along with me." I looked to the other ladies, all the ladies looked shocked and speechless. I felt apprehensive and frightened, as he had blocked my way and I could not get up from my chair without my body touching his body. I then immediately drew my chair back about a foot and half and quickly got up and turned to get out of the circle through the space between mine and Mrs. Biljlani's chair. Whereupon he slapped me on the posterior. This was done in the full presence of the ladies, and guests.[3]

Mrs. Bajaj filed a complaint alleging violations of two criminal statutes that make it a crime to "outrage" the "modesty of a woman." The investigation was slow and sluggish. By November 1988, the police were on the verge of dropping the case as "untraced" when Mr. Bajaj filed a complaint for the same offenses in the Court of the Chief Judicial Magistrate, alleging that Mr. Gill's rank in the Police Department had prevented a "fair and impartial" investigation. The Chief Judicial Magistrate asked for a report from the police. At this point, Mr. Gill filed a petition with the High Court of Punjab and Harayana to quash the complaints. Ruling in his favor, the High Court opined that the entire story told by the Bajaj couple was implausible. It would be "both unnatural and unconscionable" for a man of Mr. Gill's reputation to behave in such a manner at a dinner party at the "residential house of Financial Commissioner," an excursion into fact-finding that was later termed a "flagrant" legal error by the Supreme Court of India.[4]

The Bajaj couple filed two separate appeals to the Supreme Court. After a seven-year delay, the cases were heard in 1996. The Bajaj side was argued by Mrs. Indira Jaisingh, one of India's leading feminist lawyers and a senior advocate of the Indian Supreme Court. After a lengthy discussion of the incident and the law regarding modesty, the Court overruled the regional High Court and directed the Chief Judicial Magistrate of Chandigarh to bring the case to trial. The trial was finally held, and on August 6, 1996, Gill was convicted. He appealed, and on January 6, 1998, almost ten years after the party, Mrs. Bajaj finally won her now-celebrated case. In a packed courtroom, Judge Amar Dutt of the District and Sessions Court of Chandigarh announced, "The petition is dismissed." Gill was to pay 20,000 rupees as compensation to Mrs. Bajaj in lieu of imprisonment, and was also to pay 50,000 rupees as legal costs.[5] The judge also ordered Mr. Gill "to abstain from consuming intoxicants in public parties" during a three-year period of probationary supervision. Mrs. Bajaj was not in town to be interviewed, since she was caring for her ailing mother in Bombay. Mr. Bajaj, however, welcomed the verdict, stating, "We will not accept a single penny from the accused. We were not contesting this case for monetary compensation, but for honour."[6]

So ends a landmark victory for Indian feminists. Victory it is, but victory of a peculiar and troubling character. It called upon a Victorian law to win a remarkably Victorian case, thus enshrining in precedent the image of the working woman as married, modest, surrounded by her stalwart husband and a circle of proper "ladies."

The *Bajaj* case reveals tensions between older norms of modesty and more recent norms of women's equality that are not peculiar to India. In nations where the older norms are recognized in law, feminists are confronted with a dilemma: should they take these avenues, with the possibility that they will win some real victories for women, indirectly advancing women's equality by raising public consciousness about issues such as sexual harassment? Or should they shun them, judging that these are the wrong norms through which to move toward full legal and social equality for women? Such questions about images of gender have repeatedly been confronted by Indian feminists.[7] *Bajaj* suggests, I shall argue, that the former, pragmatic course is dangerous, since it divides women by caste, class, occupation, and marital status, ultimately strengthening norms of proper female conduct that are subversive of women's equality.

India: Legal Structure and Women's Situation

India's Constitution, closely modeled on that of the United States, contains an elaborate set of equality and nondiscrimination provisions. [8] Among these "Fundamental Rights" is sex equality: article 15 of the Constitution prohibits discrimination on the basis of "religion, race, caste, sex, place of birth or any of them,"[9] adding that this shall not prevent the state "from making any special provision for women and children,"[10] as it may also do for the lower castes. Other provisions pertinent to sex equality include article 14, which guarantees to all citizens "equality before the law" and "the equal protection of the laws";[11] article 16, which guarantees equality of opportunity for all citizens in matters of public employment;[12] article 21, which states that no person "shall be deprived of his life or personal liberty except according to procedure established by law";[13] and article 23, which prohibits "traffic in human beings . . . and other similar forms of forced labor."[14] These provisions, like other legal changes relating to women, were hotly debated at the time of independence, and represent a victory by Prime Minister Jawaharlal Nehru and his law minister Ambedkar (a lower-caste man who was a staunch advocate of women's rights) over many reactionary forces.[15]

The Constitution is a more woman-friendly document than that of the United States in several respects, especially because of its explicit affirmation of sex equality, its explicit statement that nondiscrimination does not preclude affirmative action, and its attention to problems of trafficking and forced labor. In constitutional debates the framers frequently linked the situation of women with that of the lower castes; it was clearly their intention to strike a decisive blow against both types of hierarchy.

India's legal system is in some respects similar to that of the United States, combining a basically common-law tradition with the constraints of a written constitution. The Indian Supreme Court, like ours, is the ultimate interpreter of the fundamental rights. Its role in this regard is somewhat contested, and there has been a struggle between the legislature and the Court over the procedures for amendment or modification of fundamental rights. But the current situation is that the legislature may not modify any aspect of the Constitution that alters its "basic features"; the Court is understood to be the arbiter of what those features are.[16] In interpreting fundamental rights, the Court frequently uses U.S. constitutional cases as precedents. For example, most U.S. privacy jurisprudence invoking substantive due process has been incorporated into Indian constitutional law through interpretations of article 21 that cite as precedents cases such as *Griswold* and *Roe*.[17]

There is, however, one tremendous legal difference between the systems of India and the United States. India has a uniform constitutional tradition and a uniform code of criminal law; but it has no uniform code of civil law (even within each region). With the exception of commercial law, which was uniformly codified for the nation as a whole by the British and has remained so, civil law remains the province of the various religious systems of law: Hindu, Muslim, Parsi, and Christian. There are some individual secular laws of property, marriage, and divorce, but they do not form a system, and it is difficult for individuals to avail themselves of them: ancestral property is stuck in the religious legal system of one's birth and cannot be transferred to a different system. Cases involving religious law may be appealed in secular courts, but lines of authority are very unclear.[18]

At the time of independence there was much debate about the systems of personal law. Many favored the creation of a uniform civil code. Many feminists continued to support this goal until very recently, since this seemed the only way to bring civil law into line with the constitutional norm of sex equality. A uniform code also found strong support in all religious subgroups; many liberal Muslims wrote in its favor. Today, however, the (currently dominant) BJP (Bharatiya Janata Party, the leading Hindu fundamentalist party) has made a uniform civil code one of its central campaign points, in a way that clearly links this goal with Hindu domination. Many leading Indian feminists therefore feel it important to dissociate themselves from the tactics of the BJP and to support the continued autonomy of Islamic law.[19] Even a recent Law Minister of the BJP, Arun Jaitley, now states that he favors internal reform of each of the personal codes, rather than the divisive goal of a uniform code.[20]

Because the plurality of civil systems makes progress on sex equality very difficult and laborious, women who are treated unfairly within one of the religious systems of law frequently seek help from the criminal system, which is uniform and secular, and can therefore be administered consistently with the Constitution.[21] This is why sexual harassment currently seems best addressed through the criminal law which contains a lot of material left over from the days of British rule.

I now turn briefly from law to economics, in order to set the situation of India's working women in context. India is on the whole an extremely poor nation, ranking 138th out of the 175 nations of the world on the Human Development Index of the 1997 *Human Development Report* of the United Nations Development Program, a measure that aggregates longevity, education, and income.[22] The average life expectancy at birth is 61.3[23] (as opposed to nearly eighty in the United States, Canada, Japan, and most of Europe),[24] and infant mortality is high, at 74 per 1,000 live births (although this represents a substantial decline from 165 in 1960).[25] Women do even worse than men in basic nutrition and health. It is generally believed that in nations where women and men have roughly equal basic nutrition and health care, women live slightly longer than men, with the result that the sex ratio in Europe and North America is roughly 105 women to 100 men, and in Sub-Saharan Africa (where women are major agricultural producers) 102.2:100.[26] In India, however, the sex ratio has not been even 1:1 at any time since measurements began in the early twentieth century.[27] From a high of 97 women to 100 men in 1901, the ratio dropped steadily, reaching a low of around 93:100 in 1971; after a slight rise, it has declined again even further, reaching 85:100 in 2000.[28] Experts in health and nutrition generally attribute much of this uneven ratio to differences in the nutrition of boys and girls and to unequal health care, rather than to active infanticide. But the recent availability of sex-selective abortion has clearly made things worse: counts in some regions show a sex ratio as low as 75:200. Opportunities for survival and basic health in India are in general lower than those in the developed world, but women clearly have faced unequal obstacles.

In education, the male-female gap is even more striking. In 1991, adult literacy rates for women in India were as low as 39 percent, as against 64 percent for men. (In China, the figures are 68 percent for women and 87 percent for men.)[29] While statistics are hard to interpret, since local governments tend to be boastful and since it is hard to establish a clear measure of literacy, what is unambiguously clear is that India has done very poorly in basic education across the board and even worse in basic education for women. Nor does this seem to be a necessary or unbreakable pattern, since some otherwise poor regions have done extremely well. Kerala has an adult literacy rate of 90 percent and near-universal literacy among adolescent boys and girls.[30] This remarkable record is the outcome of more than a hundred years of concerted public action,[31] involving both the state and the general public. But Kerala is an exception to the general situation. Moreover, many poor families depend on the labor of their children, including housework performed by girls. Child labor is frequently crucial to survival in families where the mother performs long days of manual labor. This pattern makes it even more difficult for women to learn skills that would equip them for nonmanual work.

An overwhelming majority (91.7 percent) of India's workers are employed in the informal sector, meaning that they do agricultural labor or craft labor, or work in businesses that employ fewer than twenty-five workers and thus are not regulated by labor unions. Within that 91.7 percent, 60 percent are women.[32] Women thus make a very significant contribution to India's economy, but in ways that are very hard for law and government to regulate. These figures show us that even if Mrs. Bajaj's case offered a good solution to problems of sexual harassment, it would be extremely difficult to enforce. But we can also see from these figures how uncharacteristic Mrs. Bajaj's situation is. She is not a wealthy woman, but she is a solidly middle-class woman, literate, and indeed highly skilled, who has advanced to a high rank in a government job (and government jobs are covered by special guarantees of equality of opportunity under article 16 of the Constitution). Her class, her marital status, her social set, the terms of her employment (in an office) — all these things define her as among the "ladies," as the Court so often called them. (Indeed, court documents frequently referred to the dinner party as a "gathering comprising the elite of the society,"[33] and linked norms of modesty and purity to that observation.) We may wonder from the start, then, how useful her victory is likely to prove to lower-caste women, women performing manual labor, or unmarried or divorced women.

How prevalent is sexual harassment in India? We have no reliable data relating to the vast majority of working women, although anecdotal evidence suggests that sexual harassment by employers is a pervasive problem, woven into the fabric of almost all laboring women's lives. A recent survey in Delhi conducted by the feminist group Sakshi reports that 60 percent of women surveyed (apparently mostly in white-collar jobs) have suffered sexual harassment, as have 55 percent of female students. Sexual harassment was defined to include "non-verbal overt sexual conduct" (54 percent of cases) and "uninvited sexual remarks" (39 percent of cases).[34] The survey reports that management usually overlooked complaints of harassment; when women did complain their morals were questioned and their complaints were derided. A recent survey in Delhi University reported that over 90 percent of female students experienced sexual harassment on campus, although this survey defined harassment very broadly to include offensive speech in the street as well as sexual coercion by teachers or fellow students.[35] We can conclude that we know very little about the incidence of sexual harassment in India, but there are good reasons to believe that it is a very serious problem.

One further point must be introduced before approaching the cases. The law in India is not the law in America. American feminists characteristically look to law for improvements in their situation, and we are right to do so, because the legal system is powerful and respected, laws are generally obeyed, and courts are significant agents of social change. All this is somewhat less true in India. India's Constitution is an admirable document, and its courts are frequently valuable agents of social progress. Yet India is a relatively anarchic nation, where law is not uniformly obeyed, and where many admirable legal guarantees have little chance of even minimal enforcement. When cases do get to court, the legal system is highly inefficient, with huge delays of a generally Dickensian character, as we see from the ten-year wait endured by Mr. and Mrs. Bajaj. Because law does not work well and because law is generally not enforced, law is considered a relatively low-grade profession to enter, by comparison with economics, business, and technology. All this colors the attitudes of feminists toward the very project of seeking remedies through law.

Harassment and Sex Equality: Halting Legal Progress

During the ten years that the *Bajaj* case wound its way through the judicial system, the law of sex equality in India was not standing still. A major sexual harassment case was decided in August 1997, after the Supreme Court's decision in *Bajaj*, though before the trial and sentencing of Mr. Gill. *Vishaka v. Rajasthan*[36] was brought by petition to the Supreme Court[37] by a coalition of women's groups and NGOs after an alleged brutal gang rape of a social worker in a village in Rajasthan. (This case was the subject of a separate criminal action, and it played no further role in the petition.) The petitioners argued that they and other working women were unsafe and unprotected from harassment in the workplace because of the failure of both employers and the legal system to address this problem. They argued that the sexual harassment of women in the workplace violated the fundamental constitutional rights of both gender equality and "life and liberty" (under articles 14, 15, and 21 of the

Constitution). They also argued that these violations entailed violations of rights to "practice any occupation, trade, or business" guaranteed under article 19. The petitioners made repeated reference to the Convention on the Elimination of All Forms of Discrimination Against Women (CEDAW),[38] which has been ratified by India, arguing that the definitions of gender equality in this document "must be read into these provisions to enlarge the meaning and content thereof, to promote the object of the constitutional guarantee."[39] They argued that this way of understanding the binding force of CEDAW is entailed by article 51c of the Constitution, which states that "[t]he State shall endeavour to . . . foster respect for international law and treaty obligations in the dealings of organised people with one another."[40] Thus, they argued, the account of rights of women in the workplace described in CEDAW was binding on India through its ratification of the treaty.[41]

The Court accepted the petitioners' argument, holding that the account of sexual harassment in CEDAW is binding on the nation, and that the relevant constitutional provisions should henceforth be read in the expanded manner suggested by petitioners, filling in the understanding of the relevant concepts described in CEDAW. (One striking example: the right to life means "life with dignity," and the nation has the responsibility of enforcing such "safety and dignity through suitable legislation.")[42] The Court issued an admirably clear and comprehensive set of guidelines, defining sexual harassment in terms of unwelcomeness and potential job disadvantage or humiliation. It described both quid pro quo and hostile environment harassment as sex discrimination. The Court then went on to outline preventive measures to be taken by employers. These include notification of the prohibition of all forms of harassment, establishment of a complaint mechanism, and appropriately set internal penalties. Internal complaint committees must be headed by a woman and at least half of their members must be women. In an especially interesting and creative step, the Court said that in order to prevent undue influence from higher levels in the business in question, complaint committees must involve a third party, such as an NGO. Finally, the Court concluded that "[t]he Central/ State Governments are requested to consider adopting suitable measures including legislation to ensure that the guidelines laid down by this order are also observed by the employers in private sector."[43]

At this point, however, the Court came up against legal reality. Court-made law in this area has limited reach and enforceability. The directives are said to be "binding and enforceable in law" until suitable legislation is enacted.[44] But what does this mean? For government employers, it really does mean something. An employer who fails to follow the directives and to set up appropriate procedures can be held in contempt of court. For large private employers covered by the Industrial Employment (Standing Orders) Act of 1946, the directives also have some force, in that the Court instructed the government to amend standing orders under the Industrial Disputes Act so that the guidelines become applicable to private employers. The standing orders, however, apply only to workers and staff, not to executives. Nor will male-dominated trade unions be likely to support the amendment process. The only value of the directives in the rest of the private sector will be to increase awareness of sexual harassment as a problem.

Recall, furthermore, that over 90 percent of India's workers, and an even higher percentage of women, are not covered by this labor legislation at all. The directives will have no impact on these workers, then, until the legislature creates new legislation. Even the Court anticipated that such legislation will take "considerable time."[45] The volatility of the current political situation (with frequent national elections and a large number of regional and caste-based parties whose support is essential to the formation of any national government) makes work on this problem unlikely in the near future. Moreover, there remains a question about where such legislation could appropriately be housed, given that most civil law remains the province of the separate religious systems. The best that can be done is to try to legislate against sexual harassment through the criminal system, but there are obvious limitations to what can be done in this way. In particular, it is not clear that the financial liability of employers that has been such an important part of Title VII in the United States could be embodied in a criminal statute.

Thus, the approach taken in the *Rajasthan* case, though in many respects promising, yields a progress that is at present largely informational and symbolic.

Bajaj v. Gill: *Modesty, Plain Meaning, and Dignity*

The *Bajaj* case, whatever its defects, at least is real. A famous man was convicted; a woman of modest circumstances won a striking and nationally famous victory. But how, more precisely, did this victory come about? Let us now examine Justice Mukherjee's fascinating opinion on behalf of the three-justice panel.

To ascertain whether the decision to quash the complaint had been appropriate, the Court had to determine whether a cognizable case had been made out under the two sections of the Indian Penal Code to which Mrs. Bajaj referred in her complaint. The relevant sections read as follows:

> 354. Whoever assaults or uses criminal force to any woman, intending to outrage or knowing it to be likely that he will thereby outrage her modesty, shall be punished with imprisonment of either description for a term which may extend to two years, or with fine, or with both.
>
> 509. Whoever, intending to insult the modesty of any woman, utters any word, makes any sound or gesture, or exhibits any objects, intending that such word or sound shall be heard, or that such gesture or object shall be seen, by such woman, or intrudes upon the privacy of such woman, shall be punished with simple imprisonment for a term which may extend to one year, or with fine, or with both.[46]

The main distinction between the two sections is that section 354 mentions force and section 509 does not. Section 354 is standardly used in cases of sexual molestation, attempted rape, and sexual assault; section 509 has a wider range, extending to verbal or gestural harassment.

Since both statutes focus centrally on modesty, the Court then felt the need to seek a definition of that term.

> Since the word "modesty" has not been defined in the Indian Penal Code we may profitably look into its dictionary meaning. According to Shorter Oxford English Dictionary (Third Edition) modesty is the quality of being modest and in relation to woman means "womanly propriety of behaviour; scrupulous chastity of thought, speech and conduct." The word 'modest' in relation to woman is defined in the above dictionary as "decorous in manner and conduct; not forward or lewd; shamefast." Webster's Third New International Dictionary of the English language defines modesty as "freedom from coarseness, indelicacy or indecency; a regard for propriety in dress, speech or conduct." In the Oxford English Dictionary (1933 Ed) the meaning of the word 'modesty' is given as "womanly propriety of behaviour; scrupulous chastity of thought, speech and conduct (in man or woman); reserve or sense of shame proceeding from instinctive aversion to impure or coarse suggestions."[47]

This section of the opinion is ironic in several ways. First, the Indian Supreme Court, in a paragraph that shows many signs of a distinctive Indian dialect of English, nonetheless interprets its own penal code by consulting not one but three British and American dictionaries of the English language. India now has the largest English-speaking population in the world, and Indian prose literature is very likely the most distinguished body of such work currently being produced in the English language. But, of course, English is only one of the seventeen official languages of India, and the BJP have at times shown opposition to its remaining even that.[48] Although English is thus more than merely the language of the colonial oppressor, there is still something culturally problematic about hanging a crucial case on the dictionary meaning of an English term, especially when it is not a dictionary that focuses on Indian English. Justice Mukherjee's procedure thus strangely and somewhat comically gestures toward India's postcolonial heterogeneity, just as, in its own way, does Mrs. Bajaj's protest of outrage, which, were it in a novel, might be reasonably ascribed either to Vikram Seth or to Jane Austen, and one hardly knows which ascription would be more appropriate.

Equally fascinating is the Court's method of statutory interpretation. In the United States, the debate over statutory interpretation has taken on political resonance, as the "plain meaning" position has come to be associated with Justice Scalia and therefore with judicial conservatism. There is of course no necessary connection between Scalia's conservatism and his interpretive approach, which he defends by reference to rule-of-law values, but in the public mind this connection is made. The *Bajaj* case shows clearly that plain meaning and a disregard for legislative history can serve a progressive agenda. Had Justice Mukherjee decided to investigate the legislative history of the statute in question, he would certainly have discovered no reference to workplace harassment, nor to official functions in which working women associate with their bosses. In terms of the conception of women dominant in India's Victorian past, it is likely that at the time of legislation a working woman such as Rupan Deol Bajaj would have been seen as by definition immodest for her very way of life, going outside the home and earning money in an office. Feminists were fortunate, then, to find in Justice Mukherjee a "plain meaning" interpreter. The plain meaning of "modesty" does not exclude someone working in an office, going outside the house, and so on. It simply refers to personal qualities that appear to be perfectly compatible with wage labor.

Justice Mukherjee then had to determine how to apply this definition to the case at hand. In order to do so, he had to answer two further questions: Is the standard of modesty a subjective or an objective standard? And does it require looking at the particular status and conduct of the woman in question? To answer these questions, the Justice turned to a 1967 case, *Punjab v. Singh*,[49] in which the putatively outraged party was a female baby aged seven and a half months, who was asleep at the time of the incident. This precedent, Justice Mukherjee argued, established that a violation of section 354 does not require any particular subjective reaction on the part of the woman in question. Section 354 is violated "when any act done to or in the presence of woman is clearly suggestive of sex according to the common notions of mankind."[50] This meant that the Court need not attend to Mrs. Bajaj's reactions, and it need not be established that she was subjectively outraged. Only Mr. Gill's conduct was pertinent, and the outrageousness of this conduct is to be judged by the "common notions of mankind." But this was not the end of the argument: "Needless to say," remarked Justice Mukherjee, "the 'common notions of mankind' referred to by the learned Judge have to be gauged by contemporary societal standards."[51]

Justice Mukherjee now demonstrated the way in which he would use contemporary norms to flesh out the notion of outrage: "When the above test is applied in the present case, keeping in view the total fact situation, it cannot but be held that the alleged act of Mr. Gill in slapping Mrs. Bajaj on her posterior amounted to 'outraging of her modesty' for it was not only an affront to the normal sense of feminine decency but also an affront to the dignity of the lady — 'sexual overtones' or not, notwithstanding."[52] In this very interesting sentence, Justice Mukherjee injected a notion of dignity into the meaning of "modesty," apparently reasoning that in contemporary terms outrageousness is understood at least in part with reference to the idea of a woman's dignity. He denied that the outrage need even be sexual in content, so long as dignity is sufficiently assailed. This is a way of extending the Victorian law into the modern era that could make the law far more relevant to and helpful in a wide range of workplace situations. The inquiry, however, does not cease to be an inquiry into "modesty." Justice Mukherjee did not replace the concept of modesty with the concept of dignity; he simply added dignity as a further factor helping us to understand the concept of modesty. Nor should we ignore the fact that the dignity in question is that of a "lady."

Justice Mukherjee also addressed in a glancing way the other important question raised by the precedent he cited: does the determination of outrage to modesty require ascertaining that the woman in question is in fact a modest woman? *Punjab v. Singh*, he argued, established that modesty is an innate possession of women: "[T]he essence of a woman's modesty is her sex and from her very birth she possesses the modesty which is the attribute of her sex."[53] He did not comment, however, on the obvious question that arises at this point: If modesty does not have to be acquired, does this also mean that it may not be lost? Nor can we derive clear illumination by consulting the case to which he referred. The case contains three separate opinions. The dissenting opinion, by Chief Justice Sarkar, agreed with the majority that the relevant standard is an objective "reasonable man" standard, but insisted that in order to establish criminal intent one must relativize the inquiry to the social norms regarding particular types of people. Thus, a "reasonable man" would not judge that a baby had "womanly modesty."[54] Justice Mudholkar argued vigorously in favor of an objective standard, and made it very clear that the age of the female is irrelevant, concluding that "when any act done to or in the presence of a woman is clearly suggestive of sex according to the common notions of mankind that act must fall within the mischief of this section."[55]

But he did not directly confront the question whether a woman of "immodest" character or reputation would also be protected. Justice Bachawat, similarly, made it clear that he thought that a sleeping or unconscious woman, an anaesthetized woman, a mentally defective woman, and a baby will all be covered,[56] but he did not comment on the issue of character. A British precedent held that a woman of allegedly bad character cannot win relief under the statute, but it is not clear that this precedent is relevant, since its use of a subjective standard was presumably invalidated by the 1967 case.[57]

The Court then addressed an objection that alludes to section 95 of the Penal Code, which reads, "Nothing is an offense by reason that it causes, or that it is intended to cause, or that it is known to be likely to cause, any harm, if that harm is so slight that no person of ordinary sense and temper would complain of such harm."[58] Citing precedent, the Court remarked that this section of the code has been interpreted to exclude from prosecution innocent actions that come under the criminal law "through the imperfection of language" but are not "within its spirit."[59] So interpreted, the section had no application to Mrs. Bajaj's complaint: the conduct alleged was indeed serious, and continued despite Mrs. Bajaj's repeated objections. "If we are to hold, on the face of such allegations that the ignominy and trauma to which she was subjected to was so slight that Mrs. Bajaj, as a person of ordinary sense and temper, would not complain about the same, sagacity will be the first casualty."[60]

What are we to make of this reasoning and its result? Modesty, we learn from the Court, is something women are assumed to have from birth. So far, so good, in a sense, for this permitted the Justice to avoid inquiring into the subjectivity of Mrs. Bajaj; that would be, he argued, no more relevant to the question of whether an offense has been committed than would the subjectivity of the seven-month-old baby in *Punjab v. Singh*. But the crucial gap in both opinion and precedent is that it is never determined that a woman cannot lose the quality of "modesty" by behavior that is inconsistent with social norms. Nor is it even clearly established that lower-class or lower-caste women possess it. Mrs. Bajaj presented herself throughout the case as a truly modest and highly respectable "lady," and it did no harm that she had Mr. Bajaj as her constant companion, both at the civil-service dinner party and at law. She was also a woman of good social class, good education, and, apparently, good caste. The dinner party was described as a gathering of "the elite of society,"[61] and the outrageousness of Mr. Gill's behavior was frequently linked to this fact in court documents. We have trouble imagining what would happen were a single woman or a divorced woman to bring a case under section 354. Wouldn't this open up avenues of inquiry into her sexual conduct that could potentially disbar her from relief under the statute? This seems all too likely, given what the *OED* and *Webster's Third International* tell us about the meaning of the statute in question. And would a lower-caste woman or a poor woman or a manual laborer have greater difficulty bringing charges than a woman of Mrs. Bajaj's standing? Certainly. Mrs. Bajaj herself repeatedly drew attention to her difference from lower-class women in statements to the press, saying, for example, "I am not a woman from the roadside. I have had 6,000 men working under me."[62]

The case, then, may be a victory for some women, but it just as surely divides women, establishing a protected and privileged class of "ladies" who can qualify as Victorian heroines, while leaving the less ladylike unprotected. (And dare we even ask what would become of a lesbian woman under this law, in one of the most determinedly homophobic nations in the world?)

Even in the United States, tenacious notions of "ladylike" conduct have proven an obstacle to women in sexual harassment cases. In *Carr v. Allison Gas Turbine Division, General Motors Corp.*,[63] for example, the lower-court judge ruled against Carr with an opinion reasoning that her "unladylike" conduct had provoked her coworkers' hostile, aggressive, and intimidating response. To this contention, the Seventh Circuit, finding in Carr's favor, made the proper reply (in an opinion by Judge Richard Posner): "Even if we ignore the question why 'unladylike' behavior should provoke not a vulgar response but a hostile, harassing response, and even if Carr's testimony that she talked and acted as she did in an effort to be 'one of the boys' is (despite its plausibility) discounted, her words and conduct cannot be compared to those of the men and used to justify their conduct and exonerate their employer. . . . The asymmetry of positions must be considered."[64] If "unladylike" conduct could make Mary Carr (initially) lose her case under Title VII, a law that nowhere mentions modesty or ladylike conduct, how much more mischief is likely to be created by a strategy of focusing on sections 354 and 509, which explicitly direct the finders of fact to inquire into these concepts and the plaintiff's standing in relation to them, in a nation in which the very fact of a woman's working outside the home is still found immodest in certain class and regional groups?

Finally, offensiveness and outrage themselves look like the wrong core categories for sexual harassment law. The international notion of a hostile work environment, invoked in *Vishaka v. Rajasthan*, directs the mind to ideas of threat, intimidation, and difference of power. The notion of outrage directs the mind only to grossness, and possibly also to unwelcomeness. The difference is parallel to the difference between the concept of obscenity, as traditionally defined in terms of sexual explicitness and appeal to prurient interest, and the feminist concept of pornography, as defined in terms of asymmetry of power, violence, and humiliation. Similarly, sections 354 and 509's notion of "modesty" focuses on the grossness and offensiveness of the male behavior in question, whereas the notion of a hostile environment would focus on power differential, intimidation, and indignity. Try though Justice Mukherjee did to read "dignity" into the old Victorian statute, such a notion does not naturally find its home there, for as John Stuart Mill shrewdly observed, Victorian women may have certain powers, but they did not have rights.[65] They may wield some influence through their delicacy and purity, but that is not the same thing as having the right to be treated equally. Indeed, although Justice Mukherjee avoided mentioning it, the dictionaries he cited inject women's *inequality* into the very definition of modesty: they refer to her (expected) conduct as "not forward" and as "shamefast," qualities that were attached to women as expressions and further reinforcements of social inequality.

Similarly problematic is the evolution of law with regard to street hassling. This is a terrible problem for Indian women of all classes and backgrounds. The problem does not only consist of verbal assaults: invasive touching of all kinds is the typical response to the presence of a woman on public transportation, or even in a taxi with an open window. Yet, once again, this conduct is legally treated as offensive in reference to a standard of womanly modesty that implicitly divides women by caste and class, treating the upper-class woman as a delicate flower who should not be sullied by any coarse suggestion. A fascinating such case is *Zafar Ahmad Khan v. State*.[66] Two young girls were being taken by rickshaw from their home in Lucknow to a neighboring town. The accused apparently followed behind them in a rickshaw. When their rickshaw broke down he stopped, and said to them words that, translated into English, were: "My sweet heart, come. Seat yourself on my rickshaw. I will reach you to the place. I have been waiting for you."[67] He was convicted under a provision of the penal code that makes it a crime to make an "obscene suggestion."[68] The opinion defined "obscene" in terms of the idea of outrage to modesty. The Court commented:

> It is not denied that the two girls to whom these words were addressed, in public, were young in age, being between 16 and 18 years. They ... belonged to a respectable, though not rich, Muslim family. ... The words addressed by the applicant were clearly offensive to the chastity and modesty of the girls. The words were likely to express and personate to the mind of the hearers, including the girls, something which delicacy, purity, and decency forbade to be expressed. The girls ... must have suffered a moral shock to hear such sensuous words addressed to them by an utter stranger. ... Teasing by Roadside Romeos is fast on the increase in cities. Unfortunately, no offence is so easy to commit yet so difficult to be booked. The victims of the offence are

mostly modest and shy girls or young women of respectable families. While on the road or passing in the by lanes, prowling desperadoes cut filthy jokes with them and pass indecent, sensuous and sarcastic remarks against them. The poor victims dare not protest in order to avoid creating a scene. . . . Publicity of such incidents sometimes leads to injurious effects against the victims themselves inasmuch as it subsequently provides material for groundless scandal and unjustified gossip against their character from interested quarters. The victims, therefore, are compelled as of necessity to silently suffer the disgrace and instinctively leave the spot as quick as they can without disclosing their identity. . . . The result is that the offenders indulge in the crime freely and with impunity.[69]

The defendant's appeal was unsuccessful, and he was returned to jail to serve out his term of three months' imprisonment with hard labor.

This case is troubling in exactly the way *Bajaj* is troubling. In one way, it does a good thing for women, by recognizing their silent suffering, the reasons why they will fear to protest, and the difficulty of stopping truly offensive behavior. And it seems likely that the defendant's remarks were not innocuous: given that he had followed the women, he may very well have had the intent at least to harass and at worst to abduct them. Nonetheless, the opinion clearly divides women into the pure and the impure, judging that the law need worry only about the suffering of women of good families. The very idea that women are so delicate as to be shocked by those particular words enshrines in law an image of woman that may subvert women's demands for equality.

Norms of womanly honor and modesty create avenues for the prosecution of genuinely offensive and bad male behavior, behavior that really does subvert women's equality. And indeed the law really did fit what was going on in the *Bajaj* case; Mr. Gill's behavior really was offensive in something like the way described, as well as being an affront to a woman's equality. Similarly in Japan, in the landmark *Fukuoka* case,[70] the female plaintiff won relief by showing a damage to her reputation and honor. In *Fukuoka*, however, the judge also introduced the concept of a "hostile working environment," and made it clear that the damaging of honor was being used as an instrument of male power. He thus at least attempted to introduce an equality element into what was really not an equality case. In *Bajaj*, by contrast, as in the Lucknow street hassling case, the outrageous behavior of Mr. Gill was never described as an instrument of power or a way of establishing hierarchy or inequality. The older norms were not supplemented by more adequate equality norms — except in the Court's glancing and obscure reference to dignity. The feminist understanding of discrimination as an equality issue that prevailed in *Vishaka* did not inform the analysis at all.

Bajaj v. Gill resulted in a high-publicity judgment for one woman, and in that sense might have encouraged other women to demand their rights. But the legal regime it resurrects and publicizes, despite the Court's clever machinations with the notion of "dignity," may make things more difficult for the many non-Victorian women of India, and for the cause of women's social equality generally.

The Future: Women's Collectives, Not the Law

I have said that the case produces a highly unsatisfactory result for working-class women. I have also said that the law in India is weak and not so highly regarded. These two elements of women's situation can now be brought together to give this paper a somewhat more optimistic conclusion than the one reached above. For women's activists in India have long recognized that the law is not the primary avenue through which they should struggle to win improvements in women's lot, where sexual harassment is concerned. And so they have devised other strategies, which are bearing fruit. The most successful strategies involve consciousness-raising, in combination with credit and other types of support for women's employment. Recall that a large majority of India's working women are either self-employed or employed in agricultural labor or cottage industries. For all such women, available credit and the support of women's collectives are absolutely crucial in making them able to stand up both against domestic violence in the home and against sexual harassment in the workplace. Let me give just one example: in Andhra Pradesh, in a very poor semi-arid region, the Mahila Samakhya project, financed by the national government, has organized women into groups to discuss their living conditions, encouraging them to demand their rights (water, electricity, bus service, a teacher who shows up, a health visitor) from the regional government. The newfound solidarity of the group has also led these women, agricultural laborers, to be much tougher against harassing conduct by their employers. One group of women whom I interviewed in March 1998[71] told me that the landlord on whose field they worked was always abusive to them, using offensive language and treating them harshly. (It was not clear how much of the bad treatment was sexual in nature, but the suggestion was that this was at least one element in it.) Before the women's collective, they told me, "We didn't have the guts to ask for anything. We didn't even have the thought that he was doing something bad." With the newfound solidarity and awareness they derived from the project, however, they decided to stop work to protest his conduct. He then stopped their wages. They all went to him as a group and negotiated. He apologized, and they resumed their work.

This is a story I have heard again and again, and I think it is from this sort of collective action that women will really win progress against harassment in India. Or, as another woman from Mahila Samakhya stated in their annual report: "A single voice is not heard. . . . We have learned to speak fearlessly. We ensured that the offender apologised in public."[72] Such strategies are more effective if the law backs them up, but they can also have at least some effect in the law's absence. The Indian government has been wise to invest in such programs, and not simply to rely on the outdated and potentially divisive concepts available through the legal system. And yet in the long run the two approaches must go together. One of the most urgent needs felt by feminists in India today is reform of the legal system and legal education, so that they more adequately perform the task of implementing the equality that has long been a constitutional guarantee.

Notes

I would like to thank Cass Sunstein for comments on a previous draft, Bina Agarwal, Indira Jaisingh, and Ratna Kapur for helpful conversations, and Sonia Katyal for fine research assistance.

1. See *Bajaj v. Gill,* A.I.R. 1996 S.C. 309.

2. See "Asia Court Upholds Police Chief's Butt Slap Conviction," *AAP Newsfeed,* January 6, 1998; *see also* "India: Court Upholds Gill's Conviction," *The Hindu,* January 7, 1998 at 9, *available at* 1998 WL 7728832. By 1998, Gill had retired from the police force.

3. *Bajaj,* A.I.R. 1996 at 312. The complaint was translated into English from Punjabi: Mrs. Bajaj speaks excellent English, but she used her regional language for the complaint. All Supreme Court documents are in English, as are the Constitution and all statutes (although they are also translated into the sixteen regional languages of the nation). India now constitutes the largest body of English speakers in the world, and its prose literature, fiction and nonfiction, is overwhelmingly written in English. (On this, *see* Salman Rushdie, *Mirrorwork: An Anthology of Indian Writing, 1947–1997* [1997]; Rushdie has been strongly criticized for unjustly denigrating vernacular literatures.) Even at the time of independence, Prime Minister Nehru's famous speech about India's "tryst with destiny" was given in English. Thus it is not very surprising that the inquiry into the *Bajaj* case turned, as we shall see, on nuances of the English language and involved consulting various English dictionaries.

4. *Bajaj,* A.I.R. 1996 at 315.

5. See "K.P.S. Gill's Conviction Upheld, Told to Pay Compensation to Bajaj," *The Times of India,* January 7, 1998.

6. "India: Court Upholds Gill's Conviction," *supra* note 2.

7. For one example, see Ratna Kapur and Brenda Cossman, *Subversive Sites: Feminist Engagements with Law in India* (1996).

8. For a more detailed account, see Martha Nussbaum, *Women and Human Develop-*

ment: The Capabilities Approach (2000); Martha Nussbaum, "India: Implementing Sex Equality Through Law," 2 *Chicago Journal of International Law* 35 (2001).

9. *Const. of India*, pt. III, 15(1).

10. *Id.* pt. III, 15(3).

11. *Id.* pt. III, 14.

12. *Id.* 16(1).

13. *Id.* 21.

14. *Id.* 23(1).

15. Nehru and Ambedkar did not get everything they wanted. Hindu opposition to proposed reforms of Hindu law giving women rights to divorce and marital consent, abolishing child marriage, and rendering women's property rights more nearly equal to those of men caused Ambedkar's resignation from the cabinet in 1951. He commented that to leave sex inequality intact was "to make a farce of our Constitution and so build a palace on a dung-heap." Nussbaum, *Women and Human Development, supra* note 8 at 171. The proposed reforms were eventually passed several years later, but they still are not well enforced. (For a detailed study, see Nussbaum, *Women and Human Development, supra* note 8, ch. 3.)

16. See the excellent discussion of this issue in Maureen Callahan Vendermay, "The Role of the Judiciary in India's Constitutional Democracy," 20 *Hastings International and Comparative Law Review* 103 (1996).

17. *Griswold v. Connecticut*, 381 U.S. 478 (1965); *Roe v. Wade*, 410 U.S. 133 (1975). The landmark Indian case that introduced a right to privacy, citing these precedents, was *Govind v. Madhya Pradesh*, A.I.R. 1975 S.C. 1378. The right was recognized in order to declare unconstitutional the remedy of forcible restitution of a woman to the conjugal home in *Sareetha v. Venkata Subbaiah*, A.I.R. 1983 Andhra Pradesh 356, a lower-court opinion that was eventually overruled by the Supreme Court. *See* Martha Nussbaum, "Sex Equality, Liberty, and Privacy: A Comparative Approach to the Feminist Critique," in *Fifty Years of the Republic* (Eswaran Sridharan et al. eds., forthcoming).

18. For discussion of current events relating to the personal laws, see *Justice for Women* (Indira Jaising ed., 1995); Flavia Agnes, *Law and Gender Inequality: The Politics of Women's Rights in India* (2000).

19. See Indira Jaising's statements in her monthly journal, *From the Lawyers Collective*, which focuses on sex equality.

20. 21. Sri Arun Jaitley, address at University of Chicago Law School (May 11, 2001).

21. One notorious example of such use of the criminal code concerned maintenance after divorce to Muslim women. The Muslim system grants a divorced woman only the dowry she brought into the marriage originally; this is less generous than the secular and Hindu systems and is frequently very hard on elderly women who are unilaterally divorced without any employable skills. Feminists found a remedy in a criminal statute making it a crime for a man "of adequate means" to allow his "relatives" to remain in a state of "destitution and vagrancy." After a vote of Parliament in 1975, it became official that ex-wives henceforth would count as "relatives" for the purposes of interpreting this statute, and many Muslim women won maintenance using this provision. This remedy became politically contentious after the highly publicized case of Shah Baho, a seventy-

four-year-old woman whose husband, a prosperous lawyer, turned her out of the house. When she won her case, the Chief Justice of the Supreme Court, a Hindu, published a strongly worded opinion criticizing Muslim practices, calling vigorously for a uniform code. The reaction provoked by this opinion was extreme, and Rajiv Gandhi solved the political problem it created by getting Parliament to pass the Muslim Women's (Protection After Divorce) Act of 1986, which deprived all and only Muslim women of their right of maintenance under the Criminal Code. *See* Nussbaum, *Women and Human Development, supra* note 8, ch. 3.

22. The aggregation involves a complex weighting process described in the 1991 Report. A summary of that discussion is found in the United Nations Development Program, *1997 Human Development Report*, 148 (1997).

23. *Id.* The data contained in the *1997 Human Development Report* are from 1994; *see* Human Development Index at 146–48.

24. *See id.* at 146.

25. *See id.* at 167.

26. Jean Drèze and Amartya Sen, *India: Economic Development and Social Opportunity* 140–42 (1995).

27. *Id.* at 151.

28. Drèze and Sen, second edition (2001).

29. Figures are from ed. 1, at 64. The *1997 Human Development Report* gives, as 1994 data, the figure 36.1 for females, 64.5 for males in India (at 151), and 70.9 (females) and 89.6 (males) for China (at 150).

30. *See* V. K. Ramachandran, "Kerala's Development Achievements," *in Indian Development: Selected Regional Perspectives* 205, 256–59 (Jean Drèze and Amartya Sen eds., 1997).

31. *See id.* at 265–70.

32. Personal communication with Ela Bhatt, founder and organizer, Self-Employed Women's Association; founder and organizer, Women in the Informal Economy Globalizing and Organizing (WIEGO), in Ahmedabad, Gujarat, India (March 18, 1998).

33. *Bajaj*, A.I.R. 1996 at 314.

34. Namita Bhandare et al., "Law: Workplace Victory," *India Today*, September 1, 1997, at 66.

35. *See* Laxmi Murthy, "Sexual Harassment: Who Will Slay the Dragon?" *The Hindu*, September 15, 1997, at 66.

36. A.I.R. 1997 S.C. 3011.

37. Article 32 of the Constitution provides for this procedure in cases involving violations of fundamental rights.

38. Convention on the Elimination of All Forms of Discrimination Against Women, December 18, 1979, 12499 U.N.T.S. 13.

39. *Rajasthan*, A.I.R. 1997 at 3014.

40. *Id.* at 3013.

41. For discussion of the case and its implications, see Rasheeda Bhagat, "Checking Sexual Harassment: A Long Overdue Measure," *Business Line: The Hindu*, September 2, 1997, at 24; Bhandare et al., *supra* note 34; "Editorial: A Welcome Recognition," *The Hindu*, September 7, 1997, at 25, *available at* 1997 WL 14057464; "India: Harassment

of Women: Complaint Cell Sought in Work Places," *The Hindu*, December 3, 1997, at 3, *available at* 1997 WL 16014223; Murthy, *supra* note 35; and Adirupa Sengupta, "Supreme Court Moves to Check Sexual Harassment," *India Abroad*, August 22, 1997, at 28.

42. *Rajasthan*, A.I.R. 1997 at 3012.

43. *Id.* at 3017.

44. *Id.*

45. *Id.* at 3016.

46. Penal Code (45 of 1860) (India).

47. *Bajaj*, A.I.R. 1996 at 313.

48. In Maharashtra, where they have been dominant, the BJP have dedicated themselves to eradicating Anglophone dominance; hence the many changes of place-names, for example, from Bombay to Mumbai.

49. A.I.R. 1967 S.C. 63. The case was an ugly one in which Major Singh masturbated over a sleeping baby, whose vagina he damaged with his fingers.

50. *Bajaj*, A.I.R. 1996 at 313.

51. *Id.*

52. *Id.*

53. *Id.*

54. *Singh*, A.I.R. 1967 at 65.

55. *Id.* at 67.

56. *Id.* at 68.

57. *See Mt. Champa Pasin v. Emperor*, A.I.R. 1928 Pat. 326. Justice MacPherson argues that the charge of offense against modesty cannot apply if the woman "has no modesty to mention." *Id.* at 332. A widow who had left her husband, the complainant was said to be "of loose moral character" because she failed to adhere to the expected behavior of widows. *Id.* at 229–30.

58. *Bajaj*, A.I.R. 1996 at 314.

59. *Id.*

60. *Id.* at 314–15.

61. *Id.* at 314.

62. *The Telegraph* (Calcutta), August 11, 1996, at 11. Bajaj granted in the same interview, however, that her case is a rare elite case, that "if it took me, with all my connections and my background as an IAS officer, eight long, arduous years to reach this stage, what chance does an ordinary woman have?"

63. 32 F.3d 1007 (7th Cir. 1994).

64. *Id.* at 1011.

65. John Stuart Mill, *The Subjection of Women* 40 (Susan Moller Okin ed., Hackett 1988) (1869) ("Her power often gives her what she has no right to, but does not enable her to assert her own rights").

66. A.I.R. 1963 Allahabad 105. Although this is a relatively old case, nothing has happened in the interim to render it obsolete.

67. *Khan*, A.I.R. 1963 at 106.

68. Penal Code (1860) Section 294, closely related to the sections under which Mrs. Bajaj pressed her complaint.

69. *Khan*, A.I.R. 1963 at 107–08.

70. Fukuoka Chiho Saibansho, Heisei Gannen 783 Hanrei Taimuzu 60 (1992) (Jap.).

71. Interview with women from Mahila Samakhya, in Andhra Pradesh, India (March 23, 1998).

72. Mahila Samakhya, *Annual Report* (1998).

37

Sexual Harassment
An International Human Rights Perspective

CHRISTINE CHINKIN

This chapter considers sexual harassment in the workplace from the perspective of international human rights law. Adopting a human rights approach locates sexual harassment in the context of women's economic and social rights and more broadly in the wider frame of international imperatives such as the maintenance of international peace and security and global economic development. Sexual harassment has come onto the international agenda comparatively recently, and the story comprises both the inclusion of prohibitions within legal instruments and significant silences, especially where breaking the silence requires intrusion into state policies relating to militarism, trade and investment liberalization, and the domestic jurisdiction exclusion from international regulation.[1] Since sexual harassment is a relatively new concept in international law there has been no significant backlash as has occurred in some national jurisdictions. Indeed it has received little attention at the international level compared with other issues of women's human rights such as other forms of violence against women, reproductive rights, and crimes committed against women in armed conflict. The challenge for international lawyers working in this area is to further the understanding of sexual harassment as constituting discrimination on the basis of sex and as violative of a range of human rights, such as freedom from degrading treatment and freedom of expression and association. These linkages emphasize that sexual harassment is committed in many locations,[2] not just in the workplace, and that international legal prohibitions must be sufficiently broad to address that fact.

The diversity and different forms of paid work undertaken by the female labor force around the world make generalizations about the types of harassment faced and the appropriate responses problematic. At the Fourth World Conference on Women in Beijing in 1995, it was accepted that women are now key contributors to the economy and to combating poverty through both remunerated and unremunerated work at home, in the community, and in the workplace.[3] The Platform for Action continues that: "Women often have no choice but to take employment that lacks long-term job security or involves dangerous working conditions, to work in unprotected home-based production or to be unemployed. Many women enter the labour market in under-remunerated and undervalued jobs, seeking to improve their household income; others decide to migrate for the same purpose."[4]

All these conditions are conducive to forms of sexual harassment that are remarkably similar worldwide. As is also recognized in this statement, across the globe women experience diverse working conditions and locations. For example, women worldwide work in enormous numbers in rural occupations. Women also form a large number of homeworkers who are constrained by isolation from being able to organize and are vulnerable to abuse from both their suppliers and sellers.[5] The U.N. Special Rapporteur on the Human Rights of Migrant Workers estimates that there are more than 130 million nonnational migrant workers in the world.[6] At least half of these workers are women, although other estimates are that since the 1980s women migrant workers have outnumbered men in large numbers.[7] Women migrant workers suffer discrimination on the basis of their race and their sex. They work largely in the informal labor market in agricultural, domestic, or factory positions where their position is one of marginalization from legal protection. Women in foreign domestic service are isolated by language and have no protection from abusive employers[8] or external events.[9] Their importance to the economies of the states they have left,[10] as well as of their families, forces them into modern forms of slavery.

Such workplace variations require recognition of forms of sexual discrimination and harassment that range from unequal pay structures and working conditions, to sexual degradation and abuse, to sweatshop labor, to isolation, vulnerability to violence, and death. These conditions are not particular to any culture and occur globally. The tension between promoting universal human rights standards and local specificities is most often experienced in the context of claims based upon cultural and religious traditions; in the context of workplace sexual discrimination and harassment local claims for the priority of economic development are also voiced. Formulating international standards against sexual harassment and discrimination requires examination of feminist theories such as those relating to the sexual and racial divisions of labor and the impact of the distinction between public and private spheres of activity and where those boundaries are properly drawn to ensure their appropriateness in particular contexts. Their application also demands consideration of gender within the ethnic, religious, race, and class contexts of each particular society.

Placing sexual harassment within international human rights law raises other dilemmas. Human rights law requires states to accept international obligations with respect to people within their jurisdiction. The importance of work performed primarily by women, both to national economies and to the global liberalization of trade and investment, undermines commitment to human rights standards—even where they formally exist—and contributes to the repression of any claims for their enforcement. State complicity in the denial of individual workplace rights ranges from asserting the priority of state economic development to exploiting the passivity and femininity of their women as a national economic resource.[11] Further, women's compliance and participation are needed for the functioning of various state enterprises, most notably the military. Discussing the well-documented connection between militarism and the presence of military forces within a vicinity and sexual harassment is beyond the scope of this essay.[12] In short, women's work is economically and socially undervalued throughout the world and is made subject to national and international policies that discount their rights. At best, their working conditions are frequently ill-regulated or poorly monitored and their vulnerability to different and often extreme forms of harassment is enhanced. At worst, women become trapped into extreme forms of sexual exploitation, including trafficking, sexual tourism, and forced prostitution, that have increased in economic and geographic terms and have become a matter of pressing international concern.[13]

Sexual Harassment and International Human Rights Law
HUMAN RIGHTS INSTRUMENTS

International law provisions relating to sexual harassment can be found within the institutional framework of the International Labor Organization (ILO), the general human rights instruments, specialized human rights instruments, and regional organizations. These have all developed separately and with less incidence of sharing institutional knowledge and experience than might have been anticipated. This section briefly examines the contribution of each.

The ILO was established for the legal protection of workers' rights. In many ways the organization is the forerunner of the United Nations human rights institutions and procedures. Its commitment to equality of opportunity was reiterated in the Declaration of Philadelphia in 1944 that represented the ILO's transition from the era of the League of Nations to that of the United Nations. Since the time of the League the ILO has concluded both protective,[14] and therefore inhibiting, treaties for women workers and those promoting equality in the workplace. The most important of the latter is its Convention 111.[15] This Convention promotes equality of opportunity in both public and private employment.[16] The Convention is subject to the supervisory and monitoring processes of the ILO. These include the obligation upon states to report to the Committee of Experts on the steps they have taken for the effective implementation of the Convention in national law. Serious issues raised by the Committee of Experts through the reporting process are chosen for public discussion at the ILO annual Conference by the Conference Committee on Standards. The Conference Committee is a political body that reflects the ILO's tripartite interests in that it comprises employer and employee representatives as well as government delegates. It can cite governments for failure to implement the conventions they have ratified.

Although Convention No. 111 is widely ratified (158 states in 2003), the ILO has been concerned about the failure of states to ratify even the core Conventions and to comply with their provisions. On June 18, 1998, it therefore adopted the Declaration on Fundamental Principles and Rights at Work. This Declaration sets out four fundamental principles binding upon states by virtue of their membership of the organization. The fourth of these is the elimination of discrimination in respect of employment and occupation, thus bringing rejection of sexual harassment into the core values of the organization.

Despite the longstanding inclusion of the prohibition of discrimination, including on the grounds of sex, within human rights law,[17] sexual harassment has not been readily understood as coming within the language of the general human rights international instruments concluded within the U.N. framework. Specific workplace rights are located within the catalogue of economic and social rights that have been accorded lesser weight, at least within Western jurisprudence, than civil and political rights.[18] The major international instrument guaranteeing economic and social rights, the International Covenant on Economic and Social and Cultural Rights (ICESCR), does not explicitly refer to sexual harassment but the assertions to equality in the workplace, of the right to "just and favorable conditions of work" and to "safe and healthy working conditions" allow it to be brought in. The false dichotomy between categories of rights has been reinforced by separate treaty monitoring bodies, the Human Rights Committee (civil and political rights) and the Committee on Economic, Social, and Cultural Rights, and has impeded a coherent approach toward addressing wrongs that fall within both categories. Harassment is not simply a workplace issue. It violates such civil and political rights as equality, freedom of movement, and freedom of association, but tends to be located within workplace rights to the detriment of consideration of how it undermines enjoyment of such other rights. The affirmation of the indivisibility of all human rights that was made at the World Conference on Human Rights, held in Vienna in 1993, should ameliorate this perception.[19] Nevertheless, in practical terms, the ICESCR has weaker language and enforcement measures than its civil and political rights counterpart.

Growing realization that the U.N.'s general human rights instruments paid insufficient attention to the forms of discrimination that are most harmful to women led to demands for a women-specific treaty. In 1979 the General Assembly adopted the Convention on the Elimination of All Forms of Discrimination Against Women (the Women's Convention).[20] Unlike the U.N. Covenants, Article 1 of the Women's Convention defines discrimination: "Discrimination against women shall mean any distinction, exclusion or restriction on the basis of sex which has the effect or purpose of impairing or nullifying the recognition, enjoyment or exercise by women, irrespective of their marital status, on a basis of equality of men and women, of human rights and fundamental freedoms in the political, economic, social, cultural, civil or any other field."

This definition contains the requisite elements of sexual harassment: the objective existence of a distinction, exclusion, or restriction on the basis of sex and the consequential impairment of the enjoyment by women of guaranteed rights.[21] It largely repeats the definition of discrimination in ILO Convention No. 111 and the Convention on the Elimination of All Forms of Racial Discrimination of 1965. In its General Comment No. 18[22] the Human Rights Committee adopted this definition, supporting a common understanding of discrimination across human rights instruments. The ILO Committee of Experts has confirmed its understanding that sexual harassment is a form of discrimination and has expounded its understanding of harassment under ILO Convention No. 111. The common definition of discrimination allows the ILO's understanding of harassment to be applied to the other Conventions. The unwanted act must show one of the following features: it is justly perceived as a condition or precondition for employment; it influences employment decisions or prejudices occupational performance; or it humiliates, insults, or intimidates the targeted person.[23] Despite the leadership of the ILO in this area there has been an unfortunate tendency for its accumulated expertise in social justice matters to be disregarded by the U.N. human rights bodies.[24]

A strength of the Women's Convention is that it contains economic as well as civil and political rights. For example, article 11 relates specifically to the elimination of discrimination in the field of employment. However although article 11 covers the right to work, the right to the same employment opportunities, the right to free choice of profession, promotion, job security and training, equal remuneration for work of equal value, the right to social security, the right to health and safety in the workplace, and measures relating to maternity and childcare, it makes no specific reference to sexual harassment. The Convention on the Elimination of All Forms of Racial Discrimination, on which the Women's Convention is largely modeled, includes the right to just and favorable conditions of work. This formula is also included in the ICESCR but is omitted from the Women's Convention.[25] This supports MacKinnon's view that race discrimination is treated more seriously and fully than sex discrimination.[26]

The omission of any explicit mention of sexual harassment from the Women's Convention is not surprising in view of its adoption in 1979, when the concept was still in its infancy in national legal systems.[27] The overall philosophy of the Women's Convention is not that of a charter of women's rights, but rather of equality between women and men in the identified areas. Thus widespread failure at that time to perceive sexual harassment as an equality issue precluded its inclusion within the Convention. In many instances human rights jurisprudence has been advanced by the regional human rights mechanisms, but in this context the same bias is found. The judicial machinery that strengthens the civil and political rights guaranteed by the European Convention on Human Rights[28] has not been extended to the rights included in the European Social Charter, including workplace rights.[29] The American Convention on Human Rights has a single provision on economic, social, educational, scientific, and cultural standards that states are obliged to achieve progressively.[30] Specific workplace rights are found in the Additional Protocol to the American Convention on Human Rights in the Area of Economic, Social and Cultural Rights,[31] which is subject to the jurisdiction of the Inter-American Commission and Court of Human Rights through individual petition.[32] In addition, the nondiscrimination clauses within the regional conventions are not freestanding in that claims of discrimination must be made with respect to rights guaranteed by the relevant convention.[33] Article 26 of the International Covenant on Civil and Political Rights is a general prohibition of discrimination, but the focus upon civil and political rights by the Human Rights Committee has militated against its application to workplace rights. However its General Comment 28, adopted March 29, 2000, does stress the need for equality in the workplace and in paragraph 9 suggests that states review their legislation and implement measures to eliminate discrimination in all fields, including by private employers. The African Charter asserts the right of all individuals to work under equitable and satisfactory conditions.[34] Coupled with its prohibition of sex-based discrimination,[35] this Convention allows sexual harassment to be brought more easily within its terms than those of the American or European Conventions on Human Rights, but again the monitoring mechanisms are rudimentary.

Within Europe, the European Community has been more effective in addressing equality than the human rights mechanisms of the Council of Europe. From the requirement in the Treaty Establishing the European Community, article 141 (formerly Treaty of Rome article 119), requiring equal pay for equal work, the institutions of the Community, have given effect to sexual equality as a matter of social justice, as well as economic principle.[36] Sexual harassment has been addressed in a number of relevant soft law measures.[37] The European Commission's Code of Practice on the dignity of men and women in the workplace provides a fuller understanding of behaviors that deny this dignity. Such behaviors include physical sexual conduct, verbal conduct of a sexual nature, nonverbal conduct of a sexual nature, and sex-based conduct such as comments about appearance, that are unwanted by the target person. Such conduct is harassment "once it has been made clear that it is regarded by the recipient as offensive," regardless of the motive of the offender.[38] Recommendations and Codes of Practice form part of the soft law of the Community, that is, nonbinding principles dependent upon self-regulation and governmental and nongovernmental pressure for compliance. However these recommendatory measures are brought within directly applicable Community law by stating that sexual harassment "may be in certain circumstances, contrary to the principle of equal treatment . . . of Council Directive 76/207/EEC."[39] A considerable jurisprudence has developed around the application of the equal treatment directive to workplace sexual harassment that is beyond the scope of this essay. While the linkage between the soft law on sexual harassment and the equal treatment directive crafts a legally enforceable framework, obstacles remain to a comprehensive prohibition of a hostile working environment and to all forms of sexually demeaning behavior in the context of work.[40]

The Community is also moving toward adopting its own human rights instrument. The Draft Charter of Fundamental Rights of the European Union agreed on July 28, 2000, goes further than the European Convention on Human Rights in that it has separate articles on equality before law (article 20); equality and nondiscrimination (article 21); and equality opportunities between men and women as regards employment and work (article 22). It also asserts the right to working conditions that respect the worker's dignity, as well as health and safety (article 29). However the form of the charter has not yet been agreed and will have no broader application than to member states of the European Union.

Strategies to Bring Sexual Harassment Within Human Rights Law

This brief survey of human rights law relating to sexual harassment presents a mixed picture. The equality provisions in the U.N. human rights treaties can be interpreted to encompass sexual harassment. Inattention to the possibility of such interpretation, however, has meant that there is little indication that the relevant supervisory bodies accept this understanding. Further, with the exception of the European Community and the regional human rights institutions, enforcement mechanisms are weak. The European Community has the most significant legal provisions against sexual harassment based upon its commitment to workplace equality, but this is a sui generis legal regime that does not constitute general international law. The slow progress within the U.N. itself toward treating seriously allegations of sexual harassment sends out another message of lack of concern at the international level.[41] The task has been to bring evolved national understandings of sexual discrimination and harassment into international standards of equality that can in turn be used to bring pressure for change in national legal systems that have not taken these steps. Formal amendment of human rights treaties is not easy, however, and other strategies to instill change have been sought.

The most obvious instrument through which to seek change is the Women's Convention. The previous lack of an individual complaints mechanism has prevented the Committee on the Elimination of Discrimination Against Women (CEDAW) from generating a jurisprudence illuminating and pushing forward the Convention's provisions,[42] including on sexual harassment. This has now changed with the introduction of an individual complaints procedure and a process of inquiry by the Optional Protocol to the Women's Convention.[43] The Optional Protocol entered into force on December 22, 2000, three months after the tenth nation ratified it.

Nevertheless the Convention's equality provisions have provided the legal basis for subsequent developments that have been crafted through two interlocking strategies: direct recognition of sexual harassment through the concept of discrimination; and its inclusion within the broader campaign to assert state responsibility for the failure by states to exercise due diligence for the prevention, punishment, and elimination of violence against women. Two forces have been primarily responsible for these advances. First, women's international nongovernmental organizations (NGOs) have effectively campaigned, lobbied, and mobilized support for the recognition of women's rights as human rights. Second, CEDAW has worked on forward-looking interpretations of individual articles of the Convention that it has published in the form of general recommendations. As these have increased in number and detail they have substituted to some extent for the lack of an international jurisprudence on women's human rights.

In 1992 CEDAW agreed General Recommendation No. 19 on Violence Against Women.[44] This recommendation is based directly upon the language of the Women's Convention, a strategy that enhances its authority and legitimacy. It affirms that gender-based violence is a form of discrimination that seriously inhibits women's ability to enjoy rights and freedoms on a basis of equality with men (paragraph 1) and thus that it violates article 1 of the Women's Convention (paragraphs 6 and 7). Paragraphs 17 and 18 apply this principle to article 11 of the Convention:

> 17. Equality in employment can be seriously impaired when women are subjected to gender specific violence, such as sexual harassment in the workplace.
>
> 18. Sexual harassment includes such unwelcome sexually determined behaviour as physical contacts and advances, sexually coloured remarks, showing pornography and sexual demands, whether by words or actions. Such conduct can be humiliating and may constitute a health and safety problem; it is discriminatory when a woman has reasonable grounds to believe that her objection would disadvantage her in connection with her employment, including retirement and promotion, or when it creates a hostile working environment.

General Recommendation No. 19 uses the language of nondiscrimination and equality to bring gender-specific violence within the ambit of the Convention. CEDAW requires states to include in their original and periodic reports to the Committee[45] details of measures taken to protect women against harassment, violence, and coercion in the workplace and has indicated that states can expect to be questioned on their progress, although this appears to have been rarely done. The coming into force of the Optional Protocol to the Women's Convention presents the opportunity for test case applications of these provisions.

Parallel to the work of CEDAW, women's NGOs mobilized around the demand for recognition of violence against women, both as a direct violation of women's human rights and as nullifying the enjoyment of all human rights, as a unifying theme of the campaign for the broader affirmation of women's rights as human rights. In the 1990s this campaign was pursued through a number of fora, including the U.N. human rights bodies, the General Assembly, and the global summit conferences held throughout the decade, notably the World Conference on Human Rights in Vienna in 1993 and the Fourth World Conference on Women in Beijing in 1995. The campaign argued the connections between the various forms of violence that are directed against women, because they are women, across the globe. By exposing the level of the incidence of such violence and by locating its occurrence within the home and the community and as perpetrated by state agencies, the view that it was a private matter of no concern to the state became unsustainable.[46] The objectives of the U.N. Decade for Women (1976–1985) were equality, development, and peace:[47] the role of women in development and the social development of women were highlighted, rather than focus upon women's human rights. In contrast, in 1993 the World Conference on Human Rights stated: "Gender-based violence and all forms of sexual harassment and exploitation, including those resulting from cultural prejudice and international trafficking, are incompatible with the dignity and worth of the human person, and must be eliminated."[48]

Later that same year in its first detailed condemnation of violence against women, the General Assembly affirmed it to be an instrument of women's social subordination.[49] The General Assembly Declaration on the Elimination of Violence Against Women stated that the roots of violence against women lie in the historically unequal power relations between women and men which have led to domination over and discrimination against women by men. This language goes beyond the concept of the equality goal of the Women's Convention by identifying the structural causes of violence, that is, women's lack of any real social or economic power in either the public or private spheres of activity. This also ensures that the problem is addressed in terms of the overwhelming disparity in commission of acts of violence against women that have not been traditionally recognized as such, either because of their occurrence in private or at the hands of family members. Emphasis on equality obscures this reality and allows for appropriation by men of provisions intended to benefit women. Continuing the progress, at the Fourth World Conference on Women in 1995, violence and fear of violence against women were seen both as obstacles to the achievement of fundamental objectives of the international community: development and peace, and as violations of women's human rights.[50]

Sexual harassment place fits squarely within this understanding. Article 2 of the Declaration states: "Violence against women shall be understood to encompass, but not be limited to, the following: (b) Physical, sexual and psychological violence occurring within the general community, including rape, sexual abuse, sexual harassment and intimidation at work, in educational institutions and elsewhere, trafficking in women and forced prostitution."[51]

Like the World Conference on Human Rights, this definition does not limit sexual harassment to that occurring in the workplace. Article 4(c) requires states to "exercise due diligence to prevent, investigate and . . . punish acts of violence against women, whether those acts are perpetrated by the State or by private persons." The Declaration, however, fails to define what behavior constitutes harassment. General Recommendation No. 19 provides a more gender-specific understanding and the Special Rapporteur on Violence Against Women[52] has also considered the question. The latter argued in her preliminary report that while the precise definition will vary with cultural values and norms, there are two vital ingredients: it is unwelcome sexual attention that is unwanted by or offensive or threatening to the recipient.[53] This puts the emphasis on its effect on the recipient and makes the perpetrator's motive irrelevant. She urged states to treat sexual harassment seriously because of its capacity to degrade women and because it reinforces and reflects the idea of nonprofessionalism on the part of women workers, who are consequently regarded as less able to perform their duties than their male colleagues.[54] Such definitions inevitably lack the context specificity and refinement that is built up through claims in national courts. In particular they leave uncertain the relationship between sex discrimination, harassment, and gender-specific violence. The Declaration includes psychological as well as physical harm, but the framework of violence against women may falsely imply the need for some form of physical violence for the action to come within its terms, an approach that has not been taken by the Special Rapporteur.

General Recommendation No. 19 and the General Assembly Declaration suggested various measures that should be taken by governments, regional and international governmental organizations, and NGOs to help achieve the objectives of elimination and punishment of violence against women. Similarly, at Beijing specific direct intervention strategies were envisaged to be taken by employers, employees, and trade unions.[55] However these amount to little more than a requirement for legal protection and workplace policies against sexual harassment. The need for training, commitment of resources, and attitudinal change toward women in the paid workforce are not stressed, although inadequate documentation and research were recognized as impediments to intervention strategies at both the national and international levels.[56]

The only binding treaty on violence against women is the Inter-American Convention on the Prevention, Punishment, and Eradication of Violence Against Women,[57] which encompasses sexual harassment within the workplace as a form of community violence against women. Most important, the obligations under this Convention are linked into the enforcement mechanisms of the Inter-American human rights system. States parties undertake to report to the Inter-American Commission of Women, requests for advisory opinions on its interpretation can be made to the Inter-American Court of Human Rights, and there is a right of individual petition to the Inter-American Commission on Human Rights.[58]

That such international developments can impact in national law is shown by the decision of the Supreme Court of India in *Apparel Export Promotion Council v. A. K. Chopra*.[59] The allegations were depressingly familiar: the alleged harassment of his private secretary by the chairman of the Apparel Export Promotion Council through unwanted overtures, insistence that she accompany him to places outside the workplace, and attempted molestation. After an internal inquiry process the chairman was removed from his post, which he challenged through the courts. The Supreme Court of India recognized the "growing social menace of sexual harassment" which "is incompatible with the dignity and honour of a female" and is not open to any compromise or debate. The Court drew upon the "message" of the Women's Convention, the Beijing Platform for Action, and the ICESCR and concluded that these require India to gender sensitize its laws. It continued that courts and counsel must never forget the core principles of such international instruments and must ensure that these do not become "drowned." This decision did not look at precise provisions of the instruments and subject them to legalistic interpretation but rather looked to their overall message and content of equality. This decision is in the spirit of the Victoria Falls Declaration of Principles for the Promotion of the Human Rights of Women, which was adopted at a colloquium of Commonwealth judges.[60] This colloquium also discussed the potential of judicial networking and of judges drawing upon decisions from other jurisdictions to support their own. It is hoped that this case will be so used to develop a similar judicial understanding of sexual harassment, at least within Commonwealth jurisdictions.

Conclusion

These instruments suggest a formal commitment to the recognition of violence against women, including sexual harassment within the workplace and elsewhere, as coming within the parameters of international human rights law that was not envisaged at the beginning of the 1990s. The *Chopra* case shows how international equality standards can be used by national courts to support the application of such principles domestically, even where there is no relevant legislation. There are nevertheless reasons for caution. The international institutions do not lead by example within their own workplace practices. The most explicit articulations of principle are contained in General Assembly resolutions and the final documents of global summit meetings. Neither type is a legally binding instrument. At best they constitute a form of soft law with programmatic and aspirational value. The model of binding obligation of the Inter-American Convention on the Elimination of Violence Against Women has not been followed elsewhere. The soft law instruments lack specific performance targets and do not contain even the admittedly inadequate monitoring and supervisory processes of the human rights treaties. These concerns have been partially addressed by General Recommendation No. 19, based as it is on the Women's Convention, but the state reporting mechanism is flawed, especially in terms of follow up to CEDAW's concluding comments. The Optional Protocol provides a mechanism for direct challenge to sexual harassment as violative of the Convention. It is to be hoped that such an application might be soon made by individuals within one of the states that is party to the protocol.

There has been progress in acknowledgment of the worldwide occurrence of sexual harassment and that this is a matter that engages state responsibility, but the limitations must be recognized. Although lip service is paid to the need to redress the social and economic subordination of women, there is little attempt at any social restructuring in any of the instruments. Even at Beijing the silences were significant. Broader issues of the impact upon women's working conditions of globalization of the economy and transnational corporate behavior were barely remarked upon.[61] There is no analysis of the structural violence inflicted by certain economic policies.[62] Sexual harassment should not be limited to sexually determined behavior but should also encompass coercion and violence directed primarily at one sex as a result of globally approved economic policies that are made operative within the workplace. Yumi Lee argues that considering that economics as practiced is clearly (male) gender-based and not gender-neutral, with the results disproportionately harming women, there is no doubt that poverty, starvation, malnourishment, suffering, and injury caused by economic policies and practices are manifestations of gender-based violence against women.[63] Desperate attempts by women to avert these consequences by accepting appalling working conditions that include, but are not confined to, unwanted sexual exploitation remain outside the discourse of human rights.

Another silence is the assumption that global security must be defined in militarist terms, despite the adverse impact this has upon women. Still other forms of harassment stem from religious or customary mores that discriminate against women in other ways, for example by restricting women's right to associate and their access to public spaces and, consequently, to paid employment. Women who persist in seeking such work, often because of lack of alternative means of support, may be subject to harassment, violence, and even death as they attempt to find work or go to their place of employment. If successful, they become especially vulnerable within the workplace because of their deviance from this imposed norm. Bringing sexual harassment into the discourse of violence against women and human rights has emphasized its global occurrence, but can deflect attention from the structural causes of that behavior that cannot be redressed by legal instrumentalities alone. The Platform for Action does suggest that developing a holistic and multidisciplinary approach to the challenging task of promoting families, communities, and states that are free of violence against women is necessary and achievable.[64] This remains the objective of international human rights law with respect to a widely understood and applied norm prohibiting sexual harassment.

Notes

1. U.N. Charter, art. 2, para. 7, prohibits United Nations intervention into matters which are essentially within the domestic jurisdiction of any state.

2. Sexual harassment in certain locations is of particular concern to international institutions that have generated policies and guidelines. The United Nations High Commissioner for Refugees has addressed harassment of displaced persons and refugees within camps, when fleeing conflict, and seeking assistance; UNHCR, Refugee Women (1999 Global Appeal and Programme Overview, December 1998, available at *www .unhcr.ch/issues/women/women.htm*).

3. *Beijing Declaration and Platform for Action* para. 49 (Sept. 15, 1995) [hereinafter *Platform for Action*].

4. *Platform for Action, supra* note 3, para. 19.

5. *See,* for example, the discussion of laceworkers in Narsapur, India. Chandra Mohanty, "Women Workers and Capitalist Scripts: Ideologies of Domination, Common Interests, and the Politics of Solidarity," in *Feminist Genealogies, Colonial Legacies, Democratic Futures* 3 (Jacqui Alexander and Chandra Mohanty eds., 1997).

6. *Report of the Special Rapporteur,* Gabriela Rodriguez Pizarro, submitted pursuant to Commission on Human Rights resolution 1999/44, Doc. CN.4/2000/82, para. 64).

7. *See Special Rapporteur on Violence Against Women, Preliminary Report,* U.N. Doc. E/CN.4/1995/42, para. 220 [hereinafter *Preliminary Report*].

8. For example, the *Report of the Special Rapporteur on Violence Against Women, Its Causes and Consequences,* U.N. Doc. E/CN.4/1996/53, para. 8, describes the plight of Sara Balabagan, a young Filipina worker who was at first sentenced to death for killing her employer. She claimed that she had acted in self-defense when he attempted to rape her.

9. On the plight of domestic workers in Kuwait after the invasion by Iraq in 1990, *see* Middle East Watch, *A Victory Turned Sour: Human Rights in Kuwait Since Liberation* (Sept. 1991); and Women's Rights Project and Middle East Watch, *Punishing the Victim: Rape and Mistreatment of Asian Maids in Kuwait* (Aug. 1992).

10. For example, there are 4.2 million migrant Philippine workers employed in more than forty states, and remittances amounted to some $5.98 billion from 1986 to 1991; in 1988 remittances were equivalent to 58 percent of exports for Bangladesh, over 20 percent for Pakistan, Sri Lanka, and India, and 14 percent for the Philippines. *See* Jan Jindy Pettman, *Worlding Women: A Feminist International Politics* 71 (1996).

11. Heng gives the example of the profile of the "Singapore Girl" designed to promote Singapore Airlines. *See* Geraldine Heng, "A Great Way to Fly: Nationalism, the State and the Varieties of Third-World Feminism," in *Feminist Genealogies, Colonial Legacies, Democratic Futures, supra* note 5, at 30.

12. *See, e.g.,* Cynthia Enloe, *Does Khaki Become You? The Militarisation of Women's Lives* (1983); Anne Orford, "The Politics of Collective Security," 17 *Michigan Journal of International Law* 373 (1996).

13. *Platform for Action, supra* note 3, para. 122.

14. *See, e.g.,* ILO Convention No. 4 Concerning the Employment of Women During the Night, 1919, *revised by* ILO Convention No. 41, 1934, *revised by* ILO Convention No. 89, 1948; ILO Convention No. 45 Concerning the Employment of Women on Underground Work in Mines of All Kinds, 1935.

15. Discrimination (Employment and Occupation) Convention and Recommendations, 1958, ILO Convention No. 111; *see also* Convention Concerning the Equal Remuneration for Men and Women Workers for Work of Equal Value, ILO Convention No. 100.

16. *See* Henrik Nielsen, "The Concept of Discrimination in ILO Convention No. 111," 43 *International and Comparative Law Quarterly* 827 (1994).

17. *See, e.g.,* U.N. Charter arts. 1, 55; Universal Declaration of Human Rights, art. 2, G.A. Res. 217 A (III) (1948); International Covenant on Civil and Political Rights, arts. 2(1), 26, Dec. 16, 1966, 999 U.N.T.S. 171; International Covenant on Economic, Social, and Cultural Rights, arts. 2(2), 3, Dec. 16, 1966, 999 U.N.T.S. 3.

18. *See* International Covenant on Economic, Social, and Cultural Rights, arts. 6–8.

19. *See U.N. World Conference on Human Rights: Vienna Declaration and Programme of Action*, pt. I, para. 5, U.N. Doc. A/CONF.157/24 (1993).

20. Dec. 18, 1979, 1249 U.N.T.S. 20378.

21. The same is true of the definition of discrimination in ILO Convention No. 111, art. 1. *See* Nielsen, *supra* note 16, at 834.

22. Human Rights Committee, General Comment No. 18, Non-Discrimination, Nov. 10, 1989.

23. *See* Committee of Experts, General Survey 1988 on the Application of Conventions and Recommendations, ILO, 75th Session, Geneva, 1988, para. 45; Nielsen, *supra* note 16, at 834. Nielsen concludes that "[a]ny act, the unwanted nature of which could not be mistaken by its author, is deemed to be sexual harassment."

24. *See* Virginia Leary, "Lessons from the Experience of the International Labour Organisation," in Philip Alston, *The United Nations and Human Rights* 580 (1992).

25. Mar. 7, 1966, 660 U.N.T.S. 195.

26. *See* Catharine A. MacKinnon, *Sexual Harassment of Working Women: A Case of Sex Discrimination* 127 (1979). Within the international arena the association between race discrimination, decolonization, and the campaign against the apartheid states in Southern Africa caused race discrimination to be consistently condemned within the General Assembly in a way that contrasts with the long silence with respect to sex discrimination.

27. The Women's Convention was adopted in 1979, the same year as the publication of Catharine MacKinnon's ground-breaking *Sexual Harassment of Working Women.*

28. European Convention for the Protection of Fundamental Rights and Freedoms, Nov. 4, 1950, ETS No. 5 and 11 Protocols.

29. European Social Charter, pt. I, Oct. 18, 1961, 529 U.N.T.S. 89, revised Strasbourg June 3, 1996, ETS No. 163.

30. American Convention on Human Rights, art. 26, Nov. 22, 1969, OAS TS no. 36.

31. Protocol of San Salvador, Nov. 17, 1988, OAS TS no. 69, arts. 6–8.

32. *Id.* at art. 19.

33. On November 4, 2000, the Council of Europe opened for signature Protocol No. 12 to the Convention for the Protection of Human Rights and Fundamental Freedoms, ETS No. 177, a general prohibition of discrimination.

34. African Charter on Human Rights and Peoples' Rights (Banjul Charter), art. 15, June 27, 1981, *reprinted in* 21 I.L.M. 58 (1982).

35. *See id.* at art. 2.

36. Catherine Barnard, "Gender Equality in the European Union," in *The EU and Human Rights* 215, 217 (Philip Alston, ed., 1999).

37. *See* European Commission Recommendation on the protection and dignity of men and women at work, Nov. 27, 1991, 92/131/EEC; Council Resolution on the Dignity of Women and Men at Work [1990] OJ C157/3; and Code of Practice to Combat Sexual Harassment, Dec. 19, 1991, 92/C 27/01; *see also* Catherine Barnard, *EC Employment Law* 200 (1995).

38. *Id.* at 253.

39. Council Directive 76/207/EEC is aimed at eliminating direct and indirect discrimination in the work context.

40. Barnard notes that the equal treatment Directive requires a more favorably treated comparator of the opposite sex and falls short of providing a principle of equality based upon disadvantage; *supra* note 37 at 254.

41. Hilary Charlesworth and Christine Chinkin, *The Boundaries of International Law: A Feminist Analysis* 187–88 (2000).

42. This is one reason behind the campaign for an Optional Protocol to the Women's Convention providing, inter alia, for the right of individual complaint. *See* Andrew Byrnes and Jane Connors, "Enforcing the Human Rights of Women: A Complaints Procedure for the Convention on the Elimination of All Forms of Discrimination Against Women," 21 *Brooklyn Journal of International Law* 679 (1996).

43. The Optional Protocol to the Convention on the Elimination of All Forms of Discrimination Against Women was adopted by General Assembly Resolution A/54/4. Oct. 6, 1999.

44. U.N. GAOR, 47th Sess., Supp. No. 38, U.N. Doc. A/47/38.

45. Article 18 of the Women's Convention requires state parties to submit a report on the progress made in implementing the Convention within one year after its entry into force for the state concerned and at least every four years thereafter.

46. *See also* Charlotte Bunch, "Women's Rights as Human Rights: Towards a Revision of Human Rights," 12 *Human Rights Quarterly* 486 (1990); Dorothy Q. Thomas and Michele Beasley, "Domestic Violence as a Human Rights Issue," 15 *Human Rights Quarterly* 36 (1993) 36; Catharine MacKinnon, "On Torture: A Feminist Perspective on Human Rights," in *Human Rights in the Twenty-First Century: A Global Perspective* (Kathleen Mahoney and Paul Mahoney eds., 1993); Rhonda Copelon, "Intimate Terror: Understanding Domestic Violence as Torture," in *Human Rights of Women: National and International Perspectives* 116 (Rebecca Cook ed., 1994).

47. *See Commission on the Status of Women, Programme for the U.N. Decade for Women: Equality, Development and Peace, 1976–1985,* U.N. Doc. E/5894 (1976).

48. *U.N. World Conference on Human Rights: Vienna Declaration and Programme of Action, supra* note 19, pt. I, para. 18.

49. *See Declaration on the Elimination of Violence against Women,* G.A. Res. 48/104 (1993).

50. *See Platform for Action, supra* note 3, paras. 112, 224.

51. This language is repeated in *id.*, para. 113(b).

52. Established by the U.N. Commission on Human Rights in 1994 to examine the causes and consequences of violence against women, Hum. Rts. Comm. Res. 1994/45.

53. *Preliminary Report, supra* note 7, para. 190.

54. *Id.*, para. 202; *cf. Platform for Action, supra* note 3, para. 161 (recognizing the experience of sexual harassment as an affront to dignity and as preventing women from making a contribution commensurate with their abilities).

55. *See Platform for Action, supra* note 3, paras. 126(a), 178(b)–(c).

56. *Id.*, paras. 120, 124(d).

57. Inter-American Convention on the Prevention, Punishment and Eradication of Violence against Women, art. 2(b), *reprinted in* 23 I.L.M. 1535 (1994).

58. *See id.*, arts. 10–12.

59. Civil Appeal Nos. 226–27, 1999.

60. Aug. 19–20, 1994, reprinted in the *Promotion of the Human Rights of Women and the Girl Child Through the Judiciary: Commonwealth Declarations and Strategies for Action,* Commonwealth Secretariat, London 1997.

61. *See* Dianne Otto, "Holding Up Half the Sky but for Whose Benefit?" 6 *Australian Feminist Law Journal* 7 (1996).

62. *See* Yumi Lee, "Violence Against Women: Reflections of the Past and Strategies for the Future—An NGO Perspective," 19 *Adelaide Law Review* 45 (1997).

63. *Id.* at 51.

64. *Platform for Action, supra* note 3, para. 119.

Afterword

CATHARINE A. MacKINNON

In the quarter century since some sex forced by power became illegal in the United States, has anything changed?

The experience has been named, its injuries afforded the dignity of a civil rights violation, raising the human status of its survivors. Resentment of unwanted sex under unequal conditions is expressed more openly and given more public respect. Women may feel more valid and powerful, less stigmatized and scared, more like freedom fighters and less like prudes, when they turn down sex they do not want in unequal settings. Many more people know that a sexual harasser is a sex bigot and see that the use of power to leverage sexual access is a tool of dominance, whether the perpetrator knows that or not. Where sex equality laws apply — most employment and education, some housing — there is someplace to go to complain. Law is considerably more responsive to survivors than it was before, whether they refuse sexual bargains, resist sexualized environments, or comply with sexual demands they cannot avoid.

But sexual harassment is still not actionable every place it occurs;[1] zero tolerance is the rule virtually nowhere; resistance is far from safe or costless; perpetrators often protect one another, and sometimes victims protect them too. Institutions are often recalcitrant in taking responsibility and are often absolved of liability when they are oblivious. Victims seldom receive the support they deserve. Complaining about sexual harassment can be more injurious, if also more self-respecting, than suffering in silence.[2] Forms of power used to force sex other than economic, educational, or governmental power of position — common sources of such power outside the context of warfare include age, familial relation, immigration status, racism, custodial position, drug addiction, and medical or spiritual authority — remain exempt from the facial reach of most equality laws. So far as is known, men sexually harass women as often as they did before sexual harassment became illegal.[3]

What has changed is the stakes. Sexually diddling the staff or the students used to be an open secret or joke, regarded as a perhaps deplorable but trivial pecadillo of some men, a tic of the person or perk of the position or both. Whatever else the man did or was outweighed the importance of whatever she said he did to her sexually. In many circles, such dismissive norms continue to reign. But, in going from a gripe to a grievance, in moving from whispers in secret to pleadings in federal court, sexual harassment went from an unnamed low-risk undertaking backed by a tacit understanding of tolerance among men to a public claim women could bring themselves under open rules with serious potential consequences for perpetrators.

The old tacit deal men had among themselves — to mutually overlook what other men did to women sexually unless an important man's claim was infringed, a deal that often encompassed the criminal law and authorities and often still does — was suddenly off. The calculation had to change. Once women could invoke and pursue civil process and sanctions for their own violation, the legality of coerced sex, and the costs to perpetrators of exposing it, newly depended on women. In a system in which even being subject to such a claim can have social weight, the fact that sexually aggrieved women were decision-makers in their own sexual grievances enhanced the civil rights law's function as a system of representation.[4] Sexual harassment became no longer something that journalists just knew about the powerful but kept quiet, or an experience by definition personal hence irrelevant to fitness for public office. Whether cynically or respectfully, as a pawn or a person, *she* suddenly counted.

Visible and audible, as an injured party, someone with relevant information, a woman can at the least make a man look bad, perhaps cost him a great deal. If the allegations are true, he is now potentially subject to real financial, reputational, and political as well as personal costs. Sexual harassment is serious business — or at least its exposure is. Women are not just bearers or objects of rights but actors in a sphere in which they had previously been acted upon. In this respect, and to this degree, women went from sexual objects of use and exchange to citizens. With women no longer absorbing the entire cost of this conduct in private, sexual politics went public, shifting the ground of political convention and becoming a visible part of politics as usual. In many instances, both on the individual level and for the polity at large, this change has made all the difference in the world.

Fundamentally, sexual harassment law transformed what was a moral foible (if that) into a legal injury to equality rights. What had been, if anything, reprehensible and deplorable, one of life's little joys or a minor rock in the road depending on your moral code or whether you were on the giving or receiving end, had real possible comeback attached. Sexually harassing conduct had been socially encouraged as masculine for perpetrators and further eroticized by being putatively but not really off-limits, while being an experience of shame for victims that kept them disempowered in the name of protection without protecting them. Now, sexual abuse remains sexualized. But sexual harassment law has changed this tut-tut no-no, a behavior that was essentially allowed while being decried only if embarrassingly displaced into public view, into an equality claim with collective meaning and the dignity of human rights that handed victims legitimate power to protect themselves, with sanctions backed by the state. To the question what is wrong with sexual harassment, previously to be answered with reference to a moral code for so-called private life, the law provided a new answer: sexual harassment is sex discrimination. That is, it is a practice of inequality on the basis of gender, an integral act of subordinate civil status because of sex, a practice of treating a person as less than fully socially human because that person is a woman or a man, a status-based treatment of hierarchy, of dominance, that is illegal.

Once the question became whether particular acts are or are not sexual harassment by legal standards—the threshold question being whether the behavior happened "because of . . . sex,"[5] meaning that it happened because of the victim's sex or gender—the question whether the behavior is morally bad was superseded, rendered obsolete and properly irrelevant to law, except perhaps for assessing punitive damages.[6] Judgments of magnitude, such as whether specific acts are sufficiently "severe" to be actionable as a hostile environment, correctly became questions of how severely discriminatory, how severely unequal, the acts are on a gendered scale, not how severely bad they are by moral compass. Judges and juries are thus called upon to ask not "is this bad?" They are called upon to ask "is this unequal?" While morality seeks to conform conduct to standards of right and wrong, whatever they may be, equality addresses the relative status and power of groups in society and is animated by an imperative of nonhierarchical treatment. Questions such as whether the other sex was subjected to similar behavior, whether the abuse was marked by gendered norms, and whether the treatment subordinated women or men as such, are determinative. How wrong, evil, or reprehensible the behavior or the parties are felt to be, becomes, within the inequality framework, properly inoperative.

Of course judgments of value remain involved. But they are equality values — not manners, civility, religion, propriety, decency, custom, or other value systems or sources of rules or codes or norms for interpersonal behavior. Once the legislative or constitutional judgment has been made to guarantee equality, whether it is good or bad to do so in particular cases is no longer a judicial question; whether a particular case presents inequalities is. Most fundamentally, the moral imperative to treat another person in a good way, *as if* they are fully human, is replaced by the requisite legal perception that, within the scope of the legal coverage, they *are* equal human beings — say, workers or students — whatever their sex or gender. In the case of sexual harassment, to use them as if they are sexual things becomes a category mistake, an instance of treating a human being as if she is not one, not a moral infraction about which people can differ, depending on their values. The argument that something is good is different from the argument that something is. While morality dwells in the normative, equality in this sense and setting is an empirical recognition, requiring not a judgment of how people ought to be treated but a cognition of the fact of their equal humanity across a specified line of particularity.

One obvious benefit of this approach, as befits a diverse society, has been that no moral agreement, community of belief, moral like-mindedness, or cultural convergence has been needed to apply sex equality standards to inequality's social harms. No particular moral sensitivity has been required to identify their existence. In any case, people with radically divergent moral commitments have to be able to implement equality laws or they will fail. While moral disagreements may underlie and be displaced onto equality questions, equality questions are properly resolved on equality grounds.

The transformation from moralism to equality, from treating people poorly or well to treating them without group rank, must occur for equality law to promote sex equality in substance. Among other reasons, this is because traditional morality upholds dominance in sex, which it genders, by defining men dominating women as "good" sex — as institutionalized, for instance, in the patriarchal family. This morality, with exceptions for extreme cases, tends to refuse to recognize that events empirically exist that it normatively rejects. Child sexual abuse, for instance, is considered exceptional rather than constant because conventional morality finds it "bad," with the result that the fact that it is done to more than a third of all girls under eighteen, and many boys, in the United States, mostly by heterosexually identified men, is regularly denied.[7] Just as traditional morality defines certain sexual behavior as right, such as male dominance in sex, even though members of powerless groups are systematically and disproportionally endangered or violated by it, sexual behavior that takes place outside favored institutional structures is defined as wrong, regardless of whether anyone is harmed. Same-sex sexuality and prostitution are both deemed "bad" by traditional morality, for instance, although the former can be not only unharmful but validating, loving, affirmatively desired, and a resistance to male dominance, while the latter tends toward the opposite on every score. Conventional morality tends to value people unequally on the basis of sex, sexuality, race, age, class, and other unequal station in life. Their sexual abuse thus is often attributed to the moral character of the actors rather than to their relative positions of inequality, making sexual injuries of inequality difficult or impossible to see.

Conservative moralism holds sex is bad, liberal moralism that sex is good — although neither fully owns up in public. Most conservatives do not want to oppose the secular religion or appear uncool or passé; most liberals do not want to be identified with sexual abuse, at least not in all of its forms. Neither morality adequately addresses sexual abuse because neither faces it as a practice of inequality: a reality of social condition, situation, status, and treatment rather than bad acts by bad people. The conventional morality of sexual regulation, whether of the Left or the Right, may at times decry the abuse of power by the powerful, but it systematically resists criticizing or undermining the fact of that power and its unequal distribution. Commonly, unequal power in private is defended, including by opposing the entry of equality law into the so-called private realm, which tends to be any place sexuality happens.[8] Most conventional morality in practice permits women and men of all ages who are seen by power as less valuable, thereby designated for use, to be sexually violated and exploited with relative impunity by those, most of them adult straight men, seen as more valuable and positioned higher up on the social food chain. Sexual morality thus traditionally entrenches what it purports to regulate or prohibit while punishing sexuality that challenges its hegemony, which is the hegemony of power itself. The misogyny characteristic of traditional morality — ranking vanishingly small numbers of women whose abuse matters and will be believed above the multitudes whose does not; imposing heterosexuality so as to make invisible anyone whose abuse either fits traditional norms (is "just sex") or deviates from them (is "perverse" rather than injurious) — puts the role of morality compared with equality in this body of case law at the heart of the question of whether anything that matters has changed.

The inquiry is thus framed: Has the sexual harassment claim, as applied, shed moralism — the normative calculus of right and wrong, good and bad —

to emerge fully as a legal injury of discrimination, an injury defined by social harm of unequal treatment? Does sexual harassment law prohibit harm to members of socially subordinated groups through sex, no more and no less? Specifically, is the inequality of power between women and men that the traditional moral approach to sex keeps in place — an approach that remains as socially dominant as sex inequality — being altered by the law of sexual harassment, or have sexual harassment law's doctrines, applications, and dynamics internalized, replicated, and extended sexual morality? If the latter, the question of whether sexual injury is a recognized wrong of discrimination is being effectively relitigated in case after case, courts finding discrimination when injuries meet the standard moral code's rules for the "bad" and not when they do not, even when the behavior is sex-discriminatory, while finding sexual behavior that they rate immoral to be sex-discriminatory even when it does not violate sex equality standards. The question is, is sexual harassment law transforming social inequality into equality of status, or merely mutating moral prohibitions into equality guise?

The concern is whether sexual harassment law updates, disguising in civil rights skin, the same underlying moral dynamics that continue to drive sexual morality in the interest of male dominance and against the interests of women and all subordinated peoples. If sexual harassment law has mapped itself onto these underlying moral dynamics, hijacking human rights rhetoric to further sexual repression and sexual stigma, while permitting the sexual abuse of power with impunity, it is morality's wolf in the sheep's clothing of equality. Read against twenty-five years of case law and political upheaval, the essays in this volume suggest that this is not the case, that the changes sexual harassment law has brought about are real if as yet incomplete.

Sexual harassment law originated the recognition that sexual abuse is a practice of inequality of the sexes, a recognition increasingly embraced and expanded, even taken as given, in the laws of nations around the world and in international forums.[9] In changing the understanding of the facts of sexual harassment's facts from morality to equality — from religious to human rights referents, from internal psychological and ideal predicates to external material ones — the cornerstone has been the conceptualization of the injury as sex discrimination.

To qualify as a legal injury of sex discrimination, the challenged behavior must be "based on sex," meaning that it happened because of the victim's gender. Ever since the breakthrough cases of the mid-1970s, in which facts of sexual harassment were first found to state a claim for sex discrimination as a matter of law, the question whether a claim is "based on sex" has not usually been extensively litigated when the alleged perpetrator is a man, the victim is a woman, and the activity complained of is sexual.[10] As a Ninth Circuit panel put the animating understanding, "sexual harassment is *ordinarily* based on sex. What else could it be based on?"[11] In practice, unless challenged, the individual parties are taken as exemplars of the sex groups of which they socially present as members, and the challenged behavior is understood as gendered on the usually inexplicit, perhaps not fully conscious, view that sexual aggression is socially gendered male and sexual victimization, female.

With the allegations thus made not by individuals as such (as they were in tort precursors)[12] but by individuals in their capacity as members of groups, and no longer of "bad" behavior but of practices integral to a social system of gendered group-based inequality that produces injuries of second-class citizenship, the typical parties become no longer bad men and virtuous women but dominating men and subordinated women. With the gravamen of the offense changed from sin to injury, its identification from moral judgment to reality perception, the questions raised change from whether anything is wrong to what has occurred, in a context that moves from private to public and from morality to politics: sexual politics.[13] Sexual harassment doctrine squarely entrenches in law the position that moral valuations of relative personal worth and sexual propriety are not the point in this legal claim. Harm because of one's membership in a gender group is.

In jurisdictions where the claim for sexual harassment is not clearly located in law as a form of sex discrimination, as in France,[14] the doctrine continues, in society as well as law, to be confused with traditional moral strictures, and to be socially delegitimated by that confusion. In this setting, laws against sexual harassment are likely to be misconstrued as repressive, as restrictions on what is reflexively considered the sexual freedom of perpetrators, rather than as liberating and enhancing to the sexual freedom of those who need no longer be their victims. Where the law construes sexual harassment as a tort but one of sex discrimination, as in Japan, the understanding is accordingly mixed.[15] India regards sexual harassment as sex discrimination but in some respects continues to treat it as a moral issue,[16] to the detriment of its effectiveness as a force for change for women, although the judicial trend is in the equality and human rights direction. Much of the shape of the claim's development can be seen to reflect the strength and focus of the women's movement in each country, specifically whether that movement has addressed the realities of sexual abuse. Many have not. To the degree that voice is absent or muted, moralism fills the void to the detriment of victims and the legal claim's development as a force for equality.

If so-called anti-sex attitudes of traditional male dominant moralism were driving the law of sexual harassment — that is, if sexual harassment has been recognized as a civil right because male-dominant moralists are sex-negative — stronger prohibitions might be expected to be applied against expressly sexual forms of harassment because they are sexual than to other forms of harassment that are not sexual.[17] This has not happened.[18] So long as they were not expressly sexual, many forms of seemingly nonsexual abuse that might be construed as gender-based harassment have been integral to sex discrimination law all along — whether as verbal abuse showing intent or motive, direct evidence shifting the burden of proof to defendants, sex stereotyping, or gender harassment itself.[19] In fact, it was the recognition that expressly sexual forms of harassment are sex-based discrimination that led to expanded judicial recognition of gender-based forms of harassment that are not expressly sexual.

Of course, the analytical relation between sexual and not-explicitly-sexual-but-gendered harassment is complicated by the reality of their near inextricability in the world. Given that sexuality is socially gendered and gender socially sexualized,[20] separating the two forms of harassment is problematic as well as difficult. Even conceptually separable facts almost always occur together and are thus adjudicated in the same cases. To say whether acts of abuse that are gendered but not sexual are ignored where the comparably severe act, if sexual, would be recognized approaches the impossible. Comparing the severity of sexual with apparently nonsexual-but-gendered abuse is an abstract and speculative venture. Distinguishing between sexist abuse that is sexual and sexist abuse that is not clearly sexual has thankfully been rendered legally unnecessary by express judicial recognition that gendered abuse need not be expressly sexual to be actionable as harassing, making gender harassment axiomatically (if not completely or always, any more than sexual abuse is) covered under sex discrimination law as sexual harassment.[21]

If sexual harassment law were animated by anti-sex hostility, that law would be unlikely to extend, as it has, to gender-based abuse that, while demeaning or derogatory or belittling, is not expressly sexual.[22] The fact that it does so extend is more persuasively explained by equality law's being anti-abuse. Surely it means something that conventional morality has been, if fairly superficially, anti-sex for easily a couple of hundred years, without being anti-abuse (sexual or otherwise), and without before seeing sexual harassment as wrong. While admitting to neither, conventional morality and its legal regime have been both pro-sex (in the hegemonic hierarchical heterosexual sense) and pro-abuse during this entire period, as the equally long absence of effective laws against sexual forms of intrusion testify. Only when the behavior became framed as a harm of unequal gender status on the basis of sex, that is, as a material injury of inequality, was its harm recognized as legally significant.

Certainly, courts and agencies often fail to recognize simple sex discrimination in particular cases, such as when women are deprived of less favorable work assignments or training opportunities because they are women.[23] This observation hardly indicts sexual harassment law as such or suggests an overweening emphasis on specifically sexual forms of abuse at work. If courts and agencies are not as sensitive as they should be to simple sex discrimination, including to gendered harassment in particular cases, they also expressly tolerate much egregious *sexual* behavior in employment and education because it resembles customary sexual practices that conventional morality tolerates, or because they see the victim as morally bad or worthless.[24] A law that was simply anti-sex would not do this. A law that was not yet sufficiently sensitive to abuse, tolerating it, including when sexual, so long as it conforms to traditional morality, would. Any emphasis on sexual abuse in sexual harassment case law over other forms of gender-based abuse, should it exist, may also be due to the particularly transparent misogyny of much harassment that is sexual, or to a choice of sexual forms of abuse by some especially misogynist perpetrators, rather than to a judicial slighting of nonsexual forms of inequality in harassment cases.

Analysis of sexual harassment law's treatment of racist sexual abuse supports the view that sexual harassment law is not moralism redux. Standing against the racist dimensions of sexual denigration that traditional sexual morality builds in are the early successful sexual harassment cases brought by women of color.[25] Far from supporting the enforced sexual availability of women of color on white men's terms, sexual harassment law in these cases opposed the stereotyping of women of color by traditional morality that stigmatizes their sexuality so as to make it insusceptible of being seen as violated. In so doing, sexual harassment law thus became a central vehicle in exposing the reality of, and cementing the legal claim for, race and sex discrimination combined. Although intersectional sexual abuse is not adequately recognized nearly as often as it occurs, traditional morality would not, and does not, support such a recognition at all. The reach of Title VII to racial and religious harassment was similarly predicated on sexual harassment precedents, opposing conventional morality's myriad racist and religious biases in both sexual and nonsexual forms.[26] The cases reveal that, while an undercurrent of traditional morality's tolerance of sexual abuse of women by men can be seen in some cases — and may even be an undertow that will have to be fought by plaintiffs in most cases on some level, so long as inequality exists — anti-sex moralism can hardly be said to be driving sexual harassment law. On the contrary, sexual harassment law stands against traditional morality's tolerance of the sexual abuse of women with less power by men with more.

Sexual harassment law also stands against the abuse of men with less power by men with more. In an area of law where precedents have so often been set by men claiming equality with women, as is the case with sex equality law, rather than the other way around, the fact that male victims of men would be seen to have the same legal rights as women victims of men might not seem like news. In sexual harassment law, it was. Traditional morality has largely suppressed the possibility of recognizing that men can be sexually violated or subordinated, at once making sexual violation of men inconceivable and naturalizing women's sexual vulnerability as biological, obscuring the social function of both forms of abuse in male supremacy. Sexual harassment law, in recognizing that men also dominate and harm men through sex, took a step traditional morality never has, indeed a step that adherence to traditional morality largely precludes. Most cases of sexual harassment are male-on-female on their facts, but given the fixation of sex discrimination law with sex differentials as the method for discerning sex-based treatment, it was by no means obvious that sexual harassment in a same-sex context of man-on-man, or men-on-man, would be found to be sex-discriminatory.

The *Oncale* case, which so found,[27] marks the first time the sex equality principle has been found to be violated in a same-sex factual setting by the U.S. Supreme Court, and one of the precious few such findings ever. Although we do not yet know if the same rule will be applied when an out gay man is harassed, it should, at pain of violating the constitutional rule of equal protection of the laws as well as sexual harassment holdings.[28] And although we do not yet know if the prohibition on same-sex harassment will extend to protect mutually desired same-sex intimacy when that is the predicate for homophobic discrimination, it also should. Thus sex equality law, having protected people with less power from unwanted sex in a same-sex setting, may, by building on sexual harassment precedent, come to protect wanted sex by groups with less power in a same-sex setting as well.[29]

In paving the way for protection of gay men from specifically sexual gay-bashing as sex discrimination (as well as for putatively nonsexual gay-bashing, which predictably will be easier to address by law as well as hard to separate from the sexual forms), and ultimately in recognizing that sex discrimination prohibitions require nondiscrimination against gay men and lesbian women as such, sexual harassment law, far from internalizing traditional morality, will have helped produce outcomes that traditional morality squarely opposes. Sexual harassment law's counter-hegemonic logic may conceivably be reversed or twisted backward by dominant moral forces, as Janet Halley fears,[30] although it has yet to. Her particular concern may more exemplify a reassertion of dominant moral rules, as Marc Spindelman suggests,[31] insofar as sexual harassment's equality rule tolls the bell on the sexual pleasures of a sex-discriminatory gender-hierarchical social order, specifically on the eroticism of the top-down unequal definition of sexuality that traditional morality has long guarded.

As with the basis of the claim in gender, tensions between morality and equality can also be discerned beneath sexual harassment law's "unwelcomeness" doctrine. The consent rule of traditional morality builds inequality of power into the criminal law of sexual abuse by tending to authoritatively assume, under conditions of inequality, that whatever sex happens is mutually desired unless proven otherwise. Apart from statutory presumptions based on age differentials, usually only physical forms of force (and typically quite extreme force) are recognized by the rape law as making sex nonconsensual.[32] The *Vinson* case exposed how inequality between a male supervisor and a female subordinate could produce sex that was consensual under this criminal law but unwelcome to the woman — hence unequal under sex discrimination law. In Mechelle Vinson's case, sex forced by inequality was found illegal.[33] Morality's "consent" was thereby exposed as consistent with inequality, as a fictional synonym for desire or choice but consistent with forced sex all along. "Unwelcomeness" was correspondingly framed as consent's equality-based, non-double-talking, meaningful alternative. The doctrine of unwelcomeness *could* become what the doctrine of consent is now: a pretend stand-in for desire and choice that in application means its opposite, sex the woman does not desire and in which she has no choice. Whether legal unwelcomeness becomes what it was created to oppose — for example, in findings that some women actually welcome abuse they could not refuse — thus becomes another facet of the question of the continuing force of moralism in sexual harassment law.

Whether a woman wants sex is a question of fact, posing the question of who proves what in a case that raises it. Why the so-called hypersensitive woman in this setting is the reviled Puritan instead of a miner's canary or a thin-skulled plaintiff has never been explained. Yet few reported sexual harassment cases reveal unwelcomeness as problematic in practice.[34] After *Harris*, courts generally assess the substance of unwelcomeness as part of whether a hostile environment was "subjectively abusive,"[35] inviting inquiry into the woman's standards and potentially her moral status as defined under male supremacy, rather than remaining focused on the harasser's actions in social context. Courts quite often find abusive conduct unwelcome even when defendants try, in customary moralistic fashion, to smear the plaintiff as a bad woman, hence uninjurable.[36] It is surprising that this attempt to turn inequality into noninjury has not succeeded more often in reported cases. Louise Fitzgerald's reflections on the litigation process pretrial support a concern that beneath the surface, traditional moralism is being smuggled into sexual harassment litigation,[37] clawing unwelcomeness back to consent, potentially devastating plaintiffs and disabling their resistance to sex forced on them by inequality and excluding them from access to justice in a way that is largely insulated from appellate review. One creative proposal would require an accused harasser to prove that the woman indicated that she wanted the sexual attention she is suing for, of which affirmative initiation and statements of desire would be good evidence.[38] Certainly, to the extent unwelcomeness is reinterpreted in traditional consent terms — violating *Vinson*, regressing to traditional moralism, and supporting dominant power — sexual harassment law becomes no longer a sex equality instrument.

Strong evidence that sexual harassment law to date is not merely replicating male dominant morality is provided by the virtual nonexistence of a defense of sexual harassment as "speech." If the law of sexual harassment was to protect this form of abuse by protecting one form dominant power takes, sexual harassment would be protected speech, as pornography is under U.S. obscenity law, and no harm done to women through it would be recognized as illegal.[39] This point is supported by Janine Benedet's discussion of the relation between pornography and sexual harassment law in Canada, where pornography's harms to adult women and its destructive effects on equality of the sexes, as well as the illegality of hate speech as a form of inequality, are constitutionally recognized.[40] Given the absence of such recognitions in the United States, the fact that U.S. law has so far approached this aspect of the experience of sexual harassment through its consequences to the unequal, rather than through speech — a legally protected artifact through which this abuse is, in part, inflicted by the powerful — is nigh on miraculous. And given the extent to which existing law of freedom of speech in the United States tracks dominant morality by effectively guaranteeing that the powerful (whether based on race, wealth, sex, age, or a combination) get what they want, unlimited by legal equality guarantees, perhaps the strongest evidence available that sexual harassment law does *not* build in power's morality is the fact that — as the essays in this volume make abundantly clear — calling sexual harassment "speech" has so little traction in sexual harassment law[41] as barely to have surfaced in case law to date. Calling sexual harassment protected speech does not pass the straight-face test. Not yet.

The major clouds on the immediate horizon are the cases on liability. They, too, can be read as shaped by a moralistic undertow. Under traditional moral rules, sexual harassment qua sexual is deemed an individual and private act, presumptively exempt from public accountability, not an act that conventional morality is comfortable referring to public authorities or attributing to group membership or to institutional entities. Intimacy guarantees impunity, and the more power the perpetrator has, the more his so-called intimacy is insulated from account. By extension, forms of violation that happen to women as women, especially the intimate kind, are deemed personal and private and cultural; forms of violation that happen also to men are more likely to be called public and institutional and political, eventually. Once the group membership hurdle was cleared in considering sexual harassment sex-based, the account-ability question loomed. In the last quarter of the twentieth century, the center of gravity in U.S. sexual harassment litigation shifted from a dispute over whether sexual harassment, if it happened, is legally sex-based to a contest over whether, given that it happened, anyone will be held responsible for it.

For decades, it has been assumed in U.S. law that if an institutional actor discriminated, the institution discriminated; if the act was discriminatory, the employer was accountable for it. In one narrowing move, many courts have now held that individual perpetrators cannot be held responsible under Title VII if they are not the employer.[42] Since Title IX arises under the Spending Clause, monitoring a contractual relation between Congress and recipient entities, only institutional recipients can be defendants,[43] focusing explicitly the question of what actions put the school on the hook. It is no accident that the Title VII cases establishing that individuals were not liable for discrimina-tion under it were brought for sexual harassment, rather than for any other kind of discrimination: traditional morality deems sex quintessentially per-sonal and as such exempt from public accountability. It is also no accident that the hurdles sexual harassment plaintiffs must clear for institutional liability in either work or school are now distinct in kind and higher in height from those any other kind of discrimination plaintiff must clear. Again, sex is morally regarded as quintessentially personal, making it uniquely difficult to attribute responsibility for it to entities. As neither Title VII nor Title IX yet runs to individual perpetrators, and institutional entities often do not meet the Court's stringent (and often unlikely) prerequisites for so-called vicarious liability,[44] current Supreme Court doctrine restricts employer or educational institution accountability so that sexual harassment by legal definition can happen and no one and nothing will be held liable for it. Under these conditions, sexual harassment can be a violation without a violator, a legal injury without a legal remedy.

The cases on liability thus track traditional morality in a number of ways. Institutions that are oblivious to what is taking place on their watch tend to be insulated from responsibility. The implicit assumption seems to be that if the institution does not know, it cannot be bad, so the victim is not injured, or at least no injury of inequality is attributable to the institution. See no evil, hear no evil, incur no liability. Apart from the disconnection between the morally based intent requirement and the unequal consequences that flow regardless of intent, the rationale for why institutions are assumed not responsible for what goes on under their aegis remains murky and elusive — particularly in the workforce, where the existence of a liability rule for sexual harassment that is different from other forms of employment discrimination has never been explained. Giving more legal power to the more socially powerful, adult working women, and less legal power to the less socially powerful, schoolgirls, the liability cases also track conventional morality by making it more difficult for children in schools to hold school districts accountable for their sexual harassment than it is for working women to hold their employers accountable for theirs.[45] These rules, by operating in reality counter to traditional morality's protectionist protestations, but consistent with its predilections for power, go far to subvert the equality principles established in the substance of the claim, smuggling conventional morality's unequal power relations in through the back door of liability.

Under the guise of a liability ruling, the Supreme Court holding in the *Ellerth* case, for example, altered the substantive law of sexual harassment for the worse. There, it held that a threat of a quid pro quo followed by a constructive discharge — a woman having to leave her job because it was discriminatorily unbearable — was what the Court termed an "incomplete" quid pro quo.[46] Under the EEOC Guidelines from 1980 through 1998, proposing an exchange of sex for a job indulgence was actionable in itself. In the language of the guidelines: "Unwelcome sexual advances, requests for sexual favors, and other verbal or physical conduct of a sexual nature constitute sexual harassment *when* submission to such conduct is made either explicitly or implicitly a term or condition of an individual's employment."[47] Most courts held accordingly, whether or not employment consequences followed from having or not having the sex.[48] Before *Ellerth*, a threat of a quid pro quo, meaning an offer or a demand to exchange sex for employment benefits, was a quid pro quo. *Ellerth* rendered sexual threats, unless sufficiently severe or pervasive to create a hostile environment, empty puffery.

Kim Ellerth's supervisor, in a sexualized context, told her that he could "make your life very hard or very easy" on the job, and followed up by making it very hard for the sexually recalcitrant Ms. Ellerth; later, he said, as he rubbed her knees at her promotion interview, that he hesitated about promoting her because she was not "loose enough" for him.[49] Rather than recognizing such sexual conditions on work as actionable discrimination, hanging like Damocles' sword over only some employees because the supervisors' power was being heterosexually deployed, the Supreme Court took the view that until the quid completes the quo, or the environment is made severely or pervasively hostile, sexual threats do no harm of discrimination at all. The case thus raised and disposed of, but barely confronted, the basic question of the nature of sexual harassment's harm — specifically of whether the employee in and at work, or only the employee's work, attracts the law's equality protection. It also raises the question of the line between the injury and its damages.

One might say that a quid pro quo statement is by definition a severe incident, making the workplace hostile. Perhaps courts will take this view. But sexual threats by superiors are also arguably injuries of sex discrimination in themselves, whether or not work is affected.[50] It may make sense to treat undelivered-upon sexual threats by coworkers under hostile environment rules, but with workplace superiors as perpetrators, a sexual threat is effectively delivered upon when uttered. As a result of the supervisor's power, the threat surrounds the worker each and every day. As Judge Cudahy noted in *Jansen*, the Seventh Circuit companion case to *Ellerth*, "quid pro quo is always a creature of power," presenting "the classic paradigm of powerful males forcing their wills on vulnerable females," whereby a "supervisor acts with actual or apparent authority when he promises employment goodies or threatens their withdrawal to extract sexual 'cooperation.' "[51] From the moment it is uttered by a supervisor, a quid pro quo statement imposes a sex-discriminatory condition of work. Such conditions are facially prohibited by Title VII's language. They are also that which makes the loss of a job when a worker leaves be considered a constructive discharge rather than a voluntary quit. In *Ellerth*, by contrast, it is as if only the job interest, not the person in the job, is protected from sex discriminatory conditions. In life, workers are harassed when harassed, not only when the consequences of that harassment further mature. In *Ellerth*, the Court did not explain why women workers should have to wait for the sword to fall, or fall on it themselves, before having a legal claim for sex discrimination.

In this light, the *Ellerth* ruling reflects a lapse in measuring sexual harassment as an injury on equality terms. It fails to grasp that sexual harassment law not only protects a person's work (the quo), but the person's equality in and at work. The same lapse is visible in the Court's differential liability rules that favor liability for sexual harassment that creates "tangible employment loss." Both *Faragher* and *Ellerth* make employers responsible for losses of this kind regardless of whether or not the victim reports, while requiring reports when the incident creates no tangible employment loss. This distinction is inadequate if it is not only a person's work but a person's equality at work, analogously not only their grades but their learning process in education, that civil rights laws exist to protect. *Ellerth* may also be read as reflecting the moral view that sexual threats in themselves are not bad enough to be illegal until they are delivered upon through employment losses. The statutory question, however, is whether such threats, executed or not, discriminate against an individual in terms or conditions of employment on the basis of sex. Is there any real doubt that quid pro quo threats do? A quid pro quo threat, from the moment uttered, is arguably a facially discriminatory "term" of employment as well as a discriminatory "condition," severe by definition. After *Ellerth*, the statement of a supervisor that "I haven't forgotten your review, it's on my desk," while patting his crotch, is either a single incident sufficiently severe to constitute a hostile environment, or it is now legally nothing.[52] One wonders if a noose hanging over an African-American's work station now must be used before it is actionable, or if a company is still liable for the fact that it is there.[53]

In the last quarter of the twentieth century, it was notably women's public accusations of sexual misdeeds by politically powerful men, not primarily cases in court, that seismically rocked public consciousness, although without the backdrop of liability for sexual harassment they would have been unlikely. The Thomas-Hill hearings of 1991 and the Clinton-Lewinsky affair of 1998 provided a field day for moralists of all stripes and decisively shaped sexual harassment thinking and adjudication. In both situations, men with power among men were challenged by other powerful men for sexual misuse of their power relative to women who had less power — far less — than they did. In neither circumstance did the affected woman sue or say that she had been sexually harassed. In both situations, the facts may or may not qualify as sexual harassment under law. In Professor Hill's case, the alleged abuse may or may not have constituted an illegally hostile environment when it happened because hostile environment law barely existed. In Ms. Lewinsky's case, the sex was apparently welcome, although the difference in power between the parties was extreme. In neither case was the man held liable for what he was said to have done. Yet both cases produced firestorms that consumed first the Right in defense of Judge Thomas, then the Left in defense of President Clinton, in rethinking whether sexual harassment — formally charged in neither instance — should be actionable. As sympathy for the exposed men surged across the political spectrum, moral outrage that their so-called private lives could be interrogated fed a resurgent defense of the sexual as such. Critique of inequality in sex was submerged, drowned.[54] The fallout is not over.

Had it not been for the development of sexual harassment law, it seems fair to say that Anita Hill's testimony, with its explosion of national and global consciousness on the issue, would be unlikely to have happened. Yet the closest controlling case to hers — the breakthrough case of Sandra Bundy holding that sexually hostile working environments were actionable as sex discrimination — may well have been too fragile, isolated, and recent to have reliably helped Professor Hill when it was handed down around the time of the injuries to which she testified.[55] Without her testimony before the Senate and the nation, Bill Clinton might not have been elected, as women enraged at Professor Hill's treatment by the Senate may have supplied his margin of victory. Without sexual harassment law, the impeachment of President Clinton, and the events surrounding it, would also not have unfolded as they did. It all began with Paula Jones's 1994 allegations of sexual harassment and proceeded fueled by, among other things, a heightened sensitivity to the place of extreme social inequality in sex that the law against sexual harassment focused, although most women continue to have sexual relations with men who have more power in society than they do.

When Paula Jones accused Bill Clinton of sexually harassing her,[56] and the Supreme Court allowed her case to proceed while he was in office,[57] the rules of power suddenly no longer outranked the rule of law, as they have since time immemorial. Droit de seigneur died, at least momentarily. Men could no longer rely on the informal (meaning real) power system safeguarded by traditional morality to get them out of the rules for treatment of women that the formal (meaning legal) power system of equality law prescribed. Panic set in. What used to be called indecent exposure by one's ultimate workplace superior coupled with a demand for oral sex and a guarded threat to keep it all quiet — Ms. Jones's allegations — were allowed to proceed toward trial in a case brought by the woman workplace subordinate subjected to it. The alleged perpetrator was no longer just a charming roué. He was a potential violator of human rights. The fact that he was the President of the United States did not exempt him. This represented real change.

What Professor Hill's allegations contributed to national consciousness on the subject of sexual harassment, the dismissal of Paula Jones's case for legal insufficiency[58] went a long way toward undermining. Given that what happened to Professor Hill was publicly perceived as sexual harassment, and what happened to Paula Jones was legally deemed not to be, it is worth observing that the acts that Paula Jones alleged — including penile exposure, physical contact, and threats — were arguably both more severe and more certainly within then-existing legal standards for sexual harassment than were the acts that Professor Hill alleged at the time that they occurred.

Under existing precedents, Paula Jones's case should have been permitted to go to trial on her quid pro quo allegations at the least, and probably on her hostile environment claim as well. The record documented that other women (specifically Gennifer Flowers) who had sex with Governor Clinton had received employment benefits.[59] This supported the issue of material fact as to whether Paula Jones was denied a job benefit as a result of her failure to have the sex Mr. Clinton proposed. Of the quid pro quo, I observed in 1979, "men with power to affect women's careers allow sexual factors to make a difference. So the threats are serious: those who do not comply are disadvantaged in favor of those who do."[60] Paula Jones allegedly did not receive a job benefit because she did not submit to sex, as evidenced by the fact that other women of record in the case did receive job benefits when they did. Although courts are not as clear as they might be on this question, one district court in dicta suggested that, under similar circumstances, if a woman plaintiff's employer "rewarded others in the office for their response to his action, she may indeed have faced an implied quid pro quo situation."[61] Supposing *Ellerth* must be satisfied, the failure to give the benefit "completes" the quid pro quo.

Although Paula Jones said sexual touching was forced on her, its accomplishment a forced submission, she did not submit to the particular sex act of fellatio demanded. She did, for a time, submit to the silence demanded: "You're a smart girl. Let's keep this between ourselves."[62] This submission may bring her circumstances in line with other submission cases in which quid pro quo has been authoritatively found.[63] Jones's case also did not present the contraindicating factors commonly used to deny a finding of quid pro quo in otherwise similar cases. Unlike in those cases, in her case there were threats at the time of the request;[64] she could reasonably have believed that he had the power to affect her job conditions;[65] and she took the implications of the threat seriously.[66] Moreover, the trial court's conclusion to the contrary, Ms. Jones did allege that adverse employment consequences flowed from her rejection of Bill Clinton's sexual advances: less challenging work assignments, a moved and less favorable work location, work by herself, an unpleasant working environment, and no work at all.[67] Such conditions have been found to be tangible enough to support a quid pro quo claim in other sexual harassment cases.[68] Finally, Mr. Clinton's requirement that Ms. Jones keep silent about his actions denied her access to a grievance process without fear of reprisals, an employment detriment in itself. A jury should have been permitted to judge the credibility of her factual allegations on these quid pro quo issues.

Arguably, Paula Jones also had a case for a hostile environment as a matter of law. Her version of the central incident included a superior's unwelcome touching of a subordinate's intimate body parts coupled with an attempted kiss, indecent exposure, and an unwelcome sexual demand or proposition.

The term "harassment" may connote to some a continuing course of conduct, as when the Third Circuit held that hostile work environments must be "pervasive and regular."[69] However, the U.S. Supreme Court's formulation of the hostile environment sexual harassment claim has squarely recognized in the disjunctive the "severe or pervasive" harassment that makes an abusive working environment actionable. This leaves room for isolated yet severe harassment alone to be enough.[70] The Court's subsequent dictum that "isolated incidents (unless extremely serious) will not amount to discriminatory changes in the terms or conditions of employment,"[71] while raising the bar on the severity of actionable isolated incidents, served further to underline the possibility that isolated incidents can be actionable in themselves if serious enough. Hundreds of acts of sexual assault were alleged in *Meritor*; two on one occasion were alleged in *Brzonkala*, where the Fourth Circuit held that "the rapes themselves created a hostile environment" for the plaintiff at school.[72] Awaiting authoritative clarification, some lower courts have thought isolated or single incidents of harassment per se insufficient to constitute hostile working environments.[73] Others have affirmed that a single discriminatory act can be enough, if sufficiently severe.[74] The question is, how severe is severe enough?

In *Clinton v. Jones*, Judge Susan Webber Wright found that the alleged incident, if true, "was certainly boorish and offensive" but not "one of those exceptional cases in which a single incident of sexual harassment, such as an assault, was deemed sufficient to state a claim of hostile work environment sexual harassment."[75] It is as if Judge Wright, rather than assessing whether the acts were unequal on the basis of sex, assimilated sexual harassment back to tort or criminal standards. As with criminal law, the injury in *Jones* was not assessed in light of the relative power of the parties. As with tort law, its gravamen was moral outrage rather than inequality. The moralism of this framing resonates with cases brought as both sexual harassment and intentional infliction of emotional distress or substantive due process together. In those cases, in analytic bleed-through, courts often hold that sexual incidents, while deplorable, are not outrageous and shocking enough to qualify as these torts.[76] Instead of measuring the severity of Paula Jones's allegations by sex equality standards — asking whether the challenged activity was gendered unequal or whether it was central to the historical subordination of women as a sex or whether men in that workplace had to work under similar conditions or whether sex equality at work could be achieved if such acts were tolerated — Judge Wright seems to have asked whether the acts were bad.

It was the wrong question, and took place in the context of a wider and equally legally irrelevant social discussion of whether Ms. Jones and her supporters were bad. Liberal moralists in particular contended that if Clinton was bad in whatever he did to Jones, the motives of his accusers were also bad in making or pursuing the claim, so it all cancelled out. Liberal moralists focused on whether Jones was in the grip of the evil Right in claiming to have been discriminated against. Conservative moralists tended to focus on how bad Clinton was rather than on whether the acts he was accused of were sex-discriminatory. In the motives morass, whether or not a woman had been discriminated against, whether or not sexual harassment — inequality on the basis of sex — had occurred, seemed not to matter much to either side. The impeachment debates foregrounded Monica Lewinsky, who did not claim forced sex and raised moral but not legal issues of equality, rather than Paula Jones, who did raise legal issues of inequality and did claim a form of forced sex. In this context, in the recurrent reflex of judges who morally decry acts while ensuring nothing will be done about them, on Judge Wright's moral scale — not a transparent one but clearly not calibrated to zero tolerance — the incident with Paula Jones became not bad enough.[77]

One virtually unnoticed case makes vividly clear that *Clinton v. Jones* may be confined to its facts and turned on the power of a powerful man rather than on legal standards applied to factual allegations. In 2001, the Eighth Circuit affirmed two rulings by Judge Susan Webber Wright in the sexual harassment case Sherry Moring brought under section 1983 against the Arkansas Department of Correction for the behavior of her supervisor, Gary Smith.[78] Smith had engaged her in a conversation of a sexual nature while they were on a business trip, then appeared uninvited at her hotel room door barely clothed, sat on her bed, touched her thigh, and attempted to kiss her. She asked him to leave and resisted his advance, pushed him back, leaned to the side to avoid him, and locked the door when he left. He also said she "owed" him for her position. Ms. Moring spoke thereafter of the incident often, avoided him, was under stress at her job, and was visibly upset over the incident. She testified that she was afraid and considered his behavior abusive and threatening. Judge Wright denied a defense motion for judgment as a matter of law and a motion for a new trial for abuse of discretion. On appeal, the Eight Circuit affirmed that a reasonable jury could find that the conduct would not have been directed at a male employee and that it was objectively hostile or abusive. The behavior was sex-based and sufficient to create a hostile working environment as a matter of law. The panel observed that "we are unaware of any rule of law holding that a single incident can never be sufficiently severe to be hostile-work-environment sexual harassment."[79]

Same judge, same statute, same state, same legal doctrine, same appellate circuit. But who ever heard of Mr. Smith? More similar facts are hard to imagine, except that Clinton's sexual aggression was alleged to have been more severe, and no evidence of similar exploits by Mr. Smith were noted. No one accused Ms. Moring of being trailer trash or a tool of the Right. She got a jury trial and no national press. She won.

Which is not to say that *Clinton v. Jones* did not have substantial effects. If, in the wake of the Hill-Thomas fiasco, sexual harassment was transformed from a back room joke into a weapon of politics as usual, after the Clinton-Jones-Lewinsky debacle, a cadre of liberal moralists seems to have decided that sex pressured by power of position is just sex,[80] not sexual exploitation or discrimination. In this respect, the discussion reverted to square one, to the time before sexual harassment was recognized as a legal claim. These critics, like their forebears who resisted sexual harassment being recognized as sex discrimination at all, and on many of the same grounds, never seem to have considered that their position might imply a critique of sex. Rather, they argued in essence that, since sexual harassment and sex are indistinguishable, the world should be made safe for sexual harassment. This missed the now rather obvious point that the sex they defend, sex that merges with sexual harassment as if that is all the sex there is, is unequal.

Epitomized by the slogan "all sex is harassment,"[81] the view seems to be that since women and men are gender unequals, all sex between them must, if sexual harassment law is right, be sex discrimination. Sexual harassment law is criticized in the name of sex; sex is not interrogated for an inequality that it and sexual harassment might share. If sex must be equal to be nondiscriminatory, they suggest, voices rising, the end of sex is at hand. Passing over the fact that there are no sex equality laws applicable anywhere in civil society except the islands of workplace and school, their point is not to try to equalize the sexes in the name of sexual mutuality and intimacy, or to provide equality rights that would promote equality in sexual relations. It is, instead, to try to make the world safe for sexual harassment by putting the political genie back into the personal bottle, de-exposing sexual exploitation by making it just another sexual practice, thus once again private, concealed, apolitical, and legally exempt.[82] The alternative of producing real sexual equality — the point of sexual harassment law — seems never to have crossed their minds.

Although Clarence Thomas was appointed to the Supreme Court, Anita Hill galvanized and inspired women. Seeing that their treatment was at least as egregious as hers, they swelled the numbers of complaints to the EEOC by coming forward by the thousands.[83] Whether women whose treatment is as egregious as Paula Jones's, who might well interpret the dismissal of her case as the reimposition of the old moral hierarchy of who counts and who does not, will stop resisting, turn their back on the courts, and return to silent subordination and despair remains to be seen.

The next twenty-five years could go one of two ways. The last twenty-five could be historicized as a "sex panic," sexual harassment law trivialized and distorted and invalidated into a hysteria and a witch hunt, sexual harassment itself diagnosed epiphenomenally for why it was spoken about rather than why it became possible finally to speak of it. Like all sexual harassment unremedied, prostitution could become ever more explicitly the model and mold for women's lives, women's life chances depending ever more entirely on their relation to power among men. Another possibility, to which this volume hopefully contributes, is that sexual harassment law becomes more meaningful in the domains to which it applies, and extends to hierarchies other than work and school — perhaps to relationships like priest-penitent, doctor-patient, lawyer-client, even to spouses and domestic partners and between parents and children. It may become more possible to address situations where the sex is the work. Understanding sexuality as a system may become standard intellectual equipment, its laws of motion seen as being as determinative, and as taken for granted, as economics. Those who report sexual abuse might no longer be targeted for destruction. Inequality may be eroticized less. If so, sexual harassment law will have been a tool in the liberation of women and a material forerunner — clear of today's sentimentality and denial — of a real equality-based sexual morality.

Notes

Insightful readings by Kent Harvey, Cass Sunstein, Marc Spindelman, and John Stoltenberg improved this Afterword. The resourceful and creative research and technical assistance of Kristal Otto, Jennifer Thornton, and Jane Yoon are gratefully acknowledged. Parts of the ideas contained in this essay were previously discussed in my "The Logic of Experience: Reflections on the Development of Sexual Harassment Law," 90 *Georgetown Law Journal* 813 (2002); "New Developments: Sexual Harassment Law," 7 *Perspectives* 8 (Fall 1998); and "Harassment Law Under Seige," *New York Times* (op-ed), March 5, 1998.

1. Places in which sexual harassment occurs but is generally not actionable include doctors' and lawyers' offices, religious settings, and on the street. See Nan D. Stein, *Classrooms and Courtrooms: Facing Sexual Harassment in K-12 Schools* (1999); Cynthia Grant Bowman, "Street Harassment and the Informal Ghettoization of Women," 106 *Harvard Law Review* 517 (1993).

2. Louise Fitzgerald et al., "Why Didn't She Just Report Him?" 51 *Journal of Social Issues* 117 (1995).

3. U.S. Merit Systems Protection Board, *Sexual Harassment in the Federal Workplace: Trends, Progress, Continuing Challenges,* 14 (1995) (42 percent of women federal employees studied in 1980, 42 percent in 1987, 44 percent in 1994 reported experiencing sexual harassment).

4. See generally Ian Shapiro, *Democratic Justice* (1999), for creative ideas on this subject.

5. This being the language of Title VII, 42 U.S.C. § 2000e-2 (West 1994).

6. Even the assessment of punitive damages is not simply based on a judgment of moral reprehensibility, but involves a more precise assessment that an employer was malicious or recklessly indifferent in knowingly violating federal law. See, e.g., *Kolstad v. American Dental Association*, 527 U.S. 526 (1999) (rejecting requirement that employer conduct must be "egregious" and clarifying malice and reckless indifference to federal law as punitive damages test under 42 U.S.C. § 1981a(b)(1)); *EEOC v. Wal-Mart Stores, Inc.*, 187 F.3d 1241, 1244 (10th Cir. 1999) (holding that punitive damages are available under Title VII where employer engaged in intentional discrimination with malice or reckless indifference to federally protected rights, citing *Kolstad*).

7. See Diana E. H. Russell, *The Secret Trauma: Incest in the Lives of Girls and Women* 61 (1986) ("Thirty-eight percent (357) of the 930 women reported at least one experience of incestuous and/or extrafamilial sexual abuse before reaching the age of eighteen years"). Similarly, because rape is inconsistent with the conventional idea of marriage and ought not happen in it by moral rules, rape in marriage has traditionally been exempted from coverage by the rape law. And, where rape in marriage can formally be charged, actual rapes in marriages are not recognized as having occurred in case after case.

8. The invalidation of the civil remedy provision of the Violence Against Women Act because it reached the "private" is just a recent example among countless ones. See *United States v. Morrison*, 529 U.S. 598 (2000).

9. See the essays in this volume on transnational sexual harassment law. See also General Recommendation No. 19, Convention on the Elimination of All Forms of Discrimination Against Women (CEDAW), 11th Sess., Agenda Item 7, U.N. Doc. CEDAW/C/1992/L.1/Add. 15 (1992), including at ¶¶ 23 and 24, and under necessary measures, ¶ 1(a). See also Europe's binding directive, Directive 2002/73/EC Amending the 1976 Directive on Equal Treatment of Men and Women, art. 1.

10. For further discussion, see Catharine A. MacKinnon, "The Logic of Experience: Reflections on the Development of Sexual Harassment Law," 90 Georgetown Law Journal 813 (2002) and Reva Siegel's introduction to this volume.

11. *Nichols v. Frank*, 42 F.3d 503, 511 (9th Cir. 1994); *Farpella-Crosby v. Horizon Health Care*, 97 F.3d 803, 806 n.2 (5th Cir. 1996) (deeming heterosexual sexual harassment "unquestionably based on gender").

12. See Catharine A. MacKinnon, *Sexual Harassment of Working Women: A Case of Sex Discrimination* 164–74 (1979); *Corne v. Bausch & Lomb Inc.*, 390 F. Supp. 161, 162–63 (D. Ariz. 1975).

13. See Kate Millett, *Sexual Politics* (University of Illinois Press, 1990) (1970).

14. See Abigail Saguy's essay in this volume.

15. See Yukiko Tsunoda's essay in this volume.

16. See Martha Nussbaum's essay in this volume.

17. Presumably, too, if traditional morality opposed abuse through sex because it was sexual, rape laws would be effective and sexual harassment would have been recognized as a legal claim long before it was.

18. In one study of almost 650 federal opinions from 1986 to 1995, physical harassment of a "sexual nature" is found to have a lower win rate at trial than physical harassment of a "nonsexual nature," a differential that climbs to 24.4 percent on appeal, where 46.2 percent of sexual cases are won compared with 70.6 percent of nonsexual cases

involving physical contact. Ann Juliano and Stewart J. Schwab, "The Sweep of Sexual Harassment Cases," 86 *Cornell Law Review* 548, 596 App. A (2001). Oral comments about individuals that are nonsexual similarly showed a slightly higher win rate at trial than oral comments about individuals that are sexual, while the win rate on appeal for the nonsexual comments is over 10 percent higher. Id. It is only through the conflation of group-based comments with nonsexual behaviors that the authors are able to suggest that they found that courts have not acknowledged harassment premised upon nonsexual behavior. See, e.g., id. at 555. Their data document the opposite. Less favorable work assignments do show a slightly lower win rate (55.9 percent) than the more sexualized forms of abuse, but requests for dates, regarded by the authors as sexual, is lower still (53.0 percent). Actually, most cases for less favorable work assignments are properly litigated as sex discrimination per se or under labor agreements; virtually no sexual harassment cases claim such behavior alone. The meaningfulness of data that separates such factors is thus questionable. Some individual judges, seeming to miss the doctrinal reality that the term "sexual" in equality law refers to sexuality and gender alike, do wrongly believe that gender-based but nonsexual harassment is not covered by Title VII. An illustration is *Williams v. General Motors Corporation*, 187 F.3d 553, 569 (6th Cir. 1999) (Ryan, J., dissenting).

19. Examples of sex stereotyping as discrimination are abundant in *Price Waterhouse v. Hopkins*, 490 U.S. 228 (1989), which also held that direct evidence shifted the burden of disproving discrimination to the defendant. The D.C. district court opinion by Judge Gesell notes that, despite considerable positive feedback, "[t]here were clear signs . . . that some of the partners reacted negatively to Hopkins' personality because she was a woman. One partner described her as 'macho' . . . ; another suggested that she 'overcompensated for being a woman' . . .; a third advised her to take 'a course at charm school.'" 490 U.S. at 235. See also *Robinson v. Jacksonville Shipyards*, 760 F. Supp. 1486 (M.D. Fla. 1991); *Nichols v. Azteca Restaurant Enterprises*, 256 F.3d 864 (9th Cir. 2001) (holding gay sexual harassment to be sex stereotyping hence sex discrimination); Nadine Taub, "Keeping Women in Their Place: Stereotyping As a Form of Employment Discrimination," 21 *Boston College Law Review* 345 (1980); 2 *EEOC Compliance Manual* § 615.6 (October 1981) (distinguishing sexual harassment from nonsexual sex-based harassment, affirming the latter is illegal).

20. For further discussion, see Catharine A. MacKinnon, "Feminism, Marxism, Method and the State: An Agenda for Theory," 7 *Signs: Journal of Women in Culture and Society* 515 (1982); Catharine A. MacKinnon, "Feminism, Marxism, Method and the State: Toward Feminist Jurisprudence," 8 *Signs: Journal of Women in Culture and Society* 635 (1983).

21. The leading case is *McKinney v. Dole*, 765 F.2d 1129, 1138–1139 (D.C. Cir. 1985). The obviousness of this position animated the U.S. Supreme Court decision in *Harris*. See *Harris v. Forklift Systems, Inc.*, 510 U.S. 17 (1993) (reversing a lower court ruling, No. 3:89–0557, 1990 U.S. Dist. LEXIS 20115 at *5–*7, that found comments including "You're a dumb ass woman" not actionable as sexual harassment). The Court also could not have been more clear that sexual desire, at least, is not requisite for a sexual harassment claim than it was in *Oncale*: "harassing conduct need not be motivated by sexual desire to support an inference of discrimination on the basis of sex." *Oncale v. Sun-*

downer Offshore Services, Inc., 523 U.S. 75, 80 (1998). On the clear coverage of gender-based but not sexual forms of harassment under sexual harassment law, see *Hall v. Gus Construction Co.*, 842 F.2d 1010, 1014 (8th Cir. 1988) ("[O]ther courts of appeals have held that the predicate acts underlying a sexual harassment claim need not be clearly sexual in nature. . . . [N]one of our previous cases hold that the offensive conduct must have explicit sexual overtones"); *Hicks v. Gates Rubber Co.*, 833 F.2d 1406, 1414 (10th Cir. 1987); *Cline v. General Electric Capital Auto Lease, Inc.*, 757 F. Supp. 923, 931–32 (N.D. Ill. 1991) (finding what it calls gender harassment to be based on sex as a form of sexual harassment of plaintiff "because she was a woman"); *Accardi v. Superior Court of California*, 21 Cal. Rptr. 2d 292, 293 (Cal. Ct. App. 1993) (finding "[s]exual harassment does not necessarily involve sexual conduct. . . . [W]e hold that sexual harassment occurs when an employer creates a hostile environment for an employee because of that employee's sex"). Cases so hold in the First Circuit, *Lipsett v. University of Puerto Rico*, 864 F.2d 881, 905 (1st Cir. 1988); Eleventh Circuit, *Henson v. City of Dundee*, 682 F.2d 897, 904 (11th Cir. 1982); Third Circuit, *Andrews v. City of Philadelphia*, 895 F.2d 1469, 1485 (3d Cir. 1990); and Sixth Circuit, *Williams v. General Motors Corporation*, 187 F.3d 553, 565 (6th Cir. 1999) ("conduct underlying a sexual harassment claim need not be overtly sexual in nature . . . harassing behavior that is not sexually explicit but is directed at women and motivated by discriminatory animus against women satisfies the 'based on sex' requirement"). See also EEOC Decision No. 71-2725, 1973 EEOC Dec. (CCH) 6290 (June 30, 1971).

22. Vicki Schultz, "Reconceptualizing Sexual Harassment," 107 Yale Law Journal 1683 (1998), advances the contrary view, arguing that sexual harassment law's focus on sexual forms of harassment has fostered neglect of gender-based but not sexual forms. At once minimizing the clarity of precedents that squarely and repeatedly hold both actionable, while missing the considerable abuse that *is* sexual that courts permit, the article, in its zeal to recoup the sexual and expand legal attention to gendered but not sexual abuse, becomes what it criticizes, as gender is disaggregated from sex. It also becomes a purported authority for the proposition it opposes, that gender harassment is not widely recognized as sexual harassment.

Some cases cited by Schultz as excluding nonsexual but sex-based acts actually include them. *Boarman v. Sullivan*, 769 F. Supp. 904 (D. Md. 1991), for example, is cited as revealing Schultz's criticized "disaggregation of the sexual from the non-sexual." *Id.* at 1713–14. The case found the acts alleged were insufficiently severe to constitute an abusive working environment. One alleged act was nonsexual ("on one occasion her supervisor remarked that a woman's film which she intended to show was stupid, and kept people from their work"); the other, however, was sexual (he "asked her to close his office door and remove all of her clothing"). 769 F. Supp. at 910. Whether or not the court was correct to find these acts insufficiently severe to be actionable, both sexual and nonsexual acts were so found. If the court was insensitive to gender, it was also insensitive to sex.

Similarly, *Raley v. Board of St. Mary's County Commissioner*, 752 F. Supp. 1272 (D. Md. 1990), is cited as authority for the proposition that "nonsexual forms of hostility escape judicial scrutiny altogether . . . Harmful acts of hazing and harassment frequently fall between the cracks of legal analysis altogether." Schultz, 107 *Yale Law Journal* at

1721. The *Raley* assignment of clerical work outside the plaintiff's job description, unsatisfactory job evaluations, and a letter of reprimand are cited as examples of nonsexual acts that neither rose to the level of hostile environment nor constituted disparate treatment. Id. at 1721 n.182. Wholly apart from their nonsexual nature, such actions may or may not be based on sex, and they may or may not constitute harassment by a variety of other measures. But incidents of *sexual* touching of the plaintiff were also found by the *Raley* court to be "isolated," hence insufficiently severe or pervasive to be actionable. 752 F. Supp. at 1280, unremarked by Schultz. No doubt much harassment is not caught by courts, but the fault may be something Schultz shares with the cases she criticizes: not seeing sexual abuse that is there.

Some cases cited by Schultz in support of the proposition that "[m]any other cases have held expressly that conduct that is not sexual in nature does not—and cannot—constitute hostile work environment sexual harassment," Schultz, 107 *Yale Law Journal* at 1718, the core thesis of the article, do not so hold. In *Holmes v. Razo*, No. 94 C 50405, 1995 U.S. Dist. LEXIS 10599 (N.D. Ill. July 18, 1995), for example, in response to the defendant's argument that the allegations do "not allege behavior of a sexual nature," the court finds, referring to plaintiff's allegation of pressure for dates, that "there is no deficiency in the sexual content of the discriminatory actions alleged in the complaint," id. at *18. That particular facts are found adequately sexual for a sexual harassment claim does not necessarily mean that only sexual facts will be found adequate. Moreover, this ruling goes only to the plaintiff's quid quo pro claim. There is no way to tell which allegations—which include threats regarding scheduling conflicts that arose from plaintiff's pregnancy—made the hostile environment claim adequate. There is no express holding of the sort Schultz contends.

Some cases say the opposite of what they are cited for. *Morrison v. Carleton Woolen Mills, Inc.*, 108 F.3d 429 (1st Cir. 1997), for example, cited for the proposition that "some courts have ruled against plaintiffs after trial on the ground that the challenged conduct is not sufficiently sexual to comprise a hostile work environment," Schultz, 107 *Yale Law Journal* at 1718, holds that frequency of discriminatory treatment (a "single, brief encounter," 108 F.3d at 439) rather than its nature as nonsexual or its gravity as insufficiently severe (plaintiff addressed as "girlie" and told to go see the "nursie," id. at 439), rendered the facts insufficient to be actionable. Strikingly, the plaintiff argued that she did not "need to show that management's conduct . . . was 'expressly sexual' in order to establish a sexually hostile work environment based on gender discrimination," id. at 441, and the court agreed: "We accept that many different forms of offensive behavior may be included within the definition of hostile environment sexual harassment. However, the overtones of such behavior must be, at the very least, sex-based, so as to be a recognizable form of sex discrimination." Id. Nonsexual-but-sex-based acts were thus not only not excluded from actionably sex-based conduct; they were potentially included in it.

23. Such acts, when based on sex, have long been recognized as discriminatory. An early example is EEOC Decision No. 71-2725, 1073 EEOC Dec. (CCH) 6290 (June 30, 1971), which found that refusal to instruct or assist or cooperate in work requiring team effort, if directed at an individual because of sex, constitutes sex discrimination. This is not to say that courts have always adequately sustained this (or any other) recognition of sex discrimination.

24. Many courts that miss gendered harassment that is not sexual also miss explicitly sexual forms of harassment. Courts routinely give short shrift to sexual acts at least as often or more often than to nonsexual gender-based abuse — including in cases Schultz, *supra* note 22, cites to the contrary. Sometimes she misses that sexual acts are sexual. Missed, for example, is the *Harris* district court's minimization of specifically sexual acts, such as the employer asking the plaintiff and other female employees to retrieve coins from his front pants pocket, and throwing objects on the ground for women to bend over and pick up as he watched. These acts were recognized by the district court as sexual but were not found to rise to the level of a hostile sexual environment; they were, instead, characterized in customary moral vocabulary as "annoying and insensitive" or "inane and adolescent," not sex-discriminatory. See *Harris v. Forklift Systems, Inc.*, No. 3:89–0557, 1990 U.S. Dist. LEXIS 20115, at *16 (M.D. Tenn. Nov. 28, 1990). The fact that these acts were sexual did *not* give them any special legal status in this court's eyes. And when the *Harris* Supreme Court reversed, it reversed for both sexual and nonsexual harassment equally.

Similarly, in *Reed v. Shepard*, 939 F.2d 484 (7th Cir. 1991), violent sexist abuse such as chaining the plaintiff to a toilet and shoving her head into it was moralistically condemned as "repulsive" by the Seventh Circuit panel, id. at 486, but found nonactionable — not because it was seen to be nonsexual, but because Reed was seen as the kind of woman who did not mind such treatment, who even "relished reciprocating in kind." Id. This was because she told "dirty jokes." Id. at 487. The Seventh Circuit, which exonerated the defendants, and Schultz, *supra* note 22, who is rightly critical of that court's dismissal of plaintiff's claims, alike miss the sexual nature of this abuse — which even the briefest acquaintance with (say) *Hustler* would reveal. The irony of using the *Reed* court's failure to find this abuse actionable as support for the critique of what Schultz terms the "sexual desire-dominance paradigm" of sexual harassment law, see Schultz, *supra* note 22, at 1729–1730, is thus lost on her. Whether she would have been as critical of the court's failure to perceive the harassment if she had grasped the sexual nature of the abuse is an open question.

25. For a few instances, see *Torres v. Pisano*, 116 F.3d 625 (2d Cir. 1997), *Watkins v. Bowden*, 105 F.3d 1344 (11th Cir. 1997), and *Hicks v. Gates Rubber Co.*, 833 F.2d 1406 (10th Cir. 1987).

26. Hostile environment sexual harassment law, initially drawing on a lone Fifth Circuit precedent that prohibited racially hostile environments, *Rogers v. EEOC*, 454 F.2d 234 (5th Cir. 1971), then became precedent for equality claims against racist bigotry in the working environment. The number of those claims then grew. Race cases include *Snell v. Suffolk County*, 782 F.2d 1094 (2d Cir. 1986); *Harris v. International Paper Co.*, 765 F. Supp. 1509 (D. Me. 1991); *Bolden v. PRC Inc.*, 43 F.3d 545 (10th Cir. 1994); *Walker v. Ford Motor Co.*, 684 F.2d 1355 (11th Cir. 1982). Religion cases include *Venters v. City of Delphi*, 123 F.3d 956, 974–78 (7th Cir. 1997); *Del Erdmann v. Tranquility, Inc.*, 155 F. Supp. 2d 1152, 1159–64 (N.D. Cal. 2001).

27. *Oncale v. Sundowner Offshore Services, Inc.*, 523 U.S. 75 (1998).

28. The leading authority for this proposition is the en banc ruling in *Rene v. MGM Grand Hotel, Inc.*, 305 F.3d 1061 (9th Cir. 2002), *cert. denied*, 2003 WL 1446593, which held that a gay man, sexually harassed as gay, can sue for sex discrimination under

Title VII. The plurality held that conduct of a sexual nature is conduct because of sex. A concurring opinion agreed for the reason that discrimination based on sexual orientation is a form of gender stereotyping. Other federal Courts of Appeals have ruled, in my view erroneously, to the contrary. See, e.g., *Bibby v. Philadelphia Coca-Cola Bottling Co.*, 260 F.3d 257, 265 (3d Cir. 2001); *Spearman v. Ford Motor Co.*, 231 F.3d 1080, 1084–85 (7th Cir. 2000); *Higgins v. New Balance Athletic Shoe, Inc.*, 194 F.3d 252, 259 (1st Cir. 1999); *Simonton v. Runyon*, 232 F.3d 33, 36 (2d Cir. 2000).

29. This largest argument is further developed in Catharine A. MacKinnon, *Sex Equality* 766–1056 (2001).

30. See Janet Halley's essay in this volume.

31. See Marc Spindelman's essay in this volume.

32. See Stephen Schulhofer, *Unwanted Sex: The Culture of Intimidation and the Failure of Law* (1998).

33. *Meritor Savings Bank v. Vinson*, 477 U.S. 57 (1986).

34. One case that raises the issue is *Trautvetter*, but on appeal the majority held that Ms. Trautvetter's sexual harassment claim was not "based on sex" because the sexual relationship she had with her superior was "personal," rather than holding that it was unactionable because welcome. *Trautvetter v. Quick*, 916 F.2d 1140 (7th Cir. 1990). Others that notably find the challenged behavior unwelcome include *Carr v. Allison Gas Turbine Division General Motors Corp.*, 32 F.3d 1007 (7th Cir. 1994); *Burns v. McGregor Electronic Industries, Inc.*, 989 F.2d 959 (8th Cir. 1993); *Jenson v. Eveleth Taconite Co.*, 824 F. Supp. 847 (D. Minn. 1993); *Cuesta v. Texas Department of Criminal Justice*, 805 F. Supp. 451 (W.D. Tex. 1991). Cases finding the challenged behavior welcome include *Reed v. Shepard*, 939 F.2d 484 (7th Cir. 1991) and *Balletti v. Sun Sentinel Co.*, 909 F. Supp. 1539 (S.D. Fla. 1995), the latter of which may have been inspired by homophobia.

35. See *Harris v. Forklift Systems*, 510 U.S. 17, 20 (1993) ("[I]f the victim does not subjectively perceive the environment to be abusive, the conduct has not actually altered the conditions of the victim's employment, and there is not a Title VII violation").

36. One good example is *Flockhart v. Iowa Beef Processors, Inc.*, 192 F. Supp. 2d 947, 967 (N.D. Ia. 2001), in which a harassed woman's occasional response to abuse by strong language "does not demonstrate that the conduct was not unwelcome," leaving the jury free to so conclude. Some courts have held that evidence that a woman " 'engaged in behavior similar to that which she claimed was unwelcome or offensive' is evidence that the behavior was not unwelcome." *Beard v. Flying J.*, 266 F.3d 792, 798 (8th Cir. 2001) (quoting *Scusa v. Nestle U.S.A. Co.*, 181 F.3d 958, 966 (8th Cir. 1999)). See, e.g., *Burns v. McGregor Electronic Industries, Inc.*, 989 F.2d 959, 963 (8th Cir. 1993) (holding that plaintiff's posing for nude pictures for magazine did not indicate that sexual advances at work were welcome); *Gallagher v. Delaney*, 139 F.3d 338, 346 (2d Cir. 1998) (holding that plaintiff's extramarital office affair did not permit court to find plaintiff was open to sexual advances). Some cases keep evidence of sexual activity outside the workplace out of workplace sexual harassment cases under Rule 412. See *B.K.B. v. Maui Police Department*, 276 F.3d 1091, 1106 (9th Cir. 2002) (remanding for new trial for failure of correctional instruction to dispel lurid prejudicial nonprobative testimony concerning victim's fantasies or autoerotic sexual practices in attempt to establish that sexual harassment at

work was not unwelcome). For further discussion, see *Wolak v. Spucci*, 217 F.3d 157, 160–61 (2d Cir. 2000) (holding that plaintiff's out-of-work viewing of pornography did not mean pornography at work did not alter her status at work, causing injury regardless of trauma inflicted by the images alone).

Of some concern are cases like *Mosher v. Dollar Tree Stores, Inc.*, 240 F.3d 662, 668 (7th Cir. 2001), in which an employer was granted summary judgment for a long-term uncomplained-of live-in relationship with a supervisor that continued after she left her job, a relationship that the court thought "can only be reasonably described as consensual." The woman, described by the court as "a willing participant," said she was afraid, that the relationship was entirely involuntary, and she agreed to the sex only because she needed to keep her job. Id. Another is *Stephens v. Rheem Manufacturing Co.*, 220 F.3d 882 (8th Cir. 2000), in which evidence of rumors of sexual affairs among company employees was excluded at trial under Rule 412, and the defendant's sexual behavior was found welcome to the plaintiff, although she argued that she tolerated it as long as she did only because the rumors led her to believe she had no recourse.

37. See Louise Fitzgerald's essay in this volume.

38. Janine Benedet, "Hostile Environment Sexual Harassment Claims and the Unwelcome Influence of Rape Law," 3 *Michigan Journal of Gender and Law* 125 (1995). This proposal is an improvement over that of Susan Estrich, "Sex at Work," 43 *Stanford Law Review* 813 (1991), which recommends eliminating unwelcomeness from sexual harassment doctrine, apparently making it possible for a woman to sue for a sexual relationship she affirmatively wanted, whether or not it was forced by inequality. This is not to say that if a wanted sexual relationship ends badly and an employee is punished for it at work, that the punishment cannot be sex-based.

39. For further discussion, see Catharine A. MacKinnon, *Feminism Unmodified* 146–62 (1987).

40. See Janine Benedet's essay in this volume.

41. In addition to the essays in this volume, see Catharine A. MacKinnon, *Sex Equality* 973–74 n.46, 1626–51 (2001); Richard H. Fallon, Jr., "Sexual Harassment, Content Neutrality, and the First Amendment Dog that Didn't Bark," 1994 *Supreme Court Review* 1.

42. *Grant v. Lone Star Co.*, 21 F.3d 649 (5th Cir. 1994); *Miller v. Maxwell's International, Inc.*, 991 F.2d 583 (9th Cir. 1991); *McBride v. Routh*, 51 F. Supp. 2d 153 (D. Conn. 1999); *Czupih v. Card Pak Inc.*, 916 F. Supp. 687 (N.D. Ohio 1996); *Wilson v. Wayne County*, 856 F. Supp. 1254, 1261 (M.D. Tenn. 1994); *Johnson v. Northern Indiana Public Service Co.*, 844 F. Supp. 466 (N.D. Ind. 1994); *Lowry v. Clark*, 843 F. Supp. 228 (E.D. Ky. 1994). Immunities and other qualifications on personal and institutional responsibility to similar effect also operate under the Equal Protection clause.

43. For discussion of this structure, see *Gebser v. Lago Vista Independent School District*, 524 U.S. 274, 285–93 (1998).

44. The essays of Deborah Rhode and David Oppenheimer in this volume analyze these rulings.

45. Compare *Faragher v. City of Boca Raton*, 524 U.S. 775 (1998) (holding employer vicariously liable for hostile environment created by supervisor but allowing employer to demonstrate that it reasonably acted to correct or prevent the harassment and that the

plaintiff unreasonably failed to correct or prevent the harm through channels offered by employer) and *Burlington Industries, Inc. v. Ellerth*, 524 U.S. 742 (1998) (same), with *Gebser v. Lago Vista Independent School District*, 524 U.S. 274 (1998) (holding that plaintiff, a female high school student who was sexually harassed by her teacher, may not recover damages against a school district where relevant school officials do not have actual notice and are not deliberately indifferent to teacher's misconduct), and *Davis v. Monroe County Board of Education*, 526 U.S. 629 (1999) (holding schools liable to students for peer harassment under Title IX only where authorities are deliberately indifferent to acts reported to proper authority in control and harasser is under the school's disciplinary authority).

46. *Burlington Industries, Inc. v. Ellerth*, 524 U.S. 742 (1998).

47. 29 C.F.R. § 1604.11 (a) (2001) (emphasis added).

48. See, for example, *Sparks v. Pilot Freight Carriers, Inc.*, 830 F.2d 1554, 1559 (11th Cir. 1987); *Robinson v. City of Pittsburgh*, 120 F.3d 1286, 1296–97 (3d Cir. 1997); *Jansen v. Packaging Corp. of America*, 123 F.3d 490 (7th Cir. 1997). *Nichols v. Frank*, 42 F.3d 503, 513 (9th Cir. 1994), and *Karibian v. Columbia University*, 14 F.3d 773, 777–78 (2d Cir. 1994), found a quid pro quo where sexually harassed women submitted to sex in employment in exchange for job benefits. See also *Cram v. Lamson & Sessions Co.*, 49 F.3d 466, 473 (8th Cir. 1995) (drawing elements of quid pro quo proof from EEOC Guidelines); *Kauffman v. Allied Signal, Inc.*, 970 F.2d 178, 186 (6th Cir. 1992) (same). The Fourth Circuit had not ruled out the possibility that a threat alone was enough to make out a quid pro quo case. *Reinhold v. Virginia*, 135 F.3d 920, 933–34 n.3 (4th Cir. 1998).

49. 524 U.S. at 748.

50. *Harris v. Forklift Systems, Inc.*, 510 U.S. 17 (1993), holds that whether or not a worker is severely psychologically affected by sexual harassment, she can be deemed injured by it.

51. *Jansen v. Packaging Corp. of America*, 123 F.3d 490, 504 (7th Cir. 1997) (Cudahy, J., concurring).

52. The facts are from *Jansen*, 123 F.3d at 503, which settled before *Ellerth* was argued in the Supreme Court.

53. Facts are from *Vance v. Southern Bell Telephone and Telegraph Co.*, 863 F.2d 1503 (11th Cir. 1989).

54. For further commentary, see Andrea Dworkin, "Dear Bill and Hillary," *Guardian* (London) (January 29, 1998).

55. The D.C. Circuit handed down its decision in *Bundy v. Jackson*, 641 F.2d 934 (D.C. Cir. 1981), on January 12, 1981; the district court opinion in the case, 19 Fair Empl. Prac. Dec. (CCH) 9154 (Apr. 25, 1979), is dated April 25, 1979. In her testimony before the Senate Judiciary Committee, Anita Hill described being sexually harassed at various points in 1981, when she was employed at the Department of Education, and throughout the fall and winter months of 1982, after she had transferred to the EEOC with Thomas. See *Nomination of Judge Clarence Thomas to be Associate Justice of the Supreme Court of the United States: Hearings Before the Senate Committee on the Judiciary*, 102d Cong. 36–48 (1991).

56. Her claim was brought under Section 1983, effectuating the Equal Protection

Clause of the Constitution, which in sexual harassment cases has been interpreted the same as, and together with, Title VII. Presumably she sued under Section 1983 rather than (or also under) Title VII because the statute of limitations had run on her potential Title VII claim.

57. See *Clinton v. Jones*, 520 U.S. 681 (1997).

58. See *Jones v. Clinton*, 990 F. Supp. 657 (E.D. Ark. 1998).

59. Flowers Declaration, ¶¶ 1, 5, 6 (March 12, 1998), Civil Action No. LR-C-94-290, *Jones v. Clinton*, 990 F. Supp. 657 (E.D. Ark. 1998).

60. Catharine A. MacKinnon, *Sexual Harassment of Working Women: A Case of Sex Discrimination* 39 (1979).

61. *Keppler v. Hinsdale Township High School District*, 715 F. Supp. 862, 868 (N.D. Ill. 1989).

62. Jones Declaration, ¶ 17 (March 11, 1998), Civil Action No. LR-C-94-290, *Jones v. Clinton*, 990 F. Supp. 657 (E.D. Ark. 1998).

63. See, for example, *Nichols v. Frank*, 42 F.3d 503 (9th Cir. 1994) and *Karibian v. Columbia University*, 14 F.3d 773 (2d Cir. 1994).

64. See *Sanders v. Casa View Baptist Church*, 134 F.3d 331 (5th Cir. 1998).

65. See *Bonenberger v. Plymouth Township*, 132 F.3d 20 (3d Cir. 1997).

66. *Highlander v. K.F.C. National Management Co.*, 805 F.2d 644 (6th Cir. 1986).

67. Jones Declaration, ¶ 32 (March 11, 1998), Civil Action No. LR-C-94-290, *Jones v. Clinton*, 990 F. Supp. 657 (W.D. Ark. 1998).

68. See *Davis v. Palmer Dodge West, Inc.*, 977 F. Supp. 917 (S.D. Ind. 1997) (altering working conditions); *Hawthorne v. St. Joseph's Carondelet Child Center*, 982 F. Supp. 586 (N.D. Ill. 1997) (moved work location and working by herself); *Reinhold v. Virginia*, 135 F.3d 920 (4th Cir. 1998) (change in work assignments, less work, different duties). The place of these gender-based but not expressly sexual conditions in sexual harassment cases is also worth noting.

69. *Andrews v. City of Philadelphia*, 895 F.2d 1469, 1483 (3d Cir. 1990).

70. For part of its test, the Supreme Court cited an Eleventh Circuit case that had limited actionability to "pervasive" harassment, *Meritor Savings Bank v. Vinson*, 477 U.S. 57, 67 (1986) ("For sexual harassment to state a claim under Title VII, it must be sufficiently pervasive to alter the conditions of employment and create an abusive working environment") (quoting *Henson v. City of Dundee* 682 F.2d 897, 904 (11th Cir. 1982)).

71. *Faragher v. City of Boca Raton*, 524 U.S. 775, 788 (1998).

72. *Brzonkala v. Virginia Polytechnic Institute and State University*, 132 F.3d 949, 959 (4th Cir. 1997). (holding claim could be founded on this showing of severity without any showing of pervasiveness).

73. Examples include *Rush v. Scott Specialty Gases*, 113 F.3d 476, 482 (3d Cir. 1997) (stating "isolated or single incidents of harassment are insufficient to constitute a hostile environment" but finding plaintiff's claim constituted a continuous pattern); *Moylan v. Maries County*, 729 F.2d 746, 749 (8th Cir. 1986) (holding prior to *Vinson* that "the plaintiff must show a practice or pattern of harassment against her or him; a single incident or isolated incidents generally will not be sufficient" in case in which plaintiff was raped); *Rabidue v. Osceola Refining Company*, 805 F.2d 611, 620 (6th Cir. 1986); *High-*

lander v. K.F.C. Nat'l Management Co., 805 F.2d 644, 649–50 (6th Cir. 1986) (dismissing hostile environment claim as not subjectively perceived to alter working environment, reiterating frequency requirement); see also *Waltman v. International Paper*, 875 F.2d 468, 483 (5th Cir. 1989) (Jones, J., dissenting) ("a hostile environment cause of action is comprised of more than one alleged offense").

74. Authorities include *Bohen v. City of East Chicago, Indiana*, 799 F.2d 1180, 1186–87 (7th Cir. 1986) (stating in sexual harassment case that "as a general matter, a single discriminatory act against one individual can amount to intentional discrimination for equal protection jurisprudence"); *King v. Board of Regents*, 898 F.2d 533, 537 (7th Cir. 1990) ("a single act can be enough"); *Smith v. Sheahan*, 189 F.3d 529, 533 (7th Cir. 1999) ("The Supreme Court has repeatedly said, using the disjunctive 'or,' that a claim of discrimination based on the infliction of a hostile working environment exists if the conduct is 'severe or pervasive' "); *Tomka v. Seiler Corp.*, 66 F.3d 1295 (2d Cir. 1995); *Brzonkala*, 132 F.3d 949 (4th Cir. 1997) (under Title IX); *Lockard v. Pizza Hut, Inc.*, 162 F.3d 1062 (10th Cir. 1998); *Vance v. Southern Bell Telephone & Telegraph Co.*, 863 F.2d 1503 (11th Cir. 1989) (holding noose hung over African-American woman's work stations on two separate occasions sufficiently severe for hostile environment claim, reversing on grounds of incorrect application of *Henson* and *Meritor* the district court's judgment notwithstanding the verdict for the company).

75. 990 F. Supp. 657, 675 (E.D. Ark. 1998).

76. See, for example, *Lillard v. Shelby County Board of Education*, 76 F.3d 716, 726 (1996) ("[T]he incident in the hallway, while deplorable, simply is not of the outrageous and shocking character that is required for a substantive due process violation. Leventhal's rubbing of Little's stomach, accompanied by a remark that could reasonably be interpreted as suggestive, was wholly inappropriate, and, if proved, should have serious disciplinary consequences for Leventhal. But without more, it is not conduct that creates a constitutional claim"); *Chancey v. Southwest Florida Water Management District*, 1997 WL 158312, *11 (M.D. Fla. Mar. 17, 1997) (finding hostile environment sexual harassment sufficiently alleged to overcome summary judgment motion but also stating that "The Court finds such behavior, while reprehensible, does not approach the extreme degree of outrageousness required to show intentional infliction of emotional distress"). See also *Leibowitz v. Bank Leumi Trust Company*, 152 A.D.2d 169, 181–82 (N.Y. App. Div. 1989) dismissing plaintiff's cause of action for intentional infliction of emotional distress and of "harassment" where it was "nothing more than component parts of her claim for wrongful discharge" under New York Labor Law 740. ("While we share in the indignation of our dissenting colleague over the use of the religious and ethnic slurs 'Hebe' and 'kike,' the particular conduct complained of in this case did not rise to such an extreme or outrageous level as to meet the threshold requirements for the tort. . . . Certainly, the use of any religious, ethnic or racial slur must be strongly disapproved and condemned. However, the fact that we view the alleged conduct as being deplorable and reprehensible does not necessarily lead to the conclusion that it arose to such a level that the law must provide a remedy").

77. One would think that, if courts were anti-sex but insufficiently opposed to gender harassment, a case in which a plaintiff was called a "dumb bitch" and "shoved . . . so hard that she fell backward and hit the floor, sustaining injuries from which she has yet to fully

recover" would not be—as it was—found sufficiently severe to create a hostile environment, see *Crisonino v. New York City Housing Authority*, 985 F. Supp. 385, 388 (S.D.N.Y. 1997), while Jones's allegations, nothing if not sexual, would not have been—as they were—dismissed as not severe enough.

78. *Moring v. Arkansas Department of Correction*, 243 F.3d 452 (8th Cir. 2001). The facts and law in the rest of this paragraph are drawn from this decision.

79. 243 F.3d at 456.

80. See, e.g., Jeffrey Toobin, *A Vast Conspiracy: The Real Story of the Sex Scandal That Nearly Brought Down the President* 172–76 (1999).

81. *Id.* at 174.

82. This is the agenda of the likes of Jeffrey Rosen; see his *The Unwanted Gaze: The Destruction of Privacy in America* (2000). That women have been subjected to centuries of unwanted gazes in what is defended as the private is not mentioned.

83. See EEOC, *Trends in Harassment Charges Filed with the EEOC During the 1980s and 1990s* available at http://www.eeoc.gov/stats/harassment.html (last modified July 11, 2000).

Contributors

Kathryn Abrams is Herma Hill Kay Distinguished Professor of Law at Boalt Hall School of Law, University of California at Berkeley, and professor of law at Cornell Law School. She is the author of numerous article on feminist jurisprudence and related forms of critical legal theory, including most recently "The New Jurisprudence of Sexual Harassment," 83 *Cornell Law Review* 1169 (1998); "From Autonomy to Agency Feminist Perspectives on Self-Direction," 40 *William and Mary Law Review* 805 (1999), and "The Legal Subject in Exile," 51 *Duke Law Journal* 27 (2001). She is now working a book entitled *Changing the Subject: Agency, Law and Feminist Legal Theory*.

Susanne Baer, habil. (Berlin), Dr. jur. (Frankfurt am Main), LL.M. (Michigan), is professor of constitutional and administrative law and gender studies at the Faculty of Law, Humboldt University of Berlin and visiting faculty at Central European University Budapest Law School. She works on gender studies, feminist legal theory, comparative constitutional and administrative law and administrative reform, and educates police and judiciary on domestic violence and gender sensitivity. Publications in English include "Violence: Dilemmas of Democracy and Law," in David Kretzmer and F. Kershman Hazan, eds., *Freedom of Speech and Incitement Against Democracy* (2000); "Equality: The Jurisprudence of the German Constitutional Court," 63 *Columbia Journal of*

European Law 5 (1999) 249; "Citizenship, Loyalty, and the Ordering of Gender: On Exclusion and the Relevance of Law in Gender Studies and Feminist Theories of the State," in Aysan Sev'er, ed., *Frontiers in Women's Studies: Canadian and German Perspectives* (1998); "A Different Approach to Jurisprudence? Feminisms in German Legal Science, Legal Cultures, and the Ambivalence of Law," 3 *Cardozo Women's Law Journal* 251 (1996); "Pornography and Sexual Harassment in the EU" in Amy Ellman, ed., *Women in the European Union* (1996).

Jack M. Balkin is Knight Professor of Constitutional Law and the First Amendment and the founder and director of the Information Society Project at Yale Law School, an interdisciplinary center devoted to the study of law and the new information technologies. His interdisciplinary work ranges widely from theories of cultural evolution to the connections between legal interpretation and musical performance. He is the author of many articles on various aspects of constitutional law, legal theory, society, and culture. His books include *Cultural Software: A Theory of Ideology* (1998), *Processes of Constitutional Decisionmaking*, 4th ed. (2000) (with Brest, Levinson and Amar), *Legal Canons* (2000) (with Levinson), and *What Brown v. Board of Education Should Have Said* (2001).

Janine Benedet is an assistant professor at Osgoode Hall Law School in Toronto, Ontario, Canada. She has an LL.B. from the University of British Columbia Faculty of Law and an LL.M. from the University of Michigan Law School, where she is currently a candidate for the S.J.D. degree. Her doctoral research, on which her essay in this volume is based, examines the use of pornography as a method of sexual harassment. She has published articles in both Canada and the United States on sexual harassment, pornography, and sexual assault.

Kingsley R. Browne, professor of law at Wayne State University Law School in Detroit, has written extensively about sexual harassment and free speech. His research has also focused on biological sex differences and their relation to the glass ceiling and the gender gap in compensation, sexual harassment, occupational segregation, and women's service in the military. He is the author of *Biology at Work: Rethinking Sexual Equality* and *Divided Labours: An Evolutionary View of Women at Work*.

Guido Calabresi was appointed United States Circuit Judge in July 1994 and entered into duty on September 16, 1994. Prior to his appointment, he was Dean and Sterling Professor at the Yale Law School, where he began teaching in 1959. He continues to serve as a member of that faculty as Sterling Professor

Emeritus and Professorial Lecturer. Judge Calabresi received his B.S. degree, summa cum laude, from Yale College in 1953, a B.A. degree with First Class Honors from Magdalen College, Oxford University, in 1955, an LL.B. degree, magna cum laude, in 1958 from Yale Law School, and an M.A. in Politics, Philosophy and Economics from Oxford University in 1959. A Rhodes Scholar and member of Phi Beta Kappa and Order of the Coif, Judge Calabresi served as the Note Editor of the *Yale Law Journal*, 1957–58, while graduating first in his law school class. Following graduation, Judge Calabresi clerked for Justice Hugo Black of the United States Supreme Court. He has been awarded more than thirty-five honorary degrees from universities in the United States and abroad, and is the author of four books and more than eighty articles on law and related subjects. Judge Calabresi is a member of the Connecticut Bar.

Christine Chinkin is professor of international law, London School of Economics and Political Science and a member of the Overseas Affiliated Faculty, University of Michigan.

Adrienne D. Davis is a professor of law at the University of North Carolina at Chapel Hill. Prior to that, she was a professor and co-director of the Gender, Work, and Family Project at the Washington College of Law at American University. Her scholarship emphasizes the gendered dimensions of American slavery, including the regulation of sexuality under slavery, and its ongoing implications for law and social norms. She is the recipient of a grant from the Ford Foundation to research meanings and representations of Black women and labor and was a resident fellow at the Rockefeller Foundation's Bellagio Study and Conference Center. She has been a Distinguished Visitor at University of Toronto, the Dean's Distinguished Lecturer in Race and Legal History at Vanderbilt Law School, and a Scholar-in-Residence in the George Mason University African-American Studies Department. She is a member of the boards of the Center of the Study for the American South and the Cultural Studies Program at the University of North Carolina and is on the editorial board of the *Law and History Review*.

Andrea Dworkin is the author of *Pornography: Men Possessing Women, Intercourse, Mercy,* and *Heartbreak: The Political Memoir of a Feminist Militant.* She is coauthor with Catharine A. MacKinnon of legislation defining pornography as legally actionable sex discrimination and coeditor of *In Harm's Way: The Pornography Civil Rights Hearings.*

William N. Eskridge, Jr., is John A. Garver Professor of Jurisprudence, Yale Law School. He is the co-editor, with Nan Hunter, of the casebook *Sexuality, Gender, and the Law* (1997). He is the author of several books, including *The*

Case for Same-Sex Marriage (1996); *Gaylaw: Challenging the Apartheid of the Closet* (1999); and *Equality Practice: Civil Unions and the Future of Gay Rights* (2001).

Louise F. Fitzgerald, Ph.D., is professor of psychology and women's studies at the University of Illinois at Urbana-Champaign. She received her bachelor's degree in psychology from the University of Maryland (1974) and her M.A. (1975) and Ph.D. in psychology from the Ohio State University (1979). She is one of the leading researchers and social science experts in the United States on the topic of sexual harassment in education and the workplace, which she was among the first to study in a scientific manner. She is the author of more than seventy-five scholarly articles, chapters, and monographs and has coauthored three books on the topic of women and work. She was the social science consultant to Professor Anita Hill's legal team during the confirmation hearings of U.S. Supreme Court Justice Clarence Thomas, and serves extensively as a behavioral science consultant and expert witness. She was the government's expert in the case of *U.S. v. Lanier,* decided by the U.S. Supreme Court, and has testified in many high-profile cases (e.g., *Jenson, et al., v. Eveleth Mines, et al.*); she assisted in developing the American Psychological Association's *amicus* brief in *Harris v. Forklift* and the National Employment Lawyers' Association brief in *Burlington Industries*. Her work has been cited not only to the U.S. Supreme Court, but also the New Jersey Supreme Court, as well as in numerous other judicial proceedings. She is consultant to both the Criminal and Housing Sections of the Civil Rights Division of the U.S. Department of Justice. Her methodology for studying sexual harassment in the workplace has been adopted by the Department of Defense for its periodic assessment of the five branches of the Armed Services. She is a member of the American Psychological Association's Taskforce on Violence Against Women, the State of Illinois Taskforce on Sexual Harassment, and the U.S. Department of Defense Manpower Advisory Committee. Most recently, she was appointed senior social science consultant to the U.S. Eighth Circuit's Taskforce on Gender Fairness in the Courts. In addition to her teaching, research, writing and consulting activities, she conducts extensive clinical work with victims of harassment and is considered an authority on the psychological consequences of sexual harassment. In recognition of her extensive scholarly contributions in this area, she was named by the American Psychological Association as the 2003 recipient of its Public Interest Award for Distinguished Contributions to Research in Public Policy.

Katherine M. Franke is vice dean, professor of law and co-director, Center for the Study of Law and Culture, at Columbia Law School. Drawing from feminist, critical race, and queer theories, she has written on a variety of subjects, including sexual harassment, African American subjectivity in the post-bellum United States, and the problem of female desire in feminist legal theory.

Sally F. Goldfarb is an associate professor at Rutgers Law School-Camden. She has also taught at Harvard, New York University, and University of Pennsylvania law schools. From 1985 to 1994, she was a staff attorney at the NOW Legal Defense and Education Fund, where she founded and chaired the National Task Force on the Violence Against Women Act and was instrumental in the drafting and passage of the Violence Against Women Act of 1994. She is the author of several law review articles and book chapters on violence against women, family law, and other topics.

Janet Halley is professor of law at Harvard University. She is the author of *Don't: A Reader's Guide to the Military's Anti-Gay Policy* (1999), and is the co-editor, with Wendy Brown, of *Left Legalism/Left Critique* (2002). She is finishing a book to be entitled *Sexuality Harassment*. She has published on sexual orientation and sodomy in various law reviews, as well as "Gay Rights and Identity Imitation: Issues in the Ethics of Representation," in David Kairys, ed., *The Politics of Law,* 3rd ed. (1998).

Tanya Katerí Hernández is a professor of law and the Justice Frederick Hall Scholar at Rutgers University School of Law-Newark. She received her A.B. in sociology from Brown University and her J.D. from Yale Law School. She is the author of "Sexual Harassment and Racial Disparity: The Mutual Construction of Gender and Race" (*Iowa Journal of Gender, Race and Justice*, 2001), among other articles, and her scholarship is devoted to issues of civil rights and the intersection of race and gender.

Orit Kamir is a professor of law at the Hebrew University, specializing in interdisciplinary cultural analysis of law, law and film, and feminist legal thought. She holds an LL.B. and a master's degree (in literature and philosophy) from the Hebrew University in Jerusalem, Israel, and earned her LL.M. and S.J.D. at the University of Michigan Law School. In her capacity as a feminist legal scholar and activist, she drafted a sexual harassment bill, which was adopted by the Israeli Parliament and legislated into law in 1998. Her publications (in both Hebrew and English) offer cultural analyses of law, society and culture, focusing on the construction of gender. Her book, *Every Breath You Take: Stalking Narratives and the Law* (2001), offers a cultural analysis that locates America's antistalking laws within the contexts of world mythology, religion, literature, film, and the social sciences. Her book (in Hebrew), *Feminism, Rights and the Law* (2002), is the first Israeli feminist jurisprudence textbook. She is currently completing a book on the emerging field of law and film.

Christopher N. Kendall is Dean of Law at Murdoch University in Perth, Western Australia. Originally from Toronto, he holds degrees from Queen's University in Kingston, Ontario (BA (Hons), LLB) and the University of Michigan Law School (LLM, SJD). In 2000, he was part of the litigation team acting on behalf of the group Equality Now in litigation before the Supreme Court of Canada in the case of *Little Sisters Book and Art Emporium*. In that case, Equality Now successfully argued that lesbian and gay male pornography, like heterosexual pornography, violates the sex equality interests enshrined in Canada's *Charter of Rights and Freedoms*.

Jane E. Larson is professor of law at the University of Wisconsin-Madison. She is the author of *Hard Bargains: The Politics of Sex* (with Linda R. Hirshman) and numerous articles on the regulation of sexuality.

Martha C. Nussbaum is Ernst Freund Distinguished Service Professor of Law and Ethics at the University of Chicago, appointed in Philosophy, Law, and Divinity. She is an Associate in the Classics Department and the Political Science Department, an Affiliate in the Committee on Southern Asian Studies, a Board Member in the Human Rights Program, and the Coordinator of the Center for Comparative Constitutionalism. Her most recent books are *Women and Human Development: The Capabilities Approach* and *Upheavals of Thought: The Intelligence of Emotions*.

David B. Oppenheimer (B.A., University Without Walls, Berkeley; J.D., Harvard) is professor of law and associate dean for academic affairs at Golden Gate University School of Law, where he teaches and writes about employment discrimination law, civil procedure, and civil rights history, and a visiting scholar at the Institute for the Study of Social Change at the University of California, Berkeley. He served as co-counsel for the National Employment Lawyers' Association in the U.S. Supreme Court in *Ellerth v. Burlington Industries, Inc.*, has litigated numerous sexual harassment cases, and was the founding director of the Boalt Hall Employment Discrimination Clinic. He currently serves on the board of directors of the San Francisco Bay Area Lawyers' Committee for Civil Rights and, until recently, Equal Rights Advocates, a California feminist public interest law firm.

Robert Post is Alexander F. and May T. Morrison Professor of Law at Boalt Hall, the Law School of the University of California at Berkeley. Among other books, he is the author of *Constitutional Domains: Democracy, Community,*

Management (1995); coauthor (with K. Anthony Appiah, Judith Butler, Thomas C. Grey, and Reva Siegel) of *Prejudicial Appearances: The Logic of American Antidiscrimination Law* (2001), and editor of *Censorship and Silencing: Practices of Cultural Regulation* (1998). He is also the author of numerous articles about the First Amendment, including "The Constitutional Status of Commercial Speech, 48 *UCLA Law Review* 1 (2000); "Subsidized Speech," 106 *Yale Law Journal* 151 (1996); and "Recuperating First Amendment Doctrine," 47 *Stanford Law Review* 1249 (1995). His most recent book, edited with Nancy Rosenblum, is *Civil Society and Government* (2002).

Pamela Y. Price received her B.A. in political science from Yale in 1978. In 1977, Price joined the landmark case of *Alexander (Price) v. Yale.* After the Court dismissed the five other plaintiffs, Price was the only plaintiff to proceed to trail in January 1979, in the U.S. District Court in New Haven. In June 1979, the Court rendered a verdict in favor of Yale; the decision was affirmed by the Second Circuit in September 1980. Price attended Boalt Hall School of Law at the University of California at Berkeley, where she received her J.D. and a master's degree in jurisprudence and social policy in 1982. In June 1991, she founded the law firm of Price And Associates in Oakland, California. She regularly represents victims of sex and race discrimination. Her victories at trial, large money judgments and settlements, and tenacity as a litigator have become legend in the Bay Area legal community. In 1993 and 2001, Price received the Charles Houston Bar Association's Clinton W. White Advocacy Award for her achievements in civil litigation. She is the youngest person to receive the award and the only two-time winner.

Judith Resnik is the Arthur Liman Professor of Law at Yale Law School, where she teaches and writes about procedure, federal courts, feminist theory, and large-scale litigation. She has written many essays on feminism, including "Categorical Federalism: Jurisdiction, Gender, and the Globe," 111 *Yale Law Journal* 619 (2001); "Asking Questions About Gender in Courts," 21 *Signs* 952 (1996); "Gender Bias: From Classes to Courts," 45 *Stanford Law Review* 2195 (1993); and "Convergences: Law Literature, and Feminism" (with Carolyn Heilbrun), 99 *Yale Law Journal* 1913 (1990). Resnik was a member of the Ninth Circuit's Gender Bias Task Force, the first in the United States to report on the effects of gender within the federal courts. She has also served as the chair of the Section on Women in Legal Education of the American Association of Law Schools. She is a Managing Trustee of the International Association of Women Judges. She is also an active participant in the processes of law. She has testified before congressional committees and is an occasional litigator. In 1987, she argued in the United States Supreme Court on behalf of a local Rotary Club's right to admit women. In 1998 she received the Margaret Brent Award from the American Bar Association's Commission on Women. She is a member of the American Academy of Arts and Sciences and the American Philosophical Society.

Deborah L. Rhode is the Ernest W. McFarland Professor of Law and director of the Keck Center on Legal Ethics and the Legal Profession at Stanford University School of Law. She is also the former Chair of the American Bar Association's Commission on Women in the Profession. In 1998 she served as president of the Association of American Law Schools, and as senior counsel to the Minority members of the Judiciary Committee, the U.S. House of Representatives, working on impeachment issues. She is a former director of Stanford's Institute for Research on Women and Gender and serves on the board of the NOW Legal Defense Fund. She writes primarily in the area of legal ethics and gender discrimination. She is the author or coauthor of ten books and more than one hundred articles. Her publications include *The Difference "Difference" Makes: Women and Leadership* (2002); *Gender and Law* (with Katharine Bartlett and Angela Harris, 2002), *Speaking of Sex* (1997), and *Justice and Gender* (1985).

Dorothy Roberts is Kirkland & Ellis Professor at Northwestern University School of Law and a faculty fellow at Northwestern's Institute for Policy Research. She has written extensively on the interplay of gender, race, and class in legal issues concerning reproduction and motherhood. She is the author of *Killing the Black Body: Race, Reproduction, and the Meaning of Liberty* (1997), which received a 1998 Myers Center Award for the Study of Human Rights in North America, and *Shattered Bonds: The Color of Child Welfare,* as well as the coauthor of casebooks on constitutional law and women and the law. She has published more than fifty articles and essays in books and scholarly journals, including *Harvard Law Review, Yale Law Journal, University of Chicago Law Review,* and *Social Text.* She is also a frequent speaker at university campuses, public interest organizations, and other public forums on topics such as race and sex equality, reproductive rights, welfare reform, and child welfare policy. She received her B.A. from Yale College and her J.D. from Harvard Law School.

Diane L. Rosenfeld is a lecturer on women's studies at Harvard University where she teaches "Women, Violence and the Law." She is also a fellow at the Harvard Law School Berkman Center for Internet and Society where she leads an On-line Lecture and Discussion Series on Violence Against Women. She formerly served as the senior counsel to the Violence Against Women Office at the U.S. Department of Justice. She received an LL.M. from Harvard Law

School in 1996. Her thesis examined the creation of batterer detention and intervention facilities.

Abigail C. Saguy is an assistant professor of sociology at UCLA and has published her work in several journals including *Law and Society Review, Qualitative Sociology, Communication Review, European Journal of Women's Studies,* and *Comparative Social Research.* In *What Is Sexual Harassment? From Capitol Hill to the Sorbonne* (2003), she examines how sexual harassment has been defined in the United States and France, drawing on legal texts, media coverage, and more than sixty interviews with American and French activists, lawyers, and human resources managers.

Carol Sanger is the Barbara Aronstein Black Professor of Law at Columbia Law School, where she teaches contracts and a broad range of courses on women, families, and children. She received a J.D. from the University of Michigan in 1976 and a B.A. from Wellesley College in 1970. She has previously taught at Santa Clara and the University of Oregon law schools. Her recent work has focused on the ways that law influences family formation, particularly relationships between parents and children. She is also the author, with E. Allan Farnsworth and William F. Young, of *Contracts: Cases and Materials* (6th ed.). In 2001, she received the Columbia University Presidential Award for Outstanding Teaching. In 2003–2004 she will be a fellow at the Woodrow Wilson School of Public and International Affairs at Princeton University, completing a book on how maternal decisions to separate from their children are regarded as a matter of cultural inquiry and as a matter of law.

Ann Scales is a feminist activist, lawyer, and teacher. She has been a legal educator for more than twenty years, teaching at various institutions including the University of Iowa College of Law, the University of British Columbia Faculty of Law, Boston College Law School, and the University of New Mexico Law School. She has published many articles on jurisprudence and gender issues. She is a member of the California and New Mexico State Bars.

Frederick Schauer is the Frank Stanton Professor of the First Amendment and former Academic Dean, and former Acting Dean of the John F. Kennedy School of Government, Harvard University. Formerly professor of law at the University of Michigan, he is the author of *The Law of Obscenity* (1976), *Free Speech: A Philosophical Enquiry* (1982), *Playing by the Rules: A Philosophical Examination of Rule-Based Decision-Making in Law and in Life* (1991), *The First Amendment: A Reader* (1996), *Profiles, Probabilities, and Stereotypes* (2003), and numerous articles on freedom of speech, constitutional law, and the philosophy of law in legal and philosophical journals. The recipient of a Guggenheim Fellowship, he is a member of the American Academy of Arts and Sciences, is a former chair of the Section on Constitutional Law of the Association of American Law Schools, was founding coeditor of the journal *Legal Theory*, and has been a vice president of the American Society for Political and Legal Philosophy.

Judy M. Shih received her J.D. in 1998 from the University of Chicago, clerked for the Hon. Diana E. Murphy of the United States Court of Appeals for the Eighth Circuit, and is currently an associate at Keker & Van Nest, L.L.P. in San Francisco.

As a member of the New Haven Law Collective, Anne E. Simon was counsel for the plaintiffs in *Alexander v. Yale University*. Since that time, she has represented clients from many areas of the United States and other countries in women's rights, international human rights, and environmental justice litigation. She was a staff attorney at the NOW Legal Defense and Education Fund and the Center for Constitutional Rights. She served as Chief Administrative Law Judge for the Massachusetts Department of Environmental Protection. She was director of the Environmental Law Community Clinic in Berkeley, California, and is currently senior attorney at Communities for a Better Environment in Oakland, California. She has been an adjunct faculty member at New York University Law School and Boalt Hall School of Law, University of California at Berkeley.

Marc Spindelman is assistant professor of law at The Ohio State University's Moritz College of Law. His current work in feminist theory, including his contribution to this collection, investigates the phenomenon of same-sex sexual violence and its relationship to male supremacy.

Cass R. Sunstein is the Karl N. Llewellyn Distinguished Service Professor of Jurisprudence at the University of Chicago. His many books include *Why Societies Need Dissent* (2003), *Risk and Reason* (2002), *Designing Democracy* (2001), *Republic.com* (2001), *The Partial Constitution* (1993), and *Democracy and the Problem of Free Speech* (1993).

Gerald Torres is H. O. Head Centennial Professor in Real Property Law at the University of Texas Law School. He received his A.B. in 1974 from Stanford, J.D. in 1977 from Yale, and LL.M. in 1980 from the University of Michigan. A leading figure in critical race theory, he is also an expert in agricultural and environmental law. He came to Texas from the University of Minnesota Law School in 1993, and has also served as Deputy Assistant Attorney General for Environment and Natural Resources in the Department of Justice and as Counsel to Attorney General Janet Reno. His many articles include "Taking and Giving: Police Power, Public Value, and Private Right" (*Environmental Law,* 1996), and "Translating Yonnondio by Precedent and Example: The Mashpee Indian Case" (*Duke Law Journal,* 1990). His book with Lani Guinier, *The Miner's Canary,* was published in 2002. He was elected to the Board of the Environmental Law Institute, appointed to the EPA's National Environmental Justice Advisory Council as well as the National Petroleum Council. He has been a visiting professor at Harvard Law School and Stanford Law School. He has also lectured in Europe and Latin American and served as a consultant to the United Nations on environmental matters. He is a member of the American Law Institute.

Yukiko Tsunoda graduated from Tokyo University in 1967 with a major in Japanese literature. Because of severe sex discrimination at that time, she was not able to find a job in her area of specialty. She changed course and was admitted to the Japan Federation of Bar Association in 1975. Since 1986, she has worked as a legal adviser for the Tokyo Rape Crisis Center and has worked in the area of women's human rights, especially rape, sexual harassment and domestic violence. She was a research scholar at the Law School of University of Michigan from 1994 to 1996. She has served as the president of Center for Education and support for Women, Japan (CESW), since April 2001. In addition to litigating cases in rape, sexual harassment and domestic violence, she has given lectures on the issue of women's rights to women's organizations and others throughout Japan.

Lea VanderVelde is Josephine Witte Professor of Law at the University of Iowa College of Law. She is the author of several articles on women, work, and legal status, including "The Gendered Origins of Specific Performance Doctrine Binding Men's Consciences and Women's Fidelity," 101 *Yale Law Journal* 775 (1992); "The Legal Ways of Seduction," 48 *Stanford Law Review* 817 (1996) and "Mrs. Dred Scott" (with Sandhya Subramanian), 106 *Yale Law Journal* 1033 (1997), as well as books on labor and property law. Her work often follows a historicist method to examine the origins and changes in legal rules involving status and power. Her current projects include a study of slavery and freedom on the American frontier and the biography of Harriet, a woman of color, Dred Scott's wife, and litigant in the notorious Supreme Court case. She is also the University of Iowa Global Scholar for 2003–2005 appointed to study of labor migration, human trafficking, and globalization.

Robin West is Professor of Law at Georgetown University Law Center, where she teaches jurisprudence, feminist legal theory, law and literature, and contracts. She is the author, most recently, of *Caring for Justice.*

Index

Abbey, Antonia, 98

Abbott, Grace, 7

abolitionist press, 3, 4

Abrams, Kathryn, 27, 86, 164, 370, 705

abuse: racist, 680; "tolerated residuum" of, 536–37, 553n4; traditional morality's opposition to, 694n17; vagueness of standard for, 443, 444

academic freedom, 300–302; used as defense, 354

accountability, 28; in educational process, 63–64, 290–91, 297, 685; employer, 442, 600n49; for sexual harassment, 683–85; standards of, 297; and status advantage, 80–81. *See also* liability

Adams, David, 549

admissibility, rules limiting, 97

adolescents, sexual identities of, 62

Advocacy Training and Treatment Center, Florida, 551

African American women, 3–4, 70, 72,

476n35, 493n55. *See also* black women; enslaved women; women of color

agency: application of, 116; attributes of, 114–15; denial of, 117; feminism and, 113–14; law of, 273, 276, 277–78, 280, 299; loss of, 142, 143; norm of, 112–13, 123n15; principles, rejection of, 278–79

Alexander, Ronni, 51–52, 54, 64

Alexander v. Gardner-Denver Company, 254–55

Alexander v. Yale University, 51–56, 61; citations of, 55–56; and Title IX, 55; Yale as defendant in, 66n28

Allen v. Farrow, 87

American Booksellers Association v. Hudnut, 383, 392

American Civil Liberties Union, 353

American Convention on Human Rights in the Area of Economic, Social and Cultural Rights, 660, 661

coercion: camouflaged as choice, 498–
99; as concept in American law, 498–
99; defined, 5122n21; law as, 511–
12n18; as opposite of free agency, 501;
protection from, 7; relationship of to
unwelcomeness, 504
Coetzee, J. M., 89
Colker, Ruth, 120, 126–27n35, 175
collective action by working-class
women, in India, 649–50
collective bargaining, 249
collective injury: and freedom of speech,
373–77; nature of, 366–69
collective interests, 134–35
Committee on Economic, Social and Cultural Rights, United Nations, 659
"common sense" test, 119, 182–83, 193
communication, defined, 384
community: services, coordination of
with criminal justice system, 546; socialization into, 388–89, 390, 391;
values, 335
comparative-equality test, in Germany,
584
compensation: insurance theory of, 313;
in Japanese tort law, 624; normative
theory of, 335
competency, sacrifice of, 142
complaint: failure to file, 104; prompt-
ness of, 127n38; structures, in education, 302
Conference of Chief Justices, 524
conflict of interest: employer, 87; standards, 296, 299
Congress, commerce clause power of,
525, 526
consciousness-raising, 68; in India, 649
consensual sexual relations, 78–79, 145–
51; agreements, 85–86; feminist case
against, 82; inequality in, 80, 146, 148;
policies on, 80–81, 87–88; prohibition
of, 87
consent: disconnected from will, 79; informed, 83; presumptive, 31nn17, 21

constitutional frameworks, variance in,
589
contract, freedom of, 598n28
Convention on the Elimination of All
Forms of Discrimination Against Wom-
en (CEDAW), 640, 659–60, 662–63
Cornell, Drucilla, 118, 122–23n14, 585–
86, 587, 593
Council of Third World Women at Yale,
55
counter-transference, 89
courtship behavior, 117–18
Crawley, Vernon, 61
credit availability, for women in India,
649
Crenshaw, Kimberlé, 175, 482
cultural practices, specificity of, 68

damages:
—compensatory, 329–31; lack of correlation of with punitive damages; 332;
quid pro quo harassment and, 332–33;
reforms of, 330, 334–35; variability in,
324, 325–26, 327, 329–30
—in harassment cases: analysis of, 325–
26; guidelines for, 335, 337; median
award of, 331; person-specific determinations in, 343–44n15; randomness
of, 337; use of exemplar cases for, 335,
337
—monetary, 250–51, 265–66n5,
321n58
—punitive, 674, 693–94n6; economic
view of, 326–27; lack of correlation of
with compensatory damages, 332; retributive view of, 326; study of, 327–
28; theory of, 326–27
Daum v. Lorick Enterprises, Inc., 331
Davis, Adrienne D., 28, 707
Davis, Angela, 463
*Davis v. Monroe County Board of Edu-
cation*, 61, 62, 298
Declaration on Fundamental Principles
and Rights at Work, ILO, 658